THE PAPERS OF
WOODROW WILSON

VOLUME 45
NOVEMBER 11, 1917–JANUARY 15, 1918

SPONSORED BY THE WOODROW WILSON
FOUNDATION
AND PRINCETON UNIVERSITY

THE PAPERS OF

WOODROW WILSON

ARTHUR S. LINK, *EDITOR*

DAVID W. HIRST, *SENIOR ASSOCIATE EDITOR*

JOHN E. LITTLE, *ASSOCIATE EDITOR*

FREDRICK AANDAHL, *ASSOCIATE EDITOR*

MANFRED F. BOEMEKE, *ASSISTANT EDITOR*

PHYLLIS MARCHAND AND MARGARET D. LINK,
EDITORIAL ASSISTANTS

Volume 45
November 11, 1917–January 15, 1918

PRINCETON, NEW JERSEY
PRINCETON UNIVERSITY PRESS
1984

INTRODUCTION

THE opening of this volume finds Colonel House in London and Paris in conference with the Allied leaders in the wake of two events catastrophic to the American and Allied war efforts—the routing of the Italian army by a combined Austro-Hungarian and German onslaught at Caporetto, in northern Italy, and the Bolshevik takeover in Petrograd and the new regime's withdrawal of Russia from the war, which of course portends the collapse of the entire eastern front. House arranges for American membership on all important inter-Allied councils; more important, at Wilson's instruction, House also agrees that the United States will appoint a military representative (but not a political delegate) to the Supreme War Council, which the British, French, and Italian leaders have recently established at Rapallo, Italy, to coordinate their war efforts. However, House is unable to persuade the Allied Prime Ministers to approve Wilson's chief objective—a joint Allied-American announcement of liberal peace terms as the first step in forcing the convening of a general peace conference.

Frustrated, and convinced that he has to act alone, Wilson resumes the peace offensive which he began in his reply to Pope Benedict of August 27, 1917. In his annual message to Congress on December 4, 1917, Wilson asks that body to approve a declaration of war against Austria-Hungary. He also denounces the military masters of Germany, who, in their grab for world domination, have plunged the world into war. Continuing, Wilson says that the United States has no desire to interfere in the internal affairs of the Austro-Hungarian Empire, and that Americans were fighting for the emancipation of the German people as much as for their own freedom and safety. "No one," he says, "is threatening the existence or the independence or the peaceful enterprise of the German Empire."

Meanwhile, conflicting and confusing reports about the ability of the Bolsheviks to consolidate their hold over Russia come from American and other diplomatic officers in that country. But one fact is clear by early December: Russia is out of the war, and there is nothing that the American and Allied leaders can do to persuade her to resume hostilities. After flirting with the idea of secretly supporting the Cossacks who are attempting to establish an independent regime in the Ukraine, Wilson decides to follow a policy of nonintervention in what is developing as a civil war in Russia and to attempt to establish informal relations with the Bolshevik government.

Representatives of the Central Powers and of the Bolshevik government meet at Brest-Litovsk in Russia on December 22. When the spokesman of the former seems to accept the Russian demand that the negotiations be turned into a general peace conference, with agreement upon liberal terms, the Bolsheviks invite the United States and the Allied powers to send delegates to Brest-Litovsk. "Everything," the note from Petrograd reads, "depends upon the Allied nations themselves. . . . The Russian revolution has opened the door to an immediate universal peace on the basis of an agreement." The British and French tell Wilson that they do not deign to reply. But Wilson, convinced that the time for universal peace might be at hand, determines to reply forthrightly. Working with Colonel House from January 4 through January 7 (and with the help of a memorandum prepared by Sidney E. Mezes, David Hunter Miller, and Walter Lippmann of The Inquiry), Wilson hammers out what has since been called his Fourteen Points Address, which he delivers to a joint session of Congress on January 8, 1918.

Wilson begins by approving the Bolshevik demand for a general liberal settlement. He then notes that the representatives of the Central Powers at Brest-Litovsk had recently made it clear that theirs was a program of the conquest and dismemberment of Russia. The voice of the Russian people, Wilson goes on, speaks with "a frankness, a largeness of view, a generosity of spirit, and a universal human sympathy which must challenge the admiration of every friend of mankind." He will respond "with utter simplicity and frankness." He then enumerates "the only possible programme" of "the world's peace" in fourteen points. The sixth demands the complete evacuation of all Russian territory, the right of self-determination for the Russian people, and a welcome of the new Russia into "the society of free nations under institutions of her own choosing." The last point demands the creation of a general association of nations "for the purpose of affording mutual guarantees of political independence and territorial integrity to great and small nations alike." As Wilson says, the "moral climax" of the war has come.

Meanwhile, Wilson is deeply involved in domestic mobilization, and still plagued by labor-management difficulties. Particularly troublesome on the home front is the plight of the railroads which, starved for capital, are unable to maintain their equipment and lines so as to transport essential materials and goods expeditiously. When a collapse of the market in railroad bonds threatens to demoralize the entire economy, Wilson nationalizes the railroads on December 28, 1917, creates a Railroad Administration, and appoints McAdoo as Director General of Railroads.

Wilson faces two momentous decisions as this volume ends. One is a response to the suggestions of the British and French leaders that American troops in France be dispersed among French and British units for training and fighting. The second is the problem of a wise policy toward Russia, in spite of the desires, already evident, of British and French leaders to intervene for various purposes in Russia.

"VERBATIM ET LITERATIM"

In earlier volumes of this series, we have said something like the following: "All documents are reproduced *verbatim et literatim*, with typographical and spelling errors corrected in square brackets only when necessary for clarity and ease of reading." The following essay explains our textual methods and review procedures.

We have never printed and do not intend to print critical, or corrected, versions of documents. We print them exactly as they are, with a few exceptions which we always note. We never use the word *sic* except to denote the repetition of words in a document; in fact, we think that a succession of *sics* defaces a page.

We usually repair words in square brackets when letters are missing. As we have said, we also repair words in square brackets for clarity and ease of reading. Our general rule is to do this when we, ourselves, cannot read the word without stopping to determine its meaning. Jumbled words and names misspelled beyond recognition of course have to be repaired. We correct the misspelling of a name in a document in the footnote identifying the person.

However, when an old man writes to Wilson saying that he is glad to hear that Wilson is "comming" to Newark, or a semiliterate farmer from Texas writes phonetically, we see no reason to correct spellings in square brackets when the words are perfectly understandable. We do not correct Wilson's misspellings unless they are unreadable, except to supply in square brackets letters missing in words. For example, for some reason he insisted upon spelling "belligerent" as "belligerant." Nothing would be gained by correcting "belligerant" in square brackets.

We think that it is very important for several reasons to follow the rule of *verbatim et literatim*. Most important, a document has its own integrity and power, particularly when it is not written in a perfect literary form. There is something very moving in seeing a Texas dirt farmer struggling to express his feelings in words, or a semiliterate former slave doing the same thing. Second, in Wilson's case it is crucially important to reproduce his errors in letters which he typed himself, since he usually typed badly when he was in an agitated state. Third, since style is the essence of the person, we would never correct grammar or make tenses consistent, as one correspondent has urged us to do. Fourth, we think that it is very important that we print exact transcripts of Charles L. Swem's copies of Wilson's letters. Swem made many mistakes (we correct them in footnotes from a reading of his shorthand books), and Wilson let them pass. We thus have to assume that Wilson did not read his letters before signing them, and this, we think, is a significant fact. Finally, printing typed letters and documents *verbatim et literatim* tells us a great deal about the educational level of the stenographic profession in the United States during Wilson's time.

We think that our series would be worthless if we produced unreliable texts, and we go to some effort to make certain that the texts are authentic.

Our typists are highly skilled and proofread their transcripts carefully as soon as they have typed them. The Editor sight proofreads documents once he has assembled a volume and is setting its annotation. The Editors who write the notes read through documents several times and are careful to check any anomalies. Then, once the manuscript volume has been completed and all notes checked, the Editor and Senior Associate Editor orally proofread the documents against the copy. They read every comma, dash, and character. They note every absence of punctuation. They study every nearly illegible word in written documents.

Once this process of "establishing the text" is completed, the manuscript volume goes to our editor at Princeton University Press, who checks the volume carefully and sends it to the printing plant. The galley proofs are read orally against copy in the proofroom at the Press. And we must say that the proofreaders there are extraordinarily skilled. Some years ago, before we found a way to ease their burden, they used to query every misspelled word, absence of punctuation, or other such anomalies. Now we write "O.K." above such words or spaces on the copy.

We read the galley proofs at least three times. Our copyeditor gives them a sight reading against the manuscript copy to look for remaining typographical errors and to make sure that no line has been dropped. The Editor and Senior Associate Editor sight read them against documents and copy. We then get the page proofs, which have been corrected at the Press. We check all the changes three times. In addition, we get *revised* pages and check them twice.

This is not the end. The Editor, Senior Associate Editor, and Assistant Editor give a final reading to headings, description-location lines, and notes. Finally, our indexer of course reads the pages word by word. Before we return the pages to the Press, she comes in with a list of queries, all of which are answered by reference to the documents.

Our rule in the Wilson Papers is that our tolerance of error is zero. No system and no person can be perfect. We are sure that there are errors in our volumes. However, we believe that we have done everything humanly possible to avoid error; the chance is remote that what looks at first glance like a typographical error is indeed an error.

Beginning with this volume, we will, for reasons of economy of space, usually print foreign-language documents only in translations and not in their original texts. Or, where it seems appropriate, we will print foreign-language documents *verbatim*, without translating them. Any person who desires to do so is welcome to examine our copies of the original documents.

We take this opportunity again to thank Dr. Mary Giunta and Anne Harris Henry of the staff of the National Historical Publications and Records Commission for their continuing and indispensable help in finding documents for us in such repositories as The National Archives and the Library of Congress. We are grateful to August Heckscher for his help in translating French documents. We also thank our editor at Princeton University Press, Ms. Judith May, for continuing assistance and Professors John Milton Cooper, Jr., William H. Harbaugh, Richard W. Leopold, and Betty Miller Unterberger for reading the manuscript of this volume and for being, as heretofore, constructively critical.

THE EDITORS

Princeton, New Jersey
May 5, 1983

CONTENTS

Interviews
A memorandum of an interview with William Howard Taft, 272
A memorandum by Lawrence Bennett about a conversation between Wilson and Vance Criswell McCormick, 366

Collateral Materials

Political correspondence, reports, memoranda, and aide-mémoire

Diplomatic correspondence, reports, memoranda, and aide-mémoire

ILLUSTRATIONS

Following page 292

Reviewing the troops at Fort Myer, Virginia
National Archives

Aboard the U.S.S. Mayflower, from left to right: Secretary Daniels,
Ambassador Satō, Viscount Ishii, Secretary Lansing
National Archives

Leon Trotsky
Princeton University Library

V. I. Lenin
Princeton University Library

TEXT ILLUSTRATIONS

ABBREVIATIONS

ALI	autograph letter initialed
ALS	autograph letter signed
Ar	archives
ASB	Albert Sidney Burleson
CC	carbon copy
CCL	carbon copy of letter
CCLS	carbon copy of letter signed
CCS	carbon copy signed
CLS	Charles Lee Swem
CLSsh	Charles Lee Swem shorthand
CLST	Charles Lee Swem typed
DFH	David Franklin Houston
EAW	Ellen Axson Wilson
EBW	Edith Bolling Wilson
EMH	Edward Mandell House
FKL	Franklin Knight Lane
FR 1918, Russia	*Papers Relating to the Foreign Relations of the United States, 1918, Russia*
FR-WWS 1917	*Papers Relating to the Foreign Relations of the United States, 1917, Supplement, The World War*
FR-WWS 1918	*Papers Relating to the Foreign Relations of the United States, 1918, Supplement, The World War*
Hw, hw	handwritten, handwriting
HwCL	handwritten copy of letter
JD	Josephus Daniels
JPT	Joseph Patrick Tumulty
JRT	Jack Romagna typed
MS, MSS	manuscript, manuscripts
NDB	Newton Diehl Baker
PS	postscript
RG	record group
RL	Robert Lansing
SG	Samuel Gompers
T	typed
TC	typed copy
TCL	typed copy of letter
TCLS	typed copy of letter signed
TI	typed initialed
TL	typed letter
TLI	typed letter initialed
TLS	typed letter signed
TS	typed signed
TWG	Thomas Watt Gregory
WBW	William Bauchop Wilson
WGM	William Gibbs McAdoo
WHP	Walter Hines Page
WJB	William Jennings Bryan
WW	Woodrow Wilson
WWhw	Woodrow Wilson handwriting, handwritten
WWsh	Woodrow Wilson shorthand

WWT	Woodrow Wilson typed
WWTL	Woodrow Wilson typed letter
WWTLI	Woodrow Wilson typed letter initialed
WWTLS	Woodrow Wilson typed letter signed

ABBREVIATIONS FOR COLLECTIONS
AND REPOSITORIES

Following the National Union Catalog
of the Library of Congress

AFL-CIO-Ar	American Federation of Labor-Congress of Industrial Organizations Archives
CtY	Yale University
DLC	Library of Congress
DNA	National Archives
FFM-Ar	French Foreign Ministry Archives
FMD-Ar	French Ministry of Defense Archives
FO	British Foreign Office
HPL	Hoover Presidential Library
IEN	Northwestern University
JDR	Justice Department Records
MH-BA	Harvard University Graduate School of Business Administration
NcMHi	Historical Foundation of the Presbyterian and Reformed Churches
NhD	Dartmouth College
NjP	Princeton University
NjPT	Princeton Theological Seminary
NN	New York Public Library
NNC	Columbia University
OCAJA	American Jewish Archives
PRO	Public Record Office
PSC	Swarthmore College
RSB Coll., DLC	Ray Stannard Baker Collection of Wilsoniana, Library of Congress
SDR	State Department Records
VtU	University of Vermont and State Agricultural College
WC, NjP	Woodrow Wilson Collection, Princeton University
WP, DLC	Woodrow Wilson Papers, Library of Congress
WU	University of Wisconsin

SYMBOLS

[December 8, 1917]	publication date of published writing; also date of document when date is not part of text
[*December 25, 1917*]	composition date when publication date differs
[[November 12, 1917]]	delivery date of speech if publication date differs
**** ***	text deleted by author of document

THE PAPERS OF

WOODROW WILSON

VOLUME 45
NOVEMBER 11, 1917–JANUARY 15, 1918

THE PAPERS OF
WOODROW WILSON

A Telegram and a Letter from Edward Mandell House

[London] 11 Nov. 4 p.m.

Paris conference has been postponed until twenty-second because of absence of principals in Italy. This has upset the plans and we will remain here until nineteenth. The Prime Minister and Chief of Staff[1] return tomorrow, and, after seeing them, I will be able to give you more definite information.

[Edward House]

T transcript (WP, DLC) of WWsh decode of T telegram (WP, DLC).
[1] That is, General Sir William Robert Robertson, chief of the Imperial General Staff.

Dear Governor,   London. November 11, 1917.

Mr. Balfour having heard that there was some friction in different parts has thought it best to send the enclosed letter to all their diplomatic agents throughout the world. I am enclosing you a copy for your information and that of Mr. Lansing.[1]

I am having an extraordinarily busy time. The difficulty with the British I find is that while one can keep in perfect agreement with them, it is exceedingly difficult to have any definite program formulated and put through. It seems no one person's business to say that this or that shall be done and then delegate it to someone to work out. The lack of this drives one around in circles. I have found this true upon every visit that I have made here.

I am urging them, as I shall urge the French, to come to some agreement as to public statements by those in authority. Up to now, both the British and French have said the things that the German Government wished them to say. I am trying to get them to adopt a policy of saying the things which the German Government does not desire them to say. A case in point is Alsace and Lorraine. The French and British, particularly Lloyd George at the instance of the French, are constantly making Alsace and Lorraine an Allied ultimatum. If Germany is beaten, France will get Alsace and Lorraine. If she is not beaten no amount of talk in British or French circles can give it to her. In the meantime, such demands weld Germany [Germans] back of their government. On the other hand there is created in all the Allied countries a sense of irritation among certain groups, that will soon begin to insist, more or less loudly, that unless the war is for some higher purpose it had better cease.

One finds this feeling in America as well as elsewhere, and I believe I can point out to the French that if they are not careful they will defeat their own purpose. I can readily see that if the war lingers on, there may come a time when there will be an irrisistible demand in all the allied countries other than France, that Alsace and Lorraine be not insisted upon as an issue.

I saw the King this morning. He sent his compliments to you and wanted you to know how much he appreciated what you had done for the allied cause. Mrs. House and I lunch at the Palace tomorrow informally.

I have found no difficulty in refusing all invitations to dinner, and my desire to work and not to frolic seems to meet with warm approval. I think, however, that it is best not to draw the line too closely with the other members of the mission. This kind of thing is new to them. They have worked very hard and I can see that they would like some diversion and I have so arranged it. Mr. Balfour will entertain them at dinner and also at the House of Commons, and the King will give them a luncheon.

Affectionately yours,   E. M. House

The Prime Minister is just back and he and I dine alone tonight. Nov. 13.

TLS (WP, DLC).
[1] This document is missing in all collections.

From Newton Diehl Baker

My dear Mr. President: Washington. November 11, 1917

You handed me on Tuesday last the emclosed [enclosed] memorandum on the General Strategy of the Present War between the Allies and the Central Powers by Major H. H. Sargent, United States Army, Retired.[1] On my return to my office I discovered that I had received an earlier copy of the memorandum, and had referred it to the War College with a request that its suggestions be studied and a comprehensive statement made of the opinion of the War College on the subject. In the meantime Senator Chamberlain in October sent me a plan submitted to him by a Mr. Rihani,[2] to which General Bliss had undertaken to prepare a reply for my signature; but which reply I did not sign because I felt that a discussion of the question involved statements to which no publicity at present could, with safety, be given. I therefore, had the letter rewritten, and sent it to you for your information.[3]

The suggestions made by Major Sargent, while not identical with those of Mr. Rihani, are in the main the same. I have reread the Sargent memorandum, and also the War College discussion of the strategy of the present war of which I enclose a copy for your information.[4]

I think you need not take the time to read the Sargent paper. In brief it is a criticism of the strategy of the Allies, on the ground that a deadlock has been reached on the Western Front, and that Napoleon, in his first campaign, and various other military Captains, broke such deadlocks by seeking new points of attack.

I think it is fair to say that Major Sargent's argument consists of pointing out that if the Western line were held by no larger force than is necessary to hold it safely, while the strength of the Central Powers was scattered by attacks upon Constantinople through Russia, and at any other point where a fresh exercise of force could be made, it would have the effect of detaching from the Central Powers their Balkan Allies, depriving them of both military resources and food supplies, and hasten peace by breaking the spirit of the German people. Incidentally, Major Sargent feels that if America were to undertake such a plan, and he prefers the Eastern Mediterranean as the place for us to strike, it would enable "America to reap her proper share of the glory" rather than to "continue to play second fiddle to England and France." The War College memorandum which I herewith enclose I have read twice throughout, and I confess I see no answer to the arguments upon which it proceeds.

Assuming that we could continue to supply additional increments of armies to France and maintain them there in sufficient number to preserve the morale of the French people, and assuming that for this purpose only a relatively small part of the total Army of the United States would be needed, we would still have to face the transportation difficulty to put a large army at any other and necessarily a more remote point. Should we take a Mediterranean point, the dangers of Mediterranean transportation are very much greater than those to which we are already subjected. Should we seek to go by a Pacific route, the length of the journey makes the whole plan inadmissible in view of the enormous tonnage necessary first to transport an adequate army, and second to keep it supplied. I think the arguments in the War College paper are quite conclusive on this point, and that the tonnage question necessarily controls the strategy of this war so far as our participation in it is concerned whatever conditions there may be on the other side.

But it is to be remembered that operation by an independent army in some other theatre of war would have to be by a large army. I should be very much alarmed indeed if we had an army of less than a half million men in Russia at this time, and I confess I would look with grave apprehension upon the situation of an army of the United States, even a half million strong, undertaking to conduct independent operations anywhere in the Balkan country. It would be surrounded by a population of very uncertain political and military stability, and might at any time be thrown wholly on its own resources and subjected to over-powering pressure by a concentrated movement against it along short interior lines from the Central Powers. General Sarrail's[5] Army at Salonica is said to have more than a half million men, and its leader is said to be an ambitious soldier, and yet it has been substantially immobile, because of the difficulties of supply, terrain and disease; the latter element having at times put as much as one fourth of his entire force out of action. I think we are obliged to assume that Salonica was as favorably a selected point as there is for such an independent force as it had the approval of the highest authorities in both the French and British Armies, and that the forces there have been of no military value beyond the fact that it has required a large contingent of Turkish, Bulgarian, Austrian and German forces to prevent its movements.

If you have the leisure to look at the War College study, I feel sure that the argument used in it will seem impressive, if not conclusive, against the undertaking of any such additional expedition, at least until the transportation question is in a different situation. In the meantime, the whole problem of equipment and supplies for the army which we have raised is at the beginning, and it would be a substantial time before we could equip, arm and supply an army of a million men in addition to those already called out, and as to the latter, of course, a substantial force must be maintained in this country and the remainder are, in some sense, pledged for use on the Western Front in cooperation with the British and French forces there.   Respectfully yours,   Newton D. Baker

TLS (WP, DLC).
   [1] Herbert Howland Sargent, "Memorandum on the General Strategy of the Present War between the Allies and the Central Powers," Nov. 2 and 4, 1917, TS MS (WP, DLC). For a summary of the "earlier copy," see WW to NDB, Sept. 22, 1917, n. 1, Vol. 44.
   [2] Ameen Fares Rihani, Syrian-born, naturalized American citizen, who specialized in studies of the history and literature of the Middle East. He was chairman of the Syria-Mt. Lebanon League of Liberation, a group with headquarters in New York.
   [3] See NDB to WW, Oct. 11, 1917, n. 1, Vol. 44.
   [4] It is summarized in NDB to WW, Oct. 11, 1917, n. 1, *ibid.*
   [5] Maurice Paul Emmanuel Sarrail, commander of the French and British forces at Salonika.

A Memorandum by Louis Brandeis Wehle,[1] with Enclosure

Washington, D. C.
MEMORANDUM FOR THE PRESIDENT: November 11, 1917.
SUBJECT: ADJUSTMENT OF LABOR DISPUTES INCIDENT
TO PRODUCTION OF MUNITIONS AND SUPPLIES.

Upon request of the President's Secretary, the undersigned will undertake to set out here, informally and as briefly as possible, some very recent developments in the relation of Organized Labor to the Government's war-production program. Of these developments, which involve all of the departments of the Government now carrying on production for war upon a large scale, it would seem that the President should have cognizance before they go so far as to conflict with some policy which the President may, perhaps, have in mind.

Review of Labor Adjustment Machinery already established, incident to Cantonment Construction, Shipbuilding, etcetera

Efforts are being made, and some of them successfully, to overcome the drift toward the compulsion of labor in wartime production. Adjustment of labor disputes by cooperation between the Government and the American Federation of Labor was carried, in the summer of 1917, into construction of cantonments, aviation fields and warehouses for the Army, and into shore construction for the Navy. (See Appendix 1)[2] Here it has been successful. With the open shop established nearly everywhere, the cantonments went up practically without interruption by strikes. This method of adjustment was then applied to labor disputes incident to construction of private shipyards and to the building of ships for the Emergency Fleet Corporation and the Navy in private shipyards. (See Appendix 2).[3] Whether this idea will prove successful as applied to ships and shipyards remains to be seen; but there are some indications that it will. This adjustment idea is also being applied to disputes of longshoremen, but results cannot yet be appraised.

*Application of idea of Voluntary Cooperative Adjustment
to Munitions and Supplies Production:*

Now the question is: Shall the Government proceed to extend this idea into the field of munitions and supplies production? Pre-

[1] Nephew of Louis D. Brandeis, at this time counsel to the Shipbuilding Labor Adjustment Board.
[2] It is printed as an Enclosure.
[3] "Memorandum for the Adjustment of Wages, Hours, and Conditions of Labor in Shipbuilding Plants," TC MS (WP, DLC).

liminary negotiations are under way for doing this. Two tentative
forms of memoranda are attached hereto as Appendices 3 and 4.[4]
It is important to note about them that they have, one or the other,
received the approving signatures of five leading presidents of international unions as individuals, and the signature of one such
president as an officer of his organization. The undersigned is bringing the representatives of the Fleet Corporation (Mr. Stevens),[5] the
Army and the Navy together, over these preliminary drafts, having
discussed them at length with Secretary Baker, Assistant Secretary
Roosevelt and Mr. Stevens. The drafts will necessarily call for much
revision. It is highly probable, on account of the large proportion
of munitions and metal supplies plants, where labor is almost or
totally unorganized, that the memorandum should expressly provide for a shop-committee system. It is also quite certain that the
provisions with reference to the Government's contracts will require
clarification and revision; and conferences with contractors themselves are now in view for that purpose. Other changes besides
these will be necessary.

Typical Features of the proposed Arrangement:
The proposed arrangement has these points in common with
either the cantonment or the shipbuilding arrangement: It provides
(1) for an Adjustment Board of three, in which the public, the
Government and labor, are represented; (2) that production shall
continue pending all disputes, and that decisions shall be final and
binding; and (3) that as basic standards the Board shall employ
such scales of wages, hours and such conditions as obtain *in each
plant* on a given date. As in the case of the shipbuilding agreement,
we have here avoided one of the bitterest points of controversy
encountered last summer in the Advisory Council of the Council
of National Defense.

New and Important Features of proposed Arrangement:
The proposed arrangement has these significant new features:
(1) The labor representative is appointed by joint action of the
Secretary of Labor and Mr. Gompers; in the other plans Mr. Gompers has been the sole nominator.
(2) The arrangement throws the work of mediation, and often of
adjustment, into the *Department of Labor* as far as seemed at all
possible. In planning this adjustment machinery, conferences extending over several months with Secretary Baker, Assistant Sec-

---

[4] "Memorandum for the Adjustment During the War of Wages, Hours and Conditions
of Labor in Production of Munitions and Supplies" (two memoranda with this title), TC
and CC MSS (WP, DLC).
[5] Raymond B. Stevens.

retary Roosevelt, Assistant Secretary Post and Mr. Gompers were borne in mind; the chief features of the plan seem to be a meeting place for the views of all interests, bearing in mind particularly that the several producing departments would be unwilling to surrender entirely to the Department of Labor the function of determining costs of production dependent upon wages. The principal features of the proposed plan are approved now also by Mr. Stevens of the United States Shipping Board as well as by Assistant Secretary Roosevelt. The attached drafts (Appendices 3 and 4) are based, in the main, on a series of trial drafts which were submitted at one time or another to all of the persons above named at such conferences.

(3) The most surprising and important feature to be noticed is in the draft marked Appendix "D."[6] It is the final paragraph, which reads as follows:

"This memorandum shall be construed by the Board, which shall adopt such procedure from time to time as may seem necessary for the fulfillment of its purpose. The signers of it hope that it will bring about an uninterrupted industrial efficiency of the Nation, during the period of the war, in the industries to which it may apply, and that it may lead to the suspension, during that period, of any established rules or restrictions which shall be actually found by the Board unreasonably to limit production for war purposes, etc."

The draft containing this significant sentence was signed by President F. J. McNulty[7] of the International Brotherhood of Electrical Workers. There is reason to believe that some of the other presidents in the metal trades would also sign it, particularly when it is balanced by the proviso which has since been drafted by the undersigned upon the suggestion and request of Mr. Stevens of the United States Shipping Board.

Changing Attitude of Organized Labor:

It is to be seen from the foregoing survey that the attitude of some of the leaders of Organized Labor has been undergoing a great change. This is probably due, in the main, to a dawning realization of what this Nation is facing. Two or three international presidents have even expressed themselves to the undersigned as viewing compulsory arbitration with favor. On the Pacific Coast a very few of the local leaders even expressed themselves as favoring the drafting of labor for shipyards, so as to establish the workers as being under the Government and not under their old foes of peace times—the employers.

[6] That is, the second of the two memoranda cited in n. 4.
[7] Frank Joseph McNulty.

Recommendations:

But it has been assumed, in building up this structure of cooperative labor adjustment, piece by piece, that the Government would, if possible, avoid the compulsion of labor. If the idea of such adjustment fails when well administered, the necessity for some form of compulsion will probably have been borne in upon Organized Labor with such force as to disarm largely its opposition to it.

It is submitted that the time is surely coming fast when the Government must have a separate centralized labor agency, having, among other functions, that of co-ordinating the work of the adjustment bodies above discussed. If they are not kept in harmony by a controlling supervision, there will come to be even a competition for labor-supply between the groups of producing agencies respectively under the jurisdiction of the different adjustment boards.

Louis B. Wehle[8]

TS MS (WP, DLC).

[8] "Please thank Mr. Wehle for this interesting memorandum which I have looked through with some care." WW to JPT, c. Nov. 21, 1917, TL (WP, DLC).

E N C L O S U R E

MEMORANDUM FOR THE SECRETARY OF WAR: August 9th, 1917

Subject: Harmonization of labor policies of War and
Navy Departments.

The construction work of the Army and the land construction work of the Navy are often in conflict, particularly as to labor supplies and as to wages and hours. A vivid instance to-day is a strike against the naval cantonment near New York, to support which, strike leaders have called sympathetic strikes at Yaphank and Mineola. Whether the Yaphank strike will occur remains to be seen. The point is that Labor knows the Government only; it can not well distinguish between Army and Navy, and it will not do so in the long run.

I have discussed the matter with Assistant Secretary Roosevelt. He has agreed that a naval officer shall sit on the Emergency Construction Committee and that the Navy will hereafter accept from the Emergency Construction Committee the names of contractors to whom contracts are to be awarded. Since it has been arranged that a representative of Organized Labor is to sit in with the Emergency Construction Committee at the selection of contractors, the contractors who will hereafter be selected for naval land work will be fairly sure to have their relations with labor upon a sound basis.

RECOMMENDATION:

I have suggested to Assistant Secretary Roosevelt, in order further to harmonize the labor policies of the two Departments with reference to land construction work, that the Cantonment Adjustment Board, as at present constituted, have referred to it all labor disputes in connection with land construction work. An officer designated by the Navy Department to replace General Garlington[1] when Navy disputes are being handled. Mr. Roosevelt heartily endorses the plan. If it meets with your approval it can be promptly referred through Mr. Roosevelt to Secretary Daniels. Please indicate your views as to this.   Louis B. Wehle

I approve the above.   Sam'l. Gompers[2]

This is entirely agreeable to me if it is to the Sec. Navy Baker.[3]

Approved   Josephus Daniels[4]

TS MS (WP, DLC).
  [1] That is, Brig. Gen. Ernest Albert Garlington. Actually, Garlington had retired from the army on February 20. Maj. Gen. John Loomis Chamberlain had succeeded him as Inspector General.
  [2] SGhw.
  [3] NDBhw.
  [4] JDhw.

An Address in Buffalo to the American Federation of Labor[1]

[[Nov. 12, 1917]]

Mr. President, delegates of the American Federation of Labor, ladies and gentlemen: I esteem it a great privilege and a real honor to be thus admitted to your public counsels. When your executive committee paid me the compliment of inviting me here, I gladly accepted the invitation because it seems to me that this, above all other times in our history, is the time for common counsel, for the drawing together, not only of the energies, but of the minds of the nation. I thought that it was a welcome opportunity for disclosing to you some of the thoughts that have been gathering in my mind during these last momentous months.

I am introduced to you as the President of the United States, and, yet, I would be pleased if you would put the thought of the office into the background and regard me as one of your fellow citizens who has come here to speak, not the words of authority, but the words of counsel; the words which men should speak to

  [1] Wilson spoke at the opening session of the annual convention of the American Federation of Labor at the Broadway Auditorium in Buffalo. He was introduced by Samuel Gompers. Governor Charles S. Whitman of New York was among the other speakers. *New York Times*, Nov. 13, 1917.

one another who wish to be frank in a moment more critical perhaps than the history of the world has ever yet known; a moment when it is every man's duty to forget himself, to forget his own interests, to fill himself with the nobility of a great national and world conception, and act upon a new platform elevated above the ordinary affairs of life and lifted to where men have views of the long destiny of mankind.

I think that, in order to realize just what this moment of counsel is, it is very desirable that we should remind ourselves just how this war came about and just what it is for. You can explain most wars very simply, but the explanation of this is not so simple. Its roots run deep into all the obscure soils of history, and, in my view, this is the last decisive issue between the old principle of power and the new principle of freedom.

The war was started by Germany. Her authorities deny that they started it, but I am willing to let the statement I have just made await the verdict of history. And the thing that needs to be explained is why Germany started the war. Remember what the position of Germany in the world was—as enviable a position as any nation has ever occupied. The whole world stood at admiration of her wonderful intellectual and material achievements. All the intellectual men of the world went to school to her. As a university man, I have been surrounded by men trained in Germany, men who had resorted to Germany because nowhere else could they get such thorough and searching training, particularly in the principles of science and the principles that underlie modern material achievement. Her men of science had made her industries perhaps the most competent industries of the world, and the label "Made in Germany" was a guarantee of good workmanship and of sound material. She had access to all the markets of the world, and every other nation who traded in those markets feared Germany because of her effective and almost irresistible competition. She had a "place in the sun."

Why was she not satisfied? What more did she want? There was nothing in the world of peace that she did not already have, and have in abundance. We boast of the extraordinary pace of American advancement. We show with pride the statistics of the increase of our industries and of the population of our cities. Well, those statistics did not match the recent statistics of Germany. Her old cities took on youth and grew faster than any American cities ever grew. Her old industries opened their eyes and saw a new world and went out for its conquest. And yet the authorities of Germany were not satisfied.

You have one part of the answer to the question why she was

not satisfied in her methods of competition. There is no important industry in Germany upon which the government has not laid its hands, to direct it and, when necessity arose, control it; and you have only to ask any man whom you meet who is familiar with the conditions that prevailed before the war in the matter of national competition to find out the methods of competition which the German manufacturers and exporters used under the patronage and support of the government of Germany. You will find that they were the same sorts of competition that we have tried to prevent by law within our own borders. If they could not sell their goods cheaper than we could sell ours at a profit to themselves, they could get a subsidy from the government which made it possible to sell them cheaper anyhow, and the conditions of competition were thus controlled in large measure by the German government itself.

But that did not satisfy the German government. All the while, there was lying behind its thought and in its dreams of the future a political control which would enable it in the long run to dominate the labor and the industry of the world. They were not content with success by superior achievement; they wanted success by authority. I suppose very few of you have thought much about the Berlin-to-Bagdad Railway. The Berlin-Bagdad Railway was constructed in order to run the threat of force down the flank of the industrial undertakings of a half a dozen other countries; so that when German competition came in it would not be resisted too far, because there was always the possibility of getting German armies into the heart of that country quicker than any other armies could be got there.

Look at the map of Europe now! Germany is thrusting upon us again and again the discussion of peace talks—about what? Talks about Belgium; talks about northern France; talks about Alsace-Lorraine. Well, those are deeply interesting subjects to us and to them, but they are not the heart of the matter. Take up the map and look at it. Germany has absolute control of Austria-Hungary, practical control of the Balkan States, control of Turkey, control of Asia Minor. I saw a map in which the whole thing was printed in appropriate black the other day, and the black stretched all the way from Hamburg to Bagdad—the bulk of German power inserted into the heart of the world. If she can keep that, she has kept all that her dreams contemplated when the war began. If she can keep that, her power can disturb the world as long as she keeps it, always provided, for I feel bound to put this proviso in—always provided the present influences that control the German government continue to control it. I believe that the spirit of freedom can get into the hearts of Germans and find as fine a welcome there as it can find in any other hearts, but the spirit of freedom does not suit the plans of the Pan-Germans. Power cannot be used with concentrated force against free peoples if it is used by free people.

You know how many intimations come to us from one of the Central Powers that it is more anxious for peace than the chief Central Power, and you know that it means that the people in that Central Power know that if the war ends as it stands they will in effect themselves be vassals of Germany, notwithstanding that their populations are compounded of all the peoples of that part of the world, and notwithstanding the fact that they do not wish in their pride and proper spirit of nationality to be so absorbed and dominated. Germany is determined that the political power of the world shall belong to her. There have been such ambitions before. They have been in part realized, but never before have those ambitions been based upon so exact and precise and scientific a plan of domination.

May I not say that it is amazing to me that any group of persons should be so ill-informed as to suppose, as some groups in Russia apparently suppose, that any reforms planned in the interest of the people can live in the presence of a Germany powerful enough to undermine or overthrow them by intrigue or force? Any body of free men that compounds with the present German government is compounding for its own destruction. But that is not the whole of the story. Any man in America or anywhere else that supposes that the free industry and enterprise of the world can continue if the Pan-German plan is achieved and German power fastened upon the world is as fatuous as the dreamers in Russia. What I am opposed to is not the feeling of the pacifists, but their stupidity. My heart is with them, but my mind has a contempt for them. I want peace, but I know how to get it, and they do not.

You will notice that I sent a friend of mine, Colonel House, to Europe, who is as great a lover of peace as any man in the world; but I didn't send him on a peace mission yet. I sent him to take part in a conference as to how the war was to be won, and he knows, as I know, that that is the way to get peace, if you want it for more than a few minutes.

All of this is a preface to the conference that I have referred to with regard to what we are going to do. If we are true friends of freedom, our own or anybody else's, we will see that the power of this country and the productivity of this country is raised to its absolute maximum, and that absolutely nobody is allowed to stand in the way of it. When I say that nobody is allowed to stand in the way, I do not mean that they shall be prevented by the power of the government but by the power of the American spirit. Our duty, if we are to do this great thing and show America to be what we believe her to be—the greatest hope and energy of the world—is to stand together night and day until the job is finished.

While we are fighting for freedom, we must see, among other things, that labor is free; and that means a number of interesting things. It means, not only that we must do what we have declared our purpose to do—see that the conditions of labor are not rendered more onerous by the war—but also that we shall see to it that the instrumentalities by which the conditions of labor are improved are not blocked or checked. That we must do. That has been the matter about which I have taken pleasure in conferring from time to time with your president, Mr. Gompers. And, if I may be permitted to do so, I want to express my admiration of his patriotic courage, his large vision, and his statesmanlike sense of what has to be done. I like to lay my mind alongside of a mind that knows how to pull in harness. The horses that kick over the traces will have to be put in corral.

Now, to stand together means that nobody must interrupt the processes of our energy if the interruption can possibly be avoided without the absolute invasion of freedom. To put it concretely, that means this: nobody has a right to stop the processes of labor until all the methods of conciliation and settlement have been exhausted. And I might as well say right here that I am not talking to you alone. You sometimes stop the courses of labor, but there are others who do the same, and I believe I am speaking from my own experience, not only, but from the experience of others when I say that you are reasonable in a larger number of cases than the capitalists. I am not saying these things to them personally yet, because I have not had a chance, but they have to be said, not in any spirit of criticism, but in order to clear the atmosphere and come down to business. Everybody on both sides has now got to transact business, and a settlement is never impossible when both sides want to do the square and right thing.

Moreover, a settlement is always hard to avoid when the parties can be brought face to face. I can differ from a man much more radically when he is not in the room than I can when he is in the room, because then the awkward thing is he can come back at me and answer what I say. It is always dangerous for a man to have the floor entirely to himself. Therefore, we must insist in every instance that the parties come into each other's presence and there discuss the issues between them, and not separately in places which have no communication with each other. I always like to remind myself of a delightful saying of an Englishman of the past generation, Charles Lamb. He stuttered a little bit, and, once, when he was with a group of friends, he spoke very harshly of some man who was not present. One of his friends said: "Why, Charles, I didn't know that you knew so and so." "O-o-oh," he said, "I-I d-d-don't; I-I can't h-h-hate a m-m-man I-I know." There is a great deal of human nature, of very pleasant human nature, in the saying. It is hard to hate a man you know. I may admit, parenthetically, that there are some politicians whose methods I do not at all believe in, but they are jolly good fellows, and if they only would not talk the wrong kind of politics to me, I would love to be with them.

So it is all along the line, in serious matters and things less serious. We are all of the same clay and spirit, and we can get together if we desire to get together. Therefore, my counsel to you is this: let us show ourselves Americans by showing that we do not want to go off in separate camps or groups by ourselves, but that we want to cooperate with all other classes and all other groups in the common enterprise which is to release the spirits of the world from bondage. I would be willing to set that up as the final test of an American. That is the meaning of democracy. I have been very much distressed, my fellow citizens, by some of the things that have happened recently. The mob spirit is displaying itself here and there in this country. I have no sympathy with what some men are saying, but I have no sympathy with the men who take their punishment into their own hands. And I want to say to every man who does join such a mob that I do not recognize him as worthy of the free institutions of the United States. There are some organizations in this country whose object is anarchy and the destruction of law, but I would not meet their efforts by making myself partner in destroying the law. I despise and hate their purposes as much as any man, but I respect the ancient processes of justice; and I would be too proud not to see them done justice, however wrong they are.

So I want to utter my earnest protest against any manifestation of the spirit of lawlessness anywhere or in any cause. Why, gentlemen, look what it means. We claim to be the greatest democratic people in the world, and democracy means first of all that we can govern ourselves. If our men have not self-control, then they are not capable of that great thing which we call democratic government. A man who takes the law into his own hands is not the right man to cooperate in any formation or development of law and institutions, and some of the processes by which the struggle between capital and labor is carried on are processes that come very near to taking the law into your own hands. I do not mean for a moment to compare them with what I have just been speaking of, but I want you to see that they are mere gradations in this manifestation of the unwillingness to cooperate, and that the fundamental lesson of the whole situation is that we must not only take common counsel, but that we must yield to and obey common counsel. Not all of the instrumentalities for this are at hand. I am hopeful that in the very near future new instrumentalities may be organized by which we can see to it that various things that are now going on ought not to go on. There are various processes of the dilution of labor and the unnecessary substitution of labor and the bidding in distant markets and unfairly upsetting the whole competition of labor which ought not to go on. I mean now on the part of employers, and we must interject some instrumentality of cooperation by which the fair thing will be done all around. I am hopeful that some such instrumentalities may be devised, but whether they are or not, we must use those that we have and upon every occasion where it is necessary have such an instrumentality originated upon that occasion.

So, my fellow citizens, the reason I came away from Washington is that I sometimes get lonely down there. So many people come to Washington who know things that are not so, and so few people who know anything about what the people of the United States are thinking about. I have to come away and get reminded of the rest of the country. I have to come away and talk to men who are up against the real thing, and say to them, "I am with you if you are with me." And the only test of being with me is not to think about me personally at all, but merely to think of me as the expression for the time being of the power and dignity and hope of the United States.[2]

Printed in *Address of President Wilson to the American Federation of Labor Convention* . . . (Washington, 1917).
[2] There is a WWsh and a three-page WWT outline of this address in WP, DLC.

To Sidney Edward Mezes

Personal   [The White House]

My dear President Mezes: 12 November, 1917

Thank you for the preliminary and brief outline of the subjects to be dealt with in the inquiry.[1] It seems to me to suggest most of the chief topics that will have to be studied, though it occurs to me that there is one omission, though it may be only apparent.

It seems to me that it will be necessary to study the just claims of the larger states, like Russia and Austria, and Germany herself, to an assured access to the sea and the main routes of commerce not only, but to a reasonable access to the raw materials of the world which they themselves do not produce.

Of course, what we ourselves are seeking is a basis which will be fair to all and which will nowhere plant the seeds of such jealousy and discontent and restraint of development as would certainly breed fresh wars.

Cordially and sincerely yours,   [Woodrow Wilson]

CCL (WP, DLC).
    [1] See the Enclosure printed with S. E. Mezes to WW, Nov. 9, 1917, Vol. 44.

To John J. Mangan[1]

My dear Mr. Mangan: [The White House] 12 November, 1917

It certainly seems a work of supererogation to deny such extraordinarily silly rumors as that to which your letter of November tenth refers.[2] Of course, there is not one iota of truth in it, and nothing but malice can have suggested it. No disloyalty of any kind has touched the inner counsels of the administration or come anywhere near the seats of authority.

It seems particularly incredible that the rumor you speak of should have been for a moment credited, when Mr. Tumulty may be seen by anybody who cares to see him at the Executive Office on any day.   Very truly yours,   Woodrow Wilson

TLS (Letterpress Books, WP, DLC).
    [1] A public stenographer of Wilkes-Barre, Pa.
    [2] It is missing. However, it concerned a rumor that Tumulty had been imprisoned in Fort Leavenworth on a charge of treason. An extreme version of the rumor had Tumulty being shot as a spy. Tumulty issued a formal statement denouncing the stories on November 13. *New York Times*, Nov. 14, 1917. See also John Morton Blum, *Joe Tumulty and the Wilson Era* (Boston, 1951), pp. 134-35.

To Josephus Daniels, with Enclosure

Personal and Confidential.

My dear Daniels: The White House 12 November, 1917

Here is a letter which I have just received from Mr. Winston Churchill which I have read with close attention and a great deal of interest. I would be very much obliged if you would read it and then either confer with me about it or express to me in any other way you please your judgment about it.

Cordially and faithfully yours,   Woodrow Wilson

From Winston Churchill

My dear Mr. President,   London, October 22nd. 1917.

During the month or so I have been in Great Britain, as an independent observer, I have had unusual and unsought opportunities to acquire a point of view on several matters, and among these on the situation as it exists between our naval Service and the British Admiralty. I have been thrown with men engaged in many different activities, I have seen the Prime Minister and other members of the Cabinet and their assistants, I have talked with naval officers of all ranks and of both Services, of progressive and conservative tendencies, including Vice Admiral Sims and Admiral Jellicoe. The opinion I have gathered I believe to be an independent one, and I send it to you for what it is worth, trusting you will not think me presumptuous in so doing.

(1) I have become convinced that the criticism of the British Admiralty to the effect that it has been living from hand to mouth, from day to day, that it has been making no plans ahead, is justified. The several Sea Lords are of the conservative school, and they have been so encumbered with administrative and bureaucratic duties that they have found insufficient time to decide upon a future strategy. The younger and more imaginative element of that service has not been given a chance to show its powers, nor has it been consulted on matters of strategy. On the other hand the British Army, under pressure of necessity, has been compelled to adopt a policy of foresightedness, and is now apparently reaping the benefits due to long preparations and the infusion of new blood.

It goes without saying that any scheme of importance of an aggressive nature requires a due period of consideration by naval strategists with the aid of civilian experts, and usually involves the co-operation of sea and land forces. Such lack of cooperation has undoubtedly been a great source of weakness during the present war. And if any such scheme is adopted many months may be necessary for the collection of the material and personnel required to carry it to a successful conclusion. Sir Eric Geddes[1] is unquestionably an able man, and apparently willing to discard precedent when necessary. There are signs that he is feeling his way, and that he is encountering a certain opposition from the Sea Lords. Not very long ago he appointed a staff of young officers who had made reputations as strategists, but both in numbers and authority it has been inadequate, and the Sea Lords have refused to support

---

[1] Sir Eric Campbell Geddes, M.P., First Lord of the Admiralty since September 1917.

it and to give its suggestions serious consideration. Its deliberations have been held in a bedroom at the top of the Admiralty building. I am informed today, however, that this staff has been increased by the First Lord, and that henceforth it will be composed of two sections, one for strategy and one for material.

(2) Because all aggressive plans hitherto proposed have been found impracticable, it by no means follows that some plan may not be hit upon, especially now that we have the combined forces of the two nations to draw upon, that will accomplish the object desired of crippling or destroying the German Fleet, or of suppressing aggressively the actions of submarines. But the accomplishment of these objects depends, first, upon due deliberation by a body of men trained for such a purpose, and who have made strategy their specialty, and second, upon the preparation of the material means called for.

I would hasten to say that I am convinced that the lack of adoption of any such aggressive plan is in no way due to a want of initiative on the part of Admiral Sims. He has urged upon the Admiralty the value of such a staff as I have described, and he w[a]s given to understand by Sir Edward Carson, before the latter's retirement as First Lord, that a staff would be established. But the Admiralty is still suffering from the inertia of a tradition that clings to the belief that the British Navy still controls the seas, and can be made to move but slowly in a new direction. In addition to this Admiral Sims has had to feel his way, he has had to build up a staff for himself, and he has been overwhelmed with work. I have visited Queenstown, I have talked with the officers of our flotilla there, with those of Admiral Sims' staff both here and in France, and the opinion is unanimous that he is the ablest officer in our Service. Their admiration for his energy and talent is unbounded, their loyalty absolute. He is extremely popular both in England and France, and his relations with the Admiralty and the French Ministry of Marine are all that could be desired. The efficiency of our flotilla, the high seamanlike qualities of our officers and their ability to make their own repairs and to keep the destroyers constantly at sea has been the subject of universal praise among British officers, and is a source of pride to Americans here.

(3) Unquestionably the most important, indeed the essential thing still to be achieved is that of a partnership between our Service and the British. It must be a full partnership. There are many good reasons why this complete cooperation has not as yet been accomplished, in addition to the situation in the Admiralty which I have described. At 30 Grosvenor Gardens I have constantly seen Admiral Sims and his staff busy from early morning until late at night, on

account of the quantity of administrative work to be done. The
machine has to be kept moving. This hampers them to such an
extent that they find themselves, in regard to strategic matters,
precisely in the condition of the Admiralty,—with this exception.
There is scarcely an officer on that staff, including the Admiral
himself, who is not keenly alive to the necessity of cooperation with
the British Navy, of making plans a long way ahead. And we have
on that staff some of the ablest strategists in our service, including
Admiral Sims and Captain Twining. Officers like Captain Twining
are wasted upon office work, which could equally well be done by
men who have a peculiar gift for it.

It is generally agreed that what is needed is a combined staff of
American and British strategists and materiel officers to sit constantly together and exert their entire energies upon making plans
for the future conduct of the war. The Admiralty, in spite of their
backwardness in creating such a staff for themselves, would welcome such cooperation, and indeed several times have requested
it. Admiral Sims could not spare the officers. He has several times
requested our Department to send him more officers. But unless
the proper men are sent to such a staff, experts in their various
specialties, the situation would be made worse instead of better. If
more officers were sent to Admiral Sims by our Department, some
of the experts on his staff could then be released for duty on the
cooperative planning staff, as he has some of the best men in the
Service with him today. He would need about eight more officers,
in order to establish such a staff in addition to the necessary administrative staff.

I take the liberty of appending a list of officers qualified for such
service,[2] each with his particular qualification indicated, a list that
practically coincides with one I made out in Washington. These
men are known to our entire Service for their abilities. I trust you
will not think I am making any reflection on our Department for
not having sent all the officers needed, but naturally they have not
the same close view of the situation as one is enabled to obtain
here.

(4) I have become convinced that whatever strategic plans are
made for the future prosecution of the war should be made on this
side of the water, subject always, of course, to the approval of our
Government. The war will be won or lost in these waters, and any
aggressive policy must be staged here. New conditions will constantly arise that have to be dealt with in conjunction with the
British and other forces. Besides, the great difficulty of commu-

[2] Not printed.

nicating in all its aspects a certain situation by cable or letter to Washington has been proved. And I may also add what seems to me the most cogent argument for the establishment of our planning staff over here that we should not merely follow the suggestions of the British Admiralty, but act with them on an equal footing. The presence on the planning staff of an energetic group of American officers and perhaps of civilian experts would strengthen the hand of Sir Eric Geddes; while any scheme they might propose, backed by our own Department and by Admiral Sims, would impel the Sea Lords to adopt it. This tendency, I think, was illustrated by their agreement to our plan of a North Sea barrage of mines, a scheme to which they were formerly opposed. We are in a position to impel them to accept new ideas of value, or at least ideas worth the trying. It will do good to infuse into their councils American blood and a fresh American view point; but we cannot act with the ocean between us, and under the circumstances the British cannot send a staff over there.

(5) The present very slight preponderance of the British Fleet over the German gives cause for a certain anxiety. The proportion of British super-dreadnaughts to German is now about 24 to 19 only, and three of the British dreadnaughts have to be withdrawn to replace as many vessels of the KING EDWARD Class now protecting the south east coast and the channel from a possible raid with heavy vessels. The latter vessels must be put out of commission in order to obtain the personnel for the manning of new destroyers. It is therefore hoped that the request of the British for four of our coal burning dreadnoughts will be complied with.

The British are badly pressed for destroyers. In the past week only forty destroyers have been with the Grand Fleet in the North Sea, and at times none at all, whereas they should have one hundred and fifty in case of being called into action. Germany has one hundred and seventy which she can bring out with her fleet at her own time. While every cruiser the British fleet is capable of sparing is at work on convoy or other duty in various localities.

(6) At present there are not enough convoying ships to take care of the merchant vessels supplying western Europe with materials and food. Except by destroyers in the zone, no ships are convoyed from Europe westward; nor, save within the zone, are those convoyed that run from the United States to Gibraltar, and from South America and the Cape of Good Hope to Dakar, on the African coast. I am also informed that none are convoyed, except by destroyers in the zone, from Gilbraltar to the British Isles.

For the merchantmen now unprotected some forty odd additional cruisers are needed, including those required to make all the present convoys safe from German raiders of high gun power. The lighter armed cruisers are of no use against such raiders as evaded the North Sea patrols during the past week and sank two destroyers and many merchant ships off the coast of Norway. The success of the war depends largely, of course, upon our giving Europe supplies, and if all ships could be convoyed and properly defended the defeat of Germany would be much more certain.

For this purpose of convoy it has been recommended to our Navy Department that our older battleships should be used, since the matter is of such grave importance that even the interference in the training of crews on these ships would in Admiral Sims' opinion be justified. The old battleships could be made into convoying vessels by the simple operation of removing the smaller batteries and of sealing up the lower ports, leaving the larger batteries, which would be ample for driving off any possible raider; while temporary bulkheads of wood could be installed to render the ships safer against torpedoes. The argument against using such vessels for convoy purposes is that a large number of trained men might be lost if a ship were to be sunk, but it would only be necessary to man them with less than one half of the ordinary crews; less than one half of the usual engineer force, since they could be steaming at convoy speed, and gun crews sufficient to man the guns remaining in use. A few of the smaller guns could be mounted on the upper deck.

(7) I think it may be said with confidence that the various plans already submitted to the British Admiralty and which have originated on this side for aggressive action against the German Navy or for making landings in the rear of the German line are now impracticable, if indeed they were not always so. Some new plan must be devised. So also is the project of blocking in the German Fleet. I have discussed these plans with many officers, American and British, with a member of the British Cabinet and with Admiral Jellicoe, who showed me all the operations on a chart of the North Sea and the Baltic.

Along the Belgian coast the work of the British monitors has been all that could be hoped for, considerable damage has been done to the enemy, and a most ingenious plan of shelling the land batteries with the aid of a smoke screen and devices for locating these shore batteries have been adopted. Such devices were necessary because of the much greater range of the shore guns as compared with the guns ships can carry. Yet the monitors have done extremely close shooting at longer ranges than would have been thought possible— over 30,000 yards. Under the most trying circumstances barrages of mines have been laid by the British, in the darkness, close to the coast, both in the Baltic and in the North Sea. According to evidence from German sources, the submarines are having considerable difficulty in finding their way through these barrages.

The plan of blocking in the German Fleet by sinking ships in the channel is regarded by military men as impracticable on account of the greater range and accuracy of the shore batteries. The question of blocking these ports has several times been seriously considered by the Admiralty, and two years preparation was made on such a plan. But it was finally abandoned because the rise of tide was found to be too great, and there was nothing to prevent the Germans blowing away the superstructures. In addition to this, eighty ships would have to be sunk in correct position at the very close range of five miles from shore under the guns of the batteries.

The plan of landing a great force behind the German lines in Belgium for the purpose of seizing the naval bases there might once have been possible before it was so strongly fortified by the Germans. Now experts of the British Army are united in discouraging it. Something like 150 ships would be needed, and they cannot at the present time be spared, while a large army would have to be put ashore. While the project of capturing Heligoland may, I think, be dismissed. If the principle that ships are powerless against strong land batteries needed to be illustrated, the unfortunate Dardanelles campaign was a case in point. And even if Heligoland could be taken it could not be held against repeated airplane attacks, since it is only 25 or 30 miles from the mainland.

The British Government are sending me tomorrow across the Channel to the front in Belgium, and I expect to remain in France for three weeks and see our American camps under General Pershing. After that I shall return to England, where my address is Morgan Grenfell and Company.

I find Englishmen of all sorts looking to your leadership, and many prominent men have expressed the hope that you might break with precedent and come over here. And Mr. H. G. Wells told me the other day that yours was the only voice that expressed what the mass of the British people felt.

Sincerely yours,   Winston Churchill

TLS (J. Daniels Papers, DLC).

To Winston Churchill

My dear Mr. Churchill: [En Route] 12 November, 1917

This is just a line to acknowledge your important letter and memorandum of October twenty-second and to assure you that it will receive the most serious consideration of the Secretary of the Navy and myself. I will not write more now until I ascertain what is possible. My own thoughts have been running along very similar lines.

Pray do not apologize for your letter. It was a pleasure to hear from you, and I value your counsel.

I hope that you are keeping well and that what you are doing now is no burden.

Cordially and faithfully yours,   Woodrow Wilson

TLS (W. Churchill Papers, NhD).

To Newton Diehl Baker

My dear Mr. Secretary: [En route] 12 November, 1917

I have read with a great deal of interest the paper by Sir Stephenson Kent[1] which you were kind enough to send me enclosed in your letter of November tenth, and it gives me matter for grave thought. I would like very much to know your own opinion as to the wisdom and feasibility of what he suggests, and I should particularly like to know whether you know of any one man who would enjoy the confidence alike of labor and capital and who could organize this matter of adjustment very much as the Food and Fuel Administrations are organizing their efforts throughout the country.

Cordially and sincerely yours,   Woodrow Wilson

TLS (N. D. Baker Papers, DLC).
  [1] It is printed as an Enclosure with NDB to WW, Nov. 10, 1917, Vol. 44.

From William Lea Chambers

My dear Mr. President: Washington November 12, 1917.

Referring to your letter to me of October 26th, 1917,[1] permit me to report that I have lost no time between engagements in actual mediation of pending cases to present the subject matter to railroad officials and to the executives of the six labor organizations immediately connected with railroad transportation. I believe I am prepared to say that the railroads will be agreeable to the principle of mediation and arbitration as suggested in your letter; also that the executives of two of the railroad labor organizations are agreeable.

At a conference held in Cleveland, Ohio, on last Friday, the 9th, partial conclusions were reached as you will see from the memorandum I am enclosing,[2] which is signed by the executives of the

Brotherhood of Locomotive Engineers, Brotherhood of Locomotive Firemen & Enginemen, Order of Railway Conductors, and Brotherhood of Railroad Trainmen and attested by my signature. From this memorandum you will observe that they have agreed that there shall be no strike or interruption of their relations with the railroads until ample opportunity shall have been afforded the United States Board of Mediation and Conciliation to bring about if possible an amicable agreement. This is a long step forward for these organizations, as they always and consistently have resisted any proposal that would commit them to compulsory mediation. It is in reality quite a victory along the lines I have been working; but you will observe that these executives are not agreeable to commit their organizations to that part of your proposal which would bind them in advance to submit to arbitration in controversies which have failed of settlement in mediation, and a personal interview with you at which they will be agreeable to discuss with you any plan of adjustment of the subject-matter is requested. You will observe that they suggest either Wednesday or Thursday, the 22nd or 23rd of November, as a date for such conference, and that any subsequent date suggested by you will be agreeable to them. Several of them had engagements which occupied all of their time up to the 21st.

Perhaps you would wish a personal conference with me at an earlier date and I can answer your summons at any time, holding all other engagements subordinate to your commands in the premises. Permit me to suggest, however, that you inform me at your convenience whether the date suggested by these executives for the conference is suitable to you and if not that you fix a date that would be satisfactory. I need not urge upon you the extreme importance of this subject, but may I not be permitted to tell you that there are conditions broadcast in the railroad world that are liable to break loose disastrously almost any moment, which I am sure the proposed conference with you will avert?

Very respectfully, W. L. Chambers

TLS (WP, DLC).
  [1] WW to W. L. Chambers, Oct. 26, 1917, Vol. 44.
  [2] Not printed. Chambers describes it well.

From William Gibbs McAdoo

My dear Mr. President: Washington November 12, 1917.

For some time past Dr. Rupert Blue, Surgeon-General of the Public Health Service, has, under my direction, been carrying forward an investigation into health and sanitary conditions in war industries and into the experience of European nations in safe-guarding the health of workers in these industries.

He has now made a preliminary report, which I append, and which I heartily approve.[1] I have been in touch with the situation for some time, and have come to the conclusion that it is necessary to the proper and effective conduct of the war that the Public Health Service undertake the supervision of health and sanitary conditions in manufacturing plants engaged in war work and among the workers themselves.

It is undoubtedly true that in the desire to produce a maximum output of war supplies in some European countries at the outbreak of the war there, industries were speeded up to the breaking point, sanitary precautions ordinarily enforced were disregarded, and the supply of industrial labor was unduly drawn upon with the result that lessened production and the occurrence of preventable deaths brought the matter so urgently to the attention of European governments that measures of governmental supervision and control were put into effect.

As you will observe by the report of Dr. Blue, there is every indication that like conditions requiring governmental supervision are arising with us. In the United States there has already been an unprecedented enlargement of industries on account of the war, and, with the increasing shortage of labor, there is every probability that the health of workers will suffer unless adequate measures are taken for its protection.

As Dr. Blue points out, the Public Health Service is already charged by Congress with the duty of investigating insanitary conditions, and, therefore, it should be comparatively easy to broaden this work so that effective control may be established and the health of industrial workers engaged on war contracts properly safeguarded, both for their own protection and to increase the efficiency of the United States in the war.

The definite recommendations of Dr. Blue are that the control of the situation should include (1) the sanitary supervision of premises, buildings and processes in industrial plants engaged in supplying war materials to the Federal Government; (2) medical supervision of workers in industrial plants; (3) the institution of a campaign of education in personal hygiene; and (4) the preparation of minimum hygienic standards for specific industries. He also suggests that there be included in Government contracts for war supplies a provision that only those supplies be accepted which shall have been produced under sanitary conditions prescribed by the Secretary of the Treasury. I have also in mind the advisability of extending this control to plants engaged in producing war supplies for the Entente Allies.

To bring about the proper cooperation along these lines, I have in mind, subject to your approval, calling a conference immediately of representatives of State, local and municipal health authorities, and of the departments having to do with war contracts, so the necessities of the situation may be explained and the best advice on the specific steps to be taken obtained. It may be that legislation may be required. Certainly a comparatively small additional appropriation will be needed.

If I receive your approval, I shall proceed immediately to call such a conference, and organize this work upon a comprehensive scale so that no time may be lost and the United States saved from the difficulties and dangers which confronted several of the European nations as a result of the lack of the proper foresight in this very important question.   Very sincerely yours,   W G McAdoo

TLS (WP, DLC).
    [1] R. Blue, "Memorandum: Desirable Federal Activities in the Field of the Hygiene and Sanitation of Industries during War," c. Nov. 6, 1917, TI MS (WP, DLC). McAdoo summarizes it well.

From Thomas Watt Gregory

Dear Mr. President: Washington, D. C. November 12, 1917.

I received yours of the 1st with attached memorandum made by Mr. Rudolph Forster[1] giving the details of a verbal statement made to him by Mr. William Bayard Hale on October 31st, Mr. Hale complaining of very outrageous treatment of his stenographer and of his family by investigating agents of the Government. Thinking that perhaps you did not retain a copy of Mr. Forster's memorandum, I herewith return it to you, keeping a copy for my own files.

I have had the matter very carefully investigated, even to the extent of having the head of my Bureau of Investigation go to New York and personally interview Mr. Hale and his stenographer. The facts developed are as follows:

First. No representative of my Bureau had made any investigation of Mr. Hale, or had had any relations whatever with his stenographer, up to the time I sent the head of my Bureau to New York last week.

Second. Mr. Hale's stenographer gave a very detailed statement of her experience with Mr. J. L. Johnson, a secret service agent of the Treasury Department. This was verified by Mr. Flynn, who is in charge of the secret service of the Treasury Department, to the extent of his stating that Mr. Johnson was one of his regular agents and had been engaged in the investigation of Mr. Hale.

Third. As the acts complained of involve a member of the secret service of the Treasury Department I thought it proper not to pursue the investigation further, as such course might be resented by the Treasury Department. I think I should state, however, that while the story told by Mr. Hale's stenographer to the head of my Bureau of Investigation in a general way substantiated the charges made by Mr. Hale, it did not sustain the statement of Mr. Hale that an attempt was made to seduce his stenographer, and that a pistol was drawn upon her.

Fourth. In case you wish the matter further investigated, I assume that you will call upon the Secretary of the Treasury to have the acts of his agent investigated and reported to you. The report made by the head of my Bureau of Investigation is quite lengthy, but can be submitted to you in case you care to glance over it.

Unless you have issued some executive orders with which I am not familiar, the investigation of Mr. Hale by a secret service agent of the Treasury Department was not only without authority of law but in defiance of the act of Congress limiting the activities of that service.

I think I should also say that on November 2nd Mr. Hale wrote a letter to Mr. Rudolph Forster[2] purporting to reduce to writing his previous conversation with Mr. Forster. Mr. Hale likewise sent me a copy of his letter to Mr. Forster and its statements differ in some very material respects from the memorandum of the conversation made by Mr. Forster which you sent to me with your letter of November 1st. As Mr. Forster has a copy of Mr. Hale's letter to him of November 2nd I presume it is not necessary for me to send you a copy.   Faithfully yours,   T. W. Gregory

TLS (WP, DLC).
[1] See WW to TWG, with Enclosure, Nov. 1, 1917, Vol. 44.
[2] It is printed as Enclosure II with WW to R. Forster, Nov. 7, 1917, Vol. 44.

From Newton Diehl Baker

Dear Mr. President: Washington. November 12, 1917.

I am very much reassured by your note of the 8th with regard to the Army and Navy football game.[1] Secretary Daniels and I last spring decided not to have the Army and Navy baseball game, deeming it an inappropriate exhibition of inter-service sport during war time. When the question of the football game came up, I felt even more strongly about it and wrote the Superintendent of the Academy that the West Point boys could not participate in such a game. Secretary Daniels and I talked it over and reached the same conclusion about it. Since then a very great deal of pressure has been brought to bear both by members of the services and various Senators and Representatives. My mind has never wavered on the subject and I have declined to allow the Academy to participate; so that there will be no football game this fall.

I shall take the liberty of showing your note to Secretary Daniels, as I feel sure he will be pleased, as I am, to know that we have anticipated your sentiment correctly in the matter.

Respectfully,   Newton D. Baker

TLS (WP, DLC).
 [1] WW to NDB, Nov. 8, 1917 (second letter of that date), Vol. 44.

From Robert Lansing, with Enclosure

My dear Mr President,   [Washington] Nov. 12, 1917.

This is an unusually illuminating review of the German political situation prepared by Mr. Grew as a part of his weekly report on the Central Powers. I think that you will find it well worth reading and so take the liberty of calling it to your attention.

Faithfully yours   Robert Lansing

ALS (WP, DLC).

E N C L O S U R E

No. 19 SECTION I.   November 5, 1917.
THE NEW CHANCELLOR.

While it is yet too early, from the fragmentary comment which has reached us from Berlin, to interpret the full significance of the change in the chancellorship, one point stands out with startling clearness: autocracy has met its first signal defeat; it has effected what the German military bulletins would have announced as a "strategic retirement" and has permitted a radical and unprecedented step forward to be taken in the political development of internal affairs in the German Empire. This step bears careful analysis.

Von Bethmann-Hollweg fell as a result of appeasing neither the Conservatives nor the Liberals, or rather of trying to appease both and finally failing owing to their ever increasing divergence. His downfall left open a gap which could be filled only by the Kaiser. Although the Reichstag caused Bethmann's retirement, it had no one to substitute for him and no majority party which could even determine upon a nominee. The choice of a successor remained with the Kaiser alone and such difficulty did he experience in making this choice that three hours before the final decision was made, it is said that the name of Michaelis had not even been brought up for consideration. There seemed to be no outstanding figure in German politics fitted to fill the chancellorship, at least none that combined ability and strength with a definite policy acceptable to a Reichstag which itself was ruled by conflicting and contradictory emotions. The Kaiser took the only course left open and appointed a politically unknown and hence irreproachable, man, Michaelis.

Michaelis, the first citizen Chancellor, untried, unversed in politics, free from all party affiliations or support, took up his monumental task on July 16th. Almost immediately the uncertain policies of the various Reichstag factions seemed to crystalize into clear-cut, well-defined lines. Each party realized that an unknown factor was coming into play and that this was the moment to force its hand and bring the new Chancellor into its own party group. The Reichstag peace resolution of July 19th was the result.[1] The oft reiterated principles of Scheidemann and the majority Socialists had at last taken root in the center of the House, and the Catholic Centrists, the pivot of the Reichstag, through their spokesman, Erzberger, swung the whole party to the Left. Though undoubtedly inspired by the Vatican, this shift was largely spontaneous and was the prelude to the formation of a parliamentary bloc which had as its guiding motive certain liberal principles to which the majority of the German people fully acquiesced. A rift appeared in the National Liberal party and a considerable section of this powerful quasi-conservative faction split away from the leadership of Stresemann[2] to join the newly formed majority bloc.

It was this bloc which confronted Michaelis from the outset of his chancellorship. On the one hand were the military autocrats, on the other the liberals. A decision for either side meant facing concerted opposition. So, like von Bethmann-Hollweg before him, he tried to temporize and avoid the issue. In his opening speech he accepted the principles laid down in the Reichstag Resolution, adding, however, that he accepted them "according to his own interpretation" of them. This proviso allowed broad discussion. The pan-Germans and annexationists at once juggled with the wording of the Resolution and claimed that it in no way bound the Chancellor to an acceptance of the liberal policy. Increasing pressure was brought to bear on him and the next three months of his

[1] About this resolution, see P. M. Warburg to EMH, July 15, 1917, n. 1, Vol. 43.
[2] Gustav Stresemann.

supremacy show acts of an inconsistent nature, calculated to appease first one and then the other faction. He tied the question of electoral reforms into a knot which could not be untied according to his scheme until next April, counteracting this by appointing two members of the Reichstag, Spahn and Müller-Meiningen[3] to ministerial posts. He did nothing to lift the political censorship or to alleviate conditions accruing from the original declaration that "a state of siege" existed in Germany. However, Kühlmann was appointed Secretary of State for Foreign Affairs and the German answer to the Pope's peace proposal was an obvious concession to the majority bloc. Thus Michaelis wavered, hoping to stall for time until some definite policy should happily fall in his way to satisfy all parties.

Michaelis was not an acute enough politician to carry on this situation long. The pan-Germans, turning to good account the food for insidious propaganda contained in the President's reply to the Pope, developed their newly-born Vaterland party into a semi-official movement and brought pressure to bear not only in the Army but on many civilians employed in government industries to accept their program of annexations and war indemnities as a proper retort to one who dared to interfere in their domestic politics. This was accomplished with the knowledge and active cooperation of certain military and government officials. It was strongly resented by the Socialists, and this resentment finally took form in an interpellation in the Reichstag on October 5th.[4] This Reichstag sitting marked the beginning of the end. In vain did von Stein,[5] Minister of War, Helfferich, Vice-Chancellor, and Westarp, the Junker leader,[6] try to explain the Government's attitude toward the Vaterland party. The evidence presented by Landsberg,[7] a social-democrat, and Haase, an extreme socialist, was too strong, and the ire of the majority bloc soon gave it a menacing complexion. Michaelis did not attend the session and his representative, Helfferich, tactless, arrogant and always mistaken in sizing up a crisis, was unable or unwilling

[3] Peter Spahn, judge and leader of the Center party, who had become Prussian Minister of Justice on August 5, 1917; Ernst Müller, called Müller-Meiningen after his election to the Reichstag from Meiningen as a member of the Liberal Peoples party in 1898. Grew is in error: Müller had not held a cabinet post of any kind up to this time. Perhaps he was thinking of Paul von Krause of the National Liberal party who became Imperial Minister of Justice at the same time that Spahn received his Prussian post. See Klaus Epstein, *Matthias Erzberger and the Dilemma of German Democracy* (Princeton, N. J., 1959), p. 212.

[4] Actually, this interpellation, which attacked the apparent connivance of the government in spreading the propaganda of the Fatherland party, was made on October 6. It is discussed in the following paragraph. See also John G. Williamson, *Karl Helfferich, 1872-1924: Economist, Financier, Politician* (Princeton, N. J., 1971), pp. 243-44.

[5] Gen. Hermann Christlieb Matthäus von Stein.

[6] Kuno, Count von Westarp, leader of the Conservative party.

[7] Otto Landsberg.

to accord the Reichstag an explanation or even the courtesy which might have smoothed over the situation.

It was accordingly a stormy Reichstag that Michaelis had to confront on October 9th. Perhaps he knew only too well the music he would have to face, for he had carefully prepared a political coup intended to divert the attention of the members from the dangerous question of government aid to the Vaterland Party. On the secret testimony of sailors, who were subsequently shot as traitors, three independent socialists were openly accused of knowledge of and conspiracy in the mutinous uprisings in the fleet during the month of August.[8] Von Capelle[9] himself, the Secretary of the Navy, furnished the details of the indictment. The effect of this thunderbolt was surprising. Instead of producing a wedge of discord between the parties of the Left, it solidified that side of the House into a unit and brought forth a series of sharp protests against Michaelis both for the injustice of the attack, the method of attack, and the attempted evasion of the question under discussion. It was a coup indeed, but one that brought about the downfall of the Chancellor.

Although the Reichstag adjourned soon after this heated session, not to reconvene until December, the party leaders and press of the majority bloc continued the attacks against the Chancellor. Never before during the war had the German press been so outspoken against a Government official. But in fairness to Michaelis it must be said that the criticism was directed against him as a vacillating, politically incapable but honest and patriotic vassal of an impossible Government, rather than as an unscrupulous trickster and clever politician. His downfall was inevitable.

When it became evident that Michaelis must go, the two men most prominently mentioned as his successor were Buelow and Kuehlmann, both eligible owing to their political ability and their experience in foreign affairs. But Buelow had permanently sacrificed the confidence of the Reichstag at the time of his downfall from the chancellorship in 1909, while Kuehlmann's appointment appeared to be out of the question owing to the opposition of the Conservatives. The problem was to find a man who could hold the

[8] Actually, the only "uprising" occurred on the morning of August 2, when some 600 members of the crew of S.M.S. *Prinzregent Luitpold*, at anchor at Wilhelmshaven, left the ship for approximately three hours as a protest against the punishment meted out to several of their colleagues as a result of earlier protests against poor food and living conditions. As later research has shown, it was the naval officer corps which, in an attempt to cover up their mishandling of the incidents, blew the affair up into a so-called mutiny involving the entire German fleet, allegedly organized by sailors who had the backing of members of the Independent Social Democratic party. The badly botched handling of the affair by both the navy and the government laid the groundwork for the much more serious mutiny of October and November 1918. See Daniel Horn, *The German Naval Mutinies of World War I* (New Brunswick, N. J., 1969), pp. 94-184.

[9] Eduard von Capelle.

parties of the Left in line, but without representing too much of a concession to them or too much of a break with the existing system. Count von Hertling was selected.

Heralded as a thorough Pan-Germanist and Junker, conservative by inheritance and nature and opposed to parliamentarianism, Hertling has apparently been able, whether through policy or conviction, to swing around half the circle of political faith to a position satisfactory to both liberal and democratic elements in the Reichstag, while leaving the Conservatives anything but pleased with the situation. At this distance, so radical an evolution in a statesman 74 years of age savors of something not quite genuine and induces one to wonder whether the leopard can really change his spots so effectually. For the moment, Count von Hertling appears to have made almost revolutionary concessions to the majority program, not only in his reported inclusion of parliamentary Ministers in his Cabinet, Friedrich von Payer,[10] Progressive; Friedberg,[11] National Liberal; Dove,[12] a Radical, and probably others, but also by his acceptance of the following demands of the Reichstag majority:

1. That Prussian electoral reform[13] be carried out.

2. That political censorship and the state of seige be abolished or mitigated.

3. That the foreign policy be conducted on the basis of the German reply to the Pope's peace note.

For the first time in German history, the candidacy of the new Chancellor was submitted to the Reichstag for its approval. But pending von Hertling's agreement with the party leaders, the press of the Reichstag majority parties, reflecting the attitude of the leaders in the inter-party conferences, adopted a distinctly hostile tone. In fact, Hertling's acceptance of the chancellorship, which he apparently made conditional upon promised support in the Reichstag, at one time seemed very doubtful. Following his conferences with the party leaders, during which von Hertling apparently acceded to their demands, this hostile tone of the press was altered to one of sceptical gratification, sceptical owing to Hertling's past antagonism to parliamentarianism. It was doubtless this scepticism which led the Socialists to refuse to bind themselves through the acceptance of a ministerial post for one of their members.

[10] Vice-Chancellor.   [11] Robert Friedberg, Prussian Deputy Prime Minister.
[12] Heinrich Dove. He did not receive a cabinet post.
[13] That is, reform of Prussia's three-class suffrage law, which dated back to 1849. Under its provisions, voters were divided into three classes according to the amounts of taxes which they paid, and their votes were weighted according to a specific formula. Hertling had just introduced a bill in the lower house of the Prussian Diet for the adoption of the Imperial equal-suffrage system. See Reinhard Patemann, *Der Kampf um die preußische Wahlreform im Ersten Weltkrieg* (Düsseldorf, 1964); see also P. A. Stovall to RL, May 4, 1918, n. 1.

The gratification of the liberal elements of the German people and press is based upon the assumption that he is entering office as the representative of the Reichstag majority rather than upon his own personality, and he evidently will last only so long as he conducts his administration as the representative of this majority. His success will depend largely upon the Reichstag majority's ability to hold together and agree upon a policy which Hertling will be willing and able to represent. In this he appears to have started well, but there will be pitfalls ahead which it will take all his ingenuity to pass successfully.

The Pan-Germanists and the large business newspapers have answered the appointment of Hertling and his concessions with loud denunciations of the change to the parliamentary system, wherein they see gross violations of the rights and dignity of the Crown. They are furthermore dubious as to his future attitude towards the question of peace terms and the belief that he will now be inclined to make peace on a basis which will permit later a rapprochement with the Western powers. His views regarding Belgium, however, at least as late as his programme speech before the Bavarian Diet on October 23, are not those which the Entente powers would be likely to find acceptable. These views intimated that a settlement of the problem of Belgium would be obtainable under an "offer to guarantee that this land in the future be no longer the object of the means of hostile intrigues," meaning that Belgium's ante bellum policy must be altered in favor of Germany, presumably by some checks inconsistent with its full independence.

Whether von Hertling is regarded as the right man to lead Germany into and through the eventual peace negotiations, or whether his appointment is considered only as of a stop gap nature, to tide over the present crisis in domestic affairs, his appointment is in any case counted upon to serve important purposes. First, there is the desire to remove all causes of friction between Berlin and Munich, both military and political. Bavarians have complained that their troops have been called upon for the hardest service, while Prussians have been spared. If any feeling of that sort persists in Bavaria, and if there are any lingering jealousies not only about the conduct of the war, but about political management, then the choice of the Bavarian Minister-President as German Chancellor must have a soothing and uniting effect. Count von Hertling himself seems to attach a significance of this kind to his selection. Second, the new Chancellor is a Roman Catholic; he enjoys the confidence of the powerful Center Party and he furthermore possesses relations with the Vatican which may well be useful in further efforts on the part of Germany to use the Pope as a tool in her peace manoeuvres. On the whole his appointment is not so surprising as it may at first have appeared.

In describing the solution of the recent political crisis, Herr Erzberger, the leader of the Center Party and therefore at present the most powerful force in the Reichstag, is reported to have said: "While the troops of the Central Powers were forcing their way across the Tagliamento, Germany at home quietly crossed the political Rubicon and in the space of five days changed from an autocracy into a democracy. This has been the most momentous week since the founding of the Empire and its achievements represent a permanent political gain for the German people. In view of the July and October happenings, the majority leaders were convinced of the hopelessness of permitting the old system to prevail. Through the Chief of the Emperor's Civil Cabinet,[14] they imparted their convictions to the Crown, urging the imperative need of a coordinated, cohesive governmental policy in foreign and domestic issues, and harmonious governmental collaboration with the Reichstag, during the war at least." Herr Erzberger then told how Count von Hertling reserved his decision to accept the chancellorship until he had conferred with the party leaders. On the advice of the latter, the Emperor's plan for separating the chancellorship and the presidency of the Prussian ministry, he said, had been dropped. Von Kuehlmann had also participated in the conferences, Erzberger said, and had urged the need of instituting a parliamentary procedure, because it was the only solution of the crisis and because of the unfavorable impression that would be made abroad if the current attempt failed to succeed.

From all reports, von Hertling, von Kuehlmann and the majority leaders are now in harmony with regard to both foreign and domestic issues and the arrangement appears to have the sanction of the Emperor who, whether voluntarily or against his will, has given the Chancellor a free hand. The Clerical Party (the Center) possesses the chancellorship, the Progressive Party will in all probability be awarded the post of Vice-Chancellor and one other important secretaryship, while the National Liberals will be represented in the vice-presidency of the Prussian cabinet. The Socialist Party, while renouncing office for itself, definitely demanded the inclusion of radical deputies in both the Imperial and Prussian cabinets and

---

[14] Rudolf von Valentini. The three cabinets—military, naval, and civil—were relics of the era of Frederick the Great. Their formal function was to advise William II in his capacity as King of Prussia on appointments and promotions. In practice, Valentini and the Chief of the Naval Cabinet, Admiral Georg Alexander von Müller, offered advice on many other matters. However, none of the cabinets had any formal authority over the civil ministries or the armed forces of Germany.

agreed to support the administration if it should keep its promises. Otherwise, according to Scheidemann, the party would fight the new government as it did the Michaelis regime. Once equal rights in Prussia were granted and control of the Reichstag majority over the composition of the Government and its policy were established, Scheidemann is reported to have said, there would be no excuse for refusing to negotiate peace with Germany on the pretext that it was ruled autocratically. Evidently the President's reply to the Pope is having its effect in the heart of German politics.

While awaiting interesting developments at the next meeting of the Reichstag, called by the Chancellor for November 22, a fortnight earlier than previously planned, we may be assured that the liberal movement in Germany, which has steadily gained momentum during the last few months, has achieved a very material victory and that new conditions for which the advocates of parliamentarianism have long been striving have at least temporarily been established. Whether these new conditions will keep pace with the increasing demands of the liberal and socialistic elements in the country remains to be seen. As power begets thirst for power, so we may be sure that the Reichstag majority and the people it represents will not be content with one step forward but will soon strike out for further capitulations from the Crown and a further expansion of democratic influence in the government of the country. The wedge between autocracy and democracy has been inserted; the rift is already visible; will it widen naturally with the momentum already started, or will it eventually encounter unyielding material which only the axe of revolution can disperse? It is the political checks and not the advances which we shall find of particular significance in the future, possibly, indeed, within the next few months.

THE DRIVE INTO ITALY.

Perhaps the most significant feature of the recent political events in Germany, described above, is that they happened in spite of, not because of, the successful drive into Italy. It is the moral effect even more than the military results of this success which must be taken into consideration, and one of the obvious purposes of the drive was to strengthen the power of the German military party. If then, the military party in spite of its Italian success was obliged to make political concessions of a far-reaching nature and if the time has arrived when such a success exerts no influence on domestic political affairs in Germany, the power of the military party must logically be considered as on the wane.

Another purpose of the drive was to stimulate the German people out of the war-lethargy, dissatisfaction and unrest which continued and increasing economic hardship is inducing. The German Government understands the psychology of the man in the street, and especially the woman in the street, in Germany somewhat better than it understands the psychology of other nations. They must have their minds taken off their troubles by distraction. This policy of providing suitable distractions at regular intervals has been only too obvious throughout the course of the war. The Russian drive, the Servian and Roumanian drives, the unsuccessful attack on Verdun, no less than the Chancellor's peace proposals of December 12, 1916, and the inauguration of the unrestricted submarine warfare on January 31, 1917, were used successively by the Government to take the peoples' minds off their difficulties and the politicians' minds off their agitations at moments embarrassing for the Government and hence embarrassing for the military party. The Italian drive was undoubtedly prepared with that end in view, but whatever effect it may have had on the people, it seems to have had singularly little effect on the politicians.

But there were still other ends to accomplish and not the least of them was to bring Austria back into the fold, from which she was, if not actually straying, at least longing for freedom. There is little question in our minds that Austria has for some time been far from satisfied with her German ally, less and less in sympathy with her methods of conducting warfare and less and less eager to carry on the conflict. By rushing to Austria's support and not only saving Trieste but pushing far down into Italian territory, Germany has re-cemented the alliance of the Central Powers.

Nor are these the only political elements in the Italian drive. Every spectacular military success increases the influence of the pacifists and pro-German elements abroad; it would be counted upon to stimulate dissension among the Italian people, no less than to strengthen peace propaganda in other countries. Just as surely, therefore, as the first German peace proposals of a year ago followed hard on the heels of the successful drive into Roumania, and the Pope's note of last summer synchronized with what the German military leaders probably believed to be the high water mark of their submarine campaign, just so surely is this drive into Italy intended to create an atmosphere favorable for further steps looking toward peace and just so surely may the steps be expected to materialize when the end of the drive, if finally successful, shall have been reached.   J.C.G.

Offset MS (WP, DLC).

Joseph Patrick Tumulty to Lillian D. Wald

Personal

My dear Miss Wald: The White House November 12, 1917

With reference to your recent telegram,[1] the President directs me to send to you for your information the enclosed copy of a self-explanatory letter from Commissioner Gardiner.[2]

Sincerely yours,   J P Tumulty

TLS (L. D. Wald Papers, NN).
  [1] It is missing.
  [2] A TC of W. G. Gardiner to WW, Nov. 9, 1917, printed as an Enclosure with WW to JPT, Nov. 10, 1917, Vol. 44.

To Thomas Watt Gregory

[The White House]

My dear Mr. Attorney General: 13 November, 1917

Thank you for your letter of November ninth about the proposed commandeering of the plants and properties of the Pacific Telephone and Telegraph Company.[1] The opinion is expressed just in the form that is most serviceable to me and I am very glad to have it. I took it for granted that your conclusion would be what it is.

Cordially and sincerely yours,   Woodrow Wilson

TLS (Letterpress Books, WP, DLC).
  [1] TWG to WW, Nov. 9, 1917, Vol. 44.

To Frank Clark[1]

Personal & Confidential W.W.[2]

My dear Mr. Clark: [The White House] 13 November, 1917

I can hardly believe that you propose in seriousness what you propose in your letter of November ninth.[3] Could anything in the history of the United States or in history anywhere justify our encouraging one nation to invade or take possession of the territory of another? I think you must have made the proposition only in half earnest.

I have not lost faith in the Russian outcome by any means. Russia, like France in a past century, will no doubt have to go through deep waters but she will come out upon firm land on the other side and her great people, for they are a great people, will in my opinion take their proper place in the world.

Very sincerely yours,   Woodrow Wilson

TLS (Letterpress Books, WP, DLC).
  [1] Democratic congressman from Florida.
  [2] WWhw.
  [3] It is missing.

Two Letters to Joseph Patrick Tumulty

Dear Tumulty: [The White House, Nov. 13, 1917]

Thank you for letting me see this.[1] You may be sure I will be on my guard.   The President.

TL (WP, DLC).
  [1] A. Brisbane to JPT, Nov. 9, 1917, TLS (WP, DLC). Brisbane asserted that the "Committee on Alcohol of the Council of National Defense" (actually, the Subcommittee on Alcoholic Control of the Committee on Hygiene and Sanitation) was composed of avowed advocates of national prohibition. They were, he charged, circulating to manufacturers throughout the country a questionnaire deliberately designed to prove that the consumption of alcoholic beverages of all kinds was impairing the efficiency of American labor. The replies, he asserted, would be used to bring pressure upon Wilson to act immediately to ban the use of all alcoholic beverages. He enclosed a copy of the questionnaire which indeed was couched in very general language, referring only to "alcohol consumption," "alcoholic beverages," and "drink consumption," and which made no distinction between light wines and beer and distilled beverages.

Dear Tumulty: [The White House, Nov. 13, 1917]

I think the best thing to do with this is for you to acknowledge it and to say that it has been placed in my hands and will of course receive my most respectful consideration.[1]

I think it would be wroth [worth] while adding that the treatment of the women picketeers has been grossly exaggerated and misrepresented.   The President.

TL (WP, DLC).
  [1] Mary Ritter (Mrs. Charles Austin) Beard to WW, Nov. 12, 1917, TLS (WP, DLC), enclosing two resolutions, T MSS (WP, DLC). The letter and resolutions, all written on behalf of a committee of 1,000 working women of New York, requested that Wilson immediately endorse the amendment for woman suffrage and take action to free the suffrage pickets imprisoned in the Occoquan workhouse. One resolution declared that the jailed women were given food "such as no human being should be forced to eat"; were "in danger of contracting syphilis and gonorrhea, and of having their health permanently injured"; and that some of the prisoners, "notably, Alice Paul," were "in immediate danger of losing their lives because of these conditions."

To Frank Lyon Polk

My dear Mr. Polk: The White House 13 November, 1917

I take real pleasure in sending you a signed photograph for Lord Reading and am very much pleased that he should desire it.
         Cordially and sincerely yours,   Woodrow Wilson

TLS (F. L. Polk Papers, CtY).

To John H. Donlin[1]

[The White House] 13 November, 1917

Your telegram of yesterday[2] has cheered me very much and I hope that you will convey my sincere thanks and appreciation to those associated with you in the patriotic action of which you give me information. You may be sure that there will be all possible cooperation at this end.   Woodrow Wilson.

T telegram (Letterpress Books, WP, DLC).
    [1] President of the Building Trades Department of the American Federation of Labor.
    [2] It is missing. However, it obviously dealt with Donlin's efforts to persuade striking workers in the building trades to return to work on federal construction projects pending a conference with officials in Washington to settle their grievances. Both A.F.L. and governmental leaders were especially concerned with strikes on shipyard construction projects in the Boston area, chiefly over the issue of the open shop. *New York Times*, Nov. 14 and 15, 1917.

To Kate Benedict Freeman Carter[1]

My dear Mrs. Carter: [The White House] 13 November, 1917

It was very gracious of you to write to tell me of your husband's death.[2] I had heard of it, of course, before your letter arrived and heard of it with unaffected grief. May I not express to you my sincerest sympathy and say with what pleasure I recall our association in the old days at Princeton? I am sure that if the recollection of fine service conscientiously rendered can comfort you, you will in part be comforted.

Cordially and sincerely yours,   Woodrow Wilson

TLS (Letterpress Books, WP, DLC).
    [1] Mrs. Jesse Benedict Carter, wife of Wilson's former colleague at Princeton, who had died on July 20, 1917.
    [2] Her letter is missing.

To James B. Regan[1]

My dear Mr. Regan: [The White House] 13 November, 1917

Thank you very warmly for your thought of me as expressed in your generous action in sending me the cases of wine. You are much more generous than I deserve.

And thank you very warmly indeed for the telegram of this morning[2] which I have just received. Your friendship is always thoughtful and most cheering to me.

Cordially and sincerely yours,   Woodrow Wilson

TLS (Letterpress Books, WP, DLC).
    [1] Proprietor of the Hotel Knickerbocker in New York. He was a friend of Tumulty.
    [2] It is missing.

From Edward Nash Hurley

Dear Mr. President: Washington November 13, 1917.

Secretary Baker has told me that you expect to call him, Secretary Daniels and myself into a conference with you some time this week. As I understand the conference will relate to some conflicting calls upon the Shipping Board by the Food Administration, the War Industries Board, and the War Department, I thought that it might be well to have before you the situation as viewed by the Shipping Board. In writing you so frankly, my whole thought is to obtain your helpful suggestions.

I know that I am merely expressing your own views when I say that our primary duty is to see to it that the war against the German government is won. So far as our direct participation in the conflict is concerned, the task with which we are confronted is the most stupendous ever imposed upon a nation in war. No nation has ever had to maintain a line of communication 6,000 miles long. Certainly no nation has ever been compelled to maintain it in the face of submarine depredations.

If there were no conflicting considerations, I would like to see America send five million men to France. There are so many things to be considered, so many interests involved, that we must consider not what we would like to do, but what we can do to make the war against the German government effective.

All the available tonnage of the world's merchant marine has been estimated at little over 30,000,000 tons. This includes the Pacific as well as the Atlantic, tramps as well as liners. It includes the tonnage of all the neutrals, and all the belligerents, South American as well as Oriental.

The submarines have been sinking approximately 600,000 dead-weight tons a month, up to October 1, 1917. We have enormously enlarged our shipbuilding capacity. Our efforts already have trebled the productive capacity of the country in 1916. We must produce 6,000,000 tons of ships in 1918. The tremendous obstacles we must overcome in order to achieve this goal are shown in the simple statement that more than eighty per cent of the contracts of the Emergency Fleet Corporation must be produced in new yards, some of which are only now under construction. Most of the space in the old established yards has been taken by the Navy Department.

The trustees of the Emergency Fleet Corporation, realizing that all red tape must be cut to accomplish the tremendous task which confronts us, has been enlarging and perfecting the organization of the corporation. We are drawing into the organization the best organizing skill and the best engineering skill that the country provides. Enormous obstacles must be overcome if we are to maintain our own line of communication and the lines of communications of our associates in the war.

Regardless of the speed with which we are able to turn our [out] new ships, we must conserve every ship that is now available, or that will be available. We must make decisions as to what services we will perform. As Mr. Baruch says, we have taken more ships out of the nitrate trade than can be spared.

We should be adding ships to this trade, instead of taking them away. We must do this if we are to continue furnishing munitions to our own army and navy and to the Allies. The same is true of the food supply. There are many products which we must bring to the United States from distant ports if we are to continue our exports for the relief of the Allies.

We must continue to bring crude oil from Mexico, or we cannot continue to produce in the United States the fuel oil and gasoline needed for our own army and navy and for export to the Allies. It is no longer a question of considering private interests. All such interests must be subordinated to the success of the war. The Allies, as well as the United States, must discontinue the shipping engaged in non-essential trade.

The main problem that confronts us right now is one of coordination and selection. The departments of the government requiring ships to perform their services must consider the war problem as a whole, and not as it affects each department. The direct needs of the War Department to transport and supply the American army in France must be balanced against the indirect, but equally essential needs of other departments. If, for instance, a ship is taken from the transportation of manganese ore, and transferred to the service of the War Department to carry supplies to our army in France, it may mean that the manufacture of steel plates will be delayed. It might mean a delay of three or four months in completing several ships near completion.

The responsibilities of the United States virtually constitute an endless chain. We are bound soon to reach the point where we must decide whether to use a ship for our own need or some imperative need of the Allies. The British, the French, the Italians, and all other nations associated with us are constantly urging us to release ships to them. We must constantly balance their needs against our own, lest in refusing them and letting their line weaken, we increase our own responsibilities and the length of the war. We must look into the future and do our part in guarding against a repetition of the Italian retreat—a retreat which might be duplicated on the French front if there were any failure of supplies from the United States.

There has been complete harmony and cooperation between the War and Navy Departments, the War Industries Board, Food Administration and the Shipping Board. All of us have been engrossed in our own responsibilities and while we have constantly conferred on separate phases of war work, some method or machinery might be adopted for coordination of the whole problem, and the balancing of one need against another. If we decide as a result of such common council just what we can do, without sacrificing any link in the chain of war efficiency, we can rely with greater certainty upon our ultimate success in the war.

Very respectfully yours,   Edward N. Hurley

TLS (WP, DLC).

From W. A. Campbell

Houston, Texas, Nov. 13, 1917.

Inasmuch as Messrs. Barrett and Musher,[1] Federal Conciliators, have failed in their efforts to bring about a settlement of the oil field strike in Texas and Louisiana and have now been assigned to other work, we the representatives of ten thousand patriotic citizens desirous of working no injustice on our government in its hour of need, earnestly appeal to you to send the Hon. W. B. Wilson in person to use his good offices to bring about an adjustment of the present controversy. Kindly wire answer.

Gulf Coast District Oil Field Workers,
By W. A. Campbell, President.

T telegram (WP, DLC).
[1] James J. Barrett and George Washington Musser.

From Henry Lee Higginson

Dear Mr. President: Boston. November 13, 1917.

You should not be troubled by a letter from me except on public affairs and, just now, about affairs which you in person have taken up.

We all know that to win this war we must have continuous production and supplies for ourselves and for our allies—supplies of all kinds, food and manufactured articles. Without this production, and without first-rate team work, we shall either prolong the war or be beaten. The latter result is not to be considered. Death would be much better.

The National Industrial Conference Board, consisting of 18,000 different manufacturers, has worked out a plan toward this end. This board has suggested that no advantage should be taken of the war to win a selfish end, and that a commission be appointed, with equal representation by the Government, the employee and the employer,—that commission to settle all questions arising. Such an arrangement would insure continuous production, as strikes and lockouts would be illegal, and would make the needed adjustments from time to time. The National Industrial Conference Board, speaking for 50,000 manufacturers, pledged that body to a loyal support of this plan, and suggested to the Council of National Defense that it ask the labor leaders also to support the plan. This suggestion went to the National Council of Defense by the hands of seventy leading men on the 6th of September, 1917. Two months have gone by and yet no acknowledgment of the receipt of this recommendation has been made, and no action has been taken toward getting the labor leaders together. I note a labor convention at Buffalo just now at which you were to be present.

I believe that the great mass of labor is loyal and ready to do its share, and that the sentiment of the country is strongly behind the suggestion made by this National Industrial Conference Board. Meanwhile, we should note that nearly 2,000 strikes have been called since we went to war. Whatever might have been said in the past, at the present time the employers are acting in a patriotic fashion, and the employees who strike are doing the contrary.

More words to you on this subject are useless, for you know the needs, the dangers, and the difficulties of the situation. Will you bring the laborers to the suggestion made as above? They cannot be hurt with the Government a third party in this conference. At the present time we may forget any difficulty of the past and all pull together, for the laborers cannot prosper unless the country prospers. I believe that you can make them see that this war is a matter of principle—of an eternal principle—and has no other purpose. You can make them see what the United States, in name and in national policy, means.

Will you forgive me for bringing up this matter to your attention? My motive in writing lies in the needs of the cause, which is dear to you as to all of us; indeed, I believe it to be our religion.

I am　　Very respectfully yours,　Henry L. Higginson

TLS (WP, DLC).

To W. A. Campbell

[The White House] 14 November, 1917

Am sorry to say that Secretary Wilson is at present on the Pacific Coast, but I appreciate the suggestion contained in your telegram and will see if it is possible for him to visit Texas.

Woodrow Wilson.

T telegram (Letterpress Books, WP, DLC).

To Joseph Patrick Tumulty

[The White House, Nov. 14, 1917]

Please let the Department of Labor have a copy of this telegram and ask them to communicate it to Secretary Wilson and seek his advice as to the possibilities, and if he cannot do it his advice as to what should be done.   The President.

TL (WP, DLC).

To Edward Nash Hurley

My dear Hurley: [The White House] 14 November, 1917

Thank you for your letter of November thirteenth handed to me by Tumulty. It is a very clear statement of the problem as it has lain in my own mind, and I am very anxious to get at the discussion of the question how we can get all counsels combined and to be able to determine the necessary priorities.

Cordially and sincerely yours,   Woodrow Wilson

TLS (Letterpress Books, WP, DLC).

To James Henry Taylor

My dear Mr. Taylor,   The White House 14 Nov., 1917

This is my contribution to the first instalment of the $5000 the church wishes to pay on the first of January.

In great haste,—with warm regards   Woodrow Wilson

ALS (NcMHi),

Two Telegrams from Edward Mandell House

[London] 14 Nov., 1 p.m. [1917]

The Prime Minister arrived to-day. I dined with him alone tonight in order to have a frank conference. The Italian situation is desperate. Venice will fall. French and British troops are being rushed to the front and they should be ready for action by November twentieth. France and England and Italy have agreed to form a Supreme War Council and believe that it is imperative that we should be represented in it because of the moral effect that it will have here. I am cabling you through the Department a copy of the agreement as signed at Rapallo. I would advise not having a representative on the civil end as designated in Article 1 but would strongly urge having General Bliss sit on the military end as described in Article 5. It is important that an immediate decision be made as to this so that it can be announced that America is in full coordination with England and France and Italy. It is necessary to do everything possible in time to encourage our friends here and in France. Your Buffalo speech came at the right time and has been enthusiastically received. We are expecting to go to Paris on Monday. It is probable that no other offensive will be made on the French front until the spring, or until the Americans are strong enough to give material assistance, or the Russians recover sufficiently to resume on the East. It looks like a waiting game. I will advise you of this further in a later dispatch.   Edward House.

T transcript (WC, NjP) of WWsh decode of T telegram (WP, DLC).

[London, c. Nov. 14, 1917]

From: Colonel House
To: The President and Secretary of State

Decisions of a conference of representatives of the British French and Italians assembled at Rapallo on November seventh nineteen seventeen.

Paragraph One: The representatives of the British French and Italian governments assembled at Rapallo on November seventh nineteen seventeen have agreed on the scheme for the organization of a supreme war council with a permanent military representative from each power, contained in the following paragraph: Scheme of organizing a supreme war council.

Paragraph Two:

Sub-paragraph One: With a view to the better coordination of military action on the Western Front a supreme war council is created composed of the Prime Minister and a member of the governments of the great powers whose armies are fighting on the front. The extension of the scope of the council to other fronts is *only* (?) for discussion with the other great powers.

Sub-paragraph Two: The supreme war council has for its mission to watch over the general conduct of the war. It is preparing recommendations for the decisions of governments and keeping itself informed of their endorsements and reports thereon to the respective governments.

Sub-paragraph Three: The General Staffs and military commands of the armies of each power charged with the conducting of military operations remain responsible to their respective governments.

Sub-paragraph Four: The general war plans drawn up by the competent military authorities are submitted to the supreme war council which under the high authority of the governments ensures their concordance and submitting if need be any necessary changes.

Sub-paragraph Five: Each power delegates to the supreme war council one permanent military representative whose exclusive function is to act as technical advisor to the council.

Sub-paragraph Six: The military representatives receive from the government and the competent military authorities of their countries all the proposals information and documents relating to the conduct of the war.

Sub-paragraph Seven: The military representatives watch day by day the situation of the forces and of the means of all kinds of which the Allied armies and the Enemies armies dispose.

Sub-paragraph Eight: The supreme war council meets normally at Versailles where the permanent military representatives and their staffs are established. They may lodge at other places as may be agreed upon according circumstances. The meeting of the supreme war council will take place at least once a month.

Paragraph Three: The permanent military representatives will be as follows: for France, General Foch; for Great Britain, General Wilson;[1] for Italy, General Cadorna.

T MS (WP, DLC).
  [1] That is, Gen. Sir Henry Hughes Wilson.

From William Lea Chambers

My dear Mr. President: Washington November 14, 1917.

I beg to acknowledge your note of the 13th,[1] in reply to my letter of the 12th, informing me that you will see the heads of the four railroad brotherhoods at 2:30 o'clock, Thursday, November 22nd.

I have accordingly notified each of the chief executives of the labor organizations and, of course, they will be at the White House on the day and at the hour stated.

Assuming that you will expect me to attend the conference I shall also make my engagements accordingly.

Very respectfully,   W. L. Chambers

TLS (WP, DLC).
[1] It is missing.

From Newton Diehl Baker

Dear Mr. President: Washington. November 14, 1917.

I have received today with great satisfaction because of the fine spirit shown by the Philippine Legislature the following cablegram from Governor-General Harrison:

The two Houses of the Philippine Legislature have unanimously adopted the following resolution.

Quote. "That the Governor General be and hereby is authorized to take all necessary steps for the earliest possible construction, under the direction of the Government of the United States and at the expense of the Treasury of the Philippine Islands, of a modern submarine and a modern destroyer, which shall, as soon as available, be offered to the President of the United States for service in Philippine waters, or elsewhere, as said President may require or authorize." End of quotation.

In forwarding this resolution I am particularly gratified to report the spontaneity and unanimity with which this offer is made and earnestly hope that its acceptance is possible. If it is impracticable to construct these vessels in the United States in the immediate future, I am informed that they could be constructed here if certain of the parts could be sent out here, and perhaps this latter course would be preferable. The funds to pay for these vessels could be taken either in whole or in part from the surplus in the Philippine treasury, or by bond issue by the Philippine Government, or, if preferred, by popular subscription. While no conditions are attached to this offer, it is generally hoped that these vessels may, wherever they are put in service, afford an opportunity for young Filipinos to serve as enlisted men on board to acquire expert education in the handling of these modern types of war vessels.

I am transmitting this to you for your information and am also sending a copy to the Secretary of the Navy.

I am,   Very sincerely,   Newton D. Baker

TLS (WP, DLC).

From John Spargo

Dear Mr. President: New York November 14th, 1917

Permit me the satisfaction of cheering your Buffalo speech. It adds the strength of several army corps to the allied forces.

It may interest you to know that all the independent Socialists I have seen are greatly stirred by the speech and hail it with satisfaction. Only one phrase—that about exporting critics—is questioned: for the rest the feeling is that you have, once again, sounded the note of a noble and generous internationalism.

With profound respect,   Sincerely yours,   John Spargo

ALS (WP, DLC).

To Albert, King of the Belgians

[The White House] November 15, 1917.

I take pleasure in extending to Your Majesty greetings of friendship and good will on this your fête day.

For the people of the United States, I take this occasion to renew expressions of deep sympathy for the sufferings which Belgium has endured under the wilful, cruel, and barbaric force of a disappointed Prussian autocracy.

The people of the United States were never more in earnest than in their determination to prosecute to a successful conclusion this war against that power and to secure for the future, obedience to the laws of nations and respect for the rights of humanity.

Woodrow Wilson.

TL (Letterpress Books, WP, DLC).

To William Gibbs McAdoo

My dear Mr. Secretary: [The White House] 15 November, 1917

I appreciate the importance of the report which Doctor Rupert Blue, Surgeon General of the Public Health Service, has made concerning the matter of health and sanitary conditions in the war industries, and also of the recommendations which he makes, but we must be careful not to get wires crossed here, as they have been in many other matters. I am going to refer your letter and the report to the Chairman of the Council of National Defense, which I know has had these very matters in mind and without whose cooperation I think it would be a mistake to call such a conference as you suggest. I expect prompt attention to this matter, because I know the interest of the Council in it.

Always   Faithfully yours,   Woodrow Wilson

TLS (Letterpress Books, WP, DLC).

To Newton Diehl Baker

My dear Mr. Secretary: [The White House] 15 November, 1917

I take the liberty of referring this important letter and report to you as Chairman of the Council of National Defense. I enclose a copy of my reply to the Secretary of the Treasury.

I would be very much obliged if you would suggest to me the best methods of cooperation.

Probably, since we already have an organized Public Health Service, it would be wise to employ it in the active investigation and correction of sanitary conditions, but I want to draw the various counsellings in this matter and actions in it together.

Cordially and faithfully yours   Woodrow Wilson

TLS (Letterpress Books, WP, DLC).

To Abram Isaac Elkus

My dear Mr. Elkus: [The White House] 15 November, 1917

I appreciate and value your letter of November fourteenth and thank you for it very sincerely. You may be sure that its suggestion will be gravely considered.

In great haste, with warmest regard,

Sincerely yours,   Woodrow Wilson

TLS (Letterpress Books, WP, DLC).

To Josephus Daniels, with Enclosure

My dear Mr. Secretary: The White House 15 November, 1917

I have such a respect for Mr. Elkus's sobriety of judgment and good sense that I attach a good deal of importance to the enclosed letter and am taking the liberty of sending it to you for serious consideration.

Cordially and faithfully yours,   Woodrow Wilson

TLS (J. Daniels Papers, DLC).

E N C L O S U R E

From Abram Isaac Elkus

PERSONAL AND PRIVATE.

Dear Mr. President: New York November 14, 1917.

A few days ago there appeared in a newspaper a statement purporting to emanate from high authority at Washington indicating that if the war was to be ended speedily by victory there must be a more determined and united attack made.

This statement encourages me to call to your attention (as I briefly did when I returned) [to] the situation in Turkey, and particularly in Asiatic Turkey, so that a favorable use might be made of that condition.

Turkey is the weakest link in the chain of the Central Powers, and Turkey is on the verge of a breakdown, for internal reasons. A confidential letter received yesterday from Constantinople, dated September 25th, confirms this information.

The Turks are extremely sensitive to any invasion of their territory, especially from the sea. The ports of Turkey in Asia on the Mediterranean, according to reports from our Consuls and others, are not well fortified, except, perhaps, Smyrna. Beirut, Alexandretta, Mersine and Jaffa are without much defense. There are no warships of the Central Powers in the Mediterranean except, perhaps, some Austrian submarines and small war vessels. It would therefore be comparatively easy to bombard all these cities.

In a letter to Mr. Polk a few days ago I gave him information which I had received, that at Adana, near Mersine, there were cotton seed oil factories which supply the Turkish and German armies, also a factory manufacturing a large part of the uniform cloth used by the Turkish army, and that these were easily subject to aeroplane attack, and indicating how they could be distinguished. This information was given by him to the English Embassy. If, in addition to bombardment, there were landing parties of sufficient size, railroad communication could be cut. Landings in that part of Turkey where many Arabs live would be met by a friendly and not a hostile population, or at least an apathetic one. A large landing party by way of Crete to Smyrna would be perhaps the most effective means of producing results. The people of Turkey only want some such excuse, as a substantial invasion would serve to compel a separate peace, if that be desired.

It is true that England is invading Palestine and also attacking from Bagdad, but that is far away from Constantinople and from Turkey's cities and territory which are useful to her and yield revenue, and, besides, the progress is slow.

I am taking the liberty of writing you this in the hope that it may serve some useful purpose. My personal knowledge of the matters referred to, and my desire to serve, must be my apology.

With kindest regards, I remain

Very sincerely yours,   Abram I Elkus

TLS (J. Daniels Papers, DLC).

To Joseph Patrick Tumulty

Dear Tumulty: [The White House, c. Nov. 15, 1917]

I suggest that you write to Mr. Long that the way to stop these things is for the Press concertedly to expose this campaign of lying.[1] You can make this suggestion with regard to this rumor even if you couldn't make it with regard to the equally atrocious one about yourself.   The President.

TL (WP, DLC).
[1] Samuel Wesley Long to JPT, Nov. 14, 1917, TLS (WP, DLC). Long, associated with a "News-Correspondence Bureau" in Philadelphia, reported that, while riding on a trolley car from West Chester, Pa., to Philadelphia, he had been asked if he had heard that Francis B. Sayre, Wilson's son-in-law, had been shot as a spy for giving information about the movement of troop ships. He demanded that something be done to put an end to such rumors. "Personally," he concluded, "I feel that a few hangings are in order."

To Henry Lee Higginson

                                         [The White House]
My dear Major Higginson: 15 November, 1917

I need not tell you that I have had very much on my mind the matter that you speak of in your letter of November thirteenth. I am not sure that it would be possible to organize such a board as the National Industrial Conference Board has worked out, or to give the adequate authority, but I am hopeful of some other arrangement which will accomplish approximately the same result. Its success depends upon my finding just the right man. That is the hardest part of every job of this sort.

Cordially and sincerely yours,   Woodrow Wilson

TLS (Letterpress Books, WP, DLC).

From Edward Mandell House

[London] Nov. 15, 8 PM

After a consultation it has been decided to postpone the Paris conference for another week. It is necessary to know whether Italy will stand or fall and to allow the French to form a new ministry[1] and have a short time in office before we meet. Otherwise the conference would be futile. Named in [I shall][2] therefore remain here until towards the end of next week. We are finding it difficult to bring these people down to a satisfactory working basis, but we will succeed in doing so shortly. The Prime Minister has just called and he promises to use all his influence in this direction. After a consultation [with] General Bliss we think that he should remain on the Supreme War Council long enough only to get a thorough knowledge of the situation and then come home and let some one else take his place. He believes [We believe] with the knowledge he has obtained here he will be more useful as Chief of Staff. The entire situation is critical & it is fortunate we are here to is intrusted to [steady] it.   Edward House.

EBWhw decode of T telegram (WP, DLC).
    [1] The ministry of Paul Painlevé fell on November 13 on the occasion of a vote of no confidence by the Chamber of Deputies. President Poincaré asked Georges Clemenceau to form a new government on November 15. Clemenceau had done so by the following afternoon.
    [2] Corrections in House telegrams from the typed copies in the E. M. House Papers, CtY.

From William Gibbs McAdoo

Dear Mr. President: Washington November 15, 1917.

I think the whole weight of the American Government should be thrown firmly and strongly in favor of the creation of the Inter-Allied Conference to consider military operations in Europe and coordinate the resources of the Allied Governments in the conduct of the war. The Inter-Allied Council I proposed for the determination of the needs and priorities of the various Allied Governments as a basis for credit to be extended to them in the United States does not, of course, go far enough, and was not intended to comprehend the major problem.

Unless we get a more effective leadership and a more effective use of the combined resources of the principal Allied Governments and of the United States, I am sure that the value of our aid will be very greatly diminished, if not entirely negatived. I believe we are facing the time when America must take the responsibilities of leadership. We alone have the power to impose our decisions upon the Allies, first, because we control the essential resources for the conduct of the war, and secondly, because we have no selfish purpose in view, and, therefore, our decisions will be regarded as impartial. The responsibilities of American leadership are very grave—I realize that fully—but, on the other hand, I think the responsibilities of a failure on our part to take that leadership are even graver.

I respectfully suggest this for your consideration.

Cordially yours,   W G McAdoo

TLS (WP, DLC).

From Robert Lansing, with Enclosure

My dear Mr. President: Washington November 15, 1917.

I think that you will find this letter of Mr. George Talbot Odell interesting reading.

Although Odell is connected with the NEW YORK EVENING MAIL, I think that his statements are reliable. I have known him for some time and have a high regard for his accuracy and powers of observation.

Will you be good enough to return Mr. Odell's letter after reading it?   Faithfully yours,   Robert Lansing.

E N C L O S U R E

George Talbot Odell to Robert Lansing

Dear Mr. Secretary: Washington D. C. Nov. 10th. 1917.

Confirming our conversation of yesterday I have the honor of stating to you in writing the message which I was asked to deliver to the United States government, a few days prior to my leaving Stockholm.

Mr. G. Sil-Vara of Vienna[1] a literary man with whom I had a previous acquaintance and whom I met again in Stockholm this summer, came to me about two days before I left that city. He had with him a letter signed by Count Czernin, Premier of the Austrian government, addressed to him, in which Czernin stated that he was exceedingly anxious that those in authority in the American government should have a clearer understanding of present political conditions in Austria and should know what changes have already occur[r]ed and what Emporer Karl is aiming to accomplish in furtherance of democratic reforms, but that under present circumstances it was practically impossible to communicate these things through diplomatic channels. Count Czernin therefore requested Mr. Sil-Vara to deliver to his American journalist friend the message with which he had been intrusted and to request me to transmit it to the proper officials of the American government when I returned to the United States. I may add that Mr. Sil-Vara offered to give me the letter from Czernin but I refused to accept it knowing that my papers would be examined in Halifax. I may also say, in order to throw some light upon the probable reason for his having been selected to deliver this message, that I know that Mr. Sil-Vara is a Corp brother of Kaiser Karl and that he has long been a close personal friend of the Emporer. The message which Mr. Sil-Vara then gave me is as follows; I quote his words as accurately as possible:

Kaiser Karl is a thorough democrat. He desires to give his people a thoroughly democratic form of government. He has abolished all forms of monarchial oppression[;] he has done away with all the court forms which pertained to the old court regime. Great stress must be laid upon the fact that he is parading before the people of Austria-Hungary as a democratic sovereign because he believes that he can thereby show his people what democracy means, educating them by showing them the difference between monarchy and democracy in terms they can understand and that his open and almost violent espousal of democratic forms will help to weaken the strength of the monarchists who are still a powerful factor. The Emporer goes about a great deal in civilian clothes. He has done away with the formalities which the old Emporer always required, such as requiring his barber always to attend him in evening clothes and having his personal aide come to him at seven in the morning with the programme of the day, in full dress uniform. Emporer Karl mingles much with the crowds on the streets and rides on tramcars in order to hear what the people are saying.

The Emporer has insisted that the Austrian Diet shall pass the government bill abolishing political censorship.[2] That bill is sure to be passed within the next few weeks. (It may have been passed by this time as the Diet was to meet early in November) It was on account of his activity in furthering the passage of the vote reform bill for Hungary that brought about the overthrow of the Tisa party in Hungary and Dr. Werkerle[3] was appointed Premier of Hungary because through him the political forces of the country could be brought together so as to create a majority in favor of the bill.[4] The bill provides nearly universal suffrage for Hungarians with the secret ballot. There are some reservations in country districts which are made necessary by racial lines.

The Emporer of Austria wishes the American government to understand that he has the same ideals of democracy which animate President Wilson and the American people. He wishes the American government to know also, that he is in a position to bring considerable pressure upon his ally the German government. The Emporer is of the opinion that at the present time, he, as the friend and ally of Germany, could exert a greater influence and be a more potent factor in bringing about the acceptance of democratic reforms by the German government than the enemies of Germany could do through threats or otherwise. He has already exerted his influence in that direction with some measure of success and he was confident that within the next weeks (this message was given to me about October sixteenth) the pressure which he could exert upon the German government would be still more potent.

Emporer Karl is anxious to do everything in his power to bring about an early termination of the war. Animated by this desire and a sincere wish to see the spread of democracy, he is seeking through this means to gain a clear understanding of the aims of the American government and would be glad to be encouraged by the President to exert the full force of his influence upon his ally to secure the acceptance of those aims.

The above constitutes the message in as nearly the words of the messanger Mr. Sil-Vara as I am able to give them. I may add that a few days later in Copenhagen, I was informed by Prof. Schulze-Gaevernitz,[5] a Progressive Liberal member of the German Reichstag, that the war aims resolution of the Reichstag of last July was passed and accepted largely through the influence of the Austrian government. I did not tell Gaevernitz anything about the above message. I may add however that Prof. Gaevernitz is publishing in a German Political Review this month an article justifying America's entrance into the war on the ground of Germany's failure to keep faith with the American government.

With sincerest regards Mr. Secretary, I have the honor to remain,
Yours very truly,   George Talbot Odell

TLS (SDR, RG 59, 763.72119/10473, DNA).
[1] "Sil-Vara," or "G. A. Sil-Vara," was a pseudonym used by Geza Silberer, an Austrian playwright.

² No such measure was enacted at this time; indeed, it was not then under consideration or discussion.

³ Sándor (or Alexander) Wekerle, Prime Minister of Hungary, 1892-1895, 1906-1910, 1917-1918.

⁴ As it turned out, the conservative opposition, led by Count István Tisza, was able to prevent the passage of any bill for reform of the suffrage at this time. Only in July 1918 was a very watered down suffrage bill enacted. Gábor Vermes, "Leap into the Dark: The Issue of Suffrage in Hungary during World War I," Robert A. Kann *et al.*, eds., *The Habsburg Empire in World War I* (Boulder, Colo., 1977), pp. 29-44.

⁵ Gerhart von Schulze-Gaevernitz.

From Champ Clark

My Dear Mr. President: Washington, D. C. Nov. 15, 1917.

One more voice will not greatly swell the acclaim with which your Buffalo speech is received; but I give myself the pleasure of saying that it is a most admirable pronouncement and I doubt not will do much good.   Your Friend,   Champ Clark.

ALS (WP, DLC).

From Herbert Clark Hoover

Washington, D. C.
Dear Mr. President: Fifteenth November 1917

In the matter of my conversation today it may be of use to you to have the data itself. As you are aware, our harvest has not been up to hopes and our statistical position without regard to savings by conservation is as follows:

Harvest of 1917, plus carry-over on July 1, 1917		704,797,000	bushels
Average yearly domestic consumption for the past three years	615,189,397		"
Additional seed requirements this year	10,190,288		"
Essential carry-over	50,000,000		"
Total exports since July 1, 1917	33,790,055	709,169,740	"
Deficiency, November 1st		4,372,740	"

Against this purely statistical position we have to consider the better grade of the wheat this year and the savings by conservation.

The practical famine in corn during the last three months and subsequent higher cost of corn meal than of flour has greatly interfered with conservation. At the utmost we can count on a saving of only 15% of the wheat, especially in view of the high wage level of the country, and this only with forced measures in mixing meal with the flour. Even so it would increase our exportable supplies by about 100,000,000 bushels of wheat. This however is a speculation on conservation measures and prudence demands we should only allow export month by month as we may be able to gauge conservation.

The Allies require a minimum of 350,000,000 bushels during the next eight months under the most drastic of rationing and substitution of other cereals, or an average of about 45,000,000 bushels per month. A large part of this must come from the Argentine and will not be available in Europe until the end of January. The Canadian surplus yet available is about 100,000,000 bushels, or, about a two-months' supply. The Canadian surplus is not available at the rate of 45,000,000 bushels—for reasons of internal collection and transportation. The Allies must be fed pending the availability of Argentine wheat and it appears that we must supply 75,000,000 bushels to attain this end, some of which we might or might not recover from Canada. This is simply a gamble on conservation. We must also furnish some wheat or flour to adjacent countries.

In these circumstances I can see no alternatives to the following courses:

1. As soon as corn is available to put the country on a mild war bread, containing about 20% of other cereals than wheat.
2. Refuse wheat (and flour) exports to all neutrals except Cuba.
3. Reduce Cuba to the minimum.
4. Instruct the Allies that they must secure all wheat from Canada, India, Australia and the Argentine and that any further exports from the United States must be replaced from Canada or the Argentine.

There is one domestic factor that we must not overlook. If we came out 10% short in our prime food this shortage would fall mainly upon the city and industrial classes as the producer always protects himself. It thus becomes 20% of their supply and as the well-to-do always live, it means 30% or 40% shortage to the poor—and our tranquility endangered.

Furthermore, it is hopeless for us to anticipate continued control of price if we are to operate food ourselves on an absolute shortage. Up to date, due to the firm control of wheat by the Food Administration, we have managed to control prices upon a visible circulating stock of wheat of only 10% of the usual amount, but it represents only ten days' supply of bread to the country and fills us with constant anxiety. We have however risked this so far in order to keep Allied ships loading without delay.

Some of the economic results of the Grain and Flour and Bread Control may interest you. Briefly, the price of wheat is today 27% greater than the farmer realized last year and 109% over a three-year pre-war normal. The price of flour at the mill is 30% less than the day the Food Bill was signed. The price of cash bread in Washington for the full one-pound loaf is six to seven cents against eight to nine cents. The farmer is today receiving 40% of the price of the loaf against under 20% in pre-war times,—the result of total elimination of speculation and extortionate profits.

Your obedient servant,   Herbert Hoover

TLS (WP, DLC).

From Louis Freeland Post

My dear Mr. President: Washington November 15, 1917.

Upon receiving from The White House copy of telegram from Texas regarding the labor situation in Southern oil fields and copy of your reply, I sent the following telegram last night to the Secretary of Labor:

"Following telegram from W. A. Campbell, President Gulf Coast District Oil Field Workers received by President. quote Inasmuch as Messrs. Barrett and Musher, Federal Conciliators, have failed in their efforts to bring about a settlement of the oil field strike in Texas, and Louisiana and have now been assigned to other work, we the representatives of ten thousand patriotic citizens desirous of working no injustice on our government in its hour of need, earnestly appeal to you to send the Hon. W. B. Wilson in person to use his good offices to bring about an adjustment of the present controversy. stop Kindly wire answer. unquote.

"The President replied today as follows. stop quote Am sorry to say that Secretary Wilson is at present on the Pacific Coast, but I appreciate the suggestion contained in your telegram and will see if it is possible for him to visit Texas. stop unquote. Please advise Kerwin or me of your action. Also wire instructions if any."

Very respectfully,   Louis F. Post

TLS (WP, DLC).

From Robert Goodwyn Rhett, with Enclosure

Dear Mr. President: Washington, D. C. November 15, 1917.

In accordance with your suggestion, the Board of Directors of the Chamber of Commerce of the United States instructs me to transmit herewith the memorandum which they had hoped to present to you in person. Their thought in coming before you at the time of presenting the written expression of their views was to convey to you by their presence an indication of their earnest desire to give you their thought for whatever benefit you might find in it. At the same time they desired to make clear the fact that they have no disposition to criticise or add to your burdens but that, on the contrary, in a moment of national crisis their sole thought was to render any help which might accrue from their practical experience and intimate acquaintance with existing conditions.

They wished also to convey again an expression of their full support and deep confidence in you in this great emergency.

Very respectfully yours,   R. G. Rhett

TLS (WP, DLC).

E N C L O S U R E

GOVERNMENT WAR BUYING

After months of close study and with intimate knowledge of the situation, the Board of Directors of the Chamber of Commerce of the United States of America is forced to the conviction that if further time is lost in planning to centralize the control of the industrial energy and the material resources of the country, serious disaster is inevitable. Only the immediate realization of actual conditions will lead to the creation of an effective organization to meet the industrial problems of the war in time to prevent great and unnecessary losses to our troops and to our Allies, and financial disaster to our country.

After seven months of the war we continue to rely upon the executive organization inherited from the times of our peaceful isolation, reinforced only by the Food Administration, the Fuel Administration, the War Trade Board, and the committees and boards formed under the Council of National Defense, the principal one of which is the War Industries Board. There has been created no Department of Munitions or War Supplies, War Supply Board, or similar agency of whatever name, able to bring about centralized control or cooperation between the various government activities engaged in procuring war materials and supplies.

It is now clearer than ever that the war can be won only with our efforts, our industrial resources and our men. We know that England and France had to create Ministries of Munitions to make effective use of their industrial resources in the war. We know that the efforts of Germany are also directed from a central body which forms general plans and controls action. With this experience and knowledge to guide us, we have not yet developed a similar directing force behind our industrial efforts or any effective substitute arrangement adapted to our conditions.

The men responsible for operating the industries of the country on which depend the production of war materials and supplies have in War Convention declared the need for such a central guiding body in order to make effective use of the resources of the country. Whether it be a new department of the Government, headed by a member of the Cabinet, whether it be a War Supply Board, or a War Industries Board with adequate power and personnel, is not vital, but it must be an agency designed to meet the emergency, to consider great problems as they arise with power to reach decisions, and to carry these decisions into effect.

To avoid any possible misunderstanding of their attitude, these men in national convention, and also by formal vote in Referenda, have made clear their readiness to submit to such control as may be necessary. They have said "it is the spirit of American Business that however fundamental may be the change in the relations of Government to business, the Government should have the power during the period of War to control prices and distribution of production for public and private needs to whatever extent may be necessary for our national purpose."

"Undismayed at the prospect of great taxes, facing the consumption of its accumulated savings, American Business without hesitation pledges our Government its full and unqualified support in the prosecution of the War until Prussianism is utterly destroyed."

These are words of far reaching import. They mean that American business in dedicating to the nation every facility it has developed and every financial resource it commands "on such terms and under such circumstances as our Government shall determine to be just," has removed any possible obstacle to such action as the occasion demands.

The subordination of all business to the war needs of the Government, imposes on the Government the duty of wise and constructive leadership. What business may do to help win the war is being determined by the Government. Concentration of industrial energy and resource will come about to the extent that the Government affords the necessary leadership. The Government faces the responsibility of exercising its control during the war in a manner to produce the results desired. There is, however, no constructive organized leadership in this direction and no central body with the authority and power to develop such leadership, and without leadership democracy can not concentrate its scattered efforts or assemble its strength for war.

This leadership is not afforded by the Council of National Defense nor by the War Industries Board. The War Industries Board has neither the power nor the opportunity to give singleness of purpose, to prevent conflict in the various activities of the Government connected with providing materials and supplies for our troops and those of our Allies, nor is it so constituted as to make it possible to do so.

Government buying is still done substantially as before the war by many independent bureaus which do not act under general control or in accordance with general policies formulated to meet great problems. In securing deliveries of purchases our Government does not make general use of the follow-up systems which have been so highly developed in commercial companies. Although our efforts in the war depend upon our shipping program, no effective method has been adopted for giving this program the full right of way without interference or of developing our other efforts with due relation to this governing program. With the [no] right to commandeer in the War and Navy Departments, the Shipping Board and the Food Administration; with no division of industries into essential and non-essential, with no program of supplying essential industries with labor and material, or of assisting non-essential business during the war in connection with the placing of orders for war requirements, there is not an effective machinery for priority in production and distribution.

Purchasing for the Government is usually by negotiation between buyer and seller, and producers are forced to protect themselves by making the best bargain they can. This is largely true even when prices have been fixed by the Government. No general practice has been adopted of buying at prices arrived at on a basis of cost, with the Government carrying the burden of risks not in the control of the seller. Although business men have gone on record that unusual profits should not be made out of the war, the Government continues in certain branches to use methods of buying that unavoidably produce high prices and frequently produce large profits.

The activities of the War Industries Board have not prevented expansion in the purchasing divisions of the War and Navy Departments. While these Departments have been developing along peace time lines, there has been established a Food Administration, a Fuel Administration, a War Trade Board—all practically independent one of another and of the Departments. The Shipping Board—a peace time institution—has spread out into a war body having charge of a problem which goes to the heart of nearly every other war problem. But although the production of ships is vital to other war time activities, the Shipping Board in this connection is not under joint control with these activities.

Central control and general planning to give singleness of purpose to conflicting activities is not entirely a matter requiring new statutes. Much can be done immediately towards establishing a central agency for all the Government's efforts to provide war supplies.

The fact that much splendid work is being done among the scattered efforts and that great accomplishments have been achieved and are in prospect must not be permitted to cloud the vision. When the safety of the Republic is involved good work is not enough. The nation must do its utmost.

Early in July it was well known in Washington that without some central body, no general plans could be formed to meet certain great problems already clearly developed. When the War Industries Board was formed in August it was evident this was at best inadequate and only a preliminary step.

After the War Convention of American Business in September and in accordance with the action there taken, a Committee of the Chamber presented the situation to the Chairman of the Council of National Defense. It was pointed out that the withdrawal for war purposes of material and labor represented by the vast sum of 19 billion dollars was creating far reaching problems, not only in connection with the actual production of the enormous quantities needed by the Government, but in connection with the usual activities of business essential to the maintenance of sound industrial life as well as of those industries non-essential during these abnormal times, but which to some extent should be preserved for development upon the return of peace.

It was made clear that pending the formation of a central agency with adequate powers, the Government cannot procure needed war materials and supplies, and that confusion exists throughout the country from uncertain price and priority policies. Great danger lies in further delay in meeting the problems of essential and non-essential industries. Undue hardship is inevitable unless comprehensive plans are promptly put into effect to determine non-essential business, and to bring about when advisable gradual contraction in the industries affected. Effort should be made to permit partial operation of these industries so that a nucleus may remain for development after the war, and in producing war essentials, the available facilities of non-essential industries should be used.

With a full sense of heavy responsibility, we have reached the conclusions herein expressed. We are appointed to represent those who operate the country's industries. They are relied upon to produce what our armies need. We do not feel that we are fully responsive to the pledge which American Business has given to our Government to support it to the utmost in the conduct of the War if we do not frankly and fully present our views as to the seriousness of the situation.

In our judgment undoubtedly the most effective method of bringing about the central agency under discussion is for Congress to create by statute a Department of War Supplies for the period of the war. To make effective use in this war of the industrial resources of the country is a great undertaking, which can be accomplished to best advantage by a member of the President's official family.

This Department should make the Government's purchases of war materials and supplies and see that delivery is made at the desired places in the United States. Decisions regarding technical questions should continue to be made in other departments, which should have full authority regarding specifications and similar matters. The general purpose would be for the Department of War Supplies to confine its activities to commercial questions: purchasing and purchasing negotiations, form of contract (other than specifications and technical matters), "chasing deliveries," storage and inland transportation.

This Department should be the only one to exercise the right to commandeer plants, material, equipment supplies; or other articles or commodities, not to include, however, completed ships or ships in process of construction. It should have full and final authority regarding all priority matters both as to production and distribution.

The organization for this Department should be created by transferring to it the various purchasing bureaus and divisions which now exist in the War and Navy Departments, the Food Administration, the War Industries Board, etc. This does not mean necessarily that the Food Administration with its great activities apart from purchasing supplies should be in this Department, or that the Shipping Board with its far-reaching and vitally important duties should be there.

Contracts for ships which might be let by the Shipping Board or the Navy Department, and all government contracts or purchases which would involve material or labor during the war, would be subordinate to the priority powers of the Department of War Supplies.

The War Trade Board, the Fuel Administration, and the purchasing for the Allies should be in this Department.

This Department should have all necessary power to concentrate the resources and industrial energy of the country toward winning the war, including the power to procure war supplies to the best advantage to the Government as to price, quality, and delivery, and to maintain essential industrial life and to preserve so far as possible the normal industrial structure until the return of peace.

Pending the securing of necessary Congressional legislation for the Department of War Supplies we favor the appointment by public Executive order of the President of a War Supplies Administrator with an Advisory Board thereby creating an organization which when clothed with all the powers now existing under present statutes will approach as far as is now possible the ultimate powers to be conferred by statute upon the Department of War Supplies.

The War Supplies Administrator to have the power to commandeer, as heretofore indicated, and whatever authority exists regarding priority in production, storage and distribution; his associates to be agreeable to him and to have such duties as he may assign. The size of the board to be determined by the number of departments and war time activities which would be affected by the acts of this board, and which should therefore be represented thereon. The governing principle should be that as demonstrated by experience, there must be an executive for action and a board for advice.

The War Supplies Administrator when appointed by the President also to receive from the Secretary of War and the Secretary of the Navy and other agencies affecting the procuring of war supplies their direct delegation of authority to the fullest extent possible, under existing statutes, so as to place under the control of the War Supplies Administrator all activities in their purchasing departments to the extent necessary fully to accord with his policies and plans.

The purchasing bureaus and divisions of the War and Navy Departments, of the Food Administration, etc. to report to and act under the supervision of the War Supplies Administrator and no withdrawal of materials and labor from the industrial market to be made by any government department without the approval of the Administrator.

The War Supplies Administrator to report directly to the President, it being the spirit and purpose of this temporary arrangement to prepare the way for the Department of War Supplies.

There are many reasons which we might present in support of certain of our suggestions but to incorporate them here would make this statement of undue length.

We should like to have an opportunity, on behalf of the business men of the country, to discuss various features of this proposal with such members of the Cabinet as you may wish to have us confer with and to that end we have appointed a special committee which is available now for this purpose.

In presenting these opinions as to the vital necessity for centralization of control with the least possible delay and suggestions as to its accomplishment we fully appreciate that there are difficulties in the way and objections to overcome. We are convinced, however, that more effective organization along these lines is necessary to the proper support of our Army and Navy and the fullest development of our industrial power.

THE CHAMBER OF COMMERCE OF
THE UNITED STATES OF AMERICA
R. Goodwyn Rhett, President.

T MS (WP, DLC).

From Robert Lansing

My dear Mr. President, Washington November 15, 1917.

Permit me to thank you most sincerely on behalf of Mrs. Foster and Mrs. Lansing, as well as of myself, for your thoughtfulness in your personal expression of sympathy in the loss we have sustained.[1]

It may be a satisfaction to you to know that Mr. Foster was one of your great admirers and a staunch believer in your policies domestic and foreign. It had been his great desire during his illness to live long enough to see the triumph of the principles which you announced believing that they were the only sure foundation of an enduring peace. I only wish that his desire might have been gratified and that he could have been spared until the world is freed from the curse of war.

With deep appreciation of your kindness, I am, my dear Mr. President, Faithfully yours Robert Lansing.

ALS (WP, DLC).
[1] John Watson Foster had died on November 15. Wilson had probably extended his condolences in person. There is no letter from Wilson on the subject. He attended Foster's funeral on November 16.

Joseph Patrick Tumulty to John Spargo

Personal

My dear Mr. Spargo: The White House November 15, 1917

The President asks me to thank you very heartily, indeed, for your kind letter of November fourteenth and for all that you are generous enough to say concerning his Buffalo address. He is gratified at the response from the public.

Sincerely yours,   J P Tumulty

TLS (J. Spargo Coll., VtU).

Sir Eric Drummond to Arthur James Balfour

Mr. Balfour,   [London] November 15th, 1917.

As you will no doubt remember, the War Cabinet recently had before them a letter from Viscount Bryce to the Prime Minister, covering a memorial from a number of representative public men, suggesting the establishment of a small Committee of British and American experts to examine the establishment of some machinery for the preservation of a permanent peace by a combination of free, peace-loving nations[.]

The War Cabinet decided:

To adjourn the matter until there had been an opportunity of discussing it with the representative of President Wilson, who was shortly expected in this country.

I had an opportunity of discussing this question with Colonel House the other day. It was clear to me that in his view it would be a mistake to set up any such Committee. He told me that the President thought it better that the Government of the United States should not in any way be committed to a cut and dried plan for the establishment of a League of Nations. The President hoped that if any Nation showed an aggressive disposition, or clearly intended to go to War Great Britain, the United States, France and perhaps some other Nations should come to an understanding between themselves as to what attitude they should adopt and that having come to a decision on this point they should then determine what steps should be taken to make it effective.

Colonel House added that the President and he were discouraging in the United States discussions as to the League of Nations etc., and that he had succeeded in employing a number of advocates of the League on various work immediately connected with the prosecution of the War.   E.D.

TCL (FO 371/3439, No. 53848, PRO).

To Edward Mandell House

[The White House, Nov. 16, 1917]

Please take the position that we not only accede to the plan for a single war council but insist on it, but think it does not go far enough. We can no more take part in the war successfully without such a council than we can lend money without the board Crosby went over to join. The war council will, I assume, eventually take the place of such conferences as you went over to take part in and I hope that you will consider remaining to take part in at any rate the first deliberations and formulations of plans. Baker and I are agreed that Bliss should be our military member. I am happy the conference is to be postponed until the recalcitrant parliaments have settled to their senses. Please insist in the conference on the imperative necessity of getting wheat first from Australia then from the Argentine and last from us. Taylor[1] has the facts and they are of the gravest significance. McCormick will show you despatch from Jones.[2] I felt obliged on principle to take the position therein stated. It is based not only on principle but on the facts and advice contained in the confidential memorandum brought over by Reading and is all the more dictated by good sense in view of the present critical situation.   Wilson.

WWT telegram (WP, DLC).

[1] That is, Alonzo E. Taylor, who represented the Food Administration on the House mission.

[2] T. D. Jones to Amembassy, London, Nov. 15, 1917, printed as Enclosure II with T. D. Jones to WW, Nov. 19, 1917 (first letter of that date).

To Joseph Patrick Tumulty, with Enclosure

Dear Tumulty: [The White House, c. Nov. 16, 1917]

I really am not in a position to discuss these matters and I would be very much obliged if Mr. Borglum might be got into communication with Mr. Coffin, the Chairman of the Aircraft Board.
                                    The President.

TL (WP, DLC).

E N C L O S U R E

Gutzon Borglum to Joseph Patrick Tumulty

My dear Mr. Tumulty: [Stamford, Conn.] Nov. 14, 1917

Regret not to find you. I want very much to see the President for a short conference on the grave and important subject of our aeronautics. The service possible and the use of this branch of our Services at the front. I am at my address at Stamford and can come at call.   Sincerely yours,   Gutzon Borglum

ALS (WP, DCL).

To Champ Clark

My dear Mr. Speaker: [The White House] 16 November, 1917

Your note about my Buffalo speech was very generous and I appreciate it deeply. Thank you with all my heart. I am always glad to win your approbation.

Cordially and sincerely yours,   Woodrow Wilson

TLS (Letterpress Books, WP, DLC).

From Edward Mandell House

Dear Governor,   London. November 16, 1917.

The Prime Minister returned Tuesday. He made an engagement with me for a conference on Wednesday. Northcliffe who had just arrived from America asked him when he was to see me. He replied "tomorrow." Northcliffe said "Sit down and write Colonel House the most cordial invitation you know how to dine with you tonight alone."

This invitation came promptly and I spent the evening with him. It had been impossible to do anything along specific lines until he returned since no one else had the authority. This, however, was true only as far as my work was concerned. The other members of the Mission immediately got in touch with the several departments corresponding with their own.

The Lord Chief Justice, Northcliffe and Wiseman are working cordially with me to force action upon important questions. Northcliffe and Reading of course are the Prime Minister's closest friends, but they realize his weaknesses.

Northcliffe has been splendid. He holds a club over the P.M. and threatens to use it unless he does as desired. Since Northcliffe has returned, the Prime Minister has repeated[ly] offered him a seat in the Cabinet which he has refused. Wiseman heard him tell George that he did not propose to relinquish the right to criticize when he thought it necessary.

We are using Reading to button things up after decisions are made. With this combination of Wiseman, Reading and Northcliffe, things are now being accomplished with more rapidity than I have ever experienced here.

The Prime Minister came to see me yesterday to urge that I consent to a postponement of the Paris Conference. I had told Wiseman and Reading that it must be held on schedule. Although I knew that this could not be done, still I did not want the P.M. to think that they could delay it indefinitely.

This postponement will not change our home-coming which I have set for December 5th, 6th, or 7th from some port in France. I found that it would be impossible to do the things necessary and have the Commission finish their work before that date.

I cannot tell you how splendidly and cordially the Commission are working together, and what a fine impression they have made here.   Affectionately yours,   E. M. House

At luncheon today L.G. asked me to say to you that if you wanted Northcliffe back he would be *delighted* to send him." He said he would even consent to take T.R. for awhile in exchange, but not for long.

TLS (WP, DLC).

From Newton Diehl Baker

My dear Mr. President,   Washington. November 17, 1917.

I had a talk with Mr. Dan'l¹ Willard a day or two ago, about the Chairmanship of the War Industries Board. His first remark to me on the subject was: "My son is fighting in France, and I cannot of course decline to do anything on this side which I am asked to do." He was, however, much concerned to solve for himself the question as to whether he could make a success of the task. The embarrassment in his mind arose from the fact that the War Industires [Industries] Board as such has no power conferred by statute, and he felt that decisions which he might make would need to be very fully backed up by the Secretary of the Navy and by me, or indeed even by you, in order to be assured of getting them executed with speed and firmness.

I assured him that, as all the executive power lay in the President, and as the President had created this Board with the idea of all of us co-operating through it, I thought he need not have any hesitation on the ground of actual power. He took the matter under advisement for several days and returned this morning to say that he had decided to accept the place.

My own favorable opinion of Mr. Willard's earnestness and efficiency was heightened by the simplicity and directness of his consideration of the problem, and his obvious willingness to do anything you desire to have him do in the matter. He asked me to say to you that he would accept the place with the understanding that his resignation would be in your hands at once upon his acceptance, so that it could be acted upon by you at any time you thought it wise to make a change without the necessity of any sort of question being raised as to the ground of your decision in the matter.

I take the liberty of enclosing a letter of appointment[2] which, if it meets with your approval, will close the matter.

Respectfully yours,   Newton D. Baker

TLS (WP, DLC).
[1] NDBhw.
[2] See WW to D. Willard, Nov. 19, 1917.

A Memorandum by William Veazie Pratt[1]

SECRET

Memorandum for Secretary. [c. Nov. 17, 1917]

1. There is something so attractive in this proposition[2] that it has been the dream of other powers than ourselves.

2. I think, possibly, and in this I have had the support of some military men, that the scene of an active offensive may lie in the Eastern Mediterranean and as a strategic move nothing looks more promising than an undertaking which seperates Turkey in Asia, from Turkey in Europe, at the Dardanelle.

3. But while this may always loom as a future move, to attempt precipitate action now, or to attempt any movement not in force would be to invite disaster for:

(a) It diverts us from our main objective which for the present is the Western front.

(b) It scatters our efforts at a time when the main body of our military forces are neither large enough, nor sufficiently well-trained to enter a new field.

(c) It starts a new enterprise with a very long line of communication, before the shorter sea line America to England and France is even secure.

(d) It contemplates a sea attack unsupported by a military force. History invariably records ultimate defeat for such undertakings. Gallipoli is a striking example of it.

(e) The bombardment of ports without their military occupation immediately, would serve only to inflame the Turks and I fear put us a little in the German class.

4. At this time, to my mind the one feasible plan to effect such a counter in Turkey lies through Japan. Their line of communication via the Gulf of Aden or Red Sea, though long, is practically secure. How willing they would be to enter into a party, having such an offensive as an objective, is not known to me. But I do believe that our every move tending to make our relations with Japan closer, is a step to the good, and through us (for I believe England is to an extent losing her influences in that quarter) such an offensive might be undertaken.

5. For Japan to undertake to strengthen the Russian front, in the present state of chaos, would be to precipitate Russia into German arms I fear. But a strong offensive by Japan in Turkey in Asia, would probably be the best move the Allies could make having the seperation of Turkey from Germany in view.   W. V. Pratt

TS MS (J. Daniels Papers, DLC).
¹ Captain, U.S.N., at this time Assistant Chief of Naval Operations.
² That is, A. I. Elkus to WW, Nov. 14, 1917, printed as an Enclosure with WW to JD, Nov. 15, 1917.

Two Telegrams from Edward Mandell House

London. November 18, 1917.

The following is short resume of general political condition: Russia: Kerensky and other more responsible officials urge Allies to make an offer of peace basis no annexations or indemnities. They believe Germany would not accept and this would help to solidify Russia. They do not believe Germany would make separate peace with Russia owing to danger of socialistic infection, but they believe Germany will take Petrograd and near provinces in the Spring. They claim this would suit German purposes better because demobilization of Russian army would produce anarchy and total stoppage of supplies.

The situation in Rumania is serious and they may be compelled to make a separate peace because of inability to get food from Russia.

The Italian situation at the present moment is better. If the line holds until the 26th there is a good chance that it may hold permanently. Tomorrow will be rather an anxious day here but I think nothing serious will happen.   Edward House.

T telegram (E. M. House Papers, CtY).

[London] 18 Nov. 7 p.m. [1917]

McCormick and Lord Robert Cecil appreciate how delicate the situation is and nothing is contemplated which will bring about a crisis in Norway and Denmark.[1] They believe Nansen[2] and the Norwegian Secretary of State for Foreign Affairs[3] are pro-German and do not represent the sentiment of either the government or the people. McCormick believes if you will allow him to go ahead as planned a speedy agreement can be secured. He proposes not to press the matter beyond the safety line.

[The getting of wheat from] Australia and Argentina first is in process and a solution will be arrived at shortly.

Edward House.

T transcript (WP, DLC) of WWsh decode of T telegram (WP, DLC).
[1] See the two letters from T. D. Jones to WW, Nov. 19, 1917, with their Enclosures.
[2] Fridtjof Nansen had arrived in the United States on July 26 as the head of a Norwegian mission charged with the task of negotiating a trade agreement with the United States. It was only on November 16, however, that serious talks began, when Nansen presented a formal proposal to the War Trade Board. See Olav Riste, *The Neutral Ally: Norway's Relations with Belligerent Powers in the First World War* (Oslo and London, 1965), pp. 198-204.
[3] Nils Claus Ihlen.

To Herbert Clark Hoover

My dear Mr. Hoover: The White House 19 November, 1917

Thank you very much for your memorandum of November fifteenth about the crop situation. It will be very serviceable to me.

In great haste

Cordially and faithfully yours,   Woodrow Wilson

TLS (H. Hoover Papers, HPL).

To William Gibbs McAdoo

My dear Mac: The White House 19 November, 1917

Here is the memorandum[1] about which I wish you would make inquiries of Flynn and your Secret Service. I think you will find that they were the ones who were active in this matter, and I hope that you will be able to get all the facts from them.

I was a bit distressed by the discussion in Cabinet the other day.[2] It made me feel derelict in not having sought a remedy at the time you suggested it, though I must say I am still in doubt as to what the best remedy is.

Affectionately yours,   Woodrow Wilson

TLS (W. G. McAdoo Papers, DLC).
¹ That is, R. Forster to WW, Oct. 31, 1917, printed as an Enclosure with WW to TWG, Nov. 1, 1917, Vol. 44.
² According to the diary of Josephus Daniels, the cabinet, on November 16, had discussed "the various secret-service agencies and the need for co-operation."

Two Letters to Newton Diehl Baker

My dear Mr. Secretary: [The White House] 19 November, 1917

The message from the Philippine Legislature which you were kind enough to send me in your letter of November fourteenth, which has just been laid before me, is indeed truly gratifying. When you reply, will you not be kind enough to request the Governor General to express to the Houses of the Philippine Legislature the profound gratification with which I learned of their action and my sincere pleasure in finding how fully they share my feeling that we are fellow-citizens?

Cordially and sincerely yours,   Woodrow Wilson

TLS (Letterpress Books, WP, DLC).

My dear Mr. Secretary: The White House 19 November, 1917

I am sincerely glad to hear Mr. Willard's decision about the chairmanship of the War Industries Board and am taking pleasure in sending him today the letter you so kindly drafted for me.

May I not thank you warmly for your own part in this matter?

Cordially and sincerely yours,   Woodrow Wilson

TLS (N. D. Baker Papers, DLC).

To Daniel Willard

My dear Mr. Willard: [The White House] November 19, 1917.

I take pleasure in asking you to accept the office of chairman of the War Industries Board.

The importance of the work to be done by the War Industries Board needs, of course, no statement from me, as you have been associated through the Advisory Commission of the Council of National Defense with its activities from the first, and realize with me the importance of the task, and its vital relation not only to our war preparation but to the maintenance of a sound economic and industrial condition of the country during the war.

Cordially yours,   Woodrow Wilson

TLS (Letterpress Books, WP, DLC).

To David Franklin Houston, with Enclosure

My dear Mr. Secretary: [The White House] 19 November, 1917

I am utterly at a loss what reply to make to this telegram and therefore turn to you, because I know that you must know about the situation and I am in entire ignorance. Do you think it is feasible for the Federal Government to act in this matter at all.

Cordially and sincerely yours,   [Woodrow Wilson]

CCL (WP, DLC).

E N C L O S U R E

Austin, Texas, November 18, 1917.

On Thursday a great meeting of cattlemen and seed crushers and state officials was held at Houston to consider ways and means for helping the cattle industry in the national and international calamity involved by the drought which is afflicting one hundred fifty out of two hundred fifty counties of Texas. An area of about the size of Germany, two million head of live stock, are involved besides an estimated money loss on grain and forage already sustained of two hundred million dollars and more than that already sustained in live stock and cotton. Farmers in large numbers are abandoning this region in despair and unless quick help comes a large part of this region will be depopulated; for months the Federal Department of Agriculture has been taking large numbers of cattle out of this territory but now they are in great part too weak to be moved. This appalling national disaster at a time when food is so sorely needed to win the war can be testified to by all the State officials, the United States Department of Agriculture, the State Chambers of Commerce, the cattle raisers association, the Farmer's Associations, the bankers associations and the United States Food Administrator. It cannot be exaggerated. We the undersigned called together this day by Governor W. P. Hobby respectfully ask you to take immediate action[.] At least fifty million dollars are needed at once as a war measure to save this situation, to help the farmer remain on the land to provide food, feed, seed, labor and credit. We respectfully suggest that this be made a revolving fund for crop and live stock mortgage loans and be carefully safeguarded and administered by a special committee appointed by you with the aid of State and County administrative officials. We greatly regret as citizens the necessity of calling for national assistance at this time but feel that it is a patriotic duty which as men we cannot shirk. We respectfully submit that you are justified in making this emergency appropriation, as it is truly a measure as any other which can be undertaken by the Government. We do not have to point to you that food is munitions and that the Government would not hesitate to use any reasonable means to save this amount of munitions. We submit that the time for extended investigation has gone by. The conditions are fully known and quick action is now needed to save the situation. We respectfully submit if this request is not heeded greater calamities will surely result and incalculable costs and discouragement to production will result.

W. P. Hobb[y],   Governor of Texas.[1]

T telegram (WP, DLC).
   [1] The signatures of twenty-two businessmen, ranchers, etc., follow.

To Joseph R. Wilson, Jr.

Dear Joe: [The White House] 19 November, 1917

I have your letter of Saturday enclosing Doctor Jordan's letter.[1]

Just between you and me, I am entirely sympathetic with the plan for a pension for the civil servants of the Government, or, at any rate, an insurance similar to that now being provided for the soldiers, but I do not think that the approaching session of Congress will be the right one in which to press the matter.

In great haste   Affectionately yours,   Woodrow Wilson

TLS (Letterpress Books, WP, DLC).
   [1] J. R. Wilson, Jr., to WW, Nov. 17, 1917, TLS (WP, DLC). The enclosure is missing.

From Daniel Willard

My dear Mr. President: Washington, November 19, 1917.

Your letter of the 17th instant, requesting me to accept the office of Chairman of the War Industries Board, is received.

I appreciate the importance of the office which you have asked me to assume, and the very great responsibility which attaches thereto. However, since you ask me to serve, I feel that in a time like the present I must accept.

The knowledge which I have concerning the development of the War Industries Board as an agency of government, enables me to understand that the basis of its strength is the confidence and support of the President. I might perhaps venture to hope that I now have that confidence, and I trust I may feel assured of your support. The issues involved are so great and in a sense so terrible, that I wish this letter to be regarded not only as my acceptance of the office, but also as my resignation thereof, to be effective at any time when it may seem to you that the interests of our country will be best served by such action.

I am not unappreciative of the honor which you have done me in this connection, and I hardly need say that I shall make every effort possible to succeed.

Very respectfully and sincerely yours,   Daniel Willard

TLS (WP, DLC).

From Thomas Davies Jones, with Enclosures

My dear Mr President: Washington November 19, 1917.

I enclose to you herewith copy of cable of November 11th which I read to you last week, together with copy of the cable that I sent to Mr McCormick at your direction. I also enclose copy of Mr McCormick's cable of November 14th relating to the same subject matter. This I also read to you, when I talked with you.

Faithfully yours,   Thomas D. Jones.

TLS (WP, DLC).

E N C L O S U R E   I

PARAPHRASE OF A TELEGRAM FROM THE AMERICAN AMBASSADOR AT LONDON DATED NOVEMBER 11, RECEIVED NOVEMBER 12, 1917.

This is intended for the information of the War Trade Board and Mr. Polk. The British and French Governments will instruct their diplomatic representatives at Christiania in the following identic language which will be sent immediately by telegraph. It is recommended by Taylor and McCormick identic instructions be at once sent to Schmedeman:[1]

"Norwegian negotiations. French and United States Governments have definitely agreed to transfer of negotiations to Christiania, you should accordingly on your colleagues receiving similar instructions open negotiations for an agreement on lines already communicated to you which may be briefly summarized as follows. We desire to obtain if possible:

"A. Cessation of all exports direct or indirect to enemy countries.

"B. Continuance of existing exports and former facilities to the Allies.

"C. Complete and reliable statistics of all exports to be furnished monthly.

"D. No landing of Norwegian fisherman's catch at other than Norwegian ports without consent of Allies. In return for acceptance of these conditions you may promise facilities for supply and importation of commodities on rationed basis estimated to satisfy Norway's legitimate home requirements.

"Detailed lists of the proposed rations as approved by the three Governments will be telegraphed within next few days.

"If you find that entire cessation of all exports to the enemy is unattainable without undue delay you may offer concession in the matter of fish exports. We should be prepared in the last resort to agree to such export up to a maximum of forty thousand tons per annum in fixed monthly installments; the term fish should include every description of fish and fish products, the weight being calculated on the basis of the amount of freshly caught fish represented in the products derived therefrom.

"Enemy armies are largely supplied with Norwegian canned goods and you should therefore make a special point of suitably limiting proportion of the fish exports to the enemy which may be sent in form of canned goods. Confidential. It is important that Norwegian negotiations shall be completed as rapidly as possible since the negotiations with Denmark are being gracefully held up till that happens."

For your information. The British will add to their telegram the following paragraph. E:

"Renewal of loan for fish purchases due for repayment next July till some month after in conclusion peace."

The hope is expressed that it will be necessary to hold here only one more conference with a view to the final determination of a scale of commodities which may be regarded as satisfying the legitimate (necessities) of Norway. It is probable that the conference will take place on Monday the 12th instant.

[1] Albert George Schmedeman, United States Minister to Norway.

ENCLOSURE   II

November 15, 1917.

For McCormick. The President sent for me this afternoon to ascertain the exact situation of Norwegian negotiations in preparation for appointment which he has made for Doctor Nansen. I explained present situation and all that led up to it and stated to him proposed negotiations to be carried on at Christiania as stated in your cable eleventh. He discussed with me the program therein outlined and directed me to cable you that he is entirely unwilling to go any farther than the principle of action already settled namely that we will supply or attempt to supply nothing to Norway except what we can be shown the people actually lack and we cannot undertake to supply them with any food elements of which they deprive themselves by exportation. He is not willing to take part in insisting that there be no export from Norway to Germany as he regards that as inconsistent with the principle upon which the United States has always insisted and the rights which she has always demanded for herself. In view of above he further directs me to say that in his judgment we cannot in good faith hold up the Danish agreement awaiting any other negotiations. Signed Jones.

ENCLOSURE III

London, Undated   Recd. November 14th

For War Trade Board November 14, 1 p.m. Our one, your five. Denmark. Prefer you continue Danish negotiations Washington, D. C. Notify Danes negotiations delayed owing to questions arising here which we hope however to straighten out satisfactorily. We will advise you when these matters are adjusted. We are most anxious that no break should occur but most important Norway be closed first.

Holland. Negotiations with Holland to be carried on in Washington, D. C. but not closed until after Norway and Denmark in order named.

Sweden. Will advise you later concerning Sweden as some Swedish delegates expected here soon from Switzerland.[1] If Sulzer[2] does not accept conditions Taylor will adjust same in Paris.

McCormick.

T MSS (WP, DLC).

[1] "*Sweden*. Will advise you later concerning Sweden as some Swedish delegates expected here soon.

"*Switzerland*. If Sulzer . . . ," From the corrected text in *FR-WWS*, 2, II, 1064-65.

[2] That is, Hans Sulzer, Swiss Minister to the United States.

From Thomas Davies Jones, with Enclosure

My dear Mr President: Washington November 19, 1917.

To supplement copies of cables which I sent to you earlier this morning, I think it would be well for you to have copy of a cable which we sent to Mr McCormick Saturday noon, after receiving a note from Dr. Nansen. I enclose copy herewith. We cabled this note in its entirety to Mr McCormick. You will see from the closing paragraph that we expressed the opinion that this note forms a fair basis for negotiations, and that negotiations should be carried on here at once. No reasons whatever have been given to us for transferring these negotiations to Christiania, hence our request for such reasons. It is increasingly evident that the Northern Neutrals have been making a concerted onset upon Washington, and while we believe that further considerable delay is dangerous, we of course are anxious to avoid any precipitate action on our part here which might interfere with what is probably the general purpose of the sending of representatives to conferences at London and Paris.

Some further developments have occurred in the Danish situation, which cannot be explained in brief, but if for your present purposes you deem them important, I shall be glad to present the facts to you, in person, if you desire.

Faithfully yours,   Thomas D Jones.

TLS (WP, DLC).

E N C L O S U R E

[Washington] November 17, 1917.

Amembassy London. For McCormick from Jones.

Quote. Our ten. Following letter delivered by Nansen late last night to Jones: Stop (Inner quote) In confirmation of my communications to you during our conversation this morning I beg you to state that my Government desire me to put the following question to the Government of the United States of America. Would the United States be able to see their way, as far as their ability goes, to secure during the length of the present war the necessary supplies for Norway, if Norway on her side in order to attain this purpose declares herself willing to lead the following unusual policy stop Norway reduces her trade exchange with Germany and her allies in the following manner, first, of food articles Norway will only export to Germany and her allies forty thousand tons a year of canned fish, fish and fish products of the kind covered by the fishery agreement with England and eight thousand tons a year of fish and fish products not covered by this agreement, consequently altogether forty-eight thousand tons a year of canned fish, fish and fish products—stop—Second, Norway will only export to Germany and her allies the following yearly quantities of the following articles, calcium carbide twenty thousand tons, ferro silicium five thousand tons, calcium nitrate eighteen thousand tons, molybdenite one hundred tons—stop—Third. The Articles covered by the copper agreement with England Norway will export to Germany only to that extent which the said agreement makes possible. Norway has already pledged herself to such an obligation by this agreement—

stop—Four. Norway will not at all export the following articles to Germany or her allies, antimony, bismuth, manganese, mica, nickel, tin, titanium and wolfram—stop—The presupposition will naturally be that Norway pledges herself to provide for that no American goods imported in accordance with an eventual agreement with you should either directly or indirectly reach the enemies of the United States and also that the Norwegian Government in all cases of export of Norwegian goods to Sweden and Denmark will procure security that such goods shall not reach Germany or her allies in any way contrary to such an eventual agreement with you. It will likewise be the presupposition of such a possible agreement that the carriage to Norway of goods for which the United States give license must not be hindered by seizure from the side of the allies—stop—As was mentioned during our conversation this morning chrome ore is not mentioned by my Government. I presume that this is due to some mistake but I am telegraphing home for new instructions on this point—stop—I sincerely hope that the above proposition of my Government may be favorably received by the Government of the United States and that we will be able to reach an agreement on this basis—stop—If this proposition will be accepted I cannot think it will give us much difficulty to arrive at a satisfactory agreement as regards the minimum supplies necessary for the Norwegian people—stop—(End Inner quote)

Letter seems to us here fair basis for negotiation and affords an opportunity for active negotiation invited by them. Our opinion clear and decided that it would be mistake to throw this matter back to Christiania and that negotiations should be carried on here at once with determination to reach best obtainable solution without delay. Board has received no detailed reasons for your recommendation that negotiations should be transferred to Christiania nor arguments of British Government in favor of this change. Please telegraph fully.

CC telegram (WP, DLC).

To Thomas Davies Jones

My dear Mr. Jones,   The White House. 19 November, 1917.

When you receive a communincation [communication] in this handwriting (!) please understand that it is done on my own typewriter by myself and is autograph,—has passed through no other mind.

Yesterday I received from House the following: "McCormick and Lord Robert Cecil appreciate how delicate the situation is and nothing is contemplated which will bring about a crisis in Norway and Denmark. They believe Nansen and the Norwegian Secretary of State for Foreign Affairs are pro-German and do not represent the sentiment of either the government or the people. McCormick believes if you will allow him to go ahead as planned a speedy agreement can be secured. He proposes not to press the matter beyond the safety line."

To-day I am replying as follows: Am distressed to differ with McCormick but inasmuch as we are fighting a war of principle I do not feel that I can consent to demand of Norway what we would not allow anyone to demand of us, namely, the cessation of exports of our own products. I am convinced that the only legitimate position is that we will not supply deficiencies which she thus creates if her exports are to our enemies.[1]

You[r] cable to McCormick stated our position admirably.

Cordially and faithfully,   Woodrow Wilson

WWTLS (Mineral Point, Wisc., Public Library).

[1] This was sent as WW to EMH, Nov. 19, 1917, T telegram (E. M. House Papers, CtY). There is a WWT copy, encoded in hand by EBW, in WP, DLC.

Two Letters from Herbert Clark Hoover

Washington, D. C.

Dear Mr. President: Nineteenth November *1917*

The temperance advocates in the country, with whose ultimate ends I have the utmost sympathy, are raising a great deal of agitation for the further enforcement of the restriction of the manufacture and sale of alcoholic beverages under the provisions of the Food Bill. This propaganda is having a re-action in some places in the refusal of the people to conserve other foodstuffs so long as food materials are being used by the brewers. The intrinsic factors in the situation as I see them are as follows:

a. The use of grains for the manufacture of distilled spirits has been stopped but there is of course available for sale for two or three years a supply of distilled spirits.

b. The world situation in grains lends considerable importance to their consumption for brewing purposes especially insofar as it affects the use of barley. At the present moment we have exhausted our theoretical wheat exports and we are compelled to refuse exports of wheat to many Neutral countries and must put sharp limitations on exports to the Allies. As we will have a practical famine in corn until the new crop is available say in mid-December, we are also compelled to refuse exports of corn. We have therefore only available at the present time barley and oats and if we are to allow barley to be exported it means an ultimate famine to the brewer. Barley is much more adapted for human food than oats and the situation of practical starvation in such places as Finland could at present be solved only by barley exports.

c. There are something like 15000 cold storage cars used for beer transport and at the present moment we are entirely short of sufficient cars to transport the vegetable crops of the country. Some waste is taking place through inability to get these products to market. In any event the brewing cars are the most important item that could be added to railway transport for this purpose.

d. It is impossible to separate the food and transport questions from social questions. These are of three orders:

The first of these from a practical point of view is that if brewing were suppressed in the country today we will have placed the country on a whiskey and wine basis unless all of the distilled spirits in the United States were seized by the Government for munitions purposes, and I am informed that the Government requirements in this particular are not sufficient to absorb the supply.

The second social phase lies around the discontent that might be created in the labouring classes.

The third,—the alternative that the efficiency of the country might be improved by the suppression of the liquor traffic entirely.

e. The use of grains for brewing purposes is not an entire loss of their food value; aside from the theoretical food value of beer itself there is the fact that some 30% of the value of the grain is recovered as cattle feed and that considerable animal industries have grown up contiguous to the breweries.

f. There is also the problem of the dislocation of business by the suppression of the brewing trade and its various industrial ramifications.

After weighing all of these complex and conflicting factors I have sought some medium course to suggest to you that would at least in part accomplish the objectives with due protection against the various dangers involved and in this connection I have sought the advice of Dr. Alsberg[1] of the Department of Agriculture.

My suggestion for your consideration is that you should (as a first step) limit the amount of grains to be used by each particular brewer to 50% of his average three-year pre-war intake and at the same time you should limit the alcohol percentage in the beer to

3%, being a reduction of 1¾% to 2%. The effect of this would be the volume of beer would be reduced from 20 to 30% with a 50% saving in the food material consumption.

I feel that the above is a compromise but that it should be welcomed by right-minded temperance advocates as a reduction of alcohol consumption and as a safeguard against a more serious evil in the increase of consumption of distilled spirits. I feel also that if the country wishes prohibition for the war such a measure should be undertaken by Congress directly as a measure on its moral grounds and that no such legislation would be effective unless the sale of all alcoholic drinks were suspended for the period of the war.   Yours faithfully,   Herbert Hoover

[1] Carl Lucas Alsberg, M.D., Chief of the Bureau of Chemistry in the Department of Agriculture.

Washington, D. C.
Dear Mr. President: Nineteenth November *1917*

I have unfortunately had a tea-pot storm in my department. Mr. Houston and I appointed a joint committee to undertake propaganda for the stimulation of animal production and I selected, amongst others, Mr. E. C. Lasater, a Texas cattle-man,[1] and Mr. Gifford Pinchot for the committee. Mr. Pinchot, whose views are followed by Mr. Lasater, instead of confining himself to stimulation of production in a patriotic way, and devising methods for a better distribution of our young cattle and other portions of the programme, took upon himself to advise me with regard to financial measures to be undertaken and more specially that we should take over the packing plants in the country and operate them for the Government, and other radical measures. These measures were practically all outside the powers of the Government aside from their visionary character. After some time he resigned and his resignation was followed by that of Mr. Lasater on the ground that we were not conducting the Food Administration for the public welfare. I have declined to answer any of the newspaper propaganda.

The fault is of course mine for having even placed them on a propaganda committee although my one justification was that their personalities could be turned to good account in this emergency.

I merely wished to inform you of this as I do not propose to take any action whatever in the matter.

Your obedient servant,   Herbert Hoover

TLS (WP, DLC).
[1] Edward Cunningham Lasater of Falfurrias, Texas, Progressive party candidate for Governor of Texas in 1912.

A Memorandum

IMMEDIATE BUSINESS.   [The White House, c. Nov. 20, 1917]

Further investigate possibility of getting food to Poland (on behalf of the Jewish Relief Committee)

Find means of forcing Britain *et al* to get wheat from Australia until the Argentine crops are ready and then get it from Argentina, reserving our supply till the last (See mem. from Hoover as to our wheat supply).[1]

To House: Take the whip hand. We not only accede to the plan for a unified conduct of the war but insist upon it. It is not practicable for us to be represented *in the same way* as the other governments on the civil side, but we will be on the military.

Bring into the conference as of the utmost importance, the food source question, as to which Taylor is fully informed, and insist upon shipping being sent to Australia and afterwards to Argentine.

The position I have taken with regard to Norway and Sweden in message sent by T. D. Jones to McCormick

QUERY.

Is the Mediterranean impracticable?

WWT MS (WP, DLC).
  [1] H. C. Hoover to WW, Nov. 15, 1917.

To Breckinridge Long

Personal.

My dear Mr. Long: The White House 20 November, 1917

You need not have hesitated to send me the memorandum which you send me under date of November nineteenth.[1] It concerns a matter which has caused me a great deal of thought and which I recognize as of capital importance.

Unfortunately, personally, I believe the proper cooperation of the newspapers to be impossible because of the small but powerful lawless elements among them who observe no rules, regard no understandings as binding, and act always as they please.

The Committee on Public Information, of which Mr. George Creel is Chairman, was created by me for the very purposes you outline, and if it had met with the cooperation of the newspaper men instead of their petty jealousy, it would have answered its purpose at once. Moreover, it has been very difficult to get one or two of the executive departments, notably the Department of State, to act through Mr. Creel's committee in the matter of publicity, and the embarrassments of lack of coordination and single management have been very serious indeed.

Such headings and colorings of the news as you quote from the Washington Post apparently nobody can control. It would be easy every day to pick out from the Washington Post glaring breaches of patriotic procedure, but I think in the long run they take care of themselves.

Your memorandum will cause me to review the whole situation in my own thoughts and to see whether anything additional can be accomplished.

With sincere appreciation,

Cordially yours,   Woodrow Wilson

TLS (B. Long Papers, DLC).
¹ It is printed as Enclosure I with the next document.

To George Creel, with Enclosures

My dear Creel: The White House 20 November, 1917

May I not send you the enclosed for your information, along with a copy of my letter in reply to Mr. Long?

In haste   Faithfully yours,   Woodrow Wilson

ENCLOSURE   I

From Breckinridge Long

My dear Mr. President: Washington November 19, 1917.

The attached memorandum is the result of my careful observation and thought on the subject for some time past. If I did not consider it of more than ordinary importance I would not presume to bring it to your attention.

It has been suggested, by one of the few gentlemen with whom the matter has been discussed, that the advice of certain well known journalists be sought before it should be presented to you. This seemed inadvisable for two reasons: first, it is not the practical operation but the theory which is primarily to be considered, for which purpose the opinion of those who have had considerable public experience, but who are not now engaged in newspaper or publicity work, is probably as valuable, and certainly as unbiased, as that of practicing journalists; second, the real object to be attained might be jeopardized by being communicated in full to one whose business, and whose freedom of action in business, might be affected by the operation of the plan proposed.

I have hesitated long before deciding to go, single-handed, to you, Mr. President, but having failed to secure the active co-operation, or operation, of the few persons with whom I have consulted, and believing in its real importance to you, to your administration, and to our country, I have determined to lay it before you.

The suggestion is for a constructive purpose, and is not a criticism of anyone.   Faithfully yours,   Breckinridge Long.

TLS (G. Creel Papers, DLC).

E N C L O S U R E   I I

The administration has, to a remarkable extent, brought the prominent and successful men of the country to its aid. The different executive departments and the extraordinary administrative boards have summoned men experienced in particular lines and qualified by peculiar training.

The response has been universal. Men who had developed a peculiar ability in various professional, industrial and economic pursuits have stopped their private endeavors and have put their ability and their training into the government service.

Almost every division of our economic structure has given its quota to the national organization. The railroads; the steel, copper, zinc, coal and other industries; the dealers in wheat, corn, and other grains; the packers and dealers in meats; the cotton merchants and the manufacturers of cotton and woolen goods; the wholesale and retail grocers and venders of foods; the medical and legal professions; the universities;—in fact, the whole producing, manufacturing and distributing apparatus of our industrial organization has yielded its representatives to help the execution of our national purpose. Co-operation and co-ordination with the federal machinery is the object.

In all the category of our industries, which have been specifically called to the aid of the government, there is one notable exception— the press. Of all the others it alone can prepare and perfect an understanding on the part of the people of the operations of the government, and, more than any other, is absolutely necessary to the proper functioning of all the parts of the machinery.

It can make the objects and purposes of the administration unders.ood, or it can make them misunderstood.

In order that it make the objects understood it must, first, itself *desire* to do so, and, second, itself *understand*. The *desire* is probably extensively extant, but can be considerably augmented. The *understanding* can be easily reached through a medium which the press will know and in which it will have confidence.

The papers fought the imposition of a censorship. The operation of the voluntary censorship leaves much to be desired—not only in the publication of news which it is not timely to publish (*vide* the "leak" from Peking on the Lansing-Ishii agreement) but in the manner of treating news which is given out for publication. A glaring example of the latter is the way in which was handled the news of the first encounter in the trenches. The first publication is that which is formative of public opinion and which effects the public emotion. The first impression is the most potent psychologically.

The Washington Post of November sixth had the following headlines: "Germans Raid Trench, Kill 3, Wound 5. Take 12 U. S. Men Prisoners * * * Losses of Germans unknown, but Americans capture one wounded prisoner * * *"

The next day the same story was treated as follows: "Americans fight Fiercely; Beaten by Superior Force. All Traditions of U. S. Army upheld against picked German shock-troops—Bravery recorded."

The impression from reading the first article was depressing—unnecessarily and unfortunately so. The impression from reading the second article would have been, had it been the original publication, stimulating—but its only function, as a second publication, was to retrieve part of the unfortunate effect of the first.

If there was a censorship to treat news items properly before releasing them it would insure the proper treatment of news or, at least, centralize responsibility for failure to do so.

Lacking such authority the government can best utilize the press by making it a part of the extraordinary war organization.

This can be accomplished by creating a board to have a Chairman, a Vice-Chairman and a small Executive Committee, resident in Washington, and of which the Chairman and Vice-Chairman would be members. The other members of the Board would be resident in various cities and would be called to Washington for consultation at intervals for the purpose of letting them, and their associates at home, feel that they were having some part in the work. Local committees, under their chairmanship, could even be organized in various sections of the country and might prove of considerable value.

The membership of the Board and the creation of any such local sub-committees would be primarily to create a psychological situation; to make the press at large feel a responsibility, and to increase the desire to be of service.

The power would be concentrated in the Chairman, or, in his absence, the Vice-Chairman. Both men would be chosen with two ideas in view:

(1) Their qualifications of a technical nature, which would include—
    (a) Experience as newspaper men.
    (b) Capacity for treating news in the proper manner.
    (c) Psychological instinct.

(2) Their *reputations* among their fellow journalists, for
    (a) Capacity.
    (b) Achievement, and as
    (c) deserving of confidence.

Unless they have the confidence of the men who are to handle the news items they prepare, their usefulness will be very limited.

Above all, however, they must have demonstrated their absolute loyalty to the administration and to the prosecution of all its plans.

The Chairman of such a board should be a man who has had a long and successful experience in the newspaper business and should be taken directly from that business. He should be such a person as could be taken into the innermost confidences of the heads of the executive department. Cabinet members should talk to him freely in confidence, for his information and to enable him to treat the news in the proper manner, so that he could get the back-ground and put out the story in the light of what might develop to be told in the future.

There are only a few men who could fill the position. It will take a man of large practical experience; loyal, just, sensitive to effects, and in whom both the newspapers and the administration have confidence.

Responsibility would be single; power would be great; obligation would be, through the administration, to the country.

The daily press would automatically become a part of the administration. They would feel that they were a part of it. Their patriotism and sense of obligation would cause them to respond to the help of the body to which they would be attached, of which they would feel themselves a part.

The advantage to the country would be great. Public opinion would respond to proper treatment. Impressions most conducive to the accomplishment of the national purpose would be scattered throughout the land. Conjecture would cease. Misunderstanding would be minimized.

T MS (G. Creel Papers, DLC).

Two Letters to Herbert Clark Hoover

My dear Mr. Hoover: The White House 20 November, 1917

Thank you for your memorandum about the relations between the food supply and the brewing industry.

I am fully in sympathy with your suggestion that the percentage of alcohol in beer should be reduced to three per cent., and I think probably it would be wise to reduce the amount of grains used by each brewer, but I am inclined to think that fifty per cent. reduction is too severe, at any rate for a beginning, because I take it for granted that such a reduction would by reducing the supply greatly increase the price of beer and so be very unfair to the classes who are using it and who can use it with very little detriment when the percentage of alcohol is made so small.

This other question arises in my mind: Is the thirty per cent. of the grain value really being saved for cattle feed systematically and universally, and if not, are there not some regulations by which we should make sure that the full saving was effected and made available in the right way?

Cordially and sincerely yours,   Woodrow Wilson

My dear Mr. Hoover: The White House 20 November, 1917

Thank you for your memorandum about Mr. Gifford Pinchot. The same thing happens wherever he is involved.

In haste   Faithfully yours,   Woodrow Wilson

TLS (H. Hoover Papers, HPL).

To William Gibbs McAdoo

My dear Mac: [The White House] 20 November, 1917

Upon receipt of the recommendations of Surgeon General Blue which you sent me,[1] I at once transmitted them to the Secretary of War as Chairman of the Council of National Defense, because I knew that that Council through several instrumentalities had been trying to deal with the same subject matter.

I am this morning in receipt of the enclosed letters and accompanying papers from the Secretary of War, one of his replies being written before and the other after the matter was brought to the attention of the Council of National Defense itself.[2] My own judgment is that the suggestions contained in the second of these two letters afford the best practicable means of dealing with this matter, and I have no doubt that when you read the Secretary's statement of the elements in the case you will be of that judgment yourself.

Always   Faithfully yours,   Woodrow Wilson

TLS (Letterpress Books, WP, DLC).
   [1] See WGM to WW, Nov. 12, 1917.
   [2] These enclosures are missing in the Wilson, Baker, and McAdoo Papers, all DLC.

To Newton Diehl Baker

My dear Mr. Secretary: [The White House] 20 November, 1917

I thank you sincerely for your attention to the suggestion of the Secretary of the Treasury concerning the supervision of matters of hygiene and sanitation for workers during the war, and I have taken the liberty of communicating your replies to the Secretary of the Treasury. My own judgment is that the method you suggest is on the whole the best practicable.

Cordially and faithfully yours,   Woodrow Wilson

TLS (Letterpress Books, WP, DLC).

To Daniel Willard

My dear Mr. Willard: [The White House] 20 November, 1917

Thank you heartily for your letter of November nineteenth. It is written in a spirit which I greatly admire, and I am very much pleased to know that you are willing to accept the important and responsible duties of the Chairman of the War Industries Board.

Cordially and sincerely yours,   Woodrow Wilson

TLS (Letterpress Books, WP, DLC).

To Thomas Watt Gregory

[The White House]
My dear Mr. Attorney General: 20 November, 1917

The writers of the enclosed letter are former colleagues of mine at Princeton,[1] thoroughly trustworthy and patriotic men, and I would be very much obliged if you would have a special inquiry made into the case of Doctor Frachtenberg.[2]

Cordially and faithfully yours,   Woodrow Wilson

TLS (Letterpress Books, WP, DLC).
   [1] The letter is missing, but (as TWG to WW, Nov. 28, 1917, reveals) it was from William Francis Magie, Joseph Henry Professor of Physics and Dean of the Faculty at

Princeton University, and George Madison Priest, Professor of Germanic Languages and Literature at the same institution.

[2] Leo Joachim Frachtenberg, on or about October 30, had been dismissed from his position as ethnologist in the Bureau of American Ethnology of the Smithsonian Institution on the grounds that he had made unpatriotic and/or pro-German remarks and that he had revealed confidential information gained while temporarily employed in censorship work for the Bureau of Investigation of the Department of Justice. See the letter cited in n. 1 above and the notes thereto. Frachtenberg had been born and reared in Austria and had received his secondary education in that country. He then studied at Cornell and Columbia universities and received the Ph.D. from the latter institution in 1910.

From Edward Mandell House

London. November 20, 1917.

A very difficult and dangerous situation has been rife here since the Prime Minister made his Paris speech announcing the formation of a Supreme War Council.[1] He ought never to have done this without consulting our Government, and the announcement along with his implied criticism of the military authorities precipitated a political crisis that threatened to overturn his Ministry.

In the very critical condition of affairs elsewhere in the Allied States this might have proved the gravest disaster of the war. The Prime Minister was constantly urging me to say something to help the situation. This I refused to do until I had heard from you. The statement I gave out[2] purposely refrained from approving the Prime Minister's plan, but merely stated the necessity for military unity and your instructions for Bliss and me to attend its first meeting following the Paris Inter-Allied Conference.

The situation had become completely composed but Tumulty's denial[3] has started everything afresh, and the Government is to be questioned in the House of Commons this afternoon.[4]

I am refraining from and am asking the Press to refrain from any further statements. If this is done the incident will be closed.

Edward House.

TC telegram (E. M. House Papers, CtY).

[1] Lloyd George had spoken on November 12 at a luncheon in his honor given by Paul Painlevé. Lloyd George had reviewed the major events of the war and had blamed Allied failures and German successes mainly on the failure of the Allied generals to coordinate plans, strategy, and the disposition of their forces. The full text of his speech was included as an appendix in House's final report on his mission to Europe and is printed in *FR-WWS 1917*, 2, I, 358-66.

[2] The text of the statement given out by House on November 18, following the receipt of Wilson's telegram to him of November 16, is printed in *ibid.*, pp. 339-40. It reads as follows:

"Colonel House, head of the American mission and special representative of President Wilson in Europe, has received a cable from the President stating emphatically that the Government of the United States considers that unity of plan and control between all the Allies and the United States is essential in order to achieve a just and permanent peace. The President emphasizes the fact that this unity must be accomplished if the great resources of the United States are to be used to the best advantage, and he requests Colonel House to confer with the heads of the Allied Governments with a view of achieving the closest possible cooperation.

"President Wilson has asked Colonel House to attend the first meeting of the Supreme War Council with General Bliss, Chief of Staff of the United States Army, as the military advisor. It is hoped that the meeting will take place in Paris before the end of this month."

³ The London *Daily Mail*, Nov. 20, 1917, printed the following item, datelined Washington, November 19: "President Wilson denies that he sent a cablegram to Colonel House stating that the United States considers that a united plan and control between the Allies and the United States is essential to a lasting peace. This denial was issued through Mr. Joseph Tumulty, the President's private secretary." *FR-WWS 1917*, 2, I, 340. For documents relating to this incident, see JPT to WW, Nov. 19, 1917, and WW to JPT, Nov. 19, 1917, both TL (WP, DLC), and [JPT] "MEMORANDUM," Nov. 19, 1917, T MS (WP, DLC). See also Ray Stannard Baker, *Woodrow Wilson: Life and Letters* (8 vols., New York, 1927-39), VII, 364, and Blum, *Joe Tumulty and the Wilson Era*, pp. 133-34.

⁴ Andrew Bonar Law easily dealt with the question in Commons. His brief remarks on the subject are quoted in *FR-WWS 1917*, 2, I, 341.

From Samuel Gompers

Buffalo, N. Y., November 20, 1917.

I am advised that the commission appointed by you of which Secretary Wilson is chairman to investigate industrial unrest in the western and inter-mountain states has reported to you on the Arizona deportations.[1] I believe that publicity of that report would be helpful in this convention and elsewhere and would inspire confidence necessary for best cooperation for our country's war needs and aims. May I respectfully suggest that full publicity be given the report.   Samuel Gompers.

T telegram (WP, DLC).
¹ W. B. Wilson *et al.* to WW, Nov. 6, 1917, Vol. 44.

From Howard Allen Bridgman

My dear President Wilson: Boston, Mass. Nov. 20, 1917

May I venture to ask if there is any statement with reference to our Government's policy concerning the conscientious objector that I could see, or has nothing final been formulated? I hope we shall be able to avoid some of the troubles in England over this matter, where from private information I judge the treatment has not been very wise or far-sighted.

I shall appreciate a word from you on this point at your convenience.   Yours very truly,   H. A. Bridgman

TLS (WP, DLC).

From the Diary of Josephus Daniels

November Tuesday 20 1917

Cabinet—What to do to help Italy. Ambas[s]ador had asked us for tank ships to carry oil, submarine chasers, mines & men to lay them, aeroplanes and men to fly them. Telegram from Italian Ambassador saying reported Germans were sending diving submarines into Mediteranean to compel Italy to sue for peace. Page said he interpreted this to mean it was Italy's request for help. It came directly when Ambassador from Italy called.

Discussed the matter of papers publishing false statements of treatment of troops on troop ships & in camps. Reports of inhumane treatment that were false. B— said suppress them. WW ask for their authority instead of suppress.

Hw bound diary (J. Daniels Papers, DLC).

To Thomas Watt Gregory

The White House

My dear Mr. Attorney General: 22 November, 1917

I take pleasure in enclosing to you a copy of the report of the commission headed by Secretary Wilson which has been doing such excellent work in composing labor difficulties throughout the Southwest and West,[1] and also their particular report with regard to interferences with the draft which were involved in the illegal actions in Bisbee to which their report refers.[2] This latter I refer to you for any action that you may think it wise or feasible to take.

Cordially and sincerely yours,   Woodrow Wilson

TLS (JDR, RG 60, Numerical File, No. 186813/50, DNA).
[1] That is, W. B. Wilson et al. to WW, Nov. 6, 1917, printed at that date in Vol. 44.
[2] That is, Appendix B, printed as an Enclosure with the letter cited above.

From William Bauchop Wilson

San Francisco, Calif., Nov. 22, 1917.

I am happy to report to you that your commission has been enabled to work out a settlement of the telephone difficulties of the Pacific Coast which has secured the approval of the representatives of the unions and of the Pacific Telephone and Telegraph company. The settlement requires the formal acceptance by referendum of the unions involved. This ratification will be urged by the leaders with every assurance of favorable action by the unions. This formal ratification is necessary in order that the strike in Washington and Oregon can legally be terminated. The settlement which the commission reached will end the present strike and interruption of telephone service and it also establishes the machinery for peace between the telephone company and its employees during the period of the war. The essential terms of the settlement are:

FIRST: Recognition of the right of girl operators to organize and to receive recognition of their unions as part of the International Brotherhood of Electrical Workers;

SECOND: Wage increase on the basis of 12½ per cent of the wage schedule for operators receiving less than $50 a month.

THIRD: A wage increase of 12½ per cent for the men.

FOURTH: Negotiations between the International and the company as to any additional wage increase and in the event of failure to agree, the question of such further increase to be determined by United States arbitrator, John E. Williams,[1] of Illinois.

FIFTH: All grievances of members of the Brotherhood shall be taken up for adjustment through the machinery of the Brotherhood with the company and in case of inability so to dispose of any grievance, its final disposition is rested with arbitrators appointed by the mediation commission designated for the various districts on the Pacific Coast.

SIXTH: The President's Mediation Commission is itself a party of the agreement with a view to securing full performance of the letter and spirit of the agreement during the period of the war.

By this adjustment an amicable settlement is effected in one of the most important transportation utilities of the country and methods established for securing and maintaining peaceful relations between the company and its twelve thousand employees[.] I am glad to be able to testify that the settlem[en]t has been effected because of the patient and wise spirit of cooperation manifested by the representatives of the unions, the girls as well as the men, and the representatives of the Pacific Telephone and Telegraph Company.   W. B. Wilson.

T telegram (WP, DLC).
    [1] John Elias Williams.

From Robert Lansing, with Enclosures

My dear Mr. President: Washington November 22, 1917.

I am enclosing to you two memoranda prepared by Mr. Williams, of the Division of Far Eastern Affairs, relative to the proposed currency loan to China and the formation of a group of American bankers to cooperate with those of other Powers in providing this financial aid.

The first memorandum treats of the matter historically and the second embodies certain recommendations as to which I would be very much obliged if you would indicate your wishes. I am convinced that unless we follow some recommendations similar to those suggested it will be impossible for us to render assistance to China, the result of which would be practically to place her in Japan's hands, which, of course, is most undesirable.

As matters are moving rather rapidly in the far east I hope you will be able to give me an answer very shortly in regard to this matter.   Faithfully yours,   Robert Lansing.

TLS (SDR, RG 59, 893.57/1840a, DNA).

E N C L O S U R E   I

November 21, 1917.

The Proposed Currency Loan to China. Historical.

The United States has been interested for years in a loan for this purpose.

1. It was proposed in January, 1903, by the Chinese Chargé that the United States investigate the fluctuations in silver exchange and aid China to stabilize her currency.

2. Dr. Jenks was sent to China for this purpose in the spring of 1903 and remained there about eighteen months.

3. He recommended a gold exchange system, which the progressives were disposed to accept, but the conservatives prevented action.

4. In 1910, however, China requested a loan of Tls.[1] 50,000,000 for currency reform and promised an American Adviser.

5. On October 27, 1910, a preliminary contract for such a loan was signed with the American Group.

6. In November, 1910, the American Group entered into an inter-bank agreement by which British, French, and German banks were to participate in the loan. This agreement was due to expire June 18, 1917.

7. In 1911, just as the final contract was to be signed, with a Dutch Adviser instead of an American, the revolution occurred.

8. The option on the loan was extended from time to time until in April, 1913, the American Group gave notice that they would not ask for further extension and in June that year this group abandoned its interest.

9. The British, French and Germans retained their interest in the project and last January, Britain and France entered into further agreements consolidating these interests with the interests of the groups in the proposed new reorganization loan. This gave Japan a share in the project since Japanese banks are interested in the Reorganization Loan.

10. It is now proposed by China, supported by Japan, to borrow for the purpose of currency reform £20,000,000. Great Britain and the United States have advised against it as the cost will be great to China. But Japan insists that it is necessary to the rehabilitation of the notes of the Bank of China. Japan has already advanced ¥10,000,000 on the proposed loan. Great Britain, therefore, has withdrawn her objections, and the loan is now about to be made. The United States Government is invited to designate a banking group to participate.

11. The matter is an urgent one, for the American Minister in a cable message received today intimates that Japan will make another advance of £2,000,000[2] upon the proposed loan and may take advantage of the present disorganized condition of affairs to insist upon terms which will restrict the financial independence of China.

Great Britain and France under pressure have agreed to this advance although neither can participate.   E.T.W.

[1] That is, Chinese taels, or Chinese silver currency.
[2] The pound sign *sic*; he probably dictated "yen."

ENCLOSURE II

RECOMMENDATIONS.   November 21, 1917.

1. Great Britain at first disapproved of such a large loan at present to China but has yielded to Japan's pleas and now approves of it. From the American point of view it would seem by far the best policy to join with Great Britain, France and Japan making a four power consortium for this particular purpose. The object would be to have the support, as members of the consortium, of Great Britain and France. The alternative would be to remain outside the consortium and to compete against Japan singly, or, against a tripartite consortium composed of Great Britain, France and Japan. It would seem infinitely preferable to be one of a four-party consortium, even if we should have to "carry" England and France, for we can reasonably presume to rely upon the support of those two countries in case Japan should show a desire to take unfair advantage of China.

2. Since 1913 the Department of State has declined to request the old American Group to participate in consortium loans. By var-

ious statements on the part of the American Group they have deprived themselves of the right to participate in the old consortium. The present proposal is to organize a new consortium for a particular purpose. It is now necessary to decide, as a matter of policy, whether the former American Group should be asked, by the Administration, to participate in the proposed new consortium or whether an entirely new American Group should be organized under the leadership of some financial concern which was not a member of the old group.

3. The Continental and Commercial Trust and Savings Bank has been approached on the subject and has expressed itself as being willing to undertake the formation of a new group but has suggested that the Department of State ask the representatives of certain members of the old group to discuss the matter in Washington at which time they should be advised by the Department that the Continental and Commercial Trust and Savings Bank has been asked to form a new group.

It may be somewhat idealistic, but it is considered probably practical to request participation in the new group by banks geographically distributed throughout the country, including members from New York, Boston, Chicago, San Francisco and, possibly, other cities. Such an arrangement probably would prevent members of the old group from obtaining domination and control of the new group and would insure that the purposes of the new group would be thoroughly in harmony with the desires and policies of the Administration.

4. It is recommended that Mr. Abbott, Vice President of the Continental and Commercial Trust and Savings Bank, which now has interests in China and which has recently been more active than any other American institution in making loans to China, be designated and authorized to organize a group as suggested above, and that he be advised in writing to the following effect:

"Dear Mr. Abbott:

"Pursuant to conversations had with the Department of State, you are hereby authorized to proceed with the formation of an American Group, composed of representative banking institutions of different sections of the country, for the purpose of joining with bankers represented in England, France and Japan to make a loan to China in the sum of $100,000,000 gold, approximately, for currency reform purposes.

"You may be assured of the coöperation of the Department of State, and the protection of the United States Government for all interests which are economic and industrial in character. Investments in China, which are designed to secure political influ-

ence or control there are not in sympathy with the policy of the Government of the United States. A loan for currency reform purposes, agreeable to the Chinese Government, has the full support of the Administration and you are authorized to form such a group and warranted in proceeding with the undertaking.
Yours sincerely, Secretary of State."
E.T.W.

TI MSS (SDR, RG 59, 893.57/1840a, DNA).

To Jacob Henry Schiff

My dear Mr. Schiff: The White House 22 November, 1917

I understand that a campaign for funds for Jewish War Relief as well as for Jewish welfare work among American soldiers and sailors is shortly to be initiated in New York, under your leadership.

From statements which I have previously made, you know how sincere my belief is that the American public, irrespective of race or creed, should respond liberally to the call for help from stricken Europe, and I feel confident that the needs of the Jewish people in the war zones will find a ready response from their co-religionists in this country.

No less important, in my opinion, is the work of the Jewish Welfare Board. Mr. Fosdick, Chairman of the Commission on Training Camp Activities, has told me of its service to soldiers and sailors in our training centers,[1] and I earnestly hope that you will be successful in your endeavor to raise the necessary money for its work. The spirit with which our soldiers leave America, and their efficiency on the battle fronts of Europe, will be vitally affected by the character of the environment of our military training camps, and by the moral stimulus which they have received while there.

Assuring you and your associates of my warm support of what you have in mind to accomplish, believe me,
Very sincerely yours,   Woodrow Wilson[2]

TLS (J. Schiff Papers, OCAJA).
[1] R. B. Fosdick to WW, Nov. 20, 1917, TLS (WP, DLC).
[2] Wilson repeated verbatim the draft of the letter to Schiff which Fosdick enclosed in his letter to Wilson, just cited.

From Frank William Taussig

My dear Mr. President: Washington November 22, 1917.

Knowing how solicitous you are to be accurate in statement, as well as fair-minded in temper, I venture to send you a memorandum concerning a passage which struck my eye in your address before the American Federation of Labor on the 12th.[1] It is possible that you will have occasion to touch upon matters of this sort again, and the memorandum may be of service to you.

Believe me, with high respect and regard,

Very sincerely yours,   F. W. Taussig

TLS (WP, DLC).

[1] F. W. Taussig, TS MS (WP, DLC). The memorandum referred to a passage in the sixth paragraph of Wilson's speech in which Wilson asserted that, if German manufacturers and exporters could not sell their goods cheaper in American markets than American competitors could sell the same goods, the former received subsidies from the German government which allowed them to undercut American competitors. Taussig stated that, to his knowledge, the German government had never paid subsidies to German manufacturers and exporters except in the single case of sugar bounties. German cartels could and did sell goods at lower prices for export than for home use, but the government did not participate in this and, besides, such practices were common in many countries, including the United States.

From William Gibbs McAdoo

PERSONAL.

Dear "Governor":   Washington November 22, 1917.

I am really deeply distressed about the attitude of the Attorney General concerning the Secret Service.[1] I have refrained from troubling you with a large amount of detail which would, I know, convince you that the attitude of the Secret Service of this Department has been generally scrupulously correct and that it has not intentionally encroached upon any other jurisdiction, nor does jealousy play the least part in its work. We have been eager only to help, and I believe that the Secretary of State, Colonel House and others will bear me out in the claim that some of the most important services rendered since the war broke out have been by the Secret Service.

I should like you to know how anxious I am to relieve all friction, and especially to spare you annoyance or trouble in this and every other direction. If you prefer to have me withdraw the Secret Service altogether from the work it is now doing for the State Department, the Food Commission, and the War Trade Board, I shall be glad to do so, although I believe that it would be very hurtful to the public interest. If, on the other hand, you would like me to try to devise some plan for getting a more effective cooperation between the various services, I shall be glad to undertake that. What I should like you to understand is that I shall be most happy to accept whatever decision you may make in the matter.

Affectionately yours,   W G McAdoo

TLS (WP, DLC).
[1] Gregory was undoubtedly very disturbed about the Hale case and probably demanded that the Secret Service stay within its jurisdiction. He may also have demanded that William J. Flynn be reprimanded or even dismissed for violating the law.

Flynn announced on December 22 that he would resign as chief of the Secret Service as of December 31. It was reported at the time that he had submitted his resignation to McAdoo a month earlier. Although Flynn stated that his decision was based on the advice of his physician, who said that he needed a rest, an unidentified friend was quoted as saying that Flynn believed that he had been hampered in his efforts to control enemy aliens "by lack of support and actual interference on the part of officials at Washington." The *New York Times*, January 4, 1918, reported that a "circumstantial story," which was circulating in Washington, indicated that Flynn had resigned because of "dissatisfaction over lack of co-operation with and support by the Department of Justice." Flynn's obituary notice in the *New York Times*, October 15, 1928, was still more precise. He had resigned, it stated, "after a disagreement with the policy of Attorney General Gregory limiting the activities of the Secret Service." "Flynn had wanted," it continued, "to use his department in running down German spies."

Flynn did not long remain out of government service. McAdoo appointed him chief of the secret service of the United States Railroad Administration on September 7, 1918, and, on July 1, 1919, Attorney General A. Mitchell Palmer made him director of the Bureau of Investigation of the Department of Justice.

Gutzon Borglum to Joseph Patrick Tumulty

Dear Mr. Tumulty: Stamford, Connecticut Nov. 22, 1917

My reason for wishing to discuss aeronautics with the President was and remains because of a desire deeper than any I have outside my immediate family's happiness, that of helping the country at this hour.

The program of the "aeronautic" board was invented by automobile production interests before they had picked their representation on that board or even before the appropriations had been passed. Patience and courtesy for these self-interested groups is running out at a terrible rate from men everywhere, who will stand by the country and the President to the last, but patience and courtesy have no effect upon inevitable failure of cheap, grandiose projects, incapable of fulfillment, which cannot but bring scandal or disaster, and which in turn can harm none but the Administration.   Yours sincerely,   Gutzon Borglum[1]

TLS (WP, DLC).
[1] "Gutzon Borglum is a sincere fellow and this letter disturbs me. Is there not somebody you can consult about how to reply to it? Perhaps you might have a few words with Baker about it." WW to JPT, c. Nov. 24, 1917, TL (WP, DLC). Tumulty sent the letter to Baker on November 26.

To George Creel

My dear Creel: The White House 23 November, 1917

Here is an ambitious scheme. If it were carried out, it would be the materials at least for the most complete and effective political machine that I have ever dreamed of! What comment do you think I ought to make upon it in replying to Mr. Hale's letter, and what part of it, if any, do you think could be acted on?[1]

Cordially and faithfully yours,   Woodrow Wilson

TLS (G. Creel Papers, DLC).
[1] This was a letter from Matthew Hale, which is missing; however, see G. Creel to WW, Nov. 28, 1917, and WW to M. Hale, Nov. 30, 1917, which probably repeated a large part of Creel's suggested reply.

To Washington Lee Capps

My dear Admiral Capps: [The White House] 23 November, 1917

It is with something more than regret that I have received through the Secretary of the Navy your letter[1] informing me of the necessity you are under to relinquish your duties in connection with the Emergency Fleet Corporation. I have admired the work you have done there most warmly, for I have kept informed concerning it, and know with what devotion and intelligence you have done it. It will be a very great loss to the Emergency Fleet Corporation that you must withdraw, and it particularly distresses me to know that the cause is your impaired health.

Of course, I will yield to your desire and assign you to other duties as soon as your health will permit you to undertake them, but I want you to know with what reluctance I do so and with what genuine personal esteem and confidence. I realize now that you have remained longer at your present post than your strength justified, and I know that you have done so from motives of patriotism. May I not express my obligation to you as a public servant?

Cordially and sincerely yours,   [Woodrow Wilson]

CCL (WP, DLC).
[1] It is missing.

To William Bauchop Wilson

[The White House] 23 November, 1917

May I not express my very great gratification at the report you make in your telegram of yesterday and convey to the commission my thanks and to those concerned in the controversy my warm appreciation of their patriotic attitude?   Woodrow Wilson.

T telegram (Letterpress Books, WP, DLC).

To Frank William Taussig

My dear Mr. Taussig: [The White House] 23 November, 1917

I am warmly obliged to you for your letter of November twenty-second, and am really chagrined that I should have conveyed a false impression by the statement to which you refer in my speech in Buffalo. One case that I had in mind was the case of the mineral dyes. Am I wrong in thinking that the Government supported the competition of the German dye manufacturers in this country by some form of subsidy or financial assistance?

Cordially and sincerely yours,   Woodrow Wilson

TLS (Letterpress Books, WP, DLC).

From Newton Diehl Baker, with Enclosure

My dear Mr. President,   Washington. November 23, 1917.

I enclose a copy of a telegram which came to the War College in code from General Judson,[1] our military attache at Petrograd.

You will observe that he asks that a copy of this be sent to the Postmaster General to be sent to you. Instead of burdening the Postmaster General with it, I am sending it direct.

Respectfully yours,   Newton D. Baker

TLS (WP, DLC).
[1] Brig. Gen. William Voorhees Judson, who was also chief of the American Military Mission to Russia.

E N C L O S U R E

Petrograd, Nov. 14, 1917.

Copy immediately to Postmaster General Burleson to show President of the United States if he sees fit:

Shock of present crisis on top of past experiences may put Russia into anarchy and out of war. In Russia 180,000,000 people, mostly ignorant as plantation negroes, scattered over one-sixth land surface of earth, exist under conditions requiring for life itself some order and system in production, transportation, and distribution. All order and system are departing. Conditions make possible cataclysm dwarfing great war and tremendous blow to democracy. Resulting world shock apt to lead everywhere to accentuated struggle between extreme socialism and severe reaction, with general setback to democratic system and civilization.

Blow to democracy, due to cataclysm in Russia, would immensely increase chance a second blow due to increased political security of autocracy in Germany.

German soldiers possess convictions Allies seek to crush Germany. This thrice arms latter in degree protecting German army from socialistic or democratic propaganda until too late.

Germany has impressed similar convictions on Russian army and on strong groups here now seeking political control. Such convictions help defeat Kerensky, make Russian army impotent and foster Russian anarchy.

Perhaps our President could solve this problem.

Apparently such solution must include effort to state practical terms peace which neither side could refuse without appearance of unfairness to simple but honest minds. German perhaps as well as Russian.

Russian socialist peace program not so (?) that advanced by President in December, 1916. Russians distrust British and think French war crazy.

Action suggested dictated in my opinion by military necessity and need not lead to undesirable peace.

Any Russian Government formed in the near future must have peace program but will remain at war if Germany does not meet fair terms unless complete anarchy prevents.   Judson.

TC telegram (WP, DLC).

From David Franklin Houston

Mr. President: Washington November 23, 1917.

I have given very careful consideration to the telegram of November 18, addressed to you by the Governor of Texas and other gentlemen. This telegram pictures a serious agricultural, and especially live-stock, situation in western and central Texas. A request is made that you immediately make available $50,000,000 as a revolving fund to assist Texas and that you[,] assisted by Texas State and county administrative officials, appoint a committee to administer the fund. I assume that you have no power to make this amount available for loans to Texas farmers. I would doubt the wisdom of action on this scale even if you felt authorized to take it. It is a question whether Congress would furnish any relief. I imagine that that body would not make an appropriation of $50,000,000 to lend to farmers and cattlemen in Texas. Such action could not be proposed without leading to somewhat similar proposals for other States, such as Montana, Alabama, Oklahoma, and possibly Kansas. The Congress might furnish some measure of relief, but I seriously doubt if it would entertain the suggestion of the Texas committee.

The situation in Texas has been under the direct observation of this Department for a long time. There has been a drought in certain sections of the States extending over a part of two years. The Department of Agriculture and its cooperative extension machinery has been rendering assistance in a number of directions. The Food Administration has cooperated in the work and the Car Service Commission of the Transportation Committee has given very active aid. In particular, the Department has undertaken, in conjunction with these agencies, to assist in the movement of cattle from the drought sections of Texas to the southeastern States where there is feed. It is estimated that 150,000 cattle have been shipped out of Texas during the last four months. About three-fourths of these were breeding cattle and would have remained in Texas under normal conditions. They were purchased outright by farmers in the eastern States. The cost to the Government of furnishing the assistance has been relatively insignificant.

Arrangements have also been made to send into the distressed areas experimental carload lots of soft corn in the ear and for return shipments of cattle. Plans also have been made to send in about 60 cars of velvet beans from the southeastern States. These are being handled by the Grain Corporation of the Food Administration. At a meeting in Houston a few days ago the cottonseed crushers agreed to limit the price of cottonseed meal and the Department understands that large quantities of cottonseed meal at Galveston were ready to move last Monday.

The Department has a list of 100,000 cattle in Texas offered for sale. This number, and perhaps a much larger number, should be shipped out of the State to areas where there is a supply of feedstuffs. We have also a list of farmers in the southeastern States who are willing to purchase large numbers of cattle. The principal difficulty is a transportation one. The Department and the Food Administration have this matter up actively with the transportation agencies. It is not improbable also that the banks of Texas which have large sums of money might be called upon for further extension of credit. The Department has taken this matter up with the Federal Reserve Board and the Reserve Bank in Texas.

I do not now see what further action can be taken. I am sending a committee to Texas to make a survey of the whole situation so that we may have further accurate first-hand knowledge.

Faithfully yours,   D. F. Houston.

TLS (WP, DLC).

From Newton Diehl Baker, with Enclosures

Information

Mr President   [Washington, c. Nov. 23, 1917]

The enclosed copy is a very helpful letter from General Pershing. It need not be returned. The Generals were sent over, in part, to get his judgment of them   Respectfully   Baker

ALS (WP, DLC).

E N C L O S U R E   I

John Joseph Pershing to Newton Diehl Baker

PERSONAL AND CONFIDENTIAL.

Dear Mr. Secretary: [Chaumont] France, November 13, 1917.

Your letter of September 10th was handed me by General Treat.[1] First of all, I wish to thank you most sincerely for your cordial expressions of approval for what has been done. It has not been easy at all times to determine the best course to pursue. The British and the French, as you know, are each watching out that the other does not receive too much attention from us. So far we have succeeded in steering fairly clear of breakers, as I have persistently tried to impress both allies that our whole purpose here is to assist in every possible way in beating our common enemy, without any thought of leaning toward one ally more than the other.

With reference to our entering the trenches for active service, I have emphasized the necessity of thorough preparation, and have been following a logical program leading up to the important final training of artillery and infantry in cooperation. This has been accepted as sound by the military authorities, both French and English, so that unless something very threatening should occur, we should not go in until we are ready. Of course, even then, there will be much to learn from actual experience.

[1] Maj. Gen. Charles Gould Treat, named commander of Camp Sheridan, Montgomery, Ala., in August. Baker's letter to Pershing of September 10, 1917, is printed, with a few omissions, in John J. Pershing, *My Experiences in the World War* (2 vols., New York, 1931), I, 223-26.

In all my conferences with General Pétain on this subject we have fully agreed that, when our troops go into their sector, they would be fully supported by the French artillery and be in close touch with their infantry. It is also our joint idea that every effort should be made to have the first clash, if possible, a victory for the Americans. Such a result would of course raise the morale of our allies and correspondingly depress the enemy. General Pétain is in full accord with this view, and I am sure that when the time comes he will cooperate to the fullest extent to bring about such a result.

The venereal and the liquor problems are both extremely difficult. The greatest danger points seem to be our ports of entry. I have recommended to the Minister of War,[2] that he declare a "state of siege," at both Bordeaux and Saint Nazaire, and he has promised to do it. Such a state practically exists in Saint Nazaire already. This corresponds to our martial law and the control of these questions would then be in the hands of the local French military commanders, who, in cooperation with our local commanders, under stringent orders, should be able to keep the ports comparatively clean. There is another serious question there, too, and that is the large number of spies that continuously infest these ports. Martial law should give us a much better control of that danger.

In the training areas men are kept busy and as this region is entirely under army control, the above problems are less difficult, although not easy there. I have established a series of medical aid stations in these areas for the sole benefit of the French people, in cooperation with the leading local French women. This effort is very much appreciated by the inhabitants who, for the most part, have been left almost without medical attention. It is also hoped that venereal cases among the women may eventually visit these dispensaries for treatment. The organization of these stations has been placed under Major Young,[3] who is one of Johns-Hopkins' most famous doctors, and who has made a specialty of this class of disease.

By publishing in orders the ravages of venereal [disease] in Europe, and the constant dangers of uncontrolled sexual relations, and by encouraging Y.M.C.A. work, and demanding the interest of officers in the welfare of their men, an excellent foundation has been laid. I feel much pleased with the attitude of the army toward this question and am gratified at what is being accomplished toward morality. I shall be very glad to have Dr. Fosdick make a visit here

[2] Paul Painlevé was still Prime Minister and War Minister as of November 13 but, as has been noted, his government fell that day and he was replaced in both capacities by Georges Clemenceau on November 16.

[3] Hugh Hampton Young, a noted surgeon who in civilian life was Clinical Professor of Urology at the Johns Hopkins Medical School. His autobiography is *Hugh Young, A Surgeon's Autobiography* (New York, 1940).

to study the situation and give us the benefit of his experience and advice. We cannot do too much to protect our young men from immorality and consequent disease, to say nothing of its effect upon our fighting strength.

With relation to the general officers, I wrote you in my letter of October 4th[4] my views in general, and my opinion of several of these officers in particular. I think you have made a good selection in General Morrison[5] in charge of training. He has been quite ill while here, but is now visiting the French and British fronts as was done by the other general officers. His illness has delayed him so that he will return a little later than the others. He is not strong enough to stand the hard field service required, as he has aged a lot since he commanded a regiment of my brigade on the border over two years ago. I would emphasize my remarks with reference to the others mentioned in my former letter, and am adding some further comment in the enclosure herewith.

Generally speaking, the young and active officers of a command look upon their division commander as their leader, and if he is inactive they lack the confidence in him necessary to his success. Such a man becomes more or less of a figurehead instead of a soldier in whom they believe. The position of a division commander is so important that it may be very truly said that the success of this war depends upon them. If a division commander does not know his work and is not up to the high standard found in the allied armies, he has no place in our army here.

The matter of recommending a Chief of Staff, and I may say of selecting men in general for important assignments, is the most difficult thing that has so far confronted me, and I can readily understand how puzzling it must be for you. Most of our officers are, of course, untried, and one's opinion of men when they were young is very apt to be wrong after those same men have grown older. I am very favorably inclined toward General Biddle,[6] and I think perhaps you will find him a broad-minded, energetic man who may measure up to your ideal. In my conversations with him it seemed that his grasp of the situation here was quite large and clear. Of course one objection is that he has not had very much to do with troops. However, I believe he has natural soldierly instincts and that he has taken every advantage that an engineer officer could take of the opportunities that have come to him.

[4] It is printed with the omission of the names mentioned in Enclosure II, in Pershing, *My Experiences*, I, 189-92.

[5] Maj. Gen. John Frank Morrison, formerly commander of Camp Sevier, Greenville, S. C.; at this time on a tour of observation of American bases in Europe. He was appointed director of training for the army in January 1918.

[6] Maj. Gen. John Biddle, at this time acting Chief of Staff in place of Tasker H. Bliss, who was in Europe.

Next to him, I have an idea that General March[7] would make a good executive. I have always had a high opinion of March and had often thought of him as timber for Chief of Staff, even before I received your letter. I think March is a strong man and that he would be of great assistance to you, especially in the possible reorganization of the War Department, which I think you are going to find necessary. I should miss him here but consider your need greater.

I shall have General March come to my headquarters at an early date in order that he may make a study of the general staff organization that I have established here. All of the visiting general officers have been impressed with the plan and especially with the very complete coordination of all staff and supply departments under one control. It might be advisable to have a study made of it for application in the War Department.

There may be other officers who would do better, but it would be a chance, so therefore I recommend to you the consideration of General Biddle as your Chief of Staff and General March as his assistant. You will then have two good men, and if General Biddle should not turn out to be the man I think he is, you would have General March there to take his place or to retain as assistant in case you should not be satisfied as to his qualifications for chief, and conclude to select someone else.

Just a word as to the supply departments. The general officers sent over complain that their divisions are not being provided with equipment, especially transportation, and say they are told that their transportation and other things that are lacking will be furnished upon arrival in France. Of course, there is no transportation here and little else that does not come from home, so that our organizations are now arriving without adequate transportation and generally none.

It seems to me quite necessary that each division should be assembled at some point near the port of embarkation, where it can be fully equipped and the division commander be given an opportunity to see that he has everything in readiness. This would insure his being prepared to take care of himself upon arrival here, and would avoid confusion in issuing initial equipment at this end and possibly the more serious inconvenience of not having it at all. I send you this as I get it, as it may not have reached you in just this light.

The War Department now has our complete project for troops and supplies, estimated on a basis of 1,200,000 men. It also has

---

[7] Maj. Gen. Peyton Conway March, at this time commander of artillery of the A.E.F. in France. He became acting Chief of Staff on March 4, 1918.

the priority schedule for both personnel and materiel. So there should be less difficulty in handling both when the personnel is organized, and if the supplies are available. In making these comments I do not fail, Mr. Secretary, to appreciate the enormity of your problems, but make them with a view to aiding you in their solution.

General Bliss and the other members of the allied conference are in London. I hope to have an opportunity to go over in detail many things with General Bliss before he returns. I am writing you in a separate letter a discussion of the general military situation.

In conclusion, Mr. Secretary, permit me to congratulate you and the country in that we have you as Secretary. You are doing a great work and doing it well. May I ask you, at your convenience, to extend to the President my most loyal greetings.

Believe me, with sincere personal and official regard,

Your humble servant,   John J. Pershing.

TCL (WP, DLC).

E N C L O S U R E   I I

COMMENTS ON GENERAL OFFICERS.

Confidential for the Secretary of War.

General Blocksom[1] is in bad shape and has been in the hospital here temporarily. He is in no sense an active man and should not be returned.

General Mann,[2] with a division, has been sent over, but as he retires very early I can probably manage to handle him until near the date of his retirement.

General Clements[3] is quite too old to command a division. I do not know his age, but he is very inactive and more or less infirm and could not begin to stand the strain.

Of the other general officers who have been sent over here, I think that Generals Parker,[4] 63; Strong,[5] 63 and Liggett[6] 61, very fat and inactive, are too old to be considered for division commanders. I presume General Scott will hardly expect to come back.

My opinion regarding General Sibert,[7] expressed to you in my letter of October 4th, is being confirmed every day.

As to other officers mentioned in my former memorandum, Generals Greene,[8] Plummer,[9] Bartlett,[10] Bell,[11] J. F., Wood[12] and Swift,[13] I am more thoroughly convinced than ever that none of them are alert or physically up to the requirements, and most of them are too old anyway to begin to learn the important duties that would be required of them. To these I wish now to add General French,[14] and I fear, General Blatchford,[15] who is now here but quite aged.

With regard to sending officers over as observers to return to their divisions, I would suggest that only those known to be entirely fit should be sent, unless you want them especially to train troops at home later.

Allow me to suggest, Mr. Secretary, that all division and brigade commanders be very closely observed at home and their attitude, their activity and prowess in training these units be fully taken into consideration and reported upon before it is finally decided to send them over with their commands.   J.J.P.

TC MS (WP, DLC).
   [1] Augustus Perry Blocksom, commander of Camp Cody, Deming, N. M. All persons mentioned in this document had the rank of major general; most of them had been promoted to this rank on August 5, 1917.
   [2] William Abram Mann, commander of the 42d Division of the National Guard, then in France.
   [3] Charles Maxwell Clement, not Clements, most recently in command of the 28th Division, Camp Hancock, Ga. He was honorably discharged from the army on December 11.
   [4] James Parker, in command of the 32d Infantry Division. Retired February 27, 1918.
   [5] Frederick Smith Strong, commander of the 40th Division.
   [6] Hunter Liggett, commander of the 41st Division of the A.E.F. He held posts of increasing responsibility and served with distinction in several of the most important campaigns of the war.
   [7] William Luther Sibert, commander of the 1st Division. He was relieved of his command on December 14.
   [8] Henry Alexander Greene, most recently in command of the 91st Infantry Division at Camp Lewis, Wash.
   [9] Edward Hinkley Plummer, most recently in command of the 88th Division at Camp Dodge, Ia.
   [10] George True Bartlett, at this time on the staff of the A.E.F. in London.
   [11] James Franklin Bell, most recently in command of the 77th Division.
   [12] That is, Leonard Wood, at this time in command of the 89th Division at Camp Funston, Fort Riley, Kan.
   [13] Eben Swift, in command of the 82d Division.
   [14] Francis Henry French, most recently commander of Camp Jackson, Columbia, S. C.
   [15] Richard Milford Blatchford, commander of the Canal Zone, Panama.

From Edward Mandell House

Dear Governor,   Paris. November 23, 1917.

I foresee trouble in the workings of the Supreme War Council. There is a tremendous opposition in England to Lloyd George's appointment of General Wilson. Neither Sir William Robertson, Chief of Staff, nor Sir Douglas Haig have any confidence in him, and they and their friends look upon it as a move to put Wilson in supreme command.

The enemies of Lloyd George and the friends of Robertson and Haig believe that George wants to rid himself of these Generals and supercede them with Wilson. They claim that Wilson is not a great general but is a politician and one that will be to George's liking.

Some of the French want a "Generalissimo" but they want him to be a Frenchman. This, too, would meet with so much opposition in England that it is not to be thought of. Any government that proposed it would be overthrown.

I have had long conferences with Bliss and Pershing on the subject and I think they see the danger as I do. I am trying to suggest something else which will give unity of control by uniting all involved rather than creating dissension.

Later.

I have just had a conference alone with Clemenceau. Without my saying a word upon the subject he practically repeated the opinion that I have expressed to you above concerning the Supreme War Council. He is earnestly in favor of unity of plan and action, but he thinks as I do that the plan of Lloyd George is not workable, and for reasons somewhat similar to those I have given.

He has nothing in mind and says that he dares not formulate a plan because it might be looked upon with suspicion. He wants us to take the initiative and he promises that we can count upon him to back to a finish any reasonable suggestion that we make.

He thoroughly approves my insistence that we work instead of accepting invitations to eat and drink and says that he refuses everything himself. He is not going to the very large luncheon given by the President tomorrow which I did not feel at liberty to upset because all arrangements were made, invitations out etc. before we arrived last night. He applauded when I told him it was my last.

I like him very much. He has put his time at my disposal and asks me to come at my pleasure unannounced and says the door will always be open.   Affectionately yours,   E. M. House[1]

TLS (WP, DLC).
[1] EMH to WW, Nov. 25, 1917, T telegram (WP, DLC, and SDR, RG 59, 763.72/7922½, DNA) is a summary of this letter.

From Herbert Clark Hoover

Washington, D. C.

Dear Mr. President: Twenty-third November *1917*

In the matter of restrictions on brewing, I am having an executive order drawn on the lines of your suggestions and am consulting the Treasury and the Department of Agriculture as to the technology and administrative measures involved. The Internal Revenue will need to take over the enforcement of the regulations.

Yours faithfully,   Herbert Hoover

TLS (WP, DLC).

A Translation of a Telegram from Fridtjof Nansen to Nils Claus Ihlen

Washington 11/23/17

Number 661. Personal. Telegram from Head of Delegation in connection with Number 633.[1] Yesterday, as anticipated in an earlier message, I had an interview with the President of the United States. I stated as strongly as possible how serious the situation was for the Nordic neutrals and how important it was to come to an agreement with his country as soon as possible, since delay tends to create needless irritation and ill feeling. He agreed with that and assured me that his policy was to avoid breaking off the negotiations and to come to an agreement. I reported that, after seeing the Norwegian government's proposal, just received, I saw the situation in a brighter light and thought we had now found a useful basis for more productive discussions. This pleased him very much. After discussing our difficulties vis-à-vis Germany in greater detail, I also stressed the strong need for the other two Scandinavian countries also to reach agreement. As he was no doubt aware, it was especially difficult for Sweden with regard to iron ore, for Swedish contracts, which were made for fifteen years ahead to deliver this ore to Germany, prevented Sweden from stopping these exports.

The President understood that breaking these contracts could in many cases create serious difficulty with Germany. So far as I knew, the Swedes were willing to limit the export as much as possible and ought not to be asked to do more, for otherwise the negotiations might break off, with serious results, especially in view of the current situation in Europe, including the Baltic. He agreed with this.

I also mentioned the forthcoming meeting of the Kings at Christiania[2] and said I considered it beneficial that the Scandinavian countries held together on a policy of neutrality and that they could then be a factor that both Germany and the Allies had to take account of. He said expressly that he agreed with this view of the matter.

I said further that the Allies must not misjudge the consequences of pressing a neutral too hard and forcing it to make a stand. So far as I can judge, Sweden, Denmark, and probably Holland will in the end have to go reluctantly with Germany. The President said that, even if Norway did not have to go with the others, the position of Scandinavia would become hopeless, something to be avoided at all costs.

The President had heard that it was rumored in Berlin that America and England would occupy Norway's south coast as a naval base; he wondered how such a rumor could start. I said that possibly I could give an explanation: before leaving, I had heard an English minister explain the advantage to England of bringing Norway into the war since its southern coast afforded an excellent base, etc., and at the same time an American admiral had spoken similarly. Thus the question was discussed openly among naval authorities.

Bryn[3]

T telegram (H4-S-4/17, Norwegian Royal Ministry of Foreign Affairs-Ar).
[1] F. Nansen to N. C. Ihlen, Nov. 15, 1917, Hw telegram (H4-S-4/19, Norwegian Royal Ministry of Foreign Affairs-Ar). Nansen reported that he had warned American leaders that pressing the neutral governments too hard on the supply question might lead them to gravitate toward Germany. There was danger of a fatal split between Norway on the one side and Sweden and Denmark on the other.
[2] Gustavus V of Sweden, Christian X of Denmark, and Haakon VII of Norway, together with their respective Premiers and Foreign Ministers, met in Christiania (Oslo) from November 28 to December 1. They agreed to maintain their neutrality in the war and to assist each other through the exchange of goods and commodities during the war emergency. *New York Times*, Nov. 28-30, Dec. 2, 1917.
[3] Helmer Halvorsen Bryn, Norwegian Minister to the United States.

To Robert Lansing, with Enclosure

My dear Mr. Secretary: The White House 24 November, 1917

Surely Mr. Hoover is right about this. I had not heard of President Menocal's intervention in this matter but take it for granted that you are handling the matter in the spirit of this memorandum of Mr. Hoover's.

Cordially and faithfully yours,   Woodrow Wilson

E N C L O S U R E

From Herbert Clark Hoover

Washington, D. C.

Dear Mr. President: Twenty-fourth November *1917*

As you know, we have formed a joint committee with the Allies for the united purchase and division of Cuban and other foreign sugars. In the meantime we had fixed a price agreement with our own sugar producers. On the basis of our domestic price the International Committee should pay approximately $4.80 per hundred, delivered New York, for Cuban sugar. This is an increase of $1.30 per 100 lbs. over 1913, the year before the war, and an increase of 25¢ over 1917, and in our view fully takes account of any increased production costs in Cuba and leaves a very wide margin of profit to the producers.

The English members of our committee contended for a price of about $4.30 New York, but, in an effort to conciliate, we offered and persuaded the English members to agree with us in offering the excessive amount of $4.90.

President Menocal has intervened and is endeavouring to force a price which works out from $5.05 to $5.25 New York and has dispatched a committee to New York to negotiate.

The President of Cuba, we understand, refuses to acceed and claims he will force us to agree through the American Government. We have endeavoured to keep the entire matter simply a commercial transaction, but they insist on interjection of governmental pressure.

I feel that we cannot, in justice to our consumers or to our own producers, acceed to their demands. It means on maximum figures demanded, about $40,000,000 to our people, and likewise a large increase of similar amounts to our Allies, which we will probably have to finance. Cuba only obtains a minor part of this huge sum because an increased price to them automatically raises the price of all the sugar of the whole world.

I trust we will, if the matter arises, have your support in our views.   Faithfully yours,   Herbert Hoover

TLS (SDR, RG 59, 837.61351/60, DNA).

From Thomas Davies Jones

My dear Mr. President   Washington Nov. 24, 1917

I had a frank but entirely friendly talk with Mr. White[1] today about the matter you spoke to me about last evening: and I believe that he will guard that unruly member of his[2] in the future, and that such drastic action as you suggested will not be necessary, at least for the present.

It seems to me probable that the relations between our Board and the Food Administration in connection with the food requirements of the hard pressed Border Neutrals will become strained, and it would be unfortunate to have any avoidable personal complications introduced. We can allot food supplies but we cannot furnish them without co-operation of the Food Administration. I do not know that the attitude of the Food Administration has been deliberately formulated. But some things have been said and done which indicate that we are not to recognize any obligation to share with those neutrals except out of our abundance. That will never do. The needs of the fighting forces must of course be met first:

but after that we should share with those who are in need all that we have whether it be scarce or plenty

Faithfully yours   Thomas D. Jones.

ALS (WP, DLC).
  [1] John Beaver White, representative of the Food Administration on the War Trade Board.
  [2] Presumably his tongue.

From Washington Lee Capps

Dear Mr. President: Washington November 24th 1917

In acknowledging the receipt of your letter of November 23rd, acceding to my request to be relieved from duty with the Emergency Fleet Corporation,—this letter having been handed to me by the Secretary of the Navy, yesterday afternoon,—I beg leave to express my very deep appreciation of your consideration and the generous terms in which you have characterized my performance of duty.

Very respectfully,   W. L. Capps

TLS (WP, DLC).

Louis Freeland Post to Joseph Patrick Tumulty

My dear Mr. Tumulty: Washington November 24, 1917.

Regarding the telegram from Norfolk of November 23rd, purporting to be signed by railway and steamship clerks, and with reference to which the President asks my advice as per your letter of November 24th, I am informed that all the signers but two are railway and steamboat employees out of work in support of the strike for the right to organize without risking discharge which railway clerks of the Atlantic Coast Line Company are making. The other two signers appear to be striking employees of the Atlantic Coast Line. Because freight clerks and freight handlers at the Norfolk transfer point refuse to handle freight destined to or coming from the Atlantic Coast Line, so long as the right of its clerks is penalized, none of the boats nor railroads at Norfolk are able to move any freight. This is the present situation at Norfolk. The best information available to the Department regarding a settlement there is that it could be secured without difficulty and by telephone if the Atlantic Coast Line dispute were adjusted.

An adjustment has been almost effected by this Department in the Atlantic Coast Line dispute as reported to us today. Concessions have been made on both sides. At the suggestion of the Department the Company had announced its abandonment, for the period of the war, of its policy of dispensing with the services of clerks for affiliating with the union, and by mutual arrangement has met a committee of its striking clerks for the purpose of discussing conditions of their re-employment. The settlement hangs fire only upon one point. While the Company is willing to re-instate 75% of these clerks witin 30 days, the clerks organization insists upon re-instatement of all within five days. I am sure that a complete and satisfactory settlement could be made if (1) the Company would re-instate all instead of 75% of those employees, or (2) could satisfy the clerks' organizations that in making re-instatements there will be no discriminations against employees who have been active in promoting organization.

In my opinion the employees ought to be protected against this possibility. It may be remote or even non existent; but fear of it is a fact, and re-instatement of all the employees seems to me the simplest as well as the surest way of establishing confidence and preventing more disputes. Inasmuch, therefore, as both sides have indicated their willingness to abide by the President's decision, and in view of the fact that the Norfolk situation as well as that of the Atlantic Coast Line itself, and the feeling of wage earners all over the country, would be most favorably affected, I suggest the following message (or one of like effect) from the President to J. R. Kenley, president of the Atlantic Coast Line Railroad, Wilmington, N. C.:

"I am much gratified to learn of the patriotic disposition of both sides to the dispute between the Atlantic Coast Line Railway and its clerks, as shown by their near approach to a settlement (period) May I not urge, in the interest of the country at this war time, and as a further means of strengthening the confidence of the wage earners of the United States in the good will of employers, that you yield the difference now remaining between you and your organized clerks by immediately re-instating all who wish to return to their former places in your service."[1]

Trusting that these suggestions may be of use to the President, I am,   Cordially yours,   Louis F. Post

TLS (WP, DLC).
  [1] Wilson repeated this *verbatim* in WW to J. R. Kenly (not Kenley), Nov. 24, 1917, T telegram (Letterpress Books, WP, DLC).

David Rowland Francis to Robert Lansing

Petrograd. Nov. 24, 1917 Recd, 27, 9:15 a.m.

2024. Translation of Trotzky's speech previously referred to[1] transmitted in full by mail. After outlining his interpretation of effect of Soviet Peace Decree upon Russias foreign relations he emphasized power of working classes and helplessness of Bourgeoisie. Referring to political attitude of other nations towards Soviet Government he stated greatest hostility thereto manifested by Great Britain, referred to opposition to war on part of French working classes and the resulting ministerial crisis, the hesitation of Italy prior to war and present despair her working class and then referred to the United States as follows: "The United States intervened in war after three years had elapsed under the influence of sober calculation of American stock exchange. America could not permit victory of one coalition over the other. America interested in weakening both coalitions and strengthening hegemony of American capital. Furthermore America's war industry is interested in war. During war America's exports increased more than twofold and reached figures which not one capitalistic state had attained. All the exports with hardly any exception go to Allied countries. When in January Germany announced unlimited submarine warfare all railway stations and docks in United States were crammed with products of war industry. To remove them was impossible. Transportation was disorganized and New York experienced hunger riots such as we have not seen here. At that time financial capital presented Wilson an ultimatum: the sale of products of industry must be guaranteed which Wilson obeyed hence the preparation for war and later the war itself. America is not aiming at territorial acquisition. America can patiently receive the fact of Soviet Government as she is sufficiently satisfied by exhaustion of Allied countries and of Germany, in addition America is interested in investing her capital in Russia." Trotzky further stated that Germany's internal economic situation forces her to adopt semipatient attitude regarding Soviet Government and finally declared that impression produced in Europe by peace decree verifies most optimistic hopes. He then gave in full the text of communication to Allied Ambassadors[2] which I have already telegraphed and also the following text of order to General Dukhonin.[3] "Citizen Supreme Commander In Chief the Council of Commissaries of the People by Commission of the All Russian Congress of Workmens and Soldiers Deputies has assumed the Government together with the obligations to propose to all belligerent nations and to their Governments an immediate armistice on all fronts and immediate opening of negotiations with a view to concluding peace on democratic principles. Now when the Government of Soviets has been confirmed in all the most important points of the country the Council of Commissaries of the People considers it necessary to make without delay a formal proposal for armistice to all belligerent countries, both to Allies and to those engaged in hostile operations against us. An announcement to this effect has been sent by Commissary of the People for Foreign Affairs to all the plenipotentiary representatives of Allied countries in Petrograd. You, Citizen Supreme Commander in Chief, the Council of Commissaries of the People, in fulfillment of the decision of all Russian Congress of the Councils of Workmen and Soldiers Deputies, Commissions, immediately upon receiving the present announcement, to address to the military authorities of the hostile armies a proposal to immediately cease military operations with a view to opening peace negotiations. Whilst charging you with the conduct of these preliminary negotiations the Council of the Commissiaries of the People orders you first to report without interruption to the Council by direct wire regarding the progress of your negotiations with the representatives of the hostile armies; second, to sign the act of armistice only by a preliminary agreement with the Council of Commissaries of the People. The President of the Council of Commissaries of the People, V. Lenin; the Commissary for Foreign Affairs, L. Trotzky; the Commissary for Military Affairs, Krylenko."⁴ As Dukhonin refused to obey instructions the following was officially promulgated on the twenty third instant. "Soldiers: the matter of peace is in your hands. You will not suffer counter revolutionary generals to destroy the great cause of peace. You will surround them with a guard in order to avoid lynching unworthy of the revolutionary army and to prevent these generals from avoiding the court that awaits them. You will preserve the strictest revolutionary and military order.

Let the regiments on the front immediately elect plenipotentiaries to formally initiate negotiations for an armistice with the enemy. The Council of the Commissaries of the People gives you the right to do this.

Inform us of every step of negotiations through all channels. Only the Council of Commissaries of the People has the right to sign the final convention for the armistice.

Soldiers: the matter of peace is in your hands. Let there be vigilance, self-control and energy and the cause of peace will conquer. In the name of the Government of the Russian Republic, the President of the Council of Commissaries of the People, Lenin. The Commissary of the People of Military Affairs and Supreme Commander In Chief N. Krylenko."   Francis.

T telegram (WP, DLC).

[1] Trotsky, in his capacity as Commissar for Foreign Affairs, spoke before the Central Executive Committee of the Soviet on November 21. Francis summarizes his remarks well. Extensive extracts from his speech are printed in Jane Degras, ed., *Soviet Documents on Foreign Policy* (3 vols., London and New York, 1951-53), I, 4-8.

[2] D. R. Francis to R. Lansing, Nov. 22, 1917, *FR 1918, Russia*, I, 244.

[3] Gen. Nikolai Nikolaevich Dukhonin, acting Supreme Commander of the Russian armies.

[4] Nikolai Vasil'evich Krylenko.

Maud May Wood Park[1] to Helen Hamilton Gardener

Dear Mrs. Gardener: Washington, D. C. November 24, 1917.

In sending you the enclosed lists I want to explain that they are based on the poll made last December, January, and February.[2]

You will remember that in consequence of the Administration's wish to limit legislation in the extraordinary session of Congress to war measures, our National Board voted that no attempt should be made by our committee to talk with members, either in the Senate or the House, about their stand on the Federal Amendment. For that reason no poll was made during the extraordinary session.

Faithfully yours,   Maud Wood Park.

TLS (WP, DLC).

[1] Wife of the late Charles Edward Park. She was a longtime suffrage leader, first in her native Massachusetts, more recently, nationwide. At this time, she was living in Washington where she served as "chairman" of the Congressional Committee of the National American Woman Suffrage Association.

[2] "POLL OF SENATE—65TH CONGRESS," "DOUBTFUL REPRESENTATIVES," "UNFAVORABLE REPRESENTATIVES November 22, 1917," and "FAVORABLE REPRESENTATIVES. November 22, 1917," T MSS (WP, DLC).

From Verner Zevola Reed[1]

Santa Barbara, Calif., November 25, 1917.

As the Honorable W. B. Wilson, the chairman of your mediation committee is enroute to Oregon and as can probably not be reached by wire until Monday I am reporting to you direct that the threatened strike in the oil industry of California was averted by an agreement reached at two o'clock this Sunday morning, the full details will be transmitted to your chairman as soon as possible. Respectfully submitted.   Verner Z. Reed.

T telegram (WP, DLC).

[1] Retired oil operator and financier of Denver; at this time a member of the President's Mediation Commission.

To Verner Zevola Reed

[The White House] 26 November, 1917

Thank you very warmly for the good news of your telegram of November twenty-fifth.   Woodrow Wilson.

T telegram (Letterpress Books, WP, DLC).

From Edward Mandell House

Paris, November 26, 1917.

The conference with Clemenceau and Petaimé [Pétain] yesterday resulted in a clear understanding as to the military situation. They gave us information about the number of fighting men left in France & what would be necessary from us.

If we send over a million men by autumn 1918 they will continue to use their own actual fighting men for offensive operations & use our responsibility [ours] for defensive purposes until then.

Petaimé believes in [that] whatever supreme War Council is created [it] should have a President or Executive officer to execute the [its] decisions. This is sure to meet with English opposition. What is your opinion of it? The English arrived by [arrive] tomorrow night, and on Wednesday Lloyd George, Clemenceau & I will have a conference.   Edward House.

EBWhw decode of T telegram (WP, DLC).

From Henry Morgenthau

New York
My dear Mr. President: November Twenty-sixth 1917.

You will recall that when I returned from Turkey in February, 1916, I was very much concerned and alarmed by the indifference displayed by the National Democratic Committee concerning the coming Presidential election.

I insisted that you permit me to resign my post and devote myself to the task of rousing the Democrats from their lethargy, and infusing enthusiasm amongst them for the campaign. I am prouder of my share in your re-election than any other service I have ever rendered.

At present I am again Cassandric in mind and want to sound an alarm as regards the coming Congressional election. It would be an irremediable calamity if you did not receive a thorough vindication of your splendid administration in the 1918 election.

Fortunately the Democratic Committee, George Creel and others are working faithfully. You are every day doing your Big Bit towards moulding public opinion. But many of our citizens are still opposed to the war, and their stand is largely based on ignorance of the causes, the scope and the results of the war.

My interest in the New York municipal election was not due to any personal affection for the candidates. It was entirely due to my devotion to good government and to my belief that the growing anti-war sentiment in New York had to be fought as vigorously as possible. I addressed a great many large and some small meetings, and mixed with Democrats, Independents and Socialists. I was greatly discouraged at the amount of outright opposition and the tremendous indifference to the war, as well as by the lack of enthusiasm among the mass of those who are supporting the war.

It has occurred to me that someone should undertake a very specific task which now presents itself to me as necessary. This task is to concentrate the public mind upon certain facts leading up to the war with a view to rallying the indifferent and winning those who oppose us. The situation requires that the story of Germany's intrigue and perfidy be adequately set down in a way to be perfectly comprehended by our people. The premeditated and carefully organized effort to interfere in the government of almost every nation in the world, to plant discord between nations, the whole outrageous scheme to dominate Europe and even America—that is the side of Germany with which Americans are not yet fully acquainted.

It can easily be shown that Turkey was the cancer in the life of the world, and, not being properly treated, has now grown into the greater cancer of Central Europe. If the Turks have, for four hundred and fifty years, constantly endangered the peace of Europe, what will happen to the world if Germany and Turkey now assume the role of tyrant and trouble-maker together?

The system of permeation through diplomatic agents and spies, which has marked the whole organization of Germany's foreign policy, is nowhere so evident as in Turkey and the Balkans.

I should like, with your approval and assistance, to undertake the preparation of this story on *a larger scale* than I have done in the enclosed articles.[1]

I am considering writing a book in which I would lay bare, not only Germany's permeation of Turkey and the Balkans, but that system as it appears in every country of the world. The German permeation of Turkey and the Balkans, their winning of Turkey and then Bulgaria, plus their destruction of Greece, placed the veritable keystone of their power on the Bosphorus. The peculiar facilities I had of informing myself upon this phase of the subject, seem to make it incumbent upon me to tell my story at this time. For in Turkey we see the evil spirit of Germany at its worst— culminating at last in the greatest crime of all ages, the horrible massacre of the helpless Armenians and Syrians. This particular detail of the story and Germany's abettance of the same, I feel positive will appeal to the mass of Americans in small towns and country districts as no other aspect of the war could, and convince them of the necessity of carrying the war to a victorious conclusion.

I have been informed that this book can be syndicated and published simultaneously over the whole country in the important daily newspapers, and in some of the larger agricultural publications.

The book should be published early this Summer and I would like your opinion as to the advisability of my giving the entire profits to a Congressional Campaign Committee; this Committee to undertake under the proper direction to assist all Congressional candidates of whose loyalty and support to the Administration, there can be no doubt.

We must win a victory for the war policy of the Government and every legitimate step or means should be utilized to accomplish it.

I am anxious to hear whether my plan meets with your approval.

With kindest regards, I remain

Yours faithfully,   Henry Morgenthau

TLS (WP, DLC).
    [1] "Emperor William Must Go, Says Morgenthau," *New York Times Magazine*, Sept. 30, 1917, p. 2, and "How the Kaiser, Weeks Ahead, Fixed Date for War to Begin, Now Revealed by Morgenthau," New York *World*, Oct. 14, 1917. See also WW to H. Morgenthau, Nov. 27, 1917, n. 1.

From Herbert Clark Hoover

Washington, D. C.

Dear Mr. President: Twenty-sixth November *1917*

As you are aware the keystone of the Food Law in its provisions as to control of distribution rests on the provisions against "unjust, unreasonable, unfair * * * profit." Now that we have the principal trades under license the interpretation of what is "unjust, unreasonable, unfair * * * profit" is arising daily.

I should like to recommend to you the adoption of the following principle for guidance of the Food Administration. That principle to be "that any profit in excess of the normal pre-war average profit of that business and place where free, competitive conditions existed is deemed to be unjust, unreasonable, unfair profit."

We have given much thought to this subject and have proposed it as a tentative principle in the great number of trade conferences held in formulating regulations and securing the co-operation of the trades in their administration. The very large profits earned from war conditions prior to our entry into the war have established a fictitious basis of commerce and at the opening of our work this principle was most strongly resented in many quarters but I believe that our steady propaganda on the line that no one has a right to take an extra profit from America at war has now proceeded so far as to enable its adoption in the food trades without consequential opposition.

If you are able to agree with this basis of interpretation it would be of the greatest help if I could have an instruction from you in somewhat the terms of the enclosed draft.[1]

If this is done I should like to ask the Federal Trade Commission to make determinations of what pre-war or normal profits were in some of the larger trades—to be determined in either of four ways as the particular business may dictate as the most facile for guidance.

1. Return upon capital invested.
2. Profit per unit of commodity.
3. Percentage upon the "turn over" of specific commodities.
4. Positive differentials for handling certain commodities between purchase price and sale price.

Yours faithfully,   Herbert Hoover

TLS (WP, DLC).
[1] See WW to H. C. Hoover, Nov. 27, 1917, n. 1.

Louis Freeland Post to Joseph Patrick Tumulty

My dear Mr. Tumulty: Washington November 26, 1917.

I have considered the following telegram received by the President from Mr. J. R. Kenley, President of the Atlantic Coast Line Railroad and submitted to me by Mr. Swem in behalf of the President:

"Your telegram of last night received this morning. While the disposition and purpose of this company is to do or to forego anything that will further the interest of the country at this time, and while it is our intention to yield to your request if you insist, nevertheless I sincerely feel that an acceptance of your present suggestion would entail results in our operation and our ability to serve the country that would be most unfortunate; it would also inflict grave injustice in displacing many loyal men who have come to the aid of the company and the country and enabled us to continue the uninterrupted operation of our property. Believing that there are aspects of the case with which you are not familiar I respectfully ask that you give us an opportunity to represent the situation to you in person. I am willing [unwilling?] to assume the responsibility for the settlement proposed without your insistance."

In response to your request that I supply the President with a tentative draft of reply to President Kenley, I suggest the following for his consideration:

"Replying to your telegram of the 25th I am sincerely grateful for your assurance that it is the disposition and purpose of your Company to do or to forego anything that will further the interests of the country at this time (period) I am all the more grateful because it appears to me important under the circumstances that your Company make the seeming sacrifice of yielding to my request of the 24th. Having considered the interests of the Company, the situation of the employees, the general labor situation and the welfare of the country with reference to them all, I feel that this course is the desirable one for your Company to pursue (period) Your assurances disclose a patriotic disposition and I have every confidence that your employees and those of the other transportation Companies affected will not fail to respond in like spirit but will cooperate fully and fairly."[1]

Trusting that these suggestions may be of use to the President, I am,   Cordially yours,   Louis F. Post

TLS (WP, DLC).
  [1] For the telegram which Wilson sent, see WW to J. R. Kenly, Nov. 27, 1917.

From William Bauchop Wilson

Oregon City, Oregon, November 26, 1917.

I am glad to report that Commissioner Verner Z. Reed of the President's Mediation Commission has succeeded in securing a settlement of the difficulties in the oil fields of Southern California between the independent oil operators and about eight thousand of their employes. The list of the settlement is as follows:

First—Recognition of the eight hour day to be effective first to the fullest extent practicable, subject only to longer working hours that may be demanded by the Federal Government to secure the necessary war requirements.

Second—A minimum wage scale for oil workers of four dollars for eight hours work effective December first, nineteen seventeen.

Third—No discrimination against union labor.

Fourth—Machinery for adjustment of disagreements between employers and employees and in case of failure to agree modes of settlement to be established by the Secretary of Labor.

This very satisfactory adjustment was due to Mr. Reed's skillful negotiation and the expert knowledge of oil matters which he was able to give to the Government as well as the splendid spirit both of the employers and the employees in subordinating their personal difference to the national good. Your Commission is on its way to Portland and after a few days there will proceed to Seattle to deal with the very important lumber situation of the Northwest.

W. B. Wilson

T telegram (WP, DLC).

From Frank William Taussig

My dear Mr. President: Washington November 26, 1917.

So far as I know,—and I believe I am as well informed as one can be,—the German government has never supported German dye manufacturers in this country, or elsewhere, by any form of subsidy or financial assistance. Financial assistance has not been needed, because the German dye manufacturers were financially strong without it. Direct export subsidy has never been given to anyone, except in the case of the sugar bounties. Indirect subsidy may be said to have been given in the form of preferential railway rates for export business; but this sort of thing, as I have remarked already, has been done by almost all countries.

Believe me, ever with high respect and regard,

Very sincerely yours,   F. W. Taussig

TLS (WP, DLC).

From the Diary of Josephus Daniels

November Monday 26 1917

Went to see the President. I had 2 cablegrams from Benson One recommended that our admiral in Europe accept position as honorary member of the British Admiralty. Very confidential & wished nothing said because if agreeable to us Geddes would see the King before it would be done An emphatic *No*.

Also Benson telegraphed plan of a Naval War Council—WW said the Military Council's plans would be changed to some extent and he suggested no action as to Naval Council be taken until changes were made known.

He said if Congress authorized acceptance by naval officers of honors &c from Grt Britain he would veto the bill. It would cause them to be trying to secure foreign favor & would be unAmerican.

Would Japs go to Russia? No, said Ishii Too far, not enough ships.

Pres. looked weary—war-worn, & said rather quizzically: "My mother did not raise her boy to be a War President—but it is a liberal education[."]

To Henry Morgenthau

[The White House]
My dear Mr. Morgenthau: 27 November, 1917

I have just read your letter of yesterday and in reply would say that I think you get impressions about public opinion in New York which by no means apply to the whole country, but nevertheless I think that your plan for a full exposition of some of the principal lines of German intrigue is an excellent one and I hope that you will undertake to write and publish the book you speak of.[1]

I am writing in great haste, but not in hasty judgment you may be sure.

Cordially and sincerely yours,   Woodrow Wilson

TLS (Letterpress Books, WP, DLC).
[1] A series of articles published in *World's Work*, XXXVI and XXXVII (May 1918-Jan. 1919) was the basis of Henry Morgenthau, *Ambassador Morgenthau's Story* (Garden City, N. Y., 1918). The book was dedicated "To Woodrow Wilson, the exponent in America of the enlightened public opinion of the world, which has decreed that the rights of small nations shall be respected and that such crimes as are described in this book shall never again darken the pages of history."

To Herbert Clark Hoover

My dear Mr. Hoover: The White House 27 November, 1917

In signing the enclosed Executive Order[1] I am acting, and acting willingly, upon your judgment, because I cannot pretend to the knowledge of the case which you have. I should have assumed that possibly it would be fair to allow a somewhat increased margin above the pre-war margin, because these dealers, like all the rest of us, have to adjust themselves to an enhanced cost of living so far as their own personal support is concerned, but I have no doubt you have taken that into consideration along with the other matters affecting your judgment.

Cordially and sincerely yours,   Woodrow Wilson

TLS (H. Hoover Papers, HPL).
    ¹ It directed the United States Food Administrator to find, for foods and feeds and their derivative products, "that a just, reasonable, and fair profit is the normal average profit which persons engaged in the same business and place obtained prior to July 1, 1914, under free competitive conditions." The Administrator was also to indicate, if he saw fit, what margin over cost would return such a fair profit and to take legal steps to prohibit the taking of any greater profit. For the text, see *Official Bulletin*, I (Nov. 30, 1917), 1.

To Maud May Wood Park

My dear Mrs. Park: [The White House] 27 November, 1917

Thank you sincerely for the list you are kind enough to send me under cover of your letter of December [November] twenty-fourth.¹ It will be of real use to me.

I also appreciate the explanation you give of when the poll was made and of the discounts therefore to be taken into the reckoning.

Cordially and sincerely yours,   Woodrow Wilson

TLS (Letterpress Books, WP, DLC).
    ¹ That is Maud M. W. Park to Helen H. Gardener, Nov. 24, 1917.

To William Bauchop Wilson

[The White House] 27 November, 1917

Your telegram of yesterday about the settlement effected by Mr. Reed in the Southern California oil fields brings me deep gratification and reassurance. Please convey my congratulations to Mr. Reed and my warm appreciation of their patriotic attitude to the employers and employees concerned.   Woodrow Wilson.

T telegram (Letterpress Books, WP, DLC).

To John Reese Kenly

[The White House] 27 November, 1917

Replying to your telegram of the twenty-fifth may I not say that I appreciate the patriotic spirit of it, all the more because I understand just the embarrassments which would be involved in complying with the request I made of you by telegram on the twenty-fourth? It would give me a great deal of pleasure to see you but I venture to suggest that that is not necessary because my request was based rather upon national considerations than upon the special circumstances connected with the present difference between the Atlantic Coast Line and its employees. I beg you to believe that

I made the request, and now renew it, only because of my familiarity with the general labor situation in the country and my conviction that a compliance with my request by the Atlantic Coast Line will distinctly contribute to the conditions upon which we must depend for the full energy and continued quiet of the country. May I not again express my warm appreciation of your attitude?

Woodrow Wilson.

T telegram (Letterpress Books, WP, DLC).

To M. Clemmons[1]

My dear Sir: [The White House] 27 November, 1917

May I not have the pleasure, in replying to your letter of the twenty-fifth,[2] of calling your attention to the following passages:

"We are such stuff as dreams are made on [of] * * *"

—The Tempest (Act 4; Scene 1; 154th line)

"What stuff wilt have a kirtle of?"

—Henry IV (Part 2; Act 2; Scene 4)

"Do not squander time; for that is the stuff which life is made of."

—Franklin (Way to Wealth; 1st paragraph)

And may I not add that that rule that a sentence shall not end with a preposition is a mere piece of rhetorical affectation?

Very sincerely yours,   Woodrow Wilson

TLS (Letterpress Books, WP, DLC).
   [1] Clemmons, of 9 Prospect Park, West, Brooklyn, N. Y., has not been further identified.
   [2] It is missing.

From Louis Freeland Post

My dear Mr. President: Washington November 27, 1917.

The resolutions forwarded to you by Mr. Hurley in his letter of November 20, 1917,[1] and transmitted by you to me through Mr. Swem with request for information and suggestion, are returned with a cordial expression of appreciation of the opportunity to advise regarding them.

The resolutions describe a more serious need. In the closing hours of the last session, Congress appropriated to the Secretary of Labor for war emergency employment service until the close of this fiscal year, $250,000. The Secretary had, upon careful estimates, asked for $750,000 and the Senate had allowed $500,000. You will see, therefore, that the actual appropriation of only $250,000 was in all probability quite inadequate for its purpose.

The shipbuilding program alone demands an approximate increase of 150,000 workers, 70% of whom must be above the laboring grade. Taking labor "turn-over" into account this means that not much if any less than half a million workers must be marshalled for ship yard employment within the next six or seven months. Even the economical U. S. Employment Service, which was operated last year at an average cost per placement of 65¢, can hardly meet this shipbuilding need with a less expenditure, considering the extra difficulties, than $1.00 per placement or half a million dollars for the desired result. And the shipbuilding program presents only one of several war labor needs. In munition production, for instance, there is evidently a great labor shortage. One munitions concern has recently applied for 8,000 workers. For all the basic war industries together, the necessary labor shift may be roughly estimated at about 12% of the wage working population—more than 5,000,000—within a year.

Without a well placed net work of placement offices and a well developed clearing system devoted primarily to war emergency employment service, this tremendous shifting of workers is likely to cause industrial chaos. It is almost certain to impose further distressing conditions upon a wage earning population already staggering under burdens of rising living costs. A national employment service, therefore, seems to me to be imperative,—one which can efficiently utilize existing State and municipal employment services and the cooperation of State Councils of Defense and other executive bodies in a federated system. This seems to me to be necessary for success in the war in so far as success is dependent upon industrial activities. I believe, also, that the system should be well financed at as early a date as possible. Such a service can not be sufficiently financed with less than a million dollars to begin with.

Such a national employment system has been started by the Department of Labor. State systems have been called upon to cooperate not only in our general employment service but especially to assist at this time in meeting the immediate needs of ship yards. Nearly every State has given hearty assent. All together this adjustment furnishes a chain of more than 200 offices operated by a considerable body of experienced employment-service workers through whom the necessary training can be provided for rapid extensions and intensifications of the whole system.

The work of the shipyard supply is being done with the small appropriation mentioned above. Utilizing the Public Service Reserve (a war emergency branch of the Department of Labor) as its registration agency, the Department has begun a campaign for finding all available shipyard workers whose transfer will not disturb other eseential [essential] industries or be in any other way detrimental to the national welfare.

If in possession of sufficient funds, the Department would immediately organize that full complement of employment offices which is necessary in my judgment to relieve the distress of workers in some places from lack of employment and the perplexity of employers in other places over lack of labor. This is a condition of labor maladjustment which such a complete employment service as the Department of Labor can create by mere extension of its present system would quickly and strongly tend to readjust.

I am, therefore, glad that Mr. Hurley has commended to your consideration the resolutions enclosed in his letter to you, and trust that early and adequate financial support for the emergency employment activities for this Department may result.

Cordially yours,   Louis F. Post

TLS (WP, DLC).
¹ E. N. Hurley to WW, Nov. 20, 1917, TLS (WP, DLC). At a conference in Washington of the Shipyard Employment Managers, a resolution was passed to ask Hurley to inform Wilson of the urgent need to strengthen the United States Employment Service. The group estimated that $1,000,000 was required for new offices to provide between 250,000 and 300,000 additional workers for shipbuilding.

From Royal Meeker

My dear Mr. President: Washington November 27, 1917.

Referring to my letter of November 12 in reply to yours of November 7,¹ asking for an approximate estimate of the cost of making the surveys suggested in my letter of November 6,² I wish to say that this morning Prof. Henry R. Seager, of the Shipping Wage Adjustment Board, called me by telephone and asked if my Bureau was in a position to proceed with studies of cost of living and family budgets in the shipbuilding centers.

The Shipping Wage Adjustment Board feels the imperative need of having these studies begun immediately. Similar wage boards are in the identical position. In order to make wage adjustments and keep up production, they must know with approximate accuracy the changes in prices and the cost of family budgets over a period of years.

I understand that labor disputes are brewing in the shipbuilding cities of Wilmington, Delaware, Chester and Philadelphia. I think it is possible to secure the price and budget data required by the Shipping Wage Adjustment Board for its decisions in these cities in a very few weeks. The practicality of this method of settling wage disputes on the basis of changes in the cost of living could thereby be demonstrated beyond cavil.

Of course, if we now had as our standard of value Prof. Irving Fisher's "standardized dollar" or commodity dollar, wage-earners and salaried employees would not now be so seriously pinched by rising prices. Even if we had the "standardized dollar," statistical studies of changing prices of commodities in terms of gold and surveys of family budgets would be just as necessary as now for only in this way can changes in the purchasing power of gold be ascertained.

As I see it, the two most important studies in the field of labor at the present time are these investigations into changes in the cost of living and the industrial surveys in order to determine the extent and possibilities of the substitution of female labor for male labor in our principal industries. As I have indicated in previous correspondence, I am doing something in both these fields, but much more needs to be done than I can possibly do even though I should break off immediately all other work of my Bureau and concentrate upon these two lines of study.

If you think my suggestions have any merit, I shall be glad to submit to you a more detailed program for one or both of these surveys.[3]   Sincerely yours,   Royal Meeker

TLS (WP, DLC).
  [1] WW to R. Meeker, Nov. 7, 1917, TLS (Letterpress Books, WP, DLC).
  [2] In the absence of Secretary Wilson, Meeker had written to Wilson on November 6 about necessary work for which the Bureau of Labor Statistics had insufficient resources. Meeker began by pointing out that the whole war was "but a series of highly specialized and enormously important labor problems," and that fighting at the front was "but a new and extra hazardous industry." "The labor of fighting the Germans face to face," he went on, "is no whit more important than any other labor in the great industry of beating the Germans, though it is undoubtedly more dangerous." Meeker noted that he was receiving requests from all over the country for information on strikes, lockouts, wages, hours and conditions of labor, employment of women to replace men, as well as on accident rates and health conditions, especially in the manufacture of explosives and other munitions of war. He was receiving "the most contradictory statements in regard to the scarcity of labor." Union leaders stoutly maintained that there was no scarcity, and employers just as stoutly held that their output was seriously reduced by stringent shortages. All these inquiries and requests for clarification were perfectly legitimate, Meeker wrote, and his bureau should have enough capable agents in the field to provide the latest and most accurate information in order to assist conciliators, arbitrators, and persons who sought new employees. The bureau should also be informed about health hazards growing out of the enormous expansion in the manufacturing of explosives, coal tar products, airplanes, and other war supplies. The war industries used large quantities of industrial poisons, some of which were new in the United States and, therefore, "especially deadly in their effects upon green and uninformed workers."
  Meeker said that he would not "indulge the passion for platitude" by pointing out that agriculture, industry, and commerce were absolutely dependent on labor; however, he did underscore the need for dependable information as to "the number of men and women in industry, the occupations they are engaged in, the feasibility of substituting women for men in certain occupations, and the possibilities of subtracting men and women from nonessential production." He concluded as follows:
  "I feel that if we are to win this war we must lay down a definite labor policy immediately and adhere to it rigorously. Price regulation and price control seem to be absolutely essential to the successful carrying on of this war. It seems to me just as essential to regulate the price of labor as it is to regulate and control the price of wheat, of sugar, and of coal. In fact, I think it wholly impossible to carry through the regulation of the prices of commodities without also working out a system for the control of wages.

Before any such wage regulation is attempted, however, it is absolutely necessary, in my judgment, that we ascertain the amount and kind of labor power in the country." R. Meeker to WW, Nov. 6, 1917, TCL (WP, DLC).

After consulting with other officials, Meeker wrote on November 12 that he was fairly confident that the program which he had outlined, together with an expansion of the work already undertaken on retail prices and the cost of living, could be carried through for $450,000. Information about the cost of living was proving to be very important in reaching settlement of labor disputes. Meeker also cited Valentine Everit Macy, chairman of the subcommittee on mediation and conciliation of the Council of National Defense, on the value of having the needed facts gathered by a permanent governmental bureau, so that the work could continue after the war and "serve as a basis in making the necessary industrial adjustments which are bound to follow upon the advent of peace." In closing, Meeker listed seven essential activities and the amounts needed for each. R. Meeker to WW, Nov. 12, 1917, TCL (WP, DLC).

³ Wilson held this correspondence in order to discuss it with Secretary Wilson upon his return from the West. WW to W. B. Wilson, Jan. 10, 1918, TCL (WP, DLC).

From William Bauchop Wilson, with Enclosure

My dear Mr. President:

At Portland, Oregon,
November 27, 1917.

Attached to the report of your Commission on the Bisbee deportations was a copy of my letter to Governor Campbell of Arizona, in which I set forth the requirements of the Federal Government as to law enforcement by state and county authorities in Arizona to terminate existing illegalities and prevent recurrences of deportations. At the time our report went to you the Governor had not replied. I now inclose, for the completeness of the record, a copy of the Governor's reply, which has since come to hand.

Faithfully yours,   W B Wilson

TLS (WP, DLC).

E N C L O S U R E

My dear Mr. Secretary: Phoenix, Arizona, Nov. 21, 1917.

I beg to acknowledge receipt of your favor, dated Bisbee, the 6th instant, which should have been replied to sooner, but for absence from the Capital and other business of an imperative nature.

Fully realizing the situation which confronted your Commission in the Warren Mining District, I desire to compliment you and the other members thereof on the fairness of your findings. I am sure that Sheriff Wheeler will fully live up to the assurances he has given and that strict observance of the requirements of the law will be absolutely adhered to by him and other county officials of Cochise County.

I am in thorough agreement with the contention that all executive officers of county and state must act in strict accordance with the laws, so that the rights and liberties of citizens may not be jeopardized or imposed upon.

Your assurance that the Federal government will cooperate with me in my endeavors to bring these ends about, to the end that Arizona may furnish its products in the fullest possible volume, for the needs of our nation during these troublous times, is appreciated.

For the State of Arizona, I desire to assure you that full cooperation will be rendered. With best thanks for your valued efforts during the five weeks' investigation of our industrial troubles, and trusting that all the details of the settlements entered into in the several mining districts visited will be carried out by all parties thereto, I am, with kind personal regards,

Sincerely,   Thomas E. Campbell Governor of Arizona.

TCL (WP, DLC).

From Frank Irving Cobb, with Enclosure

Dear Mr. President: New York November 27, 1917.

Alexander Konta and I had a little argument at dinner the other night about the question of declaring war on Austria-Hungary, he being an earnest advocate of such a declaration. Yesterday he wrote me a letter on the subject, which contains some very interesting information. There is nobody else in the United States who knows so much about the Austro-Hungarian propaganda and about the situation in Austria-Hungary as Konta; so I telephoned him this morning and asked his permission to send the letter to you for your information.   With sincere regards,   Frank I. Cobb

E N C L O S U R E

Alexander Konta to Frank Irving Cobb

My dear Frank: New York November Twenty-sixth, 1917.

Our little talk yesterday has given me food for thought. It seemed strange to me that you, with your unequalled opportunities for knowing the dangers of the present abnormal situation between the United States and Austro-Hungary, should advocate the continuance of that situation, whereas I—a Hungarian by birth, still held by many ties of sentiment to my country of origin—should hold an absolutely different view. You say that present conditions do not call for a declaration of war by the United States upon Austro-Hungary. I, on the other hand, assert that the conditions imperatively demand such a declaration. This is a striking difference of opinion. Not only that, but it first seemed to me when we talked it over that we were both on the wrong sides. It was you who should have been crying out for war—I who should have opposed the declaration.

On thinking the whole matter over, I have decided again to challenge your views—to try to show you, from facts old and new, drawn from my own observation of the times and my own intimate experience with Austro-Hungarian affairs—that a declaration is vitally necessary to the present and future interests of the United States. Before doing so, however, I just want to tell you that it is not wholly agreeable to me to write this letter. In the first place, I am too well-informed of the distress which now rules in Hungary—too saddened by the knowledge of the sufferings of my own relatives there—to wish that these sufferings should be increased by the entrance of the United States into the ranks of enemy nations. In the second place, the mere statement of my attitude—if it were publicly known—would bring upon me personally the bitter antagonisms of innumerable friends who do not realize, as I do, the very serious consequences of a mis-placed sympathy with Austro-Hungary in the present war and have not yet risen to a full conception of their duties to the country of their adoption. But I am quite prepared to face such antagonisms—even to witness the further distress of my native Hungary—if, by so doing, I can make plainer one vital truth. This truth is that, in the heart and soul of every naturalized American, the United States of America should come first—first, last, and all the time. In devotion to that idea I at least dare to declare myself, no matter what opposition comes.

But that by the way. You, at least, know pretty well that my ideas on this subject have not conduced to my personal happiness during the past three years. But let me now get straight to the point—the reasons why the United States should declare war upon Austro-Hungary. I shall take them up not so much in the order of their importance, as in the order which best suits my thoughts at the moment. This will afford me, perhaps, a better chance to tell you of some things not generally known—and in a reminiscential way—which will enforce the general argument.

First among these reasons is the one which has lately been advanced so prominently in the press—namely, that the position of the United States is anomalous—that it should regularize itself and enter the war as actively against Germany's allies as it has entered the war against Germany. The argument opposed to this, is of course, that this country is engaged in a war against Prussian militarism, and has no quarrel with the allies of Prussian militarism. I hold that there is something in this, but when the dangers of that narrow conception of the war are considered, it seems to me that all the facts prove that we ought to risk a charge of illogicality in order to obtain a safety for the nation which is daily jeopardized by our position. These facts are clear to all who know of the activities in our midst of sympathizers with Germany—Austrians, Hungarians, Bulgarians, Turks and others—who, while they are not technically enemies, are nevertheless as dangerous as and perhaps more dangerous to our welfare than those active enemy-Germans who have given our government so much unease. It is patent that, while, under our newly-passed laws covering espionage and various forms of criminality, we are able to punish enemy offenders against our institutions, we are helpless against any plots which may be hatched against us by those who work for Germany under the cloak of non-enemy nationality.

That the menace is a serious one must be known in Washington. It must also be known that the evils resulting to us from a highly-organized, though often blundering, German system of espionage, would still befall us even though the leaders of that system were all safely interned in American jails. For the Austrian spy, the Hungarian spy, the Bulgarian spy, are just as much a part of the general system of European military and naval espionage—at least in the present war—as if they were working under the direct orders of Berlin. Yet we are powerless against them, because we are not at war with them. Let us get rid of this unclean thing. Let us subject these maldoers to the same punishment that we are now meting out to our German enemies, whose malevolence we understand and whose persons are seizable under the law. Let us not, in the absence of a declaration of war against the countries which they acclaim as subjects, continue, as we have been doing, in a dangerous insecurity.

I dare say that Washington has hesitated to make declaration, not only because we have had no grievance against Austro-Hungary similar to that which we had against Germany, but also because it may have seemed unjust that Germany's allies should be warred against simply because certain subjects of those countries were acting in a hostile manner within our gates. Again there is something in this point of view. I know for a fact—and few know better than I—that a very considerable proportion of the Austro-Hungarians in America are doing their best, even since the United States went to war with Germany, to maintain a strict loyalty to their oath of allegiance. More than that, these people deprecate the efforts of those of their countrymen who are believed to be involved in enemy propaganda. But when that is said, one must admit that the propaganda still exists, that words are spoken which ring false, and that acts are performed which are inimical to American well-being. These words and acts, in their sinister objective, more than offset the patriotic labors of loyal naturalized citizens. It seems to me far better that an injustice should be done to the loyal ones than that the disloyal ones should be permitted to pursue their nefarious activities unmolested.

There is another very powerful reason why the United States should declare war upon Austro-Hungary—namely, that unless she does so, there can be no improvement in their existing relations, no alleviation of the evils which have been discussed in the foregoing paragraphs. For I must tell you that if a loyalty to Austro-Hungary exists among Austro-Hungarians in the United States rather than to the United States—that is to say, if their sympathies are with the Central Powers rather than with the United States, then this is the direct result of efforts which, for many years have been made by Austro-Hungary to retain the devotion of their immigrants oversea. This statement may surprise you, but it is true. In the same way that Germany has always tried to keep the German ideals before the Germans in America, so have Austria and Hungary ever tried to keep alive in Austro-Hungarian Americans the spirit of devotion to their native lands. This is not generally known. But *I* know it. Four years ago I had an interview with Count Tisza, then Hungarian premier, and the subject discussed between us was the furtherance of the Hungarian spirit of nationality in Hungarian-Americans. The premier expressed his anxiety that in the process of Americanization the love of these people for their native land would disappear and that when their country needed them in the future the call would not be heard. To prevent such defection of the immigrants from the Hungarian spirit, Tisza asked my aid in combating it by all the means in my power, even to the use of money. After hearing all the arguments, I informed Count Tisza that such a scheme was not only impossible of complete execution but on no account could it have my support. I informed him that it was contrary to the American spirit, which tried to make of every immigrant a good American, and was intolerable to the thought of a Hungarian who, like myself, had taken an oath of allegiance to the United States, and had received the benefits which that oath conferred.

My refusal to aid in the carrying on of such work—so anti-American, so narrowly-conceived by a statesman ignorant of real conditions here—did not prevent the scheme from being carried out. I shall now make certain statements that you will hardly give credence to, but they are true nevertheless. One of these is that there now exists in the United States, and has existed for some years, an Austro-Hungarian propaganda, insidiously carried on, the intention of which is to prevent or delay the complete Americanization of Austro-Hungarians. I state to you as a fact that every protestant Hungarian clergyman in the United States is a secret Hungarian agent, subsidized by Budapest to keep alive the love for the motherlands, to retard an immigration which results in Americanization of Austro-Hungarian citizens, and, at the present time, aims to induce them to go back to their native countries after the war. The influence of these subsidized propagandists, whose every activity is hostile to the great civilizing work among immigrants, performed by America in the past, is very great, but is carried on so skilfully that few are aware of its existence.

How is it, you may ask, that I am aware of this work. Let me then tell you that not long ago I was asked to speak in a Hungarian Presbyterian Church—the theme of my address being the demand of America on Hungarian loyalty. What was my surprise, before the address, to find myself in the midst of a group of Hungarian school-children, each one waving—the Hungarian flag! Mark you—the Hungarian flag. This so shocked my sense of what was becoming at such a moment that I was forced to enter a strong protest that such a scene should be witnessed in an American church—that loyalty to Hungary should there be taught rather than loyalty to the United States.

Was this occurrence an accident, do you think, or was it a part of a well-organized plan to defeat the great principle of Americanization? I happen to know that it was no accident. Neither was it an accident when, some years back, there was established a Hungarian bank. Behind the bank was the Hungarian government. It was that government which agreed heavily to subsidize the institution. And for what purpose? Simply to draw together the threads of various Hungarian interests, and to form a Hungarian unit in the community—a unit unassimilable with American interests and, in that sense, assimilable with interests at home. I may add, in passing, that I refused point-blank to go on the board of an institution which, in its very nature, was so anti-American.

This work, I make bolder to say, has the support of the Hungarian press throughout the United States. With one exception—that of the Cleveland "Szabadsag" which, ever since this war began, has maintained an attitude of perfect loyalty to American institutions and the American flag. As for the others, I will broadly say that there is not a member of any of the staffs of the Hungarian newspapers in the United States who is not alien in spirit and in much of his writing to the United States. He is generally anti-American—certainly unfriendly. I go further to state my strong conviction that

it would be well for the United States if every one of these papers—
except perhaps the one in Cleveland—were stopped at once. They
can do no good to American interests while they present non-Amer-
ican views and they can do infernal harm. It may be that occasionally they appear to do lip-service to our country, but their hearts
are elsewhere. Their prompt suspension would possibly damage
private interests, but the net result would be highly beneficial to
America at war.

One other point deserves your attention. This involves the question, "What will happen in Hungary if the United States should
declare war?" We all know that the United States has no technical
grievance against Hungary—except that Hungary is an ally of Germany—and we know equally well that Hungary has no grievance
against the United States. My conviction is that a declaration of
war will not greatly alter the existing relations. I except, of course,
the fact that (as I have said in previous paragraphs) such declaration
would make it easier to handle any Hungarian disloyalists who are
in our midst. It is more than probable that the eight or ten million
Hungarians in Hungary, realizing the advantages which had been
conferred upon them in the past by a friendly relationship with
America would positively refuse to go to war against us. It is only
within the past fifteen or twenty years that Hungary has grown to
be strong and prosperous, and this has been largely due to American
aid—the result of the prosperity of Hungarians in the United States
and the encouragements which America has given to Hungarian
trade. It seems hardly likely that a declaration of war which would
be made mainly to protect American interests at home, would meet
with widespread disapproval from Hungary or would result in a
greatly increased bitterness. It would, on the contrary, greatly clarify the anomalous position in which both countries are now placed,
and tend, I think, to hasten the end of the war.

There are a great many more arguments which could, if needed,
strengthen the above. But it seems to me, that I have made out a
clear case for immediate and salutary action. Anyway, whether the
declaration comes or not I hope I shall still be able to get my just
reward for my superiority at the immortal game of dominoes.

Now, will you be good!   As ever,   Alexander Konta

TLS (WP, DLC).

From Samuel Gompers

Sir: Buffalo, New York. Nov. 27, 1917

There was brought before the Convention of the American Federation of Labor which has just closed its session in this city, a resolution dealing with the pressing necessity of provision for the proper housing of workers employed in the various ship building, munition and other plants working on war orders. The Convention adopted the following:

"Inasmuch as the appointment of a permanent housing commission during the period of the war has become an immediate necessity, and as such commission to accomplish practical results should be provided with adequate funds; be it

"RESOLVED, That the Executive Council be instructed to give their support and cooperation in securing from the Government the necessary funds, and in working out with such a commission all problems which it may be called upon to consider."

This matter has already been brought to your attention through the Committee on Housing (Committee on Labor) of the Council of National Defense. As the necessity is so urgent I hasten to bring to your attention the view of the organized labor movement upon this subject as expressed by the declaration of the convention of the A. F. of L. and as above quoted in the earnest hope that the matter will be given your early and favorable consideration.

Very respectfully yours,   Saml. Gompers.

TLS (WP, DLC).

From Allyn Abbott Young[1]

Sir: Washington November 27, 1917.

I think you should have a copy of some recent correspondence with Dr. Charles D. Walcott, Secretary of the Smithsonian Institution.[2] Although this matter is really outside the proper scope of our Association's work, I am somewhat interested in Dr. Frachtenberg's case, because of widely divergent accounts with respect to the report made by the Department of Justice in this matter.

Respectfully,   Allyn A. Young

TLS (WP, DLC).

[1] Professor of Economics at Cornell University, Director of the Bureau of Research of the War Trade Board, and chairman of the committee on academic freedom and academic tenure of the American Association of University Professors (A.A.U.P.).

[2] Young had written on November 23 to Charles Doolittle Walcott about the possible interest of the A.A.U.P. in the recent dismissal of Frachtenberg. Young noted that, even though the A.A.U.P. as an academic organization was reluctant to investigate and report

on actions of governmental institutions, it nevertheless believed that the standards of research set by the Smithsonian Institution were "so high" that American universities ought to be able to look to the Institution for "proper standards in other matters." Young added that he was not precisely informed about the findings of the Department of Justice, but that he wished very much that Frachtenberg "might be given a hearing, that he might be informed as to the nature of the charges against him, and be given an opportunity to confront his accusers." This, Young pointed out, was now the procedure "in all universities of the first class," and he trusted that Walcott would agree that the Institution "ought not to take the chance of imperiling its prestige by observing standards that are in any way lower than these." A. A. Young to C. D. Walcott, Nov. 23, 1917, TCL (WP, DLC).

Walcott replied on the following day that he did not see what the standards of research or the action of universities had to do with the case in hand. The matter lay within the jurisdiction of the Department of Justice, to which he had to refer Young for information. Walcott also wrote: "I do not fear that the prestige of the Smithsonian Institution is likely to be imperiled by any action it may take in support of the government of the United States in these trying times. I quite agree with you that I do not see why this matter should be a concern to your Association." C. D. Walcott to A. A. Young, Nov. 24, 1917, TCL (WP, DLC).

Young replied as follows: "If Dr. Frachtenberg's removal was accomplished at the instance of the Department of Justice and if that Department assumes responsibility in the matter, it is entirely clear that the American Association of University Professors is not concerned with it." A. A. Young to C. D. Walcott, Nov. 27, 1917, TCL (WP, DLC).

From Charles Richard Van Hise

My dear Mr. President: Madison November 27, 1917.

On Wednesday, November 21st, Mr. Carl Vrooman, Assistant Secretary of Agriculture, made two addresses at the University of Wisconsin; the first a brief address at a patriotic convocation arranged before it was known that Mr. Vrooman was to be here, in order to assist in carrying thru the campaign to raise the amount allotted to this university for the Y.M.C.A. fund; the second at an agricultural meeting held in the Stock Pavilion.

Since Mr. Vrooman was advertised as being your personal representative, I wish to call to your attention to the character of one of these addresses. Herewith is enclosed an apparently authorized summary of this address, as published in the State Journal, the day following Mr. Vrooman's visit.[1] As showing the interpretation which was placed upon the address, there is also enclosed an editorial which appeared in the State Journal on the same day.[2]

The most objectionable paragraphs of the address read as follows: "I had the honor to review the university regiments this afternoon. I never saw a finer set of young men. But during the first fifteen minutes of my talk on patriotism before them in the University armory they were less responsive than any audience I have talked

[1] "Does University Lack Patriotic Leadership? Vrooman Asks Madison: Declares Students Are Not Responsive to Loyalty Plea; Calls America's Cause in War Holy," Madison *Wisconsin State Journal*, Nov. 22, 1917, clipping in WP, DLC. Vrooman had spoken before the convention of the Wisconsin Potato Growers.
[2] "Put Patriotism in Education," *ibid.*

before and I have talked before audiences in three-fourths of the states in the Union since war began.

"I understand this is the first loyalty meeting held at the University of Wisconsin this year. I could not help asking myself: Has the university the right kind of patriotic leadership? Is it guided by a milk and water patriotism, a kind of platonic patriotism? If this university is not most outspoken, if it does not express a militant patriotism at this time, it expresses no patriotism at all. The students on parade that I reviewed, the students I addressed are all right. I am sure of that. What they need is patriotic inspiration, patriotic leadership, patriotic education and then they'll have the enthusiasm of patriots. Is this state university giving them this kind of education at this time when it is so needed? It is the first duty of a state university to give this kind of education at this time. If the university is not doing this it is not doing its duty by our country, by the people who created it and who maintain it."

These paragraphs are an attack upon the active patriotism of the University of Wisconsin, not by direct statement, but by the far more objectionable but less courageous method of implication.

The alleged facts presented in support of the implication of lack of aggressive patriotism are first, that the loyalty meeting at which Mr. Vrooman spoke was the only one which had been held at Wisconsin in this year; second, that the student audience was not responsive to his address.

The first statement is wholly without foundation. There have been a series of patriotic meetings at the university this year, of which one of the most important was addressed by Mr. McAdoo, the Secretary of the Treasury. Among the other important patriotic meetings held the present semester are the following:

The Variety Welcome, planned especially as a patriotic meeting at the opening of the university.

Convocation address by Sherwood Eddy,[3] in promotion of the Y.M.C.A. campaign.

Liberty Loan Address, by Rev. Frank W. Gunsaulus,[4] of Chicago.

Conditions in Russia, Major Stanley Washburn and representatives of the Russian Embassy.

The World War and France, General Vignal,[5] Military Attache, French Embassy.

[3] Sherwood Eddy, a Y.M.C.A. worker since 1896, author and lecturer.
[4] The Rev. Dr. Frank Wakeley Gunsaulus, a Congregational minister since 1879, President of the Armour Institute of Technology of Chicago since 1893, and pastor of the Central Church of Chicago since 1899.
[5] Paul Vignal.

Behind the German Lines, by Rev. Newton Dwight Hillis.[6]

In addition to these and other large popular meetings, we have had lectures twice a week by members of the staff of the university, open to the entire student body and to the public. The lectures consider almost every aspect of the war. This course has been running since the opening of the semester and it is expected it will be continued thruout the year.

Since I was absent from Madison last week when Mr. Vrooman gave his address, I am unable to express a personal opinion as to whether or not the students made adequate response to him by applause.

The nature of the address of Mr. Vrooman is called to your attention for the reason that the regents, the faculty, and the students deeply resent the serious reflection made upon the patriotism of this institution by a high public official.

As giving some indication of the activity of this university in relation to the war, I present a summary of a statement which I made to the university faculty at the opening of the autumn semester in regard to the activities to that time.

When war was declared, April 6, 1917, there was not an instant's hesitation in the decision of the faculty that the university should participate in assisting to carry the war to a successful conclusion. Indeed on April 2nd, anticipating the declaration of a state of war, the faculty unanimously passed a resolution authorizing the President of the University and the military administrative committee created at that time, to inaugurate at once a course in intensive military instruction for the training of officers. The men taking the course were to be released from other studies, the military instruction being accepted as an equivalent.

Another resolution requested the regents to give leave of absence, without prejudice to rank or seniority, to members of the faculty entering the public service for national defense.

Upon the opening of the course for intensive training, April 23rd, 470 application[s] had been filed, of which 284 had been approved; this number having passed the necessary physical examination and those who were minors having obtained their parents' consent.

To the opening of the semester 351 students of the university had entered the various branches of the United States army and navy.

Also the importance of productive agricultural and industrial work

[6] The Rev. Dr. Newell Dwight Hillis, pastor of Plymouth Congregational Church, Brooklyn, since 1899; author of works on religion and other subjects. He had been notoriously anti-German before the United States entered the war.

was recognized by giving qualified students leave of absence to engage in these lines of work with credit for their studies to the end of the year on condition that they thus occupy their time for the remainder of the semester and during the summer. For these purposes 448 students were given leave of absence.

Further, on May 3rd an all-university convocation was called at which it was urged that every student of the university who had not entered military service or already entered the productive service, should devote the summer, or such part of the summer as they were not engaged in pursuing their studies, to productive work of some kind.

Reports show that no less than 1650 additional students responded to this call.

Thus the total number of students who during the summer were at work in all ways in connection with the war was at least 2450; and probably many more than that number; for doubtless many failed to report upon their summer work.

The participation of the faculty in the war has taken various directions. A considerable number of men have entered the army or navy. A number of these are line officers in the infantry or in the artillery; and others are in the special services, such as the engineers corps, the medical corps, the aviation service, quartermaster's service, interpreter's service, special scientific service, etc. Those who have entered the active service rank from lieutenants to majors.

A second group have taken position on scientific and administrative committees, created because of the war. A third group have given their time to extension or educational work directed to increasing the food production and food conservation, to the Red Cross, to teaching soldiers in the various training camps, and other activities relating to the war. A fourth group entered various lines of industrial service. A fifth group have been engaged in investigations and research in relation to the war without official enlistment.

Some of the investigations of the staff are medical; others relate to poisonous gases; others to aeroplane service; and still others to submarine detection. In the last case, for six months, there has been most intensive work of several men in close cooperation, one of whom has received a commission as lieutenant commander. Already, it has been officially recognized that the results secured are most important.

At the opening of the semester thirty-five men who were members of the university faculty last year had commissions in the army or navy and seventeen additional were attending officer's training camps or have been drafted in the national army.

The number of the faculty other than those having commissions who before the opening of the autumn semester were giving all or a large part of their time since the outbreak of the war to war work was ninety-four; and many more participated in various directions to a less extent.

Many of these men who gave the major portion of their time during this summer to war work are now back at the university; but seventy-four men will continue their service for a part or all of the year in the army and the navy, or their auxiliary branches and in official positions of different organizations devoted to war work.

In accordance with the recommendation of the faculty, it has been the policy of the regents to give leave of absence freely to men who desire to enter some form of war service for which they possess special qualifications. In most cases the leave of absence is for a year with the understanding that if the war continues the leave may be prolonged.

The present semester the war committee of the faculty, temporarily appointed last year, was made permanent for the duration of the war.

All money demands have been more than met. The faculty and students subscribed to the second Liberty Loan about $200,000. The Red Cross allotment to the university was fully met. The allotment of $20,000 for the Y.M.C.A. campaign was oversubscribed.

The military department this year is continuing vigorously to train young men to enter the army or navy. From time to time men are withdrawing to enter some branch of one service or the other. There will come before the faculty at the next meeting a recommendation of the war committee to give scholastic credit to such students to the end of the semester during which they leave.

Additional members of the faculty have been given leave of absence to take up war work; and many others are giving a part of their time to such work.

Since Mr. Vrooman's statement seems to be especially directed toward the officers of the university, I may say that I gave my entire summer, with the exception of three weeks, to the work of the Food Administration, and since the end of the vacation have continued to devote as much time as possible to that service. The particular task assigned to me is the organization of the work of the Food Administration in the higher educational institutions of the country,—universities, technical schools, and normal schools. In addition to the preparation of a set of lectures to be given in these institutions, at the request of the Food Administration, I have given numerous addresses in different parts of the country.

In short, this university has aggressively taken the initiative in many lines of effort to assist in the prosecution of the war and has given prompt and complete response to all suggestions and demands from the outside.

In view of the foregoing facts, for Mr. Vrooman, officially speaking for the government, to cast extremely objectionable reflections upon the patriotism of the University without any knowledge of what we have done or attempt to ascertain the truth, seems to us so seriously to misrepresent your position that I feel you should know the facts.

I am sending copies of this letter to the Secretary of Agriculture, to Mr. Vrooman, and to the Regents and Visitors of this university.

Very respectfully yours,   Charles R Van Hise

TLS (WP, DLC).

From the Diary of Josephus Daniels

1917 Tuesday 27 November

Cabinet—The President read speech & message of Trotsky, who said America entered war at behest of Wall Street and men whose prosperity came through making munitions. Lansing thought T— misguided but honest. Once he worked at $12 a week on N Y Socialist paper & stopped writing for it because he thought paper was unfair to President.[1] No answer now unless in message to Congress, for any answer would imply recognition WW said action of Lenine & Trotsky sounded like opera bouffe, talking of armistice with Germany when a child would know Germany would control & dominate & destroy any chance for the democracy they desire

Burleson & I advised President to take over all railroads.

WW A man said he no longer admired WW style since reading Thanksgv proclamation because he used word "stuff" & ended sentence with preposition

[1] Trotsky, after being expelled from France and Spain in late 1916, was, from January to March 1917, an editor of *Novy Mir*, a Russian-language newspaper in New York. The *Washington Post* reported on November 9 that only a few months earlier he was "working on an East Side newspaper for about $12 a week" and that he was well known among the Russians and Jews of New York.

To Josephus Daniels

My dear Daniels: The White House 28 November, 1917

I would be very much obliged to you if I might have a memorandum from you as to any legislation which you think it imperative should be considered at this session of Congress.

I assume that the Congress will prefer to confine itself entirely to matters directly connected with the prosecution of the war, and in my judgment that is the policy which it should pursue. My request, therefore, concerns only such matters as you think should be provided for at once and cannot be postponed.[1]

Cordially and sincerely yours,   Woodrow Wilson

TLS (J. Daniels Papers, DLC).
  [1] Wilson sent this letter, *mutatis mutandis*, to H. A. Garfield, Nov. 28, 1917, TLS (H. A. Garfield Papers, DLC); H. C. Hoover, Nov. 28, 1917, TLS (H. Hoover Papers, HPL); R. Lansing, N. D. Baker, T. W. Gregory, W. G. McAdoo, A. S. Burleson, F. K. Lane, D. F. Houston, W. C. Redfield, and W. B. Wilson, Nov. 28, 1917, all TLS (Letterpress Books, WP, DLC).

To Robert Lansing, with Enclosure

My dear Mr. Secretary,   The White House. 28 November, 1917.

I wish that you would be kind enough to intimate to Page (if, as I take for granted, it is your own opinion as well as mine) that we regard this a chimerical and of questionable advantage, even if it could be accomplished.

Arrangements must be made at the conference which closes the war with regard to Constantinople which could hardly be made if Turkey were first made peace with. Indeed, I suppose that peace could be made only on terms which would preclude any radical changes of control over Constantinople and the straits.

The only advantage to be gained would be to prevent the bargains of the Allies with regard to Asia Minor from being carried out.

Faithfully Yours,   W.W.

WWTLI (SDR, RG 59, 763.72119/953, DNA).

E   N   C   L   O   S   U   R   E

London, Nov. 23, 1917.

7782. STRICTLY CONFIDENTIAL for the Secretary and the President.

I learn from an authoritative source that certain of the Prime Minister's political advisers are anxious that he should persuade Turkey to conclude a separate peace and think that the recent military successes in Palestine make the present moment propitious for an attempt to buy off-hand Turks. I understand that there is considerable opposition in naval and military circles to this idea for the following reasons: First, they consider that the Turkish Government are far too deeply in the hands of Germany to be able to make a separate peace. Secondly, the Palestine operations have not yet reached their fullest development. Thirdly, they believe that other powers such as France, Italy, and Greece have ideas of their own as to future of Asiatic Turkey which might be difficult to put into effect if the Turks made peace now and the consent of these powers to such a peace might be difficult to obtain.[1]

Mr. Balfour's letter to Lord Rothschild regarding the future of Palestine[2] has awakened great hopes among the Zionist Jews of this country and press despatches indicate that it has been read with interest by the Jews of America. The Zionist feeling should no doubt be kept in mind. I should be glad of an intimation of your views on this subject for discreet use in the proper quarter should occasion arise.   Page.

T telegram (SDR, RG 59, 763.72119/953, DNA).
   [1] Lansing's reply to this paragraph was a paraphrase of WW to RL, Nov. 28, 1917, just printed: RL to WHP, Nov. 30, 1917, TS telegram (SDR, RG 59, 763.72119/953, DNA).
   [2] The letter contained the statement generally known as the Balfour Declaration. It had been decided at a meeting of the War Cabinet on October 31 to authorize the Foreign Secretary to make a declaration of sympathy with Zionist aspirations in terms of a slightly amended version of a draft submitted by Lord Milner on October 4. (This final draft differed somewhat from the one which Wilson had agreed to in WW to EMH, Oct. 13, 1917, first letter of that date, Vol. 44.) Balfour accordingly wrote on November 2 to Lionel Walter Rothschild, 2d Baron Rothschild, spokesman for the Zionist Organization, as follows:
"Dear Lord Rothschild,
   "I have much pleasure in conveying to you, on behalf of His Majesty's Government, the following declaration of sympathy with Jewish Zionist aspirations which has been submitted to, and approved by, the Cabinet:
   " 'His Majesty's Government view with favour the establishment in Palestine of a national home for the Jewish people, and will use their best endeavours to facilitate the achievement of this object, it being clearly understood that nothing shall be done which may prejudice the civil and religious rights of existing non-Jewish communities in Palestine, or the rights and political status enjoyed by Jews in any other country.'
   "I should be grateful if you would bring this declaration to the knowledge of the Zionist Federation."
   This letter was published in the London *Times* and other newspapers on November 9. About the drafting and issuance of the statement, see *The Letters and Papers of Chaim Weizmann*, Series A (7 vols., London, 1968-75), VII, 504-42; Leonard Stein, *The Balfour Declaration* (New York, 1961); and Isaiah Friedman, *The Question of Palestine, 1914-1918: British-Jewish-Arab Relations* (London, 1973), pp. 244-332.

To Royal Meeker

My dear Mr. Meeker: [The White House] 28 November, 1917

Just a hasty line in reply to your letter of yesterday. Could you give me a somewhat definite estimate of what the single investigation to which you first refer would cost; I mean that urged by Professor Seager.

Cordially and sincerely yours,   Woodrow Wilson

TLS (Letterpress Books, WP, DLC).

From Royal Meeker

My dear Mr. President: Washington November 28, 1917.

Supplementing my letter to you of the 27th instant, I quote below from a communication I have just received from Prof. Henry R. Seager, Secretary of the Shipbuilding Labor Adjustment Board:

"In connection with the wage adjustments which this Board will be called upon to make as time goes on, we shall wish to have retail price statistics for the towns and cities in which ship-yards are located. Enclosed I send you a list of all such towns and cities on the Atlantic seaboard and Gulf. I have underlined those that are of special importance from the point of view of the volume of ships under construction. I shall greatly appreciate it if you will have some one check up this list so that we may know from which of these cities you are already receiving retail food price statistics."

Prof. Seager also makes inquiry in his letter as to the prospects of this Bureau's receiving additional funds to carry out the work. He says further that unless this Bureau can undertake this work immediately the Board will be obliged to take it up independently. He adds: "The Board has been able thus far to induce dissatisfied employes in the shipyards to remain at work but next week it must begin seriously to consider the various disputes that are pending and it will desire the data as quickly as it can be secured."

I enclose copy of the list of cities, which Prof. Seager transmitted in his letter and have checked in pencil those from which this Bureau now receives reports on retail prices.[1]

Sincerely yours,   Royal Meeker

TLS (WP, DLC).

[1] "Cities In Which Shipyards Are Located," [Nov. 27, 1917], T MS (WP, DLC). It listed thirty-seven cities, of which New York, Newark, Philadelphia, Baltimore, Jacksonville, and New Orleans were checked.

Two Telegrams from Edward Mandell House

Paris. November 28, 1917.

I am having frequent conferences with the French and English Prime Ministers and we are reaching conclusions upon many matters.

The Conference itself tomorrow will not be important for there will be representatives of all Allied Powers and the discussions must necessarily be of a general and not very intimate character. Such a large conference was a mistake and has many elements of danger. Our main endeavor now is to get through with it without any mishap.

The Supreme War Council will probably meet at Versailles on Saturday. That, too, has been largely divested of its power for service by Lloyd George's insistence that General Wilson shall sit on it instead of the chiefs of staff and commanders in the field, as Clemenceau, Pétain, Bliss and I had agreed. This is because of his disagreement with Robertson and Haig. I suppose that he does not feel strong enough to depose them and is therefore using the Supreme War Council idea to supplant them in another way.

Edward House

Paris. November 28, 1917.

Yesterday afternoon at a conference of the Prime Ministers and Foreign Secretaries of England, France and Italy in which I sat, England was authorized to instruct her representatives in Switzerland to ascertain what terms Austria had to offer for a separate peace, which she has indicated a desire to make.

The Italians offered some objections but yielded. This action was taken because of the probability of Russia soon making a separate peace.   Edward House

T telegrams (E. M. House Papers, CtY).

Edward Mandell House to Woodrow Wilson and
Robert Lansing

Paris Nov. 28, 1917.

2820. There has been cabled over and published here statements made by American papers to the effect that Russia should be treated as an enemy. It is exceedingly important that such criticisms should be suppressed. It will throw Russia into the lap of Germany if the Allies and ourselves express such views at this time.

Edward House.

T telegram (WP, DLC).

Three Letters from George Creel

My dear Mr. President,   [Washington] November 28, 1917.

With regard to the "Liberty Guard" plan forwarded by Mr. Hale,[1] I would urge against its adoption on the ground that the very same idea is expressed in the State Councils of Defense. We have the Advisory Commission in Washington as the controlling body, a Chairman for each State, County Chairmen, township Chairmen, and even precinct Chairmen.

My whole effort has been to build up this organization and not only am I rejecting every suggestion that seems to threaten it, but I am gradually forcing all other organizations to acknowledge the State Council leadership. Some of the States have very remarkable Councils, while in others little or no work is being done. Too many people are prone to regard the mere fact of organization as an end in itself, but with all its faults, the plan is one in which we are *committed*, and which holds the promise of one hundred percent effectiveness.

Believe me, sir,   Very respectfully,   [George Creel]

CCL (G. Creel Papers, DLC).
[1] See WW to G. Creel, Nov. 23, 1917, n. 1.

My dear Mr. President,   Washington, D. C. November 28, 1917.

Please let me thank you for your generous reply to Mr. Long.[1] His letter is the sort of thing that used to excite me, but which I now accept as part of the regular routine. I have put the question of an advisory committee up to every prominent newspaper man in the country, not because I thought it was possible, but because I wanted *them* to admit the impossibility. The press is the only profession in the world without an organization of any kind. There is no one body to speak for it, to make bargains for it, or to enforce discipline of any kind. It is torn to pieces by ever[y] rivalry—political and commercial. An advisory committee with any authority would have to be made up of the editors of every metropolitan daily, and when these were gathered together, the only certainty as to their actions would be with regard to lack of unity.

But even were such a committee formed, only a man utterly ignorant of the newspaper business would suggest that any one individual or body could assume to exercise a direction over the treatment of matter, not to mention such technical details as the writing of heads. The things we complain about are not concerned with suggestive changes, but go to the heart of the newspaper business, involving changes in training, aims, ideals and ambitions. *News* itself must be given a new definition.

As a matter of fact, I have been surprised and gratified at the results I have been able to achieve. The volunteer censorship is being observed with few violations. Our matter goes into the papers by thousands of columns, and aside from the personal attacks of a few New York papers, like the World, feeling has grown very friendly. It is the best we can do, and it's really very good.

Mr. Long has never been near this Committee at any time, knows nothing of its work, and evidently did not think it worth while to make a single inquiry. I feel, however, that your letter closes the incident. Respectfully, George Creel

TLS (WP, DLC).
[1] That is, WW to B. Long, Nov. 20, 1917.

Memorandum: [Washington]
Dear Mr. President: November 28, 1917.

I have just received the enclosed article from William English Walling.[1] He seems to be very much excited by the continual assertion that the New Republic is the mouthpiece of the organization. I myself am somewhat in doubt as to the best attitude to adopt to Lippman[n] and his associates. The paper attacks me from time to time because I do not devote all publicity to big, constructive articles on peace plans. It demands that I should "arouse interest of public opinion in the con[s]tructive problems of settlement." I do not feel that it is wise to do this, nor my province.

Very respectfully, George Creel.

TL (WP, DLC).
[1] W. E. Walling to the Editor of the New York *Globe and Commercial Advertiser*, Nov. 24, 1917, clipping in WP, DLC. This long letter, published under the heading "High-Brow Hearstism. The Peace Agitation of the New Republic," was in fact an attack upon *The New Republic* for its defense of German Socialists and its demand for a "peace at any price" with a democratized Germany. Walling's letter concluded as follows: "The New Republic has never withdrawn its instructions to President Wilson that 'He must seek for a peace by means of diplomacy, irrespective of a military decision,' nor its statement that 'America cannot bring about a German defeat.'"

From Thomas Watt Gregory

My dear Mr. President: Washington, D. C. November 28, 1917.

I have your letter of November 20, 1917, in which you enclose a letter from Professors Magie and Priest concerning Doctor Leo J. Frachtenberg, formerly employed as an ethnologist in the Smithsonian Institution. At the request of the Chief Clerk of that Department,[1] the Bureau of Investigation, of this Department, interviewed several persons connected with the Bureau in which Frachtenberg was employed. A copy of the report of the special agent who interviewed these parties is enclosed herewith.[2] When it became known that an investigation was under way, several persons employed with Mr. Frachtenberg submitted letters in his behalf[3] and copies of these letters were forwarded to the Smithsonian Institution. In this connection, I am enclosing herewith a copy of a letter from the Chief of the Bureau of Investigation, of this Department, addressed to Mr. Hodge, Ethnolofist [Ethnologist] in Charge, in reply to a letter from Mr. Hodge to the effect that the Secretary of the Smithsonian Institution had dispensed with the services of Doctor Frachtenberg at the request of an agent of this Department.[4] The question as to whether or not this man should be retained is, of course, an administrative one for the Secretary of the Smithsonian Institution,[5] but it is understood that no hearing was accorded Doctor Frachtenberg. If such is the case, I am of the opinion that he is entitled to a hearing.

Faithfully yours,   T. W. Gregory

TLS (WP, DLC).

[1] Harry Woodward Dorsey.

[2] W. W. Grimes, "RE: DR. LEO FRAC[H]TENBERG (PROBABLE GERMAN AGENT)," Oct. 30, 1917, T report (WP, DLC). Grimes summarized his conversations on October 29 with Frederick Webb Hodge and three other members of the Bureau of American Ethnology. Hodge had said that, when a certain German appeared at the Bureau, Frachtenberg remarked to him, "We are the only Huns here." Hodge also said that Frachtenberg had "defended the Luxburg note regarding the sinking of Argentine ships, also the German atrocities in Africa." Grimes reported further that Hodge, "knowing the German character as well as he does," believed that Frachtenberg, "if given the opportunity, probably would give aid to the enemy." The other three men interviewed, Grimes went on, cited other instances; they, too, considered Frachtenberg's sentiment to be disloyal and pro-German. It was further charged that he had imparted to others information gained while he was employed by the government on confidential censorship work. Grimes concluded his report by stating that he had advised Hodge of his findings and that the latter, undecided as to whether Frachtenberg should be suspended or removed from employment, had asked Grimes' opinion. Grimes had suggested "summary removal," and Hodge had said he would so recommend to Walcott.

[3] Gregory enclosed a copy of at least one: William Addison Hervey to A. B. Bielaski, Nov. 3, 1917, TCL (WP, DLC). Hervey, Professor of German at Columbia University, wrote that he had known Frachtenberg well for eight or ten years and had repeatedly heard him express sentiments which could leave no doubt of his loyalty to his adopted country. Frachtenberg was "somewhat given to facetious remarks," and these, out of context or misrepresented, might have offended, but Hervey doubted that there had been any intentional disloyalty or disrespect. Hervey asked that Frachtenberg be given "fair play," particularly in view of his valuable services during the past summer in the

work Hervey was supervising for the Department of Justice. Frachtenberg's work there "gave repeated evidence of his undivided loyalty and zeal."

4 [A. Bruce Bielaski] to F. M. [F. W.] Hodge, Nov. 5, 1917, TCL (WP, DLC). It stated that Grimes had not requested Frachtenberg's dismissal, because this would have gone beyond the scope of an agent's authority, but, when asked, had merely stated his opinion that the matter seemed to call for dismissal. Bielaski then informed Hodge: "We feel that the matter is one for the decision of your Department and not for determination by the Department of Justice. . . . We feel that our Department is only called upon to take action in the case of employes of other Departments when its own interests in the protection of the country against activities of enemy agents seem involved." Bielaski enclosed with this letter a copy of Grimes' report (summarized above), as well as letters by various interested persons.

5 That is, Charles D. Walcott.

From John Reese Kenly

Wilmington, N. C., Nov. 28, 1917.

In reply to your telegram of yesterday, while I greatly regret that you find it necessary to insist upon a compliance with the request contained in your telegram of the twenty fourth instant, in deference thereto I am directing that the striking clerks who wish to return be employed as rapidly as practicable.   J. R. Kenly.

T telegram (WP, DLC).

Newton Diehl Baker to Joseph Patrick Tumulty

My dear Mr. Tumulty: Washington. November 28, 1917.

I have your letter of the 20th and return herewith Mr. Borglum's letter. I confess I am puzzled to know what the President ought to say in reply.

The aeronautic program was in fact made out under the personal direction of General Squier. He was advised, not only by Mr. Coffin, who at the time was the only automobile manufacturer associated with it, but also by the National Advisory Board for Aeronautics, of which Dr. Walcott, of the Smithsonian Institution, is Chairman, and upon which men of scientific distinction are numerous.

Meantime, the program of the Board, as it has been growing in the hands of the Aircraft Production Board, has been constantly submitted for criticism to the best experts abroad by representatives of the Signal Corps who are there for the purpose, and we have had the constant advice of English, French, and Italian aircraft experts sent over by their Governments for the purpose, and the progress actually made with the Liberty Engine is such as to make it unjust to refer to any of this as "cheap, grandiose projects, incapable of fulfillment."

Of course, the difficulty at the outset was that we had no aircraft experts in this country—that is to say, we had no experts in many of the types of aircraft necessary to be constructed, but I think there has been brought together in the study of this problem all of the real information both in this country and in Europe, and while one can never say in advance that so vast a project will be carried out on schedule time and without difficulties, and perhaps delays, I confess that my own belief is that our aircraft program and the progress made in it are wholly worthy of the confidence of the people. The difficulty with Mr. Borglum's letter is that it is wholly unspecific and makes no suggestion of a better course or of wiser men to be consulted.

I know Mr. Borglum personally, and admire him very greatly, but I wonder whether he has not been talked to by someone who seemed to have more information than he had, and has therefore allowed his generous and patriotic spirit to be disturbed with less cause than exists in fact.

Perhaps if the President would write Mr. Borglum and tell him of his interest in the matter, and ask him specifically to indicate either weaknesses in the present organization or men of talent who can contribute to our success but have not yet been included, it might lead to a helpful result.

Cordially yours,   Newton D. Baker

TLS (WP, DLC).

Two Telegrams from Edward Mandell House

Paris. November 29, 1917.

The first sitting of the Conference was held this morning and everything went according to programme. There were a few words of welcome from the Prime Minister and then the Conference immediately began work. Joint committees on Finance, Tonnage, Munitions and Food were formed and the needs of the several small powers will be brought before them. But merely for information, since I have requested our people to make no commitments either direct or implied.

The Supreme War Council will meet at Versailles on Saturday at ten o'clock. Clemenceau, Lloyd George, Orlando and I sitting together first to formulate plans, and the military members sitting with us afterwards.

I think it important for Bliss to return with us. He will not be needed in the Council after the first meeting as much as he will be needed at home to report and advise as to the future.

We hope to be able to sail as planned.   Edward House.

Paris. November 29, 1917.

General Foch, Chief of French Staff, who is just back from Italy tells me the Italian line will hold where it now is until Spring. He said "It is again glued together." Edward House

T telegrams (E. M. House Papers, CtY).

From Newton Diehl Baker

Information

My dear Mr. President: Washington. November 29, 1917.

From time to time I have been hearing from persons who were disturbed at the state of mind of the Jewish drafted men at Camp Upton, the reports being to the effect that they were sullen, resentful and perhaps in some sort of secret pact with one another which would be fruitful of trouble. I have had the matter so thoroughly investigated that I have now assured myself that there is no basis whatever for these reports except, perhaps, that a number of these young Jews, being Socialists, did assume a resentful attitude toward various groups of New York politicians who sought their votes for Hylan, Mitchell and Bennet. I have just had a letter from a Mr. Rosenbaum,[1] of the National Cloak and Suit Company of New York, from which I quote the following:

"We have between 50 and 60 men from our place with the colors, most of them men who have recently gone to Camp Upton on Long Island. The spirit of these men is splendid and the reports they give us are most flattering. Their letters to us show the intense earnestness of these young men and the wonderful spirit that they have brought to the work. They have no complaints to make and speak highly of the food and the treatment. I have also heard from men from other camps who talk in the same way; in fact, I have yet to hear a complaint from any of the drafted men."

I send you this item of information because it seems to me not unlikely that you may have heard some of the disquieting things which have come to me about Camp Upton.

Very respectfully, Newton D. Baker

TLS (WP, DLC).
[1] Sol G. Rosenbaum, Herman S. Rosenbaum, and William Rosenbaum were president, vice-president, and secretary-treasurer, respectively, of the National Cloak and Suit Co., Inc.

From Flora Lois Robinson[1]

Dear President Wilson,   [New York] Thanksgiving Day, 1917.

Ten years ago this very day, Jessie and I sat opposite you at your study-desk in Princeton, listening to your views on a subject which then loomed large on our horizon,—the question of college Fraternities. Even with this reminder I shall not expect you to remember me, but your friendly help at that time, the hospitality I enjoyed in your home, and my happy friendship with Jessie and Frank make it possible for me to write thus informally to you on a subject very near to my heart these days. I am writing without having consulted anyone,—not even Jessie,—as I have wished the suggestion contained in this letter to stand on its own merits.

We are all thinking in terms of the War these days, and to those of us engaged in the work of the missionary programme for the world,—(for I should mention that I have been teaching in a missionary college in India),—this has meant some readjustments to "home" relations. In consideration of all the Europeward calls for service and money, each one of us has had to decide whether he ought to sustain his relation to things so comparatively remote as "the Mission Field." Our very world-sympathies themselves have emphasised our patriotic duties, and made us anxious to serve to the best of our ability in this crisis. I do not know of a single Missionary Society that is not entering into the fellowship of suffering with Europe. The Woman's Foreign Missionary Society to which I belong, has just pledged itself to a gift of forty-five thousand dollars for French War-orphans, in addition to its annual budget of one million four-hundred thousand for non-Christian lands.

But I am sure no one will appreciate better than you, President Wilson, that there is danger of exclusive sympathies today, and that there is danger of forgetting the importance of the foreign missionary enterprise in relation to the situation that is developing and will develop because of the War. Many are ignorant of or ignore the fact that missionary influence to a large extent controls the trend of international feeling. There are, it is true, many who expect to do their share to maintain missionary work *in spite of* the War: but it becomes increasingly clear that we must not only maintain but urge on the enterprise *because of* the War.

President Wilson, I wish I might sit opposite you as we did that afternoon in Princeton, and ask you whether you believe that even in this time of national stress we dare leave the *world* needs uncared for. I feel absolutely certain you will agree that our highest wisdom,—both for the present and the future,—is that we keep our sympathies sensitive and true in response to the ever-insistent missionary challenge. Were there not sufficient resources in America, we would all expect expenditure to be made *only* in the line of direct War needs. But with the great resources there are, in spite of all the financial pressure, we have no fear of interfering with Liberty Loans, Y.M.C.A. and other Camp activities, Red Cross and other relief work, by appealing for these non-Christian countries where the War is making itself keenly felt also.

And now for my suggestion, which I prefer to present as a heart-felt wish. It is that you, as President, whose interest in the *nation* no one may question, and whose word will therefore count more than the word of any other American, give a message in your own God-given way which shall be heard throughout America, urging us to remember the less-favored countries where the missionary enterprise has been carrying on its campaign of peace these many generations; urging us not to forfeit our right to *Christian* leadership in the events that shall follow the War by setting aside Christ's world-wide programme even in this period of extraordinary national experience; urging us, perhaps, to make this gift-season of Christmas a time for very definitely contributing towards carrying the Christian message across the seas in the manifold forms through which the missionary enterprise, in all its denominations, is bringing in the "life more abundant" to the oriental and tropical peoples.

If it seems to you, President Wilson, that I should have presented this matter through some recognized religious organization, I trust you will yet give me the opportunity of requesting such a body to convey the matter to you. And yet, could your message come more personally than it would seem to come if in response to a formal request, it would, I feel, mean immeasurably more to those who read it. That is why I have taken it on myself to write this personal letter, for should the suggestion meet with the acceptance I feel led to expect for it, I can be eliminated and leave you to speak from your heart to the people of America on behalf of the countries where Christ's cause so desparately needs championing.

Should your interest in this matter make any further word from me of the slightest value, will you please consider me at your service either by correspondence or personal interview?

With deep appreciation of the fine simplicity which makes it possible for the President of our United States to be thus addressed by a "plain missionary,"—even if that missionary has in her possession an autograph portrait of yourself that you gave her ten years ago today!

I am, President Wilson,

Very sincerely yours,   Flora L. Robinson

TLS (WP, DLC).
¹ (1884-1926). A roommate and classmate (1908) of Jessie Wilson at the Woman's
College of Baltimore (now Goucher College), first identified in WW to Jessie W. Wilson,
Sept. 26, 1907, n. 1, Vol. 38. At this time, Miss Robinson was a Methodist Episcopal
missionary and the fourth principal of the Isabella Thoburn College in Lucknow, India.

To Newton Diehl Baker

My dear Mr. Secretary: The White House 30 November, 1917

What you tell me about the drafted Jewish men cheers me very
much. I had heard some such reports as you refer to and am delighted to know that there is nothing in them.

Faithfully yours,   Woodrow Wilson

TLS (N. D. Baker Papers, DLC).

To Matthew Hale

My dear Mr. Hale: [The White House] 30 November, 1917

I have discussed with my colleagues here the interesting proposal
of Mr. Max Mitchell¹ for a "Liberty Guard" organization.

The first thing that occurred to me when I looked it over was
what a splendid opportunity it would afford for misuse as a political
organization, for I suppose there has never been any national political organization quite so detailed and thorough as that which
Mr. Mitchell proposed.

We have, you know, in every state of the Union a council for
defense. At Washington we have an advisory commission in communication with these state bodies. There is a chairman for each
state, a county chairman, a township chairman, and even precinct
chairman. This seems to us practically to duplicate what Mr. Mitchell had in mind.

Our whole effort has been to build up this organization and we
are not only turning away from every suggestion that seems to
threaten it, but are gradually inducing all other organizations to
acknowledge the leadership of the state councils. Some of the states
have very remarkable councils.

I fear sometimes that in the view of some people organization is
an object in itself, whereas as a matter of fact it may be a very
serious impediment unless it grows up in a very natural and virtually spontaneous way and as the necessities arise.

Cordially and sincerely yours,   Woodrow Wilson

TLS (Letterpress Books, WP, DLC).
¹ President of the Cosmopolitan Trust Co., Boston.

To Frank Irving Cobb

My dear Cobb:　　　　　[The White House] 30 November, 1917

Thank you for the letter to you from Mr. Konta. It concerns a matter which has deeply concerned me, and I am mighty glad to have this detailed discussion of it in all its aspects.

　　　　　Cordially and sincerely yours,　Woodrow Wilson

TLS (Letterpress Books, WP, DLC).

To William Pettus Hobby

[The White House]

My dear Governor Hobb[y]:　　　　　30 November, 1917

Upon the receipt of the telegram of November eighteenth in which you joined other gentlemen in calling my attention to the distressing situation existing as to the cattle industry in some 150 of the 250 counties of Texas, I at once, of course, got into consultation with such of my colleagues as were prepared to advise me in the matter.

I learn from the Secretary of Agriculture that that department has taken the deepest and most serious interest in this problem and that it is doing everything possible to put all the instrumentalities at the command of the Government at the disposal of those who are trying to solve this question, and that the Food Administrator is also interested in it in a very practical way.

Unhappily, there is no appropriation available from which the pecuniary aid you suggest could be extended, and the extension of such aid would be a matter which I should feel in duty bound to bring to the attention of Congress before taking any action. Moreover, I believe that in view of economic situations existing elsewhere in the country the Congress would feel that it could not enter upon such enterprises without involving the national treasury in the most serious way.

All I can do, therefore, I am sorry to say, is to assure you that every sort of aid within our power will be extended. We appreciate the seriousness of the problem and are disposed to help.

　　　　　Cordially and sincerely yours,　Woodrow Wilson

TLS (Letterpress Books, WP, DLC).

To George Creel

My dear Creel: The White House 30 November, 1917

Thank you for your note of the twenty-eighth and the enclosed article from Mr. Walling. Walling seems to me to have a great deal of sense, and certainly your attitude towards what Lippman[n] and others have suggested to you is entirely correct.

Cordially and faithfully yours,   Woodrow Wilson

TLS (G. Creel Papers, DLC).

To Louis Freeland Post

Confidential

My dear Mr. Post: [The White House] 30 November, 1917

Thank you for your memorandum about developing the employment agency work of the Department of Labor.

I write to suggest this, that you prepare in the most convincing form you can give it for presentation to the Congress a request for the appropriation necessary to carry out this work on the great scale now made manifestly necessary, and that in the meantime you furnish me with an estimate of what it would cost to carry the work until, say, the first of February.

Confidentially, my idea is to supply the necessary funds to organize this work out of the Emergency Fund put at my disposal by the Congress and to continue to support it in that way if the Congress should fail to make an appropriation.

Cordially and sincerely yours,   [Woodrow Wilson]

CCL (WP, DLC).

To John Reese Kenly

My dear Mr. Kenly: [The White House] 30 November, 1917

I am sure I need not tell you how sincerely I appreciated your telegram of November twenty-eighth. The spirit in which you have acted gives me the greatest reassurance and makes me feel how sincerely the forces of the country are uniting for common action.

You may be sure that I would not have asked what I did if I had not known the necessity for it in view of the labor situation throughout the country, and that you were willing to take my word with regard to this is a matter of peculiar gratification to me.

Cordially and sincerely yours,   Woodrow Wilson

TLS (Letterpress Books, WP, DLC).

To Herbert Clark Hoover

My dear Mr. Hoover: The White House 30 November, 1917

I am very glad to receive your letter of the twenty-seventh[1] about the acquiescence of the New York State Commission and the renewal of negotiations with Cuba about the sugar.

I must say that Mr. Gonzales[2] made a very considerable impression on me with regard to the price of Cuban sugar. I took the liberty of sending him with a card to you and I am sure you were interested, as I was, in what he had to say.

Cordially and sincerely yours,   Woodrow Wilson

TLS (H. Hoover Papers, HPL).
  [1] H. C. Hoover to WW, Nov. 27, 1917, TLS (WP, DLC). Hoover reported "two troubles settled—or quieted for a time." After "breaking off relations," the Cubans had "renewed negotiations upon our basis of price." Also, the New York State Food Commission, after threatening to resign, had accepted the views of the Food Administration on the relations of the two organizations. Earlier Hoover had felt "a great deal of anxiety" because of political forces at work. As Hoover put it, "The selection of a board in New York state to control food activities, the majority of whom look towards the Governor for their inspiration is very distasteful to me and in any event, as you have so often said, boards generally do not make for efficient administration. . . . As near as I can make out the real reason behind the scene is that the Governor wishes to dominate everything in New York state and if the Food Administration is a success he wishes to add it to his laurels and if it brings criticism he wishes to be in position to lay the trouble up to the Federal Administration." H. C. Hoover to WW, Nov. 23, 1917, TLS (WP, DLC).
  [2] That is William Elliott Gonzales, Minister of the United States to Cuba. Wilson saw him at the White House on November 27.

To Samuel Huston Thompson, Jr.

My dear Thompson: The White House 30 November, 1917

I am sometimes startled to find how many things that I am deeply interested in my absorption in public work cuts me off from. I learned only last evening that you had actually been operated on for appendicitis and were out again. I was delighted to be told that you were looking unusually fit and well and had said that you felt greatly improved and strengthened. It was very delightful to get this news, and yet it caused me a pang to think that you had been in the hospital and I had not sent you any word of my sympathy and interest.

Cordially and sincerely yours,   Woodrow Wilson

TLS (S. H. Thompson, Jr., Papers, DLC).

From Joseph Patrick Tumulty, with Enclosure

Dear Governor: The White House. 30 November, 1917.

I am sending you herewith a few suggestions for your Message. About a week ago there seemed to be a unanimity of opinion that we should declare war on Austria. Now from editorial comment it appears that the matter is, as you stated a few days ago, more difficult than it seems at the first glance.

Let me call your attention to the enclosed clipping from the New York Times of today.[1]   Sincerely yours,   Tumulty

TLS (C. L. Swem Coll., NjP).
[1] Charles H. Grasty wrote in a dispatch from Paris on November 29 that reports coming via Switzerland indicated that Austria was discontented with the military situation in Italy and increasingly concerned over its own relations with Germany, which was taking a domineering role in the alliance. Grasty noted that Austria stood to lose, no matter which side won the war. He added that Emperor Charles was said to be very restless and the people "deeply embittered and distrustful of their Prussian partners." *New York Times*, Nov. 30, 1917.

E N C L O S U R E

PRESIDENT'S MESSAGE SUGGESTION

The President's address to Congress can be made the occasion for a statement of world-wide importance. It can be made the vehicle for another drive on Germany by use of the same tactics which the President has so splendidly adopted in the past in making the distinction between the German government and the German people.

There are several points that can be reiterated with advantage not only to prevent any faltering or dissension in the ranks of the allies but to infuse in them a new spirit incident to the formation of a great inter-allied council that is to mean a coordination of might.

In the first place, there is always discussion of war aims. The President can restate some of the principles which he outlined in his address to the Senate in January. And he can state that territorial interests and special matters of national concern so vital to each of the Allies cannot be discussed until the great principles for which all the allies stand are fixed and assured. He can drive home the point that discussion of war aims can without disadvantage be postponed until democracy shall have shown to the world that it *can* overcome militarism, until it has taught the lesson that great armaments avail nothing in the hands of conscience-less autocrats when the resources of the world are in the hands of free peoples, and that it is precisely to add the German people to the league of free peoples that the war is being waged against the misguided leaders of Germany whom the German people still blindly obey.

To our own people, the speech can be the occasion for an exhortation that the men who died to make America free shall not have died in vain, that the millions who already have given their lives in France to the cause of human liberty shall not sleep in their graves without a memorial from the living to carry forward the task they so heroically began, a memorial of action, of armies and navies anxious to sacrifice even more for the greatest cause the civilized world has ever known—self government and democracy. The world cannot remain half autocratic and half democratic.

There are those who pick flaws in our system of government, in the systems of government of our co-belligerents but they van [can] pick no flaw in the great principle of international honor and the sanctity of treaties and pledges for which the entente stand as opposed to the treachery, duplicity, dishonor and ruthlessness with which the German diplomatic service and the Imperial German government have now been proven to have been saturated.

As for Russia, it is timely to renew our faith in the ability of her people to right themselves. No revolution is attended without travails such as Russia is experiencing today. Misguided extremists ot [or] tools of the enemy may be in control for a time but the people will soon expel them. We must be patient and seek in the best way we can to aid and stimulate those elements which are in truth seeking democracy. It may be no military advantage immediately to us but we care more for the eventual stability of the Russian republic and the creation of democratic institutions therein than we do for a temporary military advantage because until the republic is on solid foundation and the Russian people see that no democracy which they attempt to set up can remain safe against the German menace which will endeavor to keep it in constant turmoil and confusion so that Germany may exploit and even subjugate her weaker neighbor, there can be no certain military advantages. We must bear patiently with our struggling sister republic and help where we can help.

We are just beginning to fight. We have limitless resources. We are not going to hesitate and count the pain or the sacrifice. We are going forward with one purpose—to win and to win if it takes us years instead of months more in which to do it. America with her gallant partners in the crusade for greater democracy are just girding their loins and the peoples of all the countries are going to expend as they have already every resource in the common object— the extermination of the menace of German militarism and the terrible woe that it has brought upon unsuspecting peoples.

T MS (C. L. Swem Coll., NjP).

From Edward Mandell House

[Paris, Nov. 30, 1917]

I intend 7517 [to offer] this resolution for approval of the inter-allied conference (quote) The Allies and the U States declare that they are not waging war for the purpose of aggression or indemnity. The sacrifices they are making are in order that militarism shall not continue to 22105 [cast] its shadow over the World & that nations shall have the right to lead their lives in the way that seems to them 20821 [best] for the development of their general welfare." If you have any objections, please answer immediately. It is of vast importance that this be done. The British have agreed to vote for it![1]   Edward House.

EBWhw decode of T telegram (WP, DLC).
[1] House, upon his return voyage, prepared a report of the mission to the United Kingdom and France. The report noted that, at a meeting on November 30, with Lloyd George, Balfour, Clemenceau, Pichon, Orlando, and Sonnino present, House proposed that the Inter-Allied Conference adopt a resolution substantially as above. House's account of this meeting continues as follows:
"Such a resolution as this I thought would have a wholesome effect not only in Russia but all over the world.
"Mr. Balfour strongly recommended that the Allies release Russia from her promise to continue the war. Sonnino violently opposed this suggestion. The Russian Ambassador [Vasilii Alekseevich Maklakov] was then brought into the conference, and he was in favor of some such statement as I had drafted. It was decided to request the Russian Ambassador to draw up a memorandum of what action he thought we should take and to consider the same the next day."
House recorded in the section of his report for December 1 that Lord Lansdowne's letter in the London *Daily Telegraph* of November 29 was uppermost in Lloyd George's mind. (See H. A. Garfield to WW, Nov. 30, 1917, second letter of that date.) House added that he had urged upon Reading and Lloyd George the importance of having the Inter-Allied Conference adopt a resolution along the lines indicated, but that his efforts were "fruitless." At the full meeting of the British, French, and Italian Prime Ministers and Foreign Ministers later that day, House added, his proposal and alternative resolutions by Maklakov and "the ultra-conservative Baron Sonnino" were discussed. Sonnino's proposal was favored by all but House, who "emphatically declined to subscribe to it on behalf of the United States." The refusal of the United States to be a party to this resolution "of course" effectively disposed of it. House's report, together with reports by other members of the mission and some related papers, is printed in *FR-WWS 1917*, 2, I, 334-445.

From Robert Lansing, with Enclosure

My dear Mr. President: Washington November 30, 1917.

I beg to enclose an extract from a confidential report received from the Office of Naval Intelligence which seems to me of considerable interest. I merely desire to call it to your attention.

With assurances of respect, etc., I am, my dear Mr. President,
                              Faithfully yours,   Robert Lansing.

TLS (WP, DLC).

ENCLOSURE

In regard to the labor situation in England, it is reported that the fight of labor against the Prime Minister, that is now being organized, may be very far reaching in its effects. That the Government is making strenuous efforts by sending speakers throughout the country to counteract the pacifist agitation that has sprung up in England, and that if Henderson's fight against the Prime Minister comes to a head during the war there will certainly be interesting developments. It is reported that if Henderson were to be the next Prime Minister he would be in favor of Peace. It is reported that he stated that he is of the opinion that Peace could be secured at the present time by negotiation, which would be just as advantageous to the Allies as a peace which could be secured two years from now, after half a million more lives had been sacrificed and another million [?] dollars expended. It is stated that Henderson is quite interested in Samuel Gompers and has considerable admiration for him. The report suggests that it would be of unquestionable advantage to the Allied cause to have Mr. Gompers go to England, and that an interview could be arranged without its becoming public, unless it was thought an advantage to have it known.[1]

T MS (WP, DLC).
  [1] "Would you not be kind enough to show the enclosed to Mr. Gompers in strict confidence and consult him as to whether he knows of any means by which he could help to steer Mr. Henderson?" WW to JPT, c. Nov. 30, 1917, TL (WP, DLC).

From the White House Staff

The White House.

Memorandum for the President: November 30, 1917.

Mr. Creel asks if he and Mr. Townley may see the President sometime today.[1]

T MS (WP, DLC).
  [1] Wilson saw Creel and Arthur Charles Townley, president of the Nonpartisan League, at 5 P.M. The Editors have found no record of their discussion, but Creel later wrote to Charles Edward Russell: "I sent for the heads of various agricultural bodies and unions, and among those that came to Washington in response to the call was Mr. Townley, head of the Nonpartisan League. I found him, just as I found the others, full of distrusts and suspicions born of the many lies that he had read and heard. I took him, as I took others, to the President himself, and the interview removed every doubt as to the necessity of the war and the high purpose of America. And after that I took Mr. Townley to the office of Mr. Herbert Hoover, and for three hours the two men fought out disputed points. When Mr. Townley left Washington he had not only pledged the full support of his organization to the war, but he had struck hands with Mr. Hoover and promised every co-operative effort. These pledges were kept." Creel added that it was at Townley's request that he, Creel, sent speakers into the Northwest. Charles Edward Russell, *The Story of the Nonpartisan League: A Chapter in American Evolution* (New York, 1920), pp. 243-46. For an account of Townley's views on the war (and views attributed to him, but denied), see Robert L. Morlan, *Political Prairie Fire: The Nonpartisan League, 1915-1922.* (Minneapolis, Minn., 1955), pp. 138-43, 149.

From David Franklin Houston

Dear Mr. President: Washington November 30, 1917.

I think it highly important that proper legislation relating to the development of the water power of the Nation be secured at the coming session of Congress. The present industrial situation emphasizes the need of prompt action. The scarcity and high prices of fuel and construction materials have increased the cost of steam plants and those interested in power development are turning their attention more and more to water power as a source of supply. Legislation which will make it possible to safeguard the public interests, and at the same time to protect private investors, should result in securing cheaper water power and in conserving coal and fuel oil.

It would be of advantage if the policy of the Nation with reference to water power not only on the public domain and in the National Forests, but also on the navigable streams, could be formulated in a single measure, and especially if machinery representing the three Departments concerned—War, Interior, and Agriculture— could be devised. Such coordinated machinery would have many advantages. Those interested would have a single agency to deal with in reference to all power matters. Each of the Departments has other highly important powers to administer and vital activities to direct in the areas of possible power development. With a council such as I have in mind all the interests involved could be dealt with without overlapping, duplication of effort, and friction. Especially important would be the fact that such a council could utilize highly developed existing agencies in the three Departments and save expense to the Government.

It is my thought that a water power council, consisting of the Secretary of War, the Secretary of the Interior, and the Secretary of Agriculture should be provided for in the Act, with an executive officer appointed by the President who will be charged with the duty of executing the terms of the law and the rules and regulations under the supervision of the council. It will be necessary, of course, for the council and executive officer to employ such additional assistance as may be needed to carry out the provisions of the Act. Secretary Baker, Secretary Lane and I have had a brief preliminary talk about the legislation and we propose to have another in the next day or so. Simply for your information, I enclose a tentative draft of the sections covering the machinery referred to.[1]

So far as the Department of Agriculture immediately is concerned, I have made no suggestions in the annual report for the renewal of the emergency legislation, that is, the Food Production

Act. I thought it preferable to defer consideration of this matter until later in the fiscal year when I would know more about the situation and what additional powers and appropriations, if any, should be requested.

The only other thought in my mind at this time in connection with the matters which I have to deal with in a general way is that there may be need of action by Congress to give you power directly to fix prices of essential commodities. I assume, however, that this question will be discussed either by the Secretary of War or the Secretary of the Navy or by both.

Sincerely yours,   D. F. Houston

TLS (WP, DLC).
    [1] Undated T MS (WP, DLC). The draft bill established a Federal Power Commission of three members, as described in Houston's letter, with an executive officer, a secretary, and other employees. The bill appropriated $100,000 to defray necessary expenses. So far as practicable, the commission should utilize the existing resources of the Departments of War, the Interior, and Agriculture.
    Lane had earlier suggested a similar water-power commission in FKL to WW, Dec. 9, 1916 (third letter of that date), Vol. 40.

From Maud May Wood Park

My dear Mr. President: Washington, D. C. November 30, 1917.

Your letter of November twenty-seventh has been forwarded to me from New York, and I thank you warmly for your kindness in letting me know that the lists which I sent last week may be of use.

Word has come today from our state branch in Arkansas that Senator Kirby and Representatives Caraway, Jacoway and Goodwin[1] have given definite assurance of support. I therefore enclose an amended list with their names in the proper column.[2]

Reports from a number of other states are likely to come to us within the next fortnight, and our canvass here in Washington will begin next week. If we find that further changes in the listing are needed, I shall be very glad to send you the corrections as they are made, or to give you by letter or in person any additional information that you may wish.

With sincere appreciation of your interest, I have the honor to be,   Faithfully yours,   Maud Wood Park.

TLS (WP, DLC).
    [1] Thaddeus Horatius Caraway, Henderson Madison Jacoway, and William Shields Goodwin, Democratic congressmen from Arkansas.
    [2] Polls of the Senate and the House of Representatives, Sixty-fifth Congress, showing favorable, unfavorable, and doubtful members by party as of November 30, 1917. T MS (WP, DLC).

Two Letters from Josephus Daniels

Dear Mr. President: Washington. November 30, 1917.

Replying to your request for a memorandum regarding imperative matters Congress should take up to strengthen the Navy, I am recommending authorization for such additional personnel and their thorough training as may be needed to man the rapidly increasing number of ships in service. Such authorization will be necessary. I have also recommended appropriations to complete the ships authorized in the three year building program and to add such craft as changing conditions may demonstrate to be most effective. I made this recommendation, which includes additional battle-cruisers and dreadnaughts, even though we have not begun the actual construction of the battle-cruisers and some of the dreadnaughts for which apropriations were made at the last session of Congress. Contracts for their construction have been entered into, but the paramount necessity of building a large fleet of destroyers and merchant ships made it necessary, as you know, to give priority to such ships. However, I think the money should be provided to carry out the full three year building program, and with the money provided, as soon as possible we can begin their construction. Aside from more men, and large provision for their training, and money for necessary ships, I do not think there is any naval legislation imperative enough to call for special emphasis in your message to Congress.

The splendid service of the men in the Navy, particularly on the destroyers and in the gun crews on merchant ships, dangerous and rigorous, exacting already the toll of 68 young lives, might well be included if you think suitable at this time.

                         Sincerely,   Josephus Daniels

Dear Mr. President: Washington. November 30, 1917.

Replying to your letter asking for a memorandum as to legislation imperative to be considered at this session of Congress, I addressed you a note confining myself to naval recommendations, but I notice you say "any legislation," and therefore desire to make these suggestions for such consideration as you may think they deserve at this time:

1. Next to actual military supplies and ships, transportation is the question of paramount importance. Efficient railroad transportation has broken down and the railroads have nearly killed river transportation. It is my belief that the Government must take over land and water transportation, and that the first step is government

operation of railroads for the duration of the war. I believe this would mean government ownership. This is regarded by many as revolutionary. To me it seems to be the necessary step in the evolution of transportation. The railroad managers admit their inability to meet the needs even if given the increased rate. As a by-product of government ownership would be the elimination of much of the gambling on the Stock Exchange called speculation. The railroads are run by bankers who have more interest in their bonds and stocks than in the transportation of passengers and freights. The same argument would embrace the telegraph and telephone.

2. There is a growing sentiment that all men between the ages of 21 and 31 ought to be in the draft, those who are not citizens as well as those who are. There are hundreds of thousands of men not now subject to draft who escape service and step into the positions vacated by American youths who go into the Army or Navy. The sentiment in favor of some provision of law, or treaty with allied powers, for the enrollment of these men will be tremendously stronger after the next draft. Cannot a way be provided for their enlistment?

3. The question of an extension of price fixing is one of prime importance. The wheat growers and others feel that it is a discrimination against them to fix the prices of what they sell and leave untouched the soaring prices of what they buy. Is it not necessary to make an extension of this power now, both because it is wise and right as well as because it will prevent a rising tide of feeling against the price fixing that has already justified the action?

This may not be the time for you to press these measures, even if you should approve them, but it would seem that consideration of them will be necessary as the war goes on, and you may decide that some of them should be presented now.

Sincerely,   Josephus Daniels

TLS (WP, DLC).

From Franklin Knight Lane

My dear Mr. President: Washington November 30, 1917.

I have your letter of the 28th, asking for a memorandum as to any legislation which I might think it imperative to be considered at this session of Congress.

There are two matters that I deem of primary importance. They are the water power bill and the general leasing bill. The coal situation emphasizes the need for the development of our water power. The Ferris water power bill, which has twice passed the House, is along right lines. In this connection I beg to call your attention to the following extract from a letter which I sent you on January 8th of this year.

"I had a little conference with Senator Walsh, Senator Myers, Mr. Ferris and Mr. Lenroot on Saturday, regarding the bill which I sent to you sometime ago constituting a Water Powers Commission, and giving that Commission power to make rules and regulations. I asked them if such a bill could be passed, and they said that while you doubtless would be able to do it if you insisted upon it, the Senate would not take kindly to such a delegation of power. I wonder, however, if it might not be practicable to have such a Commission of Cabinet officers as I suggested, who would make all leases; Congress to provide the terms upon which the leases would be made. It really would be better if there was but one act covering all streams and one administrative authority. This, however, is not vital, though I believe we will surely come to it eventually."

As to the general leasing bill, you know quite as much about that as I do. The difficulty is in the Senate. It has seemed to me that if any kind of a bill passed the Senate you could get out of the conference committee the sort of a bill that you would approve of, for the House Committee will stand pat for whatever you say. We need oil and need it badly. We may need it still more if the Carranza people get hold of the Tampico oil fields, which they are now driving toward. In view of this condition it may be possible to get the Senate to agree to eliminate all relief provisions touching the Naval reserves and pass a bill that would not in any way affect them. I inclose a copy of my annual report of two years ago, giving my own views on the oil matter and water power bill.[1]

Cordially yours,   Franklin K. Lane

TLS (WP, DLC).
    [1] This enclosure is missing.

From Newton Diehl Baker

My dear Mr. President: Washington. November 30, 1917.

I have received your note asking me to send you a memorandum of legislation desired by the War Department from the present Congress. There is no legislation desired outside of the usual routine of appropriations and minor amendments to existing laws; and, therefore, nothing of a sufficiently radical character to be entitled to mention in your address.

If a convenient place for it could be found in your address it occurs to me to suggest that it would be agreeble to the country to have you suggest to Congress the wisdom of passing a law authorizing suitable honors and badges of distinction as a reward for unusual service and bravery in action; and that such emblems as typify these services might be awarded by the Commander in Chief of our forces to men in the armies of other nations associated with us in the name of the people of the United States.

You have doubtless observed in the dispatches that the War Cross and some other decorations have been offered to Americal [American] sailors and soldiers by both the French and British governments, and Congress might very well authorize the acceptance of these tokens, and a reciprocal use of those devised for our own Army.

Of course, the Medal of Honor is our highest military award, and corresponds to the Victoria Cross of the British. A less distinguished honor which might be more freely distributed would seem to be highly desirable.   Respectfully yours,   Newton D. Baker

TLS (WP, DLC).

Two Letters from Harry Augustus Garfield

Dear Mr. President: Washington, D. C. November 30, 1917

I enclose a formal letter, together with draft of order, in line with my statement of Wednesday afternoon.[1]

If it meets with your approval, I should like to have both the order and the explanatory letter given to the press.

Cordially and faithfully yours,   H. A. Garfield.

[1] See WW to H. A. Garfield, Dec. 1, 1917, n. 1.

Personal

Dear Mr. President: [Washington] November 30, 1917

Lord Lansdowne's letter[1] published in the Washington Post of this morning is the most noteworthy and noblest utterance that has come out of England. It seems to me to run with your purpose and I can well believe brings you both encouragement and relief. Lloyd George and, one might well add, Roosevelt are dangerous leaders in the present emergency.

Cordially and faithfully yours,   H. A. Garfield.

TLS (WP, DLC).
[1] Lansdowne's letter to the Editor of the London *Daily Telegraph* was published in that newspaper on November 29 and was then widely reprinted. Lansdowne began by

pointing out that the number of men killed in the war could be counted in the millions, and that the total number of men engaged was nearly twenty-four million. He urged the compelling necessity to think in terms of restoring peace: "To end the war honourably would be a great achievement; to prevent the same curse falling upon our children would be a greater achievement still." Lansdowne warned that the next war would be even more dreadful than the present one and added that the "prostitution of science for purposes of pure destruction" was "not likely to stop short." In Lansdowne's words: "If the Powers will, under a solemn pact, bind themselves to submit future disputes to arbitration; if they will undertake to outlaw, politically and economically, any one of their number which refuses to enter into such a pact, or to use their joint military and naval forces for the purpose of coercing a Power which breaks away from the rest, they will, indeed, have travelled far along the road which leads to security."

Lansdowne then noted that there seemed to be "complete unanimity," in principle, on the need for security, and he quoted Wilson, Bethmann Hollweg, the papal note of August, Czernin, and Balfour to show that there existed wide agreement as to the need for some type of international sanction against aggression. Then, after reviewing various obstacles to practical agreement, Lansdowne wrote that an "immense stimulus" would probably be given to the peace party in Germany if it were understood:

"(1) That we do not desire the annihilation of Germany as a Great Power;

"(2) That we do not seek to impose upon her people any form of government other than that of their own choice;

"(3) That, except as a legitimate war measure, we have no desire to deny to Germany her place among the great commercial communities of the world;

"(4) That we are prepared, when the war is over, to examine in concert with other Powers the group of international problems, some of them of recent origin, which are connected with the question of 'the freedom of the seas';

"(5) That we are prepared to enter into an international pact under which ample opportunities would be afforded for the settlement of international disputes by peaceful means."

Lansdowne concluded by stating that he thought that, on the British side, "authority could be found for most of these propositions in Ministerial speeches." If progress could be made toward general agreement on these points, "the political horizon might perhaps be scanned with better hope by those who pray, but can at this moment hardly venture to expect, that the New Year may bring us a lasting and honourable peace." London *Daily Telegraph*, Nov. 29, 1917.

William Hepburn Buckler to Edward Mandell House

London, November 30, 1917.

Lord Lansdowne's letter, giving concise expression to what many feel, has been a fit climax to the events of the month. Notwithstanding the brilliant British advance near Cambrai, the prospect of a purely military victory over the Central Powers has during the past month become more remote than it was even six weeks ago. The condition of Italy and still more that of Russia are the obvious causes of this "hope deferred." That the heart of believers in a military knock-out should therefore be "sick" is only natural. And the result has been to turn men's minds to the other resources of the Entente, namely its power to deny Germany her imports, colonies and foreign trade.

What Lord Lansdowne suggests is not surrender of the Entente's minimum terms, but that its chief asset, economic supremacy, be used to obtain Germany's acceptance of those terms—which he sums up in the one word "security."

To induce a speedier acceptance he further proposes that on five points—now used by German militarists as bogeys to keep their fellow countrymen in the war—the disinterestedness of the Entente be made clear.

Naturally such proposals have greatly shocked all those who pin their faith to a crushing defeat and punishment of the Central Powers, to "skinning Germany" as Bernard Shaw phrases it. Lord Lansdowne points out that, though this may be possible, it is still so remote as to involve in its attainment exhaustion, perhaps ruin. And in this view the checking of the Cambrai offensive, coinciding with the events in Italy and Russia, tends to support him. Mesopotamia and Syria being "side shows," the Flanders front remains the only one on which the enemy is seriously vulnerable, and if advances here are as slow and costly as those of Cambrai and Passchendaele, Lord Lansdowne's suggestion that other than military solutions should be sought and tried seems reasonable.

The chief point of interest is to what extent the press and Parliament will accept this advice. Of course the Unionists will reject it, but the Liberal Press, including even the cautious "Westminster Gazette" have already endorsed it, and there is no doubt that former Ministers such as Buckmaster,[1] McKenna and Runciman, and probably Grey, sympathize with the Lansdowne proposals. Asquith's position is uncertain, but whatever it may be, "pro-negotiation" opinions, now that they have received such eminent support as Lord Lansdowne's, will probably become a more definite feature of the Parliamentary "opposition."

The pessimistic views to which the Prime Minister gave utterance in his Paris speech[2] have contributed no less than the Cambrai check to produce a frame of mind favorable to the reception of Lord Lansdowne's letter. I was surprized to find, at a luncheon party which I happened to attend the day after the letter was published, only one person out of four inclined to criticize it. Lord Dunluce (son of Lord Antrim)[3] now an official in the Ministry of Munitions, said he thought it the only British pronouncement which followed President Wilson's policy of appealing to and strengthening German sentiment hostile to their militarists.[4]

CC MS (WP, DLC).
  [1] Stanley Owen Buckmaster, 1st Baron Buckmaster, was Lord Chancellor in 1915 and 1916.
  [2] That is, the speech on November 13, about which see EMH to WW, Nov. 20, 1917, n. 1.
  [3] Randal Mark Kerr M'Donnell, Viscount Dunluce, son of the 11th Earl of Antrim.
  [4] Sir William Wiseman handed this letter to Wilson on December 19.

From the Diary of Josephus Daniels

November Friday 30 1917

Cabinet—Russian situation discussed. Lane thought Trotsky government might maintain itself and should not be lightly dismissed. Others thought it would fail. WW said Cossacks & others in S. Russia would not follow T. but declared for continuance of war, & had asked help and recognition. Too chaotic to act yet.

To Edward Mandell House

[The White House, Dec. 1, 1917]

The resolution you suggest is entirely in line with my thought and has my approval.

You will realize how unfortunate it would be for the conference to discuss peace terms in a spirit antagonistic to my January address to the Senate. Our people and Congress will not fight for any selfish aim on the part of any belligerent, with the possible exception of Alsace Lorraine, least of all for divisions of territory such as have been contemplated in Asia Minor. I think it will be obvious to all that it would be a fatal mistake to cool the ardour of America.

Answering your cable after conferring with Clemenceau[1] I favour the most effective war council obtainable whether directed by one man or not.

WWhw and WWT telegram (WP, DLC).
[1] EMH to WW, Nov. 26, 1917.

To Harry Augustus Garfield

My dear Garfield: [The White House] 1 December, 1917

I am giving the letter and the order to the Press today and thank you for them.[1] I am returning the document.

In great haste   Faithfully yours,   Woodrow Wilson

TLS (Letterpress Books, WP, DLC).
[1] Garfield's letter to Wilson and Wilson's Executive Order, both dated November 28, are printed in the *Official Bulletin*, I (Dec. 3, 1917), 1-2. Garfield began by referring to his letter of October 26 (printed at that date in Vol. 44) about wages and prices in bituminous coal. Most of his comments in that letter also applied to the anthracite situation, he wrote, and need not be repeated. The anthracite operators and miners had reached an agreement on November 17, Garfield noted, and, on the basis of this and detailed information on costs of production, he recommended that Wilson authorize an increase of thirty-five cents per ton for anthracite coal, except where existing contracts already provided for price increases based on wage increases. Wilson's Executive Order authorized the requested change, effective December 1, 1917.

From Edward Mandell House

[Paris, Dec. 1, 1917]

I hope you will not think it necessary to make any statement concerning foreign affairs until I can consult with [see] you. This seems to me very important.

I should be in Washington by December 17.

Edward House.

T transcript of WWsh decode of T telegram (WP, DLC).

From Robert Lansing

My dear Mr. President: Washington December 1, 1917.

Replying to your request of November 28, for a statement as to any legislation which should be considered by Congress at this session, I enclose memoranda on this subject which are self-explanatory.[1]

In addition to these memoranda I might suggest that, in my opinion, it would be wise if Congress would pass a resolution suspending during the term of the war the so-called Seaman's Act. I understand that Secretary Redfield is strongly in favor of this.[2] Many protests from foreign countries, particularly the Allied countries, have come to my knowledge complaining that as a result of this Act it is impossible to hold seamen on merchant vessels as they are free to desert whenever they please, following their own inclinations whether voluntarily or induced by German intrigue.

In this connection may I also suggest that it would be of great value to this Department if a law could be passed making it perjury for false affidavits to be presented to this Department or any Department of the Government by persons seeking action in support of their interests here or abroad. I understand that there is a provision in the Civil Service law which protects the Commission from misstatements. Such a law for the Department of State would go far in preventing it from being imposed upon by unscrupulous persons. Now, as heretofore, the Department has to rely upon statements in affidavits presented to it as the basis for communications with foreign governments. It is very important, particularly at the present time, that there should be some law requiring persons to tell the truth and nothing but the truth in the sworn statements which they present to the Department in support of their claims.

Faithfully yours,   Robert Lansing

P.S. If you approve the termination of the treaties with Norway and Sweden, I think it would be well to notify their governments in advance of any action on our part. R.L.

TLS (WP, DLC).

¹ L. H. Woolsey, "Abrogation of Treaty with Norway and Sweden of 1827 by Resolution of the Senate," Nov. 30, 1917, TI with attached MS summaries of the treaties of 1783 and 1827, T MSS (WP, DLC). Also L. H. Woolsey, "Suggested Amendment to the Draft Act of May 18, 1917," Nov. 30, 1917, TI MS (WP, DLC). The Selective Service Act provided for conscription of aliens (except enemy aliens) who had taken out their first papers for naturalization. Neutral countries had protested against such conscription, and of the War Department, with Wilson's approval, had acceded to their views. Although there was no way under the Selective Service Act to exempt nationals of neutral countries, the State Department had advised neutral governments that the President, as Commander in Chief, would discharge their subjects immediately after induction. Since this was "virtually a refusal to execute the Act of Congress in this respect," Woolsey thought that the situation should be cleared up by an amendment to the Selective Service Act to exclude from its operation "declarants of neutral nationality."

² W. C. Redfield to WW, Nov. 30, 1917, TLS (WP, DLC).

Three Letters from Herbert Clark Hoover

                                            Washington, D. C.
Dear Mr. President: First December *1917*

The purpose of Mr. Gonzales' visit is now necessarily modified by acceptance by Cuba of the terms which we proposed and as the Cuban Commission has expressed it is well satisfied I do not assume that any further opposition will be exerted. Mr. Gonzales' views were identical with those of President Menocal but I cannot bring myself to believe they were based upon such searching investigation of the cost of production as we had previously made and the figures with regard to which were practically agreed by the Cuban producers themselves.

I was very glad indeed to see him and to outline some of the difficulties that we would have to face with Cuba in the necessity to reduce the exports of bread stuffs from this country. As I have a feeling that inasmuch as every ounce of wheat products exported from the United States from now on must be by sacrificing consumption by the American people, we would be perfectly correct in asking the people of Cuba to undertake the same ration of sacrifice, that is, approximately twenty-five per cent. of their normal wheat product consumption.

                                    Yours faithfully,   Herbert Hoover

Dear Mr. President: Washington, D. C. 1 December, 1917.

As to regulating food handling concerns on a pre-war profit basis, I agree that it would work hardship if applied rigorously to small dealers. On the other hand, I have the feeling that our chief opponent to this plan—J. Ogden Armour[1]—can manage to live all right. Therefore, we will try to apply it with consideration.

We have been for two months endeavoring to come to some settlement with the packers as to regulations governing that trade. Finally we were compelled to use our own judgment as to their profit limitations. We based this judgment upon pre-war conditions with an increase of ½% for certain extra expense considerations in borrowing capital. The packers today came in a body to protest and I have written them the inclosed letter in confirmation of our discussion.[2] I trust I have your approval in the course laid down.[3]

Yours faithfully,   Herbert Hoover

[1] Jonathan Ogden Armour.
[2] H. C. Hoover to Thomas Edward Wilson, Dec. 1, 1917, CCL (WP, DLC). In this letter, Hoover recorded his understanding that T. E. Wilson, Armour, Edward Morris, Louis Franklin Swift, and Edward Aloysius Cudahy held that the rule of 9 per cent maximum profits was unjust to the packers and would prevent them from financing necessary expansions of plant. Hoover stated his understanding that prewar profits had averaged somewhat less than 9 per cent and that the bulk of the plants had been built out of profits. However, having "every desire to meet an emergency situation with every sense of justice," Hoover repeated his proposal that, if certain conditions were met, the administration would "endeavor to secure aid or alternatively adjust profits by some measure." He expressed appreciation for the willingness of the great packing firms to cooperate in the matter.
[3] Swem noted: "The President approves." C. L. Swem, c. Dec. 5, 1917, T MS (WP, DLC).

Dear Mr President: Washington, D. C. 1 December 1917

With respect to your note of November 28 on the question of legislation to be considered at this session of Congress, I have the following views:

I

It appears to me that it has now become critical, in mobilization of our productive power, our transportation, the control of labor, and the stimulation of production, that we have a general price-fixing power vested in yourself or in the Federal Trade Commission. At present, except for coal, there is no such power in the government; and by implementing exports, imports, embargoes, purchasing power for our own government and the Allies, and by making first one voluntary agreement after another, we are playing around the fringes of the problem and setting up great currents of injustice. For instance, the farmers justly complain that by these implements their income is restricted and no restraints are placed upon the goods they must purchase.

The law of supply and demand has been replaced by the law of selfishness; and while I am confident that we have eliminated profiteering in food trades it still runs rampant in other branches of commerce.

We cannot hope to restrain the constant demands of labor, with its reactions on national efficiency, unless we can bring the advances in price to a stop—and we can not do this in the food trades unless the materials of production are also controlled.

We could greatly increase the efficiency of the transportation system if we could zonalize distribution of great primary commodities, by controlling their distribution area, but as such a course would to some degree stifle competition it cannot be done without prior fixation of price. We are today saving 25% of the transport of wheat and flour by such a system, and it could be applied to the other great staple commodities.

My own views upon the economics of this question are that they should be based upon a determination of the fair price for the limited list of primary raw materials with the added power to fix the profits or differentials to be added by the various subsequent links of manufacture and distribution. Further, that this power should be backed by authority of the government to buy and sell these primary commodities if it becomes necessary to maintain regular and seasonal flow. Such legislation would enable the retail trader to be dealt with,—not now possible in the food trades.

I feel strongly that the fixing of such prices should be in the hands of somebody who can establish some sort of unity between the animal, mineral, and vegetable kingdoms, and that it cannot therefore rest in the hands of such a department as mine. It would appear to me a logical function for the Federal Trade Commission; the administration of such judgments as they might enter upon these subjects being left in the hands of the various departments which are concerned with the commerce in these commodities.

I have also the feeling that the Federal Trade Commission, being a semi-judicial body, holds the skill and independence to fix these prices, free from the great pressure to which administrative departments are now constantly subjected, and that if legislation on this line were applied for to the Federal Trade Commission it would be free from a great deal of the congressional opposition and prejudice that must arise against any particular organ of the government. We can not disguise the fact that such administrations as mine must, if we are to act with independence and justice to all sections of the community, excite the most violent opposition from individuals and minorities and that these are reflected by the direct representatives of these trades and minorities in Congress and that such prejudice would greatly color legislative action.

II

The next great problem confronting us is the stimulation of production. This rests primarily upon the fixation of prices of primary commodities at stimulative levels with consequent assurance of market at profitable levels, which would be covered by the foregoing proposals. In addition, however, I am convinced that some definite action must be taken as to agricultural labor. There will undoubtedly be a very considerable decrease in production if any further draft is made; and furthermore, the attraction of high wages in munitions plants is drawing labor from the farms. Beyond exemption from further draft, it appears to me more powers in the establishment of labor exchanges should be given to the Department of Labor, and other constructive mobilization of labor undertaken.

Another field of necessity for action has arisen if we are to promote production to its necessary level. Three sequent failures in wheat crop in the Northwest and some other points and the great drought in the Southwest with consequent cattle afmine [famine] all require constructive handling if production in those quarters is to be maintained. I would suggest a considerable appropriation, placed at the disposal of the Farm Loan Board, for advances against crops and animals. The Board at one time had worked out a constructive plan of local guarantee association.

III

The other point upon which I am convinced that emergency legislation is necessary is to give to you some general powers to control waste, to require substitution of one commodity for another in consumption, and to limit actual consumption of commodities. In other words, a broad conservation measure, capable of expression in few words, and enforcible by executive order. The necessity for forced food conservation in public places, in manufacture and distribution is evident enough; and the same necessity exists as to our other primary commodities, such as metals, and even to transport.

Such a course is the necessary complement to stimulation of production. No such powers exist today.

Yours faithfully,   Herbert Hoover[1]

TLS (WP, DLC).
[1] Two other replies to Wilson's round-robin inquiry of November 28 are TWG to WW and ASB to WW, both Dec. 1, 1917, TLS (WP, DLC). They are not printed on account of lack of substance. Neither suggested an increase in the power of the government over speech or publication.

From Louis Freeland Post

My dear Mr. President: Washington December 1, 1917.

In response to your confidential letter of November 30, 1917, I submit the following suggestion with reference to the employment agency work of the Department of Labor.

It is now manifestly necessary to provide for distribution of productive labor on a large scale. As millions of our industrial population go into the army, millions more must abandon accustomed vocations for new ones in order to make the army effective. These tremendous transformations of the labor power of the country must not be left to haphazard processes. They must be effected through a national system, thoughtfully planned and efficiently managed. Only by this means can workers be transferred with a maximum of benefit and a minimum of friction, inconvenience and suffering, from place to place and from non-essential and less essential to indispensable industries. The transfer of man power and non-essential to essential employments, is in itself a gigantic task. But through an efficient national system of labor distribution, intensive and extensive as well as systematic in its processes, dislocations of industry can be prevented, competent workers can be distributed among employers in need of help, displaced workers can be furnished suitable employment, farms can be made more productive and harvesting more secure, and fair contractual arrangements can be made between employer and employee. The nucleus of such a system already exists in the Department of Labor, where the task of labor distribution properly belongs. All that is needed is a sufficient appropriation. For adequately financing that already efficient national instrument for this highly essential war service, a minimum appropriation to the Secretary of Labor of $2,000,000 for the fiscal year 1918-19, and a deficiency appropriation of $825,000 for the remainder of the present fiscal year, are urgently recommended.

In further response to your letter of the 30th, I offer the following estimate of what it will cost to carry on this work until the first of February on the requisite scale of magnitude and efficiency:

Administration,	$ 20,000.00
100 employment offices,	165,000.00
20 district offices,	65,000.00
100 traveling examiners (salaries and expenses),	80,000.00
Total for two months,	$330,000.00

The above estimate is for two months at full scale of expenses. It is, however, quite impossible to organize on full scale immediately. The unexpended balance of the present $250,000 appropriation will probably be enough to cover all organization up to February 1. But this amount was intended to last until June 30.

Neither does the above estimate allow for the assistance that may be expected from States and municipalities.

We can furnish a more itemized statement if desired.

Faithfully and sincerely yours,   Louis F. Post.[1]

TCL (WP, DLC).
[1] A notation on this letter reveals that Wilson, on December 5, 1917, allotted $825,000 from the War Emergency Fund to the Department of Labor for the purposes which Post requested.

From Royal Meeker

My dear Mr. President: Washington December 1, 1917.

In reply to your letter of November 28, asking for a somewhat definite estimate of the cost of making needed budgetary and cost of living surveys for the use of the Shipbuilding Labor Adjustment Board, I wish to say that I arranged a conference for yesterday afternoon with Prof. Henry R. Seager and Mr. W. Jett Lauck, in which we considered the *immediate* needs of that Board.

It seemed to us that sufficient definite information could be obtained from about 14 or 15 principal shipbuilding districts. I have gone over our cost of living investigation here in Washington very carefully and have come to the conclusion that reliable results can be obtained from a smaller number of family schedules than I had hitherto assumed. Without inflicting details upon you, I figure that it will take 25 agents at $125 per month about 2 months to do the work required by the Shipbuilding Labor Adjustment Board. Our average for field expenses, including transportation, subsistence, etc., during the year 1917 has been $165 per month for each agent. This would make the cost of doing the field work $14,500. The office work of examining, editing, and tabulating the returns would cost about double what the field work would cost, or $28,000. The budgetary studies *immediately* needed could probably be completed for about $42,500. Additional investigation must be made into the retail prices of clothing, which is a most difficult study to make. I am willing to guess that we could get fairly complete information on this score for approximately $7500. This would make the total cost of the studies now required, in round figures, $50,000.

Sincerely yours,   Royal Meeker[1]

TCL (WP, DLC).
[1] A notation on this letter reveals that Wilson, on December 5, authorized the allotment of $50,000 as requested by Meeker from the War Emergency Fund.

Louis Freeland Post to Charles Lee Swem

My dear Mr. Swem: Washington December 1, 1917.

This is to acknowledge the receipt of your letter of November 30th, and inclosure, telegram received by President Wilson from Mr. J. A. Baker, President of the Brotherhood of Railway Clerks, Columbia, S. C., requesting the President to use his good offices to expedite a speedy settlement in order to avert further inconvenience to all concerned.[1] This telegram refers to the situation on the Atlantic Coast Line Railroad and I have been holding a reply to your request pending the receipt of information from our Commissioner of Conciliation, General McWade,[2] who has just wired me as follows:

"Agent King[3] informs me that Atlantic Coast Line officials have been ordered to reinstate all striking clerks in old positions and same pay. He assures me he is obeying instructions promptly, implicitly. This ends A.C.L. trouble permanently."

I suggest that you telegraph Mr. Baker stating that the Commissioner of Conciliation of the Department of Labor has reported to the Department today that the Atlantic Coast Line officials have ordered the reinstatement of all striking clerks to their old positions, thus ending the trouble on the Atlantic Coast Line Railroad.[4]

I am returning Mr. Baker's telegram, herewith.

Sincerely yours,   Louis F. Post

TLS (WP, DLC)
    [1] J. A. Baker to WW, Nov. 29, 1917, T telegram (WP, DLC).
    [2] Robert Malachi McWade, a journalist and author, United States consul and consul-general at Canton, China, 1900-1904, since August 1914 had been employed from time to time as a commissioner of conciliation in the office of the Secretary of Labor.
    [3] F. Lacy King of Wilmington, N. C., special agent of the Atlantic Coast Line.
    [4] Wilson sent Baker a telegram along these lines: WW to J. A. Baker, Dec. 1, 1917, T telegram (Letterpress Books, WP, DLC).

From Edward Mandell House

Paris. December 2, 1917.

There have been long and frequent discussions as to Russia, but the result has not been satisfactory to me. I wanted a clear declaration along the lines of my cable to you of Friday.[1] England passively was willing, France indifferently against it, Italy actively so. They were all willing to embody what I suggested if certain additions were made to which I could not agree. It was decided finally that each power should send its own answer to its Ambassador at Petrograd, the substance of each answer to be that the Allies were willing to reconsider their war aims in conjunction with Russia and as soon as she had a stable government with whom they could act.

The Russian Ambassador at Paris[2] believes it of great importance that you send a message to Russia through Francis or otherwise, letting them know of the disinterested motives of the United States and of its desire to bring a disorderly world into a fraternity of nations for the good of all and for the aggrandizement of none.

Edward House.

T telegram (E. M. House Papers, CtY).
[1] That is, EMH to WW, Nov. 30, 1917.
[2] That is V. A. Maklakov.

From Cleveland Hoadley Dodge

My dear President   Riverdale, New York City, Dec. 2nd 1917

I hesitate to butt in on matters of State, especially when I am biassed by personal considerations, and in this case what I write may be unnecessary. Still I know you will forgive me and understand my motives

Those of us who are interested in the great educational, missionary and relief work, in the Turkish Empire are worried over the possibility that the anomalous but friendly relations that now exist between this country and Turkey may be changed by a declaration of war, which would be fatal to our interests. Having my son Bayard, with his wife and two babies, at Beirut,[1] and Elizabeth and her husband in Constantinople,[2] I have a personal anxiety which is trying. In case of war, with due warning, those in Constantinople could probably get out in time, but our friends in Syria would find it almost impossible

I have recently conferred with Dr Barton of the American Board, Dr Brown of the Presbyterian Board,[3] and representatives of the two American Colleges in Constantinople & those in Smyrna & Beirut, also with Mr Elkus and Mr. Morgenthau, and the managers of the Armenian and Syrian Relief. It is the unanimous feeling of all, that war with Turkey would be a serious blow to these great American enterprises & would jeopardize many American lives besides stopping the work we are doing in saving the lives of hundreds of thousands of natives. Nevertheless we all feel that our selfish interests should not stand in the way of what you may think it best to do in carrying out your great purposes to end the war.

Mr Elkus expects to be in Washington tomorrow, and hopes to be able to see you, and has urged me to write to you to reinforce what he may say. I am therefore writing from Riverdale in hopes that my letter may reach you before you see or hear from him. He thinks it might be wise to warn Americans to leave Turkey now, but I hope that that may not be done, except in case of an actual decision to declare war. Everything is going on beautifully at present & an unnecessary warning would have a bad effect. From all accounts the Turks are treating our people with great & actually friendly consideration. They want peace badly & have no love for the Germans.

There may be good reasons for declaring a state of war with Austria, but except for the fact that Turkey and Bulgaria are allies of Germany, I do not think that the same reasons would necessarily apply to those countries. Roosevelt is lambasting poor Mr Panaretoff[4] the Bulgarian minister, & calling him a spy, but I know him so well that I have utmost confidence in him, and would vouch for his integrity.

I have thoroughly approved of your wise policy towards Austria, Bulgaria & Turkey, and whatever you decide to do now, I know will be right, but I earnestly hope that you may not be forced to change your policy, especially in respect to Bulgaria & Turkey.

I had expected to go to Washington next week, but have been lately having trouble with my insides, which does not prevent my going to my office, but necessitates daily medical treatment, which will last for some time & I am therefore obliged to postpone my trip, and fear that I cannot have the pleasure of seeing you until later in the Winter, unless you come to New York.

I am watching Col. House's great mission with keenest interest. What a wonder he is! My thoughts are constantly with you, and I devoutly trust that your health may stand the new strain when Congress gets to work. I am simply lost in admiration over all that you are doing

Mrs. Dodge joins with me in warm regards and best wishes, for Mrs Wilson and yourself

Ever sincerely and affectionately yours,

Cleveland H. Dodge

ALS (WP, DLC).

[1] Bayard Dodge continued to teach at the American University of Beirut.

[2] George H. Huntington had become Vice-President of Robert College in November 1917.

[3] That is, the Rev. Dr. James Levi Barton and the Rev. Dr. Arthur Judson Brown.

[4] Stephan Panaretoff, Bulgarian Minister to the United States since 1914.

Lessons of the War[1]

December 3, 1917.

Some months ago I had occasion to send a message to school officers urging them to increase materially the time and attention devoted to instruction bearing directly on the problems of community and national life. I called attention then to the fact that this was not a plea for a temporary enlargement of the school program appropriate merely to the period of the war, but a plea for the realization in public education of the new emphasis which the war has given to the ideals of democracy and to the broader conceptions of national life.

The American Red Cross devotes itself to the extension of our ideals and the spirit of humanity. Nowhere can its cause be exerted to better advantage than in the schools, and I am glad to know of[2] the widespread plan which brings young people into junior membership.

I am told that the articles from THE RED CROSS MAGAZINE, which in spirit explain and extend these interests, are being used as reading lessons in thousands of schools, and that the coming numbers of the magazine will contain articles especially designed for this patriotic purpose. This plan is excellent, and I look forward to a willing cooperation among school officers to carry out the idea to the fullest extent.   Woodrow Wilson

T MS (Letterpress Books, WP, DLC).
  [1] This statement was drawn from Wilson's letter to teachers and school officers, printed at Aug. 23, 1917, Vol. 44, and from his utterances about the Red Cross. Frank Nelson Doubleday, president of Doubleday, Page & Co., was also a member of the editorial board of *The Red Cross Magazine*. He sent the proposed statement to Wilson and asked his permission to print it in the next issue. F. N. Doubleday to WW, Dec. 1, 1917, TLS (WP, DLC). Wilson signed the statement on December 5, and it was printed in *The Red Cross Magazine*, XIII (Feb. 1918), 3.
  [2] In the published version, the words "am glad to know of" were changed to "have already approved."

To Edward Mandell House

[The White House, Dec. 3, 1917]

Sorry impossible to omit foreign affairs from address to Congress. Reticence on my part at this juncture would be misunderstood and resented and do much harm.

WWhw telegram (WP, DLC).

To Arthur Hendrick Vandenberg[1]

My dear Mr. Vandenberg: [The White House] 3 December, 1917

I want you to know directly from me how sincerely and warmly I have appreciated the generous support you have given the administration in these days of critical moment to us all. It has given me a great deal of cheer and reassurance and I thank you from a very grateful heart.

Cordially and sincerely yours,   Woodrow Wilson

TLS (Letterpress Books, WP, DLC).
[1] At this time editor of the Grand Rapids *Herald* and president of the Herald Publishing Co., Grand Rapids, Mich.

From Edward Mandell House

Paris, Dated December 3, 1917, Rec'd Dec. 4,
6:05 P.M.

For the President: Mr. Balfour and I (?) a conference last night. This morning he has prepared this despatch to send to the British Ambassador at Petrograd provided that his government will agree:

"I gather from your reports that the present provisional government of Petrograd has, without consulting the Allies, requested the enemy to grant an armistice on the Russian front. It is well aware that this is contrary to Russia's treaty with her allies but they argue, it seems, that inasmuch as the treaty was concluded while the autocracy was still in power it can have no binding force on the democracy which has succeeded it. I doubt whether this doctrine, inconsistent as it clearly is with any kind of stability in international agreements, will commend itself to a Russian government which can claim with justice to represent the Russian people. But, in formally repudiating it, His Majesty's Government desire to say that it is not by an appeal to treaties however binding that they desire to induce an unwilling ally any longer to contribute its share to the common effort. They base their claims on deeper principles accepted to the full by the provisional government itself. According to your report the peace which the latter desire is a democratic peace; a peace which accords with the wishes of the smaller and weaker nations which repudiates the idea of squeezing plunder out of conquered enemies under the name of war indemnities; or adding by force of arms reluctant populations to great empires. This, speaking broadly, is also the kind of peace which His Majesty's Government desire to see secured for the world; and they have always expressed their willingness to discuss the details of the allied war aims in the light of these general principles. But evidently this policy cannot be effectively carried out until Russia has established a stable government acceptable to the Russian people, a consummation which has not been reached. In the meanwhile you are at liberty to point out, should you think it expedient, that the very worst way of obtaining the sort of peace which the provisional government and His Majesty's Government alike desire is the method which the provisional government appear to have adopted. The provisional government puts its trust in an immediate armistice which it hopes will be followed by a satisfactory agreement: the Allies desire that a satisfactory general agreement may be reached (in general harmony with their declared aims) to be followed of course by an armistice. By which method are our objects most likely to be gained? When arms have failed rhetoric is not likely to succeed. So far as His Majesty's Government are aware of, no responsible German statesman has ever said a word indicating agreement either with the ideals of the provisional government or with the allied declaration of policy. Their attitude is not likely to become more accommodating nor will Russian aims be nearer of accomplishment if the Russian army is permitted to become negligible as a fighting force. The only peace which could be secured by substituting argument for action is one which would be neither democratic nor durable nor Russian. It would be German and imperialistic."[1]   Edward House.

T telegram (SDR, RG 59, 763.72/7956, DNA).
[1] House recorded the following in his Diary for December 3: "After my conference with Balfour last night, he wrote a despatch to the British Ambassador at Petrograd which goes far in the direction I have been urging. He started to bring this up at the Conference this morning, but I urged him not to do so. I thought it would only provoke discussion, and Sonnino and perhaps the French would have brought pressure upon him to modify it. Balfour agreed to send the despatch without submitting it to them, believing that he betrayed no confidence in doing so because of the resolution that was adopted on this subject at the meeting Saturday afternoon."
House noted on his retained copy of this telegram: "Balfour afterwards told me he sent this despatch without consulting London." Richard H. Ullman, *Anglo-Soviet Relations, 1917-1921: Intervention and the War* (Princeton, N. J., 1961), p. 27. On Buchanan's use of the message and the reaction in Petrograd, see *ibid.*, pp. 27-30.

From Josephus Daniels, with Enclosure

Dear Mr. President: Washington. Dec. 3. 1917.

After our conversation I cabled to Admiral Benson with reference to the Allied Naval Conference and am enclosing his answer. You will observe that Col. House approves the constitution. It would seem wise for us to wire approval. Please let me know your wishes.

                          Sincerely,   Josephus Daniels

ALS (WP, DLC).

ENCLOSURE

The following is a PARAPHRASE of a dispatch received from Admiral Benson, at Paris. 12-2-17.

Allied Naval conference convened Paris, France, November twenty-ninth-November thirtieth presided over by French Minister Marine.[1] Following countries represented: France, England, Italy, Japan, United States, and on last day Greece. Conference agreed upon following constitution for Inter-Allied Naval Council with understanding that constitution would be referred to the several governments concerned for approval and that decision would be communicated to French Minister Marine who if approved by all would inform interested parties simultaneously. Quote

Constitution of an Inter-Allied Naval Council.

Paragraph one. Council at present composed of Chiefs of Staff of English, French and Italian Navies and of Admirals designated by governments of United States and Japan; the question of representation of Russia on this board is reserved.

Sub-paragraph. Council presided over by Minister Marine of country in which council is held—the Ministers Marine of countries being at liberty to attend these meetings.

Paragraph two. The object of the Council is to watch over general conduct of Naval warfare and coordination of action at sea. It prepares projects submitted for decision of the government; keeps itself informed as regards carrying out of same; and reports to governments concerned according to the circumstances.

Paragraph three. The General Staff of each Navy and Commander-in-Chief of each power charged with conduct of naval operations remain responsible to their respective governments.

Paragraph four. The general maritime policy followed by the different Naval authorities is submitted to Inter-Allied Council in such manner that Council may be always informed of general course of events; decide on method that will insure complete cooperation; and determine best division of forces employed.

Paragraph five. The Inter-Allied Naval Council meets usually in London; it can however meet in any other place agreed upon according to circumstances. The meetings of the Council will take place as often as may be necessary and at least once a month.

Paragraph six. The Inter-Allied Naval Council will designate such permanent committees as may be considered necessary to enable it to carry out its functions efficiently period.

Sub-paragraph. The information services of the allied admiralties will supply council with all information at its disposition period. Unquote. Paragraph.

I have taken up this subject with Colonel House who approves period. I request that the matter be given immediate consideration and that I be informed at earliest possible moment of President's decision period. paragraph.

The conference prepared a Press notice which it is proposed to give out simultaneously in all countries after ratification of constitution quoted above by all governments period. Until that time it is requested that no information relative to the constitution of the Inter-Allied Naval Council be given to the press period.

Benson.

T MS (WP, DLC).
  [1] Georges Leygues.

From Lincoln Ross Colcord

Dear Mr. President: Washington December 3, 1917.

May I take the great liberty, for lack of other means, to lay before you without further introduction a thought which I hold very near to my heart? It is that a second mission to Russia should be sent from America at once, and the situation there held up until it has arrived. The Root mission went to Russia without a sympathetic understanding of the country, and returned without having acquired one. All that the members of this mission have written and said since their return, (and I am speaking of Mr. Root and Mr. Russel[l] alike), has done harm to Russia, to the American conception of the Russian situation, and to the cause of a true democratic peace. It is an absolute necessity that the mission which ought now to be dispatched immediately should be a small one, and one which had a sympathetic understanding of the Russian situation. It should be one also which really understood the true liberalism of your policies, which could in a vital sense interpret you to Russia, and which comprehended as well the tremendous international issue in its broad and active phases. I think it is hardly necessary to add that this mission should not, under the present circumstances, be a socialist one.

I have felt and written from the first that the Bolsheviki were not so black as they had been painted. Throughout the summer it has been impossible to escape a realization of the unconscious exaggeration in our press reports of Russian demoralization and anarchy, and of the equally unconscious readiness with which we have received these reports. We wished to believe them, and the wish has been father to the thought. We refused to analyze the facts as they came in; we continued to talk of demoralization and anarchy when as yet there had been no demoralization and anarchy. We refused to recognize that the Russian armies fell back from Rega in good order; we refused to bear in mind the 150 German divisions which were still being held on the eastern front; and we refused, above all, to understand or to try to imagine the terrible stress and agony under which Russia labored. It was written in our minds that revolutionists were disorganizers, and we had no eyes to see the really marvellous order, under the circumstances, which revolutionary Russia succeeded in maintaining.

But during the summer, of course, a measure of chaos came again. It came because Kerensky failed to fulfil the promise of the revolution, and because Russia therefore lost faith in Kerensky. Our popular view of this, however, was quite the opposite of the fact. We believed, and are still trying hard to believe, that Kerensky's failure lay in not assuming even more dictatorial powers than he did assume, in not crushing out the so-called radical elements, in not putting into practice his "blood and iron" policy. But Russia would not have submitted to this for a moment. We wholly misjudged the situation. Kerensky's real failure lay in not holding his ground for a restatement of the Allied war aims. It was a failure in foreign policy.

Now come the Bolsheviki, and our press and public opinion have gone quite mad. Yet the facts in the case, I firmly believe, are still quite different from our popular conception of them; and after the mists have cleared away the truth inevitably will appear. It will be seen that the Bolsheviki have brought order, not chaos, to Russia. It will be seen that they have reaffirmed the original policies of the revolution. Trotsky has published the secret diplomatic correspondence in order that there might be no dodging by the Allies this time. Personally I feel that he was wholly right in doing so, and that he was acting in close agreement with the firmly-grounded diplomatic policy of America. He has wonderfully clarified the atmosphere.

The Bolsheviki domestic policy, of course, does not concern us. It carries a radical program, but Russia is ready for a radical program. She has the village Mir, and a large majority of her people do not believe in the rights of private property. This is a fundamental difference. And although I am not a socialist, I cannot fail to note the rather cynical fact that it is this difference which really frightens the Allies when they look towards Russia. There need be no further explanation than this of our unconscious exaggeration of the menace of Russian radicalism.

Within two weeks there will be set up in Petrograd a strong

coalition government, in which the Bolsheviki will be in the majority. This government in the fullest sense will be representative of Russia. Russian policies have not changed since the revolution; it is the world which has changed. The Bolsheviki are not trying to overturn society; it is society which is overturning itself backwards. This coalition government will have to be recognized. Unless it is recognized, America and the Allies must thereafter stand frankly on a basis of imperialistic war aims. The Bolsheviki are not trying to make a separate peace with Germany. Russia does not want a separate peace. She will demand from Germany an agreement to a broad democratic peace. But if America and the Allies, in the meanwhile, refuse to recognize her government, and continue to revile it, thus fixing permanently in the hearts of the Russian people the belief that we are animated by predatory war motives, anything might happen. For Russia cannot fight much longer under any circumstances; she is in too desperate a pass. She must have either peace or faith. With neither, she cannot go on.

I am, my dear Mr. President,
Very sincerely yours,   Lincoln Colcord

TLS (WP, DLC).

From Franklin Knight Lane

Confidential

My dear Mr. President: Washington December 3, 1917.

I had a talk yesterday with Colonel George Harvey, who seemed greatly disturbed over Lord Lansdowne's letter. He said that it was a call from the Tories of England to the Tories of Germany, from Junker to Junker, to stop the war in the interest of their class; that Lansdowne felt that liberalism, and even socialism, would result from a continuance of the war both in England and in Germany, that the war was now being fought for ideals that were as antagonistic to the Tory spirit of England as to the autocratic spirit of Germany, and that therefore the property-owning classes of England were, in effect, serving notice that they wished the war to end, England relying on her diplomats to win a victory for them in conference, rather than on the soldiers in France.

Harvey thought that a new statement of the war aims of the Allies should probably be made, but that you would have to make this statement and that you alone could make it. He says that the Tories of England expect a Cabinet crisis within the next three months and hope to be restored to power and to put the Lloyd

George-Lord Northcliffe combination out of business, and that the Tories also hope to get the credit of having stopped the war. I asked him for his authority, and he said that it was his knowledge of English politics and English politicians, of whom he says Lansdowne is the most shrewd and far-sighted.

Faithfully and cordially yours,   Franklin K. Lane

TLS (WP, DLC).

George Creel to Edgar Grant Sisson

[Washington] December 3, 6 p.m., 1917

1878 For Sisson from Creel:

"Drive ahead full speed regardless expense. Coordinate all American agencies in Petrograd and Moscow and start aggressive campaign. Use press billboards placards and every possible medium to answer lies against America. Make plain our high motives and absolute devotion to democratic ideals. Deny that supplies are going to be stopped and state America's eagerness to help. Have Breshkovskaya and others issue statements and translate pamphlets. Engage speakers and halls. Urge Red Cross and Y.M.C.A. to fullest effort. Cable if send motion pictures and give necessary details. Sending thousand words daily from Sayville via Eiffel Tower to Bullard Moscow. Try to have Westnik[1] get it at Petrograd. Family well."   Lansing.

T telegram (WP, DLC).
 [1] Cable name for the Petrograd Telegraph Agency, which was the official Soviet press bureau.

An Annual Message on the State of the Union

December 4, 1917.

Gentlemen of the Congress: Eight months have elapsed since I last had the honour of addressing you. They have been months crowded with events of immense and grave significance for us. I shall not undertake to retail or even to summarize those events. The practical particulars of the part we have played in them will be laid before you in the reports of the Executive Departments. I shall discuss only our present outlook upon these vast affairs, our present duties, and the immediate means of accomplishing the objects we shall hold always in view.

I shall not go back to debate the causes of the war. The intolerable wrongs done and planned against us by the sinister masters of

Germany have long since become too grossly obvious and odious to every true American to need to be rehearsed. But I shall ask you to consider again and with a very grave scrutiny our objectives and the measures by which we mean to attain them; for the purpose of discussion here in this place is action, and our action must move straight towards definite ends. Our object is, of course, to win the war; and we shall not slacken or suffer ourselves to be diverted until it is won. But it is worth while asking and answering the question, When shall we consider the war won?

From one point of view it is not necessary to broach this fundamental matter. I do not doubt that the American people know what the war is about and what sort of an outcome they will regard as a realization of their purpose in it. As a nation we are united in spirit and intention. I pay little heed to those who tell me otherwise. I hear the voices of dissent—who does not? I hear the criticism and the clamour of the noisily thoughtless and troublesome. I also see men here and there fling themselves in impotent disloyalty against the calm, indomitable power of the nation. I hear men debate peace who understand neither its nature nor the way in which we may attain it with uplifted eyes and unbroken spirits. But I know that none of these speaks for the nation. They do not touch the heart of anything. They may safely be left to strut their uneasy hour and be forgotten.

But from another point of view I believe that it is necessary to say plainly what we here at the seat of action consider the war to be for and what part we mean to play in the settlement of its searching issues. We are the spokesmen of the American people and they have a right to know whether their purpose is ours. They desire peace by the overcoming of evil, by the defeat once for all of the sinister forces that interrupt peace and render it impossible, and they wish to know how closely our thought runs with theirs and what action we propose. They are impatient with those who desire peace by any sort of compromise,—deeply and indignantly impatient,—but they will be equally impatient with us if we do not make it plain to them what our objectives are and what we are planning for in seeking to make conquest of peace by arms.

I believe that I speak for them when I say two things: First, that this intolerable Thing of which the masters of Germany have shown us the ugly face, this menace of combined intrigue and force which we now see so clearly as the German power, a Thing without conscience or honour or capacity for covenanted peace, must be crushed and, if it be not utterly brought to an end, at least shut out from the friendly intercourse of the nations; and, second, that when this Thing and its power are indeed defeated and the time comes that we can discuss peace,—when the German people have spokesmen whose word we can believe and when those spokesmen are ready in the name of their people to accept the common judgment of the nations as to what shall henceforth be the bases of law and of covenant for the life of the world,—we shall be willing and glad to pay the full price for peace, and pay it ungrudgingly. We know what that price will be. It will be full, impartial justice,—justice done at every point and to every nation that the final settlement must affect, our enemies as well as our friends.

You catch, with me, the voices of humanity that are in the air. They grow daily more audible, more articulate, more persuasive, and they come from the hearts of men everywhere. They insist that the war shall not end in vindictive action of any kind; that no nation or people shall be robbed or punished because the irresponsible rulers of a single country have themselves done deep and abominable wrong. It is this thought that has been expressed in the formula 'No annexations, no contributions, no punitive indemnities.' Just because this crude formula expresses the instinctive judgment as to right of plain men everywhere it has been made diligent use of by the masters of German intrigue to lead the people of Russia astray—and the people of every other country their agents could reach, in order that a premature peace might be brought about before autocracy has been taught its final and convincing lesson, and the people of the world put in control of their own destinies.

But the fact that a wrong use has been made of a just idea is no reason why a right use should not be made of it. It ought to be brought under the patronage of its real friends. Let it be said again that autocracy must first be shown the utter futility of its claims to power or leadership in the modern world. It is impossible to apply any standard of justice so long as such forces are unchecked and undefeated as the present masters of Germany command. Not until that has been done can Right be set up as arbiter and peace-maker among the nations. But when that has been done,—as, God willing, it assuredly will be,—we shall at last be free to do an unprecedented thing, and this is the time to avow our purpose to do it. We shall be free to base peace on generosity and justice, to the exclusion of all selfish claims to advantage even on the part of the victors.

Let there be no misunderstanding. Our present and immediate task is to win the war, and nothing shall turn us aside from it until it is accomplished. Every power and resource we possess, whether of men, of money, or of materials, is being devoted and will continue to be devoted to that purpose until it is achieved. Those who desire to bring peace about before that purpose is achieved I counsel to carry their advice elsewhere. We will not entertain it. We shall regard the war as won only when the German people say to us, through properly accredited representatives, that they are ready to agree to a settlement based upon justice and the reparation of the wrongs their rulers have done. They have done a wrong to Belgium which must be repaired. They have established a power over other lands and peoples than their own,—over the great Empire of Austria-Hungary, over hitherto free Balkan states, over Turkey, and within Asia,—which must be relinquished.

Germany's success by skill, by industry, by knowledge, by enterprise we did not grudge or oppose, but admired, rather. She had built up for herself a real empire of trade and influence, secured by the peace of the world. We were content to abide the rivalries of manufacture, science, and commerce that were involved for us in her success and stand or fall as we had or did not have the brains and the initiative to surpass her. But at the moment when she had conspicuously won her triumphs of peace she threw them away, to establish in their stead what the world will no longer permit to be established, military and political domination by arms, by which to oust where she could not excel the rivals she most feared and hated. The peace we make must remedy that wrong. It must deliver the once fair lands and happy peoples of Belgium and northern France from the Prussian conquest and the Prussian menace, but it must also deliver the peoples of Austria-Hungary, the peoples of the Balkans, and the peoples of Turkey, alike in Europe and in Asia, from the impudent and alien dominion of the Prussian military and commercial autocracy.

We owe it, however, to ourselves to say that we do not wish in any way to impair or to rearrange the Austro-Hungarian Empire. It is no affair of ours what they do with their own life, either industrially or politically. We do not purpose or desire to dictate to them in any way. We only desire to see that their affairs are left in their own hands, in all matters, great or small. We shall hope to secure for the peoples of the Balkan peninsula and for the people of the Turkish Empire the right and opportunity to make their own lives safe, their own fortunes secure against oppression or injustice and from the dictation of foreign courts or parties.

And our attitude and purpose with regard to Germany herself are of a like kind. We intend no wrong against the German Empire, no interference with her internal affairs. We should deem either the one or the other absolutely unjustifiable, absolutely contrary to the principles we have professed to live by and to hold most sacred throughout our life as a nation.

The people of Germany are being told by the men whom they

now permit to deceive them and to act as their masters that they are fighting for the very life and existence of their Empire, a war of desperate self-defense against deliberate aggression. Nothing could be more grossly or wantonly false, and we must seek by the utmost openness and candour as to our real aims to convince them of its falseness. We are in fact fighting for their emancipation from fear, along with our own,—from the fear as well as from the fact of unjust attack by neighbours or rivals or schemers after world empire. No one is threatening the existence or the independence or the peaceful enterprise of the German Empire.

The worst that can happen to the detriment of the German people is this, that if they should still, after the war is over, continue to be obliged to live under ambitious and intriguing masters interested to disturb the peace of the world, men or classes of men whom the other peoples of the world could not trust, it might be impossible to admit them to the partnership of nations which must henceforth guarantee the world's peace. That partnership must be a partnership of peoples, not a mere partnership of governments. It might be impossible, also, in such untoward circumstances, to admit Germany to the free economic intercourse which must inevitably spring out of the other partnerships of a real peace. But there would be no aggression in that; and such a situation, inevitable because of distrust, would in the very nature of things sooner or later cure itself, by processes which would assuredly set in.

The wrongs, the very deep wrongs, committed in this war will have to be righted. That of course. But they can not and must not be righted by the commission of similar wrongs against Germany and her allies. The world will not permit the commission of similar wrongs as a means of reparation and settlement. Statesmen must by this time have learned that the opinion of the world is everywhere wide awake and fully comprehends the issues involved. No representative of any self-governed nation will dare disregard it by attempting any such covenants of selfishness and compromise as were entered into at the Congress of Vienna. The thought of the plain people here and everywhere throughout the world, the people who enjoy no privilege and have very simple and unsophisticated standards of right and wrong, is the air all goverments must henceforth breathe if they would live. It is in the full disclosing light of that thought that all policies must be conceived and executed in this midday hour of the world's life. German rulers have been able to upset the peace of the world only because the German people were not suffered under their tutelage to share the comradeship of the other peoples of the world either in thought or in purpose. They were allowed to have no opinion of their own which might be set up as a rule of conduct for those who exercised authority over them. But the congress that concludes this war will feel the full strength of the tides that run now in the hearts and consciences of free men everywhere. Its conclusions will run with those tides.

All these things have been true from the very beginning of this stupendous war; and I can not help thinking that if they had been made plain at the very outset the sympathy and enthusiasm of the Russian people might have been once for all enlisted on the side of the Allies, suspicion and distrust swept away, and a real and lasting union of purpose effected. Had they believed these things at the very moment of their revolution and had they been confirmed in that belief since, the sad reverses which have recently marked the progress of their affairs towards an ordered and stable government of free men might have been avoided. The Russian people have been poisoned by the very same falsehoods that have kept the German people in the dark, and the poison has been administered by the very same hands. The only possible antidote is the truth. It can not be uttered too plainly or too often.

From every point of view, therefore, it has seemed to be my duty to speak these declarations of purpose, to add these specific interpretations to what I took the liberty of saying to the Senate in January. Our entrance into the war has not altered our attitude towards the settlement that must come when it is over. When I said in January that the nations of the world were entitled not only to free pathways upon the sea but also to assured and unmolested access to those pathways I was thinking, and I am thinking now, not of the smaller and weaker nations alone, which need our countenance and support, but also of the great and powerful nations, and of our present enemies as well as our present associates in the war. I was thinking, and am thinking now, of Austria herself, among the rest, as well as of Serbia and of Poland. Justice and equality of rights can be had only at a great price. We are seeking permanent, not temporary, foundations for the peace of the world and must seek them candidly and fearlessly. As always, the right will prove to be the expedient.

What shall we do, then, to push this great war of freedom and justice to its righteous conclusion? We must clear away with a thorough hand all impediments to success and we must make every adjustment of law that will facilitate the full and free use of our whole capacity and force as a fighting unit.

One very embarrassing obstacle that stands in our way is that we are at war with Germany but not with her allies. I therefore very earnestly recommend that the Congress immediately declare the United States in a state of war with Austria-Hungary. Does it seem strange to you that this should be the conclusion of the argument I have just addressed to you? It is not. It is in fact the inevitable logic of what I have said. Austria-Hungary is for the time being not her own mistress but simply the vassal of the German Government. We must face the facts as they are and act upon them without sentiment in this stern business. The government of Austria-Hungary is not acting upon its own initiative or in response to the wishes and feelings of its own peoples but as the instrument of another nation. We must meet its force with our own and regard the Central Powers as but one. The war can be successfully conducted in no other way. The same logic would lead also to a declaration of war against Turkey and Bulgaria. They also are the tools of Germany. But they are mere tools and do not yet stand in the direct path of our necessary action. We shall go wherever the necessities of this war carry us, but it seems to me that we should go only where immediate and practical considerations lead us and not heed any others.

The financial and military measures which must be adopted will suggest themselves as the war and its undertakings develop, but I will take the liberty of proposing to you certain other acts of legislation which seem to me to be needed for the support of the war and for the release of our whole force and energy.

It will be necessary to extend in certain particulars the legislation of the last session with regard to alien enemies; and also necessary, I believe, to create a very definite and particular control over the entrance and departure of all persons into and from the United States.

Legislation should be enacted defining as a criminal offense every wilful violation of the presidential proclamations relating to alien enemies promulgated under section 4067 of the Revised Statutes[1] and providing appropriate punishments; and women as well as men should be included under the terms of the acts placing restraints upon alien enemies. It is likely that as time goes on many alien enemies will be willing to be fed and housed at the expense of the Government in the detention camps and it would be the purpose of the legislation I have suggested to confine offenders among them in penitentiaries and other similar institutions where they could be made to work as other criminals do.

---

[1] That is, Wilson's proclamations of April 6 and November 16, 1917. The first proclaimed that a state of war existed between the United States and Germany and directed all officers, civil or military, to exercise vigilance and zeal in discharging their duties relating to enemy aliens, "being males of the age of fourteen years and upwards." This proclamation and that of November 16 specified various regulations governing the conduct, location, and movements of these enemy aliens. Section 4067 of the Revised Statutes was based on the Act of July 6, 1798. The texts of the two proclamations were printed in the *Washington Post*, April 7 and Nov. 20, 1917, and in other newspapers.

Recent experience has convinced me that the Congress must go further in authorizing the Government to set limits to prices. The law of supply and demand, I am sorry to say, has been replaced by the law of unrestrained selfishness. While we have eliminated profiteering in several branches of industry it still runs impudently rampant in others. The farmers, for example, complain with a great deal of justice that, while the regulation of food prices restricts their incomes, no restraints are placed upon the prices of most of the things they must themselves purchase; and similar inequities obtain on all sides.

It is imperatively necessary that the consideration of the full use of the water power of the country and also the consideration of the systematic and yet economical development of such of the natural resources of the country as are still under the control of the federal government should be immediately resumed and affirmatively and constructively dealt with at the earliest possible moment. The pressing need of such legislation is daily becoming more obvious.

The legislation proposed at the last session with regard to regulated combinations among our exporters, in order to provide for our foreign trade a more effective organization and method of cooperation, ought by all means to be completed at this session.

And I beg that the members of the House of Representatives will permit me to express the opinion that it will be impossible to deal in any but a very wasteful and extravagant fashion with the enormous appropriations of the public moneys which must continue to be made, if the war is to be properly sustained, unless the House will consent to return to its former practice of initiating and preparing all appropriation bills through a single committee, in order that responsibility may be centred, expenditures standardized and made uniform, and waste and duplication as much as possible avoided.

Additional legislation may also become necessary before the present Congress again adjourns in order to effect the most efficient coordination and operation of the railway and other transportation systems of the country; but to that I shall, if circumstances should demand, call the attention of the Congress upon another occasion.

If I have overlooked anything that ought to be done for the more effective conduct of the war, your own counsels will supply the omission. What I am perfectly clear about is that in the present session of the Congress our whole attention and energy should be concentrated on the vigorous, rapid, and successful prosecution of the great task of winning the war.

We can do this with all the greater zeal and enthusiasm because we know that for us this is a war of high principle, debased by no selfish ambition of conquest or spoliation; because we know, and all the world knows, that we have been forced into it to save the very institutions we live under from corruption and destruction. The purposes of the Central Powers strike straight at the very heart of everything we believe in; their methods of warfare outrage every principle of humanity and of knightly honour; their intrigue has corrupted the very thought and spirit of many of our people; their sinister and secret diplomacy has sought to take our very territory away from us and disrupt the Union of the States. Our safety would be at an end, our honour forever sullied and brought into contempt were we to permit their triumph. They are striking at the very existence of democracy and liberty.

It is because it is for us a war of high, disinterested purpose, in which all the free peoples of the world are banded together for the vindication of right, a war for the preservation of our nation and of all that it has held dear of principle and of purpose, that we feel ourselves doubly constrained to propose for its outcome only that which is righteous and of irreproachable intention, for our foes as well as for our friends. The cause being just and holy, the settlement must be of like motive and quality. For this we can fight, but for nothing less noble or less worthy of our traditions. For this cause we entered the war and for this cause will we battle until the last gun is fired.

I have spoken plainly because this seems to me the time when it is most necessary to speak plainly, in order that all the world may know that even in the heat and ardour of the struggle and when our whole thought is of carrying the war through to its end we have not forgotten any ideal or principle for which the name of America has been held in honour among the nations and for which it has been our glory to contend in the great generations that went before us. A supreme moment of history has come. The eyes of the people have been opened and they see. The hand of God is laid upon the nations. He will show them favour, I devoutly believe, only if they rise to the clear heights of His own justice and mercy.[2]

Printed reading copy (WP, DLC).

[2] It is impossible to know when Wilson began to draft this address, since virtually all the entries in the Head Usher's Diary for November and early December indicate that Wilson worked some part of the day in his study. The following versions of this address are in WP, DLC: a WWT outline; a WWsh draft; a WWT draft, "Dec. 1917"; the final WWT draft, "December, 1917"; the galley proofs of the address, with Wilson's changes and additions; and the printed reading copy. The page proofs, with a few additional WWhw changes, are in the G. Creel Papers, DLC.

A comparison of these drafts reveals that Wilson based them all substantially on the shorthand draft, and that later changes involved only the transposition of sentences and portions of paragraphs and changes to improve the style of the text.

From Louis Kopelin

Chicago, Ill., December 4, 1917.

Personally and as editor of the Appeal to Reason, Girard Kansas, the oldest and largest American socialist publication, I heartily congratulate you on your inspiring address before Congress today. Your open-hearted espousal of a democratic peace after the central European peoples have been freed from the yoke of Prussian militarism removes the last possible suspicion against the cause of the entente allies. I earnestly trust that the peoples of Germany and Russia, particularly the socialists, will now realize that they have been badly duped by the scheming Prussian military masters. Your address today should convince the liberals of all lands that the cause of fundamental democracy in national and international affairs is boldly championed by the American President and ruthlessly throttled by the Kaiser. On which side will they line up? I am on your side.

Louis Kopelin.[1]

T telegram (WP, DLC).
[1] "Please find out from Postmaster General if this Appeal to Reason is one of the papers which have gotten into trouble and been denied the mails. Please return to me." T MS (WP, DLC).

From George Foster Peabody

Dear Mr President   [New York] Dec 4th 1917

The deep thrill which has possession of my mind after the second careful reading—at the quiet hour of midnight—of your great message to the peoples and the Statesmen of the World—through the Congress—must have the outlet of a line of expression to you of my prayers and hope that the blessing of Infinite power may accompany to the minds and hearts of the German and Austrian peoples the simple statement of the profound purpose and desire of these United States in their relation to this world conflict.

I am sure that all the shot and shell and other agencies of destruction have not had the potency of these words of yours in accomplishing the winning of the War.

I rejoiced exceedingly to have you remind the Congress as well as the Statesmen of the World of that immortal January address to the Senate. My faith has never faltered in counting upon the "Peace without victory"—alas that so few have been able to understand the deep thought. The words are forever true I believe—your wisdom—Gods greatest gift—is so shown in the brief but sympathetic reference to Russia. I believe Gods mysterious work will bring out of this passion for Peace of the ignorant Russian peasant the most persistent dynamic to enforce the highest human knowledge of these greatest of State papers. I bow in enthusiastic reverence before your use of "words" as elucidating thought and recall that "Logos" was the name of the perfect revelation of the Divine. I hail you as ever true leader of the opinion of mankind.

It seems to me that I would be lacking in view of the unlimited quality of my admiration, if I did not ask the privilege of frankly telling you of my sharing with many of your truest and finest supporters and admirers a poignant regret that you include the company of rare souls, who accept the Sermon on the Mount as being the essence of the revelation of God in Christ, among those who "strut their uneasy hour" and of those for whose mind you said at Buffalo you had "contempt." I know of a surety to my own soul that you could not mean what very many have felt keenly as seeming "vindictive." So I hope that at some not far distant day you will elucidate your distinction between those who feel they must keep before the public eye and be martyrs if possible, no matter what aid is given to the enemy, and those many who serve in manning the Mine Sweepers and facing any danger that does not conflict with their being true to the light as God gives them to see it. In this country there are many such who recognize "the powers that be as ordained of God" in a democracy at any rate, and trust and admire you largely and give you much surer support than many of those who tender their business ability—in all sincerity though that be.

My enthusiasm for your far sightedness and much wisdom Mr President is a passion, and I am jealous for anything that may be misinterpreted by the true minded.

I could not let these words of grateful appreciation and hearty thanksgiving go to you in a telegram. I felt that I had to write with my own hand, and I have to beg your pardon for the length to which my ardor and intensity of regard have led me

I am with highest respect

Faithfully Yours   George Foster Peabody

ALS (WP, DLC).

A Statement by Robert Lansing

I drafted this as a public statement
but after conferring with the President
did not use it   R.L.

December 4, 1917.

This Government has found it impossible to recognize Lenine, Trotsky and their associates as the *de facto* government of Russia since there is inadequate evidence that they are the real agents of the sovereignty of the Russian people. When the Bolshevik faction under the leadership of Lenine seized by force the public offices at Petrograd and Moscow arresting or expelling the provisional ministers and military commanders who had obtained authority through legal succession from the revolutionary body which had come into power on the abdication of the Czar, they set up in those two cities arbitrary and irresponsible authority based solely on physical control over the residents.

Dedicated as the Government of the United States is to the principle of democracy and to a social order based on individual liberty and the supremacy of the popular will operating through liberal institutions it cannot but consider that the attempt by any class of society, whether distinguished by birth, wealth, occupation or poverty, to arrogate to itself superior political authority to be inimicable to democracy. Such class despotism differs only from autocratic monarchy in that the sovereign authority is in the latter case exercised by an individual without sanction of the popular will while in the former case it is exercised by a group of individuals. Upon despotisms of every nature the people of the United States have looked invariably with disfavor as subversive of the rights of man, and hostile to justice and liberty.

Holding these views this Government has watched with deep concern the overthrow by force of the provisional authority representing the revolution at Petrograd, and that on the eve of the popular election of a Constituent Assembly called to establish a constitutional government based on the principle of democracy.

The American people have rejoiced with the people of Russia in the dawn of a democratic era and the prospects of an orderly exercise of popular sovereignty through agencies lawfully and peaceably created. They have been prepared to give every moral and material aid to Russia in her period of transition from absolutism to constitutional democracy; and this sympathetic spirit has been increased by the conviction that the Russian nation, like this nation, recognized in the Imperial German Government the greatest peril to liberty and democracy in the world and especially threatening to new-born freedom in Russia. Convinced of the mutual appreciation of the German menace this Government naturally anticipated that the Russian democracy would with the zeal and determination of a people jealous of their rights resist the intrigues of German agents and prosecute with courage and vigor the war which the free peoples of the world are waging against Prussian militarism.

Relying upon a full realization by the Russian people of the imminent danger to their political and territorial integrity from autocratic Germany and upon their faithful adherence to their cobelligerents, this Government has watched with disappointment and amazement the rise of class despotism in Petrograd and the open efforts of the leaders of the Bolsheviki to withdraw from the conflict even at the expense of national honor and the future safety of democracy in Russia.

It has been justly claimed that democracies sacredly perform their treaty obligations whatever the cost may be, that they are hostile to autocracy and are unswervingly loyal to nations which have befriended them in their time of need. Russia, as the world knows, is overwhelmingly democratic in spirit and purpose, and yet those, who today claim to represent the nation, threaten to violate treaties made with other free peoples, to make friends with the most inveterate enemy of Russian aspirations, and to abandon the faithful friends of Russia in the great struggle against the Prussian autocracy.

In the light of this program, so contrary to democratic ideas of honor and duty, it cannot be that the Bolshevik leaders represent the Russian people or express their true will. The men who have seized the public authority in Petrograd, have gone further and threatened that, in the event that the governments of the nations at war with Central Powers refuse to recognize them as the *de facto* government of Russia and decline to receive their initiative for an armistice and peace, they will follow the course which they have proposed "appealing to the peoples after the governments." This arbitrary and irregular method of conducting foreign intercourse is a further evidence of the despotic spirit of the Bolshevik faction and of their utter disregard of constitutional and representative government, which is the very foundation of national independence and the safeguard of individual rights. Without submission to government resting upon the rule of majorities democracy is an empty word, and personal liberty becomes a prey to tyranny and lawlessness.

The Republic of the United States, which has proven to the world by one hundred and forty-one years of national growth in prosperity and power the benefits of free institutions, expresses now, as it did immediately after the abdication of the Czar, its friendship for the great democracy of Russia and its sympathy with [the] Russian people in their aspirations; it repeats its belief in the loyalty of Russia to her treaty obligations and affirms its confidence in the continued resistence of the national power of Russia to the sinister Government of Germany which by its very existence imperils the liberty and territorial integrity of the Russian nation; and it declares its conviction that upon a full expression of the sovereign will of the Russian people, uninfluenced by class-hatreds and unconstrained by class-despotism, there will arise a strong and stable government founded on the principles of democracy and the equality of man which will defend every citizen of free Russia in the enjoyment of his inherent rights of life, liberty and the pursuit of happiness from all foes of freedom both foreign and domestic. To that end the Government and people of the United States have sought and will continue to seek to render aid in every way which they are able provided their aid is acceptable to the Russian nation.

T MS (R. Lansing Papers, NjP).

From the Diary of Josephus Daniels

December Tuesday 4 1917

Pres. spoke to Congress. No tickets for wives of cabinet officers.
. . .

WW looked serious, confident, compelling. He had given much thought to his message—read it deliberately & calmly, letting its logic and strength make all the impression. It was received with marked approval & evoked enthusiasm. After delivery we discussed it at cabinet meeting—all gave warm commendation. WW seemed relieved & was plainly pleased at its reception.

Because of Roberts College & such institutions he hoped we would not have to declare war upon Turkey, but must be prepared for any eventualities. He wished a plebiscite on Alsace & Lorrain[e]. Suggested that many who had owned & still owned land should be entitled to vote. Not certain all wish to go to France. Children speak German. Wished to let the world know we stood for no such treaties as would call for land or money beyond repairing Belgium and Northern France.

To Newton Diehl Baker, with Enclosure

My dear Baker,   The White House [c. Dec. 5, 1917].
    Is such a programme *possible*?   W.W.

ALI (N. D. Baker Papers, DLC).

E N C L O S U R E

London. December 4th.
Number 10. For the Acting Chief of Staff. CONFIDENTIAL.

All military authorities here since my arrival in England have represented with growing urgency the grave possibilities of the military situation early in 1918. This culminated in a conference between the British and French Chiefs of Staff and General John J. Pershing and myself immediately after the first session of the Inter-allied conference here in France on November 29th. As a result of this conference I have submitted to the Committee on Maritime Transportation, appointed by the Inter-allied Conference, the following communication.

Paragraph 1. "At a conference between General Tasker H. Bliss, Chief of Staff of the American Army, General John J. Pershing, Commander in Chief of the American Expeditionary Forces, General Robertson, Chief of the Imperial General Staff of Great Britain, and General Foch, Chief of the General Staff of the French Army, the military situation on the Western Front and its requirements as to man power from the United States was carefully considered. As the result of this conference it was unanimously agreed that the United States should, as its minimum effort send to France, as rapidly as possible, 4 complete corps of 6 divisions each or 24 divisions in all, the last division to arrive not later than the end of June 1918.

Paragraph 2. In order to accomplish this program, and after making every possible reduction in the personnel of the divisions, in the number of animals to be transported, and the amount of reserve supplies to be on hand in France not later than June 1st next, it is estimated there must be added to the tonnage now available for the transportation of American troops, 1,500,000 gross tons by January 1st, 1918, 300,000 gross tons by March 1st, 1918, and 200,000 gross tons by June 1st, 1918, or two millions gross tons in all. The foregoing is presented to the Committee on Maritime Transportation with the earnest request that it receive immediate and most careful consideration. For any assistance that they may be able to give, Gen. Tasker H. Bliss and General John J. Pershing place themselves at the disposal of the committee, Tasker H. Bliss (General) Chief of Staff of the American Army."[1]

I assume that the transportation thus made available will continue to bring troops until at least the Fifth Corps, making a total of at least 30 divisions, shall have arrived in France by the end of the summer. The military situation for 1918 is undoubtedly critical and grave. All Chiefs of Staff of the armies of the Western front and the representatives of the commanders in the field at the conferences here urge that the United States must be prepared to make a great effort as early in the year as possible. With this end in view and in order to insure the equipment with artillery and ammunition of the American troops as fast as they arrive in France, the Minister[s] of Munitions of France and England and Perkins[2] representing the United States, have exhaustively examined the situation and adopted the following resolutions for their respective Governments. "The representatives of Great Britain and France state that their production of artillery (field, medium and heavy) is now established on so large a scale that they (are?) able equip completely all American divisions as they arrive in France during the year 1918 with the best make of British and French guns and howitzers. The British and French ammunition supply and reserves are sufficient to provide the requirements of the American Army thus equipped at least up to June 1918 provided that the existing 6 inch shell plants in the United States and Dominion of Canada are maintained in full activity and provided that the manufacture of 6 inch Howitzer *carriages* in the United States is to some extent sufficiently developed. On the other hand the French and to a lesser extent the British require as soon as possible large supplies of propellants and high explosives and the British require the largest possible production of 6 inch howitzers from now onwards and of 8 inch and 9.2 inch shells from June onwards. In both of these matters they ask the assistance of the Americans. With a view therefore first to expedite and facilitate the equipment of the American armies in France and second to securing the maximum ultimate development of the ammunition supply with the minimum strain upon available tonnage the representatives of Great Britain and France propose that the American[s]' field medium and heavy artillery be supplied during 1918 and as long after as may be found convenient from British and French gun factories and they ask (A)

[1] Clemenceau enclosed a copy of this memorandum in G. Clemenceau to D. Lloyd George, Dec. 14, 1917, TLS (D. Lloyd George Papers, F/50/1/26, House of Lords Records Office). In his letter, Clemenceau also enclosed a TC of his letter to House of December 6, 1917, approving the terms of Bliss' memorandum.

[2] That is, Louis Loucheur, Winston Leonard Spencer Churchill, and Thomas Nelson Perkins. Perkins, a lawyer of Boston, was the representative of the War Industries Board in the mission led by House.

that the American efforts shall be immediately directed to the production of propellants and high explosives on the largest possible scale and (B) Great Britain also asks that the 6 inch 8 inch and 9.2 inch shell plants already created for the British service in the United States shall be maintained in the highest activity and that large additional plants for the manufacture of these shells shall at once be laid down.

In this way alone can the tonnage difficulty be minimized and potential artillery developments both in guns and shells of the combined French British and American armies be maintained in 1918 and still more in 1919.

With regard to very heavy artillery and certain special classes of long range guns the representatives of France and Great Britain recommend a separate and original manufacture by the United States. They also recommend that the existing production of 8-inch and 9.2 inch howitzers equipment in the United States shall be continued.

Finally if the above general principles are approved by the Governments of the three countries the precise measures of manufacture and supply with programs and time tables shall be concerted by a technical commission composed of representatives of the three great powers concerned."

Paragraph 3. The situation will be quite different in 1918 from what it has been in 1917. In 1917 the British and French guns and howitzers output has been below the ammunition supply. In 1918 the reverse will be true. The situation as to guns and ammunition supply and capacities now are as follows. The French can and are willing to supply the American army as it arrives in Europe with its full quota of 75 millimeter field guns and with adequate supplies of shells for this size provided that the United States furnish raw materials propellants and explosives in advance. The British have capacity to manufacture 6 inch howitzers sufficient to supply their own needs and to supply the American army as it arrives in Europe with its full quota if United States can supply 400 carriages for such howitzer. The British have not sufficient 6 inch shell capacity to supply their own requirements to say nothing of American requirements unless the supply of such shells which they have been obtaining from United States and Canada is continued at least to the extent available before United States entered the war. That is to say the British have relied upon getting this shell from United States and Canada and have concentrated upon increasing their supply of this howitzer and need this shell to carry out the 1918 program. The British have reserves of propellants and explosives sufficient to complete United States full quota 6 inch shells if American army should adopt that howitzer provided that United States can replenish those reserves beginning July 1st, 1918. The French capacity for making 155 millimeter howitzer and shells is sufficient to enable France to supply the American Army as it arrives in Europe with its full quota for 1918 of both howitzers and shells of this size provided that the raw materials for both howitzers and shells and propellants and explosives are furnished in advance by United States. Inventory shows requirements due to recent losses must however be met either by British or French to a very substantial amount. The British can furnish 8 inch and 9.2 inch howitzer to equip the American army for 1918 as it arrives. They urge continuance American activities in the manufacture of howitzers and shells of these sizes. I am satisfied that only by coordination of all available capacities in the three countries can American troops here and troops of British and French be fully equipped for the great effort necessary in 1918 and urge that development of independent American program be subordinated to the making of this effort.

Paragraph 4. Specifically it is recommended that (A) sufficient 75 millimeter field guns and ammunition be purchased from the French to equip the first 30 divisions sent to France. The home program for manufacture of this material should be continued. The home output for 1918 will probably all be required for equipping and training of troops at home. The home manufacture of 75 millimeter ammunition should be expedited as far as possible and troops in France supplied from home as soon as home production is on an assured basis. (B) That the factories of the United States and Dominion of Canada heretofore engaged in the manufacture of British 6-inch howitzer ammunition be continued indefinitely and extended if necessary to meet British requirements. This is of vital importance as these shells are essential to 1918 campaign from every point of view. Serious consideration should even now be given the question of our adoption of the British 6-inch howitzer in place of the French 155 millimeter howitzer. The answer must depend to a large extent upon the extent to which American program for manufacture 155 guns and shells has advanced. British and French are agreed that 1 howitzer is substantially as easy to make as the other. French are confident we shall have no difficulty in manufacture of shell. British have had difficulty in making French shell and fear that we will whereas they point out that we have been making British shell for several years with great success and have men as well as plants that have proved they can turn them out. We can not urge too strongly the importance of producing the largest possible amount of shells of this size and recommend that the amount of shell which can certainly be produced be given great weight in determining type to be adopted. Subject to your decision as to type we recommend that sufficient howitzers of the type selected be purchased from the French or the British to equip the first 30 divisions to arrive in France. We now have bought 260 155 howitzers from the French and must start with these. Home manufacture of the piece selected and its ammunition should be continued, the 1918 output being used for the equipping and training of troops at home. When the home output of ammunition is on an assuring basis troops in France should be supplied with ammunition from home *sources*. If the British 6 inch is adopted provision should be made also for developing the manufacture of British 6 inch howitzer carriages in the United States to the extent of 400 for the year 1918. (C) Sufficient 175 millimeter Filloux guns and ammunition for the first 50 divisions to arrive in France should be purchased from the French. Home manufacture of this piece and of the 4.7 guns and of ammunition for both these pieces should be developed energetically. No guns of these calibers are obtainable from British sources. (D) Concerning heavy howitzers of the 9.5 inch type the outright adoption of the British 8 inch and 9.2 inch howitzer is considered *imperative*. These calibers are of great and increasing importance. There is no hope of home production of 9.5 inch howitzer before 1919. Sufficient 8 inch and 9.2 inch howitzers can and should be obtained from British sources to equip the first 30 divisions to arrive in France. The existing capacity for manufacture of British 8 inch and 9.2 inch howitzer in the United States must be continued and existing plants for the manufacture of ammunition for these pieces must be maintained and others laid down in order to insure a sufficient supply of ammunition not only for our own needs but to provide a part of the needs of the British. Present plans for the manufacture of 9.5 inch howitzer should be entirely subordinated to the preceding. Box(es) of trench mortars and ammunition of 3 inch Stokes 6 inch Newton Stokes and 240 millimeter type are obtainable from the British and French sources to meet American demands until these demands can be supplied from home sources. Particular efforts should be made to develop home manufacture of 6-inch Newton Stokes ammunition and 240 millimeter trench mortars and ammunition. (F) With regard to super heavy artillery great efforts should be made for home production of railroad mounts for 12-inch mortars and 10 inch 12 inch and 14 inch seacoast guns. It is imperative that sufficient number of these calibers be withdrawn from seacoast forts to supply our armies in France and if necessary to assist the British and French.

Paragraph 5. The whole question as to how England France and the United States can put forth their maximum efforts during the critical year of 1918 has been considered in great detail by the Minister[s] of Munitions of Great Britain and France and by Perkins representing the United States and by their technical assistants and the preceding plan was fully and cordially agreed upon by all parties.

Paragraph 6. It is most urgently recommended that the plan as outlined above be adopted by the United States and that existing plans be subordinate where necessary for the purpose of carrying out these specific recommendations and espe[c]ially that all plans for the development of an independent program by the United States be subordinate to the idea of the strongest possible joint effort and that in every instance where we have established capacity and ability to manufacture no experiment(s) be tried.

Paragraph 7. You will see that the foregoing leaves everything in the hands of the Americans and British who must furnish the necessary tonnage. The commander in the field wants our troops as fast as they can come. If you accept program of supply proposed by Allied Minister[s] of Munitions then troops can be equipped as fast as they come. As to the necessary tonnage, the Interallied Conference at final session afterwards adopted a resolution of its Committee on Maritime Transportation as follows "The Allies, considering that the means of maritime transport(s) at their disposal, as well as the provision(s) which they dispose of, should be utilized in common for the pursuit of the war, have decided to create an inter allied organization for the purpose of co-ordinating their action to this effect and of establishing a common program, constantly kept up to date, enabling them by the maximum utilization of their resources to restrict their importations with a view to liberating the greatest amount of tonnage possible for the transpor[t]ation of American troops."

Paragraph 8. But to secure results there must be continued insistence by our War Department.   Bliss

T telegram (N. D. Baker Papers, DLC).

To Gutzon Borglum

My dear Mr. Borglum: The White House 5 December, 1917

Your letter of November twenty-second to Mr. Tumulty he was kind enough to show me, and I had meant to write to you sooner about it. Of course, what you say disturbs me not a little and I write to ask you if you will not do me the great favor of indicating as specifically as possible the weaknesses you see in our present organization in the matter of aeronautics. I would also appreciate it very warmly if you would tell me what men of practical gifts not now connected with the service of the Government you think could be serviceable to us in working towards a successful result.
                    Cordially and sincerely yours,   Woodrow Wilson

TLS (WC, NjP).

To Flora Lois Robinson

My dear Miss Robinson: [The White House] 5 December, 1917

It is not at all necessary for you to recall yourself to my recollection. I remember with the greatest pleasure meeting you, and my daughter Jessie and I have often since spoken of you and I have through her kept track in some degree of your own work.

I entirely agree with you with regard to the missionary work. I think it would be a real misfortune, a misfortune of lasting consequence, if the missionary programme for the world should be interrupted. There are many calls for money, of course, and I can quite understand that it may become more difficult than ever to obtain money for missionary enterprises. It may be, too, that the extension of those enterprises is for the present impracticable, but that the work already undertaken should be continued and should be continued as nearly as possible at its full force seems to me of capital necessity, and I for one hope that there may be no slackening or recession of any sort.

I wish that I had time to write you as fully as this great subject demands, but I have put my whole thought into these few sentences and I hope that you will feel at liberty to use this expression of opinion in any way that you think best.
                    Cordially and sincerely yours,   Woodrow Wilson

TLS (Letterpress Books, WP, DLC).

To Cleveland Hoadley Dodge

My dear Cleve: The White House 5 December, 1917

Just a line to say that I sympathize with every word of your letter of the second about war with Turkey and am trying to hold the Congress back from following its inclination to include all the allies of Germany in a declaration of a state of war. I hope with all my heart that I can succeed.

In a tearing haste, but with the warmest affection,

Faithfully yours,   Woodrow Wilson

TLS (WC, NjP).

From Josephus Daniels

Dear Mr. President: Washington. Dec. 5, 1917.

Enclosed you will find a cablegram just received referring to the inter-allied Naval Council.[1] The papers this morning carried reference to this Council.   Sincerely   Josephus Daniels

ALS (WP, DLC).

[1] The enclosure is missing. However, it was, as the *New York Times*, December 5, 1917, reported, a dispatch from Paris announcing the full agreement of the Allied governments in regard to the creation of the "Inter-Allied Naval Committee."

From Harry Augustus Garfield

Dear Mr. President: [Washington] December 5, 1917

Your address to Congress is wonderfully luminous. I do not see how it is possible for anyone to misunderstand your program of immediate action and ultimate aim.

The jingo press will doubtless emphasize the first and try to forget the second, but, as Gilbert Murray is reported to have said concerning the Lansdowne letter, it will do harm only to the cause of the German Government.

As always, with affection and high regard,

Faithfully yours,   [H. A. Garfield]

CCL (H. A. Garfield Papers, DLC).

Roger Culver Tredwell[1] to Robert Lansing

Petrograd Dated December 5th, 1917 Recd. 6th, 3:22 p.m.

Deliver the following message from S. Lemel, Sonneberg[2] to Creel. "December 4th. Actual Russian situation is a disturbing surprise to me. It is my duty and yours to see that the facts are laid before President as clearly, strongly and as soon as possible.

Statements the result of rigid though rapid investigations, not impressions. Have conferred with Embassy staff, heads military and Red Cross missions, and Consular Officers. Submit hard facts, *unavailing* (unbiased?), unyielding and joint conclusions therefrom. The conclusions are two fold.

Russia is out of the war. She cannot be counted on as a fighting factor. There is no possibility of a war party gaining power. If new revolutionary army organized it will be in indefinite future and more likely to be used for internal than external warfare. But now no military aid is to be expected. Refer to General Judson reports on conditions of Russian army. This should be no surprise to the Allied Governments for Tseretelli,[3] of former Kerensky cabinet, tells me that several months ago he told American and British Ambassador[s] that Kerensky could not hold power unless he advanced peace program. Pressure of Allied diplomacy forced him to hide the facts from Russia and the world.

Bolsheviki played peace card, combined with popular land program and swept country. Even if they fail on the administrative side and are forced out, any new party to gain democratic support must accept their formula, "peace and land."

Sequel of armistice agreement and of future negotiations of the most importance. Armistice should be technically guarded, no transfer of troops to other fronts, no exchange of prisoners, no reestablishment of trade relations and other points of immense military interest, to assure *belligerency*, a (ceded?) rather than German neutrality in the event of separate peace.

Obviously logical deduction for us is importance of practical contact between our official representatives and those in actual power here so that these points let us be treated in conference as friendly as possible. Formal recognition not involved. The question has not been raised and need not be now considered.

Found Ambassador without policy except anger at Bolshiviki, unamenable to arguments or entreaties of his official advisers, military and civil, and General Judson very anxious to meet Trotsky for conference on terms of armistice. My own work was hopelessly involved in this situation. Can hope to accomplish nothing if there is open break between the Embassy and de facto Government.

Risked using what pressure I could muster, helped to secure from Ambassador wavering consent to single conference Judson and Trotsky and by virtue of unofficial status arranged for that meeting.

Judson has reported to Washington, D. C. the satisfactory results of his conference.[4] Trotsky referred to the conference in a public meeting December second which I attended and had reported as follows: "When General Judson told me that we have to be careful with the Germans as they are a very crafty people I told him that we were the stronger because we do not have to delude anyone" Trotsky spoke further "The negotiations will go on for several weeks. The demand will be made by us that during the armistice the Germans do not transfer any troops to the western front as Russia cannot consent that the armistice shall be used for crushing England and France. We demand an honest armistice." These sentiments were applauded by audience and Bolshiviki leaders *or* [are] publicly pledged to insist upon honest armistice and to resume war if the negotiations [prove] *to be a failure*. Trotsky's reference to the fact that he had conferred with Judson gave us the only favorable press comment since my arrival.

This is summary of arguments for immediate establishment of working, informal contact with de facto power by official representatives here and I recommend such instructions.

My second conclusion is *intimately a part of claim made. Have been* reluctantly convinced that no fruitful work can be done here by any division of our Government as long as Francis remains in charge of *Embassy*. Not only does he impress every one as a sick man absolutely unfitted to the strain physical and mental of his great post but also he has allowed himself to become subject of public gossip and of investigation by the secret police of the Allied nations because of open association with a woman suspected (?) perhaps without sufficient evidence, of espionage. Importance is in suspicion to the association with *Harriot de Cram* (Matilda Cramm?),[5] said to have made his acquaintance on the boat coming over, has established herself on terms of free access to the Embassy, where the Ambassador lives alone. Bullard was informed month ago that the British secret service was making an investigation. A representative of the French Government informally presented few days ago to one of our officials memorandum which contained a paragraph asserting this woman had had at least one meeting with a man arrested last summer in New York charged with espionage, that she had boasted that she had free access to the American Embassy in Petrograd and that she could get what she wanted from the Ambassador. Part of her alleged boast certainly true. Some information on this subject has reached Washington, D. C. On the day I arrived, the Department of State *reminded* Francis that this woman was an undesirable person to have in the "employ" of the Embassy and that the connection should be severed at once. Yet she was in the Embassy on Sunday December second one week later and was alone with the Ambassador until after midnight. It is possible that the Ambassador's erratic actions of the last few weeks is due to the disturbing force of this personal entanglement. However the important point, agreed on by all in a position to know, is that an exceedingly humiliating scandal is momentarily imminent. There will be no frank interchange of views between the Allied Ambassadors and Francis.

If my representations are not sufficient to secure immediate action I ask that request be made upon military mission and Embassy staff for report upon these serious charges. Information will be given as a matter of duty to nation, though with personal unwillingness. However such an inquiry would take time.

I therefore urge that to prevent public humiliation formal orders be sent to Ambassador to hasten to Washington via Japan to report in person to the President on Russian situation and that Embassy be left with Charge d'Affaires. Then while he is enroute make inquiries. There is not a boat for a month or more and it is above all important that he should leave here at once with the least possible scandal."   Tredwell

T telegram (R. Lansing Papers, NjP).
  [1] American Consul at Petrograd.
  [2] Code name for Edgar Sisson.
  [3] Irakli Georgievich Tseretelli, a Menshevik.
  [4] Judson reported in telegram No. 110, December 1, that, with Francis' assent, he had just had a long interview that morning with Trotsky about the armistice negotiations which were to begin the following day between the Bolshevik regime and the Central Powers. Judson, emphasizing that he was speaking unofficially, had pointed out that in many ways the interests of Russia and of the Allies still ran parallel. He had recommended that, if Russia agreed to any armistice, it should be "of long duration with no exchange of prisoners or of products and with enemy troops remaining in position." Trotsky was "very responsive" and implied, Judson wrote, that "his principles and desires for peace left him wide latitude in armistice negotiations." Trotsky said further that he would be glad to have Judson cable to the United States that he, Trotsky, would "observe and endeavor to protect the interests of Russia's Allies," that the points which Judson raised "appealed to him or had already been in his mind," and that he would instruct his armistice commission accordingly. Trotsky also told Judson that the armistice protocol would not be signed for at least a week and that the Allies would be given further opportunity to protect their interests. Judson reported further that the Bolsheviks would soon control the army field headquarters (Stavka) at Mogilev, just as they already controlled the War Ministry and General Staff. The peace program was strengthening them. "No important elements here oppose peace," he summed up, "except to annoy Bolshevicks."
  On the day following the Judson-Trotsky exchange, the Petrograd newspapers printed a statement by Trotsky. It described the interview and said that Judson had made it clear that he had no right to speak in the name of the United States Government since it had not yet recognized the Soviet regime. However, Judson added (according to Trotsky), "he had come in order to start relations, to explain certain circumstances, and to clear up certain misunderstandings." "The time of protests and threats addressed to the Soviet Government," Judson allegedly said in conclusion, "has passed, if indeed there ever was such a time."

In a second telegram, No. 111 of December 2, Judson said that Trotsky's newspaper statement about the interview was "less inaccurate than might have been expected." Judson noted that the British had just issued a "semi-official conciliatory statement." He then summarized information received from Lt. Col. Monroe Crawford Kerth, U.S.A., as follows: "Kerth, from Stavka, reports unanimous opinion there armistice a certainty; advocates discussing concrete peace terms with Russia now, saying United States wishes nothing Russia will not agree to, including acceptance of peace terms by German people; that majority of other Allies could also be reasonably satisfied now; that Russia would continue to fight if enemy rejects fair terms; that now be no time to sacrifice all by standing on dignity; that such stand on dignity will result in successive steps as follows:—separate Russian armistice, separate Russian peace, reorganization Russian Government and administration with Germany's assistance, Russia neutral, assisting Germany, Russia ally of Germany." Judson then commented: "In my opinion Kerth states matter correctly."

In telegram No. 115, December 4, Judson reported that Gens. Aleksei Alekseevich Manikovskii, Assistant Minister of War, and V. V. Marushevski, Chief of the General Staff, had been arrested in Petrograd and that Gen. Nikolai Nikolaevich Dukhonin, the Acting Supreme Commander, had been murdered by a mob at Stavka. He had been killed despite the efforts of Nikolai Vasil'evich Krylenko, the Soviet Commissar for War and Supreme Commander, who took possession of Stavka on December 3 without resistance. Judson then commented: "Any plan to form fronts with Roumanians, Ukrainians, Kaledines [followers of Gen. A. M. Kaledin, about whom see M. Summers to RL, Dec. 6, 1917, n. 2], et cetera, appears most chimerical. Might start ineffectual civil war possibly ending in reestablishment of monarchy but no conceivable benefit Allies. No Russians have or can sustain a War Policy. Russia is past carrying on war although if Bolsheviks do not succeed in armistice or peace they might be able to hold troops awhile. Many Russians especially landed classes desire use [for] political purposes. Any allied policy involving Civil War would probably soon throw Russia into arms of Germany." After noting that Dukhonin had appointed General D. G. Shcherbachev, formerly commander on the Rumanian front, to succeed him, Judson concluded: "No foreign marines or troops should attempt to come in under present conditions. This important and opposed to naval attache's recent (pledge?)."

Judson's three telegrams were received in the War College Division of the Office of the Chief of Staff in the War Department on December 4, 5, and 6, respectively. He had sent copies to Pershing, and, in Washington, copies were sent to the State Department. W. V. Judson to War Department, Dec. 1, 2, and 4, 1917, T telegrams (WDR, RG 165, Office of the Chief of Staff, 10220-D-39, 40, and 41, DNA).

5 For an account of the charges, largely unverified, against Matilda de Cram (originally von Kram?), see George F. Kennan, *Russia Leaves the War* (Princeton, N. J., 1956), pp. 38-41, 114, 126-28, 387-88, and 416.

A Translation of a Telegram from
Jean Jules Jusserand to Stéphen Jean Marie Pichon

Washington, without date [Dec. 5, 1917], received December 6, 1917.

CONFIDENTIAL.

Nos. 1501-1502. Having been received today by the President, I complimented him upon the success of his message of yesterday, which is as great in the press as in Congress, the Republican newspapers joining their approbations to those of the Democratic.

I took advantage of his good humor to ask him about the implications of certain passages of his speech, particularly the one relative to the universal peace which he would desire, in light of the fact it could not be that the present German government is of the kind that he would wish to have make it. He replied that he would wish, upon every occasion, to make it clear to the German masses that, contrary to what is repeatedly told them in order to stiffen their resistance, it is not a question of the destruction of their country. He repeated to me, in the same terms as before: that type of peace must be avoided because a peace of this nature could only be sources of war. Such a one was the one of 1871, when Alsace-Lorraine was torn from you.

It is a useful reaffirmation to note, that he recognized the unjust as well as the impolitic character of the act committed then.

On the subject of a passage in which he speaks of the necessity of assuring to the nations access to maritime routes, Mr. Woodrow Wilson told me that he thought specially of Poland and Danzig, whose sovereignty it will, without doubt, be difficult to consign to the new state on account of the German population situated between this city and the Polish territories. But it would be necessary to assure the Poles with appropriate guarantees of access to this port and the right of usage. Special arrangements must be envisaged for numerous other ports, Constantinople, for example. It is certain that he is not thinking of an Austria, if she ought to survive, without access to the sea.

The President told me that he had taken particular precautions in order that the complete text of his message would be telegraphed to Paris in French, in order to avoid the serious misunderstandings that he had experienced at the time of his response to the Pope. He expressed to me his surprise at the quick and brusque termination of the conference at Paris, which he attributed to the difficulty of working effectively with so many countries represented by so many people.

Relative to the Bolsheviks, the President told me that, in his opinion, the attitude should be one of the most absolute caution (reserve), limiting intercourse to current necessary affairs and avoiding everything which could give the appearance of encouragement and abstaining from protests which are a form of recognition of the existence of this group. Protests could, moreover, incite the Bolsheviks to turn the animosity of their partisans against our nationals.

A note in friendly terms sent to the Bolsheviks by Colonel Judson, chief of the American military mission, and appearing to approve the idea of a general peace, is completely the opposite of Mr. Wilson's idea. I have it from Mr. Polk that it was sent without either authorization or forewarning, that it very much surprised the Department of State, and that explanations have been asked of Mr. Francis.   Jusserand

I have signaled this note to Colonel House who has responded by telegram that it was, without doubt, "an absurd fable."

T telegrams (Guerre 1914-1918, États-Unis, Vol. 509, pp. 146-48, FFM-Ar).

To Harry Augustus Garfield

My dear Garfield: The White House 6 December, 1917

I wrote the address in the spirit of our conversation of the other day and I was in hope that you would like it and feel that it really said what I then tried to say. I need not tell you, therefore, that your letter of yesterday has given me the greatest pleasure.
          Cordially and faithfully yours,   Woodrow Wilson

TLS (H. A. Garfield Papers, DLC).

To Joseph Patrick Tumulty

Dear Tumulty: [The White House, c. Dec. 6, 1917]

I don't want to mix in with this thing.[1] I don't think it was very wise of Vrooman to say what he did, but I am afraid he has a good deal of justification for it, and yet it would not be wise for me to take sides in the matter and I am wondering if you might not just acknowledge these two letters for me in the way you think best.
          The President.

TL (WP, DLC).
    [1] That is, the controversy about the loyalty and patriotism of members of the University of Wisconsin. Wilson referred to C. R. Van Hise's letter of November 27, printed at that date, which strongly defended the university's actions, and to an opposing letter by Richard Lloyd Jones, editor of the Madison *Wisconsin State Journal*, who supported Vrooman's strictures. Jones, who as chairman of the Board of Visitors had received a copy of Van Hise's letter, wrote to Wilson that the university did in fact "lack patriotic leadership." He dismissed most of Van Hise's "concrete cases" as irrelevant or misleading and said that he had "statistical evidence" that Wisconsin was "the most Germanized university in America, maintaining for years a German faculty so out of proportion to academic needs that it became evident propaganda 'put over' on a guileless and unsuspecting administration." Jones also wrote that the loyalty of certain leading professors had been called into question and that Van Hise had permitted a resolution to the effect that the faculty was not in favor of La Follette's position on the war to slumber in a committee. R. L. Jones to WW, Dec. 1, 1917, TLS (WP, DLC).

To William Phillips

My dear Mr. Phillips: [The White House] 6 December, 1917

I am grateful to your [you] for your letter of yesterday.[1] I prepared my address to Congress without consultation with anyone and went up to the Capitol with a very serious doubt in my mind as to the effect it would have on the international situation. I knew that I was bound in conscience to say what I did and I did not hesitate to say it, but I have been greatly relieved by what appears to have been the reception on both sides of the water, because even the truth spoken out of season is sometimes harmful.

Cordially and sincerely yours,   Woodrow Wilson

TLS (Letterpress Books, WP, DLC).
    ¹ It is missing.

To Lincoln Ross Colcord

Personal.

My dear Mr. Colcord: [The White House] 6 December, 1917

May I not say, first, that I read with genuine appreciation your letter to the Public Ledger about my address to the Congress.¹ It was one of the most generous and comprehending of the notices I have seen.

I have your letter of December third, which I have read with a great deal of interest and upon which I have thought a good deal since reading it. I do not believe that at present, at any rate, I could send such a mission to Russia as you suggest. For one thing, I do not know where I would find the men suited to the purpose, but your interpretation of what is going on over there corresponds with so much that has come to me in one way or another, directly and indirectly, that I have been very much impressed by it and thank you for it very warmly.

Cordially and sincerely yours,   [Woodrow Wilson]

CCL (WP, DLC).
    ¹ Lincoln Colcord, "MESSAGE MAY SWING RUSSIANS INTO LINE," Philadelphia *Public Ledger*, Dec. 5, 1917. "The magnificent liberalism of President Wilson's address in Congress this afternoon will uplift the failing hearts of the Russian people, as indeed it will uplift the failing hearts of the whole world," this dispatch, dated December 4, began. Wilson had raised the war again to "a plane of true democratic idealism" by reaffirming "outright" the "policies" of his "Peace without Victory" address of January 22, 1917. In Wilson's address, Colcord went on, the world had "stepped from the shadow of defeat to the sunlight of victory."
    The war will go on to a true democratic victory and peace. The President has shown that the true liberal and man of peace is one who, in "justice, generosity and idealism," stands ready to forgive.
    This message, "this gift," will come to the Russian people at a critical juncture in their affairs. Americans had been misinformed over and over about Russia. They had refused to recognize that Russia engaged 150 German divisions on the eastern front and the "terrible stress and agony under which Russia labored."
    "We have refused to do all this because we did not in our hearts support the Russian revolution." Now we must face the facts before it is too late. The Bolsheviks are not anarchists; they have brought order, not chaos. It is the only government in the democratic camp which has dared to expose Allied war aims. "The tone of the President's speech today in Congress is a direct result of Trotzky's publication of the secret diplo-

matic correspondence, and is a definite and encouraging answer to the Bolsheviki foreign policy."

The Bolsheviks have called upon the proletariat of the world to rise against their governments. Italy is now broken, "and the Italian disaster is a wholly political one." France is on the brink of revolution; the French people have lost faith in their government and are not willing to fight for Alsace-Lorraine. Clemenceau is an arch-tory and imperialist. The situation in England is more stable, but nothing else can keep the peoples of England, France, and Russia in line except "the firm and uncompromising liberalism of the President's speech today." The Russians will listen to this message. "With the war aims of the Allies guaranteed by President Wilson's message, Russia will be held to the camp of the Allies. She cannot do much fighting but she will be held."

To Josephus Daniels

My dear Mr. Secretary: The White House 6 December, 1917

As I understand it, Admiral Benson understands that we are entirely agreeable to this plan, inasmuch as it is now acquiesced in by all of the Allies. Thank you very much for having let me see the enclosed.

In haste   Faithfully yours,   Woodrow Wilson

TLS (J. Daniels Papers, DLC).

To Thomas Watt Gregory, with Enclosure

The White House
My dear Mr. Attorney General: 6 December, 1917

This telegram from the Bohemian National Alliance of America makes a very strong appeal to me. Do you think it would be possible in any way to comply with the request contained in the last part of the telegram which I have marked?

Faithfully yours,   Woodrow Wilson

TLS (JDR, RG 60, Numerical File, No. 189497/1a, DNA).

E N C L O S U R E

Chicago, Ill., December 5, 1917.

Above the thunder of guns, above the storms of war the clear voice of our President resounds throughout the world. Your stern voice declares war upon the family and the ruling German [and] magyer [Magyar] caste now holding down central European peoples. It will encourage these peoples to fight tyrants who had abdicated their own sovereignty in favor of the Hohenzollern. Like the voice of Lincoln calling for defence of the Government of the people, for the people and by the people so your voice gives new strength to millions of oppressed, for their fight is now led by the President of the world's premier republic. As Americans of Bohemian de[s]cent we have double interest in your decision. We believe that America's declaration of war on Austria[1] signals a happy turn in this great tragedy of humanity when America defines the issues and leads the fight for the autocracies of the old world are doomed. We welcome America's declaration against Austria-Hungary. It will encourage wonderfully our loyal allies in the very heart of Europe, the Czchosl[o]vak people in their defiance of oppressor We welcome America's declaration because we are convinced that from now on the cause of small nations of [is] sure of victory regardless of events on the battlefield. You, Mr. President, have always been just to those who were loyal to the American Government and to the great ideals of democracy, you represent. We therefore request you to give special *statutues* [status to] those Czechs and Slovaks who have as yet been unable to obtain the privilege of American citizenship. Great Britain, France, Russia and all the allies do not treat the czechs and slovaks as Austrians and enemies. This request is made in the name of thousands of members of the Bohemian national alliance, who voluntarily join the American army, even though they were not citizens. All citizens of Bohemian descent join in the petition that the stigma of enemies should not be branded on the Bohemian people, Czechs and Slovaks deprived even before the war of consular protection beg the President to become their protector. Our organization promises on behalf of all its members that there shall be no more loyal and devoted element of the American people than the men and women of Bohemian blood.

Bohemian National Alliance of America,
by Dr. L. J. Fisher,[2] President.

T telegram (JDR, RG 60, Numerical File, No. 189497/1a, DNA).

[1] The United States Congress on December 7 passed a resolution declaring that a state of war existed between the United States and the Imperial and Royal Austro-Hungarian Government. Seventy-four senators voted for the resolution, none against, but La Follette, who had missed the signal for the vote, said shortly afterward that he would have offered an amendment stating that the United States would not be bound by, or join in, any agreement by the Allied powers to deprive Austria-Hungary of any territory it had held on August 1, 1914. Without such an amendment, La Follette said, he would have voted against the resolution. In the House of Representatives, the vote was 365 to one. Meyer London, Socialist of New York, voted against the resolution, and Ernest Lundeen, Republican of Minnesota, was paired against it. *Cong. Record*, 65th Cong., 2d sess., pp. 67-68 and 99-100. Wilson approved the resolution the same day, and, on December 11, he proclaimed that a state of war existed. The proclamation imposed less stringent restrictions upon subjects of Austria-Hungary in the United States than Wilson's previous proclamation had imposed upon German subjects. See WW to TWG, Dec. 11, 1917, n. 1.

[2] Ludvik J. Fisher, a Chicago physician, president of the Bohemian National Alliance of America since its formation in 1915.

To George Foster Peabody

Personal.

My dear Mr. Peabody: [The White House] 6 December, 1917

I am grateful to you for your letter of December fourth, and I am none the less grateful because of the feeling you express that I have been doing injustice to some very rare souls. I dare say it must seem so, and nobody regrets more than I do that the generalization to which I was obliged to confine myself sweeps within it those who do not deserve the condemnation which my words imply. I feel, however, my dear Mr. Peabody, that I could not have discriminated without offering a refuge of excuses and protestations to men who do not deserve consideration. I have not known in this instance how to do definite and particular justice.

In great haste
Cordially and sincerely yours,   Woodrow Wilson

TLS (Letterpress Books, WP, DLC).

From William Gibbs McAdoo

Dear Mr. President: Washington December 6, 1917.

For some months I have been studying the railroad problem as an essential part of our financial, credit and war problems. The communication just sent to Congress by the Interstate Commerce Commission[1] has precipitated the issue, and makes it necessary, in my opinion, to deal with it promptly and decisively.

I came to the conclusion some weeks ago that the only solution compatible with the genuine interests of the great masses of the American people was the prompt assumption by you of the control and operation of the railroads during the period of the war. Your power to do this is ample, and you can exercise it without waiting for further legislation. If you exercise it immediately, you will have control of the situation, and such additional legislation as you may require can easily be secured. If you do not, and the matter of policy is to be determined by the Congress, there will be protracted debate, with an aggravation instead of an improvement in existing conditions both economic and financial.

What the railroad managers and capitalists of the country seem to want is legislation which will give to a committee of railroad executives power to control the railroads as a "unit" during the war and to put upon the Treasury the burden of financing the railroads, the character of the improvements and expenditures represented by that financing to be under the control of the railroads themselves. In addition to this, they want an increase of rates. This, if carried out, would merely be running around a vicious circle. Increased freight rates would not alone be sufficient, as admitted by the railroad executives at the hearing before the Interstate Commerce Commission recently, to rehabilitate the credit of the railroads to such an extent that they can finance their own problems without Government aid. Increased rates would add to the cost of food and all the other essentials of life and put a large additional burden upon the already overburdened people, without compensating benefits. The efficiency of the railroads for the purposes of the war and for the service of the public would not, in my judgment, be measurably increased. The same management and methods growing out of the long established practice of preserving the integrity and business of each system of railroads as an independent unit would predominate and control their policies and their operations, and the advantage of unified control and operation, which is imperatively demanded if the present emergency is to be met, would not be gained. The load they would place upon the Federal Treasury would be a very burdensome one. I am not at all sure that we could afford to assume it unless the Government itself controlled absolutely the expenditures by determining the character and extent of the improvements to be made and became incidentally an operating partner in the railroads. Even then we should not get the benefits of actual control and direction. However well intentioned the railroad managers may be—and I believe they are well intentioned and earnestly patriotic in their desire to serve the country at this time— the inherent defects of the present system make it impossible for private management to accomplish the task. The Government alone can meet the situation.

I believe that the masses of the American people are irreconcilably opposed to strengthening the power of the railroads under private management, to the increase of rates, and to the use of the Federal Treasury to support their credit.

Opposed to this is the solution which is in your own hands and which can be brought about by a stroke of the pen. Under your control, the railroads could be operated with great efficiency, with a large reduction in operating costs through the elimination of wasteful expenditures now necessitated by the maintenance of unnecessary competitive conditions and jealously guarded rights and prerogatives of the various systems, which, no matter how praiseworthy their intentions, are unable to subordinate completely their interest to the paramount interest of the public. No increase of rates would be needed immediately, if at all, and the new capital expenditures required could be largely financed by the savings that would be effected through Government control and operation. Economy and efficiency could be enforced all along the line, and a signal demonstration could be·made to the country of the emptiness of many of the claims of the railroad managers and of the value of a larger unification and Governmental direction and control of the transportation facilities of the country, which are so vital to the best interests of the people.

The effect of Government control upon the whole mass of railroad securities, a very large portion of which will be found among the assets of the commercial and savings banks of the United States, would be highly beneficial. It would strengthen every financial institution in this country and enlarge its ability to help finance the Government's necessities in this time. Under Government control, the reserves now kept by the various independent railroad systems could be greatly diminished, and the expenditures of these reserves for necessary betterments and improvements could be enforced under Government direction. The general improvement of railroad credit would enable the railroads, under the aegis of the Government, to finance in large part, if not altogether, their requirements.

We should also have the power to determine their financial needs, and to say when and how they should be satisfied. This would prevent any needless conflict with the Government's own financial operations, and effect a harmonious cooperation of infinite value to the Treasury Department in carrying forward the great operations in which it must engage during the progress of the war.

I wish with all my heart that you would immediately exercise the existing powers conferred upon you by law and take control of all the railroads of the country. I would omit none. If, after experience gained in the operation of the railroads as a whole, it should be found that some portions are not needed, they could be released. Confidence would be restored in a marked degree in financial and industrial circles if you should take this action and you would be absolutely in command of the entire situation. I am confident, from my two recent trips throughout the entire country, that the great mass of the people from one end of the land to the other would rejoice if you should take this problem vigorously by the throat in the exercise of the powers you already possess and with your characteristic courage and foresight. The control, management and operation of the railroads under your direction is a much simpler matter than would ordinarily be imagined. I know it can be handled.

This is just a hasty letter touching only the fundamentals of the problem. I should be glad to submit a more elaborate argument if you care to have me do so.

Cordially yours,   W G McAdoo

TLS (WP, DLC).
[1] The commission stated that the war emergency necessitated unified operation of the railroad systems of the country. This could be done either by the railroad companies themselves or by the President, using the authority granted him by the Adamson Act of August 29, 1916. In the former case, legislation would be needed to repeal existing antitrust and antipooling laws. In either case, it would be necessary to provide adequate yearly return and proper upkeep for the railroads. The commission did not recommend one course or the other, but, in a minority report, Charles Caldwell McChord said that the companies had not risen to the emergency and that governmental control was the only answer. For the text of the commission's report and excerpts from McChord's dissent, see the *New York Times*, Dec. 6, 1917.

From Herbert Clark Hoover

Dear Mr. President: Washington, D. C. December 6, 1917.

I submit herewith a proclamation[1] limiting the alcoholic content of beer to 2.75% by weight, and the amount of grain which may be used by each brewer to 70% of his 1917 consumption of grain. My letter of November 19 recommended that the alcoholic content of beer be reduced to 3 per cent by volume, or 2.4 per cent by weight. At the urgent request of leading brewers who represented that the low alcoholic content proposed would substantially alter the character of beer and render it unpalatable, I have raised the percentage from 2.4 by weight to 2.75 by weight. The latter figure represents a reduction from the present average content of from 25 to 35 per cent.

The reduction of 30 per cent in the amount of material used should result in a saving of approximately eighteen million bushels of grain during the year 1918 without reducing the barrelage of beer from that of the year 1917.

The Commissioner of Internal Revenue has approved the form of the proclamation, and is preparing regulations for its enforcement.   Faithfully yours,   Herbert Hoover

TLS (WP, DLC).
[1] A typed note on this letter reads: "(Proclamation signed and sent to State Dept. Dec. 8, 1917)."

Maddin Summers[1] to Robert Lansing

Moscow. Dated December 6, 1917. Recd 9th, 7:55 P.M.

Strictly confidential. General Brusiloff who was recently wounded by Bolsheviki yesterday called me to hospital and asked me to state to the American Government that General Alexieff as Commander

in Chief and General Kaledin the Lieutenant Governor[2] at (*) a
man [in command] of the combined Cossacks troops have formed
a well equipped army of fifty thousand cavalry and a trustful infantry force. A union will be effected with the Ukrain troops and
loyal elements of the army and people who are flocking to the South.
Rodzianko[3] and other leaders of the constitutional regime supporting them. In case Bolsheviki dissolve or terrorism (*) constitutional assembly with a cabinet will be determined upon. In case
they cannot control same Alexieff and members of the partisan
Government will proclaim seat Government in Cossacks country
and will then send forces to Moscow and St. Petersburg to reestablish order. Brusiloff thinks armies Alexieff and Kaledin more
than sufficient to reestablish order and avert further anarchy but
thinks several weeks will elapse before active operation can be
begun. Brusiloff states that there are still loyal troops in Russia
which will continue to fight Germany and hold German troops on
this front. He says that Prince Troubetzkio[4] has communicated
Alexieff's plans to British Embassy and that financial support has
been promised. He asks that the United States support them morally and financially. He strongly urged that unless such an important movement is successful Russia will become a prey to anarchy
and civil war.

General Alexieff sent a trusted friend to inform me confidentially
of his movements. He confirmed Brusiloff's statements that Alexieff
had formed a union with the Ukrain forces and a part of the army
of the south western front. He stated that Alexieff strongly recommended the occupation of the Siberian railway by the Allies in
order to insure arrival of supplies and prevent liberation of large
numbers of German prisoners who may do irreparable harm by
stirring up civil war, organizing massacres of foreigners and destroying the railway.

The Consulate General would greatly appreciate the confidential
aims of the Department as to its attitude with respect to the Bolsheviki who have violently seized the power and the Government
which has been recognized as that of the Russian people.

Summers.

T telegram (WP, DLC).
   [1] American Consul General at Moscow.
   [2] Gen. Mikhail Vasil'evich Alekseev, who had been Chief of Staff to Nicholas II, 1915-
1917; Supreme Commander, March-May 1917, and Chief of Staff to Kerensky, September 1917; and Gen. Aleksei Maksimovich Kaledin, who was the first elected Ataman
of the Don Cossack Voisko.
   [3] Mikhail Vladimirovich Rodzianko, who had been President of the Fourth Duma and
Chairman of the Temporary Committee of the Duma.
   [4] Prince Grigorii Nikolaevich Trubetskoi, who had been in the Foreign Ministry under
Nicholas II.

To the Duke of Devonshire

[The White House] December 7, 1917.

In presence of the awful disaster at Halifax[1] the people of the United States offer to their noble brethren of the Dominion their heartfelt sympathy and grief, as is fitting at this time when to the ties of kinship and community of speech and of material interests are added the strong bonds of union in the common cause of devotion to the supreme duties of national existence.

                                        Woodrow Wilson.

T telegram (Letterpress Books, WP, DLC).
    [1] Over 1,000 persons were killed and thousands more were injured when munitions aboard the French Line steamship *Mont Blanc* exploded on December 6, after a collision in Halifax harbor with the Belgian Relief steamship *Imo*. A large section of the city was laid waste, and relief efforts were hampered by a blizzard. *New York Times*, Dec. 7-9, 13, 1917.

To David Benton Jones

My dear Friend: [The White House] 7 December, 1917

I was genuinely disappointed not to see you while you were here. If I had known sooner that you were coming, I would have kept a place open on my day's calendar. Please let me know next time.

I hope that you found your brother stronger. I must admit I have been a bit anxious about him and a bit conscience-stricken to have put such heavy work upon him.

                    Cordially and sincerely yours,   Woodrow Wilson

TLS (Letterpress Books, WP, DLC).

To Newton Diehl Baker, with Enclosure

My dear Mr. Secretary: The White House 7 December, 1917

You need not read the whole of the enclosed letter unless you wish to. The part that concerns both you and me is the last part, in which Mrs. Cuyler, an old acquaintance of mine, urges that we consider the advisability of exempting school teachers from the draft until the end of this scholastic year. Have you thought out any method by which we can safeguard the schools against serious interruption?

                    Cordially and faithfully yours,   Woodrow Wilson

TLS (N. D. Baker Papers, DLC).

ENCLOSURE

From Juliana Stevens Cuyler[1]

Princeton, New Jersey.

My dear Mr. President, Dec. 4th [1917].

I must take my courage in both hands and think of you not as one of the greatest men in the world today, but as the Mr. Wilson I remember in old Princeton days or this letter never could be written. I must think even further back before I was married and you were young and uncelebrated, to the time when some Princeton people went to the unveiling of the Soldiers Monument in Trenton. Some of us who were invited to lunch at Mr. Charles Green's[2] found ourselves at luncheon time in the Green house down town, which was an office building, and the wrong side of the parade. It stretched like an impenetrable and endless river between us and Mrs. Green's[3] residence. You won't remember it, probably, but I love to think of it now. As our exigency grew more acute you offered to go out and forage for food, but came back unsuccessful. Meanwhile, I had corralled some paté-de-fois gras sandwiches from some friends of my Aunt's, Mrs. Baker,[4] who was with us. You were grateful to me then. I'm afraid you won't be now, but having harked back so far I feel more in a position to tell you why I am writing. I want to ask for your consideration in the case of exempting school masters from the draft until the end of this scholastic year, only till June 1918. I think we mothers of America are facing through our boys a serious and critical condition.[5] England is regretting the mistake she made in letting her school masters volunteer the first year of the war, with the consequent demoralization of many of her educational centers. Germany has not allowed her young school masters to go into active service until this year. This is all I want to ask. Will you give it your consideration, and forgive me for taking so much of your time?

Yours very sincerely, Juliana Stevens Cuyler.

ALS (WP, DLC).

[1] Mrs. John Potter Cuyler, about whom see EAW to WW, July 24, 1899, n. 2, Vol. 11.

[2] Charles Ewing Green. See the index references to him in Vol. 13.

[3] Mary Livingston Potter Green.

[4] Emelia Jane Stubbs (Mrs. Alfred Brittin) Baker, wife of the long time rector of Trinity Episcopal Church of Princeton.

[5] Her son, Richard Mathä Cuyler, was then a student at the Kent School.

To Juliana Stevens Cuyler

My dear Mrs. Cuyler: [The White House] 7 December, 1917

It was a real pleasure to receive your letter, and you may be sure that I will give very serious attention to the suggestion it contains.

My thought often runs back to the old comparatively care-free days in Princeton, and I beg to assure you that it was not necessary to recall to me the incidents of our very delightful acquaintance.
Cordially and sincerely yours,   Woodrow Wilson

TLS (Letterpress Books, WP, DLC).

From Edward Mandell House

Paris. December 7, 1917.

Your message to Congress has been favorably read here in governmental circles although there is an uneasy feeling concerning the phrase "It must liberate nations [peoples] which were once happy in Belgium and Northern France from the Prussian grip."

They fear you designedly said "Northern France" to make it clear that you did not have Alsace and Lorraine in mind.

I have told the Minister for Foreign Affairs your real feeling and I hope this will compose them.   Edward House.

TC telegram (E. M. House Papers, CtY).

From Joseph Patrick Tumulty

Dear Governor: The White House December 7, 1917

In our talk today you said that your mind was still open with regard to the question we were discussing, but you seemed to have some doubt as to whether the responsibility of administering the American railways, super-added to the duties with which the Secretary of the Treasury is already charged, would not be too great for him. In the case of a weak man or of a man who had not shown the ability that Mr. McAdoo has demonstrated to deal with such matters, this would undoubtedly be true; but there is an old maxim in the business world which says that if you want to get a thing done, the best man to apply to is to a busy man, and this maxim applies to Mr. McAdoo most conspicuously. Of course, it is not to be expected that he would burden himself with the details of managing the American railways, but in the administration of the Treasury Department, his capacity for decision and his discrimination in the selection of his subordinates is the secret of his success, and

I have not the slightest doubt that these qualities would enable him to deal with the railway proposition with equal competency. Inasmuch as the railway problem is essentially a financial and economic problem, and inasmuch as the Treasury Department is the Department of our government that has to deal with problems of this character, the relation between the two propositions seems to me self-evident. Of course, Mr. McAdoo would procure the assistance and cooperation of the ablest experts that he could find. To serve the country in these positions would be a great distinction, but the essential thing is that the head of the organization should be a man with vision, energy and willingness to secure able lieutenants and leave to them a wide latitude of action in the discharge of their duties.

This, my dear Governor, if you will permit me to say so, is exactly what you are doing in your capacity as President of the United States. Congress has given you the widest possible powers, and practically all the activities of our government and our nation are under your direction and control. This direction and control is not less intelligently exercised because of the multiplication of the responsibilities that have been put upon you. You are discharging them satisfactorily simply because you exercise the authority with which you are invested wisely and show great intelligence in the selection of your subordinates. This is what Mr. McAdoo would have to do.   Sincerely,   Tumulty

TLS (WP, DLC).

From Daniel Willard

My dear Mr. President: Washington December 7, 1917.
I am directed by the War Industries Board to say to you that we are advised that there is now no law authorizing the fixing of prices for the public or the Alllies on lumber and no means of compelling obedience to such prices if disregarded. The prices imposed upon the steel manufacturers and copper producers, if resisted, could have been enforced by seizing the mines and factories under power conferred upon the President and upon the Secretary of War and the Secretary of the Navy in certain Appropriation Acts; and the existence of this power was sufficient to compel obedience to prices without exercising the power. But it is obviously impossible for the Government to seize and manage lumber mills, forests, etc. The Board therefore feels that it should not undertake to fix the prices of lumber and like products of industries which it is impracticable for the Government itself to take over and operate, because if such

prices should be disregarded when there is no law providing penalties or other means for enforcing obedience to the order, the result would be to discredit the whole price-fixing program. In short, we think it wise to fix prices only in those cases where there is some means, direct or indirect, of compelling obedience.

For these reasons we are not submitting for your approval prices to be charged the public on lumber.

This situation has led the War Industries Board to make a report to the Council of National Defense (which if approved may reach you) recommending legislation investing the President with power through such Agencies as he may select to fix prices during the period of the war on such articles and commodities as he may deem necessary.   Very respectfully,   D Willard

TLS (WP, DLC).

From William Bauchop Wilson

Seattle, Washington, December 7, 1917.

You will be happy to hear that the Western Pine Association guided by a broadminded conception of patriotism has just advised your Commission of the voluntary adoption of the eight hour day within its own lumber field to become effective on January first, nineteen eighteen. In addition the Association will initiate in the new year a farsighted program of dealing with the complex problems of industrial relations peculiar to the lumber industry of the Northwest. This means that the national policy as to working hours, conditions conducive to stability and standards justifying expectations for maximum productive efficiency have been introduced into the great inland empire embracing vast sections of the States of Washington, Idaho, Montana and Oregon, having an annual cut of two billion two hundred million feet of timber and employing sixteen thousand men. The pioneer action thus taken by the Western Pine Association makes your Commission confident that the lumber industry of the Northwest in its entirety will soon adopt a policy which will be a unique contribution toward the effective execution of the war program.   W. B. Wilson.

T telegram (WP, DLC).

From William Christian Bullitt

Dear Mr. President: Washington 7 December, 1917.

Mr. Colcord has shown me your letter to him. May I take the liberty of saying to you that of all the men I know, Mr. Colcord himself is the fittest to explain to the leaders of Russia the aims and hopes of liberal America.

The thought in my mind is not of a large mission but of one man. I believe fervently that one man should be sent to explain to the Russians how very closely akin are your hopes for the world and their own. One true liberal with letters from your hand might be able to win the leaders of Russia to belief in the truth that their program can be carried out only by the most understanding co-operation with the United States.

Mr. Colcord is a true liberal.

Very respectfully yours,   William C. Bullitt

TLS (WP, DLC).

From Pleasant Alexander Stovall

Dear Mr. President: Savannah, Ga. December 7, 1917.

It has given me great pleasure to read the announcement that the project for the provisioning of Switzerland has been signed by Mr. Vance McCormick in Paris.[1] Since my return to the United States, in accordance with the instructions of the Department, it has given me pleasure to testify that Switzerland is playing the War game under difficult circumstances, with great fairness. So far as I could see when in Berne, the country is neutral and the people are very jealous of their neutrality and national integrity. I tried to impress this fact upon Mr. Vance McCormick and upon the State Department.

I am so glad to know that this act of justice and of generosity to Switzerland has been consummated. I am sure that we will have much to ask of Switzerland when we have American prisoners interned in Germany, and you will pardon me for taking this view, that our relations in Switzerland will be greatly improved, and that my influence when I return to my post in Berne will be immeasurably advanced. Switzerland as you know, is the Good Samaritan of Europe, and all the belligerents are acting through Berne in behalf of their prisoners of war. This is not the reason, of course, which influenced our action; but this is one of the effects which I cannot help realizing.

The action of our Government in formally recognizing the neutrality of Switzerland, to which you remember I called your attention in my short interview with you, was a splendid thing.[2] It not only helps and heartens Switzerland, but it strengthens our own position in Europe, where we have become an active bel[l]igerent.

Since I have returned to Georgia on my leave of absence, Mr. President, it has been my good fortune to meet the people in many places. I have spoken before audiences in Savannah, Augusta, Atlanta, Athens and Statesboro. In every place I have made patriotic appeals, and you would have been gratified, had you been there, to see the instant and hearty response which the audiences gave. Any mention of your war policies were applauded with enthusiasm, and I have yet to find a single town or city where the people were not ready and willing for any call or any sacrifice.

At the same time, I recognize that in many of the rural counties and in the back country the same conditions do not prevail. There is much to be done in the way of campaigns of education. I have spoken twice in Florida, and the same conditions which I have noticed in Georgia, also prevail there, viz: hearty and spontaneous endorsement of the President's policies.

I expect to return to Washington about the first of the year, and with your permission, to assume my duties in Switzerland as soon thereafter as possible.

With best wishes, I remain

Respectfully yours,   Pleasant A Stovall

TLS (WP, DLC).
[1] See n. 3 to the memorandum by W. E. Rappard, printed at Nov. 1, 1917, Vol. 44.
[2] See n. 5 to *ibid*.

Edward Thomas Brown to Mary Celestine Mitchell Brown

Dearest: The White House Dec. 7th 17.

I have played golf almost every morning this week with the President. We leave the House promptly at 8:30, arrive at the course in ab't twenty minutes, play twelve holes, and back in the car at 10:15 or 10:20, the difference being attributed to my loss of balls. I don't think the President ever lost a ball in his life. He doesn't play what "we golfers" call a long game, but his direction is simply remarkable. He is almost invariably straight down the course.

I almost always outdrive him, but this week he has beaten me three out of four games. Tomorrow morning (being Saturday) we will play eighteen holes.

I rise at 7 oclock, dress & have my breakfast at 8, & always ready to start right on the dot—8:30.

Mrs. W. has gone out with us every morning this week, but has not played golf. She takes part of her morning mail, the paper & her knitting and waits for us in the car. This week, is the first time I have noticed we have secret service men stationed at different parts of the course. I have always thought this ought to be done & am delighted now they have begun it.

We are now playing altogether at the Washington Country club, on the Va. side. I am sending a copy of the President's address to Congress delivered on last Tuesday. I wish you could have been with me. It was a wonderful & impressive scene & I know what you think of the speech itself, but Congress was more responsive than I had ever seen it.

Time after time the Senate, House & Galleries rose as one man & cheered to the utmost. The only Senator who kept his seat & did not applaud was La Follette. I have been told this was also true of Hardwick, but I did not see him. . . .

Yrs as always,   Edward

ALS (RSB Coll., DLC).

From the Diary of Josephus Daniels

1917 Friday 7 December

Cabinet

McAdoo said bankers were telling munition makers to depend on Federal treasury & it could not finance everything. "If banks refuse to transact the business for which they were created after awhile banks will wake up to find they have no business to transact," said W.W.

"What is law? Is it not to promote [and] secure justice?" asked W.W. God forbid. It is to fix a system said lawyer who was steeped in learning and stupidity. WW: To quote my father: "You cannot reason out of a man what reason did not put into him"

Discussed what to do with Austrians & others in that Empire. The Bohemians are loyal,—so are others in that Empire. They are not to be troubled. Only the German-Austrians to be interned. Suggests that legislation be obtained by which they can be made citizens. Many Bohemians volunteered in Canada. When captured by Germans they *are* invariably shot.

An Address to the Gridiron Club[1]

[Dec. 8, 1917]

Mr. Toastmaster: I have no speech to deliver tonight which I have prepared. Before I say the very few words that I want to say, I have a very great pleasure in announcing that our fears, at any rate a part of our fears, about the lives lost on the destroyer which was sunk are removed by news which has just come. Secretary Daniels has just phoned that Mr. Bagley and Mr. Cranford were not lost but saved, and that almost all the men of the crew were saved also.[2]

It is pleasant, gentlemen, to think of some of the fine things that go along with war. One of them you have just illustrated yourselves. We now feel ourselves comrades of all the men who are fighting for us. We feel towards these men who risk their lives on the sea, in the ship that has just gone down, as if we knew them personally and with our own hearts involved in their destiny.

That is really the only theme that I wanted to suggest to you tonight.

It has always seemed to me that democracy is a more practical thing than we have generally allowed our thoughts to realize. Patriotism, gentlemen, is not a sentiment. It is a principle of action. The action breeds the sentiment. The impulse of the sentiment is born in the demonstration, is in the action, not in the sentiment.

I have had some very grim resolutions to make since we entered this war. I have had men profess their patriotism to me and not proved it. I have made up my mind that I am not going to listen any more to the words. I am going to wait for the proof in the action. I am able to say that I have not been disappointed in the action, but I have had illustrated for me the fact, over and over, that a man's principles do not reside in his professions but in his performances.

And with regard to that great thing which we call democracy, it is not a form of government. It is a vital nexus or connection. It is something which literally unites us in purpose and in sympathy with all our fellow men. One of the happy circumstances of this war is that men who formerly enjoyed wealth and privilege and exemption from any onerous duty are now in the ranks as privates, and men who formerly were their servants, in a sense, are officers and command them. And there is no jealousy either way. The men in the ranks are proud to be in the ranks. They know that the rank of the army and the navy is not a class distinction but a distinction of duty only, an assignment of the difference of function.

And if this war teaches us nothing deeper than that, it will be a valuable lesson to learn, that among us there are no ranks except the ranks of performance and function, that men are all of the same kinds and all have the same hearts under their jackets, and we ought not to take the word "democracy" upon our lips unless we feel that it has an intimate and profound character.

Don't you feel what is happening in this world?

We used to talk about our sympathy with other nations. We used to talk about the comradeships which run round the wide globe because we are all human beings of like sort. But we never felt it before as we feel it now. We never had it translated into duty before as it is translated now—the duty that has translated itself also into a sort of zest and glory for us, that we are fighting for something much greater than concerns merely ourselves.

We are very lavish in the use of many words and don't discriminate very nicely, but there is one word about which we are rather careful, and that is the word "noble." We call all sorts of men great for all sorts of performances, but we call only one sort of man noble, and that is a man who has some great surplus of energy which he spends on others than himself. We don't erect monuments to all our great men, but we love to erect monuments to those noble men who thought first of others and only afterwards of themselves.

Now we are put in that position as a nation. The war does not touch us as intimately now as it touches France, for example, and struck Belgium and threatened England and invaded Italy, but we have the same zest in it that any Frenchman or Belgian or Italian or Englishman can have. Thus we know that we now all understand what the conflict means. It means the choice between genuine liberty and a servile submission.

And I know that you will forgive me if I confess a certain impatience at some of the obstacles still remaining—very subtle obstacles, very intangible obstacles, but very real and stubborn obstacles. We haven't yet, in the service of this government, really learned this lesson of equality. Sometimes I fancy myself in a position just about as delicate as Mr. Hammerstein,[3] surrounded by prima donnas and embarrassed by having to wonder what is the best way to do a thing so as not to hurt anybody's feelings, whom I ought to speak to first, what combination of gentlemen I ought to consult, whom I ought to compliment before I find somebody whom I can use.

I had a dream the other night, that one of those prima donnas was showing some very much lacerated feelings because he had been overlooked in some matter. I couldn't remember which one it was when I waked up, but I remembered the rest of the dream. I remembered, I am sorry to say, that I lost my temper, and that I told this gentleman I was sick and tired of this business of hurt feelings, and that I had formed a definite resolution that I was going to publish a list of gentlemen who preferred their private sensibilities to their public duties, and I was going to give that list an international circulation, and then we would know whom to give the leading parts to and who were willing to constitute the chorus.

I don't want you to take this as a piece of ill temper. It is not a real imprimatur that I am talking about. It applies in no single quarter, it applies in every quarter. I am perfectly willing to take orders if somebody will give me intelligent orders. And I think that there ought not to be a man in the United States who isn't now willing to take orders and not ask any questions. Because we are all in a great work for an extremely great object. The man who places his own interests, the man who thinks what is going to be his situation when the war is over, the nation which calculates what is going to be its advantage or its disadvantage when the war is over, is unworthy of the great partnership we have formed.

The thing that buoys me up every day is the consciousness that the people of the United States would lose heart in this war if they thought we were fighting for anything selfish at all. It is a glorious thing, gentlemen, that we should represent such a people.

When I addressed the Congress the other day, I was, I hope, expressing my own individual opinion, but that wasn't what I was trying to do. I was trying to express what appeared to be the real mandate of the people who put me in my present office. I was trying to express what appeared to be the spirit and the principles of the American people, and they are disinterested principles and disinterested purposes.

And, as we hear these voices of humanity that ring louder and louder through the world, we know that we are not single and distinct in that matter. We know that the hearts of men everywhere are suffering with that great hope that men shall come into a real brotherhood of freedom and equality of privilege, that they shall not rival each other in the effort after selfish privilege and exclusive advantage, but that, matching wit with wit, they shall go together in a great brotherhood of industrial competition in which they shall not envy each other and in which they shall help each other.

I pray in my heart that this war is going to bring a great emancipation to the human spirit. I am only sorry—genuinely sorry— that I can't go with the boys that are going away on the other side. When the orders go forth sending these lads abroad, my heart aches that I can't go with them, because I can't imagine any greater distinction than to end my life for the only purpose that gave life.

JRT transcript (WC, NjP) of CLSsh (C. L. Swem Coll., NjP).

[1] Patriotism was the theme of the dinner at the New Willard Hotel attended by 300 men and Jeannette Rankin, congresswoman from Montana. For the first time in the club's thirty-three years, the dinner was "dry," and it was also wheatless and meatless, a feature that was noted in a song for "Herb" Hoover, who was present. There were various skits, including one about the war-revenue bill in which this exchange took place: "What is a domestic partnership? Woodrow Wilson and 100,000,000 Americans. What is a foreign partnership? The kaiser, Bob La Follette, and Jeremiah O'Leary." At another stage in the proceedings, Henry Ford and Frank Vanderlip arose and sold several thousand dollars worth of war certificates to those present, and Wilson asked permission to subscribe. *Washington Post*, Dec. 9, 1917.

[2] Lt. Commander David Worth Bagley, commanding officer of *U.S.S. Jacob Jones*, a new destroyer, which had been torpedoed and sunk by a German submarine on December 6. Bagley was the brother of Mrs. Josephus Daniels. "Cranford" was Clifton Cranford, an electrician's mate. About fifty officers and enlisted men were lost. Most of the survivors were taken to the Scilly Islands, off Cornwall, but two were taken prisoner on the submarine. *New York Times*, Dec. 9, 10, 12, and 19, 1917.

[3] Oscar Hammerstein, the well-known operatic impressario in New York, and grandfather of Oscar Hammerstein II, later celebrated as a lyricist and librettist.

To Frank Irving Cobb

My dear Cobb: The White House 8 December, 1917

Thank you for the suggestion of your letter of yesterday.[1] I shall act upon it at once.

And thank you very warmly also for your generous words about the address. I hope with all my heart that it may have some effect in the enemy countries on the other side of the water.

Cordially and faithfully yours,   Woodrow Wilson

TLS (IEN).

[1] The letter is missing, but Wilson in forwarding it to Creel (in the next letter) referred to Konta, presumably in connection with patriotic work among Hungarian Americans. Later, describing the work of the Committee on Public Information, Creel wrote: "Work among the Hungarian population was intrusted to Mr. Alexander Konta of New York, who gave time, money, and finest faith to a difficult and thankless task. It was not only that certain vicious factional elements threw every possible obstacle in his path, but he was equally attacked by *The New York Tribune* and similar papers that made a business of chauvinism. Undismayed and undiscouraged, Mr. Konta continued the work, and the American-Hungarian Loyalty League played no small part in our national unity, for men of Magyar stock figured importantly in the coal and steel industries." George Creel, *How We Advertised America: The First Telling of the Amazing Story of the Committee on Public Information that Carried the Gospel of Americanism to Every Corner of the Globe* (New York, 1920), p. 187.

To George Creel

My dear Creel: The White House 8 December, 1917

Here is a letter from Cobb of the World containing a suggestion which I think we ought to act on. I hope you will see some opening through which we can do so.

So far as I know, his judgment of Mr. Konta is a just one.

In haste

Cordially and faithfully yours,   Woodrow Wilson

TLS (G. Creel Papers, DLC).

To Elizabeth Merrill Bass

Personal.

My dear Mrs. Bass: [The White House] 8 December, 1917

I realize the importance of the circumstances to which you call my attention in your letter of yesterday and will see if it is possible to do anything about the matter, though it does seem to me sometimes that any direction in which we move is fraught with difficulties of the most serious sort.

In haste   Faithfully yours,   Woodrow Wilson

TLS (Letterpress Books, WP, DLC).

To Albert Sidney Burleson, with Enclosure

My dear Burleson: The White House 8 December, 1917

There is a great deal of force in what Mrs. Bass says in the enclosed letter. Don't you think that it would be well for you to discuss the matter with Kitchin and Webb? It would be too bad to make a mess of this important thing and do it in the way that will do the most harm, if Mrs. Bass is right in her impressions as to the effect it would have to bring the question to an immediate and forced vote.   Faithfully yours,   Woodrow Wilson

TLS (A. S. Burleson Papers, DLC).

E N C L O S U R E

From Elizabeth Merrill Bass

My dear Mr. President: Washington, D. C. December 7th, 1917.

I am wondering if it has been called to your attention that Chairman Webb of the Judiciary Committee has announced in the newspapers that suffrage is to be reported out of the Judiciary Committee on to the floor of the House next Tuesday for a vote. Democratic Floor Leader Kitchen has concurred publicly. I went to see Mr. Webb and Mr. Kitchen, not as a suffragist, but as Chairman of the Woman's Bureau in charge of Democratic organization, and told them that while they were entitled to vote their particular convictions in any way they chose when the question of suffrage came up in the natural way, that to report it out for a vote in the beginning of the session when the women were neither ready nor asking for it, would be construed by the women of the country and the newspapers as a distinctly unfriendly act, and would react perhaps fatally on the Democratic party in the coming elections for Congress. The New York women who are making ready for an active suffrage campaign among their own congressional delegation would particularly resent this.

I also told them that the militant group,[1] backed as we believe by the Republican National Committee, would welcome this action with joy, as furnishing them with material for their campaign against the Democratic party.

I am enclosing the poll of the Congress, which has already been sent you,[2] but I have had it classified so that it can be more readily counted, and I think it shows that even though there may be a number of changes in favor of suffrage by now, still a forced vote would easily defeat the measure by Democratic votes, and we would have to go to the election next year with that handicap. Mr. Kitchen seemed partially convinced by what I said, that it would be a fatal party move at this moment, and agreed to talk it over with Chairman Webb, who is quite obstinate.

I am writing this in hope that you will see Mr. Kitchen and convince him that purely from the standpoint of party expediency it would be a fatal move.

May I also call your attention to the fact that Chairman Webb is claiming sole jurisdiction in the matter of submitting suffrage amendments, even though the House voted for a committee on suffrage at the close of the last session: that also is stirring women to the depths. It seems to me that no matter how the Democrats of the South finally vote on the question of the Federal Amendment, it is a fatal party move to make overt offensive moves against the women of the country.   Faithfully yours,   Elizabeth Bass

TLS (WP, DLC).
  [1] That is, the National Woman's party, led by Alice Paul.
  [2] In Maud M. W. Park to WW, Nov. 30, 1917. Mrs. Bass' further revision is missing.

To Robert Lansing

My dear Mr. Secretary   The White House. 8 Dec., 1917

This despatch disturbs me.[1] Had you heard from any other source of such conduct on the Ambassador's part?   W.W.

ALI (R. Lansing Papers, NjP).
  [1] That is, R. C. Tredwell to RL, Dec. 5, 1917.

To William Bauchop Wilson

[The White House] 8 December, 1917

The action of the Western Pine Association gives me the deepest gratification and I hope that you will have occasion to express that gratification to the officers of the Association. Please accept my warmest congratulations on the extraordinary work you and your associates are doing. I sincerely hope that you are entirely well and strong again. Was distressed to learn that you were unwell.

Woodrow Wilson.

T telegram (Letterpress Books, WP, DLC).

To Daniel Willard

My dear Mr. Willard: [The White House] 8 December, 1917

Thank you sincerely for your letter of December seventh. I dare say that the action of the War Industries Board in determining that it is not wise to attempt to fix prices where the prices fixed cannot be enforced is a wise one.

I shall look forward with great interest to the recommendations of the Council of National Defense with regard to legislation intended to establish a control over the prices of all commodities.

Cordially and sincerely yours,   Woodrow Wilson

TLS (Letterpress Books, WP, DLC).

To Edwin Robert Anderson Seligman

The White House

My dear Professor Seligman: 8 December, 1917

It was a very friendly thought that led you to send me these letters of the ages before the flood.[1] The flood being now upon us, I dare say that most things will seem to us antique that antedate it.

It recalled many interesting memories to me to read these letters, and I thank you most sincerely.

I hope that I have not entirely got over the modesty of these letters; indeed, oddly enough, I remember the particular paper referred to in the second letter and still retain the opinion of it which I had then.

Cordially and sincerely yours,   Woodrow Wilson

TLS (E. R. A. Seligman Papers, NNC).
[1] Probably WW to E. R. A. Seligman, March 16, 1886, April 19, 1886, and Nov. 11, 1886, all printed in Vol. 5. What Wilson called "the second letter" was the one dated Nov. 11, 1886.

From William Gibbs McAdoo

Dear Mr. President: [Washington] December 8, 1917.

Concerning the permanent Inter-Ally Council in Europe, now in process of formation with your approval, I received, through the State Department, the following message from Mr. Crosby:

No. 11. French Finance Minister[1] proposes that instead of having one Inter-Ally Council as originally proposed, its functions shall be divided between two councils, one to deal with questions relating primarily to purchases and supplies and the other primarily with financial questions, trade council to have headquarters in London and finance council to have headquarters in Paris. It is suggested that I be chairman of each council as representative of United States. Only suggestion of extending powers is to include questions relating to finance and war trade with neutral countries. These questions particularly those relating to exchange necessarily involved in the main questions for consideration of which council was formed. It seems probable that to some extent at least the two councils will have the same personnel. Colonel House and I favor the proposed division principally as means of satisfying apparent strong desire of French that portion of work originally planned for Inter-Ally Council should center at Paris instead of having all center at London. It is distinctly understood that the work of both councils will be recommendatory only and that finance ministers of Governments represented in Council will retain full freedom of action. Of course European powers would in any case be free to have their delegates in these councils consider the extension of authorization above indicated but before taking part as United States representative in such organization prefer to have matter distinctly understood by you and to have your approval. Please cable promptly whether you concur.

I immediately on December 3rd asked the Secretary of State to forward the following reply to Mr. Crosby:

My own judgment is against two councils. Concentration instead of diffusion is the need of the hour, it seems to me, but am willing to accept your and House's judgment whatever it may be.

Yesterday I received, through the State Department, a message from Mr. Crosby containing the following passage relating to the organization of the Inter-Ally Council:

Referring to my number 11. Think very desirable to have authority to proceed with organization of two councils as indicated therein. Reading will recommend plan to Bonar Law and expects approval by this, all now recognize absolute interdependence of neutral purchases international exchange and our advances to Allies, hence extreme desirability of consideration of all these questions in two central bodies.

I think it wise to accept the recommendation of Mr. Crosby which seems to be concurred in by Colonel House, and I propose to cable Mr. Crosby accordingly. May I ask whether the course proposed meets with your approval?

Cordially yours,   Wm. G. McAdoo

CCL (SDR, RG 59, 763.72/8095, DNA).
[1] That is, Louis Lucien Klotz.

From George Creel

Memorandum to the President.

Dear Mr. President: [Washington] December 8, 1917.

I enclose circular[1] that has aroused a good deal of criticism owing to its use of the words "Our Allies." It is a term that I have avoided myself. The people who are protesting are undoubtedly pro-German, and I would like to have your view before I answer any of the numerous letters.   Respectfully,   George Creel

TLS (WP, DLC).
[1] It was a poster (WP, DLC) showing a large fish, with a lemon and assorted vegetables. It bore the caption: "U. S. Food Administration. Eat More Corn, Oats and Rye Products— Fish and Poultry—Fruits, Vegetables and Potatoes   Baked, Boiled and Broiled Foods   Eat Less Wheat, Meat, Sugar and Fats To Save for the Army and Our Allies."

From William Cox Redfield

My dear Mr. President: Washington December 8, 1917.

The Secretary of War has sent me a copy of Mr. Hoover's letter to you of the 1st instant on the question of legislation for this Congress.

At the last meeting of the Council of National Defense, Mr. Hurley spoke with regret and anxiety of the delays caused in our shipping work by labor troubles. I am convinced these two matters are largely one and that Mr. Hoover's suggestion about regulating prices lies at the heart of Mr. Hurley's problem.

It seems to me there are two ways in which the matter of labor stoppages must be approached, and that each is insufficient without the other. I use the word "must" because it seems to me that conditions exact from us both ways and that neither will do alone.

The workman suffers most from high retail prices. His margin of safety is least. Against what may seem such excessive demands as an increase of 40% in wages, he knows there has been an increase of 100% or even 200% in retail prices of food.

Mrs. Redfield paid twelve cents a pound for beans and perhaps twenty cents a pound for pork to cook with them. Now she is asked forty cents a pound for beans and sixty cents a pound for pork. This may not trouble her seriously but it is ruinous to a man on a daily wage.

The root of the labor trouble lies in the trouble in the workman's home arising from high retail prices. If we can control these we control the heart of the matter.

When these are controlled, and hardly until then, we can appeal to his patriotism to keep busy as a producer for the Nation's sake. This is the second thing and ought to be done, but just as we can hardly preach religion to a starving man, so patriotism is a cold thing when the breakfast is scant and a strike seems the only way to make it sufficient.   Yours truly,   William C. Redfield

TLS (WP, DLC).

From Albert Shaw

Dear Mr. President: New York December 8, 1917

I greatly appreciated your confidence and frankness in talking to me on Wednesday[1] about the larger aspects of the world war. I have very strong convictions regarding some things that have to do with international policy and some other things that have to do with the practical conduct and prosecution of the war itself. It was very gratifying to me to feel that your sense of the application of principles to measures is as sound as your statements of the principles themselves.

This latest Congress message of yours has won great approval, not only from newspapers but from men of independent mind and judgment who think for themselves and who have sometimes been opposed to you. I have spoken with a good many such men, and they are now completely in accord with what you say.

You are being urged, naturally, by men who think in terms of their own special activity, to lay chief stress upon things which mutually antagonize one another. I do not really think you have a "single track mind," and I believe you realize fully that a number of things may be operating at the same time. Thus I attach great importance to your message to the Austrian people at the very moment when you joined Congress in declaring war against Austria. You notify them that you are not proposing to dismember

[1] December 5.

Austria or to bring about a future crushing or humiliation of the Austro-Hungarian aggregation of peoples.

At the same time that you arouse enthusiasm among the Italians, by making war upon their chief enemy and by planning to send some help and relief to the defenders of Italy, you are serving notice that the bargain which Italy exacted from the Allies, before going into the war, is no longer binding. If the Italians accept aid from you, they must admit at the same time that your aid is not to be used to bring about an unwarranted dismemberment of Austria. France, furthermore, in constantly soliciting and eagerly accepting American aid, is by necessary implication also accepting your principles regarding the aims and objects of the war.

In respect to the nature of our participation in the war, you could not naturally say very much in public. But I feel that you have a wise sense of the apportionment of effort. For my part, I am thoroughly opposed to the policy of sending very large masses of infantry to France. I believe that those civilian leaders who advocate this policy are totally mistaken, and that the Army men who are working for it are blind to the facts of the situation as a whole.

If this is to be a very long war, we must conserve our resources in order to apply them at a time of our own choosing. We can defend ourselves against the whole world for a thousand years if we choose our own times and places. We can produce everything that we need, within our own continental area. We were brought into the war by interference with our rights on the sea; and we cannot develop the Navy too fast or advocate too energetic a naval policy on the part of England and the Allies.

Our great contribution to the immediate cause abroad should be supplies of all kinds and the highly specialized services such as aviation, surgery and Red Cross aid, and ships without limit. We have many who say arbitrarily that the war is to be won by fighting on the siege line of the Western front. On that line the Germans are operating a series of buzz-saws, and the Allies are operating a series of wood-piles. The buzz-saws are occasionally dulled and put out of order, but the wood-piles melt away much more rapidly than the buzz-saws wear out.

I do not think you could make a greater mistake than to take a million or two of American boys, from all over the United States, and merely feed them into the German machine along this siege line that extends from Hamburg to the Adriatic. The Allies already have far more men than the Teutons have on that line. Naturally we must be represented there. But the Allies need from us, chiefly, the certainty that we can continue to give them surplus food and supplies and can find the shipping as against the submarine peril.

I believe that while this siege line is being held, flank operations could detach Turkey in comparatively short order, and that Bulgaria could next be brought to rights. Of the four people in the Balkans— namely, the Serbians, Greeks, Bulgarians, and Rumanians—the Bulgarian people are the best and most reliable. Unfair treatment and stupid Allied diplomacy forced the Bulgarians in the wrong direction. The Italian reverses ought to make it much easier to deal with the Bulgarian problem on wise political and diplomatic lines.

I have not hesitated, while supporting your policies with good will and sincerity, to express my own views to the readers of the Review from month to month. We have many more readers now than ever before, and they are in every county in the United States. I find these elements of public opinion with which I am in touch to agree with me that the development of our Navy, the development of our aviation policy, the tremendous development of our land and sea transportation, and your policies of finance, of thrift, and of large agricultural and mechanical production, are of relatively greater importance than the policy of taking out of industry millions of men for immediate standing armies.

We have done well thus far, because we need to train many officers and to create a system under which, if necessary, we could rapidly train five millions or even ten millions of soldiers. But with this machinery at work, we ought naturally to keep as many men as possible at work in the mines, in the shipyards, and on the farms. If we transport too many of them to France, we shall not only cripple our ability to produce the food and supplies that our allies demand, but we shall greatly increase the unrest and anxiety of the country by reason of the disadvantages under which our boys are to be placed in fighting at great distance, on foreign soil.

The war has two great aspects to be considered. One of these is the worldwide aspect. The other is the strictly European. The first of these is what has most engaged your thoughts. Of course the two are intimately connected. But, generally speaking, it seems to me that American effort should be guided by America's relation to the worldwide war, while Europe's effort is more directly engaged with the line fighting within European points. The problem of the seas and of ships is worldwide. The doctrines of justice, good will, honesty, are of worldwide bearing. The future of the Turkish Empire as well as the future of China is of worldwide concern.

I am troubling you with a set of our "Presidential Messages and State Papers,["] in ten volumes.[2] This is the first set that has come

---

[2] *Presidential Messages and State Papers; Being the Epoch-Marking National Documents of All the Presidents from George Washington to Woodrow Wilson, Collected and Arranged, with Brief Biographical Sketches*, Julius W. Muller, ed., with an introduction by Albert Shaw (10 vols., New York, 1917).

from the printers. I shall a little later have a specially bound set for you, and this first one can be passed over to Mr. Tumulty or some-body else. The old Richardson set[3] did not, of course, cover several recent administrations, and it is not convenient for ordinary use.

If you have a few moments to glance cursorily at the set, you will see that the first nine volumes are occupied with the Messages and Addresses of all the previous Presidents, and the tenth volume is exclusively devoted to your utterances. This makes it possible to continue to expand the tenth volume. While binding the tenth volume uniformly for the purposes of this set, we shall also bind it separately and distribute it independently of the rest.

We are now bringing the Wilson volume up to date by adding the Buffalo Labor speech, two or three briefer utterances, and the great Message to Congress of the present week. In a short time we shall have the revised edition ready, with these documents in-cluded. I have taken the liberty to write to Mr. Rudolph Forster, to have him ascertain if there were other utterances of recent date that ought to be included. We think that it is well to put in the little message to Brazil on her entering the war, your Thanksgiving proclamation of this year, and one or two other such matters. If there should be anything else that belongs appropriately, we would be glad to have further word from Mr. Tumulty or Mr. Forster.

Besides this Brazil message there is one that relates to Greece, and another to the Liberty Loan. These things, while brief, seem to us to have a permanent historical value and to enrich, therefore, the collection we are making—although this collection of course does not pretend to be exhaustive. The Taft-Roosevelt material has been very much cut down by our editor of the volumes, because while it was very voluminous much of it did not seem for our purposes to have permanent reference value for the ordinary citizen or student.

Please pardon so long a letter, and believe me, with great respect and regard,   Faithfully yours,   Albert Shaw.

TLS (WP, DLC).
    [3] James D. Richardson, ed., *A Compilation of the Messages and Papers of the Presidents, 1789-1897* (10 vols., Washington, 1896-99).

From Lincoln Ross Colcord

Dear Mr. President: Washington, D. C. 8 December, 1917
    Your generous and kindly letter made me very happy, both on a personal score and on the score of world-mutation in which all our hearts are so deeply engaged. But from your towering address the

other day I had of course derived the greater joy, and for it I had given the greater thanks. Permit me now to thank you for having taken time to be so generous on the lesser issue.

The terrible danger towards which the Bolsheviki are heading is clearly defined by their anti-capitalistic program. There is plain disaster even in their domestic application of this program. I said the other day that Russia is ready for radical measures, and so she is; I said there is no anarchy in Russia, and until now there has been no anarchy in the sense in which we use the word. But real anarchy there has been and is, after all, for Lenine and Trotsky are real anarchists or communists. And they cannot put through even their domestic program in the face of the democratic institutions of the world, much less in the face of German autocratic institutions. But when they insist on applying this anti-capitalistic and anti-institutional program not only to the internal affairs of Russia but also to international foreign policy, the fearful danger is self-evident. If Russia is not ready for this program, surely the western democracies are not ready for it.

But there remains a hope. Lenine and Trotsky, under the pressure of responsibility, will suffer a change of heart. This will come about most powerfully with respect to domestic affairs, since these will be the motive instruments. Perhaps, balked at home, they will attempt to spend their anarchistic ardor upon their foreign policy. This must be anticipated and offset. They must be persuaded to modify their program most of all upon the side of foreign policy. They must be shown that such a course would not be one of compromise, but that the real compromise would be contained in their proposal to force social revolution upon nations which fundamentally are not prepared for it.

The course of events in Russia seems fairly plain. There will be civil war, and the Allies are fostering it; they will do anything, lose the war, rather than support an anti-capitalistic program. There are of course powerful forces in Russia which will support a counter-revolution. But I doubt if the Allies realize the fundamental radicalism of Kaladines' program also. Two weeks before the Bolsheviki uprising Kaladines as hetman of the Cossacks submitted to Kerensky a strong protest against his failure in foreign policy, and an equally strong representation that Russia required immediate peace. The Allies are chasing the illusion of a dictatorial power which can never appear in Russia now.

Not being a socialist myself, I cannot contemplate with equanimity the frightful measures which are surely imminent in the world to-day. I am afraid of France, where revolutionary blood has run so often, so wonderfully, and sometimes so disastrously. Ultimately, of course, there can be no disaster in revolution. But I believe with all my heart that there could always have been an orderly way to accomplish what revolutions have accomplished. The history of the world is the history of revolutions, and the history of revolutions is the history of evil and stupid authority. The new world which is plain before us, which is inevitable, cannot and must not come through anarchy. Yet that, too, is plain before us as the next step, if wise and brave things are not quickly done.

I have been very close to the Russian Ambassador during the last few weeks; Colonel House introduced me to him in Magnolia last summer. He gives me his heart and mind on this subject. I think he is half-right and half-wrong. He is wonderfully sympathetic towards the lowly people of Russia, but he is not one of them himself. He has been a member of revolutionary societies in his student days under the old regime, yet his family belonged to the bourgeoise. He has suffered only for freedom, never for bread. His knowledge of socialism and of Russian history is profound, and he points out very clearly the steps which are inevitable. And yet he is not ready to admit that these steps are right unless there is a change of heart throughout the west, and that only be [by] these steps can the truth finally be won. He is not ready to admit the deep significance of the contradictory fact that Lenine and Trotsky, the anarchists, the wild and wrong, have struck the first blow of outright *truth in action* which has been delivered during the summer. And he is not ready to recognize the extreme carefulness, the actual wisdom, with which they have so far conducted their negotiations.

It is impossible to define in words the shades of difference which separate my belief from his; we have had fine talks in the attempt to clear up this issue between us. But the difference, slight in its definition, is vast in its results. If there is no other way, and if the time has come, then I am for revolution. He wants still to compromise.

I have also cultivated the acquaintence of Baum,[1] the representative in America of the Council of Soldiers' and Workingmen's Delegates. He was at hard labor in Siberia when the revolution freed him, and is, of course, a Jew. He is one of the people; but there seems to be a last analysis which the Russian Jew cannot face. Baum wants peace now whether or no. Maybe he is right; I am not too sure.

My other friends who purport to know Russia—Mr. George Kennan, for example—are all living in a past day. And perhaps all of us are living in a past day. The world seems unaccountably to have distanced its inhabitants. The future actually is the present, through the strength and meaning of potentialities. Only imagination can see what already has arrived.

M. Bakhmeteff knows both Lenine and Trotsky personally, Lenine better than Trotsky. He tells me that Lenine has a simple mind, but a powerful and dogged character. Trotsky is more the theorist, a better thinker than Lenine, frankly an anarchist, and an effective orator.

I am, my dear Mr. President,

Faithfully yours,   Lincoln Colcord

TLS (WP, DLC).
    [1] Unidentified.

From the Duke of Devonshire

Ottawa, Ont., December 8, 1917.

I desire to thank Your Excellency for your message which the Canadian Government and I have received with profound appreciation and gratitude. We recognize in it and in the generous offers of assistance to the stricken city of Halifax which have been received from many quarters of the United States a further proof of that community of feeling which unites the two people in a bond of mutual sympathy and interest so particularly appropriate at the present time, when both are engaged in a common purpose to vindicate the principles of liberty and justice upon which the foundation of both governments rest.   Devonshire.

T telegram (WP, DLC).

From William Pettus Hobby

My dear Sir: Austin, Texas December 8, 1917.

Permit me to thank you for your good letter of November thirtieth, assuring your cooperation in an effort to relieve the very serious conditions which have arisen in western Texas on account of the unprecedented drouth that has visited this State.

Very respectfully yours,   W P Hobby

TLS (WP, DLC).

From Cleveland Hoadley Dodge

My dear President   Riverdale-on-Hudson Dec. 8th 1917

Just a line to thank you for your reassuring letter—that, coupled with the action of Congress, in not pressing the Turkish question, has made me very happy.

It is needless for me to tell you how profoundly grateful I am for your wonderful message to Congress. Your little typewriter must have been inspired. I see all sorts of people and there is only one sentiment—that of warm appreciation & admiration. Thoughtful people consider it the greatest of all your state' papers & feel that it will have a great effect in clearing the atmosphere & ought to bring a righteous peace nearer than perhaps we dare hope.

Harry Fine was in my office yesterday & we had a little love feast, celebrating you & all you are doing. He said that he doesn't see much of Dean West & is not sure what he thinks of the message

May God bless you & all your's is the earnest prayer of
                Your devoted friend   Cleveland H Dodge

Don't bother to answer this

ALS (WP, DLC).

From Newton Diehl Baker

Dear Mr. President: Washington. December 9, 1917.

I have your note of the 7th inclosing a letter from Mrs. Cuyler with regard to the exemption of school teachers from the draft until the end of this scholastic year.

The first draft is now substantially completed; the second, which will take place under the new classification, will probably bear even less heavily upon the teachers' class than the first. I have no data as yet at hand to show how many teachers have actually been drawn into the military service, but it must have been a very small number. Indeed, it is likely that the first disturbances in this field have been from the volunteering of young teachers, which is a thing we had no right to discourage and could not have prevented. So far as primary schools are concerned, they are so largely in the hands of women that the total number of men withdrawn from them must have been exceedingly small.

I have made arrangements which keep medical students and a selected number of engineering and technical students in schools; beyond that it has not seemed possible to go in academic exemptions. I will, however, examine the matter in the light of the new classification and also upon the statistics of the present draft and, if the interruptions of education seems serious, will take up with General Crowder the matter of devising a remedy.

Respectfully,   Newton D. Baker

TLS (WP, DLC).

From Sir Cecil Arthur Spring Rice

Dear Mr President   Washington. 9 Dec 1917

I have been instructed to send you the inclosed in strict confidence. The sender of the telegram (Rumbold) was in charge of the British Embassy in Berlin at the time of the despatch of the Austrian ultimatum.[1]

My father in law[2] who knew the Kaiser very well thought that he probably agreed to the ultimatum to Servia, and then was sent to the North Sea to keep him out of any peace influences. On his return it was too late to retrace his steps although he certainly shrank at the last moment.

The arrangements with the Bank and Krupps, were—the withdrawal of large sums from abroad and of course the supply of the *secret* guns (the big ones). It was not necessary to inform the Foreign Office lest the diplomats should get wind of what was intended.

I was so glad to have had the great pleasure and privilege of hearing you speak last night.

I remain, with the most profound respect

Your obedient servant   Cecil Spring Rice

ALS (WP, DLC).
[1] The Editors have been unable to find this dispatch by Sir Horace George Montagu Rumbold, Chargé d'Affaires in Berlin in July 1914, or any reference to it.
[2] Sir Frank Cavendish Lascelles, British Ambassador to Germany, 1895-1908.

From Samuel Huston Thompson, Jr.

Dear Mr. President: [Washington] Dec. 9th. 1917.

I cannot help but regard your note to me as a great compliment. To think that I could have crept into your mind when you were the center of this world chaos! This certainly did please me and yet I felt quite guilty of taking any of your time when my trouble was so light compared with the rest of humanity.

This sort of kindness towards others as well as me reveals your kinship with your great predecessor, Lincoln, as much as does your patience and wisdom.

I only wish the world knew how often you have helped the other fellow to "carry on." It is my earnest desire that men will some day learn of this "sweetness and light" which you dispense so generously and yet so secretly.

While I was in bed I read a book that found a quickened response. It is called "Wilson and the World's Peace."[1]

What pleased me was that the author explained many of your actions and processes in a way that I have tried to delineate them in talks I have been making about the "why and wherefor" of the war.

Some day when peace comes, leisure is an actuality and we see "face to face" I shall hope for an opportunity to check many points with you and see whether my intuitions have been correct.

This day finds me physically as strong as ever and eager for the future, with some of my crabbed disposition forever removed, I trust, and so does Mrs. Thompson[2] though she is too kind to ever hint at it.

My brother,[3] a medical Captain in the trenches with the English Expeditionary Forces in France in a letter today says "the English regard Wilson as the great man of the war." They will some day round this sentence out by adding—and in peace.

Your sincere friend   Huston Thompson.

ALS (WP, DLC).
  [1] George D. Herron, *Woodrow Wilson and the World's Peace*, about which see WW to M. Kennerly, Oct. 1, 1917, n. 2, Vol. 44.
  [2] Caroline Cordes Thompson.
  [3] William McIlwain Thompson, Princeton 1890.

To William Cox Redfield

My dear Mr. Secretary: [The White House] 10 December, 1917

Thank you for your letter of December eighth about wages and prices. You certainly have analyzed the case very correctly indeed.
Cordially and sincerely yours,   Woodrow Wilson

TLS (Letterpress Books, WP, DLC).

To Herbert Clark Hoover

Personal.

My dear Mr. Hoover: The White House 10 December, 1917

I have noticed on one or two of the posters of the Food Administration the words, "Our Allies." I would be very much obliged if you would issue instructions that "Our Associates in the War" is to be substituted. I have been very careful about this myself because we have no allies and I think I am right in believing that the people of the country are very jealous of any intimation that there are formal alliances.

You will understand, of course, that I am implying no criticism. I am only thinking it important that we should all use the same language.

Cordially and sincerely yours,   Woodrow Wilson

TLS (H. Hoover Papers, HPL).

To George Creel

My dear Creel: The White House 10 December, 1917

I have your memorandum of the eighth about the circular using the word, "Our Allies." I have written Mr. Hoover a line about it, but don't think you need answer the letters you speak of, but if you do, just say no significance is to be attached to the words, they are merely used for short.

Faithfully yours,   Woodrow Wilson

TLS (G. Creel Papers, DLC).

To Albert Shaw

My dear Shaw: The White House 10 December, 1917

You may be sure I greatly enjoyed our talk the other day. It is a long time since we had one.

I am sincerely glad to have your views, for you may be sure they carry a great deal of weight with me, and no excuse was needed for the length of your letter. It was not too long.

I am very much interested in what you tell me about the edition of messages of the Presidents and am very much complimented by the care you are taking to make a fair representation of my own utterances. I shall look forward with a great deal of interest to seeing the volumes.

Cordially and sincerely yours,   Woodrow Wilson

TLS (A. Shaw Coll., NjP).

To Witter Bynner

My dear Mr. Bynner: [The White House] 10 December, 1917

I have no doubt that I owe it to your kindness that I received the other day a copy of your poem, "The New World."[1] May I not thank you for it very warmly and say with what pleasure I shall hope for an opportunity to turn aside from the rush of the day and read it?
Cordially and sincerely yours,   Woodrow Wilson

TLS (Letterpress Books, WP, DLC).
[1] Witter Bynner, *The New World* (New York, 1915). The copy is in the Wilson Library, DLC.

From Louis Freeland Post

My dear Mr. President: Washington December 10, 1917.

This is in reply to your question relating, as I understand it, to the desirability or not of withdrawing the recommendation which the Secretary of War as Chairman of the Council of National Defense telegraphed on the 4th inst. to the Governor of Minnesota,[1] copied below and heretofore brought to your attention.[2]

It seems to me that it might prove unwise to withdraw the recommendation of the Secretary of War's telegram unless its withdrawal were followed promptly by State action in substantial harmony with it. My present judgment, influenced by subsequent events and information, confirms my original opinion that the Secretary of War's telegram suggested a simple and dignified as well as friendly and effective solution of the controversy.

The Department of Labor had offered its friendly services in aid of Conciliation. It had advised arbitration. The employees had accepted its advice. The Street Railway Company had taken the ground that they were no longer a party to the controversy, but were merely executing orders of the Public Safety Commission of the State, to which they therefore referred the Department of Labor. The De-

[1] That is, Joseph Alfred Arner Burnquist.
[2] The issue of recognition by the Twin City Rapid Transit Company of a union sponsored by the American Federation of Labor had been the subject of much agitation in Minneapolis and St. Paul since the late summer of 1917. A conspicuous form of this agitation was a so-called button war (a competitive display of insignia) between members of a company-sponsored union and the carmen affiliated with the A.F.L. local. On November 19, the Minnesota Commission of Public Safety, which had been granted sweeping powers by the legislature to protect life and property for the duration of the war, ordered the discontinuance of the use of buttons or other insignia. It also banned all solicitation for all unions on company property and instructed the transit company to discipline violators of the orders. Trade unionists throughout Minnesota rallied behind the embattled A.F.L. local: there were demonstrations, mass protest meetings, and discussion of a general sympathy strike. This was the setting for the events described by Post below. See Carl H. Chrislock, *The Progressive Era in Minnesota, 1899-1918* (St. Paul, Minn., 1971), pp. 131-32, 157-60.

partment of Labor had thereupon placed its conciliation service at the disposal of the Public Safety Commission. The Chairman of said Commission (the Governor of the State) had replied with assurances that Federal interference at this time would "result in an attempt to defy a duly constituted authority of Minnesota," that he would use every power at his command "to uphold the dignity of the State and to protect the rights of all concerned," and that if the time were to arrive when Federal assistance were needed to maintain the laws of Minnesota he would call for it. The Department of Labor had acknowledged this reply with its assurances that there neither had been nor was any intention on its part of embarrassing the Public Safety Commission of Minnesota. It had accompanied this with a statement of a possibility that the dispute might spread injuriously to national interests beyond Minnesota. It had also referred the Governor to the Department's Commissioner of Conciliation at St. Paul[3] if he (the Governor) should think the Department of Labor might "be helpful at any turn in the situation." Since this communication the Department of Labor and its Commissioner of Conciliation have taken no active part in the controversy, except to be represented upon request at the conference in the office of the Secretary of War which resulted in the telegram referred to above as having been sent by the Secretary of War to the Governor of Minnesota.

This conference, held December 4, was attended by Representative Van Dyke,[4] of the St. Paul district, and Mr. Ames,[5] one of the members of the Minnesota Public Safety Commission. Representative Van Dyke explained the dangers of the situation: that the controversy was no longer a local street railway strike; that it involved a question of labor union rights of wide recognition which would probably soon develop a Federal problem of serious character; and that a meeting of local members of various organized trades was to be held on the following morning at St. Paul to determine upon the advisability of a general strike on the ground that important labor union prerogatives were being thrust aside by the Public Safety Commission. Apparently impressed by this statement, and also influenced by the fact, which he stated, that the Commission's action to which the labor unions especially objected was the result of an innocent misunderstanding, Mr. Ames suggested an adjustment which the Secretary of War thereupon phrased for a telegram to the Governor, and to which all the conferees, includ-

3 Robert S. Coleman.

4 Carl Chester Van Dyke, Democratic congressman from St. Paul.

5 Charles Wilberforce Ames, president and general manager of the West Publishing Co. of St. Paul, publishers of law books.

ing Mr. Ames, agreed. For convenience of reference I quote the telegram:

"The Department of Labor and the Council of National Defense have been considering with Mr. Ames of the Public Safety Commission and Representative Van Dyke the situation existing in Minneapolis and St. Paul with regard to the orders made by the Public Safety Commission of Minnesota in the matter of the street railway controversy. Grave national interests are involved in the present situation and we concur in believing that this controversy ought not to be allowed to create the serious situation which would exist if widespread sympathetic resistance to these orders occurs. Recognizing the fact that the Governor of Minnesota is primarily authorized to deal with this situation, we nevertheless join in earnestly recommending that you request the Public Safety Commission to suspend the further execution of its order and that the street railway company restore the status quo existing at the time the order was made so far as it affects employees not now at work by reason of the enforcement of the order by the company; that you further request the Public Safety Commission to announce at once that it will reopen the entire question and will invite proper representatives of the Federal Government to be selected by the Department of Labor in Washington with the Council of National Defense to advise and consult with the Public Safety Commission in a comprehensive effort to adjust all grievances and restore a situation satisfactory to all concerned."

It was supposed by all that Secretary Baker's above recommendation would be accepted by the Governor. I and my associate (Mr. Kerwin), at any rate, were confident that thereupon the whole controversy would be adjusted in a spirit of good will which would favorably affect industrial relationships throughout the country. We were, therefore, surprised and deeply concerned when upon the following day the Department of Labor received the following message from its Commissioner of Conciliation at St. Paul:

"Failure of authorities here to accept suggestion of Secretary Baker results in very grave and tense situation. Some guard companies from throughout the State have been called here and are arriving. I fear possible bloodshed with consequent wider differences. Over all looms danger of sympathetic strike. Any action to be taken should be immediate."

Subsequent information has disclosed the fact that the anticipated meeting was held in St. Paul, that the attendance was enormous, that thousands had quit their work in important industries, resolved to abandon it indefinitely if so decided by the meeting, and that the issue was the supposed attack by the Public Safety Commission upon a general trade-union custom. At the solicitation, however, of Representative Van Dyke, an adjournment was taken by this meeting until December 11, in order to afford opportunity for amicable adjustment.

If at this adjourned meeting, to be held tomorrow, it were to appear that the Federal Government has stepped aside and left the controversy to be settled locally, by the forcible methods indicated by the Governor's telegram to the Department of Labor, the Federal government might be obliged to interfere with an armed force after blood had been spilled and bitterness intensified.

Even if that necessity did not arise, it is certain that the labor situation throughout the country would not be improved, and highly probable that it would be greatly prejudiced, if the present pacific overtures of the Federal government were withdrawn and no other basis for a friendly settlement were substituted.

You should be advised, however, that some of the influences among the employees in this controversy may be of a questionable character. The Department has advices from trustworthy sources to the effect that I.W.W., pro-German and obstructive-pacifist influences are active. They may even have prompted the dispute, although that is only a bare possibility. They seem at any rate to have promoted it. But to the extent that any of this is so, I have good reason for believing that it is only incidental. There appears to me to be a very real labor dispute, likely to generate and intensify industrial bitterness among working man [men] who are not unpatriotic but are acting in good faith. In my judgment it cannot be settled by sheer force, such as to labor interests both within and without the State, the State authorities will probably appear to have unnecessarily invited if force should be used.[6] And yet it is a dispute which can in all probability be easily and harmoniously adjusted along the lines of the Secretary of War's letter to the Governor.

If I might venture a suggestion, I would advise (1) that either directly or through the Secretary of War or the Secretary of Labor you secure in some appropriate way the advice of ex Gov. John Lind, who is the member of the Public Safety Commission of Minnesota whom the Governor has publicly declared to have been designated to deal with labor subjects; (2) that prior to December 11, 1917, (tomorrow), steps be taken to allow the adjourned labor meeting to be informed that a friendly adjustment is desirable for national reasons, to the end that the meeting may be inclined to take a further adjournment in expectation of a friendly settlement meanwhile; (3) that some means be devised whereby the Public Safety

[6] This sentence *sic*.

Commission of Minnesota may act in substantial accordance with the recommendation of the Secretary of War but in freedom from any appearance of doing so under Federal coercion.

With great respect,

Faithfully and sincerely yours,   Louis F. Post

P.S. Since dictating the above, our Commissioner of Conciliation at St. Paul, pursuant to Departmental instructions of the 8th, has arrived in Washington. He has a thorough understanding of the situation and is a man of good judgment. It is our purpose to detain him here for the present. Meanwhile any other department of the government may have the benefit of his information, advice or other service if this should seem desirable to you.

TLS (WP, DLC).

From Charles Lee Swem

Mr. President: The White House [Dec. 10, 1917].

In connection with one of Mr. Post's suggestions,—Mr. John Lind is now in Washington, at the Powhatan.   C. L. Swem

ALS (WP, DLC).

To Joseph Patrick Tumulty

Dear Tumulty   [The White House, Dec. 10, 1917]

Please get Gov. Lind and Mr. Kerwin (separately or together) into immediate conference with the Sec'y of War.   W.W.

ALI (WP, DLC).

A Translation of a Telegram from Victor Emmanuel III

Rome (Received December 10, 1917. 3:30 pm.

By declaring war on Austria Hungary, the United States of America has fulfilled its position on the world war, that is, to secure the triumph of Right. The Italian nation launched in the struggle in the name of a supreme ideal of Justice and for the achievement of her legitimate aspirations. She was ever confident of the full adhesion and unconditional support of the United States. The brotherhood of arms strengthens, so that shall never be loosened the bonds already so strong that united our nations. The people, army and navy of Italy join me in sending their fervent and hopeful applause to you, Mr. President, who so worthily represent and so wisely guide in these troublous time[s] the noble and generous nation of North America.   Vittorio Emanuele

Hw MS (WP, DLC).

From Robert Lansing

My dear Mr. President: Washington December 10, 1917.

I have been considering the Russian situation and, although our information is meager and to an extent confusing, I have reached the following conclusions:

That the Bolsheviki are determined to prevent Russia from taking further part in the war.

That the longer they continue in power the more will authority in Russia be disorganized and the more will the armies disintegrate, and the harder it will become to restore order and military efficiency.

That the elimination of Russia as a fighting force will prolong the war for two or three years, with a corresponding demand upon this country for men and money.

That with Bolsheviki domination broken the Russian armies might be reorganized and become an important factor in the war by next spring or summer.

That the hope of a stable Russian Government lies for the present in a military dictatorship backed by loyal disciplined troops.

That the only apparent nucleus for an organized movement sufficiently strong to supplant the Bolsheviki and establish a government would seem to be the group of general officers with General Kaledin, the hetman of the Don Cossacks.

These conclusions present the problem as to whether we ought to take any steps to encourage the Kaledin party, and if so the nature of those steps.

I think that we must assume that Kaledin and his Cossacks know less about us and our attitude than we know about them, that through Bolshevik and German sources they are being furnished with false information and very probably have been told that we have recognized the Bolshevik Government and so are coming to the conclusion that further resistance is useless. Of course to have this group broken up would be to throw the country into the hands of the Bolsheviki and the Germans could freely continue their propaganda which is leading to chaos and the actual disintegration of the Russian Empire.

A possible way of checking this is to get a message through to Kaledin (probably via Tiflis and courier) telling the true state of affairs, and non-recognition of the Bolsheviki and our readiness to give recognition to a government which exhibits strength enough to restore order and a purpose to carry out in good faith Russia's international engagements.

Whether such a communication is advisable is, I think, worthy of consideration, but if it is to be sent it ought to be done without delay as I am convinced that German intrigues and Bolshevik false representations will speedily impair the morale of Kaledin's followers unless something is done to give them hope that they will, if their movement gains sufficient strength, receive moral and material aid from this Government. It seems to me that nothing is to be gained by inaction, that it is simply playing into the Bolsheviki's hands, and that the situation may be saved by a few words of encouragement and the saving of Russia means the saving to this country of hundreds of thousands of men and billions of dollars. I do not see how we could be any worse off if we took this course because we have absolutely nothing to hope from continued Bolshevik domination.

In regard to Kaledin and the Russian generals, Alexieff, Brousiloff and Korniloff, who appear to be with him or about to join him, I have inquired of Major Washburne, who knew them personally and more or less intimately. From him I gained the following:

Kaledin is a man of ponderous determination, who is unaffected alike by victory or defeat. He is a strong character who carried through his purposes regardless of opposition. As a commander he resembles Grant. He radiates force and mastery.

Alexieff is a modest, quiet man, but the most skillful strategist in Russia, if not in any of the allied countries. He listens patiently, talks little and reaches his decisions alone.

Brousiloff is the most brilliant general in the Russian armies and arouses the enthusiasm of the soldiers and his subordinates by his ability and forceful personality. As a strategist he is only second to Alexieff. While Kaledin is a man of the people, Brousiloff is of the aristocracy.

Korniloff is not equal to any one of the three other generals in military skill or in personal popularity with the troops. He has, however, considerable influence with soldiers recruited in Siberia and Turkestan.

The foregoing indicates the elements of strength in the military group which seem to be gathering about Kaledin, and which will in all probability obtain the support of the Cadets[1] and of all the bourgeoisie and the landowning class.

I would like to talk this matter over with you after Cabinet meeting tomorrow if that meets your convenience.

Faithfully yours,   Robert Lansing

TLS (WP, DLC).
[1] That is, members of the Constitutional Democratic party.

From Newton Diehl Baker

Dear Mr. President: Washington. December 10, 1917.

I return herewith the letter sent you by Mr. R. G. Rhett, President of the Chamber of Commerce of the United States.[1] To it you will find attached a letter from Mr. Daniel Willard to me,[2] and I have also taken the liberty of adding the letter for you to write Mr. Rhett if it meets with your approval.

I think it will not be necessary for you to read Mr. Willard's letter if you glance over the one I have prepared for your signature addressed to Mr. Rhett.[3]   Respectfully,   Newton D. Baker

TLS (WP, DLC).
[1] R. G. Rhett to WW, Nov. 15, 1917.
[2] D. Willard to NDB, Dec. 7, 1917, TLS (WP, DLC).
[3] Wilson sent Baker's draft as WW to R. G. Rhett, Dec. 12, 1917.

From George Weston Anderson[1]

Dear Mr. President: Washington December 10th, 1917.

Saturday night I left New England in a driving northeast snowstorm. New England, more than any other section, is dependent upon transportation for coal and other supplies of vital necessity. I have some special knowledge of conditions there, and naturally feel some special responsibility for that section. I therefore feel it my duty to say to you that I think the situation is one of critical danger. If we should have a month or two of mild, open weather, we may get on. If the reverse, the situation would beggar description. I am confident—I think sure—that the country has adequate transportation facilities if they could only be competently and coordinatingly used. But the problem is not being dealt with with efficiency or vision. It will not be so dealt with until the roads are treated as national roads and put under national control of a man or men having national vision. This means a radical change at the top, but no radical change in the general organization and personnel of the operating forces.

Yesterday I had a long and very satisfactory talk with Judge Sims.[2]

It is clear that the Executive may rely on full and cordial support from him.

If you have come to the question of men, means and methods, let me suggest that Director Charles A. Prouty[3] has a wider knowledge of railroad executives and a greater familiarity with governmental machinery than any other one living man. It seems to me he could render the greatest kind of service, whoever should be put in general control of the problem.

Pardon this letter, but the situation in New England and the forecasting attitude of the New Englander's mind compel me to write it.   Very respectfully yours,   George W. Anderson

TLS (WP, DLC).
  [1] Wilson had appointed him a member of the Interstate Commerce Commission on September 29.
  [2] That is, Thetus W. Sims, chairman of the House Committee on Interstate and Foreign Commerce.
  [3] Charles Azro Prouty, member of the Interstate Commerce Commission, 1896-1914; chairman, 1912-1913; Director of the Bureau of Valuation of the I.C.C. since 1914.

From Gutzon Borglum

New York, December 10, 1917.

Have just arrived from the West and find your letter. I will give it immediate and most careful attention.

Faithfully,   Gutzon Borglum.

T telegram (WP, DLC).

To William Procter Gould Harding

[The White House]
My dear Governor Harding: 11 December, 1917

May I not acknowledge the receipt of your letter of December eighth enclosing the resolutions of the Federal Reserve Board in favor of the establishment of a War Emergency Finance Corporation?[1] I have several times discussed a similar suggestion with the Secretary of the Treasury and with others who are as deeply interested as the rest of us in the proper financial arrangements for the conduct of the war, and have been awaiting the recommendation of the Secretary himself with regard to the matter. I am sure that it will soon be forthcoming, and I shall be very glad indeed to give the whole matter my most careful consideration.

Cordially and sincerely yours,   Woodrow Wilson

TLS (Letterpress Books, WP, DLC).

¹ W. P. G. Harding to WGM, Dec. 8, 1917, TLS, enclosing resolutions, TS MS, both in WP, DLC. The significant resolution reads as follows: "That the Federal Reserve Board recommends the organization of a corporation with adequate capital, to be known as The War Emergency Finance Corporation, to be owned entirely by the Government of the United States and managed by a board of directors appointed by the President, composed principally of representatives of various departments and of government boards; this corporation to make loans on approved security to savings banks and industrial enterprises entitled to such accommodation, so far as such relief cannot be obtained through existing financial channels."

McAdoo enclosed the resolutions and their covering letter in WGM to WW, Dec. 10, 1917, TLS (WP, DLC). He urged Wilson to defer a decision in the matter until he had settled upon a policy for the operation of the railroads during the war. He noted that a corporation such as the one proposed by the Federal Reserve Board might require as much as $500,000,000 from the United States Treasury. He suggested the form of reply to Harding's communication which Wilson followed in the above letter.

To George Weston Anderson

My dear Mr. Anderson: [The White House] 11 December, 1917

Thank you for your letter of December tenth. I realize very keenly the gravity of the situation and am now trying to work out a somewhat radical solution. Your suggestions were most welcome.

Cordially and sincerely yours,   Woodrow Wilson

TLS (Letterpress Books, WP, DLC).

To Sir Cecil Arthur Spring Rice

The White House.

My dear Mr. Ambassador,   11 December, 1917.

Thank you very much for your kindness in sending me the confidential memorandum which accompanied your note of Sunday, which Miss Benham has handed me. It has interested me very much. It is quite in line with all other authentic accounts of the actual way in which this wretched war was started.

I warmly appreciate your kind reference to my little speech on Saturday evening. May I not say how much I was gratified by your exceedingly generous reference to me in the very interesting and suggestive speech with which, I am sure, you delighted the whole company?   Cordially and sincerely Yrs.   Woodrow Wilson

WWTLS (FO 115/2348, p. 224, PRO).

To Victor Emmanuel III

[The White House, Dec. 11, 1917]

The gracious and friendly message which Your Majesty was kind enough to send me on December tenth has given me genuine gratification. I am sure that I speak for the people of the United States when I say that it has given us deep satisfaction to unite with the people of Italy in fighting for the great cause which is the heart of the present war, and that I also speak for them in expressing the most sincere admiration of the spirit and valor with which the people of Italy are sustaining this great struggle for liberty and justice and humanity. The great sacrifices the friends of liberty are now making will bring their perfect fruitage of peace and security and friendship among the nations in the years to come and every man who lays down his life in this war will be entitled to participate in the lasting glory of the ultimate triumph.

Woodrow Wilson.

T telegram (Letterpress Books, WP, DLC).

From Newton Diehl Baker

Dear Mr. President: Washington. December 11, 1917.

I have your note[1] returning to me the confidential copy of General Bliss' telegram of December 4th. You ask "is such a program possible"; it can only be made possible by sacrificing other things, which up to now we have believed to be of equal, if not of greater, importance.

As General Bliss will be home now in a few days, perhaps the relative importance of these things can be determined and a conclusion reached as to just where our strength can best be exerted.

Respectfully yours,   Newton D. Baker

TLS (WP, DLC).
[1] WW to NDB, Dec. 5, 1917.

To Thomas Watt Gregory

[The White House] December 11th, 1917.

To the Attorney General of the United States:

You are hereby charged with the duty of execution of the proclamation issued by me, dated December 11th, 1917,[1] and of the regulations therein contained regarding the conduct of natives, citizens, denizens or subjects of Austria-Hungary, being males of the age of fourteen years and upwards, who shall be in the United States and not actually naturalized, and you are specifically directed to cause the arrest of any of such persons as in your opinion is subject to arrest or deportation or removal or restraint under said regulations, and to issue or cause to be issued such permits or licenses as are therein provided for and to take any other action prescribed or authorized therein. Woodrow Wilson

TLS (Letterpress Books, WP, DLC).
[1] This proclamation, in accordance with the joint resolution of Congress of December 7, declared that a state of war existed between the United States and Austria-Hungary. As was customary in such declarations, it enjoined "all natives, citizens, denizens, or subjects of Austria-Hungary, being males of 14 years and upwards, who shall be within the United States and not actually naturalized" to preserve peace toward the United States, to refrain from crime against the public safety and from violating the laws of the United States and of the states and territories thereof, and also to refrain from "actual hostility or giving information, aid, or comfort to the enemies of the United States." All such persons who complied with these injunctions were to be left undisturbed in their lives and occupations. Those who failed to comply would be subject to the penalties provided by law. In addition, the proclamation declared that no such person as described above could leave or enter the United States except as the President prescribed and that any such person of whom there was reasonable cause to believe that he was aiding or about to aid the enemy, was violating or about to violate any presidential regulation or criminal law, or was dangerous to be at large, was subject to summary arrest by federal officials and to such confinement as might be directed by the President. *Official Bulletin*, I (Dec. 13, 1917), 1, 7.

From Samuel Gompers

Sir: Washington, D. C. Dec. 11, 1917.

I am in receipt of authentic information that a most serious and far reaching suspension of coal mining operations is imminent in the State of Alabama. Some two weeks ago Dr. H. A. Garfield, of the United States Fuel Administration, invited representatives of the United Mine Workers and the Alabama Coal Operators to Washington for conference, and urged that all differences be submitted to arbitration with a representative of the Fuel Administration as umpire. To this request the Mine Workers agreed unqualifiedly. The operators asked time to return home for consultation with their associates which was granted and Dr. Garfield fixed Thursday, December 6 as the date for both parties to again meet in Washington.

The Miners' delegation were present on that date and are still waiting, but the Operators have not yet appeared. The latest telegram from their spokesman[1] in reply to a direct telegram from Dr. Garfield sent on Saturday last to be here today, advises he is to be in this city on December 12 on other business and may be consulted at that time.

The Miners of Alabama, feeling further delay intolerable, are on the verge of inaugurating an immediate suspension of mining, thereby curtailing a daily production of 175,000 tons of coal and are already vested with full authority to do so by the International Executive Board of the United Mine Workers of America.

It seemed to me to be my duty to call this critical situation to your attention for such consideration and action which you may deem most wise in the premises. Mr. McCormack, President of the Alabama Mine Operators' Association, is to be in Washington tomorrow, December 12, and Dr. Garfield will be in communication with him.   Very respectfully yours,   Saml. Gompers.

TLS (WP, DLC).
¹ George Bryant McCormack of Birmingham, Ala., president of the Pratt Consolidated Coal Co. and the Birmingham Terminal Co.

From Grenville Stanley Macfarland

Personal

My dear President Wilson: Boston December Eleventh 1917.

Thank you very much for the appointment which you have given me out of your crowded moments.¹

I thank you also for the appreciation which you expressed of the editorial on your recent message to Congress.² The basis of the editorial was an enthusiastic communication from Mr. Hearst to me while in Washington. Indeed the editorial was not as enthusiastic as Mr. Hearst's message, probably because I have not his enthusiastic temperament.

It seems to me unfortunate that men in a position like that of Senator Lodge of Massachusetts should take public occasions to interpret our policy as one of extinction of the German people. These extremists very largely nullify the good effect of your attitude. It makes the German-Americans suspicious of the sincerity of our expressed purposes and, of course, it gives an opportunity for the German government to make the German people themselves suspicious.

I talked yesterday with one of the most intellectual and pestiferous of the German propagandists in this country, one with whom you personally discussed the situation last year.³ He has been a social aquaintance of mine for a long time, being originally a fellow townsman. He told me that he was convinced that if the German people felt that you were sincere and that your message expressed our whole program, the war would be over in six months, or just as soon as the German people could liberalize their government. Thus you can see how men like Lodge and James M. Beck and all that crowd, who not only opposed you for re-election, but opposed you with some of the vilest methods, are deliberately trying to "gum the cards."

I was greatly delighted to see a statement in the morning dispatches that you are probably contemplating taking over the operation of our railroads. Not even the Declaration of Independence nor the Emancipation Proclamation would equal for liberty and democracy your act in taking the operation of these railroads out of private hands, for economic independence, economic liberty, are more fundamental than political and social independence and liberty, because you can have the forms of political and social independence and liberty without the substance, but you cannot have economic independence and liberty permanently without having the substance of political and social independence and democracy.

I have almost a superstition that you will now or soon take the great step, for in my day dreams ever since I was a boy at Harvard,[4] I have imagined the President of the United States freeing the people from the menacing chicanery of the railroads as a great act of war like Lincoln's emancipation of slavery. If as an act of war we take the railroads, I believe it will be the first time in all history that a nation waging an extra-territorial conflict ever helped to make democracy more secure at home.

Yours sincerely,   G. S. Macfarland.

TLS (WP, DLC).
[1] Wilson saw Macfarland at the White House on December 13.
[2] "President Wilson's Epoch Making Message Comes as a Reply to Lord Lansdowne's Demand to Restate War Aims," *New York American*, Dec. 6, 1917. This editorial declared that Wilson's message to Congress was "probably . . . his best in form and substance." "It breathes the spirit of Lincoln's second inaugural," Macfarland wrote, "and will take its place beside that great document." Most of the editorial simply summarized the main points of Wilson's speech and stressed the argument that the German people were not to blame for the war and could have a just peace whenever they established a new government with which the United States could negotiate. Peace with the United States meant peace with the world, for the Allies would be unable to continue the war if the United States withdrew from it as the result of a satisfactory peace settlement with Germany.
[3] Probably William Bayard Hale.
[4] He was a member of the Class of 1900.

From the Diary of Josephus Daniels

1917 Tuesday 11 December

Cabinet

WW. Hate to do nothing about Russia but puzzled to know how to take hold. Lane Perhaps Constituancy [Constituent] Assembly may point the way. No, neither party will have majority. Lansing: The Bolsheviks permit soldiers to vote wherever they are & charge them so they will have a majority for their party—Civil war possible. Everything now too chaotic to make any move.

Gregory presented proclamation as to Austrians, not along line of Germans, calling them denizens & not alien enemies Sentiment not to regard Bohemians & others who came to this country to escape Austrian rule as alien enemies.

Burleson wanted us to call 5 million men at once. Baker & WW: Could not transport them & it would make it impossible to feed & equip our allies.

Redfield urged construction of concrete ships Said Norway had built them. I thought still experimental. Hurley was watching experiment. Red: We are not using sailing ships. The President said he had talked it over with shipping board not once but several times.

Decided to ask Congress to make $1,200 the lowest pay for stenographers.

A Memorandum of an Interview with William Howard Taft[1]

[Dec. 12, 1917]

Mr. Taft described to the President Dr. Buttrick's recent visit to Great Britain at the instance of the American Ambassador, and with the approval of the British Government. He further outlined the plan presented to him by Dr. Buttrick by which American speakers were to be invited by the British Government to visit Great Britain, spend a few days in getting an idea of what the nation is doing under war conditions, and then by talking with individuals and groups and by making public addresses, to give the public of Great Britain a clearer and truer conception of the institutions and ideals of the American people.

On the return of these Americans to the United States, it was hoped that they would be a means of giving their fellow-countrymen a more accurate idea of the British people, their part in the war, and their loyalty to the causes for which the Allies are fighting. It was made clear that the general purpose was to promote mutual understanding and good will and thus to draw the two nations into closer relations of sympathy and cooperation.

Mr. Taft further stated that he had received through Dr. Buttrick, from the British Government, an invitation to be a member of one of the groups which it was planned to send, from time to time, unostentatiously to Great Britain. He pointed out that the general aim had seemed to him desirable and that he had expressed his willingness, at some financial sacrifice, to accept the invitation, provided that an official invitation were received from the British Government and provided that he might submit the matter to the President, not to secure from the President authority to go in any representative capacity but only to be assured that his going would not seem to the President unwise for any reason.

After listening to Mr. Taft's statement, the President expressed a judgment adverse to Mr. Taft's going and to the plan in general. He based his objections upon the following grounds:

1. He questioned the desirability of drawing the two countries too closely together. He said that there were divergencies of purpose and that the United States must not be put in a position of seeming, in any way, involved in British policy. He cited the treaty between Great Britain and Italy as one example of British governmental policy to be heartily disapproved. He intimated that the motives of the United States were unselfish while those of the British Empire, as disclosed in this treaty, seemed of a less worthy character. In connection with the idea of a closer understanding between the two countries, the President said that there were too many Englishmen in this country and in Washington *in the interests of Great Britain*, and that he had asked Col. House to say to the British leaders informally that it would be desirable to have many of them return to their homes.

2. He added that the American people knew already what England was doing in this war and that it was not necessary to take this step to advise them.

3. The President pointed out that there were centers in the United States heartily opposed to England and that such conspicuous attempts to draw the countries more closely together would arouse antagonism and resentment.

4. He also made the point that Mr. Taft's prestige as a visitor to Great Britain would further arouse the jealousy of France and the other Allies which the United States Government was already finding embarrassing. He stated that the larger loans to Great Britain, rendered necessary by the situation, were criticized by the French Government.

When Mr. Taft suggested that the plan had originated with the American Ambassador to Great Britain whose letters to Dr. Buttrick and others, urging this action, Mr. Taft had had an opportunity to read, the President replied: "Page is really an Englishman, and I have to discount whatever he says about the situation in Great Britain."

When Mr. Taft summed up the situation by saying that he understood the President to oppose the idea, the President reiterated his statement as follows: "I think you ought not to go and the same applies to the other members of the party. I would like you to make my attitude on this question known to those having it in charge here."

T MS (R. A. Taft Papers, DLC).
[1] At the White House at 4:30 P.M. on Dec. 12. This document was drafted after a conversation with Taft on December 13 by George Edgar Vincent, former President of

the University of Minnesota and (since May 15, 1917) President of the Rockefeller Foundation. According to a typed note on the document, Taft authenticated the memorandum on December 13, 1917.

To Robert Lansing, with Enclosures

My dear Mr. Secretary The White House. 12 Dec., 1917
This has my entire approval. Woodrow Wilson

ALS (SDR, RG 59, 861.00/804D, DNA).

E N C L O S U R E I

From Robert Lansing

My dear Mr. President: Washington December 12, 1917.

After consultation with Secretary McAdoo today, and in line with our talk last evening, I have prepared the enclosed telegram which Secretary McAdoo approves.

If it meets with your approval will you be good enough to send it to the telegraph office of the Department so that it can immediately be put upon the wires?

Faithfully yours, Robert Lansing.

TLS (SDR, RG 59, 861.00/804D, DNA).

E N C L O S U R E I I

NOT FOR DISTRIBUTION December 12, 1917.
Amembassy LONDON.
Confidential

For CROSBY. The Russian situation has been carefully considered and the conclusion has been reached that the movement in the south and southeast under the leadership of Kaledine and Korniloff offers at the present time the greatest hope for the reestablishment of a stable government and the continuance of a military force on the German and Austrian fronts. While there can be no certainty of the success of Kaledine it is not improbable that he may succeed. From Moscow and Tiflis come very favorable reports as to the strength of the movement and as to the weakening power of the Bolsheviki.

Paragraph. In view of the policy being pursued by Lenine and Trotsky which if continued will remove Russia as a factor in the war and may even make her resources available to the Central Powers, any movement tending to prevent such a calamity should be encouraged even though its success is only a possibility.

Paragraph. It would seem unwise for this Government to support openly Kaledine and his party because of the attitude which it seems advisable to take with the Petrograd authorities, but it is felt that the Kaledine group should be shown that the Allied Governments are most sympathetic with his efforts. Without actually recognizing his group as a *de facto* government, which is at present impossible since it has not taken form, this Government cannot under the law loan money to him to carry forward his movement. The only practicable course seems to be for the British and French Governments to finance the Kaledine enterprise in so far as it is necessary, and for this Government to loan them the money to do so. In that way we would comply with the statute and at the same time strengthen a movement which seems to present the best possibility of retaining a Russian army in the field.

Paragraph. You will, after conferring with the Ambassador, take this matter up with the proper British and French authorities having charge of financial matters and report as soon as possible their views and whether or not they are willing to adopt the course above outlined and if so, to what extent financial aid will be required.

Paragraph. In view of the fact that this matter relates to credits to foreign governments and at the suggestion of Secretary McAdoo, who approves of the policy, I am addressing this telegram to you directly assuming that you will before taking the matter up with representatives of Great Britain and France confer with the Ambassador as to the politic course to pursue.

Paragraph. I need not impress upon you the necessity of acting expeditiously and with impressing those with whom you talk of the importance of avoiding it being known that the United States is considering showing sympathy for the Kaledin movement, much less of providing financial assistance.[1]

CC telegram (SDR, RG 59, 861.00/804D, DNA).
[1] This was sent as RL to WHP, Dec. 13, 1917, T telegram (SDR, RG 59, 763.72/8200a, DNA).

To Joseph Patrick Tumulty

Dear Tumulty: [The White House, c. Dec. 12, 1917]

I really have not time to see these gentlemen before Monday and I should like very much to keep out of the prohibition mix-up.[1] Will you not express my regret at being tied up by engagements?

The President.

TL (WP, DLC).
[1] Guy Edgar Campbell, a Democratic congressman from Pennsylvania, had requested a brief appointment with Wilson for a nonpartisan committee composed of himself and six other congressmen to discuss "the advisability of action at this session of Congress regarding national prohibition." [JPT] to WW, Dec. 12, 1917, TL (WP, DLC).

To Samuel Gompers

My dear Mr. Gompers: The White House 12 December, 1917

I am very much obliged to you for calling my attention to the mining situation in Alabama. I have been in communication with Doctor Garfield and am putting myself at his disposal to help in any way that is possible.

In great haste
Cordially and sincerely yours,   Woodrow Wilson

TLS (S. Gompers Corr., AFL-CIO-Ar).

To Robert Goodwyn Rhett

My dear Mr. Rhett: [The White House] December 12, 1917.

In November you were good enough to present to me a copy of the conclusions and recommendations of the Board of Directors of the Chamber of Commerce of the United States upon the then existing arrangements of the War Industries Board and the coordination of purchasing for the Army and Navy.[1] As I was at the time considering the addition of Mr. Daniel Willard to the War Industries Board and desired to have any change in these arrangements worked out under his direction, I have delayed more than a formal acknowledgment of your letter until now.

Mr. Willard informs me that he has had conferences with the members of your Board and discussed the conclusions and recommendations which you presented to me, developing some difference of opinion as to the wisdom of an immediate substitution of the different agencies for those already existing, but in the main Mr. Willard tells me that he has been greatly helped by the views you have expressed and is being constantly aided by the generous work which the Board of Directors is carrying on for his benefit. From it all I gather that Mr. Willard and the War Industries Board are progressing toward a much more satisfactory situation than at first existed and that the judgment and knowledge of the Board of Directors and the Chamber of Commerce is being consulted to enable him and his associates to reach a sound and effective system. I am, of course, happy to know that this helpful relation between Mr. Willard and the Chamber exists, and beg you to thank your associates for their cooperation with him in the matter.

Cordially yours,   Woodrow Wilson

TLS (Letterpress Books, WP, DLC).
[1] R. G. Rhett to WW, Nov. 15, 1917.

Reviewing the troops at Fort Myer, Virginia

Leon Trotsky

V. I. Lenin

Aboard the U.S.S. Mayflower. From left to right: Secretary Daniels, Ambassador Satō, Viscount Ishii, Secretary Lansing

From Elizabeth Merrill Bass

Washington, D. C.
December 12th, 1917.

My dear Mr. President:

The latest development in the suffrage situation, as you may know, is that the Judiciary Committee, not waiting for the organization of the new suffrage committee has reported suffrage out on to the floor of the House without recommendation. We may not be able to delay a vote until after the holidays, but we shall try. Floor Leader Kitchen and Mr. Webb, who have not in the least the interests of your administration or the Democratic party at heart, are in spite of remonstrances from all of the Democratic Congressmen of the suffrage states, taking this adverse action and striking this blow at the women.

On Friday evening I am to deliver an address to the convention of the National American Woman Suffrage Association at Poli's Theatre on every phase of the war work. I am to be presented as speaker for the Liberty Loan Committee by our Chairman, your daughter.[1] I am not asked to make a suffrage talk and shall only refer to suffrage in general terms, unless you should wish to make me your mouthpiece to add another phrase to your Atlantic City speech.[2] The suffragists of the country enthroned you in their hearts when you said "I fight with you and in the long run we shall not differ as to methods."

We are in danger of being defeated in the House on an early, forced vote, and you may desire to give the Convention assembled here this week another sentence of encouragement. I am enclosing a list of eleven senators who will vote "No" without doubt.[3] They may be among those with whom your influence would be paramount.   Faithfully yours,   Elizabeth Bass

TLS (WP, DLC).
[1] Eleanor Wilson McAdoo.
[2] See the address printed at Sept. 8, 1916, Vol. 38.
[3] This enclosure is missing.

From Joseph Patrick Tumulty, with Enclosure

The White House
December 12, 1917.

Memorandum for the President:

Mrs. Gard[e]ner of the Woman's Suffrage Society called this afternoon and left the attached polls. She stated that the poll of the Republicans in the Senate showed—

                    29 sure
                    2 probable

         2 possible
        10 against;
and that the Democratic poll in the Senate showed—
        23 sure
        3 possible
        26 against.

Mrs. Gardner stated that the following were listed as uncertain and that a word from the President would probably cause them to vote favorably: Senator James

                King
                Phelan
                Simmons
                Martin
                Swanson
                Fletcher
                Trammel[l]
                Overman
                Walcott.[1]

Mrs. Gardner stated that the friends in the Senate thought it would be well if the vote could be taken next week—before the vote in the House—as they felt that a large majority in the Senate might influence the House vote. As the poll now stands it would appear almost like a Republican victory, and, for this reason, Mrs. Gardner expressed the hope that the President could persuade at least eight of the ten Senators named above to vote favorably.

[1] Josiah Oliver Wolcott, Democrat of Delaware.

ENCLOSURE

Yeas	Nays
Ashurst	Bankhead
Chamberlain	Beckham
Gore	Broussard
Hollis	Culberson
Hughes	Fletcher
Johnson, S. Dakota	Gerry
Jones, N. Mexico	Hardwick
Kendrick	Hitchcock
Kirby	James
Lewis	King
Myers	McKellar ?
Newlands	Martin
Owen	Overman

Pittman

Ransdell

Robinson

Shafroth

Sheppard

Smith, Ariz.

Stone ?

Thomas

Thompson

Vardaman

Walsh

Phelan ?

Pomerene

Reed

Saulsbury

Shields

Simmons

Smith, Georgia

Smith, Maryland

Smith, South Carolina

Swanson

Tillman

Trammel ?

Underwood

Williams

Wolcott[1]

T MSS (WP, DLC).

[1] All senators listed in this enclosure were Democrats. Those not previously identified were Joseph Eugene Ransdell of Louisiana, John Crepps Wickliffe Beckham of Kentucky, and Peter Goelet Gerry of Rhode Island.

From Newton Diehl Baker

Information only

Dear Mr. President: Washington. December 12, 1917.

Secretary Post and I had a long talk with Governor Lind about the St. Paul and Minneapolis Street Railroad situation. So far as that particular controversy is concerned, I am satisfied that the Governor of Minnesota and Governor Lind are write [right] in believing that the Federal government has no right to intervene and could serve no useful purpose by attempting intervention. The difficulty is not the present controversy, but the long and agitated history of obstinacy and oppression by the Street Railroad Company, which has given the Union the support of public opinion, even in unjust demands. I hope soon to be able to make a suggestion to you, at least for consideration, which will cover the St. Paul and Minneapolis situation, and also a wider field, which may help to prevent greater difficulties in the spring.

Respectfully yours,   Newton D. Baker

TLS (WP, DLC).

From Gutzon Borglum

My dear Mr. President: [New York] 12 December, 1917.

Thank you for your letter of December fifth. I was in Dayton or it would have been answered earlier.

America's production program has lowered quality and crushed initiative—a result inevitable to general standardization, and the requirements of mechanical production. I feel that at this hour of the world's crisis, when Europe has exhausted her ingenuity and has turned to us to solve the unsolved problem, this inelastic policy, regardless of efficiency is suicidal. Europe waits on our thought. She reaches for our inspired, youthful initiative—instead we fumble crudely over her mechanics, clinging blindly to our lagging development, then madly commission the immature product.

Six Hundred and Forty Millions were appropriated to accomplish in the air what the armies seemed unable, without too great sacrifice of life, to do on land, and "not a dollar was allotted or specified for investigation or experiment." Close upon the heels of this unprecedented appropriation appeared the policy "No money shall be spent or time lost, or encouragement given to any plans or projects not tried and established." Had we pled expediency and swiftly adopted the last word in aeronautics from the front, and in our haste to rescue Europe, trampled our own abilities, there would have been a larger justification. But no such plea exists, and Europe's proffered aid rebuked prevents the claim.

We have been caught squarely between the wheels of thoughtless, ill-considered production.

The present Board has shown one great merit—it gets things under way. But after we forgive its ways and means we yet sit with what it has done and question the war value of the product.

I unhesitatingly state it is so far below the standard of our competitors in Europe, that we shall meet with further disappointments if even allowed by the Boards at the front to risk or compete with our resourceful antagonist. Our Board seems utterly indifferent to the fact that aeronautics is not over twenty-five percent efficient, that planes have practically no innate stability, are unfitted for extended flight and that engine alone cannot correct these faults. The reason for this is natural, as suggested in my letter to Mr. Tumulty, the whole power of our present committee has slipped into, rather never was in other than the hands of one or two men whose interest and training is outside the knowledge of the great subject they control until finally a definite condition of mind has grown up derogatory to anything but quantity production.

If this Aeronautic Board were split and rebuilt into a creative Executive Board of Design and a separate Board of Production, leaving the Military Board, including the Army and Navy to designate precisely such flying machines as they desire, they specifying sizes, purposes and armaments, all would be simpler. This would strip the Production Board of all power not strictly confined to delivery of the article designated by the Army and Navy, designed and supervised by the Executive Board of Design. The advisory function of the aeronautic committee would disappear and become instead, creative and executive. They would design and order. This Board need not be made up of over three Americans, and should have associated with it representatives from England, France and Italy, that would place at our disposal in the most authoritative manner, the last word in aeronautics, and, in fact, establish an International Board. This suggestion I believe, would have the effect of getting round pegs into round holes, and jolting the machinery down to a close fit. This organization would be logical— not very different from at present—and at once accomplish very serious changes without surgical operation, which every constructive man dreads.

You further asked me to suggest "men of practical gifts not now connected with the Government service." There comes to mind several brilliant laymen, who have but book-knowledge of the subject, or mere theorists, without vision, who know nothing, execute less, yet discuss wisely the "slip and drift" or "whether the vacuum created maintains the plane in the air, or the force that creates the vacuum." Our way to destroy militarism is blocked mainly by these ineffectual abilities. There is, however, a Professor Galloup[1] (?) at Worcester, about whom I hear the kind of things that makes me think worthy of consideration. You are seeking a man of "practical gifts" with a fine constructive imagination, not buried beneath too much old knowledge, executive, bold yet wise and again bold. I wish I could tell you of such a man. Such a man should serve you. He might coordinate all this work without interfering, and possibly designated as an Assistant Secretary of War, he might so benefit by that authority necessary to much that he would be privy to.

There should also be created a very active subsidiary group whose whole business would be to go directly to the form and character of the great weaknesses in aeroplanes and, as far as possible, correct them.

While I may let me express to you my gratitude for the high standard of public service you have definitely inaugurated.

Very sincerely yours,   Gutzon Borglum

TLS (WP, DLC).
[1] Perhaps, Robert Hutchings Goddard, professor of physics at Clark University; pioneer in the development of rocket propulsion. Borglum probably garbled the name both here and in G. Borglum to WW, Dec. 25, 1917.

From William Henry Roberts[1]

                                            Philadelphia, Pa.
Honored and Dear Friend: December 12, 1917.

Permit me to draw your attention to the fact that on December 18th, at the Richmond Hotel, Richmond, Va., the Committees on Union of this General Assembly and of the General Assembly of which your beloved father was for so many years Stated Clerk,[2] will meet in joint session to consider the matter of Reunion between these two branches of the Presbyterian Church. If you could find it feasible among your many pressing and burdensome duties to send me word at Philadelphia, between this and the afternoon of December 17th of your views on this very important subject, I should value the same highly. We here are standing firmly by the President and the Government of the United States, and are doing all in our power to awaken the people to the consciousness that we are engaged in a most righteous war, involving the happiness and well being of generations yet unborn.

With great respect,   Yours loyally,   Wm H. Roberts.
                    Chairman Committee on Union.

TLS (WP, DLC).
[1] Wilson's old friend, still the Stated Clerk of the General Assembly of the Presbyterian Church in the United States of America.
[2] That is, the General Assembly of the Presbyterian Church in the United States, commonly called the southern Presbyterian Church.

From Samuel Reading Bertron

My dear Mr. President: New York December 12, 1917.

During the past two weeks I have been in close touch with the Russian Ambassador and have given a great deal of my time to studying the Russian situation. It is apparent that with Germany's present method of procedure she is planning to dominate Russia as soon as complete disorganization of the Russian Army is effected. Should she accomplish this purpose, with the resources of Russia back of her, she could continue the war indefinitely, or she could make such peace terms on the West as the Allies might require and amply repay herself from the resources of Russia, and thus end the war the real victor.

Notwithstanding the demoralization of Russia, a large portion of the population is sound and can be utilized as a basis for the redemption of Russia, if not as a fighting force, in any event as a permanent great Democracy. To accomplish this purpose however, immediate and far-reaching efforts by ourselves and our Allies will need to be undertaken and carried through at a great expense. A practical method of carrying out such a procedure I think has been worked out by the Ambassador and by me. I have discussed the situation with several members of our Russian Commission and they agree with us. I have also briefly discussed it with Mr. Lansing and Mr. McAdoo who concur. The necessity of undertaking immediate and far-reaching plans is very pressing.

I wonder if you could see me for a few moments on Thursday, if not any other day you may name, or, if you prefer, a meeting with several members of the Commission could be arranged. I think you know that I would not suggest intruding upon your time now, except for the vital importance of this matter. My address in Washington will be the Shoreham Hotel.[1]

Please believe me,   Faithfully yours,   S R Bertron

TLS (WP, DLC).
[1] "It is literally impossible for me nowadays to have interviews such as Mr. Bertron here suggests, and I am not the proper one for him to bring it to. Please urge him to seek an interview with the Secretary of State and discuss the whole matter with him in order that the Secretary of State may advise me regarding its feasibility." WW to JPT, c. Dec. 13, 1917, TL (WP, DLC).

To William Gibbs McAdoo, with Enclosure

Dear Mac.,   [The White House, c. Dec. 13, 1917]

You will be interested in the enclosed   W.W.

ALI (W. G. McAdoo Papers, DLC).

E N C L O S U R E

MEMORANDUM FOR PLACING THE TREANSPORTATION AGENCIES
OF THE NATION IN TRUST
FOR THE NATION AND THE SECURITY HOLDERS.

I.   The proposal is to create an operating trust or operating committee, appointed by the President, or an operating corporation like the Shipping Board, to operate the railroads either temporarily or permanently as a unit, and in trust for owners and the nation. The earnings to be disbursed:

(1)   to pay operating expenses;
(2)   for depreciation and maintenance;
(3)   for interest and dividends on securities at a rate equal to the average rate of interest received by the security holders during the preceding —— years.

If the net earnings have been diverted to improvements, then a payment to the security holders equal to such diversion.

(4)   Any balance to be disposed of as the President shall direct.

II.   The operating trust (which should represent industry and agriculture as well as transportation) should have power to consolidate all transportation agencies, unify or dispense with offices, operating staffs, clerical forces, etc., classify freight—irrespective of existing schedules—fix rates, charges, tariffs, and operate the property as fully and as freely as at present.

III.   Competition would be ended, as *would the struggle for long hauls*. Motive power and cars could be mobilized for use where most needed. Empty trains would no longer be carried from city to city to secure return freight. Great terminals could be consolidated at little expense. Hundreds perhaps thousands of needless trains could be abandoned, now operated to secure a share of passenger traffic. Cars could be operated at full capacity. It is believed that the carrying capacity of the railroads could be increased fully one hundred present. [percent.] by ending the competition of a hundred different railroads, not only for traffic but for needless long hauls.

The unification under government control would bring about other colossal economies. Hundreds of offices in cities could be closed. Thousands of clerks, freight solicitors and agents could be dispensed with. There would be an end of advertising, of press bureaus, of publicity. The fast freight lines which now secure the cream of the traffic would be brought under government control, as would the refrigerator car lines, private car companies, etc. Law departments engaged in fighting cases before the Interstate Commerce Commission, and railway commissions of the states, could be utilized in other ways. Immense economies would be realized in the financing of securities. There would be other gains from interest upon deposits. Hundreds possibly thousands of high salaried officials could also be dispensed with.

IV.   *Freight rates could be immediately simplified.* There are millions of classifications in this country. In Europe freight schedules are so simple and so few in number they can be understood by anyone. This would mean colossal saving in clerk hire alone. It would be a great help to shippers. It would end dishonest discrimination.

V.   Rebates, discriminations, and privileges of all kinds would be ended. Cars would be distributed equitably. *Small industries would be stimulated. Government ownership of the railroads would undoubtedly do more than any other thing to break the stranglehold of the larger trusts, and stimulate independent business.* Cars could be supplied the farmers. They complain that facilities are provided the middle men and speculators but are not obtainable by the farmers. The same complaint is made by independent coal operators and many business men.

VI.   The political activities of the railroads would come to an end. Something must be done to identify the talent of the nation with the nation. Today a great part of it is aligned against the state. This is inevitable under private ownership. Government ownership would do more to free the talent of America than any other one thing.

VII.   Coal mines, over 100,000,000 acres of forect [forest] lands, oil and mineral resources would immediately pass to the government. This would cheapen fuel, oil, timber.

VIII.   Increasing land values are enriching the railroads to the extent of hundreds of millions each year. This is being capitalized, and higher rates are being demanded upon this increment.

Hundreds of millions are also being collected from the public and passed into betterments and improvements. The shippers and consumers of America are really financing the railroads at excessive transportation costs. These should be saved to the nation, they can only be saved through public ownership.

The net earnings of the railroads in 1916 amounted to over a billion dollars. A reduction in interest rates would save a large part of this sum to the government.

IX.   The great gain is the substitution of service for profit; the ending of the struggle of hundreds of competing lines for their share of the traffic; the stoppage of the wastage of competition, almost as wasteful in transportation as would be the having of a score of competing water companies in a town, a score of competing fire departments, or a score of different armies. *It would free shippers, business men, manufacturers, and farmers from fear. It would change the psychology of America. It would also probably stimulate and increase production more than any other thing that could be done.*

Under the proposal there need be no change in the machinery of operation other than that incident to unification and mobilization; the present employees to be retained, except where unnecessary.

Frederic C. Howe.

T MS (W. G. McAdoo Papers, DLC).

From Robert Lansing

My dear Mr. President: Washington December 13, 1917.

There is being brought considerable pressure for the issuance of a declaration in regard to this Government's attitude as to the disposition to be made of Palestine. This emanates naturally from the Zionist element of the Jews.

My judgment is that we should go very slowly in announcing a policy for three reasons. *First*, we are not at war with Turkey and therefore should avoid any appearance of favoring taking territory from that Empire by force. *Second*, the Jews are by no means a unit in the desire to reestablish their race as an independent people; to favor one or the other faction would seem to be unwise. *Third*, many Christian sects and individuals would undoubtedly resent turning the Holy Land over to the absolute control of the race credited with the death of Christ.

For practical purposes I do not think that we need go further than the first reason given since that is ample ground for declining to announce a policy in regard to the final disposition of Palestine.

Faithfully yours,   Robert Lansing[1]

TLS (SDR, RG 59, 867n.01/13½a, DNA).
 [1] "The President returned me this letter at Cabinet Meeting December 14, 1917, saying that very unwillingly he was forced to agree with me, but said that he had an impression that we had assented to the British declaration regarding returning Palestine to the Jews RL." RLhw memorandum (SDR, RG 59, 867n.01/13½a, DNA).

To William Henry Roberts

[The White House]
My dear Doctor Roberts: 14 December, 1917

Not being in touch with any of the practical aspects of the question of reunion between the Northern and Southern Presbyterian Churches, I do not feel that I am entitled to a judgment. I can only say in reply to your letter of December twelfth that I would greatly rejoice to see the reunion brought about.

Sincerely yours,   Woodrow Wilson

TLS (Letterpress Books, WP, DLC).

From William Gibbs McAdoo, with Enclosure

CONFIDENTIAL.

Dear "Governor":   Washington December 14, 1917.

The security markets in New York are very much demoralized. The declines in the past few days have produced a situation which contains very evil potentialities. Confidence has been badly impaired for various reasons. A great deal of unreasonable fear enters into the situation and wild rumors are in circulation. One of the contributing factors is the uncertainty about the railroad situation. The report of the Interstate Commerce Commission brought the issue to a head before provision could be made by the Administration to meet the situation which that report developed. I am told that rumors are in circulation that if the Government takes over the railroads, the rights of bondholders and stockholders will not be protected. Foolish as this is, it is making an impression.

I am inclined to think, therefore, that we ought to take action in the railroad matter at the very earliest possible moment, even before the holidays. Meanwhile, some sort of statement emanating from the Administration might have a very helpful effect in allaying apprehension, checking panic tendencies and reviving confidence in New York. I am concerned about the continued declines, because if they reach a point where a panic would set in, grave injury would result and the financial operations of the Government would be seriously imperilled. I think we might be able to arrest the existing demoralization if something reassuring could be said.

I have been asked to make a statement in reply to a telegram which may be sent to me and to which the enclosed would be responsive. Will you not be good enough to look over it and tell me if you would approve my saying something along these lines?

Affectionately yours,   W G McAdoo

TLS (WP, DLC).

ENCLOSURE

In reply to your telegram, I see no reason for the pessimism which seems to prevail in the security markets of New York. The financial situation is inherently sound and strong and the operations of the Government will continue to be conducted with the utmost regard for the maintenance of prosperous conditions throughout the country. The railroad situation is going to be dealt with promptly, and the rights of stockholders and bondholders will, of course, be fully and justly protected. There is no ground for alarmist rumors about conditions here or on the military fronts in Europe. This is no time for nerves or nervous people. We are going to win the war and solve all our difficulties if we keep our heads and courage.

PS. I may not use this. I merely want to be armed for the Emergency.   W.G.M.

T MS with WGMhw PS (WP, DLC).

From Joseph Patrick Tumulty, with Enclosure

The White House 14th December [1917].
Memorandum for the President:

Mr. Bertron called to see me yesterday and left with me the attached memorandum prepared by the Russian Ambassador. He said they had discussed the matter of Russian affairs with the Secretary of State and seemed to feel piqued that nothing had been done. He made a request for an appointment to see the President with the other members of the Commission.

The Secretary

TL (WP, DLC)

E N C L O S U R E

The situation in Russia with all its chaos, conflicting aims and movements, threat of civil war and irreparable action is of the greatest complexity and pregnant of the greatest dangers.

It must be admitted that the Bolsheviki, how ever unrepresentative of the true spirit of Russia and preposterous in aims and methods of statesmanship, have succeeded through demagogic and energetic action to attain a degree of triumph which, although temporary, is nevertheless capable to incur irreparable consequences in the way of the final disorganization of the fighting powers of the nation.

How ever unpopular is the idea of any separate peace as such, and despite the fact that the doings of the Bolsheviki can not be recognized as binding and representative of Russia's aims, one still has to anticipate the worst of possibilities and admit as a fact that under certain conditions the Bolsheviki, through the irresistible force of events, will bring a suspension of active military operations at the Russian front and thus practically will lead Russia out of the war.

But the very bitterness of the happenings imperatively obliges to face the real bearing of the events in Russia and not only to consider them from the point of view of active warfare. One should not regard Russia solely as a military factor, as a presumably "lost" link in the Allied war machine. The deepest wisdom of the advice "in the very heat and ardor of struggle" not to lose from sight the final goal for which democracy is conten[d]ing necessitates to visualize the Russian problem in the light of final settlement and ultimate achievement.

No matter how distressing and resentful are the present features of the process in Russia, dangers of far more reaching character are to be foreseen; dangers which luminously appear when the very aims of the war are visualized, when the purposes and principles of this world struggle are taken into account.

Russia, if withdrawn from the war, is left face to face with a Germany which has not yet consumed the process of democratization and the Masters of which are full of aspirations for economic, if not direct, conquest.

Russia's material exhaustion, increasing disorganization and spreading spirit of anarchy creates conditions which will furnish to autocratic Germany a splendid field for most propitious activities. The work of the extremists and their propaganda has already revealed itself in confused tendencies towards a dismemberment of Russia. The perpetuation and the deepening of this process of disunion would fully answer to the actual plans of the rulers of Germany which they are concealing so hypocritically under quasi democratic utterances of Foreign Minister Kuehlmann, declaring Germany's acquiescence to the principles of settlement formulated by the Russian Democracy.

The self-determination of nations, revealed in the creation of an independent Kurland, Lifland,[1] Lithuania, and Russian Poland, and followed by a further process of dismemberment of Russia would, under certain circumstances, mean a replacement of the United Empire by a congregation of small weak commonwealths, devoid of any political weight or economic independence. This vulgar and illusory realization of a sound and just democratic idea would create a field where political intrigue and economical control would allow the performance of the greatest of Germany's imperialistic dreams. Intensive political and economical penetration will be energetically pursued by Germany while war is waging in the West and every thought, effort, attention and resources are concentrated by the Allies on warfare. A commercial conquest of disrupted Russia would

---

[1] That is, Livonia, now divided between Latvia and Estonia.

be probably started with all vigor as soon as conditions at the Front allow a penetration into Russia for German merchandise. This process would be enhanced in Russia by the critical state of exhaustion, the lack of commodities, which has been the result of the 3-years war strain of the country under inefficient administration. The gift of commodities would infiltrate with the insidious propaganda tending to perpetuate, under quasi democratic forms, the poison of political disunion and dismemberment of Russia and serve to consolidate the clutch of Prussian military and commercial autocracy over a people, which will thus have the misfortune to fail to achieve the great aim of the Russian Revolution—the establishment on the East of Europe of a Great Unified Democratic State. Thus, not only the aims of the Russian revolution will be frustrated, but the heaviest blow will be struck to the cause of the world's democracy.

Not only will the elimination of Russia from the scene of active warfare and German control of her resources bring new insurmountable difficulties to the goal of military victory; but, moreover the process of Russia's political disintegration and the grip that the Rulers of Germany might have over her, could seriously enforce the "claim autocracy has to power or leadership in the modern world."

The President in his speech has considered the possibility of "The worst that can happen to the detriment of the German people," being that, "if they should still, after the war is over, continue to be obliged to live under ambitious and intriguing masters interested to disturb the peace of the world." This situation, the President said, sooner or later will "cure itself by processes which assuredly would set in."

This setting in of an actual democratization is inevitable for Germany as for any other autocracy left to outlive the results of the war within its own borders and present means. The financial and economic burden caused by the expenditures of the war imposes problems of a character and magnitude which cannot be solved through prevailing means of economic and political statesmanship. These problems will have to be met everywhere by political and social measures, which are incompatible with any form of autocratic government.

It must be admitted, however, that things will look far different if autocratic Germany would be able to make use in this process of the unlimited material resources of Russia and her vast territories. Russia's riches under the control of Prussian rulers would permit them to employ the country's wealth to encounter the financial and economic liabilities imposed on the German Government by the war, and the territories of the East would easily serve to unload the tension of psychological strain which the sufferings of the war have created in the mentality of the people. Moreso, a situation can be conceived when the German autocracy, relying on the resources of Russia and Asia Minor, will be able to conserve political stability, while the pressure of the inheritance of the war will reveal itself to her Western democratic neighbors in political instability and internal reverse.

It should be recalled on this occasion that through actual administration, financial assistance and political intrigue the Masters of Germany have already accomplished their ambitious desire of practical control of the Balkans and Asia Minor. If gaining further control of the resources of Russia and if being able to frustrate any active political opposition of her democratic elements Germany would realize a domination which by far supersedes the most ample imperialistic dreams.

Under such conditions Germany can be very liberal in the future settlement of matters on the Western Front, and a reverse of arms in the West and a conclusion of peace with the Allied Belligerents on most easy terms would [not] in the slightest way affect her imperialistic ambitions if her actual grip on the East is not discontinued.

This imminent danger of a success of German autocracy can be paralyzed only in case the process of further political disintegration and economic chaos in Russia is stopped and followed by an active and constructive movement for political unity, democratic stability, economic progress and welfare.

The consolidation of Russia, therefore, into an efficient and independent democracy, capable with all the strength of democratic action to weigh on the balance of the destinies of the world's democracy, is a most important factor of far-reaching democratic "war policy."

This imperative and urgent necessity of not losing Russia as an indispensible partner in the society of democratic nations is being felt vaguely—although every day more distinctly and persuasively—in the voice of public opinion. Help to the Russian people, active propaganda of the Allied and democratic cause in Russia, are revealed in different thoughts and suggestions, which all rally in a sound of vigorous desire not to remain inactive, to oppose German plans and German vigilance by energetic and efficient measures. This understanding is accompanied by an emphatical distinction between the Russian people and its passing rulers of violence,— those who are leading the country to disaster and, by deliberate action or through blindness of fanati[ci]sm, are contributing in fact to the strengthening of autocracy in Germany.

There arises a genuine feeling of necessity to help the Russian people in their present distress and to actively assist the reconstruction of the Russian democracy. Support has to be given to the sound and constructive forces which arise throughout the present chaos in Russia, so as to enable them to vanquish the destructive and demoralizing activities of extremism backed by fraudulent German plans. To leave these forces isolated in their strife for organized and legal democracy would be an irreparable error.

This is not only an expression of sentiment. It is a deep and obvious political necessity. In order to avoide the imminent dangers of German domination on the East, an active, deliberate and far-reaching policy of assisting Russia in her democratic consolidation should be adopted and carried through with all vigor and efficiency. But Democratic stability is inconceiveable without economical organization and a certain rate of welfare in everyday life, which would give the people a feeling of security against suffering and exhaustion and prevent the destructive action of despair, which drive people into extreme action and enslave them to any Master who bring relief from starvation and annihilation.

Effective policy to be adopted in assisting the process of consolidating the Russian democracy involves, therefore, the necessity of economic reconstruction and expedient relief.

The object of the policy to be adopted toward Russia is to enable the Russian people to achieve, with the greatest possible expediency, a desirable status of political stability. An orderly democratic government has to be consolidated out of the present chaos, and material exhaustion has to be replaced by a well-working economic system. To enable the constructive elements of the nation to achieve these ends, assistance in a systematic form has to be exercised along the following lines:

1) Propaganda.
2) Economic organization.
3) Relief.

Under propaganda, one has to understand the complex of educational activities, using all means of persuasion and enlightenment, which outside of regular campaign work by Russians themselves, devoted to the consideration of Russian internal problems, should involve a wide publicity by the United States and other Allied countries, explaining to the people of Russia the real aims and intentions of the world democracies and picturing, in all their reality, the aspirations of German autocracy.

Work of political character should be completed by action of moral relief and comfort of which the activities of the Y.M.C.A. show such a beneficial example.

Economic organization presumes the accomplishment of certain measures, which would result in restituting the shaken system of production and distribution and reinstalling, to a certain degree, normal economic activities within the parts of the country which are being politically consolidated.

Two elements are of the greatest importance:

A) Railway transportation: supply of rolling stock, repair shops, etc., as well as efficient management.

B) Reestablishment of agricultural production. In this respect it should be noted that the terrible losses of men and cattle during the war have greatly undermined the productive capacity of Russia and an abundant supply of agricultural implements and tractors has to replace the deficiency of man and horse power.

As to relief, this would mean supplying the people with everyday commodities as boots, clothing, etc., the complete lack of which in the country creates untold suffering. Restitution of an orderly government is closely connected with relief and a certain guarantee of security in the supply of elementary commodities. It is not only impossible to vouchsafe any political stability under threat of suffering or starvation. But the promise of relief and the hope of adequate supply and proper distribution of commodities is in itself an effective factor for the reestablishment of order, a most attractive argument in favor of orderly authority and organization against detrimental anarchistic elements.

Possibilities for effectuating economic organization and relief should be widely accorded to elements, carrying authority and endeavoring to restore order. We approach now the most delicate part of the problem: To whom such assistance should be given, and through what channels?

It is clear that pouring a stream of material assistance into a sea of chaos would not only be a useless waste but, under circumstances, could encourage disorderly factors. Assistance, therefore, should accompany in all cases the consolidating work of democratic elements of constructive character, rendering a material basis for their eventual activities.

At this moment it is impossible to foresee in detail the character of the elements and the form of their activities which will finally succeed in reestablishing unity and democratic order in Russia. The very vastness of Russia's territory, the diversity of its population and of its economic and intellectual features do not allow to designate, beforehand, any specific path or leader of salvation. The complexity of the situation will probably determine that the reconstruction of Russia will appear as a final result of manifold concur[r]ing activities of national character: Constituent Assembly; the consolidation and reunion of the, at present, independent "commonwealths," (Caucases, South Russia, Siberia, etc.), which, in order to retain legality and organization, have seceded for the time being into self-dependent communities; revolutionary, military dictatorship, effectuating strong rule for a clear defined aim of saving the liberties of the people.

All these promises of national consolidation will inevitably reveal themselves in different ways in the qualms of national suffering which the young democracy is undergoing in its birth. In each particular case, it will be necessary to use judgment and to decide the form and the extent of assistance to be rendered.

For this purpose a special body should be formed, authorized to take decisions as to the policy to be followed and determining the action which would be taken. To allow effective and expedient accomplishment of its decisions, this body must have under control sufficient means of material assistance and of relief in direct disposal of its executive organs.

The magnitude of the work and its momentuous political importance excludes any other possibility of performance except that on governmental lines. The proposed task can be only accomplished on a basis of determined policy with the appropriation of necessary State funds.

A special committee, named by the Government and representing different factions of public thought and activity should be formed in order to deal with the whole of the Russian situation. This committee, acting on behalf and on account of the United States Government, should be given the disposal of the necessary funds and authorized to carry out the whole of the material and executive work in regard to Russia.

As to supplies, the Committee should inherit the whole complex of orders actually executed or contemplated in behalf of the Russian Government. The Committee would have to decide which of these orders should be suspended or reduced and which, on the other hand, such as railway material, boots, agricultural implements, etc., should be continued and if necessary amplified with all expediency.

This Committee should naturally accept the further control of contracts, the disposal of manufactured articles, as well as assume the handling of credits allot[t]ed by the United States Government for these orders in the process of war cooperation.

It should be noted that decisions as to the general course to follow have to be taken without possible delay. The present situation of expectant attitude in regard to running and proposed contracts can not be continued for any length of time on account of the approaching lack of funds for current payments as well as the impossibility of prolonging incertitude in the programs of production.

CC MS (WP, DLC).

From William Bauchop Wilson

Seattle, Washn., Dec. 14, 1917.

Wednesday your commission was assured that the lumbermen of the Pacific northwest would submit a program acceptable to us and the adoption of which would create conditions essential for the needed production in the Pacific northwest lumber industry. Overnight the situation changed through influences known to me and as to which I shall advise you upon my return. We are leaving here with the announcement that the commission has reached definite conclusions and will report them to you with recommendations for action. I regret to burden you with a message other than one announcing accomplished results but I deem it necessary that you personally be advised of what I am confident will be many an intervening step to the right final solution of a very serious situation. We are leaving for the east this evening and, agreeable to your wishes, we shall stop off at the Twin Cities.

W. B. Wilson.

T telegram (WP, DLC).

Two Letters from Samuel Gompers

Sir: Washington, D. C., December 14, 1917.

On one occasion I took the liberty of addressing you upon a subject which was then imminent but which is now assuming proportions so threatening and so dangerous that I feel it an incumbent duty upon me, as a man and a citizen, to bring to your attention a thought upon the pending Joint Resolution now before the House of Representatives, being a proposed amendment to the Constitution of the United States, commonly known as the nationwide prohibition amendment.[1]

Did I for a moment feel that the subject matter were of but passing or momentary interest, or that it did not involve grave injury and dangers, I should hesitate long before asking your consideration of what I hope to present to you; but, because I am so apprehensive of the consequences to our people, our country and the tremendous enterprise in which we are engaged, I feel it incumbent upon me to trespass upon your time so that you might in your own way use your good judgment and great powers to avert what I am fully convinced would be the greatest cause of dissension and discontent among our people, if the pending prohibition constitutional amendment were passed by Congress and submitted for ratification.

The Congress has passed, and you have approved, the law prohibiting the manufacture of spirituous liquors (whiskey, etc.) during the period of the war. Existing law places within your power the modification, limitation and, if necessary, the prohibition of the manufacture of beers and light wines. You have already exercised that power in part, and whenever or wherever it shall appear to you that either of these powers conferred upon you shall be necessary to be exercised, no one whom I know will find the slightest cause of dissent or disapproval.

The advocates of the proposed prohibition amendment have disingenuously declared that the amendment is necessary as a war measure. How fraudulent is this pretense is best understood when it is known that the amendment cannot become effective until after the Legislatures of three-fourths of the States shall have ratified it, and, as is known, it is hoped that the war will have been successfully fought and won and come to an end long before the proposed constitutional amendment could come into operation.

But in the meantime, that is, between the time of the passage of the amendment by Congress (if it should pass) and until its ratification or defeat, covering a period of from six to seven years, and during the time when it is most essential that there shall be unity of spirit and action among the people of our country, the apple of discord will be thrown among them and the minds of the people will be diverted from the essential subject of winning the war to a proposition which can only become operative after the war has been concluded.

Beer is the general beverage of the masses of the people of our country. Light wines are used among large groups of our people. Many of them have acquired the habit by heritage of centuries and generations. The workers—the masses—no more than others in their indulgence in beers or light wines have found them a healthful part of their daily diet, particularly with their meals. With the cosmopolitan character of a large mass of our people, their divers habits and customs, I submit that it is neither wise, practical nor beneficial to divide them into opposite camps upon a non-essential to the winning of the war, when its effectiveness—even if it is advantageous—could only become operative after the war is closed.

In the countries of our Allies liquors—spirits, beer and light wines—are under control and regulation. Not one of our Allies has attempted either during the war or proposed thereafter to prohibit their manufacture or sale. Indeed, the regulations provide as part of the rations to the fighting men some portion of beers or light wines, and in some instances a limited quantity of spirituous liquors.

Upon the proposed constitutional amendment neither the Senate Committee nor the Committee of the House of Representatives having this proposed constitutional amendment under consideration has given one moment of time for the purpose of hearing those who are vitally interested in this question. Requests for hearings of those vitally and primarily interested have been disregarded, ignored and denied.

Hundreds of thousands—aye, perhaps more than two millions of wage earners would be affected and thrown out of employment were nation-wide prohibition forced upon our people. It is not difficult to understand how disaffected would they become during the war when the question would be forced upon their attention that, at some particular time after the war, they would be thrown into a state of unemployment and be bereft of the opportunity of maintaining themselves and their dependents.

Of course you know that the States which have elected to have prohibition within their borders are secured their full right and protection thereunder by State and Federal law, and the Supreme Court of the United States has recently guaranteed and strengthened that protection. The States, however, which elect and prefer not to avail themselves of that course should not, I submit, be coerced into becoming prohibition territory against their will.

My life has been thrown among the masses of our people. Whatever other characteristic has been developed in me from that mingling with them, I am vain enough to believe that I understand men; and in addition to and quite apart from the direct injury which this proposed prohibition amendment would inflict upon the workers primarily involved, I am constrained to say that the turmoil and dissension which are sure to be generated in the minds of our people as the result of this prohibition proposition causes me great mental and conscious disturbance.

Of course I am conscious of the delicate position in which you are placed in this matter, but the projectors of this scheme of prohibition are neither wise, practical nor patriotic. They are eaten up with egotism and fanaticism. Their project is not calculated to unite our people. They interject a subject calculated to divide and to cause dissension by advocating a measure which could only become operative after the war.

And it is because of the threatened danger which is involved in the entire scheme that I appeal to you as my leader, in common with the leadership of all our people in the great cause of justice, freedom and Democracy, to interpose whatever influence and power you can exert that this imminent danger shall be averted.

Respectfully,   Samuel Gompers.[2]

[1] That is, S.J. Res. 17, which was to become the Eighteenth Amendment. Introduced by Morris Sheppard on April 4, it had passed in the Senate on August 1 and was to pass in the House on December 17.

[2] "Please acknowledge and say that I appreciate the very great weight of the arguments he uses." WW to JPT, c. Dec. 17, 1917, TL (WP, DLC).

Sir: Washington, D. C. December 14, 1917.

It is with great pleasure that I submit to you herewith copy of resolutions adopted by the recent convention of the American Federation of Labor held in Buffalo, November 12-24, 1917. They are as follows:

["]RESOLVED, That we, the deleagates to this Thirty-seventh Annual Convention of the American Federation of Labor, herewith and hereby convey to the Honorable Woodrow Wilson, President of the United States, our profound appreciation of his presence upon the opening day of the convention and for the direct frankness with which he addressed us.

RESOLVED, That there is particular gratification in the fact that the first President of the United States to honor and inspire by his presence a convention of the American Federation of Labor should be so staunch a defender and so able an interpreter of the fundamental principles of practical democracy.

RESOLVED, That after sober, serious minded consideration of the industrial problems arising as the result of our country's participation in the war for human rights and the perpetuation of democratic institutions we pledge to him our undivided support in carrying the war to a successful conclusion, in supporting him in his efforts to apply the principles of democracy to the solution of the problems which arise in industry and in conducting the war so that it shall be a war of the people, continued in defense of the fundamental institutions for human liberty transmitted to us by the forefathers of our country."

Respectfully yours,   Saml. Gompers.

TLS (WP, DLC).

From Robert Goodwyn Rhett

My dear Mr. President: Washington, D. C. December 14, 1917

I have your letter of December 12th. Our Board was gratified to learn of the selection of Mr. Daniel Willard as Chairman of the War Industries Board, and desires to do all in its power to aid him in the task he is undertaking.

As Mr. Willard has explained to you and as we undertook to make clear in our memorandum sent you on November 15th, we have the very definite view that the weakness of the present situation lies in the fact that real power to control and thus effectively co-ordinate the buying is not centralized. The War Industries Board has no power under the statute, and no authority which in practise must be recognized by the various bureaus. Mr. Willard hopes that the necessary measure of coordination may be brought about by developing an effective spirit of cooperation. This may be possible, but our feeling is that the experience thus far indicates clearly that the necessary coordination of effort is not likely to be secured by this method, and that the delay involved in prolonged effort in this direction carries the possibility of very great harm.

I find that our memorandum sent to you, copies of which were placed in the hands of the Secretary of the Navy, the Secretary of War, and Mr. Willard, gave the impression in some directions that we believed a Department of Munitions or of War Supplies was the only cure for the present situation. We did not intend to convey that idea or to declare that it could be accomplished only by the creation of such a Department. Our plea is for adequate machinery of coordination carrying with it unquestioned power of supervision and decision, thus positively fixing responsibility for action or in-action.

We will be glad to cooperate with Mr. Willard in the efforts he is making and with all other agencies of the government. Our Board cannot escape the conclusion, however, that it is necessary to have sharper concentration of authority and that prompt action in this direction is a pressing need.

Very truly yours,   R. G. Rhett

TLS (WP, DLC).

Two Letters from William Kent

My dear Mr. President: Washington December 14, 1917.

In accordance with your suggestion, I send you herewith notes concerning the parliamentary and practical situation of the proposed water power bill. Before going into detail, I wish to again emphasize my view, first, that one coherent and consistent bill is not only needed but has a better chance of passage than bills representing divided authority, and second, that such a bill, with proper backing, can be passed without making concessions to those shortsighted or with selfish motives.

I understand that the first necessary step—that of agreement by the Secretaries of War, Interior and Agriculture—has been taken, and that Merrill's bill[1] was satisfactory, with a few amendments, which were unanimously agreed upon.

Mr. Lenroot next figures in the program. He suggests that you request of the Rules Committee, that a special joint committee be created from the Lands, Interstate and Foreign Commerce and Agriculture Committees. If the rule went on to specify that the members of this Committee should consist of the Chairman and the ranking member in each case, you would have Ferris and Lenroot in Lands, Sims and Esch[2] in Interstate and Foreign Commerce, and Lever and Haugen[3] of Agriculture. It occurs to me that inasmuch as Ferris has had the introduction of several water power bills on his hands, that he would be the natural person to head the Committee and introduce the bill. Sims is a new chairman, and would doubtless concede this courtesy. Lever, of course, would do anything to help the situation. Your suggestion that, before asking the Rules Committee to act in this way, the Committees themselves be consulted could, I believe, be easily answered by requesting Ferris, Sims and Lever to meet you to discuss the general question and this phase in particular.

As a matter of course, there should be the earliest information given to those really important in passing the legislation, as to the form and substance of the proposed bill to be introduced. Lenroot is the most important man in the situation, but owing to Ferris' position as Chairman, I imagine he would be peeved if he were not immediately taken into consultation.

At the present time there has been appointed in the Lands Committee a sub-committee on this water power situation, consisting of Ferris, Lenroot, Taylor, Raker, and La Follette.[4] Ferris, Taylor and Raker would doubtless do anything that Secretary Lane requested, and I do not think in any event Taylor, Raker and La Follette would resent being left off such a joint Committee as is suggested. If this plan works out satisfactorily and Ferris introduces the bill, there will be no question of its passing the House. Lenroot's leadership would give it a strong majority on the Republican side, and the States' Rights Democrats have been beaten so often on this proposition that there will be no trouble. The only insistence necessary would be to secure its passage without any considerable amendment.

As to the Rules Committee, Foster is strongly in sympathy with proper water power control and development; Garrett knows little about it, but is all right; and I presume Pou would, as a matter of course, act with the Administration. If there were to be any doubt in this Committee, Foster could doubtless straighten out the kinks.

Now, as to the Senate, the two leaders in water power legislation have been Walsh and Shields, although of course Myers, as Chairman of the Public Lands Committee, has been considerably in evidence. I should not be surprised if Shields would get in line, if given an early opportunity by Secretary Baker. Walsh is a difficult man to argue with, but would probably work in if consulted. Fletcher, Chairman of the Committee on Commerce, would, I am sure, be all right, but I do not believe he has given the matter much attention. As to representation on the Agricultural Committee on the Democratic side, that matter should be left to Secretary Houston. I feel sure that, between Lenroot and others of us, we can get some first class Republican backing on that Committee. Chamberlain figures on both the Committee on Commerce and the Public Lands Committee, and would, without any doubt, help us along. I feel sure that Senator Johnson, of California,[5] on the Commerce Committee would be glad to help fight this matter through on the floor, and know he would do it well. On Public Lands, you could rely on Myers, Pittman and Chamberlain, who doubtless ought to be consulted. Baker should see Chamberlain on the predominant war measure issue. Lane should see Myers and Pittman. As a general on the floor, I should strongly recommend Senator James, of Kentucky. He has the right general attitude and would run over petty opposition and look out for jokers. Senator Hughes, of New Jersey, would be another of a similar sort.

Just as soon as Lenroot, Ferris and Sherley have had a chance to see the bill, if they are satisfied with it, I shall be glad to assist in following up the Rules Committee and Joint Committe procedure in the House.

You know more about the discretion of Senator James than I do, but I believe it would be well to consult with him in confidence as to methods of procedure in the Senate. He has asked me to call on him and talk it over, which I can do without in any way implicating you. It is to my mind most essential that the program be laid out and followed just as fast as is possible by the Secretaries.

Yours truly,   William Kent

[1] This was the bill summarized in DFH to WW, Nov. 30, 1917, n. 1. Oscar Charles Merrill was Chief Engineer of the Forest Service in the Department of Agriculture.

² John Jacob Esch, Republican congressman from Wisconsin.
³ Gilbert Nelson Haugen, Republican congressman from Iowa.
⁴ Edward Thomas Taylor, Democratic congressman from Colorado; John Edward Raker, Democratic congressman from California, and William Leroy La Follette, Republican congressman from Washington.
⁵ Hiram W. Johnson.

Dear Mr. President: Washington December 14, 1917.

I happened to find in the Congressional Record that Senator Shields had introduced his water power bill yesterday, and is urging it for passage today. I just talked with Lenroot over the telephone, and he tells me that he sees no way of heading it off. I suggested that Baker might communicate with Chamberlain, and you with James, and he said that something of that sort might possibly work.

The situation is entirely changed by this procedure. If the bill is passed, and it probably will be, it will never get by the House, and not even by the Interstate and Foreign Commerce Committee, but there will be every reason to communicate with the leading people on the Interstate and Foreign Commerce Committee of the House at an early date, and get them familiar with the situation. I am not surprised at Senator Shields' action, but had hoped that he might see his own interest in different behavior. The bill as up for passage is extremely unsatisfactory, and could never be accepted.

It is barely possible that Senator James or some other man in whom you have confidence might do something toward stopping the passage, but I understand how delivate [delicate] the situation is.   Yours truly,   William Kent

TLS (WP, DLC).

From William Graves Sharp

Paris Dec. 15th 1917

2900. For the President. This afternoon Mr. Clemenceau, President of the Council, telephoned asking if I could meet him on a most important matter. On seeing him he handed to me to read the following communication expressing a very earnest desire that I at once cable the same to you. This I promised to do and to follow the same line by cabling you to the Department the chief points set out in the statement to which he refers:

(Blue) "From President of Council Clemenceau to President Wilson concerning gasoline supply of France. Just at the critical moment of the war, when the year 1918 will begin in the midst of military operations, of great magnitude and of crucial importance, on our front, the armies of France must never be exposed to run short of gasoline which is necessary for the motor lorries, for the field artillery with tractors and for aviation.

The shortage of gasoline would cause the sudden paralysis of our armies and drive us all into an unacceptable peace.

Now, the stock gasoline which has been fixed by the French Commander-in-Chief as a minimum amounts to forty-four thousand tons and the monthly consumption of the French armies alone average to thirty thousand tons.

Today, fifteenth December, he said that stock has fallen down to twenty-eight thousand tons and should exceptional measures not be taken at once by the Government of the United States, it will very likely fall to nothing in a short period of about two months.

These measures may and must be taken without a single days delay for the common safeguard of the Allies. The only thing is that President Wilson should obtain from the American oil companies the extra hundred thousand tons of tank steamers which are necessary to France for the supply of her armies and people and which must be put at her disposal for the direction of the war.

These tank steamers exist, some are plying in the Pacific Ocean instead of sailing in the Atlantic, others can be provided from the new fleet of tankers which is now being built in the United States.

Therefore, President Clemenceau asks President Wilson personally to act with authority of head of the Government for the immediate sailing for the French ports of said hundred thousands extra tons of tankers.

There is for the Allies a question of public salvation. If they are determined not to lose the war, the fighting France must, by the hour of supreme Germanic blow, have large supplies of gasoline which is, in the battle of to-morrow, as necessary as blood."

(Green) Knowing something of the grave concern which everybody in France looks upon the military situation for the ensuing few weeks and being familiar with the drastic regulations which are being made to conserve the gasoline supply throughout France I am sure that Mr. Clemenceau does not overstate the seriousness of the situation.

As a suggestion of some possible value may it not be feasible for a larger number of the smaller boats sailing on the Great Lakes to be sent through the Canal for the ocean carrying trade in this particular service. Lake navigation has now closed and will not be resumed for several months.   Sharp

T telegram (SDR, RG 59, 763.72/8181, DNA).

Two Letters from William Gibbs McAdoo

Dear Mr. President: Washington December 15, 1917.

Further reflection and study have convinced me that the basis of compensation and guarantee to owners I suggested the other day if the Government takes over the railroads is not fair to the Government. The year 1916, taken alone, was an exceptionally prosperous one for the railroads. For the Government to guarantee that basis for the remainder of the war, in view of the uncertainties as to cost of material, labor, etc. would be unwise, and would probably cause great dissatisfaction among the people of the country, notwithstanding the favorable effect it might have upon the general financial situation. I believe we can accomplish both these objects, however, by the adoption of a fairer basis to the owners of the railroads and the public.

First: Let the Government agree to pay into the treasury of each road each year a sum sufficient to pay existing fixed charges and dividends on the outstanding capital, at the rate of dividend paid during the year 1916, *provided* the average annual net earnings of the years 1915, 1916, and 1917 have been sufficient for that purpose. If not, then the rental should be the average annual net earnings of said years 1915, 1916 and 1917.

Second: Future surplus earnings under Government operation, over and above the suggested "rental," to go into a common fund to be used by the Government for the improvement, development and betterment of the properties, in such manner as the Government may determine.

The purpose of this is to avoid having to keep accounts of the earnings of the various systems as independent properties while under Government control. Railroads earning a surplus over the rental may object to this, but, since the Government takes all the risk and guarantees a specific return to stock and bond holders, it should be free to make use of the surplus, if any, for the improvement or betterment of all or any part of the properties that it may deem essential to the efficient operation of the railroads for war purposes. I cannot see that the railroads have any right to consider surplus earnings or deficiencies if the Government guarantees to each of them a fixed return.

Third: Where the roads have recently built extensions, the results of which have not yet been reflected in the earnings of the three year period, there should be added to the ascertained annual earnings a sum equal to say 5% on the cost of such extensions.

Fourth: As to extensions, permanent improvements, additional terminals, equipment, etc, made by the Government during its occupation of the properties, it should be stipulated that the Government shall be reimbursed by the beneficiary railroad upon final accounting, upon an agreed basis.

Fifth: As to obligations of the various railroads maturing during Government occupation, it should be stipulated that the railroads shall finance such maturing obligations by refunding them or otherwise, under Government approval, or, if the railroads should be unable to do it, that the Government will finance such maturing obligations and become subrogated to all the rights of the holders of such obligations.

I have no doubt whatever as to your power to enter into *agreements* with the roads or any of them for the "leasing," so to speak, of their properties for the duration of the war on such terms as you may agree upon with them. In the absence of agreement, or inability to make agreement with the roads, they will be remitted to the courts, as a matter of course, for their remedy in securing compensation under the rules appertaining to the taking of property by eminent domain.

I would suggest, therefore, that, in your message, you state that you are advised that under the present authority your powers are ample for the purpose of making terms with the railroads by voluntary agreement as to the "rentals" to be paid for their use, but that legislation will be necessary to enable the Government to aid the railroads in financing maturing obligations, if that should become necessary, and for expenditures outside of the surplus funds that may be realized from the operations of the railroads themselves, for new equipment, further improvement, including enlarged or additional terminals, etc, and that, as to these features the Secretary of the Treasury will advise with the Committees of the Congress, etc. I much prefer to use the word "rental" or something equivalent to it than to use the word "guarantee," because clearly you have the power to agree with the railroads for the payment of rental out of the earnings of the properties and go to Congress for an appropriation to cover deficiencies, if any should result, whereas I am in doubt as to whether or not you would have the power to *guarantee* the payment of interest charges on bonds of the railroads, dividends on their stocks, etc. without a more express authorization from the Congress.

It is of the utmost importance, so far as the financial situation is concerned, that the question of terms should be spared a long and protracted debate in the Congress, with all of the uncertainties and anxieties that would produce in the minds of the many thousands of owners of railroad securities throughout the country. It is not necessary that the terms should be agreed upon before possession of the property is taken—we shall have time to work that out—but an indication in a general way of your ideas as to what terms you consider fair would have a very re-assuring effect, and would, I believe, instantly restore confidence, now badly impaired, throughout the entire country in the future of the railroads and the stability of railway securities.

It would be necessary to exempt expressly all trolley lines and electrically operated lines that are not a part of the standard steam railroad systems of the country.

It will be essential also to issue, simultaneously with your address to the Congress, a proclamation which will have to be most carefully drawn to cover the situation. It would help me immensely if you would let me know who is preparing the proclamation and if you will ask them to confer with me about it. If no one has yet undertaken it and you want me to proceed with the preparation of it I shall be glad to do so.

Affectionately yours,   W G McAdoo

P.S. On the question of "rentals," please read enclosed memorandum from Williams.   WGM

TLS (WP, DLC).

Dear Governor,   [Washington] Dec 15/17

This is a very important paper from Williams[1] and I wish you would consider it in connection with my two letters of today.[2]

Affy Yrs   WGM

ALI (WP, DLC).

[1] J. S. Williams to WGM, Dec. 14, 1917, TLS (WP, DLC), a detailed analysis of problems involved in the government's takeover of the railroads.

[2] The one not printed is WGM to WW, Dec. 15, 1917, TLS (WP, DLC), which argued strongly for taking over all railroads, rather than those in certain geographical areas and not others.

From Joseph Patrick Tumulty

The White House

Memorandum for the President: December 15, 1917.

Mrs. Gard[e]ner and Mrs. Park called this afternoon and left the attached House poll on the Suffrage question. The following is the result of this poll:

Favorable	235
Unfavorable	155
Doubtful	42
Vacant	3

These ladies asked if the President could speak to the following Representatives:

> Hull of Tennessee
> Glass of Virginia
> Heflin of Alabama
> Lee of Georgia
> Larsen of Georgia
> Crisp of Georgia
> Stedman of North Carolina
> Snook of Ohio
> Welty of Ohio
> McKeown of Oklahoma
> Sterling of Pennsylvania
> Nicholls of South Carolina
> Robinson of North Carolina
> Garrett of Texas
> Harrison of Virginia
> Wilson of Texas
> Campbell of Pennsylvania
> Flynn of New York—[1]

all of whom are understood to be willing to vote for the amendment if they can be assured that the Administration wishes it.[2]

T MS (WP, DLC).

[1] Those congressmen not heretofore identified were Gordon Lee, William Washington Larsen, John Stout Snook, Benjamin Franklin Welty, Thomas Deitz McKeown, Bruce Foster Sterling, Samuel Jones Nicholls, Leonidas Dunlap Robinson, Daniel Edward Garrett, Thomas Walter Harrison, James Clifton Wilson, and Joseph Vincent Flynn. All were Democrats.

[2] There is nothing in WP, DLC, or in the appointment diaries, to indicate that Wilson got in touch at this time with any of the congressmen mentioned in this memorandum.

From Robert Lansing, with Enclosure

My dear Mr. President: Washington December 15, 1917.

I am enclosing you a confidential dispatch from Minister Reinsch which you have no doubt seen, and which it seems to me deserves special attention.

I wrote you on October 20th in regard to the proposal to send Chinese troops to Europe.[1] If you will refer to my letter it may recall the situation to your mind.

Would you be good enough to advise me as to your wishes in this matter in order that I may make reply to Mr. Reinsch?

Faithfully yours,   Robert Lansing

TLS (WP, DLC).

[1] Lansing either misspoke or else the "October 20th" was a typographical error. The Editors have been unable to find a copy of a letter from Lansing to Wilson of October 20, 1917, about the use of Chinese troops in Europe in any collection or archive. A number of documents relating to this subject are printed in FR-WWS 1917, 2, 1, 691-703.

E N C L O S U R E

Peking Dec. 12th, 1917

December 12, 6 p.m. Confidential. Your cipher telegram November 24, 1 a.m. my telegram November 23, 9 p.m. and previous telegram. I have the honor point out that by supporting the despatch of Chinese troops to Europe the American Government would not only secure the direct military benefits for the Allies but would so influence the situation here that any attempts weaken the allegiance of China to our cause would become futile and that serious internal dissensions would disappear. The local political situation would be immensely relieved if General Tszen could be given the high commissionership in connection with the despatch of troops.[1] Liberal leaders have great confidence in General Tszen personally and would willingly support him after he should be made independent through temporary elimination from local affairs by an important mission abroad. In this manner alone could Tszen be extricated from harmful relationship with military reactionaries and become the trusted leader China needs. On the other hand his assuming charge of the expenditures [expedition] would give dignity and efficiency to China's participation in the war. Nothing could contribute more towards the reestablishment of national union [unity]. The American Government could thus without the least interference contribute powerfully to the welfare of China and make war participation a blessing to all parties.

As China took the decisive step at the suggestion of the United States and as the hope of American Government financial support was held out to the Chinese Minister at Washington, the friends of America and the constructive leader[s] of China hope that the United States will not deny its assistance considering their deep desire that China should be used in this war and that the opportunities of participation should not be lost in local conflicts and turned into dangers to all for the lack of a moderate support which only the United States can supply. For the sake of the welfare of China, the avoidance of a possible breakdown such as the Russian and the realization of Chinese active war assistance I have the honor to ask your support.　　　　　　　　　　　　　　　　　Reinsch

T telegram (WP, DLC).
[1] Actually, Tuan Ch'i-jui, who in fact was soon appointed to this post.

From Edward Mandell House

On Board U.S.S. Mount Vernon,
Dear Governor,   December 15, 1917.

We expect to land this afternoon and if convenient to you I will take the 11.08 Monday morning reaching Washington at 4.40 P.M.

I have had the Mission working all the way over on a report for their respective Departments, and a summary for your information and that of the State Department. These are ready and go forward along with my own to Washington by Gordon tonight.

I hope you will find that the Mission has been successful and well worth while.

Looking eagerly forward to being with you again, I am,
Your devoted,   E. M. House

TLS (WP, DLC).

From Frederic Clemson Howe

Ellis Island, N. Y.
My dear Mr. President: December 15, 1917.

When in Washington on Thursday last I outlined with Mr. Creel a proposal for placing the railroads in trust for the owners and the Government through an operating-holding trust or company.[1] He asked me to prepare a memorandum on it for transmission to you, which I did; but it may not have been sent to you, as Mr. Creel left the city in the afternoon. I am, therefore, taking the liberty of enclosing a copy of the same.

I have made something of a study of railroad transportation in Germany, Switzerland, Belgium and Denmark, which brings into sharp relief the gains which come to a people when their transportation agencies are operated for service. I wish there was some way in which I could portray this. In these countries railroads are run for industry and agriculture, for producers and consumers. Operating officials are thinking of the state, rather than of directors, stock-holders, speculators. Their whole psychology is reversed. They introduce all kinds of conveniences, services, economies. They build up industries instead of killing them. They encourage anriculture [agriculture] instead of discriminating against it. They carry fuel cheaply in order to aid industries. They aid export trade in the same way. They encourage water transportation to get rid of bulk freight, which can be much more cheaply carried by water. They consolidate and build great terminals and wide flung yards convenient for factories and industries. They eliminate all kinds of hurdles which exist in this country. The operating mind is a different mind altogether. It is more like that of a scientist, who is thinking in terms of state. There is no struggle for the long haul. Rather the aim is the short haul. There is no struggle between different roads for traffic. Germany build[s] up her export trade by these means. She also stimulates all kinds of agriculture, cattle-raising, and gar-den [garden]-trucking round about the cities. In Denmark trans-portation is designed for the promotion of agriculture; for getting the goods out of the country as cheaply and expeditiously as pos-sible. In Belgium the main lines are co-ordinated with the water-ways. They are also connected up with light railways similar to our inter-urban lines. Belgium's export trade is, I believe, the largest per capita of any country in the world. Switzerland brought about tremendous improvements when she took over the railroads a few years ago. Australian railroads transport cattle from feeding place to feeding place. They carry settlers out into the country at prac-tically no charge. They haul agricultural implements at a low rate. Every freight agent is connected with the food control board. He receives anything from a bunch of rabbits up to a car-load of hay, receipts for it, and sends it on to its destination.

In other words, in these countries the railroads are integrated into the life of the country and serve it much as the circulatory system serves the human body. It is merely incidental to the social organism. In all these countries, too, the railroads are *consciously* used to develop the country, to aid its upbuilding. There is none of that conflict that exists all over this country by virtue of the irrec-oncilable conflict between profits and service.

And I think that one of the biggest gains from such an integration of the railroads with the nation is political and social. Today the large majority of the men of big talents that I meet have an indif-ference, a dislike, or a contempt for the state. They are divorced from it because of their conflict with it. I have no desire to see the Prussian conception of the state introduced in this country; but I do feel that we cannot go on as we have in the past with the wealth, and the press, and the powerful talent of the nation in one camp, and with the state bereft of its best ability as it is at the present time. We are in a state of almost continuous war within ourselves, and as a result the state is so much weaker than the private interests within the state. And the big gain that I see in Government own-ership is the identification of the *mind* of our powerful men with the state rather than against it. And I do not see how we can have a functioning democracy until this is brought about.

The proposal which I enclose leaves the question of purchase to be determined later. It allows perfect freedom of re-organization,

but it saves to the people all of the tremendous economies which
will result from consolidation, unification of lines, the full use of
cars and terminals, and the speeding up of the equipment which
we now have. It also frees us from the necessity of spending billions
for new equipment when we are not using the equipment that we
have, because of the competition of different lines. Possibly even
more important, the providing of adequate transportation will probably increase the production of wealth by thousands of millions
annually.

    I have the honor to remain,

Very sincerely yours,   Frederic C. Howe

TLS (WP, DLC).
  [1] It is printed as an Enclosure with WW to WGM, Dec. 13, 1917.

From Robert Scott Lovett

My dear Mr. President: Washington December 15, 1917.

    I called on Attorney General Gregory Thursday afternoon to put
before him some of the legal aspects of the present railroad problem,
and subsequently summarized in a memorandum for him the points
I made, with some additions, and sent it to him yesterday. He was
about to leave town—for Chicago, as I understood—and as you are
doubtless considering this problem even now, it has occurred to
me that there might be something helpful to you in these suggestions; and I feel it my duty to send you a copy of the memorandum.[1]

    The only apology I can offer for this intrusion is a rather over-
whelming sense of the gravity of the problem and a desire to assist
you wherever I can.   Very respectfully,   R. S. Lovett.

TLS (WP, DLC).
  [1] R. S. Lovett, "Memorandum," c. Dec. 14, 1917, T MS (WP, DLC). This document
outlined in some detail the legal problems involved in a federal takeover of the railroads.
In general, Lovett believed that the situation of the railroads was not as critical as others
had portrayed it, and he urged that Congress be requested to pass suitable enabling
legislation before any takeover of the roads occurred.

Sir William Wiseman to Edward Mandell House

[London] December 15th. 1917.

Very Secret:

    (a) Effect of United States Mission to Europe has been to give
new encouragement to the Allies at a time when they are sorely
tried. Everybody recognizes that success means complete understanding between America and Allies.

(b) The most urgent problem at present is man-power to secure our Western line against formidable German attacks which may be expected throughout winter. When these have failed, military party will have lost the great temporary prestige which they now hold, and strong liberal reaction may be looked for. It is of vital importance that the United States should come to the assistance of the Allies with man-power immediately, that United States troops now in France should take their places by companies in the line with our men as suggested to you in Paris, and also that reinforcements should be hurried from America at all costs. The next few months will be critical.

(c) The President's speech to Congress enthusiastically received in England. It expresses perfectly British sentiment and is excellent antidote to Lansdowne letter, which is now generally recognized as an unfortunate blunder.

(d) Tardieu has made a statement that America desires a Generalissimo. This has caused considerable surprise in England. It should be unofficially denied in the United States.

(e) Cambrai battle started with British success. During week following Nov. 20th. numerous German counter-attacks were repulsed with heavy enemy losses. Germans brought up large reinforcements on Nov. 30th. and launched heavy attacks against all three sides of salient. Those against Northern and Eastern faces were repulsed but Southern attack succeeded and penetrated as far as Gouzeaucourt. Our counter attack cleared that village and as far as La Vacquerie, but we evacuated eventually eastern part of the salient and withdrew owing to impossibility of supplying troops in the Bourlon area so long as Latreau ridge remained in the enemy's possession. The Germans have engaged nineteen fresh divisions at Cambrai since Nov. 28th. and now have four fresh divisions in reserve in that area. It is therefore probable that their attack will be continued.

(f) Statement from Washington that United States revised shipping estimate is only one third of original estimate causes us dismay. If true, it is most serious news. Uncertainty also shows necessity for permanent American War Mission in Europe which can speak with authority on such subjects.

(g) All Russians desire peace and there seems little hope of obtaining assistance for Roumanian army either from Poles, Cossacks or Ukraines, though we are keeping in touch with movements. We did not feel able to protest against armistice between Roumanian and enemy forces, and if Russia makes a separate peace, Roumania will be compelled to follow suit. Russian armies, except in Caucasus where position is steadier, are melting away. We shall do all we can to secure that no supplies shall in any event be sent to Germany from Russia. The War Cabinet have asked Mr. Balfour and the D.M.I.[1] to form a Committee to handle Russian affairs.

(h) Italy seems to be fighting well and holding their present line. Political situation, however, is giving some cause for anxiety as Giolitti[2] is working against present Ministry. The need of wheat and coal is great, and our information is that civilian morale is largely dependent on adequate supplies. We are doing our best, but dif[f]iculties, especially of shipping, are great.

(i) Personal investigation of Austria's peace terms discussed at Paris has made little progress, but there may be something definite to report shortly.

Mr. Balfour adds personally that shipping always has been and still remains his chief preoccupation.

(j) No decision yet regarding Lord Reading or Northcliffe's return to America.

(k) Deeply grateful for kind thoughts expressed in your letter to me.

What the Presd. does earnestly desire to cooperate in securing is the most effective possible unity of military direction that can be secured by mutual agreement. There has been no such expression of opinion as T. expressed.[3]

T telegram (E. M. House Papers, CtY).
  [1] The Director of Military Intelligence, Maj. Gen. Sir George Mark Watson Macdonogh.
  [2] Giovanni Giolitti (1842-1928), Prime Minister of Italy, 1892-1893, 1903-1905, 1906-1909, and 1911-1914. Opponent of Italian intervention in the war.
  [3] EMHhw marginal note at Paragraph (d).

To Edward Mandell House

White House Dec 16 1917

Delighted that you are safely back Will look forward with to [the] greatest pleasure to seeing you tomorrow Hope you will stay with us   Woodrow Wilson

T telegram (E. M. House Papers, CtY).

From William Gibbs McAdoo

Dear Governor,   [Washington] Dec 16/17

We have encountered some insuperable obstacles in the RR matter and I see no way to overcome them except by legislation. I dont see how you can address the Congress until a more definite program is decided upon. I am at your call any hour today.

Affectionately   WGM

ALI (WP, DLC).

To Joseph Patrick Tumulty

Dear Tumulty: [The White House, c. Dec. 17, 1917]

I have forgotten who is directly in charge of the aviation pro-gramme, but I would be obliged if you would find out and see that this letter[1] is placed in his hands. The statements in it are so serious, though I must say so vague, that I don't see how I can absolutely pass them over; although I take little stock in them.

The President.

TL (WP, DLC).
[1] G. Borglum to WW, Dec. 12, 1917. The chairman of the Aircraft Production Board was Howard E. Coffin.

To Robert Scott Lovett

My dear Judge: [The White House] 17 December, 1917

Thank you for your letter of the fifteenth with its enclosure. You may be sure I welcome all the light I can get on the exceedingly difficult question to which your letter refers.

Cordially and sincerely yours,   Woodrow Wilson

TLS (Letterpress Books, WP, DLC).

From Edward Nash Hurley

Dear Mr. President: Washington December 17, 1917.

I have some encouraging news regarding the building of ships which I know will prove interesting. I have had Lloyd's agency make a thorough investigation of the possibilities for the production of steel tonnage and you will note by the attached statement[1] that they estimate we will produce 3,712,000 deadweight tons of steel shipping during 1918. This is a conservative estimate. In addition to this we have 1,600,000 deadweight tons of wooden ships under contract which are being built very rapidly. The entire program for 6,000,000 tons is well under way. In 1916 there were about 520,000 deadweight tons of ships built in this country, and in 1917 there will be turned out about 900,000 tons. As the labor situation in our shipyards at the present time seems most favorable, I am hopeful that our goal of 6,000,000 deadweight tons of shipping for 1918 will be reached.

Very faithfully yours,   Edward N. Hurley

TLS (WP, DLC).
[1] It is missing.

From John Wilbur Chapman

Jamaica, New York.
My dear Mr. President: December 17th, 1917

When the representatives of the National Service Commission of the Presbyterian Church in the U. S. A. had an audience with you by appointment June 19th, you were pleased to accept the resources of our Church, as we tendered them to you, for the period of the war.[1]

You also expressed your pleasure in the pledge of loyalty which we gave to you in the name of the Church.

You were good enough to make certain suggestions to us at that time, and these suggestions we have sought faithfully to carry out.

Inasmuch as I am just at the close of the first six months of my Moderatorial year, I am sending you this brief report, realizing that you cannot of course be burdened with much correspondence, but feeling at the same time that you would be pleased to know what we have been trying to do.

It has been my privilege to visit eight of the Synods of the Church, and also to hold meetings in 25 of the leading cities of the country East of Omaha.

The burden of my message, and of those associated with me, has been, first,—the absolute necessity that support should be given to yourself and to the Government in these times of war. Second,—that the Church should keep herself as you have suggested, "at the flood tide of her spiritual power." Third,—that the Church should emphasize the righteousness of the warfare in which we are engaged.

In all the cities visited we have found great enthusiasm for yourself and the influence you are exerting throughout the world, and we have also found a spirit of loyalty to the Goverment in the prosecution of the war.

I would like to have you know, Mr. President, that we feel that our Church has responded magnificently to the ideals which you have set before us, and I wish to pledge you anew the support of the Church, of which you are so honored a member.

In behalf of the Presbyterian Church in the U. S. A., with great respect I am,   Yours faithfully,   J Wilbur Chapman

P.S. There is being sent to you from our offices in New York samples of the literature which we are sending out to our ministers in which we think you will be interested. J.W.C.

TLS (WP, DLC).
[1] About this meeting, see the address and reply printed at June 19, 1917, Vol. 42.

Sir Cecil Arthur Spring Rice to the Foreign Office

[Washington] 17 Dec 1917

S of S thinks that it would be extremely dangerous for U S to entirely lose touch with Russian revolutionary party and he is afraid lest cutting off supplies would give new material for German anti-ally propaganda. The USG are therefore continuing all supplies except arms & ammunition. S of S does not believe in possibility of acting on revolutionary party through the N Y Jews who are in close touch with them. This element of the population is he fears not to be relied on. He thinks it possible that Germany by withdrawing troops, contrary to the terms of the agreement with present Russian govt may excite anti-German feeling in Russia, but he has not much confidence.

Hw telegram (FO 115/2318, p. 238, PRO).

Sir Cecil Arthur Spring Rice to Edward Mandell House, with Enclosure

Dear Colonel House   Washington, Dec: 17, 1917.

I have been instructed to communicate the enclosed to you as soon as possible. Please acknowledge receipt.

The Military advisers here suggest that possibly a suitable arrangement would be for one American Regiment to be attached to each division and for one of each of the 3 battalions to be attached to each of the 3 brigades in the division. This would keep the men under the orders of their own battalion commanders. This is merely a suggestion, which may be useful.

We are all so delighted to greet you here

The tel: is a *"personal message"* to you from the Prime Minister.

Yours sincerely   C S. R.

HwCL (FO 115/2203, p. 121, PRO).

E N C L O S U R E

Having regard to Russian situation and the fact that both guns and troops are being rapidly transferred from the Eastern to the Western front, the Cabinet are anxious that an immediate decision should be come to in regard to the inclusion with British units of regiments or companies of American troops, an idea which was discussed with you at Paris. In the near future and throughout the earlier months of next year the situation on the Western front may become exceedingly serious, and it may become of vital importance that the American man power available in France should be immediately used, more especially as it would appear that the Germans are calculating on delivering a knockout blow to the Allies before a fully trained American army is fit to take its part in the fighting.

T MS (FO 115/2203, p. 122, PRO).

David Lloyd George to Edward Mandell House

To Colonel House,   [London, Dec. 17, 1917]

We are receiving information from very trustworthy sources to the effect that the United States shipbuilding programme for 1918 is not likely to exceed 2,000,000 tons. You will realise from our discussions here and in Paris, which were conducted on basis that United States would produce 6,000,000 tons—afterwards increased to 9,000,000 [—] how serious a view the War Cabinet takes of this news. The American shipbuilding programme is absolutely vital to the success in the War. May I urge that immediate steps be taken to ascertain the real situation in respect of shipbuilding as all depends upon estimate being realised.

Lloyd George.

T telegram (A. J. Balfour Papers, FO 800/209, p. 422, PRO).

From the Diary of Colonel House

The White House, December 17, 1917.

I came to Washington today on the 11.08 train. Bill Nye of the State Department Secret Service accompanied me. He read the riot act to the railroad officials and succeeded in having the train arrive on time. Janet, Louise,[1] Frank Polk, Grayson and Gordon met me. I drove by the White House first, intending to leave my bags and go on to Janet's, but I found the President in his study waiting for me. We had a conference which lasted from five until seven o'clock.

It was then too late to dress for dinner and we postponed that formality until afterward when we dressed and went to the theater.

I gave the President a report of my activities in London and Paris and he seemed deeply interested. I shall not go into detail, but I recommended that he send General Tasker H. Bliss over as soon as he could make ready to act as our Military Adviser in the Supreme War Council. I explained the formation and working of that Council and how inefficient it had been made because of Lloyd George's determination to eliminate the British Chief of Staff and the General Commanding in the Field.

In reply to his query as to how matters could be remedied, I thought it would be necessary to wait until we had a sufficient force on the firing line to give us the right to demand a voice in the conduct of the military end of the war. I suggested that I should return to Europe around the first of April, or whenever it was thought the right time, to sit in with the Prime Ministers of Great Britain, France and Italy on the Supreme War Council. He gave cordial assent to this proposal, remarking "I could not possibly send anyone else, for no one knows my mind as you do. Quick decisions are necessary, and it is often useless to try and consult by cable. Someone must be there who knows what to do without referring back to me, and you are the only one whom I would trust to do this, for you and you alone know what I should do in like circumstances."

The President knows, as I do, that it is necessary to have someone who will act on his own initiative and who will receive his unqualified support.

Mrs. Wilson, the President and I dined alone and after the theater went to bed without further discussion.

T MS (E. M. House Papers, CtY).
[1] House's granddaughter, Louise Auchincloss.

To Joseph Patrick Tumulty, with Enclosure

Dear Tumulty: [The White House, Dec. 18, 1917]

I don't like to answer this in writing. Perhaps you will be kind enough to seek out Senator Lewis and tell him.

First, that I do not think it would be wise for me to send for Debs. I suspect, as he does, that the leadership of the Socialists is in some way involved, and the rivalry between Debs and Hillquist, and there might be serious embarrassments connected with involving myself in any way.

Second: My judgment is that it would be very unwise to introduce or press at this time any bill for the national ownership of the railroads. It would inject an element into the situation which need not just now be injected, and would seriously conflict with any solution that I am able to think out as a war solution. The purchase of the railroads during the period of the war would, of course, be a financial impossibility.   The President.

12/18/17 Read to Senator Lewis over telephone by T.W.B.[1]

TL (WP, DLC).
[1] Thomas W. Brahany.

From James Hamilton Lewis

Dear Mr. President,   Washington, D. C. Night Dec. 13, 1917

Knowing your many engagements, and the oppression it would be to add to them by personal interviews, I beg to submit the matters of this note as calling for your consideration.

First. When some weeks ago I telegraphed from Chicago asking a conference, it was to put before you that I had been of Counsel for Eugene Debs, in a matter his atty engaged me for in an appellate Court. By this association this attorney came to me while I was lately on speaking tour in Ill. and *saying* that he spoke on *authority*, said that if I would say to the presdt to send for Debs, and ask Debs to aid in support of this war, *that Debs would come to White House*, confer, then go out and oppose all Socialists who were using Socialism as opposition to the nation's war. (The desire of Debs to wrest leadership from *Hillquist* may be involved) but I inform you that these men are waiting my reply to their offer to me. Of course they beseech that *if not invited no* word of the suggestion go forth.

May I suggest that no invitation be sent to Debs except with the assurance given beforehand to one of your friends, of his *sure* course. He must not be left to say that you invited him, and he declined. We must have a man who will be able to say Debs asked that he be invited by you, if the dignity of the matter should make necessary the divulgence of the fact caused by any *unexpected* course of Debs. (Your judgement on this matter controls any course of mine)

2d. I beg to inform you that while atty gen'l of Chicago and acting mayor (Corporation Counsel) I prepared and pressed thro' the Council, and afterwards the Courts[,] the public ownership system now existing as to Chicago Street Railways. I have had a bill before my committee (Interstate Commerce) duplicating the method as to Railroads. I am anxious to amend the bill and *press* it for action. It contemplates ownership by Government leaving operation to be determined as a business arrangement.

I am anxious *not* to conflict with any purpose *you* have, and in no wise to run in any way counter to purposes the war necessities demand. If you have no view conflicting with my object I will press the measure, of course as my *independent*, uninspired action. If you think any inconvenience to any plan you have would be occasioned I will *not* press the measure.

Anxious for your view that I may serve such in the matters herein stated, I beg to be   Your servant   Jas Hamilton Lewis.

ALS (WP, DLC).

To Joseph Patrick Tumulty, with Enclosure

Dear Tumulty: [The White House, c. Dec. 18, 1917]

I very much appreciate this letter of Mr. Brisbane's and hope that you will tell him so. I hope you will tell him, at the same time, that I really think the best way to treat Mr. Roosevelt is to take no notice of him. That breaks his heart and is the best punishment that can be administered. After all, while what he says is outrageous in every particular, he does, I am afraid, keep within the limits of the law, for he is as careful as he is unscrupulous.   The President.

TL (WP, DLC).

E N C L O S U R E

From Arthur Brisbane

My dear Mr. President: Washington, D. C. December 18, 1917

I enclose two clippings from today's Washington Times that I thought might perhaps interest you.[1] I know that you are too busy to read newspapers for yourself and I want you to see these clippings. I believe that it would be extremely popular if you, as an individual or through one of your departments, should remind Mr. Roosevelt that the United States at war is not a playground for ex-presidents to display their foolish egotism.

I think that it has a bad effect to permit Mr. Roosevelt in all the papers of the United States to say unrebuked that which would put in jail some little Socialist editor, and cause his newspaper to be suppressed.

The clippings which I enclose in this go to one thousand of the principal newspaper editors of this country who receive the Washington Times every day. If there is anything that you think might be said officially or semi-officially through the Washington Times, I should be very glad to print it.

Colonel Roosevelt should be ashamed of his conduct. He is trying to build up a following, using inevitable difficulties at the beginning of the war for his own selfish purposes. A public letter of rebuke from you would bring him to his senses in a moment. He sometimes thinks soberly.   Yours very sincerely,   Arthur Brisbane

P.S. May I call your attention, respectfully, to the following facts in which I have no personal interest.

The attacks that Mr. Roosevelt makes today upon you and the efficiency of this country, belittling us in the eyes of European nations, will be cabled to England passed BY THE CENSOR THERE AND PRINTED EVERYWHERE.

The statement that Mr. Hearst makes today, under the British ruling, is not allowed to go over the cables to England or through the mails. And Mr. Hearst is not allowed to send from England telegrams or letters to his newspapers published in the United States—because in the opinion of England, those newspapers have not been edited to suit *England.*

Lord Northcliffe mentioned to me the fact that a cable which he had sent to me was returned by the censor on the ground that it could not be delivered, because as an editorial writer I was in the employ of W. R. Hearst. I hope the time will come when this government will tell England that the United States Censor is the censor for the press of the United States, and that England should be contented with censoring her own press, and not refuse to an American citizen the use of papers and mail unless requested to do so by United States government.

If England is justified in forbidding Mr. Hearst to use the mails and the cables between England and the United States, because Hearst is alleged to have said some things not flattering to England, would not the United States be justified in refusing Roosevelt permission to send to England by mail or by cable his statements that are intended to bring the United States government into contempt and inspire the Allies with distrust and dislike of the Americans and those that direct American affairs.

TLS (WP, DLC).
    [1] Only one has survived. It was "Republican Stones Thrown from Glass Houses," *Washington Times*, Dec. 18, 1917. This was a reprint of William Randolph Hearst to the Editor of the *New York American*, December 16, 1917. Hearst argued that the Republicans had little right to criticize the Democratic administration's conduct of the greatest war in history in view of their own bungled management of the Spanish-American War of 1898, "a small war against a small, weak nation."

From Jeannette Rankin

My dear Mr. President: Washington, D. C. December 18, '17.

I am still receiving petitions by letter and telegram from my constituents in Montana urging a federal investigation of the mining conditions in Butte. Another general strike is threatened by the miners, with the possibility of a sympathetic strike throughout the west. Such a demonstration at this time would not only be a calamity in so far as the productivity of the west is concerned, but the psychological effect upon the patriotism of the workers whose loyalty is essential during the present crisis might prove demoralizing.

It is reported that the Anaconda Copper Company is trying sur-reptitiously to fill its mines with Greeks shipped in from other parts of the country. "Yet the Federal Commission," to quote a letter received today from a Butte constituent, "says that nothing needs to be done—with thirteen of the Company's mines closed tight as a drum, and the deadly gas dropping the men in the mines like cattle in the shambles."

I cannot represent to you too strongly the necessity for immediate action, and I urge you, as I have urged in previous letters and in person, to instruct the Secretary of Labor to look into the conditions in Butte.   Respectfully,   Jeannette Rankin[1]

TLS (WP, DLC).
[1] "I would be obliged if you would acknowledge this letter for me and say that I have been diligently trying to find out what was the best thing to do about the Butte situation; that I was largely following the counsel of Secretary Wilson." WW to JPT, c. Dec. 19, 1917, TL (WP, DLC).

Edward Mandell House to Sir William Wiseman

No. 06. VERY SECRET: New York. 18.12.17.

Following is for W.W. from BRUSSA [HOUSE]:

(A). I have worked out something regarding Paragraph B. of your cable, and cable goes to PERSHING today and copy of it will go to your Government through British Embassy for information of Brit-ish Government. PRIME MINISTER sent me personal message yes-terday through British Embassy, consequently had to reply through same channel.

(B). President is delighted to read what you say of his message in your Paragraph C. I shall cable you something further in that connection in a few days.

(C). Regarding your Paragraph D., President earnestly desires to co-operate in securing the most effective possible unity of military direction that can be secured by mutual agreement. There has been no such expression of opinion as TARDIEU expressed.

(D). I am getting at the facts as to shipping programme, and will cable fully in a few days. I have impressed upon PRESIDENT to do his best for the greatest possible effort in that direction. Please advise PRIME MINISTER.

(E). Regarding Paragraph G., PRESIDENT believes it is essential to give whatever aid is possible to the Polish, Cossacks, and others that are willing to fight Germany, and while he has no power to lend money direct to such un-organised movements he is willing to let France and England have funds to transmit to them if they consider it advisable.

(F). Please keep me advised so that close co-operation along all lines may be possible.

T telegram (W. Wiseman Papers, CtY).

From the Diary of Colonel House

[The White House] December 18, 1917.

I have had many consultations today with the President, Lansing, Polk, Bliss, Baker, Benson, McCormick and others. I have received several cables from Lloyd George and Wiseman, some of them relating to one thing and some to another. Lloyd George's chief trouble is the shipping and the keen desire of both the British and the French to have our men amalgamated with their troops in companies and regiments.

In talking this over with the President, I thought it advisable to settle the matter at once and not allow it to drag along. I told him pretty much what I recommended in my report, therefore I shall not repeat it here. He said he would send for Secretary Baker and discuss it with him. While he was at the telephone, I suggested that General Bliss be also invited, which was done. Bliss and Baker came to the White House immediately and, as I anticipated, Bliss did all the explaining, for Baker knew but little of the subject under discussion. Bliss' advice was almost identical with what I had already given the President, and it was decided that Baker should draw up a cable to General Pershing indicating our decision.

The President asked me to see Secretary Baker later and advise him as to the substance of his cable, which I did. The President also thought I had better let both the British and French Governments know what had been cabled to General Pershing, since it was a complete answer to their requests. Instead of doing this, I got Lansing to paraphrase the Baker cable and take it up personally with the British and French Ambassadors. In telling the President of this afterward, and of my reasons for bringing Lansing and the Ambassadors into it, he smiled and said, "I suppose it is well to let them feel they are doing something now and then."

An important decision the President and I made was to formulate the war aims of the United States. I never knew a man who did things so casually. We did not discuss this matter more than ten or fifteen minutes when he decided he would take the action I told some of the Interallied Conference he would take as soon as I returned to America. It will be remembered that I urged Lloyd George, Reading and Balfour at Paris to join me in formulating a broad declaration of war aims that would unite the world against

Germany, and would not only help the Russian situation, but would knit together the best and most unselfish opinion of the world. I could not persuade them to do this, and now it will be done by the President. It would have been better if the Interallied Conference had done it for reasons which are apparent.

The President asked me to have Mezes give a memorandum of the different questions which a peace conference must necessarily take up for solution. I told him I already had this data in my head. He replied that he also had it, but he would like a more complete and definite statement such, for instance, a proper solution of the Balkan question.

I suggested that I cable Sir William Wiseman to return to New York at once in order to have the benefit of his advice regarding the way England would receive what we have in mind to say. The President said he thought it would not be well to consult with anybody. If we consulted with the British we should have to consult with the French etc. I combatted this by saying it was not for the purpose of consulting Wiseman but merely to have him look over what was decided upon and judge if there was anything offensive to the British point of view which we had overlooked. The President did not reply, but later in the day asked how soon I thought I could get Wiseman here. I cabled Wiseman to start immediately. My cables to him and his replies are a part of the record. It will be remembered that Wiseman is now acting as liaison officer between me personally and the British Government.

I complimented the President upon his message to Congress, telling him it was practically what I should have advised if he had waited until my return, although I should have made a more thorough job of it. I should have said all he said, but should have added what is now proposed. It should have been done in one document rather than in two. He did not agree as to the wisdom of this, although he did not dissent.

We took up the discussion of the railroad question. He had made up his mind to take over the railroads and put McAdoo in as Administrator. The legal difficulties involved were holding him back. He had found he could not take over the funds which the railroads had on hand, and without them, he could not run them (railroads) unless Congress made an appropriation for that purpose.

I have been so engrossed with foreign affairs that I have not given this question any attention, but since it is a matter of such burning importance, I shall try to help find a way by which immediate action may be taken without referring it to Congress. I told the President I hoped he would do for the railroads what he had done for the banks. That is, he should make them conduct their business honestly and then see that they had a fair deal.

He surprised me by saying that the only constructive thought he had applied to any of the great measures was in the Federal Reserve Act. My opinion is, he gives himself too much credit in that case and not nearly enough in the others, for I know myself of suggestions and thoughts he has put into other great measures enacted during his administration which made the difference between a good law and an inferior one.

At lunch we had an interesting conversation which I brought up by saying that I found myself thinking of Lloyd George's secretaries and was wondering why I had thought of them. The process was as follows: There were some Virginia apples on the table and I speculated upon whether they were the kind Mrs. Dana Gibson[1] had promised to send us. This took me to her sister in London, Mrs. Astor,[2] and Waldorf Astor being the Secretary of Lloyd George brought up the line of thought.

I mentioned this to the President and asked if he ever thought how the roads of destiny turned. For instance, he was now in a position to influence, for good or for evil, a large part of humanity, and I wondered if he had followed the turning in the road which had brought him to this position. If he had not had the quarrel with the authorities at Princeton, he would not have securing [secured] the nomination for the Governorship of New Jersey. In ordinary years, New Jersey would have elected a republican rather than a democrat. If Roosevelt had not fallen out with Taft, Taft would probably have been re-elected. And so it goes.

The President thought these things were not chance, but were well worked out conclusions which had reached a conjunction. He admitted that there was such an element as chance. For example, if one were walking down the street and a brick fell from a chimney on him that, he thought, was purely chance. We finally decided that Providence had direction in human affairs because one could not account for the conjunction of circumstances otherwise.

The President spoke of how much he was handicapped by not having a secretary whom he could trust with his confidential work. He said Congress, he was sure, would be willing to give him an additional secretary, but that Tumulty's heart would be broken if he asked for one. I expressed regret that he did not have such a secretary as Newton Baker. I told of how efficiently I was served while abroad on my mission, and how often I thought of him and wished he could be served so well. He said, "I suppose you had nothing to do but to steer, and that is what I should be in a position to do."

[1] Irene Langhorne Gibson, wife of the famous magazine illustrator, Charles Dana Gibson.

[2] Nancy Witcher Langhorne Shaw (Mrs. Waldorf) Astor.

He said he had offered Tumulty another place, that of Customs Appraiser, at a salary of $9000.00 for life, but he had declined it. He thought Tumulty wanted a Cabinet place but he considered him utterly unfit for it and therefore he could not dispose of him in that way. I disagreed with him. I thought Tumulty wanted the position he has now, and his refusal to be forced out, and his determination to hold it even at the expense of his pride, made me suspicious of him. He said "suspicious in what way?" I replied that perhaps the Catholic Church insisted upon his remaining. To this he answered "they do not like him." "Perhaps not,["] said I, "nevertheless, they would prefer him to a Protestant."

I have no such prejudice against the Catholic Church as the President seems to have. I have tried repeatedly to get him to put them in the Cabinet and other high places, not, indeed, because they were Catholics but because they were best fitted for the positions for which I suggested them. The reason I think it a mistake to keep Tumulty as Secretary to the President is because of the feeling Protestants generally have on the subject.

The President could not see in what way the Catholics could benefit by Tumulty's position since he never told him anything of value. He spoke of the folly of the Catholic Church trying to force itself into politics. He thought the country had gotten the impression that he did not treat his friends with consideration and that he was not grateful. He thought a man could not serve his country well and allow personal friendships to enter into any of his acts.

I know where the President got this idea. It was from Tumulty himself. He has been driving it into the President for the past three or four years in fact, ever since his position became precarious. He has made the President believe that under no circumstances can he afford to break with any of his other friends, citing McCombs and Harvey as two instances. I disagreed with the President and said he was more criticised for sticking to his friends than he was for breaking with them. He replied, "I suppose you refer to Daniels and Tumulty. The country now seems to realize that Daniels is making good."

I told the President that as far as Tumulty was concerned, he went with the wrong people. The President knows this and realized they were trying to use him, but he did not believe Tumulty had anything of value to give them. In this again he is mistaken. By some means, Tumulty is aware that the President contemplates taking over the entire railroad system of the United States. This information is of enormous value to the men with whom Tumulty associates, many of whom are merely paid agents of Wall Street operators.

In speaking of the dinner at the Elysee Palace given by President and Madame Poincare to the Interallied Conference, I told the President that they made me the guest of honor. He replied, "They should have done so as you were my personal representative." In answer to this I answered that they did not know it since I had not shown my credentials to anyone in England or France. This astonished him. I do not see exactly how I should have preceded the Prime Ministers of other countries even though I was the President's personal representative. It was an honor the French desired to pay the United States, and neither the President nor I were thought of.

I informed him that I had arranged with the French Government to have all the members of our Mission sit in the Interallied Conference and also Ambassador Sharp. I explained that it did not make any difference whatever how many sat in; that the real work was done by the Prime Ministers of Great Britain, France, Italy and myself at private conferences. I thought I now understood how to handle the peace conference most effectively when it came, but I did not go into details.

I saw Vance McCormick today, and after some discussion with him I decided to ask Admiral Benson to call the Mission together tomorrow after I had gone and have them work out a plan for better coordination between the Allies; particularly as to our representation. I did not mention this to the President for I prefer to see what they recommend before bringing it to him.

After dinner tonight the President and I went inot [into] executive session until half past nine o'clock when we went to bed.

I find the President still antagonistic to Lansing. Lansing constantly does something to irritate him, and generally along the line of taking action without consultation. In this instance, it was sending a despatch to John W. Garrett at the Hague concerning the rece[i]ving of some peace overtures which Garrett thought the Germans were about to make, but in which the President had no confidence.

I have about come to the conclusion that it is George Creel who is prejudicing the President against Lansing.

I thought the President or Lansing should give out a report of the Mission's work at the Paris Conference, and the President agreed to it except that he preferred to give it out himself.[3] I try my best to keep him from being so secretive. It would be much better to take the public into confidence whenever it can be done without injury to the public welfare. I should inaugurate an entire new policy if I were President. I should do away, as far as possible, with secret diplomacy. In most instances it could be done with entire safety.

[3] See RL to WW, Dec. 27, 1917, and WW to RL, Dec. 31, 1917.

From Newton Diehl Baker, with Enclosure

Dear Mr. President   [Washington, Dec. 18, 1917]
    This is a copy of the dispatch as sent.
                        Respectfully,   Newton D Baker

ALS (WP, DLC).

E N C L O S U R E

[Washington] December 18, 1917.

Both English and French are pressing upon the President their desire to have your forces amalgamated with theirs by regiments and companies and both express belief in impending heavy drive by Germans somewhere along the line of the Western Front. We do not desire loss of identity of our forces but regard that as secondary to the meeting of any critical situation by the most helpful use possible of the troops at your command. The difficulty of course is to determine where the drive or drives of the enemy will take place; and in advance of some knowledge on that question, any redistribution of your forces would be difficult. The President, however, desires you to have full authority to use the forces at your command as you deem wise in consultation with the French and British commanders in chief. It is suggested for your consideration that possibly places might be selected for your forces nearer the junction of the British and French lines which would enable you to throw your strength in whichever direction seemed most necessary. This suggestion is not, however, pressed beyond whatever merit it has in your judgment, the President's sole purpose being to acquaint you with the representations made here and to authorize you to act with entire freedom in making the best disposition and use of your forces possible to accomplish the main purposes in view.

It is hoped that complete unity and coordination of action can be secured in this matter by your conferences with the French and British commanders.

Report result of any conferences you may have with French and British commanders and line of action that may be agreed upon.
                    Newton D. Baker   Secretary of War.

TC telegram (WP, DLC).

To Franklin Knight Lane

My dear Lane: [The White House] 19 December, 1917

I will be very much obliged if you would drop me a line as to what you think about the suggestion which Kent makes in the enclosed letter.

In haste

Cordially and faithfully yours,   Woodrow Wilson

TLS (Letterpress Books, WP, DLC).

To Breckinridge Long

My dear Mr. Long: The White House 19 December, 1917

I have read very carefully your letter of December fifteenth[1] and need hardly say that I sympathize with the object you have in mind in the matter of organizing the newspaper men in some serviceable way to put the news service upon a higher plane of intelligence and public duty, and I sincerely hope that something may come of the organization which is being formed in Paris.[2] Certainly, its personnel would promise good results; but I do not believe, from experience which I hope some time to have an opportunity of narrating to you, that anything of the same sort would be possible on this side the water. There are too many irregular, irresponsible and unmanageable forces amongst us, and while the members of a particular group would no doubt be honorably bound by their engagements, they could bind nobody else and control nobody else. If there should by any chance come a breathing spell when I can talk this matter over with you, I shall be very glad to do so.

Cordially and sincerely yours,   Woodrow Wilson

TLS (B. Long Papers, DLC).
[1] B. Long to WW, Dec. 15, 1917, TLS (WP, DLC).
[2] In his letter, Long discussed the formation by American journalists and others residing in Paris of the American War Publicity League in France. He attached a clipping from the *New York Times*, November 22, 1917, which stated that the purpose of the organization was to "facilitate the sending of proper and accurate information concerning the military and political situation." He also enclosed W. G. Sharp to RL, Dec. 12, 1917, T telegram (WP, DLC), which said that the object of the group was to place "information on the war on a higher and more helpful plane before American readers." Long went on to suggest that a similar organization on a larger scale should be formed in the United States in order to "inspire the membership of the press to treat news in a manner which would tend to increase confidence in the plans for the prosecution of the war and in the persons who are charged with that prosecution."

To John Wilbur Chapman

[The White House]

My dear Doctor Chapman: 19 December, 1917

I value your letter of December seventeenth and am very much cheered by it. I did not doubt that the Church would respond in the finest way to the patriotic appeals made to it, and I thank you very warmly for the very encouraging report which you so generously made.

Cordially and sincerely yours,   Woodrow Wilson

TLS (Letterpress Books, WP, DLC).

From James Cardinal Gibbons

My dear Mr. President: Baltimore. December the 19th, 1917.

Some time ago I received a letter from the Cardinal Secretary of State[1] of His Holiness, informing me of the great solicitude of the Holy Father for the very sad and in fact critical condition of the Serbians and Syrians, who on account of the lack of foodstuffs are facing starvation.

The Holy Father has made unceasing efforts, especially with the British Government by which under guarantees of neutrals, foodstuffs could be introduced into these countries to relieve the situation, but so far, to no avail.

It now appears that the Pope has been informed that the American Red Cross would be disposed to assume the burden of providing, especially for the Serbians, by sending into Switzerland the necessary provisions which would be sent into the territory of the Austro-Hungarian Monarchy to be from there forwarded into Serbia. On its side, of Course the American Red Cross would wish to be assured that these provisions would really be distributed to the Serbian people, and this by means of a regular control to be exercised by some neutral organization with the consent of the Austrian Government.

The Holy Father has wished me to lay this matter before you with the hope that by your valuable influence some relief may reach these suffering people, and offers his co-operation.

I am certain, Mr. President, that any action you would take in furthering these humane efforts would be grateful to His Holiness as you know they would be to me. I would appreciate very much a reply from you so that I may inform the Holy Father.

With sentiments of the most profound respect, I am

Very sincerely Yours,   J. Card. Gibbons

TLS (WP, DLC).
¹ That is, Pietro Cardinal Gasparri.

From Alexander Jeffrey McKelway

My dear Mr. President: Washington, D. C., December 19, 1917.

In spite of all the demands upon your time, I am presuming, at the request of our General Secretary, to ask you to write us a letter endorsing the efforts of the National Child Labor Committee in upholding the standards of protection for the working children of America. From the experience of Great Britain, we have been persuaded to believe that these efforts are not only in the interest of the childhood of America, but also tend to efficiency and economy of production.   Cordially yours,   A. J. McKelway.

TLS (WP, DLC).

From Newton Diehl Baker

Information

Dear Mr. President: Washington. December 19, 1917.

You will be interested to know that last week we received, completed, 125 training airplanes, and that our weekly production will increase. That means that we are now getting more airplanes a week than the Army had altogether before we entered the war.

Other parts of the airplane program are progressing satisfactorily.
                    Respectfully yours,   Newton D. Baker

TLS (WP, DLC).

From William Bauchop Wilson

                    Minneapolis, Minn., December 19, 1917.

At the request of the Presidents Mediation Commission the representatives of the Trades Unions of the Twin Cities have agreed unconditionally to withdraw the sympathetic strike order they have in contemplation so that the Commission may handle the street car problem unhampered by the danger of a sympathetic strike in other industries. It will take some little time to work out an adjustment of the street car situation but in view of the attitude of the leaders of the labor movement the Commission is enabled to leave here tonight and proceed to Chicago to deal with the difficulties in the meat packing industry.   W. B. Wilson.

T telegram (WP, DLC).

Edward Mandell House to Sir William Wiseman

New York. 19. 12. 17.

VERY SECRET. *Following is for W.W. from BR.* [HOUSE]

(A). It is important that you come over immediately for consultation, and that you reach New York before January 1st. This is confidential between us.

(B). Regarding tonnage: PRESIDENT says we are just as alive to the importance of it as you are, and that we will do our utmost. What you have heard is inaccurate. We will presently be in a position to tell you exactly what to expect in figures. Conferences are going on today about the matter and President is giving it his personal attention.

TC telegram (W. Wiseman Papers, CtY).

From the Diary of Colonel House

[The White House] December 19, 1917.

Secretary Lane called today and complained rather bitterly that the President no longer trusted him and did not take him into his confidence. I combatted this and thought the work the President was doing in other departments relating to the war, was the reason for his reticence. As a matter of fact, I think the President has cooled considerably toward Lane. He mentioned him but once yesterday and that was to say that Lane had told him something about George Harvey, showing that Lane had been in conference with Harvey about certain matters.

I have had up with Lansing and the President the question of representation in Switzerland. I believe, and so does Lansing, that Abram Elkus should replace Stovall. The President hesitates to displace Stovall although he knows he is not equal to the work there. I suggested as a compromise sending Elkus as Commercial Attache or some such minor position, and have him keep in touch with the situation.

I told the President I would return the $2500.00 he gave me for expenses abroad since I had not spent any of it. Brown Brothers paid me $5.42 in interest on the amount so my check on the Guaranty Trust Company is for $2505.42.

The President was interested in my conversation with General Pershing and that I believed I had won him over to our side.[1]

I am leaving on the four o'clock train for New York after a busy and profitable stay in Washington. It is agreed that I shall return Sunday to remain four or five days. I shall then stop with Janet and Gordon for the holidays, but will doubtless see something of the President in order that we may get up the statement he is to make as to our peace terms.

[1] Actually, House had two conversations with Pershing on December 4 and 6, both of which may be relevant to his rather cryptic remark above.

House wrote of the first conversation in his diary entry of December 4 as follows:

"I had a long talk with Pershing and called attention to what I considered the difficulties of his position. I wished him to know how much I desired his success. If he were a failure, it would reflect upon the President, and it could be said if he had sent Roosevelt or Wood or someone else, things might have been different. I called his attention to the importance of his task and urged him to attend strictly to the military part and leave the semi-diplomatic end of it to others. Some of this I thought Sharp could do and I advised him to get a trusted friend, who had some knowledge of politics and diplomacy, to do the rest. He said he had selected Robert Bacon for that purpose but had found him incapable of doing it properly. He thought, too, he had made a mistake in getting an ex-Ambassador and for reasons which can readily be understood.

"I promised Pershing to talk with his father-in-law, Senator Warren, upon my return and then select some man to help him. I thought if this was not done, his troubles would accumulate and he would find himself seriously hampered in the discharge of his military duties and his influence generally lessened.

"He took occasion to tell me that he had no political ambition whatsoever and that the stories being told about his desire to be a candidate for President were wholly false. I encouraged him in this position. I said we had never had a military President who had been a success or who had added to his prestige, excepting General Jackson who was more of a politician than an army man. Grant, I thought, would be considered greater today if he had not touched politics or business. Washington, too, lessened rather than added to his reputation when he entered politics. Pershing agreed to all this and I hope he will hold to his resolution."

Before his second conversation with Pershing on December 6, House had spoken with General Pétain and Premier Clemenceau, who had complained of Pershing's allegedly "narrow" point of view and his refusal of offers of French assistance and facilities. House discreetly informed Pershing of their feelings and urged the General to deal with Pétain and Clemenceau as diplomatically as possible. The remainder of the conversation appears in his diary as follows:

"I told Pershing of the French and British desire to have our troops go into their ranks for training. He thought the situation might require it, but he was of the opinion that if the American troops went in, very few of them would ever come out, and that it would be foolish to expect to build up a great American army by that method. He was very fair and open-minded about this.

"When I pressed upon him the difficulties of the situation and how nearly impossible it was for one man to do both the military and diplomatic end of it, he agreed and urged me to come back and sit on the Supreme War Council in order to take over that part of the work. He thought there was no one else who could do it so well because there was no one who knew the situation as I knew it, and held the confidence of the President to such an extent. He said it would be particularly gratifying to him if I would do this; that he had learned to have a sincere regard for me, and that he thanked me from the bottom of his heart for the frankness with which I had talked to him, which had been and would be of inestimable benefit. I promised again to help in every way possible and suggested that he write me from time to time when anything occurred which he thought I might bring directly before the President, or that would be of service to him and his great work in Europe."

To Alexander Jeffrey McKelway

My dear Doctor McKelway:

[The White House]
20 December, 1917

As the labor situation created by the war develops, I am more interested than ever, if that were possible, in throwing all the safeguards possible around the labor of women and children in order that no intolerable or injurious burden may be placed upon them. I am, therefore, very glad indeed that the National Child Labor Committee is diligently continuing its labors and extending its vigilance in this important matter. By doing so it is contributing to efficiency and economy of production, as well as to the preservation of life and health.

Cordially and sincerely yours,   Woodrow Wilson[1]

TLS (Letterpress Books, WP, DLC).
[1] This letter was published widely by the National Child Labor Committee.

To Frederic Clemson Howe

My dear Howe: [The White House] 20 December, 1917

Thank you for the memorandum about the railroads. I always value your thinking about such matters and just now I am doing a great deal myself about the railroads.

Cordially and sincerely yours,   Woodrow Wilson

TLS (Letterpress Books, WP, DLC).

To James Cardinal Gibbons

The White House
My dear Cardinal Gibbons: 20 December, 1917

Your letter of December nineteenth concerns a matter which I have thought about a great deal and in which I am sincerely anxious to help. The difficulties in the way are many, largely because we find that we cannot rely upon the promises of the belligerents opposed to us in the matter of the transmission and distribution of relief. But you may be sure that if any way can be found, I shall be glad to find it.

With sincere regards,

Cordially yours,   Woodrow Wilson

TLS (Baltimore Cathedral-Ar).

To George McLean Harper

My dear Harper: The White House 20 December, 1917

Thank you for your little note.[1] As a matter of fact, the copy of the Alumni Weekly which contained your too generous article[2] did get through the mill and reach me, and I read the article aloud to Mrs. Wilson with genuine appreciation. Thank you very warmly.

You are quite right. I take no stock at all in the Alumni Weekly. It has been full of falseness from the first, and so I had not seen a copy of it for a long time. I am very glad I saw this copy.

With warmest regards to you both,[3]

Cordially and faithfully yours,   Woodrow Wilson

TLS (G. M. Harper Papers, NjP).
    [1] It is missing.
    [2] George M. Harper, "Woodrow Wilson, Man of Letters," *Princeton Alumni Weekly*, XVIII (Dec. 5, 1917), 222-24. As the title suggests, Harper provided a brief analysis of Wilson's formal literary works from *Congressional Government* through *Constitutional Government*, with a few comments on Wilson's major statements on the World War. He attempted a capsule summary of the essence of Wilson's political thought, but he was primarily concerned to set forth the essential elements of Wilson's literary style.
    [3] Belle Dunton Westcott (Mrs. George McLean) Harper.

From William Kent

Dear Mr. President: Washington December 20, 1917.

I have just returned from New York, and have made inquiry concerning the proposed water power legislation. Mr. Lenroot informs me that the Shields bill has been turned over to the Interstate and Foreign Commerce Committee, Mr. Sims, Chairman, and that Mr. Sims is not particularly favorable to joint action, but has followed the suggestion of the Lands Committee in appointing a subcommittee to confer. Mr. Lenroot also informs me that no one in the House has been recognized by the receipt of the proposed bill or a request to confer with anyone in connection therewith. It is extremely important that Mr. Lenroot, who remains in town, should be consulted, and also Messrs. Ferris and Sims, if they can be reached. Delay in action will be apt to greatly complicate matters. I believe that, as soon as possible, you should call in the three Chairmen, Messrs. Ferris, Sims and Lever, and the ranking members, Messrs. Lenroot, Esch, and Haugen.[1] Time is of the essence of any legislative program. I believe that early action would have put Senator Shields in a position where he could not have pushed his bill, and further delay in recognizing and consulting with those in charge in the House will lead to complication and lack of coherent endeavor.   Yours truly,   William Kent

TLS (WP, DLC).
    [1] Wilson met with the men above mentioned and twelve other members of the House Committees on Agriculture, Interstate and Foreign Commerce, Public Lands, and Rules at the White House at 8 P.M. on January 4, 1918.

From John Avery McIlhenny and Others

The President: Washington, D. C. December 20, 1917.

The Commission has the honor to present for your consideration a matter which is regarded as of vital importance in the Commission's work of recruiting the civil service under war conditions.

The great influx of war workers is overtaxing the living accommodations of the city of Washington. Since a state of war was declared aproximately 20,000 clerks and other employees have been added to the civil service in Washington. Probably more than that number of persons have taken up residence in the city for other reasons. The prospect is that the coming year will witness a further increase in the population of the city of, perhaps, 50,000. Reports of unpleasant experiences met by newly appointed Government employees in their efforts to obtain rooming and boarding places are being circulated broadcast throughout the country, with the result that the Government's work is being hampered.

Notwithstanding the excellent work done by several organizations which have been trying to solve the problem, the situation is so serious that the Commission feels it to be its duty to call it to your attention with the suggestion that the whole matter be placed in the hands of the Council of National Defense, with sufficient funds to bring about the needed relief.

We have the honor to be:

Very respectfully,   John A McIlhenny
Chas M Galloway
H. W. Craven

TLS (WP, DLC).

Sir Cecil Arthur Spring Rice to the Foreign Office

Washington 20 Dec 1917

S of S told me Japanese had a large colony in Vladivostock who might be attacked. In that case Japan had a force ready. China had taken necessary measures and he was in consultation with Chinese Minr.[1] He was afraid landing of Japanese might cause a violent outbreak of feeling in Russia and strengthen hands of Bolshevists.

Russian Ambr. here notes a change in the direction of sympathy for Bolshevist party but I gather that this is rather due to desire of USG not to adopt non possumus attitude.

Hw telegram (FO 115/2318, p. 248, PRO).
[1] That is, Ku Wei-chün (Vi Kyuin Wellington Koo).

To John Avery McIlhenny

My dear Mr. Chairman: [The White House] 21 December, 1917

Allow me to thank you and the other Commissioners for your letter of yesterday about the situation with regard to living accommodations for the vastly increased number of employees of the Government. I have been very much concerned about the matter myself and will look still further into it.

Sincerely yours, Woodrow Wilson

TLS (Letterpress Books, WP, DLC).

From Georges Clemenceau

My dear Mr. President,   Paris. le dec. 21 1917.

Allow me, when my good friend Mr. Tardieu leaves Paris on his way to Washington, to take advantage of the occasion to tell you directly, from man to man, that we are doing our very best to be equal to all this dreadful time requires. You did set us such a magnificent example that we need only follow you and you may be assured that we will spare nothing to do as well as America is doing. Great our intentions are, great also is our good will and courage to put to its right end the greatest historic labour for justice and right that was ever undertaken by nations down to this day. All I can say is that we will do our best to be worthy of our cause, being certain that the great American Republic means, as we do, to accomplish the utmost in view of the mighty achievement. My friend Tardieu, in whom we place full confidence, will tell you that your name is pronounced every day here by all Frenchmen as the name of a friend whom it would be a great joy for us all to greet on our national soil.

He will also tell you that we see in the great country who has chosen you as her chief a people of brethren in the highest sense of the word, with whom our firm hope is to pursue, hand in hand, the highest work of civilization, grounded on the firm principle: to each man his right.

Believe me, My dear Mr. President,

Most truly yours   G Clemenceau

ALS (WP, DLC).

From Elizabeth Merrill Bass, with Enclosure

Washington, D. C.

My dear Mr. President: December 21st, 1917.

Senator Hollis, of New Hampshire, sent me the enclosed letter this morning. He has been polling the Democratic members of the Senate, and Senator Smoot has been polling the Republican members. You will note the Democratic result.

The first list in the letter and the last list contain some of the same names, but it is the first list whom he thinks might be changed, or at least the eight or nine of them that are needed.[1]

Respectfully yours,   Elizabeth Bass

[1] There is nothing in the appointment books or Wilson's correspondence for this period to indicate that he made any immediate effort to influence any senators on the matter.

ENCLOSURE

Henry French Hollis to Elizabeth Merrill Bass

Dear Mrs. Bass: [Washington] 20 December, 1917.

I gave the following list to my stenographer this morning to be given you over the telephone in case you call up:

Beckham	King	Swanson
Culberson	Martin	Trammell
Fletcher	Pomerene	Williams
Gerry	Smith (of Maryland)	Wolcott
James	Simmons	

Nine of this fourteen would carry the day for us.

It takes sixty-four. Smoot guarantees twenty-nine Republicans. I guarantee twenty-two Democrats, including Stone. Pittman tells me that Phelan is all right but I have not asked Phelan personally. Counting Phelan, we have fifty-four, so we need ten others. The following Democrats are in favor, with Phelan doubtful:

Ashurst	Lewis	Sheppard
Chamberlain	McKellar	Smith of Ariz.
Gore	Myers	Stone
Hollis	Newlands	Thomas
Hughes	Owen	Thompson
Johnson of South Dakota	Pittman	Vardeman
Jones of New Mexico	Ransdell	Walsh
Kendrick	Robinson	
Kirby	Shafroth	

The following Democrats are against, with Trammell doubtful:

Bankhead	King	Smith of Md.
Beckham	Martin	Smith of S. C.
Broussard	Overman	Swanson
Culberson	Pomerene	Tillman
Fletcher	Reed	Underwood
Gerry	Saulsbury	Williams
Hardwick	Shields	Wolcott
Hitchcock	Simmons	
James	Smith of Ga.	

so it is exactly an even break,—twenty-five to twenty-five, with one doubtful on each side.   Sincerely yours,   Henry F. Hollis

TLS (WP, DLC).

From George Creel

MEMORANDUM

My dear Mr. President,   [Washington] December 21, 1917.

Major Stanley Washburn, of the State Department, has proposed a speaking tour of the United States in the interests of Russian understanding, and the Secretary of State strongly approves of the plan.

Mr. Washburn asks two private cars, press representatives, magazine reporter, a representative of National Security League,—all approximating a cost of $40,000 for a 40 day trip.

I have decided against the plan on account of its extreme expensiveness.

Respectfully,   George Creel

TLS (WP, DLC).

From Vance Criswell McCormick

Dear Mr. President: Washington December 21st, 1917.

At your suggestion I am enclosing a sketch[1] giving very roughly my idea of what I think would be an effective way of handling the Inter-Allied Tonnage question. I consider this question the paramount one of the war, as I explained in the memorandum I gave Col. House.

I have discussed this proposal fully with the other members of the Mission and I can say that they are all unanimously in favor of it, except Mr. Colby, who explained his objections to you yesterday.

Sincerely yours,   Vance C. McCormick

TLS (WP, DLC).
¹ Actually, a diagram of an organization to have complete control over the disposition of tonnage.

Bainbridge Colby to Joseph Patrick Tumulty

My dear Mr. Tumulty: Washington December 21, 1917.

I am sending you herewith a copy of the letter written by Mr. H. G. Wells about which I spoke to you yesterday.¹

I mentioned to the President the other day that I had this very interesting expression of Mr. Wells' views, and said I would send it to him. It follows pretty much the lines of a long and rather intimate conversation I had with Mr. Wells in London, and his conception of America's role at the present time, and his ardent admiration of the President led me to suggest that he set forth his views in writing. I told him I should like to convey them to "a very illustrious person," and I have no doubt that Mr. Wells assumed that I would show his letter to the President. In this sense his letter may be regarded as a communication addressed to the President, who I think will find the letter of more than passing interest.

Yours faithfully,   Bainbridge Colby

TLS (WP, DLC).
¹ The letter, H. G. Wells to B. Colby, is printed in H. G. Wells, *Experiment in Autobiography* . . . (New York, 1934), pp. 605-11. In this long letter, Wells set forth his ideas about the necessity for a new world order, to be embodied in a league of nations, and his conviction that only the United States, and more particularly, Woodrow Wilson, could force the Allies into a clear statement of war aims, a commitment to a just peace, and participation in a conference to organize the league.

Frank Irving Cobb to Edward Mandell House

(*Personal*)

Dear Colonel House: New York December 21, 1917.

You doubtless saw the interview with Penrose in The Times this morning, attacking the Administration and threatening, in effect, to make a partisan issue of the conduct of the war.¹ William R. Willcox, Chairman of the Republican National Committee, was in to see me this morning and he is much disturbed over the situation. The Old Guard crowd in the Republican Party is trying to compel Willcox's retirement, the real reason being that he has supported the Administration in the war, and has refused to play politics with it. Willcox finds on the part of the Penrose-Smoot Republicans a determination to make a party fight hereafter, and naturally is apprehensive as to the damage that they can do. Incidentally, in the course of the conversation, Willcox said that it would help considerably if the President would strengthen the loyal faction by taking a few more prominent Republicans into the War Administration. He was not referring to a coalition cabinet or any nonsense of that kind. He said that the appointment of Root had been a very great help to them in keeping down this other element, and that if they had a little more help of that kind he believed that they could retain control of the party. I have known Willcox for many years, and believe he is a man of the highest character and integrity who is earnest in his support of the Government in this war and will be glad to do anything that he can to help. If the President could find a way to work a little more closely with Willcox and Republicans of that type, I am sure that the results would be extremely beneficial. I do not know how he feels about it, but my own opinion is that some of them are far more trustworthy than many of the Democrats in Congress with whom he is compelled to work.

It is plain from the Penrose interview that the Old Guard Republicans are going to make their appeal for Republican support on the ground that the President's appointments are mainly partisan, that the war is incompetently conducted, and that Republicans have been excluded from the conduct of the war. It is a fake issue, but nevertheless dangerous on that account, and it will, of course, have the support of Roosevelt, who is eager to attack everything that has been done or left undone, and their combined capacity for injury is very great.

With sincerest regards,   As ever, yours,   Frank I Cobb.

TLS (WP, DLC).
[1] "Republicans Plan an Early Campaign," *New York Times*, Dec. 21, 1917. Senator Boies Penrose stated that there were abundant issues for the Republicans to use in the congressional campaign of 1918. Among them, he said, were "the conditions of the War Department, the neglect of the camps and cantonments, and the failure to supply sufficient arms." Penrose charged that political considerations had dominated the administration's appointments to positions important for the conduct of the war. "The Republicans have not been partisan in this war," he asserted, "but the time has come when they must be consulted and men of experience and ability placed in places of responsibility." As an example of political appointments, he cited the sending of Colonel House to represent the United States in conference with the Premiers of the Allied nations: "If President Wilson did not wish to send his Secretary of State I think some other man versed in big problems and international usages should have been sent." "As a party," he concluded, "the Republicans have loyally supported the Government but we are now going to ask for an accounting and propose to carry our fight to the people in the next Congressional elections."

From the Diary of Josephus Daniels

1917 Friday 21 December

WW read telegram that British censor had sent from N. Y. Tribune to Trotsky asking him for Christmas message.[1] Why will an

American paper be guilty of such stupidity or worse. B. said it has been supporting the war policy. "Yes" said WW, "it was for war all the time, and cannot change, but it is not genuine in its real support." WW read telegram from Russian Commissionaire Minister of Foreign Affairs[2] who proposed that consuls be given passports to America & other countries to propose the overturning of all governments not dominated by the working people.[3] "The impudence of it" said WW. And the impotence. Should his message be printed. Lansing Lane "Yes," Baker & I no. Baker said it would do no good & might encourage men of IWW type in America. WW said it was his reaction not to make it public. Why did American censors permit Tribune telegram to go out? I am to see.

By the way, WW said Crane's cook & housemaid said Trotsky owed them $10 & 20 each—money they had given to some sort of club he organized.

[1] This telegram was not printed in the *New York Tribune*; it was undoubtedly suppressed.

[2] That is, Leon Trotsky (Lev Trotskii).

[3] Daniels referred to a telegram which discussed diplomatic couriers, not consuls. On December 14, the Commissariat for Foreign Affairs sent the following communication to all embassies and legations in Petrograd:

"For the information of the Allied and neutral embassies and legations: Certain embassies have refused to visa the passports of the diplomatic couriers of the National Commissariat for Foreign Affairs. The institutions concerned have given as the motive that the council of the National Commissaries is not yet 'recognized' as the government. The question of recognition is one of form, and the government of the Soviets treats with entire indifference this detail of the diplomatic ritual. Nonrecognition does not free, however, from the necessity to reckon with the Soviet government as with a fact. Statements to the effect that 'unrecognized government' cannot have diplomatic couriers are unfounded if only because the Soviet government considers necessary diplomatic relations not only with the governments but also with the revolutionary socialist parties which are striving for the overthrow of the existing governments. Finally, it is impossible not to point out that the above-mentioned embassies are conducting the policy of 'nonrecognition' in an extremely one-sided manner as they themselves are constantly applying to the National Commissariat for Foreign Affairs with requests for giving them such and such authorizations and certificates for securing free passage for their diplomatic couriers, etc.

"Considering the further maintenance of such an order of things entirely inadmissible, the National Commissariat for Foreign Affairs has given instructions that henceforth no permits are to be issued, in general no facilitating to be done for the representatives of those embassies which view it as their task to create for the Soviet government petty chancery difficulties." *FR 1918, Russia*, I, 303-304.

From Daniel Willard

My dear Mr. President: Washington December 22, 1917.

On the 10th instant, in response to a general invitation sent out by the War Industries Board, representatives of the different steel interests—about 40 in number—met with the Board in Washington, and through Judge Gary, who acted as their spokesman, discussed the present condition of the steel industry and particularly the schedule of prices now in effect by agreement.

Briefly, it was claimed that the actual cost of manufacturing steel had advanced upon the average about $2.00 per month since September, when the present prices were made effective. Notwithstanding this, however, Judge Gary stated that they were willing to agree that the present schedule of prices which terminates by agreement on January 1st, should continue in effect for a further period.

The War Industries Board has received from the Federal Trade Commission a carefully compiled statement showing the cost of the essential elements entering into steel, such cost figures having been based upon data available as of November 1st.

This whole matter was given full consideration today by the War Industries Board, after conference with representatives of the Fuel Administration and Federal Trade Commission, and the Board unanimously adopted the following resolution:

RESOLVED, That the present prices previously fixed by agreement with the steel interests and approved by the President for ore, coke, pig iron, steel and steel products be continued until March 31st, 1918 and that no contracts for delivery running beyond that date be entered into which fix specific prices.

The Board is of opinion that owing to the uncertainty which will result from insufficient and irregular transportation during the next three or four months and other causes which will affect the cost of manufacture, particularly the unsettled labor condition, that the existing prices should remain in effect until the first of April, but that no new contracts which include prices, should be entered into by the manufacturers extending beyond that period.

In case the conclusion which has been reached by the Board, as indicated in the above resolution, should meet with your approval, it is suggested that a statement similar in effect to the one shown on attached sheet should be given out for the information of the public.

The War Industries Board will be glad to furnish, either in person or by letter, any additional available information which you may desire in this connection. We have not asked for a personal conference with you concerning this matter because it seemed unnecessary to take your time for that purpose, providing you should be willing to approve of the continuation of the existing arrangement until April 1st, which course seems to the War Industries Board the wisest one under all the circumstances.

We shall await your further instructions.

Very respectfully submitted,   Daniel Willard

TLS (WP, DLC).

To Joseph Patrick Tumulty, with Enclosure

Dear Tumulty   The White House [Dec. 22, 1917].

Please acknowledge receipt of this and send it, as at my request to Chairman Willard of the War Industries Board.   W.W.

ALI (WP, DLC).

E N C L O S U R E

December 22d, 1917.

The President today approved the recommendation of the War Industries Board that the maximum prices heretofore fixed by the President upon the recommendation of the Board upon ore, coke, pig iron, steel and steel products, subject to revision on January 1, 1918, be continued in effect until March 31st, 1918. No new contracts calling for delivery of any of said commodities or articles on or after April 1, 1918 are to specify a price unless coupled with a clause making the price subject to revision by any authorized United States Government agency, so that all deliveries after that date shall not exceed the maximum price then in force, although ordered or contracted for in the meantime. It is expected that all manufacturers and producers will observe the maximum prices now fixed.

T MS (WP, DLC).

From George Creel

My dear Mr. President: Washington, D. C. Dec. 22nd, 1917.

I think it absolutely necessary and of the highest importance that Mr. Hoover's statement, prepared for the Congressional Committee, and also sent to you this morning,[1] should be given to the press at once for publication in Monday morning's papers. I went to see him about it this afternoon to urge this course upon him, and found that you had thought the course unwise, inasmuch as it might be construed as a discourtesy to the Committee. Senator Kenyon and Senator Jones, our friends, want to see the report printed, and the three who might regard it as a discourtesy—Reed, Vardaman, and Lodge—are the ones who are doing everything in their power to keep this report from the public until such time as their own lies may have had time to sink in and take on color of fact. I feel very strongly about this. The papers are waiting for it. Tomorrow's issues will have the story of how Mr. Hoover was flouted from day to day and denied at the last moment the privilege of appearance that had been promised him. The statement, issued from the White House, with a notation by you, would cap a splendid climax.[2]

Unfortunately, I am compelled to leave town in a little while to meet my wife and children[3] who are coming from California. If you agree with me, will you be kind enough to have some one at the White House telephone Mr. Hoover and we will make the necessary arrangements together tomorrow.

Respectfully,   George Creel

TLS (WP, DLC).

[1] Henry Cabot Lodge, on December 11, had offered a resolution (S. Res. 163) calling for an investigation of shortages in supplies of coal and sugar. The Senate Committee on Manufactures, headed by James A. Reed, a severe critic of Hoover, began its hearings on December 14. The first witness, Claus August Spreckels, president of the Federal Sugar Refining Co., charged that the sugar shortage had been "created" by Hoover himself through an agreement with all sugar refiners not to import any raw sugar during the war except through the agency of the International Sugar Committee, a subdivision of the Food Administration. Spreckels further asserted that the Sugar Committee was "a mere adjunct" of the "sugar trust," that is, the American Sugar Refining Co., and that, by setting the price to be paid for imported raw sugar too low, the committee effectively prevented any importation at all and thus kept supplies of raw sugar away from the independent refiners. The results were shortages and high prices. The testimony during the following week produced heated rebuttals of Spreckels by George Morrison Rolph, head of the California and Hawaiian Sugar Refining Co. and chairman of the International Sugar Committee, and Earl D. Babst, president of the American Sugar Refining Co. and also a member of the committee. Hoover repeatedly requested either to testify before the committee or to be allowed to submit a formal statement on behalf of the Food Administration and the International Sugar Committee. Reed either refused the requests or postponed action until some later time. See the *New York Times*, Dec. 12, 14-16, 18-23, 1917.

[2] See the news report printed at Dec. 25, 1917.

[3] Blanche Lyon Bates Creel, George Bates Creel, and Frances Virginia Creel.

From Minnie Bronson[1]

Your Excellency: Washington, D. C. December 22, 1917

One of our members in Wisconsin has sent us the enclosed extracts from the Milwaukee Leader, edited by Victor L. Berger, the socialist, in which it is alleged that a representative of the administration recently visited Miss Alice Paul and told her that "the President would not mention suffrage in his message at the opening of Congress, but would make it known to leaders of Congress that he wanted it passed and would see that it passed."[2]

In the Milwaukee Leader of December 18, Victor Berger declares that this story "has every appearance of being true," and urges it as a proof of "effective picketing."

The syndicate writer quoted originally with this allegation has his material published in many newspapers throughout the country; and while we have no doubt that the story is untrue, a statement from you, Mr. President, would at once stop any further circulation of this canard, and make it impossible for men like Victor L. Berger to intimate that the President of the United States "secretly favors" suffrage methods he has publicly condemned.

Thanking you for a reply at your early convenience, Mr. President, I am   Respectfully yours,   Minnie Bronson

TLS (WP, DLC).
    [1] General Secretary of the National Association Opposed to Woman Suffrage.
    [2] TC of article and editorial in the *Milwaukee Leader*, Dec. 18, 1917, T MSS (WP, DLC).

From Alexander Jeffrey McKelway

Dear Mr. President: Washington, D. C., December 22, 1917.

We are greatly indebted to you for your kindness in sending me your letter of December 20th, which we shall be able to use with great effectiveness in the prosecution of our work.

With best wishes for a happy Christmas and for a New Year which shall bring to fruition your great plans for the peace of the world, I remain,   Cordially yours,   A. J. McKelway.

TLS (WP, DLC).

From Joseph R. Wilson, Jr.

My dear Brother: Baltimore, Maryland December 22, 1917.

Thank you so much for another year's subscription to "Littell's Living Age." I especially appreciate your thought at such a time as this when your mind is so burdened with international problems.

We three decided some weeks ago to forego the pleasures incident to even an exchange of gifts in our own home, feeling as we do that the money so spent can be put to better use at a time when there are so many demands for funds.

Kate and Alice join me in wishing you, sister Edith and the members of your household a very, very happy Christmas. Our prayer for you is that God, during the year to come, may continue to give you strength of mind and body and lead you as He has in the past along the paths of righteousness for His Name's sake.

With deep love to you all,
                Your affectionate brother,   Joseph R. Wilson.

TLS (WP, DLC).

Sir Cecil Arthur Spring Rice to the Foreign Office

Washn. 22 Dec 1917

Your tel No. 5502

S of S told me today that of course he recognized the great danger of allowing the B to hold control of E. Siberia, and the stores at Vladivostock. At the same time he feared that Jap intervention, solely regarded from the Russian point of view, would provide German anti-ally propaganda with a powerful weapon and this would certainly be more powerful if the U S joined Japan in occupying Russian territory.

On the other hand sole Jap. intervention from the point of view of general policy constituted a great danger.

He hoped that it would not be necessary to take any action. In the meanwhile the U S warship was at hand should foreigners be threatened. But the port would shortly be closed by ice & the icebreakers were in the hands of the B.

I gather from the official in charge of U S Russian department that altho no news had been received from Vladivostock for four days there was reason to believe that the B were far from being in complete control in E. Siberia.

S of S shares your views but wishes me to impress on you the danger likely to result, from point of view of the Russian internal situation, from joint U S & Jap intervention. I am sure that USG, though they are evidently anxious that the allied R R[1] in Petrograd should act in closer accord than at present, cherish the hope that the U S has an exceptional position among the Russian masses, and that this capital should be husbanded as much as possible.

It is also probable that USG does not believe that an expedition to the Far East would be popular in this country, or even pos[s]ible.

Hw telegram (FO 115/2318, pp. 266-67, PRO).
  [1] Railroad representatives.

From Herbert Clark Hoover

Dear Mr. President: Washington, D. C. 23 December 1917

As you are aware, the Senate inquiry on the sugar shortage has been in session for a matter of ten days. I have repeatedly requested permission to appear before the Committee in order that I might make a complete statement of the matters at issue from the Administration's point of view and give the very cogent reasons for each step taken in the protection of the American people from profiteering and excess prices. I was informed yesterday that I should be heard today at twelve o'clock and had prepared a complete and impersonal statement of the entire sugar question, copy of which I have already sent to you. I was informed late this morning that I would not be heard and that the Committee had adjourned over Christmas. I thereupon sent the statement to the Committee and asked that it be introduced into the record and through Judge Lindley[1] requested that it might be given to the public in order that many mis-impressions might be dispelled.

Senator Jones moved that the Committee place it in the record and give it to the public but the Committee refused and also refused to say whether they would consider it discourteous or not if we issued it to the Press. I cannot but feel that here is a double attempt to stifle truth and to leave prejudice in the minds of the public. Senator Jones authorizes me to say to you that he thinks this statement should be given to the Press and that nothing will alter the mind of the majority of this Sub-Committee.

May I request that if you can spare a moment to glance over the statement to witness its impersonal nature, and if you find it in order, that you would consider whether or not it could be issued as from you through Mr. Creel's bureau to the public, as the statement was forwarded to you as much as to the Senate Committee.

Yours faithfully,   Herbert Hoover

TLS (WP, DLC).
   [1] That is, Curtis Holbrook Lindley.

To George Creel

My dear Creel: The White House 24 December, 1917

I think you were quite right not to authorize the tour of Mr. Stanley Washburn. It would have been a very great mistake to do it. I shall take occasion to speak to the Secretary of State about the matter.

Always   Faithfully yours,   Woodrow Wilson

TLS (G. Creel Papers, DLC).

Two Letters to Samuel Gompers

My dear Mr. Gompers: The White House 24 December, 1917

Your letter of December fourteenth has just been handed me emobdying [embodying] the admirable resolutions passed by the recent convention of the American Federation of Labor, held in Buffalo, November 12-24 last. I hope that you will have some early opportunity of conveying to the members of that convention the very deep gratification which those resolutions have given me. They have done not a little to keep my heart strong.

Cordially and sincerely yours, Woodrow Wilson

My dear Mr. Gompers: The White House 24 December, 1917

Thank you for your letter of December twenty-first[1] about the housing situation and the additional facts which Mr. Hiss[2] submits. I hope that we shall very early have from the Council of National Defense systematic suggestions about this exceedingly important matter. Cordially and sincerely yours, Woodrow Wilson

TLS (S. Gompers Corr., AFL-CIO-Ar).
[1] It is missing.
[2] Philip Hiss, architect of New York, chairman of the Section on Housing of the Advisory Commission of the Council of National Defense.

To Newton Diehl Baker

My dear Mr. Secretary: [The White House] 24 December, 1917

I am writing to you as Chairman of the Council of National Defense to lay before you the enclosed.[1]

I know that the Council has had this exceedingly important matter up, and I hope it is beginning to see its way to systematic suggestions as to how it is to be dealt with, at any rate so far as the Government is concerned.

Cordially and sincerely yours, Woodrow Wilson

TLS (Letterpress Books, WP, DLC).
[1] That is, Gompers' letter of December 21 about the housing situation.

From Robert Lansing

My dear Mr. President: Washington December 24, 1917.

I did not fail to communicate to Mr. McCormick[1] the inquiry contained in your memorandum of the 19th,[2] regarding the amount of financial relief which would be permitted to go to Poland from the United States.

Mr. McCormick has told Mr. Phillips that the whole question is one which the War Trade Board would like to consider carefully before recommending a figure which in its opinion is desirable as a maximum. This opinion Mr. McCormick hopes to be in a position to send you in a month's time. Meanwhile the War Trade Board is willing that the applications for license should be continued as received at a rate not to exceed $600,000 per month, it being under-stood that this arrangement is a temporary measure.

With assurances of respect, etc., I am, my dear Mr. President,
Faithfully yours,   Robert Lansing.

TLS (WP, DLC).
[1] W. Phillips to V. C. McCormick, Dec. 19, 1917, CCL (SDR, RG 59, 861.48/591b, DNA).
[2] It is missing.

From Thomas Davies Jones

My dear Mr. President: Chicago December 24, 1917.

I have been for some months past resisting a growing conviction that I am not really up to the work of the War Trade Board. I have sought the best advice I could get here at home, and I can no longer delay asking you to relieve me of the work. I believe this step is necessary.

I have felt it a privilege to have a part in the public service during these trying times, and I very deeply regret the necessity of giving it up. But there is no escape from it.

I am writing today to Mr. McCormick and to the Secretary of Commerce.   Ever gratefully yours,   Thomas D. Jones.

TLS (WP, DLC).

From Verner Zevola Reed

Denver, Colo., Dec. 24, 1917.

The strikers of the oil fields of Louisiana and the Gulf Coast of Texas voted their strike off as of Christmas Eve in order that you might take it as a Christmas greeting from them and an additional proof of their undivided loyalty to you and the national defense. I purposely withheld until to-day the statement that the oil operators of California during the Santa Barbara conferences held a meeting and instructed their chairman, L. P. St. Clair,[1] to offer to you through me all of their properties their treasuries and their services without condition, if you at any time should deem them necessary for the national defense. I respectfully offer to you my best Christmas wishes.   Verner Z. Reed.

T telegram (WP, DLC).
[1] Leonard Pressley St. Clair, president of the Independent Oil Producers' Agency of California.

From William Gibbs McAdoo

Dear Mr. President: Washington December 24, 1917.

I have received the following cable message, through the State Department, from Assistant Secretary Crosby:

In an interview proposed by Italian Ambassador[1] am informed that present shipping arrangements provide for only three hundred thousand tons coal for Italy in each of the two following months as compared with the requirements of six hundred fifty thousand for reasonably effective operation of industries, railways and ships. Country threatened with famine and revolution because food in railway cars at ports cannot be transported to other points where bread lacking. Ninety per cent all cities having gas plants in Italy represented as being now wholly without illuminating gas, generally condition approaching breakdown. The Ambassador has represented these facts to British authorities. Lord Robert Cecil suggested his interview with me. English shipping authorities acting alone, appear to be unable to better situation though recognizing its absolutely critical importance as it seems highly probable that Italy must change her position in war if better situation cannot be created. Only practical step now suggesting itself and approved Italians English and other American advisers here is that inter-ally shipping board should be immediately organized with a view to placing Italian situation before French and English thus [Those] brought together under conditions and guided by principles indicated in Paris Conference believe it would be wise to let me temporarily represent our government in bringing this organization into being so that situation may be immediately clarified. In my judgment this is most important immediate subject presented in war situation. Strongly impressed with importance of immediately obtaining neutral tonnage in all pending cases. Slight advantage in matter of blockade seems less important that [than] cure of situation which is all war operations. Cravath[2] fully concurs. Please advise action as soon as possible.

In view of the great urgency of the matter as represented by Mr. Crosby, I ask that your consideration of the proposal that an Inter-Ally Shipping Board should be immediately organized with a view to placing the Italian situation before the French and British Governments under conditions and guided by principles indicated at the Paris conference, and that Mr. Crosby be designated temporarily to represent our Government in bringing this organization into being.

I am sending a copy of this letter to the Secretary of State.

                              Cordially yours,   W G McAdoo

TLS (WP, DLC).
    [1] Marquis Guglielmo Imperiali.
    [2] Paul Drennan Cravath, corporation lawyer of New York, at this time counsel to and member of the United States Treasury Mission to the Inter-Allied Council on War Purchases and Finance.

From George Parmly Day[1]

Your Excellency: New Haven, Connecticut December 24, 1917.

The Yale University Press will before long begin the publication of a series of fifty volumes of American History, to be called "The Chronicles of America." These have been in preparation for some time and have been written by authors selected with the approval of the Council's Committee on Publications of Yale University. No manuscript has been accepted for the series until it has been approved both by the editor of the series, Professor Allen Johnson, of the Department of History, Yale University, and by the Council's Committee on Publications of the University. It will be evident from what has been said that the greatest care has been used and that every precaution has been taken to make it certain that the work shall be in every way a scholarly contribution to the general public's knowledge of American History. It is our belief that you will share with us the feeling that this will be of the greatest benefit to our country.

We shall feel highly honored if you will permit the series to be dedicated to you and if you will accept, with our sincere compliments, copies of the volumes as published in the first special edition, which in such case would more properly be described as the President's Edition.

In the hope that you will grant our request, which is endorsed by the Council's Committee on Publications of Yale University, and with all good wishes, believe me

Yours sincerely,   Geo. Parmly Day

TLS (WP, DLC).
    [1] Treasurer of Yale University; founder, president, and treasurer of Yale University Press.

A News Report

[Dec. 25, 1917]

WILSON GIVES OUT REPLY
BY HOOVER THAT REED BARRED

Washington, Dec. 25.—President Wilson today indicated his disapproval of the manner in which the Senate Investigating Committee, headed by Senator Reed of Missouri, has inquired into the sugar shortage, by authorizing the publishing of an explanation by the Food Administrator, Herbert C. Hoover, of the sugar situation.

The Senate committee by a majority vote last week sustained the objection of Senator Reed against making the statement public or permitting it to be read into the official record until Mr. Hoover himself was called to the witness stand. Feeling that he had been treated discourteously by the committee, Mr. Hoover carried the matter to the President, who today took the unusual course of giving the statement, prepared for a Senate committee, to the press through the Committee on Public Information.

This unprecedented action on the part of the President, it is predicted, may arouse the ire of Senator Reed and some of those members of the Investigating Committee who thus far have refused to give Mr. Hoover a hearing. Before adjourning over the Christmas holidays the committee announced that Mr. Hoover would be called later. The Food Administrator and his counsel have maintained that an early hearing was promised them by the committee and that it was unfair to them to permit the impression created by antagonistic witnesses, particularly Claus A. Spreckels, to go abroad that the Food Administration had been a party to what has been termed a "sugar corner."

Mr. Hoover's statement attributes the sugar shortage here to the heavy movement of sugar from the Western Hemisphere to Europe, and asserts that without the fixing of prices by agreement sugar would have been selling for 25 or 30 cents a pound, and more than $200,000,000 probably would have been profiteered from the American people by this time. According to the statement, the Allies before the war took only 300,000 tons annually from the Western Hemisphere. This year they have taken 1,400,000 tons.

Since the food administration was created in August the United States has exported to the Allies 110,356 tons of refined sugar and Cuba has shipped to Europe 246,133 tons of raw product. This, it is declared, is just the amount of the shortage in the United States. Even with these shipments, it is pointed out, consumption in England has been reduced to twenty-four pounds a year for each person and in France to fourteen pounds, against a consumption in America of fifty-five pounds.

The shortage, the Food Administrator declares, will continue during next year, as it is the duty of the United States to continue to feed the Allies.

"Next year," he says, "our supplies will be short 250,000 to 300,000 tons unless the Allies go to Java for supplies. This amounts to an economy of about 70 per cent. on our part. If the Allies are forced to go to Java it will require an extra amount of shipping which if used to transport troops will move 150,000 or 200,000 American soldiers to France."

Charges that the Food Administration has permitted sugar stocks to remain in parts of the country unmoved are denied, as are statements that sugar was left in Cuba while an effort was made to beat down Cuban prices.

"There are no sugar stocks in this country," it is declared, "which are not in course of distribution."

As to the fixing of sugar prices, the Food Administrator had this to say:

"There was no other way under the law to prevent profiteering except by voluntary agreement, as the food bill carried no power to fix prices. These agreements have of necessity been made with the old manufacturers, including the sugar trust. Independent refiners are represented by a majority on a committee whose duty it is to divide the imported sugar between all equitably. This committee has no price-fixing power; it has solely to do with distribution. The independent refiners who have been fighting the trust for years could be depended on to watch any unfair action."

The statement recounts the Food Administration's efforts to reduce consumption to avert the shortage which was foreseen in the Summer, and continues:

"The reduction has shown in the decrease in candy sales, &c., but, on the other hand, a similar campaign for the preservation of fruit has increased consumption in that direction—but will reduce consumption later on. * * * Taking into consideration all factors, it is not certain that there has been any increase in actual consumption, and, considering the increased canning use, there may have been a decrease."

Mr. Hoover emphatically denies charges that George M. Rolph, head of the Food Administration's sugar division, endeavored to benefit the California refinery of which he is head through the arrangement of the Cuba price. The text of the Food Administrator's statement is appended:[1]

Printed in the *New York Times*, Dec. 26, 1917.
    [1] The foregoing is a good summary of Hoover's statement.

From Robert Lansing

My dear Mr. President: Washington December 25th, 1917.

You have doubtless been impressed, as I have, in reading the various reports on economic conditions in Germany by the increasing anxiety of German financiers and commercial and industrial leaders as to what will happen to their foreign trade after the war.

They evidently feel that the more the conflict is prolonged so much the more lasting will be the bitterness against Germany, with the possible result that it will cause discrimination against German trade at least by individuals if not by governments and by international agreements. I have the impression that the repeated efforts of the Imperial Government for peace-negotiations are due in considerable measure to pressure by these economic interests in order to prevent as far as possible the commercial isolation which is more and more feared as the war goes on.

Whether these fears are or are not justified seems to me of less importance than the fact that they exist. If they do, and I think that that can hardly be doubted, ought we not to turn to advantage this mental state of the influential business class in Germany by making their fears as to the *post-bellum* trade conditions more intense?

Just how we should do this I am uncertain but I feel certain that we should not lose this opportunity to increase German dissatisfaction with the Imperial Government's war policies. One method would seem to be to threaten commercial retaliation or reprisal after the war. Personally I do not believe such a method of imposing penalties could be carried out as it would be against the almost irresistable processes of trade, but the threat might have the desired psychological effect in Germany and prevent the conditions on which the adoption of the method is predicated.

In any event I am convinced that this subject should receive very careful consideration at this time when the German people are beginning to realize the consequences which may result from continuing the present policies and practices of their Government, and when we should leave no stone unturned to weaken the control of that Government over the people.

Faithfully yours,   Robert Lansing.

TLS (WP, DLC).

From Newton Diehl Baker, with Enclosure

Information

Dear Mr. President: Washington. December 25, 1917

This telegram closes happily the most menacing labor dispute in the country. Secretary Wilson started the negotiation and left his associates to conclude it. The result is fine beyond anything I believed possible, after hearing the passionate statements of the men.

Respectfully,   Newton D. Baker

ALS (WP, DLC).

ENCLOSURE

Chicago, Ill. Dec. 25, 1917.

An adjustment has been effected of the difficulties in the packing industry the basis of settlement is as follows: first the establishment of machinery through the appointment of a United States administrator whereby all pending and future questions affecting employment in the packing industry will be settled by peaceful process instead of by conflict; John E. Williams of Chicago is named as administrator; second prohibition against discrimination for a membership or nonmembership in a labor union; third the abandonment of the lockout and strike at least for the period of the war; fourth the Government through the President's mediation commission is itself a party to the arrangement and thereby undertakes to secure its enforcement stop This adjustment affects the plants of the packers located in Chicago, Kansas City, Sioux City, St. Joseph, St. Louis, East St. Louis, Denver, Oklahoma City, St. Paul, Omaha, and Fort Worth, and involves about one hundred thousand employees.   Felix Frankfurter

TC telegram (WP, DLC).

From Gutzon Borglum

Stamford, Connecticut

My dear Mr. President: December 25th, 1917.

Since writing you I have visited two other factories and attended several aeronautic conferences. This, with the present investigation, so disturbs me that I must write further, with the hope that congressional investigation of the aeronautic bodies may be avoided—at this time. At the aeronautic conferences I alone am emphatically against congressional investigation, on the ground that nothing must happen while there is time to correct conditions from within, and so avoid repetition of the ship and ordinance scandals. There is little mood to accept this.

If the opportunity arrives, I will tell you of conditions I personally know, which strike at the root of honest, disinterested public service; of irregularities, graft, self-interest and collateral profiting in the very heart of our production department, but general public knowledge of actual aeronautic conditions would be as a military disaster to American arms as well as an unwarrented blow at our government.

The world's war is at our door, aiming at the phenomenon of self-governed humanity. Every belligerent government except ours has broken down under criticism and investigated scandal. Every government has self-interests and incompetency somewhere—it's human, and governments—good ones—are human. But good governments correct their own disorder. Therefore, I suggest, not as a substitute to my first letter, but as preparatory to any change advisable and to inform and safeguard:

The immediate selection of three competent, fearless and incorruptible men, whose loyalty to you is above question. Give them authority, without publicity, to go quickly over the present aeronautic plan and accomplishment in our aircraft and report on

Engines, planes and propellers, the general and special character of all and each, general and specific service of all and each.

Contracts placed and system employed in selecting contractors.

Supply sources, by whom held.

Relation of members of Production Board to supply controls, also to contractors—direct and collateral.

Test experiments, when made, purpose and result. Why are our planes inferior generally to all foreign planes and vastly poorer than German planes.

What use is made of the excellent data constantly sent here covering all necessary information relating to Germany's planes.

Such inquiry should not audit accounts—a larger principle is at stake.

For this report you need a highly trained, broad guaged [gauged] engineer; an expert, efficiency production man; and a man, who knows the art of machine flying and the history and possibilities of machines.

Your engineer should be an internal combustion engine man, who knows airplanes and that an airplane engine is not simply a refined truck engine. Elements enter into flying two to ten thousand pounds of balanced, inert material, that will not be bulled into space by simply machine force. He should also be a man who knows propellers. This latter item has almost been forgotten and today no reliable propeller exists that can safely be standardized for even one machine!! This has gone so far that the D.H. No. 9,[1] tried recently at Dayton is without a propeller that can lift its 3600 pounds with any efficiency, Wright's, Curtis', the American Propeller Co.'s and Lang's[2] propellers all failing. Prof. Gallopp, I believe, is the man for that position—a man, whose knowledge has not hurt his intelligence. I find he is, at present, consulting engineer to an established, high-class automobile company in Indiana.

The second should be any trained specialist on efficiency organization. I could possibly get a half dozen names of men with this special training. Our nation runs that way.

The third position I should like to fill personally. There are no principles in aeronautics related to flying the "heavier than air" machines that I am not thouroughly familiar with and there are many principles I have discovered not known generally. I feel, however, as De Vinci did, when seeking a commission. He wrote: "as for that art, I know all that is known." The open-mindedness of this carries its own forgiveness. I observe accurately, avoid prejudices and have no fears that I know of, and I am not afraid of failing or being wrong. I know I'm a good organizer and I can handle and keep the confidence of men. I am not only anxious but I am prepared to serve you and the great service to the world you, for America, have undertaken.

I could put into your hands, in the briefest possible time, a report—with a digest—of our aeronautic condition to date, together with war needs that would carry its own conclusions, index our immediate course, and avoid scandal. Investigation, I believe, during war time, should be periodical and automatic. This would rob them of abnormal interest and make them, if properly framed, great policy affecting functions.

I earnestly hope you will let me contribute to your great work.
                Faithfully and sincerely yours,   Gutzon Borglum

TLS (WP, DLC).
    [1] That is, the English-designed De Havilland model No. 9, a day bomber.
    [2] The Dayton-Wright Airplane Co., formed by Edward A. Deeds, Orville Wright, and others in April 1917, and the Curtiss Aeroplane and Motor Corp., formed in 1917 by Glenn Hammond Curtiss, the aviation pioneer. Both of these concerns were among the largest contractors for military airplanes. The Editors have found no reference to Lang or his company; he was probably a small subcontractor.

A Proclamation[1]

[Dec. 26, 1917]

WHEREAS the Congress of the United States, in the exercise of the constitutional authority vested in them, by joint resolution of the Senate and House of Representatives, bearing date April 6, 1917, resolved:

That the state of war between the United States and the Imperial German Government which has thus been thrust upon the United States is hereby formally declared; and that the President be, and he is hereby, authorized and directed to employ the entire naval and military forces of the United States and the resources of the Government to carry on war against the Imperial German Government; and to bring the conflict to a successful termination, all of the resources of the country are hereby pledged by the Congress of the United States.

    [1] Words in italics in this document added by Wilson; words in angle brackets deleted by him.

And by joint resolution bearing date of December 7, 1917, resolved:

That a state of war is hereby declared to exist between the United States of America and the Imperial and Royal Austro-Hungarian Government; and that the President be, and he is hereby, authorized and directed to employ the entire naval and military forces of the United States and the resources of the Government to carry on war against the Imperial and Royal Austro-Hungarian Government; and to bring the conflict to a successful termination, all the resources of the country are hereby pledged by the Congress of the United States.

And whereas it is provided by section 1 of the Act approved August 29, 1916, entitled "An Act making appropriations for the support of the Army for the fiscal year ending June 30, 1917, and for other purposes," as follows:

The President, in time of war, is empowered, through the Secretary of War, to take possession and assume control of any system or systems of transportation, or any part thereof, and to utilize the same, to the exclusion as far as may be necessary of all other traffic thereon, for the transfer or transportation of troops, war material and equipment, or for such other purposes connected with the emergency as may be needful or desirable.

And

WHEREAS, it has now become necessary in the national defense to take possession and assume control of certain systems of transportation and to utilize the same, to the exclusion as far as may be necessary of other than war traffic thereon, for the transportation of troops, war material and equipment therefor, and for other needful and desirable purposes connected with the prosecution of the war;

NOW, THEREFORE, I, WOODROW WILSON, President of the United States, under and by virtue of the powers vested in me by the foregoing resolutions and statute, and by virtue of all other powers thereto me enabling, do hereby, through Newton D. Baker, Secretary of War, take possession and assume control at 12 o'clock noon on the *twenty-eighth* day of *December*, 1917, of each and every system of transportation and the appurtenances thereof located wholly or in part within the boundaries of the continental United States and consisting of railroads, and owned or controlled systems of coastwise and inland transportation, engaged in general transportation, whether operated by steam or by electric power, including also terminals, terminal companies and terminal associations, sleeping and parlor cars, private cars and private car lines, elevators, warehouses, telegraph and telephone lines and *all* other equipment and appurtenances commonly used upon or operated as a part of such rail or combined rail and water systems of transportation;—to the end that such systems of transportation be utilized for the transfer and transportation of troops, war material and equipment, to the exclusion so far as may be necessary of all other traffic thereon; and that so far as such exclusive use be not necessary or desirable, such systems of transportation be operated and utilized in the performance *of such other services as the national interest may require and* of the usual and ordinary business and duties of common carriers.

⟨I hereby direct⟩ *It is hereby directed* that the possession, control, operation and utilization of such transportation systems hereby by me undertaken shall be exercised by and through *Wm. G. McAdoo, who is* hereby appointed and designated Director General of Railroads. Said Director may perform the duties imposed upon him, so long and to such extent as he shall determine, through the Boards of Directors, Receivers, officers and employees of said systems of transportation. Until and except so far as said Director shall from time to time by general or special orders otherwise provide, the Boards of Directors, Receivers, officers and employees of the various transportation systems shall continue the operation thereof in the usual and ordinary course of the business of common carriers, in the names of their respective companies.

Until and except so far as said Director shall from time to time otherwise by general or special orders determine, such systems of transportation shall remain subject to all existing statutes and orders of the Interstate Commerce Commission, and to all statutes and orders of regulating commissions of the various states in which said systems or any part thereof may be situated. But any orders, general or special, hereafter made by said Director, shall have paramount authority and be obeyed as such.

Nothing herein shall be construed as now affecting the possession, operation and control of street electric passenger railways, including railways commonly called interurbans, whether such railways be or be not owned or controlled by such railroad companies or systems. By subsequent order and proclamation, if and when it shall be found necessary or desirable, possession, control or operation may be taken of all or any part of such street railway systems, including subways and tunnels; and by subsequent order and proclamation possession, control and operation in whole or in part may also be relinquished to the owners thereof of any part of the railroad systems or rail and water systems, possession and control of which are hereby assumed.

The Director shall as soon as may be after having assumed such possession and control enter upon negotiations with the several companies looking to agreements for just and reasonable compen-

sation for the possession, use and control of their respective properties on the basis of an annual guaranteed compensation, above
accruing depreciation and the maintenance of their properties,
equivalent, as nearly as may be, to the average of the net operating
income thereof for the three year period ending June 30, 1917,—
the results of such negotiations to be reported to me for such action
as may be appropriate and lawful.

But nothing herein contained, expressed or implied, or hereafter
done or suffered hereunder, shall be deemed in any way to impair
the rights of the stockholders, bondholders, creditors and other
persons having interests in said systems of transportation or in the
profits thereof, to receive just and adequate compensation for the
use and control and operation of their property hereby assumed.

Regular dividends hitherto declared, and maturing interest upon
bonds, debentures and other obligations, may be paid in due course;
and such regular dividends and interest may continue to be paid
until and unless the said Director shall from time to time otherwise
by general or special orders determine; and, subject to the approval
of the Director, the various carriers may agree upon and arrange
for the renewal and extension of maturing obligations.

Except with the prior written assent of said Director, no attachment by mesne process or on execution shall be levied on or against
any of the property used by any of said transportation systems in
the conduct of their business as common carriers; but suits may
be brought by and against said carriers and judgments rendered
as hitherto until and except so far as said Director may, by general
or special orders, otherwise determine.

From and after twelve o'clock on said *twenty-eighth* day of *December* 1917, all transportation systems included in this order and
proclamation shall conclusively be deemed within the possession
and control of said Director without further act or notice. But for
the purpose of accounting said possession and control shall date
from twelve o'clock midnight on December 31, 1917.

IN WITNESS WHEREOF, I have hereunto set my hand and caused
the seal of the United States to be affixed.

Done by the President, through Newton D. Baker, Secretary of
War, in the District of Columbia, this 26th day of December, in the
year of our Lord one thousand nine hundred and seventeen, and
of the independence of the United States the one hundred and
forty-second.

By the President: Woodrow Wilson
Robert Lansing   Newton D. Baker
    Secretary of State   Secretary of War

TS MS (WP, DLC).

Two Letters to William Gibbs McAdoo

My dear Mac: [The White House] 26 December, 1917

The matter referred to by Crosby in the enclosed, which I return so that I may refer to it more briefly, has been brought to my attention repeatedly and I have discussed it very fully with Colby, who was especially sent over there to acquaint himself with it and who wishes to accomplish something similar to that which Mr. Crosby proposes.

Frankly, I think Crosby is concerning himself in too many matters and is apt to get things very much confused. You know how we suffer from that on this side of the water, different agents of the British Government all undertaking the same thing, and I hope sincerely that you will give Crosby some kind of kind warning.

Always   Affectionately yours,   [Woodrow Wilson]

CCL (WP, DLC).

Dear Mac.,   The White House. 26 December, 1917.

The proclamation is all right. I will have it copied here and copies made for the press, to be released to-morrow morning, along with a statement from me. If you are thinking of making a statement, too, you had better bring it over this afternoon (say about 5.30) so that we can compare the two and have them gee in every particular.

Meanwhile I will show the proclamation to Baker and make sure that he is in entire accord with us in all respects.

In haste,   Faithfully Yours,   W.W.

P.S. I have inserted the date Noon, 28 Dec., as the date on which the act is to take effect. W.W.

WWTLI (RSB Coll., DLC).

To George Parmly Day

My dear Mr. Day: [The White House] 26 December, 1917

I am very much interested in what you tell me of "The Chronicles of America," which the Yale University Press is about to publish, and very much complimented that you should wish to dedicate the series to me and send me copies of the volumes as they appear; but I must say in frankness that I should be greatly embarrassed by such a gift and dedication, for similar dedications have been suggested in a great many instances and rather than discriminate between one case and another, I have uniformly declined. I could not now consistently or without giving very great offense consent in this case.

I am sure that you will understand and will believe that there is in this not the least lack of appreciation of the very high honor you propose. Sincerely yours, Woodrow Wilson

TLS (Letterpress Books, WP, DLC).

To Jeannette Rankin

My dear Miss Rankin: [The White House] 26 December, 1917

The potato was certainly a conclusive evidence of the prowess of Montana and we took great pleasure in including it in our menu. It was a meal in itself and a very palatable one.

With warm appreciation,
Very sincerely yours, Woodrow Wilson

TLS (Letterpress Books, WP, DLC).

To Bainbridge Colby

My dear Mr. Colby: The White House 26 December, 1917

It was kind of you to remember to send me H. G. Wells' letter. I shall read it with the greatest interest.

Thank you also for your telephone message from New York which Tumulty has conveyed to me.

May I not wish for you and all of yours the best things of the season and of the New Year?
Cordially and faithfully yours, Woodrow Wilson

TLS (B. Colby Papers, DLC).

From Newton Diehl Baker, with Enclosure

Dear Mr. President: Washington. December 26, 1917.

I take pleasure in transmitting to you the attached cablegram from General Pershing in accordance with his request.
Cordially yours, Newton D. Baker

I have sent a suitable response.

TLS (WP, DLC).

ENCLOSURE

[Chaumont] December 25, 1917.

To the Adjutant General, Washington.

Number 415, December 25th, for Chief of Staff:

Please extend to the President and the Secretary of War Holiday Greetings, and best wishes for the success of our arms during the coming year, and convey to them from all ranks of the American Expeditionary Forces renewed pledges of devotion to our sacred cause. Likewise express our greetings to our comrades at home coupled with full confidence in their patriotism, courage and devotion to the flag.

Pershing.

TC telegram (WP, DLC).

From Newton Diehl Baker

Information

Dear Mr. President,   Washington. December 26, 1917.

I have conveyed to the Secretary of State your suggestion, and he today notified the British, French and Italian Governments of the determination of the United States to participate in the Supreme War Council, and of the designation of General Bliss as our representative.

It is the intention of General Bliss to leave on the first available transportation.   Respectfully yours,   Newton D. Baker

TLS (WP, DLC).

From Robert Lansing

My dear Mr. President: Washington December 26, 1917.

It appears that there are a number of hospital units in training at Allentown, Pennsylvania, which have been ready to go to France for some time. The War Department, however, has for some reason decided not to send them to France. They are fully equipped, ready for immediate action and comprise, I believe, several thousand men.

It has occurred to me that it might be a good political move to let them, or at least some of them, go to Italy. I have sounded the War Department and am advised that neither the Secretary nor the Surgeon General sees any difficulty from the point of view of the War Department to sending the units to Italy immediately. The

Secretary of War, however, defers to the judgment of this Department as to whether it would be in the general interest to send them to Italy.

I believe that the appearance of American hospital units in Italy would make an excellent impression at the present time and would hearten the Italian people. Will you be so kind as to let me know whether the suggestion has your approval?

With assurances of respect, etc., I am, my dear Mr. President,

Faithfully yours,   Robert Lansing

TLS (WP, DLC).

A Translation of a Telegram from Jean Jules Jusserand to Stéphen Jean Marie Pichon

Washington, without date [Dec. 26, 1917], received December 27, 1917

No. 1593. In the course of a long interview that I just had with Colonel House I am able to say without any doubt whatsoever that he reported from France exactly the impressions that we would have wished him to. "Never," he told me, "have I found morale higher and the national spirit firmer." The results of the conference seem to him excellent. He congratulated himself many times upon the relations that he was able to establish with Your Excellency and with the President of the Council. He gives the warmest praise to both.

He expressed himself along the same lines as the President did.

On the question of Alsace-Lorraine, he confirmed to me anew, what I had been told repeatedly by the Department, that Mr. Wilson believes that the war must not end until these ancient territories have been returned to us. It is the last question that the President talked to him about just before his [House's] departure for France.

These completely parallel impressions have been reported by Admiral Benson, himself, who is ordinarily silent and not very communicative. He came to me the first time that I saw him again and expressed himself on our side with a warm approbation which is rare with him.   Jusserand

T telegram (Guerre 1914-1918, États-Unis, Vol. 509, p. 183, FFM-Ar).

A Memorandum

[Washington] December 27, 1917
For Mr. McCormick

At their meeting on December 27, 1917, Mr. McCormick reported to the War Trade Board the results of the conference he had had with the President that afternoon as follows:

The President approved the commandeering of the Dutch vessels lying idle in our harbors, if their use could not be secured by charters pursuant to some fair proposition made to the Dutch, it being understood that such proposition would be submitted forthwith and that if it should not be accepted within a reasonable time, the commandeering should then take place. The President at the same time stated that the vessels so commandeered should be put into safe trades.[1]

The President also stated his approval of this principle, namely, that, it being understood that the neutrals would be supplied with the foods necessary to their subsistence as a matter of humanity, it would be proper to make the exportation of all other commodities the subject of bargaining and reciprocal arrangements. For example we could say to Norway that we would send them no copper unless they furnish us with molybdenum, and we could say to the Dutch that we would send them no cotton unless they furnish us with linen.   L.B.[2]

T MS (V. C. McCormick Papers, CtY).
  [1] For documents on the status of Netherlands vessels, see "Negotiations with the Netherlands," *FR-WWS 1917*, 2, II, 1117-58, and "The Taking Over of Dutch Ships—Agreements Regarding Exports to the Netherlands," *FR-WWS 1918*, 1, II, 1377-1480.
  [2] Lawrence Bennett, Secretary of the War Trade Board.

To Newton Diehl Baker

My dear Mr. Secretary: [The White House] 27 December, 1917

Will you not upon the proper occasion send to General Pershing some such message as the following:

"The President requests me to send to you and to all the American officers and forces associated with you the most cordial New Year's greetings and to express his unqualified confidence that the American forces under your command may be counted upon to render the name of their country still more glorious, both by feats of arms and by personal conduct characterized by the highest principles of bravery and honor."[1]

Faithfully yours,   Woodrow Wilson

TLS (Letterpress Books, WP, DLC).
  [1] Baker sent this telegram to Pershing on December 31, 1917. See R. A. Hayes to JPT, Dec. 31, 1917, TLS (WP, DLC).

To Thomas Davies Jones

My dear Friend: The White House 27 December, 1917

Your letter of December twenty-fourth deeply distresses me. I have found your counsel and aid invaluable in the extremely important work of the War Trade Board and it is not going to be possible to replace you, but I haven't it in my heart to ask anything which would demand of you sacrifice of your health and, therefore, I must yield with a very heavy heart.

I hope it will be possible for you to recuperate rapidly, and my thoughts shall follow you with genuine affection.

With the warmest good wishes for the New Year to you all.
                                    Faithfully yours,   Woodrow Wilson

TLS (Mineral Point, Wisc., Public Library).

From Howard Elliott[1]

                                    At Washington, D. C.,
My dear Mr. President: December 27, 1917.

I have had an abiding faith that, when you acted on the difficult and complicated railroad question, you would do so with a full appreciation of all the necessities of the situation.

I think it is a good thing for the country that the suspense is over, and I hope and believe that every railroad man,—whether officer or employe,—will do his utmost to carry out the views and orders of yourself and Mr. McAdoo.

With every desire to do what I can personally, and with great respect, I am,   Yours very sincerely,   Howard Elliott

TLS (WP, DLC).
[1] Former head of the New Haven System; at this time, chairman of the executive committee of the Northern Pacific Railway Co.

From George Creel

                                    Washington, D. C.
My dear Mr. President: December 27, 1917.

Sisson cables that your message[1] has been printed and widely circulated, and that a very sound service has been formed for the handling of our wireless and cable news.

I gathered a half million feet of film for the Y.M.C.A. for exhibition in the soldiers' houses on the firing line. These pictures show our social, industrial, and war progress. They should be in Russia now, and I have cabled Sisson to take as much of the film as he wishes, using it in cities for our publicity purposes. This will obviate the necessity of a separate expedition.

Sisson understands he is not to touch the political situation, to avoid all personal entanglements, and that while he is not to consider himself an attaché to the Embassy, he must maintain the most friendly relations with the Ambassador.

The Secretary of State, any number of Senators, and practically every other citizen interested in international affairs, deluge me from day to day with the suggestion that we send to Russia men of Russian birth for the purpose of explaining America's meaning and purposes. I have not thought this wise because the Russian situation changed so from day to day, and demanded such extreme caution in every approach. I have now, however, a list of very remarkable people that it might be well to send; men born in Russia, successful Americans in every way, and able to write and speak authoritatively. What do you think of sending them over?

Propaganda, of course, goes hand in hand with policy. It is impossible for me to do very much in Russia or with Russians until certain decisions are made. Even were it proper for me to advise, I do not feel that I am sufficiently in possession of facts to give intelligent advice. The people that come to see me, and to whom I attach most importance, however, feel strongly that some definite statement should be made that we stand ready, as in the past, to give whole-heartedly of all that we possess, to relieve distress, to aid in restoration, and to build foundations under military strength, but that this spirit of generous helpfulness can only be given effect in cooperation with a Russian movement that is expressive of the whole people, that has its source in democratic procedure, and its authority from a free electorate.

These portions of Russia where the German prisoners are, where the coal fields are, where the grain belt is—all are in possession of anti-German, anti-Lenine forces. Such a statement would strengthen these forces even while cutting away Bolsheviki supports.

I am not trying to be "ambassadorial," but simply searching for some light that will enable me to see my own way clearer.

Respectfully,   George Creel

TLS (WP, DLC).
[1] That is, Wilson's Annual Message of December 4.

From Robert Lansing

My dear Mr. President: Washington December 27, 1917.

I enclose for your consideration a summary of the results of Colonel House's mission to Europe[1] which, if it meets with your approval, I would like to make public as I said to the newspapermen some time ago that a statement would be made in regard to the work of the Mission.

May I have a word with you after Cabinet meeting tomorrow in regard to this matter?[2]

Faithfully yours,   Robert Lansing

TLS (WP, DLC).
[1] A summary in general terms (undated T MS, WP, DLC) of the reports by House and other members of the American war mission to England and France. The summary is printed in the *Washington Post* and the *New York Times*, Jan. 3, 1918.
[2] See WW to RL, Dec. 31, 1917.

From Joseph Patrick Tumulty

Dear Governor: The White House December 27, 1917.

An editorial in the Times of this evening reminds me that tomorrow you will celebrate another birthday. Just a line to congratulate you and to shake you by the hand.

A few evenings ago I said to a friend of mine while watching the soldiers guard the White House, "Those sentries tonight are standing guard over the man who is alone the hope of a suffering world."

You know the depth of my admiration and affection for you.

These lines from Zangwill's "The Mantle of Elijah"[1] draw a better picture of you as I know you than anything I have ever seen.

With affectionate regard,   Sincerely yours,   Tumulty

TLS (WP, DLC).
[1] Tumulty quoted (T MS, WP, DLC) from Israel Zangwill, *The Mantle of Elijah, A Novel* (New York and London, 1900), pp. 17-18.

Two Telegrams from Sir Cecil Arthur Spring Rice to the Foreign Office

Washington 27 Dec 1917

No. 4030   S of S told me he thought the only policy to be followed in Russia by USG was one of abstention. He said you were fully informed as to his views namely that the U S was the only one of the allies who could hope to exert any influence, and that it would be dangerous and unwise to sacrifice this chance, however slight. He told a friend in confidence that short of an intolerable outrage on the U S he hoped to maintain a neutral & expectant attitude. (This of course does not affect the policy already commd. to you and French govt.) Private arrangements have been made for the despatch of certain U S socialists, whose character could be absolutely relied on, vouched for by Rabbi Wise and S of S hopes that their representations would not be without effect. House seemed to be less hopeful and agrees with Buchanan that we should regard Russia as a possible German colony, unless some radical change takes place. He thinks however that this situation will help allies in maintaining close & friendly relations with Japan.　CSR

Washington 27 Dec 1917

No. 4031　S of S told me today that he had just seen Jap Ambr.[1] who had assured him that Japan had no intention of landing a force in E. Siberia. Their view (which entirely coincided with S of S's) was that such action would have a disastrous effect on Russian popular opinion. S of S observed to me that a joint Japanese-American action would have a still more disastrous effect and it was a great relief to him that the Japanese Gvt had refused to yield to the pressure of public opinion, which appears to have demanded vigourous action.

Colonel House whom I also saw told me that he was personally convinced of the friendliness of all the Jap. Rep'tives whom he had seen and that he hoped & believed Japan's policy would continue friendly to the allies and the U. S. He said he called on the Japanese Ambassador this afternoon.

The point of view of the USG is that a Japanese expedition to Siberia would arouse hostile sentiment both in Russia and the U. S.: there would be pressure here for American participation which the USG is strongly opposed to on political & military grounds. The USG is also in receipt of more reassuring news as to the failure of the B[olsheviks] to obtain control in E. Siberia. Repeated to Tokyo.
CSR

Hw telegrams (FO 115/2318, pp. 297-98, PRO).
[1] That is, Aimaro Sato.

To William Bauchop Wilson

My dear Mr. Secretary:　　The White House 28 December, 1917

It was good to see a letter from you written in Washington, because I have been anxious about your health and am delighted that you are back. I hope with all my heart that you are feeling better and will take the rest necessary entirely to restore your health.

It was kind and thoughtful of you to write me on my birthday[1] and you may be sure I appreciate it as coming from one whom I count a real and invaluable friend.

Cordially and sincerely yours,　Woodrow Wilson

TLS (received from Mary A. Strohecker).
[1] W. B. Wilson's letter is missing.

To Joseph Patrick Tumulty

Dear Tumulty: [The White House, c. Dec. 28, 1917]

There is no such photograph but I am willing to undergo the trial if a first-rate photographer can be assigned to this.[1]

The President.

TL (WP, DLC).
[1] The Rev. Dr. Howard A. Bridgman, editor in chief of the Boston *Congregationalist and Advance*, had requested a standing, full-length portrait of Wilson. Bridgman wrote: "I do not want to ask too much, but we have a splendid full length portrait of Lincoln and another of Washington and would like to put President Wilson beside them early in February just before the Lincoln and Washington birthdays." H. A. Bridgman to JPT, Dec. 21, 1917, TLS (WP, DLC). Arrangements were made with the Clinedinst Studio, and the portrait appeared on the cover of *The Congregationalist and Advance*, CIII (April 4, 1918).

To Howard Elliott

My dear Mr. Elliott: [The White House] 28 December, 1917

I warmly appreciate your letter of December twenty-seventh. I have never had any doubt that we could count on men like yourself to the uttermost to back the Government and serve the country.

Cordially and sincerely yours,   Woodrow Wilson

TLS (Letterpress Books, WP, DLC).

To Charles Edward Russell

My dear Mr. Russell: [The White House] 28 December, 1917

It is with a very unusual sense of gratitude that I thank you for your letter of December twenty-sixth.[1] These are days when cheer such as your letter gives me is a necessary tonic in the day's work, for there is much to break the spirit down. I thank you all the more because I trust your judgment in such matters of observation with the greatest confidence. You have done me a real service by such a message.

Sincerely your friend,   Woodrow Wilson

TLS (Letterpress Books, WP, DLC).
[1] It is missing.

From Raymond Poincaré

Translation

Mr. President,   Paris, le December 28, 1917.

The Government of the Republic has asked me to thank you for the decision which you have been so good as to take, concerning the mode of action of the American army. The fate of the war may depend on the conditions in which your valiant troops will be engaged on the battle front. The sad events in Russia shall soon liberate a very large number of enemy divisions which are already on the move towards our frontier, and the Anglo-French lines will have certainly to sustain, in the course of the year 1918, a formidable and prolonged pressure.

France is resolved, in spite of the heavy sacrifices which she has been bearing for more than three years in the cause of universal liberty, to hold against every onslaught, until final victory. But a number of months will still elapse before the complete formation of the American army. When that army has been entirely transported to Europe, it will of course, if such is your desire, compose an indivisible whole. Until then American valiance would certainly not rest content with total inactivity. The troops, landing in succession, would not consent to stand mere spectators of the battles which will be fought and in which our common hope will be at stake.

The sooner the American flag will float on the very front by the side of our own tricolor, the sooner will become apparent, in all its significance and grandeur, the historical role assumed by the United States under your guidance. There is therefore a paramount interest in the American troops being engaged with ours, the moment they reach the battle zone.

But the divisions will sooner be formed into effective forces than provided with their staff, their artillery and their horses. On the other hand, whatever the bravery of American soldiers, they cannot acquire, from one day to the next, the experience of a difficult fight which we have had for more than three years to conduct as a counterpart to that of the enemy. There may be grave risks in allotting separate sectors to divisions either grouped or isolated, before they have been supplied with all they need and have mastered the methods of present warfare.

In the interest of the American army as well as in the common interest, the system which the Government of the Republic has proposed to you and which you have been so good as to accept, is greatly to be preferred. It reserves entirely the future, and during the period which will precede the definitive constitution of the army of the United States it will allow your tactical units, that is your regiments, to become with ours component parts of divisions to quickly benefit from that fraternity of arms and to brilliantly distinguish themselves, from the coming months on, in the European battles.

The turning into practice of your decision has unluckily met, up to now, with some difficulty, and an agreement has not proved possible between the commander in chief of the French army and General Pershing. The Government of the Republic sees a serious danger in the prolongation of this incertitude. The transfer of German troops from Russia to the Western front will apparently continue without cease, and all forebodes violent attacks. The success of the next campaign depends on the rational utilisation of all the allied forces. I doubt not that, under your high inspiration, the valorous American army will contribute to the victory, heartily conforming itself, like the French troops, to the necessities of the struggle.

Accept, Mr. President, the expression of my faithful friendship.
                              (Signed)   Raymond Poincaré.[1]

T MS (WP, DLC).
  [1] This translation was supplied by the French embassy in Washington.

From Samuel Reading Bertron

New York, Dec. 28, 1917.

Permit me to congratulate you upon the wise and constructive measure which you announced publicly yesterday and which will have a wonderful reassuring effect upon the business interests of the country and most helpful in restoring transportation so essential to winning the war.   S. R. Bertron.

T telegram (WP, DLC).

From Hale Holden[1]

Sir: Washington, December 28, 1917.

I beg to send you an expression of appreciation of the action you have taken in the interest of the country in dealing with the transportation question. You have not failed to see the matter with the clear vision and high purpose which the country has come to anticipate in your public utterances; the anxiety of the public in behalf of the great underlying investments in railroad securities has been relieved by the basis for Government control which you have defined and the appointment of Mr. McAdoo has met general approval.

The railroads will omit no effort to loyally support your administration of the properties and in common with all officers and employes, I hope to render to you full measure of service, according to my ability, in this very important matter.

With great respect, I beg to remain

Very sincerely,   Hale Holden

TLS (WP, DLC).
¹ President since 1914 of the Chicago, Burlington & Quincy Railroad Co.

From Thomas Watt Gregory

Dear Mr. President: Washington, D. C. December 28, 1917.

Notwithstanding the many large matters before you, I feel that I must burden you with a brief statement of what has developed in regard to the California oil situation.

Last February, at your suggestion, I took up with Senator Swanson, the Secretary of the Navy, and the Secretary of the Interior, a suggestion of Senator Swanson of a plan for granting some character of relief to those who had taken up, for oil purposes, land withdrawn by President Taft in 1909 and 1910. The measure suggested by Senator Swanson was as follows:

"That any claimant, who either in person or through his predecessor in interest, entered upon any of the lands embraced within the executive order of withdrawal dated September 27, 1909, prior to July 3, 1910, honestly and in good faith for the purpose of prospecting for oil or gas, and thereupon commenced discovery work thereon, and thereafter prosecuted such work to a discovery of oil or gas, shall be entitled to lease from the United States any producing oil or gas well resulting from such work, at a royalty of not less than one-eighth of all the oil and gas produced therefrom, together with an area of land sufficient for the operation thereof, but without the right to drill any other or additional wells; provided, that such claimant shall first pay to the United States an amount equal to not less than the value of one-eighth of all the oil and gas already produced from such well; and provided further, that this act shall not apply to any well involved in any suit brought by the United States, or in any application for patent, unless within ninety days after the approval of this act the claimant shall relinquish to the United States all rights claimed by him in such suit or application; and provided further, that all such leases shall be made, and the amount to be paid for oil and gas already produced shall be fixed by the Secretary of the Interior under appropriate rules and regulations."

The Secretary of the Interior acquiesced in this measure "in so far as it relates to the naval oil reserves." As to the withdrawn lands outside of the naval reserves, he thought the provision should be more liberal. The Secretary of the Navy, while regarding the proposition as a liberal one, acquiesced in it. In the letter addressed to the Secretary of the Interior on February 21, 1917, a copy of which was also sent to the Secretary of the Navy, I stated that in case those two Departments were satisified with Senator Swanson's suggestion I would make no objection to its adoption. On February 26, 1917 I wrote a letter to Senator Swanson, copies of which were mailed on February 27th to the Secretary of the Interior and the Secretary of the Navy (enclosing a copy of my letter above referred to, addressed to the Secretary of the Interior on Feb. 21st) in which I stated the attitude of the Secretary of the Interior and the Secretary of the Navy and myself in regard to Senator Swanson's proposition. In this letter I also said "The President authorizes me to say to you that he has fully discussed with me your suggestion, contained in my above mentioned letter of February 21st, and that it is the limit of liberality in which he is willing to go in dealing with these oil claimants."

Nothing was done at that session of Congress, and I inferred from a conversation I had with you that you had some character of understanding with the Land Committee of the House or with the Chairman thereof which enabled you to control the situation at that session. At the present session, and just before adjournment for the Christmas holidays, the bill "To encourage and Promote the Mining of Coal, etc." was taken up on the floor of the Senate with a favorable report[1] by Senator Pittman, of the Committee, and Section 16 of this bill was then amended to read as follows:

"Sec. 16. That upon relinquishment to the United States within ninety days from the date of this Act or within ninety days after final denial or withdrawal of application for patent, of any claim or subdivision thereof asserted under the mining laws prior to July third, nineteen hundred and ten, to any unpatented oil or gas lands included in any order of withdrawal the claimant or his successor in interest shall be entitled to a lease for each asserted mineral location of one hundred and sixty acres or less or any subdivision thereof upon which such claim is based and upon which said claimant, his predecessors in interest, or those claiming through or under him, have, prior to the date of this Act, drilled one or more producing oil or gas wells, such lease to be upon a royalty of one-eighth of the production of oil or gas produced and saved therefrom after first deducting from the gross

[1] The report from the Senate Committee on Public Lands to accompany S. 2812 is printed in *Cong. Record*, 65th Cong., 2d sess., pp. 290-94.

production such oil or gas as may be used in development and operating such land, and otherwise on the same terms and conditions as other oil and gas leases granted under the provisions of this Act: Provided, however, That no claimant who has been guilty of fraud in the location of any oil claim or gas bearing lands shall be entitled to any of the benefits of this section, nor shall his assignee be entitled thereto unless he affirmatively shows that prior to the passage of this Act he purchased such lands in good faith, for a valuable consideration and without actual knowledge of such fraud: Provided further, That upon the issuance of said lease and prior to the delivery thereof the applicant therefor shall pay to the United States for one-eighth of the oil or gas produced and saved from the lands included in said claim at the current field price at the time of production, which shall be in full satisfaction for all oil or gas extracted from said land prior to said lease; And provided further, That none of the provisions of this section or of this Act shall be applicable to or affect lands or minerals included within the limits of any naval petroleum reserve; Provided further, That the provisions of this section shall be applicable in all cases provided for herein, including cases where court actions have been heretofore commenced or may hereafter be commenced by the United States Government affecting the title to such lands or the product thereof; Provided further, That any bona fide occupant or claimant of oil or gas bearing lands in the Territory of Alaska, who prior to withdrawal had complied with the requirements of the mining laws, except as to discovery of oil or gas in wells, and who prior to withdrawal expended not less than $1,000 in permanent improvements on or for each location, shall be entitled to the benefits of this section."

It was agreed (my understand[ing] is that with only some 7 or 8 senators present) that the bill should be voted on January 7th with a very limited debate as to amendments.[2] I should add that Senator Pittman's report which accompanied this bill is utterly and absolutely unfair, and fails to present the facts, and indeed utterly distorts many of them.

By the amendment of Section 16, the Naval Reserves are excluded from its effect, and Senator Pittman stated in the recent debate that this amendment would eliminate the main contest over the bill and also that "which the late Senator from Wisconsin, Mr. Husting, supported so earnestly and so ably." This statement is exactly the reverse of the truth. Senator Husting, at the time of his

[2] This was agreed upon on December 18, 1917. *Ibid.*, pp. 489-90.

death, had in course of preparation a strong minority report against the bill, opposing any character of relief to those who had violated the withdrawal order except such as courts of equity would give them in disposing of their suits. Unfortunately, the minority report had not been fully prepared and signed by Senator Husting, and hence does not appear in the record. Also in the course of the debate, Senator Swanson stated that with the Naval Reserves eliminated from the bill he would make no opposition to its passage. Senator Pittman's report to the Senate contains the following: "The language of the compromise provision contained in Section 16 was prepared and submitted by the Interior Department at the request of the Joint Committee composed of members of the Public Lands Committee of the Senate and the Public Lands Committee of the House."

An analysis of Section 16 shows that it goes far beyond what you fixed last February as the limit of liberality to which you were willing to go in giving relief to these oil claimants. In the first place, it furnishes relief to any of these claimants, even after their application for patent has been denied by the Government. In the second place, it gives to such claimant a lease for each asserted mineral location of 160 acres or less, or any subdivision thereof. In the third place, it gives a lease, with a royalty of one-eighth to the Government, to each claimant who up to the time of the passage of this act had developed an oil or gas well, provided he proceeded under a claim asserted prior to July 3, 1910 (which would mean that the mere posting of notice under which no work whatsoever was done, even for several years, could, even within the last few weeks, have been purchased and for the first time money spent thereon, in case this resulted in the production of gas or oil). In the fourth place, the benefits of the act would accrue to those who claim through dummy locations or through fraudulent claims, (and I should say just here that practically all of these claims are now in the hands of assignees of these claimants, certainly in all cases where fraud is charged). The act does provide that these benefits shall not[3] accrue to those who "purchased such lands in good faith for a valuable consideration and without actual knowledge of such fraud." This gives them relief far beyond what the well established rule of law gives to the man who affirmatively establishes that he has paid value in good faith and without actual or constructive knowledge of any fraud, and without being put on notice of such facts as would, if followed up, reveal such fraud. Under the terms of the section as drawn, practically all it would be necessary for the claimant to

[3] *Sic.*

assert to gain the benefit of the act would be that in purchasing the fraudulent location he had done so without actual knowledge of the fraudulent intention of the party who made the location. It should also be observed that the well established rule of law as to constructive notice is actually done away with. In the fifth place, the section gives the benefit to the defendants in all cases where the Government has heretofore brought suits, including those in which it has secured judgments, and it would apply to some $7,000,000 already impounded by the Government by receiverships in suits relating to lands outside of the Naval Reserves.

To state the proposition broadly, the effect of the operations of this section is to give to practically all claimants of lands outside the naval reserves located in violation of the withdrawal order of President Taft seven-eighths of the oil they have heretofore produced and seven-eighths of all that may be produced in the future, without making any real distinction between fraudulent and bona fide claims and without requiring any improvements to have been made upon the lands before or after the withdrawal orders, with the single exception that at the time of the passage of this bill gas or oil shall have been developed.

There is, of course, not the slightest distinction between the rights of parties within the Naval Reserves and those outside of the Naval Reserves, nor can any reason founded on justice be stated why those claiming within the Naval Reserves should not benefit while those outside of the Naval Reserves shall benefit. It was frankly stated by Mr. Pittman that he acquiesced in the amendment eliminating the Naval Reserve because otherwise he could not get the bill enacted into law. My information is that the Public Lands Committee of the House has reported a bill which, while differing in verbiage from Section 16 of the Senate bill, is substantially to the same effect.[4]

The value of the lands outside the Naval Reserves which are affected by this relief measure is roughly estimated to be about double the value of the lands inside the Naval Reserves.

Faithfully yours,   T. W. Gregory

TLS (WP, DLC).

[4] See *Exploration for and Disposition of Coal, Oil, Gas, Etc.*, 65th Cong., 2d sess., House Report No. 206, submitted by S. Ferris, Chairman of the Committee on Public Lands, to accompany H.R. 3232.

From William Kent

Dear Mr. President: Washington December 28, 1917.

Concerning the procedure in water power legislation, Mr. Lenroot states that, in his opinion, it would be well for you to have an early interview with Mr. Sims, Chairman of the Interstate and Foreign Commerce Committee, so as to smooth the way for the action of a special committee, of which, as a matter of course, he would be a member. I understand that he is somewhat jealous of his jurisdiction, especially since the Shields bill has been referred to his Committee.

Following a meeting with Mr. Sims, it would seem advisable that you should meet Messrs. Ferris and Lenroot, to discuss further procedure.

The latter suggests that the Rules Committee should be urged to pass a special rule creating a new Committee, to be appointed by the Speaker. The Speaker would doubtless, as a matter of course, appoint the Chairman and ranking members of the two Committees; he might also appoint the Chairman of and ranking member of the Agricultural Committee, making six, and, if a seventh man seemed desirable, it would be well to have Mr. Sherley appointed, or, if he did not wish to serve, Dr. Foster, both of whom have taken great interest in the subject and are men of large influence.

If there were a chance of selection from the Committee membership other than the Chairman and ranking member, Mr. Sidney Anderson,[1] as minority member of the Agricultural Committee, would be particularly valuable, both on account of his influence, and on account of the intense interest he has taken in this subject. Mr. Lever would doubtless coincide in this view, if spoken to about it, and I am quite sure that Mr. Haugen, the ranking member, would not object. If desired, I could look into this matter.

The rule should cause to be referred all matters concerning water power legislation to the new Committee, which would put the Shields bill before them, where the new bill could be made a substitute.

Mr. Lenroot believes that Mr. Ferris should be the man to introduce the bill, but that he should not take this action until the new Committee shall have been formed (of which he would doubtless be Chairman) and until that Committee shall have formally passed on and adopted the bill.

After examination of a copy of the bill, which has just reached him, Mr. Lenroot believes that in essentials it is a good measure. His suggestions for changes are concerned with minor matters, and, in my opinion, would be gladly accepted by the Secretaries, as improvements. Yours truly, William Kent

I am told that Mr. Sims is here in town as are Messrs Ferris and Lenroot. I sincerely hope that you can take this matter up before you have a return of the vacating Congress[2] WK

TLS (WP, DLC).
  [1] Sydney Anderson, Republican congressman from Minnesota.
  [2] Wilson saw Sims at the White House at 5 P.M. on December 31.

From William Gibbs McAdoo

Dear Governor: Washington Dec. 28. 1917

My warm and affectionate greetings and congratulations on your birthday. It signalizes a momentous event in the history of our country today—an event for which your vision and superlative statesmanship are responsible. My prayer is that you may be spared many more years for the service of your country and humanity and that I may prove worthy of your confidence and capable of performing the great task you have entrusted to me.

Affectionately Yours   W G McAdoo

ALS (WP, DLC).

From William Cox Redfield

My dear Mr. President   [Washington] Decr. 28. 1917

The months have been so full that I hardly realize you can have another birthday due in what seems so short a time. But the calendar seems inflexible and as the one I use was published by the Dept. of Commerce 'twould be a grievous fault to doubt its truthfulness. What a year of years, a year of cares this has been to you! How little, after all, can we who love and honor you relieve you of the heavy burden. The most we seem able to do is to watch with you while the great world drama unfolds about us.

But we may, indeed we ought to tell you on these anniversaries of the faith that is in us, of our trust in God and in you His servant, doing His work, speaking to our people as I verily believe in His spirit. More or less, I suppose we are "in the wilderness" but the Promised Land must be ahead and each hard, troubled day must bring it nearer.

May I hope for the coming year that we shall at least see the dawn of peace, of peace that shall bring you the reward of work well done, of the consciousness of having led your country safely through. In what the year shall bring of effort and of anxiety it will be a privilege to me to do all in my power to help and to cheer.

I cannot wish you many more *such* birthdays but many glad ones I earnestly do wish you   Sincerely   William C. Redfield

ALS (WP, DLC).

From Felexiana Shepherd Baker Woodrow

My dear Tommie: Columbia, S. C., Dec. 28, 1917.

Not a letter, but just a line to let you know that I am thinking of you, and that my daily prayer for you is
"As thy days, so shall thy strength be."
With love to you and your dear Wife,

Affectionately,   "Aunt Felie."

ALS (WP, DLC).

A Memorandum by Lincoln Steffens

[c. Dec. 28, 1917]

The war is dividing men along the class line. It is becoming a class war.

This is the conviction I got on my lecture trip across the country.

Business men and the upper class generally are for the war, honestly, but passionately; aggressively. Accused of sordid motives and conscious of making money, they are developing a moblike madness which is understandable but harmful. Officials and the press are catching it.

Labor and the lower classes are not exactly against the war, but they are not for it; not yet; and the attitude of the upper class and the policy (or some acts) of some parts of the government and press are packing the workers back into a suppressed, sullen opposition.

This can be cured. More. I believe that this evil tendency can be turned into a force for good. And the principle to apply is that of good politics as distinguished from good morals.

A democratic government must not only *be* right; it must *appear* right.

The Administration is not making a class war. Let it show that it isn't. It's no use resenting the imputation and pointing to scattered acts and facts which will set the Administration right in history. This is no time for argument and controversy. Act.

Accept openly the fact that there is this growing feeling. Say so. Call it by its names: doubt, confusion, suspicion, hate. And don't rebuke it. Understand it, sympathetically, and then—melt it into something akin to love and faith.

Ask the pro-war people to be more patient with the anti-war folk.

Ask the pacifists to be more considerate of the fighters; and to put their minds, not on peace, but the terms of a permanent peace.

Ask the soldiers again, as Baker did once, not to deal with the I.W.W.'s in the I.W.W. spirit. Ask this of the employers also.

Ask all editors, writers and speakers,—all—to remember that the war psychology is a little like a sickness; that it makes men's minds sensitive and sore; and that to say things that give pain to this state of mind is like being rough with the wounded.

Ask official prosecutors of war-time offenses to be fairer; they must do their duty, but they should do it less personally than some of them are doing it now; and more gently, much more justly.

Ask the President to practice mercy, as Lincoln did; only, in this later day, more systematically, on a larger scale. He could pick from among his personal friends some humane spirits (like Fremont Older)[1] to go about for him "visiting them in prison" and calling on the families of the convicted, and recommending pardons, many, many pardons.

I would reverse the policy as to free speech and a free press, but I will not urge this. I have seen Russia, and I learned there to trust "the mob"; to put in "the people" a faith which I did not have before. I know now that liberty works. The final effect of free speech in Petrograd was to make the speakers moderate their tone and consider the feelings of their auditors!

But certainly the President can repeat his assurance now that after the war, the war measures limiting our liberties will be repealed. And he can clinch this by letting us hope that some bad practices (notably in the Post Office) which grew up before the war, may be stopped when we make peace.

All these things should be done in one proclamation; and this also: the most important of all:

Stop the appearance of "war on Labor." Stop or suspend labor prosecutions. Declare an amnesty in the class struggle and pardon all labor convicts in prison for "labor crimes"; all.

Too much? Hear me out.

The President is acting in the Mooney case now, and for Berkman, I hear. That is good, but it's too quiet, too slow. What we need now is an act of clemency so big, so loud, so unmistakable that all men will get it and feel it. I would have the President and Governors, too, join in a declaration of amnesty and pardon *as an attempt "to win back a faith that Labor had no right ever to lose in their government."* In other words, I would handle it as an emergency; and it is an emergency to be faced as such.

Labor thinks this is a class war; that capital is getting the better of labor in it; that the employers are using the situation to gain advantages; and I heard groups of workers and one group of business men declaring that the Administration was in the "plot" to "fix" Organized Labor now for good and all!

I tried to reason with this state of mind, and failed. It's that terrible war psychology, which takes a few incidents that have no relation to one another, and darkens them into a conspiracy. Officials are doing the same thing. This is the day of "conspiracies." The prosecution of the I.W.W.'s is for conspiracy; a pro-German plot; and no doubt there are "proofs" which will appeal to a jury in war-time. But I happen to know that Arturo Giovanniti, Gurley Flynn, Tresca,[2] and other Eastern I.W.W.'s quarrelled a year ago with Haywood and the Western I.W.W.'s and not only could not have conspired with them; they "did not speak." And the rank and file of labor know this. And they think that the detectives didn't investigate far enough to learn of it. Nor did the investigators find out, apparently, that Giovanniti, for one reason, and Haywood, for another, are fiercely pro-Allies and anti-German.

If there was a conspiracy in the I.W.W. it was to use the war, as Labor thinks their bosses have, to raise prices and improve their condition.

And so on the other side: Labor's suspicion that the administration is in a conspiracy with the employers' associations to make war on Labor under cover of the war in Europe! Labor has "proofs." They point to this wholesale indictment of I.W.W. leaders at this time. I happen to know that employers' associations were preparing for this and other labor battles before the war on Germany was declared; and I don't know it, but I am as sure as I am of President Wilson's democracy, that the Administration is not in any such "conspiracy."

But I do see that the Administration seems to think that Mr. Gompers and the Central Organization of the A. F. of L. represent labor. They don't. There are over 100,000 workers in the I.W.W. and a great majority of the A. F. of L. has a silent, but deeply class-conscious sympathy with the I.W.W. and other radical labor groups. I know this from leaders close to Gompers; and I know it from having seen with my own eyes contributions by A. F. of L. unions of moneys for the defence of I.W.W. and other radical cases, which represent to Labor "the fight of their class against the Government, the War and Capital."

And so, knowing this and knowing what the "proofs" are that the agitators use, I can see that one flash of lightning might clear the whole atmosphere, disarm the suspicious and inspire all men with the President's spirit. Let me sound Haywood and the I.W.W.'s on an amnesty; and the pacifists; and, yes, the farmers and big employers' associations. All men are capable of great things, if only they are asked for great things. I believe that with half a chance, I could show you that with a generous, candid, kindly, democratic proclamation of a labor-peace policy such as the President is always disposed to make, he can mobilize America for what he is after— one last war for an everlasting peace.

Anyhow, get me a hearing. Or, if you can't or won't, please don't scorn my faith. It is good. I got it in the muck.

Lincoln Steffens.

I forgot to give you this from Steffens   E.M.H.

TS MS (WP, DLC).
    [1] Managing editor of the San Francisco *Bulletin*, prominent liberal and reformer.
    [2] Arturo Giovanniti, Elizabeth Gurley Flynn, and Carlo Fresca, all eastern leaders of the I.W.W.

Hugh Robert Wilson[1] to Robert Lansing

Ponta[r]lier
(Berne) Dated Dec. 28, 1917
Rec'd Dec. 30, 9:25 PM

2308 Dec. 28. 4 PM For Polk and Colonel House. "Concerning peace maneuver. German government believes situation the duplicate of that of one year ago, German people demanding universal peace. I believe safe to conclude that demand for peace is so great in Germany that government is being forced to make some attempt as it was forced last December by Socialists.

December last military authorities did not want peace as they wished to begin submarine war, and they hoped that Allied reply to this offer would unify German people. This hope was realized and Germany was enabled to begin her U-boat war and defy the United States.

Today military authorities more confident than a year ago but they realize must have people behind them.

Method different this year. Last year an overture was made, this year it takes form of address delivered at Russo-German peace conference,[2] object to embarrass Allied governments and to draw from them a reply which will unite German and Austrian people. Then offensive in west can begin.

Cannot overemphasize importance this maneuver. Internal conditions very bad and prospects for spring worse. German government cannot stop pay attention movement itself and is dependent on Allies to do it. If Allies make report similar to a year ago Germany will be united and confidence will be placed in military leaders. On the other hand, if the Allies appreciate meaning and importance this peace move they will answer in a way to divide people and government.

I believe we must add something to our position that we cannot make peace with irresponsible government. This not only because of situation in Germany but because of peace sentiment in France and England among great masses of people, and because of peace desires of neutrals who fear Germany on the one hand and desire friendship of Allies and United States on the other; we must make some public reply to Germany's peace offers, and in so doing must have in mind one supreme object which is to break the detirmination within Germany, to win at any cost. The importance of such detirmination, which is dependent on the will of the German people, is acknowledged by Hindenburg in a statement to Cologne editors 'If the people at home rema[i]n unbroken behind us we shall win.' Therefore suggest no American or Allied official make public statement regarding this maneuver until after careful discussion between Allies, and that in framing reply, the following be borne in mind. One Importance dividing German sentiment and two, importance of uniting allied people for great battles of coming months. More we divide Germany easier for our armies in the West. More we unite Germany more men's lives will be lost (signed) Ackermen.["]3

I am in accord with sentiments Ackerman expresses and desire to add that German government allowing until January fourth for participation of Allied nations, probably indicates beginning of offensive shortly after that date which offensive they hope will change political aspect and unify peoples. I therefore consider it of paramount importance that reply if made by Allied governments be made at earliest possible moment, and that it be of such a nature as to strengthen liberal sentiment in Germany, and defeat plans of Pan-Germans for unifying country behind military leaders for further prosecution of war. Venture to suggest that statement made along following general lines would tend to accomplish purpose indicated; that the Allied governments have declared they could not treat with the present German government, that therefore they could listen to no peace proposals from germany which were not created by the Reichstag and which were not proposed by the German government at the instance of the Reichstag and as the agent of this body.   Wilson

T telegram (WP, DLC).

¹ The American Chargé d'Affaires in Switzerland.

² A peace conference had convened on December 22 in Brest-Litovsk as arranged in an armistice agreement signed there on December 15 between representatives of the Bolshevik regime on one side and of the German, Austro-Hungarian, Bulgarian, and Turkish armies on the other side. The principal delegates at the conference were, for Germany, Kühlmann and Major General Max Hoffmann, Chief of Staff to the Commander in Chief in the East; for Austria-Hungary, Czernin; for Bulgaria, Christo I. Popov, Minister of Justice; for Turkey, Achmed Nessimy Bey, Minister of Foreign Affairs; and for Russia, Adolf Abrahamovich Joffe (or Ioffe), who had been recently released from a Siberian prison. At the first public session, on December 22, Joffe called for open meetings and proposed the discussion of peace terms involving, in general, no forcible annexations of territory, self-determination for nationalities, protection of the rights of minorities, and no indemnities. At the next session, on December 25, Czernin replied that the Russian proposals formed a discussable basis for "a general and just peace," provided that all the belligerent powers accepted them. Czernin, speaking in the name of the delegations of the Quadruple Alliance, then went on to say:

"This having been stated beforehand, the following observations must be made regarding the six points which are proposed by the Russian delegation as a basis for negotiations.

"(1) It is not the intention of the Allied Governments to appropriate forcibly territories which are at present occupied. The question of the troops in occupied territories must be settled in the sense of the withdrawal of troops from such and such places.

"(2) It is not the intention of the Allies to rob of its independence any of the nations which in the course of this war have lost their political independence.

"(3) The question of the State allegiance of national groups which possess no State independence can not, in the opinion of the Quadruple Alliance, be regulated as between States, but is, if required, to be solved by every State with its peoples independently in a constitutional manner.

"(4) Likewise, according to the declaration of the statesmen of the Quadruple Alliance, protection of the right of minorities forms an essential component part of the constitutional right of peoples to self-determination. The Allied Governments also grant validity to this principle everywhere in so far as it is practically realizable.

"(5) The Allied Powers have frequently emphasized the possibility that not only could both sides renounce indemnification for war costs, but also indemnification for war damage. Accordingly, every belligerent Power would only have to indemnify for the expenditure for its nationals who have become prisoners of war, as well as for damage done in their own territory by illegal acts of force committed against civilian nationals belonging to the enemy. The Russian Government's proposal for the creation of a special fund for this purpose could only be taken into consideration if other belligerent Powers were within a suitable period to join in the peace negotiations.

"(6) Regarding this point Germany is the only one of the four allied Powers that disposes of overseas colonies. On this subject, the German delegation, in full accord with the Russian proposals, makes the following declaration:

"The return of colonial territory, forcibly occupied and captured, during the war, is an essential component part of the German demands, which, under no circumstances, can be departed from. The Russian demand for the speedy evacuation of such regions as are occupied by the enemy likewise corresponds with German views. In view of the nature of the German colonial territory, the form proposed by the Delegation on the basis of the principle previously discussed, seems at present impracticable. The fact that the natives of the German colonies, despite the greatest difficulties and the slight prospects of success in the struggle against an enemy many times superior, and disposing of unlimited overseas reinforcements, have, through thick and thin, loyally adhered to their German friends, is proof of their attachment and their resolve under all circumstances to remain with Germany, a proof which in seriousness and in weight far exceeds every possible demonstrations of wishes by voting. The principles for economic intercourse propounded by the Russian Delegation in association with the six points just discussed meets with the unconditional agreement of the Delegations of the Allied Powers, which have always advocated the exclusion of all economic oppression, and which see in the restoration of a regular economic intercourse, which takes fully into account the interests of all concerned, one of the important requisites for consolidating friendly relations between the present belligerents.

"We are ready to enter into negotiations with all our enemies; but, in order to avoid unnecessary loss of time, the Allies are ready to enter upon the consideration of those special points the examination of which seems in any case necessary for both the Russian Government and the Allies."

The reports of Joffe's speech as translated from *Pravda*, December 23, and of Czernin's speech as translated from a telegram, December 25, via Vienna, were printed in the London *Daily Review of the Foreign Press*, Dec. 27 and 29, 1917. They were reprinted in U. S. Department of State, *Proceedings of the Brest-Litovsk Peace Conference: The Peace Negotiations between Russia and the Central Powers, 21 November, 1917–3 March, 1918* (Washington, 1918), pp. 38-41, from which the above quotation is taken (p. 41). This publication stated that the Berlin *Deutscher Reichsanzeiger*, December 27, 1917, contained an account of the meeting of December 25 practically identical with the one in the London publication.

3 That is, Carl W. Ackerman, at this time a correspondent in Switzerland for the *Saturday Evening Post* and other publications.

Two Letters to George Creel

My dear Creel: The White House 29 December, 1917

Thank you for your letter of the twenty-seventh about the Russian propaganda. You are taking just the right position. It must be our position for the time being, at any rate, and we must wait to see our way before pushing forward any faster than we are now doing or in any different way.

Cordially and faithfully yours,   Woodrow Wilson

TLS (G. Creel Papers, DLC).

My dear Creel,   The White House. 29 December, 1917.

I wonder how this "got past" the censors?[1] Fiske, as you probably know, is a perfect old granny most of whose ideas are perfectly negligible. What the merits of this one are I do not know; but it was a serious indiscretion on his part to go into print about it and an equally serious indiscretion on the part of the censors to let it get by them, do yow [you] not think so? Maybe it happened in some other way, however. I am merely sending this for your information, and for inquiry.   Faithfully Yours,   Woodrow Wilson

WWTLS (G. Creel Papers, DLC).
1 The Paris edition of the London *Daily Mail* had reported on December 25 as follows: "Rear Admiral Bradley Fiske states that the American navy has evolved a plan for finishing Germany's fleet by means of aircraft. In this he sees the road to victory with a minimum cost of money, time and human life. Wireless press." Ambassador Sharp quoted this comment in telegram No. 2953 and commented that, even though the statement was not specific and not directly official, he considered it as "exceedingly harmful." It conveyed the kind of information which "ought to be stowed away in the back of the head until time to strike." W. G. Sharp to RL, Dec. 26, 1917, T telegram (WP, DLC). Wilson sent the telegram to Creel, who returned it on January 3 with the statement that the Censorship Office frankly confessed a mistake. He pointed out, however, that the original dispatch read: "Rear Admiral Bradley Fiske says *he* has plan to end German Fleet with aircraft." Creel added that he was taking up this distortion with the *Mail*'s correspondent and had also given "more stringent orders" to the censors, and that these mistakes would not occur again. G. Creel to WW, Jan. 3, 1918, TLS (WP, DLC).

To Robert Lansing, with Enclosure

My dear Mr. Secretary,   The White House. 29 December, 1917.

What do you think about this? To have anything at all to do with it is certainly to play with fire and to risk incurring the suspicion of every state in Latin America; and yet, if the man is sincere, what he purposes (always provided his programme does in all good faith include a free and constitutional election) must of necessity claim our sympathy.   Faithfully Yours,   W.W.

WWTLI (SDR, RG 59, 818.00/287½, DNA).

E N C L O S U R E

Panama, Dec. 26, 1917.

Confidential. Supplementing my December 22, 6 p.m.[1] Alfredo Volio,[2] accompanied by British Minister,[3] called upon me today asking that I inform Department of his intentions. The following is a summary of these and of his responses to my questions.

As the leader he expects to invade Costa Rica from Nicaragua through Guanacaste to overthrow Tinoco, hold a free election. He has no personal ambitions but is willing to be a candidate for the Presidency. He has organization and counts on uprising in every province when he starts and anticipates no effective opposition except in the city San Jose. He stated that he expected Nicaraguan President[4] to favor him but would like Department to intimate to him to do so which would assure it, that Julian Irias is a friend of Tinoco and has procured commissions for some ten Nicaraguan leaders in the Costa Rican army, that he would assure pro-American, pro-Ally administration; that the Germans would favor him but only because of their considerable investments and of confidence of stable government under him; that he has ample funds including drafts on the Mercantile Bank of America and will remain here a week or more and in the meantime wishes to communicate by cable with Manuel Castro Quesada requesting that I procure for him transmission of his cables; that Rafael Cannes, the third designado, is closely connected with the family of Tinoco but would be an acceptable president; that Augustine, brother of Manuel Castro Quesada, instead of the latter, was with his party and had gone to Sinaola; that Monge[5] arrived yesterday with him. Others expected tomorrow.

Later He has filed following cablegram addressed to Alfredo Gonzalez, Manuel Castro Quesada, Costa Rican Legation, Washington or New York. "Flag of rebellion raised, country back of us, let Gonzalez influence Department to favor us. Have Castro come to Panama. I will tell about Nicaragua later. Answer to Panama."

Censor is withholding transmission until he hears from me. Please instruct immediately whether it should be forwarded. British Minister says Volio is a personal friend but that he believes him to be pro-German. He impresses me as not yet having effective organization but seeking one and especially the countenance of the Department.   Price.[6]

T telegram (SDR, RG 59, 818.00/280, DNA).
  [1] It is missing in the State Department files.
  [2] A member of the upper-class group who had supported Tinoco's coup. See Alberto F. Cañas, *Los 8 Años* (n.p., 1955), pp. 12-13.
  [3] Sir Claude Coventry Mallet, the British Minister to both Coast Rica and Panama, resident in Panama.
  [4] Emiliano Chamorro.
  [5] Colonel Ricardo Monge.
  [6] William Jennings Price, United States Minister to Panama.

To Samuel Reading Bertron

My dear Mr. Bertron: [The White House] 29 December, 1917

It gratifies me very much indeed that you should approve as you do of my action in the railroad matter and I hope with all my heart that things will turn out as we hope in that great and critical matter.

With the best wishes for the New Year,

Cordially and sincerely yours,   Woodrow Wilson

TLS (Lettterpress Books, WP, DLC).

To Addie Worth Bagley Daniels

My dear Mrs. Daniels: The White House 29 December, 1917

The cake was perfectly beautiful and as palatable as it was good to look at, and I am deeply and sincerely grateful to you for thinking of me in such a delightful way on my birthday. The sixty-one candles on the cake did not make so forbidding a multitude as I should have feared they would, and our little family circle had a very jolly time blowing them out and celebrating. It was a regular "blow-out."

With warm regard and appreciation and the best wishes for the New Year for you all,

Cordially and faithfully yours,   Woodrow Wilson

TLS (J. Daniels Papers, DLC).

From Joseph Patrick Tumulty

Dear Governor: The White House 29 December 1917.

No matter how we may try to explain it, the testimony of both Generals Crozier and Sharpe[1] has made a very bad impression upon the country. The testimony developed at yesterday's yearing [hearing] with reference to the lack of supplies, clothing, etc., and the number of deaths, which came from men who were reluctant to testify, is bound to make a decidedly bad impression. For instance the testimony of Major Generals Wright and Greble, commanders at Camps Doniphan, Oklahoma, and Dowie, Texas,[2] is particularly to be feared because of its affect. General Greble testified that for a time they had sixteen deaths a day and that eight thousand men were crowded into hospitals that could only accommodate eight hundred. He said he telegraphed General Gorgas[3] and Charpe [Sharpe] in September, last, telling them that the sanitary conditions ought to be remedied. General Greble said that he could get no results until after there was much sickness in camp.

I am convinced from what I hear that the Committee is going to make a very radical report. Coming from a Committee dominated by Democrats, I am afraid this will be looked upon, unless we anticipate it in some way, as a wholesale denunciation of the War Department, which of course would be most unfair to the Secretary of War. My suggestion is that you take some action of a radical character by way of anticipating the action of this Committee.

I beg to call your attention to the enclosed clipping from the New York Times of today.[4]   Sincerely yours,   Tumulty

TLS (WP, DLC).

[1] Responding to widespread complaints that the army had failed to supply sufficient clothing, ordnance, and heating facilities for soldiers in training, the Senate Military Affairs Committee on December 12 began hearings on the situation. The chairman, Senator Chamberlain, said that the hearings were intended to inform Congress and were not undertaken in any spirit of criticism. Maj. Gen. William Crozier, the Chief of Ordnance, testified on December 12, 13, 14, 15, and 17 on shortages of weapons, powder, and ammunition. Maj. Gen. Henry Granville Sharpe, the Quartermaster General, on December 21 told of delays in providing clothing, equipment, and shoes, with the result that some soldiers were still in khaki summer uniforms. Baker, after a long conference with Wilson, had announced on December 15 the formation of a War Council of seven members, headed by himself, to deal with problems of supply. Crozier and Sharpe would be relieved of their administrative duties and become members of the council. Baker let it be known on December 18 that General Goethals had been recalled to active duty as Acting Quartermaster General and that Brig. Gen. Charles Brewster Wheeler would be Acting Chief of Ordnance. *New York Times*, Dec. 12-22, 1917. For further information about the hearings conducted by Chamberlain, see Daniel R. Beaver, *Newton D. Baker and the American War Effort, 1917-1919* (Lincoln, Neb., 1966), pp. 88-93, 96-104.

[2] Maj. Gens. William Mason Wright and Edwin St. John Greble. Camp Doniphan was at Fort Sill, near Lawton, Okla.; Camp Bowie, at Fort Worth, Tex.

[3] That is, Maj. Gen. William C. Gorgas, Surgeon General.

[4] Under the headline "Camp Epidemics Laid to Want of Winter Equipment," this account described testimony by Generals Wright and Greble at the hearing on December 28. They reported sanitary deficiencies, lack of adequate hospital facilities, overcrowding,

and shortages of winter clothing and blankets. Many of these conditions had been corrected, they said, but both camps still had serious shortages of military equipment needed for training. In the hearing, it was brought out that there had been many cases of measles, meningitis, scarlet fever, diptheria, tuberculosis, pneumonia, hookworm, and other diseases. The clipping from the *New York Times*, Dec. 29, 1917, is in WP, DLC.

From Thetus Wilrette Sims

Dear Mr. President: Washington, D. C. December 29, 1917.

I beg pardon for making the following suggestions for your consideration. I have read, of course, closely your proclamation taking over the railroads and your statement issued in connection therewith, and naturally I infer that your address to Congress will in no way differ from the proclamation. But the suggestion I want to make is that in your address you refrain from making any statement fixing any date as to when the government operation of the railroads shall cease. Your proclamation, as I read it, names no date. I apprehend that there will be attempts to place in the legislation a statement to the effect that operation of the railroads by the Government shall cease at a specific date after the close of the war, and that perhaps there will be a strong effort made to put such a statement into any bill we may report. Believing, as I do, that it is not wise at this time to name any specific date as to when the Government shall cease to operate the railroads, I want to be in a position to fight any amendment that may be offered in Committee to that effect. Of course you will take this only as a suggestion.

I beg further to say that I would be very glad indeed to have a copy of the bill that you desire introduced and passed delivered to me at least a day or two before it is to be introduced so that I may study the same and familiarize myself with its provisions. I know that immediately upon introducing the bill that the newspaper correspondents will ask for a statement from me as to the contents and purposes of the bill, which I will be unable to give in a satisfactory way if I have not had time to study it prior to its introduction. I desire to introduce the bill on the same day, but after you have delivered your address to Congress. Of course I will treat the copy given to me as entirely confidential and give out no statement concerning it to any newspaper man or any other person.

With all good wishes for the success of this great undertaking, I am,   Very sincerely yours,   T. W. Sims

TLS (WP, DLC).

From Sir Cecil Arthur Spring Rice, with Enclosure

Personal and secret

Dear Mr President   Washington. December 29th 1917.

I saw the Japanese Ambassador today and had an entirely informal and private conversation with him. The general gist of his language is embodied in the rough memorandum annexed to this letter. It does not represent the result of official instructions and is merely in the form of a personal impression which is conveyed as a purely personal communication, which may be of interest.

Sato has received orders to proceed to Japan and he does not know whether he will return. He is a friend of Ischii who may possibly succeed him but of this he is not certain. Sato is sixty years old and is anxious to retire on personal grounds although he would have gladly stayed here to the end of the war. Although very reserved he has the most friendly sentiments to this country and as far as I can penetrate his reserve seems to be a good and sincere friend of the United States and the co-belligerents.

He was greatly pleased and touched by the visit of Colonel House who called at the Embassy and expressed in the most friendly terms his gratitude for the most useful co-operation afforded to him and the allies by the Japanese representatives in Europe. Sato is anxious to explain the American situation to his government and looks forward to the privilege of an audience before his departure.

There is always great difficulty, even for one who like myself have had very close and intimate relations with Japanese statesmen in past times, in getting at the bottom of the Japanese mind. There is always a strong suspicion of the East for the West. But I think that there is sincerity in what Sato says about the imperative nature of the rule of honour and its acceptance as an essential condition of life by the central direction of Japanese policy. There is also sincerity in what he and other Japanese say about the necessity of according equal treatment to Japan if other nations desire to be treated on a basis of equality and not in an atmosphere of mutual distrust and suspicion.

I venture to send you this at once, and in this personal form in case you should accord him an audience in the immediate future.[1] I am sure you will appreciate my motives. I am informing the State Department of the general sense of the memorandum

With the deepest respect I have the honour to be
                    Your obedient servant   Cecil Spring Rice

P.S. Sato did not seem to know of the recall of Japanese reservists from the U S.

TLS (WP, DLC).
¹ Wilson saw Sato at the White House on December 31. There is no report by Sato on this conversation in the Japanese Foreign Ministry Archives.

E N C L O S U R E

MEMORANDUM.

PRIVATE AND SECRET.

Japan is quite contented with the present condition of affairs in East Asia. Russia under a popular and democratic government in the hands of Russians is no danger to Japan. On the other hand, if Germany obtains control of Russia as she has done of Austria and Turkey the situation is fraught with danger. The ports of Eastern Asia would become German submarine bases. German instructors would organise the vast masses of Russians and Chinese and use them under German officers in the same way as they have used the Turks. There would be a regime of aggression and wholesale murder and Japan would have to face a danger threatening her existence. She was bound to make preparations to resist this danger. But she is quite conscious that if she takes action before the moment has come when action is imperatively necessary she would only precipitate the danger. It is not yet absolutely certain that Germany will obtain control over the whole of Russia including Siberia. If Japan takes action before the danger has taken form she would be giving strength and new material to the German propagandist who would point out to the Russians that the Yellow Peril was threatening the Eastern horizon and that Germany's help was necessary in order to fight this peril.

Japanese public opinion is quite convinced of this but is more alive to the Russo-German peril than it is to the possible effects of Japanese action on Russian public opinion. It must also be remembered that there is a strong suspicion in Japan of the Allies and especially of the United States who are suspected of designs on Eastern Asia. There is undoubtedly a fear of American action in the same way as in the United States there is a fear of Japanese action.

Although no authoritative statement can be made it is probable that the Japanese government is making every preparation in view of the possibility of German control in East Siberia but at the same time is very reluctant to take premature action. It would be important however that Japanese public opinion should be re-assured as to the possibility of sole American intervention.

With regard to the future the following general considerations may be cited as probably governing the situation.

There is a strong feeling in the Japanese Army of admiration for the German military system and for the bravery devotion and skill of the German officers. But there is little chance of a militarist government on the German model obtaining control of the Japanese government. For one thing there is a very strong democratic sentiment due partly to American influences among the people of Japan. For another thing the Japanese military system, that is the spirit of the military caste, is based upon the principles of BUSHIDO that is the rule of honour and chivalry. Here there is a profound and fundamental divergence from the German military spirit which acknowledges no rule but force. Japan has certain engagements which she cannot break without forfeiting her honour and losing face. Even were these engagements formally and officially ended the obligation would remain to remain faithful to her former friends and allies and not because of some motive of convenience to turn against them and requite their services with open or secret wrong. Both the United States and England have stood by Japan when Japan was powerless and both have refused in times past to join the Kaiser's wished for world coalition against the yellow race. It must not be forgotten that Japan for years suffered under the restrictions of the treaties which prevented her exercising the rights of sovereignty on her own territory. From a military and naval point of view, there was no impediment whatever to denunciation as foreign powers would not and could not have interfered. Japan however preferred to obtain the modification of the treaties not by force, but by friendly negotiation. In despite of the most violent pressure from Japanese public opinion and the representations of the naval and military authorities, Japan preferred to remain faithful and loyal to her promises, and her written engagements. It is out of the question that Japan should depart from the role of honour either at this moment or at any other unless the entire character of the Japanese people and government is radically changed.

What could effect this change? If the Japanese people were persuaded that they were regarded as outside the pale they also would regard the rest of the world as also outside the pale. If the world accepts the word of Japan as the word of an equal to an equal then Japan will have no desire to depart one iota from her engagements. She must have absolute equality of treatment not as like to like but as equal to equal. If, for instance, the United States and England claim certain rights in countries not belonging to them on geographical or other grounds, then the United States and England must allow Japan to claim similar rights on similar grounds. The Monroe doctrine, as interpreted by President Wilson's words and still more by his actions, implies no derogation of sovereignty, no exclusive political or commercial rights but embodies in a clear and definite form the natural doctrine of self preservation and the protection of American territory by common action from a common danger. A similar doctrine finds favour in Japan. The geographical position of Japan imposes on her certain duties by right of self defence. She cannot allow certain vital points to fall into the hands of a possible enemy. Her geographical position gives her certain obvious commercial advantages of which she proposes to take full advantage. She would resent any attempt to curtail her liberty of action or to prevent her commercial development by engagements or action giving other countries an advantage over herself.

President Wilson's action and words as regards both the American and Asiatic questions are accepted as entirely satisfactory and as a firm and good basis for the continuance of the most friendly relations.

With regard to the future Japan is alive to the immense danger of the establishment of a huge military empire under one central control extending from the North Sea to the Yellow Sea. This threatens her existence and it also threatens the existence of the independent nations of the world and of the principles of freedom on which those nations govern their polity. The liberty of the Pacific from submarine warfare and German sea policy is as essential to Japan as it is to the United States and as the liberty of the Atlantic is to the United States, France, England and Italy. Japan is willing to accept the position of the outpost of the free nations on the Western Pacific as France and England are willing to accept a similar position as the outpost and barrier on the Eastern Atlantic. But the essential thing is that the free nations should accept the comradeship of Japan on a basis of mutual respect, mutual confidence and entire and perfect equality.

T MS (WP, DLC).

From John Palmer Gavit

Dear Woodrow Wilson: Englewood, N. J. December 29. 1917

I did not know until this morning that your birthday had intruded upon your other responsibilities. Thus I am behindhand in offering my felicitations and good wishes. I shall deserve no credit for, but shall none the less accept all and more than my share of joy in, the fact that the year 1918 will be a very great year for Woodrow Wilson, and perhaps through him more than any other living human being, for all the rest of us.

My own acquaintance with the said Woodrow Wilson has been

a source of considerable inspiration to me personally. He has averaged rather better, on the whole and according to my standards of judgment, than any other public man that I have known; and I have known some rather fine ones. I derive comfort from the belief that he will do well to the end. Just now, I think, he is approaching a crucial opportunity and a period of great temptation. In my own fashion I am praying that he will recognize and know what to do in the day of his visitation; that no smallness or self-pride, or stubbornness of opinion or any other human narrowness or frailty on his part or that of his advisers will palsy his hand or misdirect his choice. What ought he to do? God bless my soul, I don't know; if I did, I'd tell him instanter!

Anyway, be sure that there is nothing within your gift that I want, except your friendship.   Faithfully,   John P. Gavit

ALS (WP, DLC).

Translations of Two Telegrams from Jean Jules Jusserand to Stéphen Jean Marie Pichon

New York, without date [Dec. 29]
received December 30, 1917

CONFIDENTIAL

No. 1613. I reply to your telegram 2381 and following and refer to my 1339.

I have just sent to the Congress of the United States the translation I have had made of the letter from the President of the Republic. Mr. Wilson, who kept me for an hour,[1] told me that he had already been kept *au courant* with our divergences of views by General Bliss, and that they put him in a state of great embarrassment. I can, he said, appoint and, in the event of a grave situation, replace a commander in chief, but I would not know myself how to find a substitute for him. He is on the spot and of the (group missing)

The argument of General Pershing is that, if the troops are parceled out, they would lose their individuality and their esprit de corps, their healthy rivalry among themselves. He seems persuaded that the best service that they could render would be to act as reserve troops, stationing themselves at points still unknown, where the great German offensive might begin.   Jusserand

[1] Jusserand conferred with Wilson at the White House from 2 P.M. to 3 P.M. on December 29.

New York, without date [Dec. 29],
received December 30, 1917.

No. 1615. I have strongly insisted that the President might well wish to take up again an examination of the question, showing him that it was so grave as to cause the personal intervention of the French chief of state. I urged him to have sent to General Pershing new instructions which, even if they not be absolute orders (which we would prefer) should be of such a sort as the Entente so happily establishes with our military chiefs, whose greater experience is incontestable.

The President is going to reflect and consult his advisers about this matter, the great gravity of which he understands. He will not fail to respond to the President of the Republic. I do not believe that the value of the ministerial presentations (word passed) conveyed by Mr. Poincaré, and which I have emphasized verbally, have escaped him.   Jusserand.

T telegrams (État-Major de l'Armée de Terre, Service Historique, 14 N 25, pp. 50-51, FMD-Ar).

To Joseph Patrick Tumulty

Dear Tumulty: [The White House, c. Dec. 30, 1917]

What did you find out about these matters that Mr. Borglum is so excited about?[1] I think it important that we should get at the root of this thing and find out if there really is anything lagging or anything the matter. I had a very full report about it not long ago and things seemed going very satisfactorily. If Mr. Borglum has a grievance or has any personal element in it, it is rather important that we should know.   The President.

TL (WP, DLC).
[1] See G. Borglum to WW, Dec. 25, 1917.

From the Diary of Colonel House

December 30, 1917.

I have done nothing with the diary for a week. It has been impossible not only because I spent nearly a week in Washington, but the time has not been propitious. However, I made notes each day while in Washington and will now dictate from them.

Loulie and I went to Washington on the 12.08 train Sunday the 23rd to spend Christmas with Janet and Gordon at No. 1827 Nineteenth Street. We had a delightful and quiet trip. A White House motor was waiting to take me to the White House where I had a few minutes with the President. I gave him the data I had prepared for his information and to use in his forthcoming message to Congress upon the United States' war aims.[1] We did not discuss these, but took up the railroad question which is the burning issue at the moment.

I urged him to take over the railroads as soon as possible. He thought he could not do so before Wednesday or Thursday because the papers would not be ready until Monday night the 23rd, and he did not wish to make the announcement Christmas Day. Besides, there was a long statement to prepare which would probably take the matter over until Wednesday or Thursday.

Sunday evening for dinner Janet and Gordon had the Attorney General and Mrs. Gregory, B. M. Baruch, Chas. R. Crane and Mrs. Crane and their son Richard and his wife.[2]

My day on Monday was largely spent at the State Department consulting with Lansing, Polk, Phillips and with different members of our Mission whom I had asked to come to the Department to meet me. Now that Gordon is in the Counsellor's office, I receive everyone there rather than at the White House. It is just as convenient and less conspicuous.

We have gotten our report in final shape. It has gone to Lansing, who, in turn, will transmit it to the President for whatever action he may see fit.

Monday night while we were all busy with Loulise's [Louise's] Christmas tree, the President called unannounced. He had a package of papers with him about which he said he wished to consult me. He remained for a half hour or more, but there was nothing, as far as I could see, that required immediate attention, and I am at a loss to know why he should have called. He must have done it merely as an act of courtesy rather than for any advice he wished to get upon the matters he presented.

Christmas Day was cold and wet and I did not leave the house although a number of people called. Among them was Secretary McAdoo with whom I had a long conference regarding the railroads. McAdoo showed an almost childish delight in assuming this new and great responsibility. He already has more than he can do, particularly with his methods. He has ability, vision and an enormous amount of energy, but he lacks both the ability and the desire to delegate authority to others as fully as he should with the amount

[1] The memorandum by S. E. Mezes, D. H. Miller, and W. Lippmann printed at Jan. 4, 1918.
[2] Ellen Douglas Bruce Crane.

of work he has to do. Not only that, he is a poor judge of men, which is a great drawback and, in a measure, justifies his disinclination to delegate full authority to his subordinates.

For Christmas dinner we had Sam Auchincloss, Sam Sloan Colt, Mrs. Lewis Hancock, Dorothy and Margery.[3]

On Wednesday I had a quiet day. I undertake to use my visits away from the White House to see a number of my friends. I find it difficult to get in touch with them ordinarily. I also saw a number of people at the State Department, among them Herbert Hoover who asked me to recommend some good man for Counsellor for the Food Administration. I recommended Sherman Whipple of Boston who declined. I afterward suggested William A. Glascow of Philadelphia,[4] who accepted. The man he has is incapaci[ta]ted by over-work. I find with Hoover, as with others, that the matter he is working on is the most important in the world. Hoover believes that food should be moved at the expense of coal or other necessary commodities. He does not think it matters much if the people are a little cold just so the Allies have food. I find this characteristic in nearly all self-centered individuals having a particular specialty. One finds in France, for instance, that Petain believes we should send men at the expense of everything else, Tardieu believe[s] we should send steel and supplies of a like nature, even thought [though] we have to curtail the supply of men.

Gordon and Janet had invited Sir Cecil and Lady Spring-Rice with several other important personages to dine Thursday evening but an invitation came about midday from the President and Mrs. Wilson inviting us all to dine at the White House. Janet's dinner was called off and we went to the White House.

The President and I went to his study after dinner for a half hour. I could see some signs of weariness in him and I begged him to take, as nearly as possible, a week's rest before we got at the war aims message. He promised to do the best he could. I know him so well that I detect, almost sooner than anyone, I think, signs of fatigue or nervousness. I am enabled to do this because I am not with him constantly, but frequently enough to note the difference in him from time to time.

We went through a great many things which are of passing importance and which were decided with unusual celerity. The only matter we differed on was the appointment of Mayor Mitchel to the Army. Mitchel has been trying in every creditable way to get

[3] Samuel Sloan Colt, a banker since 1914 with the Farmers Loan and Trust Co. of New York, at this time in Washington as a lieutenant with the Ordnance Department of the army; Attilia Aldridge Anderson (Mrs. Lewis) Hancock, wife of a banker and former Mayor of Austin, Texas, and her daughters, Dorothy and Margery.
[4] That is, William Anderson Glasgow, Jr.

into the service even in a subordinate capacity, and the President has instructed Baker not to permit him to do so on the ground that it would be injecting politics into the army. As a matter of fact, his real reason is his personal dislike of Mitchel. The President carries these dislikes to a degree which is not creditable to him.

We argued about Mitchel for some ten or twelve minutes, and he finally concluded to reconsider the matter, although he did not agree to pass upon it favorably. It is not because of my high regard and sincere friendship for Mitchel nor that I fail to realize that he deserves the President's disapproval for some of his actions toward the President personally, but I do not approve of mixing personal feeling with public service. If Mitchel wishes to go into the army at this critical time, he should be permitted to do so, and in such capacity as he is fitted, for he has had military training. A refusal to permit him to volunteer will make a martyr of him and the President by his action will help Mitchel rather than hurt him.[5]

The President asked me to return Friday of next week. He plans to address Congress on the railroad question on the 4th and after that we will prepare together his address on war aims which he hoped to deliver to Congress, Tuesday, January 8th. We think the peace terms upon which Germany is insisting at Brest-Litovsk will give him the proper opportunity to state our war aims.

In talking to the Wilson family about the Sargent portrait, we practically all agreed that it did not do the President justice; that it gives him rather a weak face. I again suggested that Sargent had pictured him as the esthetic scholar rather than as the virile states-man, but my conclusion was that it did not make much difference what kind of face a portrait gave a man, but it was what the man had accomplished that counted. If he did great deeds in a masterly way, it made but little difference what posterity saw in his face. We then fell to citing instances of men we had known with strong faces who had no strength of character or ability.

We left the White House early not only because I knew the President was tired and needed a rest, but also because I had to take the midnight train to New York. We have had a delightful Christmas holiday with Gordon, Janet and little Louise. They seemed so glad to have us with them and they have done everything in their power to make our stay happy and comfortable.

[5] Mitchel announced on January 11 that he had accepted a commission as major in the Aviation Service of the army.

To Robert Lansing

My dear Mr. Secretary,   The White House. 31 December, 1917.

I have read this and entirely approve of it.[1] It contains the whole fact and I do not see that anything could profitably be added, except the comment I suggested over the telephone this morning, namely that we feel that a great deal has been accomplished and are very much gratified by the results.   Faithfully Yours,   W.W.

WWTLI (WP, DLC).
[1] That is, the summary report described in RL to WW, Dec. 27, 1917.

Two Letters to William Gibbs McAdoo

Personal.

My dear Mac: The White House 31 December, 1917

You know of coure what I am going to recommend to Congress with regard to guarantees to the roads. It would be of great service to me if the lawyers who are serving you would have ready for me by the time Congress opens, if possible, a bill embodying the guarantees which I could place in the hands of the Chairmen of the committees concerned.

   In haste   Affectionately yours,   Woodrow Wilson

TLS (W. G. McAdoo Papers, DLC).

My dear Mac.,   The White House. 31 December, 1917.

Here are the papers I spoke to you about the other day,[1] and suggested that you have them carefully considered. They come from the Brotherhood chiefs through their counsel, Mr. Plumb and have made a considerable impression on my mind.

                    Faithfully,   W.W.

WWTLI (W. G. McAdoo Papers, DLC).
[1] Glenn E. Plumb, *Brief Filed on Behalf of the Brotherhood of Locomotive Engineers Brotherhood of Locomotive Firemen and Enginemen Order of Railway Conductors and the Brotherhood of Railway Trainmen before the Interstate Commerce Commission in the Matter of the Tentative Valuation of the Atlanta, Birmingham & Atlantic Railroad Company* (n.p., n.d.).

To Franklin Knight Lane

Personal.

My dear Lane: [The White House] 31 December, 1917

I have seen a copy of the newly-formulated leasing bill and am distressed to find that it goes practically as far as was proposed the last time in the matter of indulgence of the oil men in the disputed districts. I have gone over this matter so often and with such close attention that I am very clear in my conviction about it, and personally I cannot go an inch further than was embodied in the proposals of Senator Swanson, with which I think you are familiar, and my conclusion affects not only the naval reserve, so-called, but the other areas under discussion. I wish very much that you could exert your influence to get this modification of the proposed concessions adopted, not as your own judgment, for I know it is not, but as my judgment, and one which must necessarily be reckoned with in the final settlement. I am suggesting this to you because I think you may have some more open and tactful approach to the matter than I could have. My intervention at this stage would seem a bit blunt.

The measure suggested by Senator Swanson was as follows:

"That any claimant who, either in person or through his predecessor in interest, entered upon any of the lands embraced within the executive order of withdrawal dated September 27, 1909, prior to July 3, 1910, honestly and in good faith for the purpose of prospecting for oil or gas, and thereupon commenced discovery work thereon, and thereafter prosecuted such work to a discovery of oil or gas, shall be entitled to lease from the United States any producing oil or gas well resulting from such work, at a royalty of not less than one-eighth of all the oil and gas produced therefrom, together with an area of land sufficient for the operation thereof, but without the right to drill any other or additional wells; provided, that such claimant shall first pay to the United States an amount equal to not less than the value of one-eighth of all the oil and gas already produced from such well; and provided further, that this act shall not apply to any well involved in any suit brought by the United States, or in any application for patent, unless within ninety days after the approval of this act the claimant shall relinquish to the United States all rights claimed by him in such suit or application; and provided further, that all such leases shall be made, and the amount to be paid for oil and gas already produced shall be fixed by the Secretary of the Interior under appropriate rules and regulations."

Faithfully yours,   Woodrow Wilson[1]

TLS (Letterpress Books, WP, DLC).
[1] Lane replied: "I am heartily in favor of your solution of the oil problem as set out in your letter of December 31st, and shall at once make an effort to secure its adoption." Lane added that he had asked Senators Myers and Pittman and Representatives Ferris and Taylor to meet with him on the morning of January 3. FKL to WW, Jan. 2, 1918, TLS (WP, DLC).

To George Wylie Paul Hunt

[The White House]

My dear Governor Hunt: 31 December, 1917

I congratulate you upon your return to your gubernatorial duties.[1] It is a matter of great regret to me to lose your advice as conciliator, but the regret is more than offset by my gratification at your return to the important office of Governor of your state.

May I not send you my warmest greetings and best wishes for the New Year?

Cordially and sincerely yours,   Woodrow Wilson

TLS (Letterpress Books, WP, DLC).
[1] The Supreme Court of Arizona had decided on December 22 in favor of Hunt in his contest with Thomas E. Campbell over the governorship of Arizona. Hunt resumed the office on December 25, 1917. *New York Times*, Jan. 28 and Dec. 23 and 26, 1917.

To Hale Holden

My dear Mr. Holden: [The White House] 31 December, 1917

Your very generous letter of December twenty-eighth has given me a great deal of pleasure and I want to thank you for it very sincerely. I hope and believe that by hearty cooperation, which I do not for a moment doubt, we shall be able to work out something that will be for the real and permanent benefit of the railroads. The difficulties are many and tremendous, but we shall overcome them.

In necessary haste,

Sincerely yours,   Woodrow Wilson

TLS (Letterpress Books, WP, DLC).

To Thetus Wilrette Sims

My dear Mr. Sims: [The White House] 31 December, 1917

The suggestions contained in your letter of December twenty-ninth are most welcome and you may be sure will be acted upon.

This is just a brief note but it means just what it says.

Cordially and sincerely yours,   Woodrow Wilson

TLS (Letterpress Books, WP, DLC).

To Hiram Woods, Jr.

My dear Hiram: [The White House] 31 December, 1917

Charlie Mitchell's death has grieved me most deeply,[1] as you may imagine, and you may be sure that I would have got over to his funeral if it had been possible for me to do so; but it was impossible, and the fact that I could not be there adds to my grief. Thank you very warmly, my dear fellow, for sending me the sad news.[2] I am writing to Mrs. Mitchell today. The old circle is broken and I am very sad.

Always   Faithfully yours,   Woodrow Wilson

TLS (Letterpress Books, WP, DLC).
[1] Charles Wellman Mitchell had died on December 28.
[2] Woods' letter is missing.

To Florence Crowe Mitchell

                                        [The White House]
My dear Mrs. Mitchell: 31 December, 1917

I am sure I need not tell you how my heart aches at the news of Charlie's death. He was very near and very dear to me, one of the best and truest friends I ever had, and while I know that the loss to his profession[1] has been very great, what fills my heart just now is my own personal loss and, above that, your own irreparable bereavement. My heart goes out to you in the deepest and truest sympathy. I wish there were some great word of comfort that I could speak to you. The only comfort I have for myself is that the memory of him will always be exceedingly sweet.

Sincerely and faithfully yours,   Woodrow Wilson

TLS (Letterpress Books, WP, DLC).
[1] He was a physician.

To Felexiana Shepherd Baker Woodrow

My dear Aunt Felie: The White House 31 December, 1917

Your little note of the twenty-eighth gave me the greatest pleasure and cheer, and I want to send you in return for myself and from all my little household the warmest and most affectionate greetings of the New Year.

I wish I had time for a real letter but you will know how much this message means, even though it is short.

Affectionately yours,   Woodrow Wilson

TLS (received from James Woodrow).

From David Lloyd George

London, Dec. 31 [1917].

At this season I wish in behalf of the British War Cabinet to send to your Government and people a message of good will. Every day that passes must make us realize more clearly that the hopes of the human race centre upon the triumph of our cause.

Every day proves to us that our friendship for one another is becoming more and more the cement of that league of free nations which now stands as the guardian of justice and liberty throughout the world.

We wish in particular to send a message of thanks to the United States Navy for the great services it has rendered in the past year and of greeting to the young American army now training to take its place in the battle for human freedom. We are relying upon the great addition this army will make to strengthen the Allies in their joint struggle for free civilization, and we are confident that when the time of battle comes they will sustain the great traditions set by their own forebears by helping to win a complete triumph for the cause to which they have dedicated themselves.

Printed in the *New York Times*, Jan. 1, 1918.

From Robert Lansing

Dear Mr. President: Washington December 31, 1917.

Upon receipt of the confidential telegram from Panama in regard to Volio's revolutionary plans against the Tinoco Government, I at once cabled our minister to give no encouragement to armed revolution and to prevent the censor from sending the filed cablegram to Castro Quesada, who is the moving spirit in this affair.[1]

This I did in accordance with our policy not to countenance the use of force in gaining control of the government, a policy, which you may remember, I declared to Gonzales and Quesada when they called upon me several months ago.[2] It seemed to me that we could not do less than pursue this policy in the case of the present movement.

We are in a peculiarly embarrassing situation in regard to Costa Rica, since our settled policy as to non-recognition of Tinoco, which I feel we ought to continue, runs directly contrary to our interests in prosecuting the war. There seems little doubt (although I hope to be absolutely certain in a short time) that Castro Quesada and his party are pro-German and receiving financial support from the Germans in their revolutionary activities. Tinoco, on the other hand, by inclination or for politic reasons, is pro-Ally. Gonzales, the deposed President, counts little, Quesada being the strong man. He is of notoriously bad character, worse I believe than Tinoco.

In these circumstances I do not feel that we should give encouragement to Quesada or, on the other hand, protect Tinoco. I, therefore, adopted the course which I have stated and which is consistent with our announced policy. I think until we are fully satisfied about Quesada and the Germans we should maintain this attitude.   Faithfully yours,   Robert Lansing

TLS (SDR, RG 59, 818.00/280, DNA).
    [1] RL to W. J. Price, Dec. 29, 1917, TS telegram (SDR, RG 59, 818.00/280, DNA).
    [2] See RL to WW, Feb. 19, 1917, Vol. 41.

From Franklin Knight Lane

My dear Mr. President: Washington December 31, 1917.

I have had a conference with Mr. Ferris and Mr. Lenroot regarding the water power bill. They tell me that there is danger that the Shields bill, which has passed the Senate, will come up for action soon in the House, and that there is necessity for some immediate step if we are to get our composite bill, which you have before you, passed. Mr. Lenroot advises that the wise procedure is for you to call Mr. E. W. Pou and Dr. Martin D. Foster, of the Rules Committee in the House, and ask them to bring in a special rule for the appointment of a special committee by the Speaker, with the understanding that it will be composed of Representatives of the Public Lands Committee and the Interstate Commerce Committee of the House, to sit together upon this bill so that each of the Committees can feel that it has a hand in its production, and that if those Committees together report in favor of this bill there is no doubt that the House will pass it. You will, of course, have to make it known specifically that you desire this bill passed. This procedure will head off the Shields bill and will present to the Senate, when it has passed the House, the necessity of dealing with this matter as a whole. The Senate then would have to take some method by which it could deal with the bill that had already passed the House, perhaps through a combination of its Committees. The one thing Messrs. Ferris and Lenroot think is now necessary is for you to ask Mr. Pugh [Pou] and Dr. Foster to see you and tell them that you wish a rule brought in by which this consolidation of Committees will take place and pass upon this particular bill.
                         Cordially yours,   Franklin K Lane

TLS (WP, DLC).

From George Creel

My dear Mr. President: [Washington] December 31, 1917.

I have drawn up a statement of war progress that I am very eager to submit for White House issuance as a New Year's statement to the people. Secretary Baker agrees with me as to its importance. May I bring it over, or shall I send it?

Colonel Thompson, who gave a million to Kerensky, is in Washington to-day with Mr. Lamont of the firm of Morgan. They saw the whole of official England with respect to the Russian situation, conferred with Mr. McAdoo yesterday, and are now with the Secretary of State. Colonel Thompson has more first-hand information than any one yet reporting. Will it be possible for me to bring them over today?   Respectfully,   George Creel

TCL (RSB Coll., DLC).

From George Creel, with Enclosure

Dear Mr. President: [Washington] Dec. 31, 1917.

This is the statement to which I referred in my former note. If we are to use it we must have it by six o'clock at the latest. The thought came to me at the last moment, hence the effect of hurry.

May I beg the favor of a decision before six, if possible?
          Respectfully,   George Creel

TCL (RSB Coll., DLC).

E N C L O S U R E[1]

⟨The Old Year bequeathes a heritage of confidence to the New. Our war progress has been as remarkable as it is inspiring, and stands as a guarantee of swift future accomplishment that shall express completely the iron determinations of a free people fighting in defense of all that national existence has taught them to hold dear.⟩

⟨It is now⟩ Nine months ⟨since this republic was⟩ *have elapsed since we were* driven to accept the aggressions of the Teutonic allies as constituting a state of war. Devoted to peace, unarmed, and not unfriendly, we sought with determined patience to avoid a quarrel. We tried, by every worthy means, to appeal to ⟨their⟩ reason and ⟨their⟩ *to manifest* interest. ⟨and,⟩ *In* order that our acts

[1] Words in angle brackets in the following document deleted by Wilson; words in italics added by him.

might not give the lie to our words, we carefully avoided *even* the appearance of making ready for war while we offered them peace. We waited until every fair-minded citizen of our pacific democracy was aware that peace was impossible. ⟨before we so much as began to prepare reluctantly to defend ourselves.⟩

⟨It followed that⟩ On the day when war was declared, *therefore,* we had little ready but our new resolve. We had at last a united people, ⟨at last⟩ a people ready to turn from the pursuits of peace that have been our great pride and our sole ambition, and eager ⟨to surrender⟩ in the interests of military necessity *to surrender* personal liberties that we have been most jealous to preserve. But the very legislation needed to organize us for war still had to be prepared and enacted. We had still to recruit a whole nation to arms, convert it to unnatural aims, train it in alien industries and find not only the tools of war but the machinery to make those tools and the workmen to direct that machinery.

The record of achievement *therefore* ministers equally to our pride and courage, attesting unity and affirming high resolve.

The Navy, our first line of defense, has leaped from a personnel of 73,000 to a fighting strength of 293,000. ⟨Over⟩ *More than* 1,000 war vessels are now in commission whereas there were only 300 in the early days of 1917. There ⟨is⟩ *are* building now, under night and day driving, 424 capital and important ships, ⟨not including⟩ *besides* submarine chasers and small craft. The seized German vessels, supposedly damaged for the duration of the war, were quickly repaired by Navy engineers, and within five months were again in commission under the American flag.

The Regular Army, from a scant 150,000 has grown to 500,000; the National Guard has expanded from ⟨107⟩ 120,000 to 425,000, and a half million young Americans, first selections for the National Army, are in the training camps.

In Regular Army, National Army and the National Guard, we have today over 1,500,000 picked men under arms, and a machinery of selection is in smooth operation that will add steadily to the number until, if need be, the whole ten million registrants are fitted for the firing line.

A great and proper pride is to be taken in the speed and precision of this progress, for at every point were involved new undertakings of unparalleled magnitude that tested our competence and our determination.

On May 18 the selective service act became law ⟨of the land⟩ by an almost unanimous vote of Congress.

On June 5, ten million⟨s of⟩ young Americans between the ages of 21 and 31 were registered, and on June 30, 4,557 local boards were ready to begin the task of examination and exemption.

For the training of these men there had to be provided almost instantly sixteen cantonments, great cities of wood and steel complete in every municipal detail.

On May 7, the order to select sites was given; on June 15 building began, and within 90 days after the driving of the first nail, the selected men entered new homes that did not fail in a single *essential* comfort or convenience.

Sixteen cities were also brought into swift being for the training of the 400,000 men of the National Guard, called into Federal Service on July 3.

The business of officering the Army went hand in hand with its creation. Sixteen officers' training camps were rushed to completion, and on May 15 received 30,000 volunteer entrants. Of this number, 27,341 qualified. A second series was started August 27, and in January a third series will commence. These men, drawn from civil life to lead *armed men*, constitute democracy's answer to the fear of militarism.

The Navy faced this problem of training no less splendidly than the Army, and buil⟨ded⟩t over 250 new training stations for its eager volunteers.

No greater or more expert care was ever given than *has been given* to our soldiers and sailors. Over 12,000 of the foremost physicians, surgeons and sanitarians have been taken into the Medical Service, and while the civil population is called upon for every denial, no single complaint has come from an encampment with respect to the quantity and quality of food. Clean, fine, sound and strong, the splendid wellbeing of these young thousands, ⟨assured⟩ *attained* in the face of seemingly impossible ⟨accomplishment⟩ *tasks*, serves as ⟨an answer⟩ *sufficient reassurance* to ⟨the singular indecency that attempts to play upon⟩ natural fears and anxieties.

On June 15, ⟨scarce⟩ *only* two months after our entrance into *the* war, General Pershing and staff arrived in France, and on July 3 the first division of American soldiers reached the land of La Fayette and Rochambeau.

Every man in the expeditionary force must carry supplies for six months, so that each 100,000 represents an equipment for half a million. The strain of this effort, ⟨compelled to be⟩ *necessarily* undertaken months in advance of expectation, has entailed certain inadequacies in connection with the home forces, yet not one of these is vital or ⟨resultant⟩ *has resulted* in more than a minimum of physical discomfort.

Our determination to carry this war of self-defense to a successful conclusion has not stopped with the upbuilding of an Army and Navy expressive of our strength and high resolve.

Two great Liberty Loans have been launched. The first called for $2,000,000,000 and over three billions was subscribed; the second for three billions and almost five billions were pledged. Of these amounts, over four billion has been loaned already to other nations at war with the Imperial German Government.

That we might discharge our duty to the peoples of other countries by sharing our supplies with them, generously and honestly, a Food Control Act was passed on August 10, and is in efficient operation.

No scandal has shamed our faith, and greater proof of a peoples' devotion to declared ideals could not be given than the expenditure of billions without ⟨such revelations⟩ *any instances* of dishonesty *such* as have humiliated every nation in every other war.

Under the strain of terrific necessities, not a single social or industrial standard has been lowered but rather ⟨it is the case that⟩ an even larger protection has been thrown about the workers of the nation, our women and our children.

It may not be said that these achievements have surprised America, for we are a people of large and confident expectations, but it is true that the record is one that has amazed and gratified those nations⟨, who⟩ *that* await our aid in the great struggle that is to decide between freedom and autocracy for the world.

⟨No finer resolves for the New Year can be made than that solid fact shall not be clouded by noisy assertion, our pride lessened by petty irritations or our courage weakened by slanderous exaggerations.⟩[2]

T MS (WP, DLC).
[2] Creel seems to have deleted this paragraph himself. Wilson suppressed this statement for the reasons given in WW to G. Creel, Jan. 2, 1918.

From Robert Bridges

Dear Mr. President: New York December 31, 1917

I have sent you in another parcel the first copy of "The United States and Pangermania," (Chéradame)[1] which will be published in about a week. This book has been made especially for America and I believe that it will interest you, particularly in view of what you have said on many occasions. At any rate, I want you to have an early chance at it.

With best wishes for the New Year, and confidence in the great part you are to play in it, I am

Faithfully yours,   Robert Bridges

P.S. It was a sad day, yesterday when we put Charley Mitchell away. Talcott, Lee, Webster, Henderson, Hiram[2] and I carried him from the house and church. We had had so many good times together that I could almost hear his cheering voice with some remark about Hiram or the rest of us. What we were doing did not seem to be the reality—but all the happy past was the real, permanent thing. And so I shall try to keep it. Hiram is the one who will feel it most, as they went through a good many serious crises together. Hiram thought they would save him this time—but the tide suddenly turned. Good old Hiram had almost his last conscious word and look.   Bobbie

TLS with Hw PS (WP, DLC).

[1] André Chéradame, *The United States and Pangermania* (New York, 1918). On the title page was a quotation from Wilson's address of June 14, 1917: "From Hamburg to the Persian Gulf the net is spread." In an introduction, "To My American Readers," Chéradame wrote: "Germany no longer exists. In her place stands Pangermany, whose existence is incompatible with the independence of the United States and the Freedom of the World."

[2] That is, Charles A. Talcott, William B. Lee, James E. Webster, Robert R. Henderson, and Hiram Woods, Jr., M.D., members of the Princeton Class of 1879.

David Rowland Francis to Robert Lansing

Petrograd Dated Dec. 31st, 1917
Recd. Jan. 1st, 1918, 3:03 p.m.

2163. Following is textual translation of address:[1] "To Peoples and Governments of Allied Countries," mentioned in my 2169. "The peace negotiations which are being conducted in Brest-Litovsk between the delegation of the Russian Republic and the delegations of Germany, Austria-Hungary, Turkey and Bulgaria have been suspended for ten days until December twenty sixth in order to give to the Allied countries a last possibility to take part in the further negotiations and thus secure themselves against all the consequences of a separate peace between Russia and the enemy countries.

"At Brest-Litovsk two programs have been presented, the one expressing the point of the all Russian Congresses of Councils of Workmen's Soldiers' and Peasants' Deputies—the other in the name of the Governments of Germany and her Allies.

"The program of the Republic of the Soviets is the program of consistent socialistic democracy. This program has for its purpose the establishment of conditions under which, on the one hand, every nationality independently of its freedom and the level of its development would receive an entire liberty of national development, and on the other hand, all the nations might be united in an economic and cultural collaboration.

"The program of the countries at war with us is characterized by their statement that: It does not enter into the intention of the Allied powers (namely Germany, Austria, Turkey and Bulgaria) to violently incorporate the territories seized during the war. This means that the enemy countries are ready to evacuate at the peace treaty the occupied territories of Belgium the northern departments of France, Servia, Montenegro, Roumania, Poland, Lithuania, Courland in order that the subsequent destiny of the contested provinces may be decided by the population concerned itself. The step which the enemy Governments are making towards the program of the Democracy under the pressure of circumstances and chiefly of their own labouring masses, lies in their renouncing new violent annexations and contributions. But in renouncing new conquests, the enemy Governments proceed from the idea that old conquests, old acts of violence of the strong over the weak are rendered sacred by historical prescription. This means that the fate of Alsace Loraine, Transylvania, Bosnia and Herzegovina et cetera on the one hand, Ireland, Egypt, India, Indochina, et cetera on the other, are not subject to revision. Such a program is profoundly inconsistent and represents a project of an unprincipled compromise between the pretensions of Imperialism and the opposition of the labouring Democracy. But the very fact of the presentation of this program is an enormous step forward.

"The Governments of the Allied nations have hitherto not joined the peace negotiations for reasons which they have obstinately declined to exactly formulate.

"It is now impossible to repeat that the war is going on for the liberation of Belgium the northern departments of France, Servia, et cetera for Germany and her Allies announce their readiness to evacuate these provinces in the event of an universal peace. Now after the presentation of peace terms by the adversary it is impossible to get off with general phrases concerning the necessity of carrying on the war to the end. It is necessary to say clearly and precisely what is the peace program of France, Italy, Great Britain, The United States. Do they demand along with us the giving of the right of self determination to the peoples of Alsace Lorraine, Galicia, *Posnonia* [Poznán], Bohemia, the Southern slav provinces? If they do, are they willing on their part to give the right of self determination to the peoples of Ireland, Egypt, India, Madagascar, Indochina, et cetera, as the Russian Revolution has given this right to the peoples of Finland, Ukraine when Russia et cetera? For it is clear that to demand self determination for the peoples that are comprised within the borders of enemy states and to refuse self determination to the peoples of their own state or of their own colonies would mean the defence of the most naked, the most cynical imperialism. If the Governments of the Allied countries were to manifest the readiness—along with the Russian Revolution—to construct peace on the basis of an entire and complete recognition of the principle of self determination for all peoples and in all states, if they were to begin with the actual giving of this right to the oppressed peoples of their own states—this would create international conditions under which the compromise program internally contradictory, of Germany and in particular of Austria-Hungary would manifest all its inconsistency and would be overcome by the pressure of the peoples concerned.

"But up to now the Allied Governments have decidedly not manifested in any way their readiness to enter upon a really democratic peace, nor could they owing to their class character. Their attitude towards the principle of national self determination, is not less suspicious and hostile than that of the Governments of Germany and Austria-Hungary. On this point the conscious proletariat of the Allied countries has just as little illusion as we. With the Governments now existing all that can be considered is to set up in opposition to the Imperialistic compromise program which the peace terms of Germany and her Allies represent another Imperialistic compromise program on the part of Great Britain, France, Italy and the United States. What is the program of the latter? In the name of what aims could they require the prolongation of the war? To these questions now after the two programs of peace have been presented in Brest-Litovsk a clear precise and categorical answer must be given.

"Ten days separate us from the resumption of the peace negotiations. Russia in these negotiations does not bind herself to the consent of the Allied Governments. If the latter continue to *saboter* [sabotage] the cause of universal peace the Russian delegation will appear all the same for the continuation of the negotiations. A separate peace, signed by Russia, would without doubt inflict a heavy blow on the Allied countries, chiefly on France and Italy. But the prevision of the inevitable consequences of a separate peace must determine the policy not only of Russia, but also of France, Italy and the other Allied countries. The Soviet Government up to now has struggled in every way for an universal peace. No one can deny the significance of the results attained in this direction. But in the future everything depends upon the Allied nations themselves. To bring their own Governments to immediately present their peace programs and to participate on their basis in the ne-

gotiations—this has now become a question of national self preservation for the Allied nations.

"The Russian revolution has opened the door to an immediate
universal peace on the basis of an agreement. If the Allied Governments are ready to take advantage of this past possibility general
negotiations can open immediately in one of the neutral countries.
In these negotiations with the indispensable condition of their complete publicity the Russian delegation will as heretofore defend the
program of the International Socialistic Democracy as against the
Imperialistic programs of the Governments both of the enemy and
of the Allied countries. The success of our program will depend on
the extent to which the will of their imperialistic classes will be
paralyzed by the will of the Revolutionary Proletariat in each country.

"But if the Allied Governments in blind obstinacy which char-
acterizes the falling and perishing classes, again refuse to participate in the negotiations, then the working class will be confronted
with the iron necessity of tearing the power out of the hands of
those who cannot or will not give peace to the nations.

"In these ten days the fate of hundreds of thousands and of
millions of human lives hangs in the balance. If on the French and
Italian fronts an armistice be not concluded at once a new offensive
just as senseless, as merciless and as resultless as all the preceding
ones will engulf fresh innumerable victims on both sides. The automatic logic of this slaughter, let loose by the governing classes,
is leading to the complete destruction of the flower of the nations
of Europe. But the nations wish to live and they have the right to
do so. They have the right, they are bound to throw aside all who
impede their living.

"Whilst addressing to the Governments a last proposition to take
part in the peace negotiations, we at the same time promise entire
support to the working class of each country which will rise up
against its national imperialists, against the jingoes, against the
militarists—under the banner of peace, of the brother-hood of nations and of the socialistic reconstruction of society."

Francis

T telegram (SDR, RG 59, 763.72119/1059, DNA).
 [1] About the circumstances surrounding this declaration by Trotsky, which was issued
on December 29, see Kennan, *Russia Leaves the War*, pp. 221-24. The Soviet leaders
had just learned from Hoffmann that, in the German view, the "no-annexations" formula
did not mean that the Central Powers would withdraw their forces from the Baltic
countries and Russian Poland before the end of hostilities with the western powers as
well as with Russia. December 26, mentioned in the first paragraph, was January 8 in
the western calendar.

To Robert Lansing, with Enclosure

My dear Mr. Secretary,   The White House. 1 January, 1918.

I have just read with a great deal of interest the despatch from Berne dated the twenty-eighth of December and numbered 2304 in which there is an extended report of interviews with one Julius Meinl.[1] Those views advance a long stride, in fact nearly all the way, towards our position, and I am anxious to learn what is known of Meinl and what importance may be attached to his statements.

Faithfully Yours,   W.W.

WWTLI (SDR, RG 59, 763.72119/10068, DNA).
[1] In response to an inquiry from the State Department, H. R. Wilson reported in telegram No. 2363 on January 7 that Meinl was a wealthy importer of coffee, tea, and chocolate who lived in Vienna and was a member of the Commercial Advisory Council. Meinl was active in Austrian politics, Wilson went on, and had been criticized for his partisanship of England. Meinl was known to oppose a close alliance between Austria and Germany. He had been the leader of the Politische Gesellschaft, a discussion group in Vienna. Wilson wrote further that both his informant, an Austrian, and the British legation in Switzerland believed that Meinl was "very ambitious to play role in political affairs." Wilson concluded by stating that there was no doubt that Meinl was "in a situation to be in touch with leading persons in Austria and Germany," but that (as indicated in the last paragraph of telegram No. 2304, printed below), Wilson "doubted the sincerity of Meinl's statements, especially concerning Ludendorf's earnest desire for peace." H. R. Wilson to RL, Jan. 7, 1918, T telegram (WP, DLC).

E N C L O S U R E

Pontarlier (Berne) Dated December 28, 1917.
Rec'd   "   30, 1:50 P.M.

2304. Julius Meinl, Austrian Kommerzien (?), friend of Emperor Charles, and Hausmann,[1] progressive Reichstag member, held a conference with Consul Agent Geneva[2] and expressed a desire speak about America and were referred by agent to Edelman.[3]

Vice consul stated, answering their inquiry concerning America's intentions, that country united behind President and determined to carry out war to end, that if Germany wants peace she must state in definite and tangible form her demands.

Meinl replied Von Kuhlmann already renounced all claims to Belgium. Entente committed error in failure to act on July peace resolution of Reichstag. This refusal weakened claims of German people and strengthened pan-Germans. Hausmann added complete change has taken place in Germany within past few months. Reichstag is governing body, indicated by Hertling's consultation before accepting chancellorship. Even Von Valentini inclined to liberalism. Von Bulow[4] endeavored to become Chancellor but failed to despite known favoring of Crown Prince. Real leader appears to be Ludendorf and he, Hertling and Von Kuhlmann are earnest in their desire for peace.

Meinl made following memorandum concerning kind of peace desired: "Society of nations, international arbitration, proportional and mutual disarmament on *that* basis Minister's statement about Belgium, evacuation of France, submission of all outstanding questions of European peoples and nationalities to the Peace Congress on this basis of consideration of the wishes of the people."

Vice Consul explained he could speak in no official capacity but felt certain that too many questions were reserved for Peace Congress and that clearer statement should be made of more vexing problems. He inquired about Alsace Lorraine. Meinl replied autonomy was promised these provinces in Reichstag resolution of July 22. Statement to that effect could be included in general peace proposals.

Meinl added Germany would not make serious objection to Turkish question, would not object to withhold conquered territory from Turkey, would consent to make Constantinople free port and Dardanelles free passage. Austria has no desire to dominate Balkans. Bulgaria should be permitted to rule territory inhabited by Bulgarians and no other. Austrian Reichsrath has declared for no annexations and would stand by this. Poland would be a separate kingdom. As to Kurland and other occupied territories they should be left for the people themselves to decide within three year period.

Belgium would be evacuated, certain of its losses to be repaid but not in the form of indemnities.

According to Meinl's statement Germany is ready to make concrete proposals to America provided they were sure American Government would receive them and treat them confidentially. He considered, in the meantime, it would cause excellent impression in Germany if President would include in some speech a declaration somewhat as follows: "We have heard some time ago the voice of the German people but we have not yet heard the voice of the German rulers who, so far as the world knows, have nearly absolute power in their country. Those rulers, who in the minds of the rest of the world are associated with militarism and autocracy, have up to November last failed to reveal their real war aims. If they are really in accord with their people they would do their country and the whole world a great service if at least they would unequivocally declare what their opinion is and what their aims are with regard to the great issues of this war. We do not even know whether they unreservedly indorse the peace resolution of July nineteenth of the German Reichstag."

See my 2282, December 22, 10 A.M.[5] While it is apparent from these two interviews that Meinl has been instructed to make feelers, I do not believe that too much weight can be attached to his interpretation of the views of the ruling class of Germany, especially in his characterization of Ludendorf as a peace angel.

Wilson.

CC telegram (SDR, RG 59, 763.72119/10068, DNA).
  [1] Konrad Haussmann, a leader of the Progressive party in the German Reichstag.
  [2] Lewis Wardlaw Haskell, the United States Consul in Geneva.
  [3] Samuel Edelman was an American vice consul in Geneva.
  [4] That is, Prince Bernhard von Bülow.
  [5] In this dispatch, Wilson reported that Meinl, who was visiting Prince Alexander Hohenlohe, had approached Harold F. McCormick (then in Bern as coordinator of purchasing for the A.E.F. in Switzerland) and asked whether he could get a message to President Wilson. McCormick replied that he could answer no questions. "Meinl stated," the telegram continued, "it would be good to know within eight days what terms would be seriously considered by President Wilson" if the Central Powers openly proposed them, for they "did not care again to make proposals which would not be seriously considered." Wilson also reported that Meinl's mission was "known to authorities although he came in private capacity"; that he "claimed to have arrived after consultation with Kuhlmann in Berlin"; and that Meinl had told McCormick that any communication could be sent through Prince Hohenlohe. H. R. Wilson to RL, Dec. 22, 1917, T telegram (SDR, RG 59, 763.72119/10068, DNA).

To Robert Lansing

My dear Mr. Secretary,   The White House. 1 January, 1918.

You ondoubtedly took the right course in this,—indeed the only course honourably open to us.[1]   Faithfully Yours,   W.W.

WWTLI (SDR, RG 59, 818.00/288½, DNA).
  [1] See RL to WW, Dec. 31, 1917.

To Robert Lansing, with Enclosure

My dear Mr. Secretary,   The White House. 1 January, 1918.

This seems to me a sensible programme,—except the bribery of Persia,—and I am writing to ask your opinion as to the most feasible and least objectionable way (if there is any) in which we could establish similar unofficial relations with the Bolscheviki.

Faithfully Yours,   W.W.

WWTLI (SDR, RG 59, 861.00/936½, DNA).

E N C L O S U R E

London December 29, 1917.

8090. Very Confidential. The Foreign Office has given me the following memorandum. "Confidential. The Secretary of State for Foreign Affairs presents his compliments to the United States' Ambassador and has the honor to transmit herewith for His Excellency's confidential information a copy of a memorandum regarding policy of the Allies in Russia which was agreed to at the conference held at Paris on the twenty-second instant.

Foreign Office December twenty-eight, 1917. Circulated to the King and War Cabinet.

Memorandum prepared for Lord Milner and Lord R. Cecil on suggested policy in Russia and accepted by M. Clemenceau and M. Pinchon on December 22nd, 1917.

At Petrograd we should at once get into relations with the Bolsheviki through unofficial agents, each country as seems best to it.

We propose to send Sir George Buchanan on leave for reasons of health but we shall keep a Chargé d'Affaires there. We do not suggest that our Allies should follow our example. Sir George Buchanan's long residence in Petrograd has indelibly associated him in the minds of the Bolsheviki with the policy of the Cadets and he stands to them for much the same as say M. *Miliakoff.*

We should represent to the Bolsheviki that we have no desire to take part in any way in the internal politics of Russia and that any idea that we favor a counter revolution is a profound mistake. Such a policy might be attractive to the autocratic governments [of Germany] and Austria but not to the Western democracies or America. But we feel it necessary to keep in touch, as far as we can with the Ukraine, the Cossacks, Finland, Siberia, the Caucasus, et cetera, because these various semi-autonomous provinces represent a very large proportion of the strength of Russia. In particular we feel bound to befriend the Ukraine since upon the Ukraine depends the feeding of the Roumanians to whom we are bound by every obligation of honor. As for the war, we should carefully refrain from any word or act counter to condoning the treachery of the Russians in opening peace negotiations with our enemies but we should continually repeat our readiness to accept the principles of self determination and this includes that of no annexation or indemnities. We should present [impress] on the Bolsheviki the importance of not being satisfied with empty phrases from the Germans and point out that unless they get specific undertakings from them as to such questions as Poland, Bohemia, the Roumanian parts of Transylvania, not to speake of Alsace Lorraine and the Trentino, they will get nothing. Meanwhile their powers of resistance are melting away and they will soon be, if they are not now, at the mercy of the German Kaiser who will then snap his fingers at all their fine phrases and impose on them any terms he pleases. They should be told that it is now probably too late to do anything to save the personnel of the Army but the material of the artillery can still be preserved and at the very least it should not be transferred to our enemies to be used against the Western democracies. Most important of all, the Bolsheviki should prevent if they can the wheat districts of Russia, such as the Ukraine, falling into the control of or being made available for the Central Powers. This makes another reason why we are anxious to support and strengthen Ukraine and why we urge on the Bolsheviki that far from trying to coerce the Ukranians they should enter into close cooperation with them in southern Russia. Our principal object must be, if we can, to save Roumania. Next we must aim at preventing Russian supplies from reaching Germany. Finally we are bound to protect if possible the remnant of the Armenians not only in order to safeguard the flank of our Mesopotamian forces in Persia and the Caucasus, but also because *unless an* Armenian union, if possible with a Georgian autonomous or independent state, is the only barrier against the development of a Turanian movement that will extend from Constantinople to China and will provide Germany with a seaport of even greater danger to the peace of the world than the control of the Bagdad Railway.

If we could induce the Southern Russian Armies to resume the fight that would be very desirable, but it is probably impossible to secure these objects. The first thing is money to *recognize* (reorganize?) the Ukraine, to pay the Cossacks and Caucasian forces, and to bribe the Persians. The sums required are not, as things go, very enormous but the exchange presents great difficulties. If the French could undertake the finance of the Ukraine, we might find the money for the others. It is understood that the United States will assist.

Besides finance, it is important to have agents and officers to advise and support the provincial governments and their armies. It is essential that this should be done as quickly as possible so as to avoid the imputation as far as we can that we are preparing to make war on the Bolsheviki.

We would suggest that the Ukraine should be *again in this matter* (dealt with?) by the French while we would take the other southeast provinces. A general officer from each country would be appointed to take charge of our respective activities but they would, of course, keep in the closest touch with one another through carefully selected liaison officers in order to ensure the utmost unity of action.

It is for consideration whether we should facilitate the return to Southern Russia of the numerous Russian officers at present in France and England.

Paris 22nd, December, 1917."

T telegram (SDR, RG 59, 861.00/3478, DNA).

Lord Robert Cecil to the British Embassy

URGENT. VERY SECRET.   [London] Jan. 1st. 1918.

War Cabinet are very uneasy about Vladivostock. There are lying at the port 648.000 tons of very valuable military stores including 136.000 tons railway material; 60.000 tons nitrate of soda; 15.000 tons explosive; 58.000 tons barbed wire; 70.000 tons shells of Russian pattern; 43.000 tons phosphate; 27.000 tons metal, including copper and aluminium, and 78.000 tons tea, rice, cotton and rubber. All accounts that we receive agree in describing the situation at Vladivostock as very uncertain. A large proportion of troops there are certainly Bolshevick and it is quite possible at any moment they may seize the stores and send them to Petrograd to be sold to the Germans. In these circumstances the British Government feel the question of landing a sufficient force to guard these stores should be re-considered. Such a force would necessarily have to be mainly Japanese, but it is important from many points of view that it should contain an element of other nationalities, lest the Bolshevick should be enabled to say it was an attempt to invade Russia. Unfortunately available British force in the neighbourhood is very small and most we could provide would be two (?) companies from troops now stationed at Hongkong. It seems therefore of great importance that the United States Government should send a contingent to co-operate in any military proceedings of the kind indicated.

I spoke this afternoon to the Japanese Ambassador on the subject. He did not receive the suggestion very favourably and expressed the hope that everything would be done by peaceful means such as conceding local Government in that part of Siberia, to avoid intervention. I agreed with him that it would be better to avoid intervention if we could be sure the stores would be safe, but that their amount and value seems to render it necessary not to run any risk of their being transferred to the enemy. He promised in any case to give these views to his Government.   Robert Cecil.

TC telegram (WP, DLC).

From the Diary of Josephus Daniels

Jan 1 [1918]

Spent all the morning at Attorney Generals. Senator Swanson present and we discussed how to conserve the Naval Reserves and agreed on a bill giving the President power to take them all over, those in litigation as well as others, and operate them by Secy of the Navy, & pay over just & equitable sums to the owners and if they demanded more for them to be allowed to go into the courts. Land office & Int. Dept manned by Western men who think all land & oil lands in the West ought to belong to the West and resent the idea that the Fed. governt has any right to them. This tinges their point of view against the Governt

To Edward Mandell House

The White House, January 2, 1918.

Papers indicate that George is about to consult the Prime Minister of France about peace proposals and the best way to counter on the German proposals.[1]

Do you think there is any danger of their anticipating me? I should be afraid of the formulating.   Woodrow Wilson.

T telegram (E. M. House Papers, CtY).
[1] E.g., the New York *World*, Jan. 1, 1918.

To David Lloyd George

[The White House] January 2, 1918.

I am sure that I am expressing the feeling and purpose of the people of the United States as well as my own in sending you and through you to the Government and people of Great Britain a message of good will, and of resolution to continue to put every man and resource of the United States into the imperative task and duty of winning for the world an honorable and stable peace based upon justice and honor, and securing to the peoples of the world, great and small alike, the blessings of security and opportunity and friendly and helpful intercourse. Your own message on behalf of the British War Cabinet is deeply appreciated and our spirits respond to its friendly challenge.   Woodrow Wilson.

T telegram (Letterpress Books, WP, DLC).

To Newton Diehl Baker

My dear Mr. Secretary: The White House 2 January, 1918

Apparently this *is* a serious matter to which my friend, Gavit, managing editor of the New York Evening Post, calls our attention, and I hasten to send his letter to you.[1] You will know how to find out the facts and deal with them.

In haste, with the warmest good wishes for you and yours for the New Year,   Faithfully yours,   Woodrow Wilson

TLS (N. D. Baker Papers, DLC).
     ¹ J. P. Gavit to WW, Dec. 30, 1917, TLS (WP, DLC). Gavit wrote that many young men were being shipped north from southern camps who were barely convalescent from the measles. This disease, he added, left adults particularly susceptible to pneumonia, and this was the principal reason for the prevalence of pneumonia in the new army.

To George Creel

My dear Creel: The White House 2 January, 1918

I couldn't get hold of you yesterday afternoon and, therefore, had to arrange for the "killing" of that statement, because the more I thought about it the more it seemed to me an unnecessary risk to make such a statement while uncertain in my own mind of the effect it would have, not upon our own people, for that would be easily calculable, but upon the international situation, coming in the midst of peace intimations of every kind.

You can see that it might be construed as a note of defiance and as if calculated in time to operate as a rebuff of all peace offers.

I would like a little more time, too, to consider the scope and character of the statement, and a short delay, if we should ultimately determine to issue it, will not be of great disadvantage.

     Always
               Cordially and faithfully yours,   Woodrow Wilson

TLS (G. Creel Papers, DLC).

To John Joseph Fitzgerald

My dear Fitzgerald: [The White House] 2 January, 1918

I was heartily sorry not to get another glimpse of you before you left, and I want you to know how warmly I appreciate your letter of the thirtieth.¹ We shall miss you very much here, where so many tasks remain to be accomplished, but I do not doubt that it was necessary for you to withdraw,² and you may be sure I wish for you the best things that can be earned and won, at the same time relying with entire confidence upon your generous friendship.

               Cordially and sincerely yours,   Woodrow Wilson

TLS (Letterpress Books, WP, DLC).
     ¹ It is missing.
     ² Fitzgerald had announced on December 3 that he would resign from the House of Representatives on December 31 and return to New York to resume the practice of law. He said that the requirements of a large family and the need to meet his growing obligations and provide for the future compelled him, before it was too late, to devote himself to his profession. *New York Times*, Dec. 4, 1917.

To John Palmer Gavit

My dear Mr. Gavit: [The White House] 2 January, 1917 [1918]

Thank you warmly for your birthday letter, which you may be sure I appreciate, and also for the letter which accompanies it about the men who you think are being sent too soon away from the camps after suffering from measles. I have called the Secretary of War's attention to what you tell us and am sure that he will promptly take the necessary steps.

With best wishes for the New Year.

Cordially and sincerely yours,   Woodrow Wilson

P.S. House told me that he would gladly get into communication with the lady[1] about whom you spoke in a recent letter to me and whose ideas you wanted us to consider. Just at this writing I can't put my hand on your letter and recall her name.   W.W.

TLS (Letterpress Books, WP, DLC).
    [1] There is a cryptic reference to a Miss King of the New York *Evening Post* in the House Diary, entry for Dec. 31, 1917. She might have been Caroline Blanche King, nutritional expert, later the first dietician appointed to serve with the United States Army.

To Robert Bridges

My dear Bobbie: The White House 2 January, 1918

Thank you for the book, "The United States and Pangermania." I have heard a good deal of Cheradame's articles in the Atlantic Monthly but have never had time at the right moment to turn to them. I hope I shall have better luck with this book.

It was a deep distress to me that I could not get over to Charlie Mitchell's funeral. His death has affected me very deeply. My thought, like yours, goes back to the old days of our delightful comradeship, and those memories, thank God, are a permanent possession. Death seems to me in such instances a very unreal thing, but it has this terrible aspect of reality, that it does take the dear fellow away from us for the days to come, and I grieve with all my heart.

It would have been a pleasure to see the rest of the crowd even in such distressing circumstances and to have the benefit of sharing their sympathy would have been a great comfort to me.

With the best wishes for everything that is good in the New Year,

Affectionately yours,   Woodrow Wilson

TLS (G. von L. Meyer Coll., DLC).

From William Gibbs McAdoo

Dear Mr. President: Washington January 2, 1918.

I received your letter of December 26. I have, of course, cabled Crosby as you direct. I confess, however, that it has been my own view that the Inter-Ally Council must concern itself with matters of this character, and that, if the United States is to bear successfully its part in financing the war, Crosby must be given the support of our own Shipping Board and of our War Department as well as of the Allies in the effort to coordinate demands upon our Treasury. The Inter-Ally Council was organized, so far as my purposes were concerned, with a view to relating the demands for loans to the Allies to the demands for munitions, supplies and ships. Ships are the crux of the whole situation. The United States Treasury can, I hope, meet the demands of the United States and of the Allies, if those demands are limited to expenditures which can be made promptly effective at the scene of war. But expenditures cannot be made effective without the necessary ships, and the question at once arises as to whether or not the Allies shall be permitted to continue to make purchases of supplies, requiring immediate advances by the Treasury for their payment, without reference to the question whether tonnage can be found to send the supplies forward. The same question is presented in relation to the expenditures of our own War Department. According to the best information I am able to obtain, it is unlikely that tonnage will be available to make effective at an early period the military establishment we are organizing here. Unless the demands of the Allied Governments and of the United States itself are coordinated with reference to the shipping problem and the financial problem, I am in grave doubt of the ability of the Treasury to meet the situation. The only organization which gives hope of producing such coordination is the Inter-Ally Council. I feel, therefore, that it is imperative that Mr. Crosby's activities be not limited, but that his hands be strengthened by adding to the American representation of the Council representatives of our War Department, of our Navy Department, of the Shipping Board, and of the Food Administration. The financial problem of the United States is not so much one of resources as it is of the speed with which these resources can be safely mobilized. I have no doubt of the ability of the United States to bear the stupendous burden of financing the war if reasonable time is given for the effort. What gives me grave concern is the expenditure of money without apparent reference to the date when it can be made effective toward winning the war, and the consequent danger that it may be necessary to withhold financial assistance desired for immediate use because of the expenditure of the United States and of the Allies for purposes which cannot be made effective, because of shipping, for many months to come.

With reference particularly to Mr. Crosby's cable concerning the Italian tonnage situation, I am concerned not so much about the method of dealing with the matter as I am about the vital importance of the situation, as presented to Mr. Crosby by the Italian Ambassador in London. May I direct your attention again to that portion of Mr. Crosby's cable (copy enclosed) referring to the critical situation of Italian industries, etc., for lack of shipping? Time being of the essence, it seemed to me that Mr. Crosby's suggestion was a very wise one, namely, that an Inter-Ally Council on Shipping should be formed, even if organized as a temporary expedient until a permanent organization can be effected, of which Mr. Crosby might act *temporarily* as the head.

Of course, I do not want to cross any of Mr. Colby's wires, and if he has the matter in hand and an organization can be effected quickly to meet the situation, that would, of course, satisfy all that I have in mind.

The impressive fact is this: That the credits we are asked to extend to Great Britain, Italy and France must be predicated upon the ability to ship the supplies, materials, etc., which those credits are to purchase in America. Therefore, unless the shipping situation is considered along with the application for such credits, it is impossible to determine them intelligently. Mr. Crosby ought to be put in position quickly to consider credits with relation to the ability to ship supplies, as well as to consider credits with relation to the ability to secure the supplies themselves in our markets.

I am sorry to trouble you with this again, but the matter is of such gravity that I am obliged to beg your further consideration of it.   Cordially yours,   W G McAdoo

TLS (WP, DLC).

From Newton Diehl Baker, with Enclosure

My dear Mr. President: Washington. January 2, 1918.

I enclose you a cablegram which has just come to me from General Pershing. I have not handed it out to the newspapers, but beg leave to suggest your asking Mr. Tumulty to do so.

Respectfully yours,   Newton D. Baker

Okeh W.W

TLS (WP, DLC).

E N C L O S U R E

London, January 2, 1918.

All officers and men of this command extend to the President as our commander-in-chief most sincere thanks for his message of confidence and we heartily return his New Years greetings and trust that his health and strength may be conserved. All ranks extend to him and our people at home new pledges of loyalty and devotion.   Pershing.

TC telegram (WP, DLC).

From Newton Diehl Baker

Dear Mr. President: Washington. January 2, 1918.

I return herewith the letter from Mr. Borglum, which Mr. Tumulty has just sent me. The fact that we have necessarily, for military reasons, suppressed much publicity about the aircraft program should be remembered in considering such a letter; and yet Mr. Borglum's high character makes it quite impossible to take otherwise than very seriously the suggestions he makes. I have attached to my own office here Mr. Stanley King,[1] a capable, upright, and disinterested business man. Would it not be wise to have Mr. Borglum urged to come to Washington, talk freely with me, let me associate Mr. King with him, and give them an absolutely free hand to investigate every suggestion which Mr. Borglum can make, for the purpose of reporting directly to you, or to you through me, so that on the basis of such an immediate and thorough-going inquiry we can remedy what is wrong or set right any unjustified apprehensions.

Some of the statements made in Mr. Borglum's letter are difficult to accept, in view of the fact that there is at present in Washington an international staff of experts, consisting of officers deemed of the highest experience and sent by the various Allied Governments to consult with us, and this body is in daily conference with General Squier and his associates. In addition to that, we have in Paris a very strongly manned aircraft section which is in daily cable communication with General Squier, and in France and England is in constant and intimate touch with aircraft work in those countries and, so far as it can be learned, with the German activities. And yet I never feel it safe to rely on any situation so long as there is one upright, responsible doubter, and for this reason I earnestly hope that Mr. Borglum can be asked to come to Washington to see me. I have taken the liberty of dictating a note, which I herewith enclose, to Mr. Borglum for your approval.[2]

Respectfully yours,   Newton D. Baker

TLS (WP, DLC).
[1] A lawyer of Boston and secretary and director of W. H. McElwain Co., shoe manufacturers. He had been appointed as special assistant to the Secretary of War on October 4, 1917.
[2] It is printed as the next document.

To Gutzon Borglum

My dear Mr. Borglum: The White House January 2, 1918.

I have your letter of December 25.

Knowing the earnest and loyal purpose with which you have written me, I have conferred with the Secretary of War and, at his request and my own hearty concurrence, I urge you to come at once to Washington, lay the whole matter frankly and fully before the Secretary, and by your own investigation discover the facts in this business. The Secretary of War assures me that he will be delighted to clothe you with full authority to get to the bottom of every situation, and that he will place at your disposal the services of Mr. Stanley King, a member of his own personal staff, if you desire to have his counsel in your inquiries. The Secretary further says that he will bring you into personal contact with General Squier, whom you doubtless already know personally, and will direct that every facility of inquiry be placed at your disposal. When you have thus investigated, if the other experts whom you suggest in your letter of December 25 still seem desirable to be appointed you can say so to the Secretary; and in the event of any difference of judgment between you, which seems to me impossible, I would be most happy to have a report from you personally to me on any phase of the matter which remains in the slightest degree doubtful in your mind.   Cordially yours,   Woodrow Wilson

TLS (photostat in G. Borglum Papers, DLC).

From Robert Lansing

My dear Mr. President: Washington January 2, 1918.

The communication of the Bolsheviks to "the peoples and governments of the Allied countries," contained in Mr. Francis' telegram No. 2163 of December 31st, impresses me with the adroitness of the author whose presentation of peace terms may well appeal to the average man, who will not perceive the fundamental errors on which they are based.

The address from beginning to end is to a class and not to all classes of society, a class which does not have property but hopes to obtain a share by process of government rather than by individual enterprise. This is of course a direct threat at existing social order in all countries.

In the second place the address discusses the rights of nationalities (though it does not use the term) without defining what a nationality is, and at the same time advances doctrines which make class superior to the general conception of nationality. Is the Bolshevik idea of nationality based upon blood, habitation of a particular territory, language, or political affinity? Accurate definition of the word is necessary to interpret the terms proposed, otherwise they are too vague to be intelligently considered.

If the Bolsheviks intend to suggest that every community (though they state no unit as a basis for independent action) can determine its allegiance to this or that political state or to become independent, the present political organization of the world would be shattered and the same disorder would generally prevail as now exists in Russia. It would be international anarchy.

Though founded entirely on the assertion of legality, the right of communities within a constituted federal union to determine their allegience was denied by the Government of the United States in 1861 and the denial was enforced by military power. We, as a nation, are therefore committed to the principle that a national state may by force if necessary prevent a portion of its territory from seceding without its consent especially if it has long exercised sovereignty over it or if its national safety or vital interests would be endangered.

I can see that, where a particular region lies between the territories of two nations which the world has recognized as sovereign states, there may justly arise the question as to which nation should incorporate the region into its territory and that the decision may properly rest with the inhabitants of the region, but I do not see that the same question arises in the event that the inhabitants of a territory already under the sovereignty of a nation have the same right to become an independent state and to be admitted into the family of nations by a mere expression of popular will. Such a theory seems to me utterly destructive of the political fabric of society and would result in constant turmoil and change. It simply cannot be done if social order and governmental stability are to be maintained.

The suggestions of the Bolsheviks in regard to Ireland, India, and other countries which have been and are integral parts of recognized powers are in my opinion utterly untenable if it is desirable to preserve the present concept of sovereign states in international relations. However justified may be the principle of local self-government, the necessities of preserving an orderly world require that there should be a national authority with sovereign rights to defend and control the communities within the national boundaries.

It is apparent, as I said at the outset, that the Bolsheviks are appealing in this address to a particular class of society, which they seek to arouse against the present order of things, enticing them with the possible abolition of the institution of private property and the possible control by that class of accumulated wealth and of its distribution. The document is an appeal to the proletariat of all countries, to the ignorant and mentally deficient, who by their numbers are urged to become masters. Here seems to me to lie a very real danger in view of the present social unrest throughout the world.

Of course the enforcement of the will of the ignorant, indifferent to all save their own pleasures, would be the worst form of despotism, especially as that class has always been controlled by violent and radical leaders. It would be a species of class-despot, which would have far less regard for private rights than an individual despot. This seems to be the present social program of the Bolsheviks, and they appear to be putting it into operation in Russia. It is essentially anarchistic rather than socialistic in character and will, wherever adopted, break down every semblance of social order and public authority.

I think in considering this address it might properly be asked by what authority the Bolsheviks assume the right to speak for the Russian people. They seized the Government at Petrograd by force, they broke up opposition in the army by disorganizing it, they prevented the meeting of the Constituent Assembly chosen by the people because they could not control it,[1] they have seized the property of the nation and confiscated private property, they have failed to preserve public order and human life, they have acted arbitrarily without pretense of legality, in fact, they have set up over a portion of Russia a despotic oligarchy as menacing to liberty as any absolute monarchy on earth, and this they maintain by force and not by the will of the people, which they prevent from expression.

In view of present conditions I believe it would be unwise to

[1] Elections had been held throughout Russia, beginning on November 25, to select delegates to a constitutional convention. Of the 707 deputies elected, 410 were Social-Revolutionaries, and less than a third supported the Bolsheviks. The Constituent Assembly had been scheduled to meet on December 11, but the Soviet authorities prevented this and set a new date of January 18 for its meeting.

make reply to this insidious address; but, if it seems advisable not to ignore it, I think the only course should be to state frankly the false premises upon which it is based and the vagueness of the unit of independent communal power which they propose to set up. In view of the threat against existing governments and the promised aid to revolutionists I would personally prefer to see the communication unanswered whatever the consequences might be. Lenine, Trotsky and their colleagues are so bitterly hostile to the present social order in all countries that I am convinced nothing could be said which would gain their favor or render them amenable to reason. I feel that to make any sort of reply would be contrary to the dignity of the United States and offer opportunity for further insults and threats, although I do not mean that it may not be expedient at some time in the near future to state our peace terms in more detail than has yet been done.

Faithfully yours,   Robert Lansing.

TLS (WP, DLC).

Ronald Hugh Campbell[1] to Edward Mandell House

London, January 2, 1918.

Mr. Balfour would be grateful if you would convey the following personal message from him to the President.[2]

As Col. House will have informed you the Paris Conference authorized us to carry on informal conversations on peace terms with the Austrians should a fitting occasion arise.

In accordance with this policy a British and an Austrian representative met in Switzerland last week with every precaution of secrecy; and interviews of a friendly and unofficial character were held on two successive days.[3]

The British representative acting on instructions refused on this occasion to discuss the question of a general peace which should include Germany. The Austrian representative acting also on instructions held out no hopes whatever of Austria separating herself from Germany during the continuance of the war. In these circumstances no conclusions could be even provisionally arrived at sufficiently precise to lay before the Allied Governments. Nevertheless our representative returned with some very definite impressions and was able to convey some important suggestions.

He gathered that Austria was undoubtedly anxious for peace and that though she would not and could not abandon her ally, she would be prepared to exert the strongest pressure to induce that ally to accept a "reasonable settlement." He further gathered however close Austria might be bound to Germany during the war, she had no desire to be Germany's vassal when the war was over.

His statement that the destruction of Austria was no part of the British war aims was received by the Austrian representative with much satisfaction and his expression of our strong desire to see the various nationalities of which the Empire is composed given an opportunity for autonomous development was received with much sympathy—a sympathy which was said to reflect opinions in "highest quarters."

The Austrian representative expressed the earnest wish that these conversations should be renewed at an early date, a wish with which the British Government will probably comply.

Nothing has so far been said to any of the Allied Governments about these conversations: and for obvious reasons it is most desirable that as few persons as possible should know of them until they issue into something definite and tangible.

Campbell.

TC telegram (WP, DLC).
[1] Private Secretary to Baron Hardinge of Penshurst, the Permanent Under Secretary of State for Foreign Affairs.
[2] The original document is "Private telegram to President Wilson prepared after today's Cabinet, 2 Jan. 1918," T telegram (A. J. Balfour Papers, Add MSS, No. 49738, British Library). This telegram was drafted by Balfour on December 28, 1917, reviewed and edited by Lord Robert Cecil, and shown to Lloyd George and Smuts, who approved the revised draft. The drafts and commentaries are in *ibid.*
[3] General Smuts had met quietly in Geneva on December 18 and 19, 1917, with Count Albert von Mensdorff-Pouilly-Dietrichstein, who had been the Austrian ambassador to Great Britain from 1904 to 1914. Smuts' report to the War Cabinet about his meeting with Mensdorff is printed in David Lloyd George, *War Memoirs of David Lloyd George* (6 vols., Boston, 1933-37), V, 21-35. A note about Smuts' mission was published in the London *Justice* on February 7, 1918. *New Europe*, VI (Feb. 14, 1918), 160. See also Sterling J. Kernek, *Distractions of Peace during War: The Lloyd George Government's Reactions to Woodrow Wilson, December, 1916-November, 1918* (Philadelphia, 1975), p. 79.

Sir Cecil Arthur Spring Rice to the Foreign Office

Washington 2 Jan 1918

President was on point of sending a new years message to all the co-belligerent and neutral governments explaining the reasons why the U S had gone into the war, and the steps which had been taken. Except for a rather exaggerated paragraph about shipping there could be no exception taken to what was said. The last para was to the effect that: "The paths of peace have led us into field of battle. But we shall not swerve from that path either for lust of revenge or hunger for spoil. Nor shall our judgement be beclouded by the desire for victory." At last moment message was withdrawn by President's order.

French Ambr. is rather perturbed at effect here of news that allies are contemplating a joint official answer to German-Russian peace terms and there are rumours that USG may come forward with proposals which would be difficult for allies to accept. The N Y World of yesterday had an article which some think was inspired from White House laying stress on President's former statements as to the acceptance of peace terms if proffered by a German govt truly representative of the people, if the terms in themselves repudiated ideas of conquest.[1]

S. of S has evidently not received any instructions from President, as he made no statement to me today, and best opinion here is that President's views are unchanged as to vigorous prosecution of war.

Hw telegram (FO 115/2371, p. 274, PRO).
[1] The story in the New York *World*, Jan. 1, 1918, bore the dateline of Washington, December 31, 1918, and follows:
"A confidential exchange of views concerning possible joint action when the peace proposal of Count Czernin, the Austrian Foreign Minister, has been officially received is now in progress between Washington, London, Paris and Rome. This lends greater significance to the announcement from London that Premier Lloyd George will shortly go to Paris for a conference with Premier Clemenceau. The Entente Allies have an agreement not to entertain any peace proposals from the enemy without consultation with each other.
"It is felt that the efforts of the Germans to involve the United States and the Allies in the peace negotiations proceeding with the Russian Bolsheviki have developed to such a stage that notice of the propaganda must be taken and an attempt made to neutralize it.
"Germany is believed to be prepared to offer almost any conceivable bait to an individual enemy in order to drive a wedge into the Allies and cause its disruption and having succeeded measurably with Russia is trying to get that nation to influence her late allies.
"Rumors that have existed for the past fortnight to the effect that another peace proposal was about to be launched by the Central Powers either through the Vatican or some neutral state, are believed to have their foundation in the attempt of the German negotiators to use the Russian delegates for that purpose. But, if there is to be another peace proposal through those channels, or if the Russian negotiations are to be made the vehicle to carry forward the German designs, it is believed in some quarters here that the time is ripe now for a strong and well-considered declaration by the Entente Powers and America that will effectually anticipate and counter this attack.
"It has been stated repeatedly that the Allies and the United States could not ignore any genuine peace offer which the Central Powers might make.
"The fact that when Count Czernin's proposal is officially received it will be given serious consideration here and in Allied capitals does not mean that it will be accepted. It does mean that a reply will be sent either to the Bolshevik Government at Petrograd, which presumably is to transmit it, or to Vienna, through neutral diplomatic channels, if the offer is sent formally by the Austro-Hungarian Government.
"Whatever reply is sent by the United States and the Allies will be an effective one. It may be no more than a specific declaration of war aims.
"General Staff officers here are understood to attach great significance to the attempt of the Central Powers to force the Entente Powers into peace negotiations. To their mind it is a clear indication that the German military leaders have not accomplished all that they feel capable of doing in the field. They can 'hold on' for a long time yet, it is suggested, but they cannot extend fields of occupation without an enormous loss of men and time at the risk of a terrible defeat. Therefore, the Teuton diplomats seek to realize everything possible from what the German armies have done, and the Brest-Litovsk negotiations are the first steps toward that end."

To Franklin Knight Lane

My dear Mr. Secretary: [The White House] 3 January, 1918

Thank you for your letter of December thirty-first about the water power bill. I am going to have a conference with representatives of the committees concerned tomorrow evening if I can get them together.[1]

In haste   Faithfully yours,   Woodrow Wilson

TLS (Letterpress Books, WP, DLC).
[1] Wilson met at the White House at 8 P.M. on January 4 with Representatives Ferris, Foster, Sims, Lever, Pou, Garrett, and others. The House, on January 11, approved a resolution (H. Res. 220) which provided for the appointment of a special committee to consider bills and resolutions relating to water power. *Cong. Record*, 65th Cong., 2d sess., pp. 844-51.

From David Rowland Francis

Petrograd. Dated January 3, 1917.
Recd. 6th, 5.17 a.m.

2187. For the President.

I cabled Secretary Lansing in my 2166, December 29, 10 p.m.,[1] requesting that you or he address some communication to the Russian people explaining why it is impossible or inexpedient for the Allied countries to join in the peace negotiations begun between Russia and the Central Empires and adjourned for ten days to enable Russia's allies to participate. It was my conviction at that time that the Allies would not respond and that separate peace between Russia and the Central Empires was a foregone conclusion. Such an eventuality now seems less probable—in fact exceedingly doubtful, because Germany notwithstanding her agreement to negotiate separate peace with no annexations, no indemnities, is with characteristic evasion endeavoring to forestall the untrammeled self-displeasure[2] the people of Courland, Lithuania and other sections of Russia now occupied by German invaders, by claiming that inhabitants of those sections have already expressed their desire to become German provinces. Such claim was set forth in the first of the sixteen articles of peace proposed by the Central Empires. The peace commissioners of the Soviet Government readily saw the German chicanery in this article, discussed it at length and made a counter-proposal which the Austro-German peace commissioners said they would be compelled to refer to their respective governments before replying thereto. Adjournment was then had for ten days. Commissioners of Soviet Government returned to Petrograd accompanied by representatives of fifteen broken and depleted armies, and made report to a joint meeting of the Central

Committee of the People's Commissaries, with the Petrograd Soviet and with the Committee on Army Demobilization.

The Russian Army wearied with three years of horrible struggle and looking forward with relief and joy to a cessation of hostilities, almost within their grasp, were so open to doubt in feeling by this German move that their representatives in the Petrograd meeting, of practical unanimity, courageously asserted their willingness and determination to continue the struggle rather than yield to the unjust demands which the Central Empires sought to impose. The resolutions passed by the joint meeting above described were transmitted in my cable 2178 to the Department.[3]

Having received no reply to suggestion in my 2166, I now respectfully request that you reiterate in some public manner the noble expressions of your address to the United States Senate of January 22 last. Assumed message was delivered and promulgated before America entered the war, but it portrayed in impressive terms the kind of a peace that would be enduring, the kind of a peace all just-minded and right-feeling peoples could join in a league to enforce. That was the same kind of a peace that Russia championed after the revolution of March last and the same kind of a peace that the Soviet Government of Russia and the worn soldiers of this afflicted country feel is now jeopardized by German trickery.

I am not suggesting the formal recognition of any government in Russia that is not founded upon the will of the free people of this great country. My cables to the Department bear testimony to my opinion of any power established by force among a people who had made wise provision for the organization of a government deriving its just powers from the consent of the governed. It is our duty, however, to use any legitimate means to combat the merciless methods of an unscrupulous enemy whose success would be a catastrophe to civilization and a manifest injury to mankind.

The psychology of war justifies and demands the repetition of the noble humanitarian thoughts expressed in your great message to the Senate. Failure to reiterate those sentiments at this juncture may possibly cause Russia to take a step which will not only sacrifice the gains of the revolution, but would be a stain upon her honor which the efforts of generations could not eradicate. The tired people of this country will not fight for territory; they need status quo ante. Nor for commercial advantage, for their enormous resources will insure commercial prosperity for years to come. Nor will they fight for treaties made by governments they had overturned, but they possibly will struggle for a democratic peace for the fruits of the revolution if appealed to by a country whose unselfish motives they recognize as they do ours.

There are numerous parties in Russia and many plans as to the future welfare of these peoples, and also, several would-be governments, but all are advocating provisional government and doing so for the reason, as they claim, that Russia by occupation fight no more. In my judgment the only hope for Russia remaining in the war is from the failure of the separate peace now being negotiated by the Soviet Government with the Central Empires. Consequently we should spare no effort to bring about such a consummation. Such a communication as you, and you only can make, whether it prove successful or not, will make a deep impression on the heart of Russia and will demonstrate again what is universally admitted, and that is, that your utterances concerning the object of this war and the enduring peace that should follow it together with the armament limitation which will be realized if such peace is secured, mark a new era or an end of warfare and throw a new light on the relations of governments and peoples finally. If Germany will slight a democratic peace it spells German defeat and the world is safe for democracy.   Francis

T telegram (SDR, RG 59, 763.72119/1072, DNA).
[1] D. R. Francis to RL, Dec. 29, 1917, *FR 1918, Russia*, I, 405.
[2] "self-determination of."
[3] D. R. Francis to RL, Jan. 2, 1918, *ibid.*, 419-21.

Two Letters from Joseph Patrick Tumulty

Dear Governor: The White House. January 3, 1918.
  Mr. Creel submits this[1] to see if it meets your approval.[2]
                                                          J.P.T.

TL (WP, DLC).
  [1] A version of the statement (printed as an Enclosure with G. Creel to WW, Dec. 31, 1917, as emended by Wilson) with the following additional changes: In the (new) first paragraph "pacific" was replaced by "peace loving." Before the paragraph on Liberty Loans, a new paragraph was inserted: "The Shipping Board facing a task of unparalleled magnitude and complicated by every difficulty, now has under way a program that meets our expectations and our needs." A new concluding paragraph was added: "Our satisfaction in these achievements, heightened as it may well be by the expressions of appreciation from those nations who await our aid in the great struggle, is fundamentally, however, not in the things done, but in the larger purpose for which they are done. It must not slacken our efforts in grappling with the greater tasks yet before us in this New Year. It should not be diminished by the unthinking whose standards of military preparation and achievement are those of the predatory powers who have devoted the years of peace to the purposes of armed conquest. No man who goes forth to battle for America, no home from which he has been taken, can now or in years to come, be robbed of the priceless comfort of knowing that he defends the cause of a nation whose ways were the ways of peace and whose purposes may be read in its devotion to freedom, justice and the rights of our common humankind." T MS (WP, DLC).
  [2] This statement was not published.

Dear Governor: The White House January 3, 1918

I spent last evening in examining carefully the editorial comments in the principal journals of the country with reference to the effect on editorial opinion of the German peace proposals recently laid down by Count Czernin.[1] A summary of this opinion is as follows:

From the NEW YORK EVENING POST:

"Comments of the English press on the peace proposals of Germany and Austria, as reported in today's cables, are highly significent. The Northcliffe papers, to be sure, go on foaming at the mouth; but the opinion of such diverse organs, such intensely warlike and anti-German newspapers as the DAILY EXPRESS, the DAILY TELEGRAPH, and the CHRONICLE, is quite of another tenor. None of them admits that the terms of peace put forward at Brest-Litovsk are admissible as they stand. All point out deficiencies. All specify matters that must be insisted upon. But all agree that the offer is of such a nature as to demand a response. It would seem clear that the Teutonic advances are exactly of the kind to give the Allies that opportunity to make a joint and public statement of their war-aims and of their minimum demands which Lloyd George has just assured the labor unions that he has been seeking.[2] It is not a question of either accepting or rejecting outright and in toto the German proposals. *All that the situation requires is a discriminating answer, pointing out what is satisfactory, what is dubious, what is impossible, and what other things must be stipulated and agreed to before there can be peace.*"

Continuing, this editorial calls attention to the fact that Bismarck began in 1871 by demanding Belfort as well as Metz from France and that he afterwards yielded Belfort to the entreaties of Thiers.

"* * * And all the more reason is there for merely laying down a cautious basis for peace parleys when neither side is victorious. The important thing to bear in mind is that Germany has made the advances. She has taken the step which she has said it was impossible for her to take—make explicit and detailed proposals of peace. It is now for the Governments of the Allies and of the United States to press through the opening thus made for them. It is, thus far, only an opening. But the enemies of Germany may well take heart at this tacit confession of her unwillingness to keep on fighting and utilize the splendid opportunity they now have both to set their case clear and fair before the world and to press their advantage over German negotiators."

In a sense, the editorial from the SPRINGFIELD REPUBLICAN seems to support the attitude taken by the NEW YORK EVENING POST. The REPUBLICAN says:

"* * * Lloyd George's letter to the labor unions, while pointing out the difficulties, is a fairly plain hint that the Allies are well on the way to a revised statement to fit the altered conditions of the war."

The SPRINGFIELD REPUBLICAN goes on to say that a statement is needed

"because peace terms are as much a part of strategy as the planning of battles. In diplomatic maneuvers the Germans have a great advantage, and the reply to Russia is at least adroit. If not countered it might be dangerous, but when the Allies are ready to speak they should be able to make it perfectly clear that the real blame for continuing the war, like the blame for beginning it, does not rest with them."

The attitude of the NEW YORK EVENING POST and the SPRINGFIELD REPUBLICAN is supported by such papers as the BALTIMORE SUN, by the NEW YORK SUN, by the NEWARK NEWS, and by "Uncle Dudley," a very, very able writer in the BOSTON GLOBE, who says:

"* * * The Allies can forestall any such acrimonious debate by meeting the German peace offensive at once. They must now get together and formulate a definite counter-offensive. With the political unison equal to that of the Central Powers, they can either formulate their own set of peace proposals, or they must ask the German Government categorical questions as to the exact meaning of its latest proposals and other questions vital to the Allies' consideration of peace. Such questions, or a counter-peace proposal on the part of the Allies, would put the Germans on the defensive again regarding peace and prevent any disruption of the Entente. The Allies must meet the powerful peace offensive of the Central Powers promptly and courageously with a unified and high-minded policy."

Such papers as the CHICAGO DAILY NEWS, the PHILADELPHIA RECORD, the WASHINGTON POST, and the NEW YORK HERALD take the position that no reply of any kind should be made.

Sincerely, Tumulty

TLS (WP, DLC).

[1] See H. R. Wilson to RL, Dec. 28, 1917, n. 2.

[2] Lloyd George, in a letter to a "Special Conference of the British Labour Movement," which met at Central Hall, Westminster, on December 28, said that Britain was still fighting for the same goals as had prompted her to enter the war in 1914—"in order to free the world once and for all from the intolerable menace of a militaristic civilization, and to make possible a lasting peace by restoring the liberty of the oppressed nationalities, and by enforcing respect of those laws and treaties which are the protection of all nations, whether great or small." However, Lloyd George added, Great Britain could not discuss peace terms except in consultation with its allies. London *Times*, Dec. 29, 1917.

From Newton Diehl Baker, with Enclosures

Dear Mr. President: Washington. January 3, 1918.

After the conference with you, in which Colonel House, General Bliss, and I participated, I sent a dispatch to General Pershing and then sent you a copy. In order to save your time I enclose a second copy, with General Pershing's reply.

The French Ambassador came to me yesterday with the suggestion that our troops be added, by regiments or smaller units, to French Divisions, "in order to protect our troops while they are learning fighting conditions at the front." This is in effect the same suggestion. The French Ambassador had a cablegram from M. Clemenceau to the effect that General Petain and General Pershing were in disagreement on the subject. I will take the whole matter up by cablegram with General Pershing and ask him to see M. Clemenceau and work out any misunderstanding which has arisen with regard to any earlier conference with General Petain. It seems to me entirely clear that if our regiments are integrated with either French or British Divisions the difficulty of getting them back when we want them would be very great, and that the ultimate effect of such a course would be practically to put our troops here and there in French and British Divisions under the command of French and British Commanders, with a corresponding weakening of the forces under General Pershing's command for independent operations. The disinterested ground urged by the French Ambassador, to the effect that it was for our good and was merely an accommodation on the part of the French, seems hardly to cover the whole case.

I am assuming that we ought to rely upon General Pershing to decide this kind of question, as he is on the ground and sees the needs as they arise and, of course, will desire to preserve the integrity of his own forces for independent operations unless the emergency becomes overruling.

Respectfully yours,   Newton D. Baker

TLS (WP, DLC).

E N C L O S U R E   I

Pershing, Amexforce, Paris.   Washington, December 24, 1917.

Number 558. December 24. Confidential.

Both English and French are pressing upon the President their desire to have your forces amalgamated with theirs by regiments and companies and both express belief in impending heavy drive by Germans somewhere along the line of the Western front. We do not desire loss of identity of our forces but regard that as secondary to the meeting of any critical situation by the most helpful use possible of the troops at your command. The difficulty of course is to determine where the drive or drives of the enemy will take place; and in advance of some knowledge on that question, any redistribution of your forces would be difficult. The President, however, desires you to have full authority to use the forces at your command as you deem wise in consultation with the French and British commanders in chief. It is suggested for your consideration that possibly places might be selected for your forces nearer the junction of the British and French lines which would enable you to throw your strength in whichever direction seemed most necessary. This suggestion is not, however, pressed beyond whatever merit it has in your judgment, the President's sole purpose being to acquaint you with the representations made here and to authorize you to act with entire freedom in making the best disposition and use of your forces possible to accomplish the main purposes in view. It is hoped that complete unity and coordination of action can be secured in this matter by your conferences with the French and British commanders. Report result of any conferences you may have with French and British commanders and line of action that may be agreed upon. Baker, Secretary of War.   McCain.

E N C L O S U R E   I I

Received at the War Department January 2, 1917 [1918]. 10:33 A.M.

No. 433. January 1st, Confidential.

For the Chief of Staff.[1] Reference confidential cablegram 558 from Secretary of War. Do not think emergency now exists that would warrant our putting companies or battalions into British or French divisions, and would not do so except in grave crisis. Main objections are first, troops would lose their national identity; second, they probably could not be relieved for service with us without disrupting the allied division coming up especially if engaged in active service; third, the methods of training and instruction in both Allied armies are very different from our own which would produce some confusion at the start and also when troops return for service with us. Attention should be called to prejudices existing between French and British Governments and armies, and the desire of each to have American units assigned to them to the exclusion of similar assignments to the other. Also each army regards its own methods as best and they do not hesitate to criticise each other accordingly. We have selected what we consider best in each and added to our own basic system of instruction. After consultation with both French and British commanders, have arranged to take every advantage of aid from both Allies *if they desire* pushing forward our instruction as rapidly as possible * * * availing ourselves of additional instructors and units to assist. Shall probably place first division in trenches by brigades about the middle of January for further trench experience and training. This will permit continuance of special training by brigade not in trenches. Period of time to be kept in line not yet definitely determined, but will be followed by active assignments to temporary sector as circumstances may dictate. Other divisions will follow as rapidly as their proficiency in any training will warrant. Believe that this action will stimulate morale of French and will satisfy clamor for our entry into line(s) which have become very persistent. Sector scheduled for this training quiet now and full cooperation with adjacent French troops arranged to prevent serious mishap. Will wire definite location(s) of sector in separate cable. Further conference with French and British Commanders in Chief being arranged to definitely determine eventual American sector, and manner of employing American troops in general.   Pershing.

TC telegrams (WP, DLC).
   [1] Bliss had retired as Chief of Staff on December 31, 1917, his sixty-fourth birthday, and Maj. Gen. John Biddle was Acting Chief.

From Frank William Taussig

My dear Mr. President: Washington January 3, 1918.

   I hesitate much to intrude and to submit views on general questions. My practice since I have been in Washington has been not to give an opinion on any subject until it is asked. But in times like these it may be that you will wish to know what men of my sort are thinking about, and therefore, without further ado, I will submit some opinions on the immediate problems of peace and war.

   1. We cannot afford to neglect such statements of possible peace terms as Czernin recently made. The principles of settlement which he states are in essentials so similar to those which the United States, through yourself, has laid down, that we must recognize a possibility of settlement.

   2. We can insist that these principles be carried out with sincerity; and insistence on their sincerity is the note that should be struck by us. So long as it appears that there are no pretenses or intrigues or concealed manoeuvers, we shall be willing to negotiate. We can

state this courteously, but firmly and unmistakably. There must be no princes or governors named by the Central Powers, provisional or temporary; there must be no provisional or temporary occupations. Any provisional occupation or government should be of international creation, and administration should be in the hands of officials or appointees from neutral nations.

3. I am firmly of the opinion that we should not continue the war in order that France should get Alsace Lorraine, or Italy the Trentino. These are matters on which we may have our sympathies, but which can form no part of our principles of settlement. A settlement by popular vote (plebiscite) would be most welcome to us. But we cannot fight for this sort of readjustment of the map of Europe.

4. The Germans are entitled to get back their colonies. The principle of no annexations is applicable both ways. Some rearrangements of colonial territories are desirable and probably manageable: rearrangements to minimize rivalry, contact, friction. The principle of political self-determination, or popular vote, is obviously not to be applied to Hotentots and South Sea Islanders.

5. We cannot insist upon the democratization of Germany, or upon overt political changes in Germany, as a condition of peace. The more we insist upon such changes, the less likely are they to come in the early future. The endeavor of foreigners to oust the autocratic regime tends to strengthen that regime; it arouses all the ardor of patriotism in favor of what is attacked from outside. I am confident that great political changes in Germany are bound eventually to come. Peace terms which are in the nature of a draw will promote the change. But we must let the Germans settle their institutions for themselves.

There are further matters of detail on which I might dilate, but I will not weary you by stringing them out. What my general attitude is you will gather easily enough. I am sure it represents the attitude of untold numbers of thinking men.

Believe me to be always, with high respect and regard,

Very sincerely yours,   F. W. Taussig

TLS (WP, DLC).

From William Boyce Thompson

My dear Mr. President: Washington Jan. 3, 1918.

Your letter,[1] handed to me by Mr. Sisson in Petrograd, came as a deeply appreciated honor. I would have answered it before this but for the fact that I wished to accompany the acknowledgement with some report of progress.

I cannot help but feel that you will be very proud of our very real accomplishment, for while the situation, on its surface, may seem to be hopeless, it is far from that in reality.

With small funds, and working without explicit instructions, we have counteracted the German propaganda to such an extent that the German peace was not only delayed but is today not an accomplished fact by any means.

I will be in Washington for some time and hold myself at your command in the event that you wish any personal report. My views in this whole matter of Russia are expressed in the memorandum that Mr. Creel is forwarding.[2]

Believe me, sir,   Very respectfully,   Wm B Thompson

TLS (WP, DLC).
    [1] WW to W. B. Thompson, Oct. 24, 1917, Vol. 44.
    [2] It is printed as the next document.

A Memorandum by William Boyce Thompson

January 3, 1918.

MEMORANDUM OF THE PRESENT SITUATION IN RUSSIA
SUGGESTED MEANS TO PREVENT GERMAN DOMINATION OF RUSSIA

Extract from President Wilson's message to Congress December 4, 1917:

"But the congress that concludes this war will feel the full strength of the tides that run now in the hearts and consciences of free men everywhere. Its conclusions will run with those tides.

"All these things have been true from the very beginning of this stupendous war; and I cannot help thinking that if they had been made plain at the very outset the sympathy and enthusiasm of the Russian people might have been once for all enlisted on the side of the Allies, suspicion and distrust swept away, and a real and lasting union of purpose effected. Had they believed these things at the very moment of their Revolution, and had they been confirmed in that belief since, the sad reverses which have recently marked the progress of their affairs toward an ordered and stable government of free men might have been avoided. The Russian people have been poisoned by the very same falsehoods that have kept the German people in the dark, and the poison has been administered by the very same hands. The only possible antidote is the truth. It cannot be uttered too plainly or too often."

William B. Thompson, commissioned as Lieutenant-Colonel, on

the Red Cross Mission to Russia, has just returned via London from Petrograd, having spent four months there in close touch with almost all elements of the situation.

Colonel Thompson, under the general approval of Mr. Creel, carried on certain educational work in Russia, designed (a) to acquaint the Russian people with the evil aims of German autocracy, and (b) to demonstrate the fundamental sympathy of America and of her Allies with the aspirations of the new Russia. Thompson's opinions, based upon the results of his work and upon his general observations in Russia, are, roughly, as follows:

1. No matter how hopeless the situation looks, it is still well worth our while to make a distinct effort to keep the Germans from dominating the Russian situation. Russia as a fighting force may well be gone, but if the Allies handle the situation wisely and vigorously they can still maintain it as a menace to Germany. Moreover, America's attitude toward Russia at this critical moment will be proof to the whole world (including perhaps the liberal groups in Germany) of the sincerity of America's aims in this war.

2. The Germans have made rapid strides in getting hold of the Russian situation, employing all sorts of methods, corrupt and otherwise, in the attempt to render the dominating elements (shifting from day to day) their own.

3. Germany has been trying to make hers, one party after another in Russia, and is now making her most vigorous attempts with the Bolsheviks. Let us make the Bolsheviks our friends.

4. The Bolsheviks are not the wild-eyed rabble that most of us consider them. Even the present group, under the questionable leadership of Troitzky and Lenin, have maintained more stable order in Petrograd than that under any other previous regime that Thompson witnessed. Most of them are kindly, earnest men, heartily desiring to live at peace with their fellow men, and being absolutely unwilling to fight each other or to enter into any form of civil war. Most of the sentiments expressed by the Bolsheviks are common to ninety per cent. of the population of Russia, and, in some form, they have come to stay.

5. The British Embassy, and, in some measure, all the Allied embassies, have failed to realize that autocratic rule in Russia has gone, never to return. Their sympathy has been somewhat with the old regime, and they have been unable to see clearly that this great democratic feeling sweeping over all Russia is bound, sooner or later (no matter how unstable its form today) to become crystallized and to work out the situation.

6. Owing to this failure, complete on the part of certain of the Allies, and partial on the part of others, the Allies have either openly

or secretly tried to bring back elements of the old order, or else they have failed to try to keep on friendly terms with the newer ruling elements, whatever they might be.

7. The British Military Attaché,[1] as Mr. Lloyd George said, made a very bad break, in helping to get rid of Kerensky, who at least was the firm friend of the Allies, and opposed to a separate peace. The policy of the British Government has been, until recently, to give heavy support to the Korniloff and Kaledin movements, although it should be obvious that these movements representing force can never be permanently successful in the Russia of today.

8. It should be well understood that a complete re-orientation of parties has taken place, the Miliukoffs, etc., who were the leaders in deposing the Czar, now being moved over to the extreme Right, and the elements formerly represented by Kerensky now forming the Center.

9. Kerensky was in reality a strong man, but his regime was tolerated purely on sufferance, and because he could not compose the whirling elements he had to give way and be succeeded by a still more radical element, namely, the present Bolsheviks. These facts should be remembered, because the general elements which were back of Kerensky still contain the best hope for final stable government in Russia, and it is not unlikely that there will be a partial swingback from those at present in power (the extreme Left) to the elements in the Center.

10. Lenin and Troitzky may be in German pay, but despite the most vigorous efforts, it has never been possible to prove this. Furthermore, it is certain that their present course as Internationalists is consistent with that which they have followed for fourteen or fifteen years.

11. All the foregoing leads to the conclusion (which President Wilson made clear in his message to Congress) that if the Allied program had possessed more insight into, and sympathy with, this great movement of democracy, we should be in a much stronger position today. The problem is to try to win back to such a position, and in so doing to cut down German influence.

12. Thompson's friend Lamont,[2] finding that the authorities in London were in practical despair over the Russian situation, were doubtful of the wisdom with which they had handled it, and were desirous of securing any new light upon it, cabled to Thompson at Petrograd to come to London as soon as he had finished acquainting Mr. Sisson, Mr. Creel's representative who had arrived at Petrograd,

---

[1] Lt. Col. Alfred William Fortescue Knox, British military attaché in Russia since 1911.
[2] That is, Thomas W. Lamont.

with the work which Thompson was carrying on there. The hope was that Thompson could reach London prior to Colonel House's departure. Colonel House had, however, sailed for America before Thompson's arrival. Consequently, Lamont arranged for Thompson to see the leading members of the British Government and give them his view of the Russian situation; roughly as outlined above; at the same time keeping Secretary Crosby of the Treasury and also (whenever possible) Ambassador Page informed as to his interviews.

13. In this manner conferences were arranged with leading members of the British Government, including the following: Sir Edward Carson of the War Cabinet; Admiral Hall, head of the Naval Intelligence; Lord Reading; Colonel Buchan, head of English propaganda work; Sir George Clarke[3] of the Foreign Office (representing Mr. Balfour, whose views were later explained by the Prime Minister); and Mr. Lloyd George. The Prime Minister discussed the matter privately at luncheon with Thompson and Lamont, and the gist of his views may be summed up as follows:

"Colonel Thompson, you have given me a picture of the Russian situation far more clear than anything I had received hitherto, and I am much impressed with the analysis which you have made. I have had, in the back of my head, the feeling that there was a lack of understanding, and we must in some way get at the situation.

"I want you to tell President Wilson of this talk with me. Tell him that we are most sympathetic here in the idea of trying to handle Russia with greater insight, and that I will co-operate along these lines to the full with the President. I think it would be wise if the President were to see fit to make a concrete suggestion, but in any event I do not wish you to feel that your visit here has been anything but helpful.

"I have been pleasantly surprised to find that Mr. Balfour is already rather sympathetic with this idea of a radical change in the policy of dealing with Russia."

14. The members of the British Government mentioned above had shown throughout the week of interviews their growing sympathy with the point of view presented by Thompson. Sir Edward Carson, for instance, when asked whether he had any message to send to America, replied—"Tell President Wilson, please, that I will go just as far as he will, and further, and that there will be no question about money to be contributed to this educational work." These various governmental authorities all seemed to feel that the old methods had utterly failed, and that there was at least a fair

---

[3] Sir George Russell Clerk, a Senior Clerk in the Foreign Office.

hope in Thompson's suggestion. They all expressed a hope that the Prime Minister would see the matter in the light that he apparently did in the final interview with him. (Of course since the departure of Thompson and Lamont from England, the British views may have changed somewhat with the changing conditions in Russia, but in Thompson's judgment there has been no radical change in Russia itself.)

15. It is absolutely necessary that instant proof should be given of America's continuing interest in Russia. The most effective method is the inauguration of measures of practical relief. A flow of supplies, exclusive of munitions, should be started to Russia at once. Such supplies have been purchased and are now under control of the Russian Embassy here. Let the Red Cross be asked to become agents for the distribution of them in Russia. The details can be worked out after the Red Cross accepts this duty.

16. The suggestion is proffered for the organization of an informal committee in Petrograd, with necessary branches, vested with the largest possible amount of discretionary power. Recognition of the Bolsheviks is not essential. CONTACT IS. This contact, gained informally and unofficially, permits the changing situation to be followed exactly, and not by guesswork. At the same time it does not bind the Government in any degree, and cannot conceivably work embarrassments. This committee would deal with conditions. It would work through any and every group in the attempt to arouse Russia to the German menace, to make the peace terms impossible of acceptance by Germany, and to scatter the seed of Revolution throughout Austria-Hungary. Enough has already been done to prove the tremendous possibilities of the plan.

17. If Thompson were asked today to outline in detail a complete formula for work in Russia, he would be unable to do it, but he is convinced that, as just suggested, with a wise committee on the ground, backed by practical relief measures, great progress in the right direction can be made; that Russia is best disposed towards America, for, as Mr. Lloyd George pointed out, the English there are "in wrong." Thompson makes no claim to diplomatic knowledge and procedure. From the time he spent in Russia, however, he believes that the President of the United States can speak to the Russian people almost as well through a message to the American Congress as by formal communication to those representing the Russian Government. Thompson believes that, should America now declare herself in agreement with certain of the basic Russian peace terms as quoted, such as no punitive indemnities, etc., and suggest the necessity of the Russian people ascertaining from Germany more precise definitions as to what the vague German terms mean,

it is not at all impossible that Germany should outline in detail clauses substantially satisfactory; or, failing so to do, might furnish proof to the Russians that the German pretenses towards peace are empty. (Since this clause was dictated, the Germans have apparently become more specific in their proposals.)

18. Thompson does not wish to return to Petrograd, but he holds himself in readiness to serve in whatever way he can, and will do anything that the President wishes. He has spent upwards of a million dollars of his own money in the effort to postpone the present chaos, and believes that his work did result in several weeks of postponement. He is prepared to undertake any work that may be asked of him.

19. The conclusions as to the Russian situation reached herein by Thompson, were reached, of course, before he had read the striking passage in the President's message quoted at the beginning of this memorandum. That passage describes exactly the policy which Thompson has understood from the very beginning that the President would have wanted followed in Russia. So many people abroad, however, seem to be unable to comprehend this policy that Thompson began himself to doubt, until he read upon his return to America this clear reiteration of the only policy which, in Thompson's opinion, can possibly succeed in Russia.

20. Finally, it is criminal folly to proceed upon the assumption that Russia is lost to us. Russia is NOT lost. But we are forcing Russia into German power by our silence and our refusal to display the slightest interest in the deep convictions that possess the Russian people. They want peace, but they do not want a German peace, nor will they submit to one if given any intelligent aid or support in the negotiations.

It is possible even now to take entire charge of the Russian situation, bringing it around to our point of view absolutely. We have given Germany a free hand for her lies and plots; it is time to start a truth drive.

The English have become committed to this idea. Buchanan, the Ambassador at Petrograd, has already been withdrawn, and his successor will be a man of larger democracy and greater vision.

T MS (WP, DLC).

From Josephus Daniels

My dear Mr. President: Washington. 3 January, 1918.

The situation with reference to the oil reserve seems to the Attorney General, Senator Swanson and myself to call for the immediate adoption of a plan. We have, therefore, drawn up a bill approved by Senator Swanson, acting for the Naval Affairs Committee, the Attorney General and myself to take over all the lands in the three oil reserves and give authority to the Secretary of the Navy to operate them and make such disposition of proceeds as is legal, and in such cases where there [are] equities to make an offer of an equitable adjustment. The Attorney General and Senator Swanson believe this is the best solution, and I have long entertained this opinion. After our conference and after we agreed upon a bill, we decided, before Senator Swanson introduces it, to ask for a conference with you so that we can discuss it. As the matter is the unfinished business in the Senate and as the Ferris Bill in the House, which bill is not at all satisfactory, may come up at any minute I hope you can arrange to give us this conference very soon. In the meantime, if you cannot make an appointment today, could I request Mr. Ferris to hold up his bill until next week?[1]

Faithfully yours,   Josephus Daniels

TLS (WP, DLC).
[1] The Ferris bill, H.R. 3232, was not acted upon further. 65th Cong., 2d sess., *House Journal*, p. 632.

From the Diary of Josephus Daniels

Jan 3 1918

Council of Nat. Defense. Labor question up [?] Lane wanted Labor War Council of 3—Wilson (WB), one named by Gompers & one by Manufacturing organization. Baker wanted a Labor Director, one man, & thought that best. Decided to take the matter up with the President & obtain his view

An Address to a Joint Session of Congress

4 Jan'y, 1918[1]

Gentlemen of the Congress: I have asked the privilege of addressing you in order to report to you that on the twenty-eighth of December last, during the recess of the Congress, acting through the Secretary of War and under the authority conferred upon me by the Act of Congress approved August 29, 1916, I took possession and assumed control of the railway lines of the country and the systems of water transportation under their control. This step seemed to be imperatively necessary in the interest of the public welfare, in the presence of the great tasks of war with which we are now dealing. As our own experience develops difficulties and makes it clear what they are, I have deemed it my duty to remove those difficulties wherever I have the legal power to do so. To assume control of the vast railway systems of the country is, I realize, a very great responsibility, but to fail to do so in the existing circumstances would have been much greater. I assumed the less responsibility rather than the weightier.

I am sure that I am speaking the mind of all thoughtful Americans when I say that it is our duty as the representatives of the nation to do everything that it is necessary to do to secure the complete mobilization of the whole resources of America by as rapid and effective means as can be found. Transportation supplies all the arteries of mobilization. Unless it be under a single and unified direction, the whole process of the nation's action is embarrassed.

It was in the true spirit of America, and it was right, that we should first try to effect the necessary unification under the voluntary action of those who were in charge of the great railway properties; and we did try it. The directors of the railways responded to the need promptly and generously. The group of railway executives who were charged with the task of actual coordination and general direction performed their difficult duties with patriotic zeal and marked ability, as was to have been expected, and did, I believe, everything that it was possible for them to do in the circumstances. If I have taken the task out of their hands, it has not been because of any dereliction or failure on their part but only because there were some things which the Government can do and private management cannot. We shall continue to value most highly the advice and assistance of these gentlemen and I am sure we shall not find them withholding it.

It had become unmistakably plain that only under government administration can the entire equipment of the several systems of transportation be fully and unreservedly thrown into a common service without injurious discrimination against particular properties. Only under government administration can an absolutely unrestricted and unembarrassed common use be made of all tracks, terminals, terminal facilities and equipment of every kind. Only under that authority can new terminals be constructed and developed without regard to the requirements or limitations of particular roads. But under government administration all these things will be possible,—not instantly, but as fast as practical difficulties, which cannot be merely conjured away, give way before the new management.

The common administration will be carried out with as little disturbance of the present operating organizations and personnel of the railways as possible. Nothing will be altered or disturbed which it is not necessary to disturb. We are serving the public interest and safeguarding the public safety, but we are also regardful of the interest of those by whom these great properties are owned and glad to avail ourselves of the experience and trained ability of those who have been managing them. It is necessary that the transportation of troops and of war materials, of food and of fuel, and of everything that is necessary for the full mobilization of the energies and resources of the country, should be first considered, but it is clearly in the public interest also that the ordinary activities and the normal industrial and commercial life of the country should be interfered with and dislocated as little as possible, and the public may rest assured that the interest and convenience of the private shipper will be as carefully served and safeguarded as it is possible to serve and safeguard it in the present extraordinary circumstances.

While the present authority of the Executive suffices for all purposes of administration, and while of course all private interests must for the present give way to the public necessity, it is, I am sure you will agree with me, right and necessary that the owners and creditors of the railways, the holders of their stocks and bonds, should receive from the Government an unqualified guarantee that their properties will be maintained throughout the period of federal control in as good repair and as complete equipment as at present, and that the several roads will receive under federal management such compensation as is equitable and just alike to their owners and to the general public. I would suggest the average net railway operating income of the three years ending June 30, 1917. I earnestly recommend that these guarantees be given by appropriate legislation, and given as promptly as circumstances permit.[2]

I need not point out the essential justice of such guarantees and their great influence and significance as elements in the present financial and industrial situation of the country. Indeed, one of the strong arguments for assuming control of the railroads at this time is the financial argument. It is necessary that the values of railway securities should be justly and fairly protected and that the large financial operations every year necessary in connection with the maintenance, operation and development of the roads should, during the period of the war, be wisely related to the financial operations of the Government. Our first duty is, of course, to conserve the common interest and the common safety and to make certain that nothing stands in the way of the successful prosecution of the great war for liberty and justice, but it is also an obligation of public conscience and of public honor that the private interests we disturb should be kept safe from unjust injury, and it is of the utmost consequence to the Government itself that all great financial operations should be stabilized and coordinated with the financial operations of the Government. No borrowing should run athwart the borrowings of the federal treasury, and no fundamental industrial values should anywhere be unnecessarily impaired. In the hands of many thousands of small investors in the country, as well as in national banks, in insurance companies, in savings banks, in trust companies, in financial agencies of every kind, railway securities, the sum total of which runs up to some ten or eleven thousand millions, constitute a vital part of the structure of credit, and the unquestioned solidity of that structure must be maintained.

The Secretary of War and I easily agreed that, in view of the many complex interests which must be safeguarded and harmonized, as well as because of his exceptional experience and ability in this new field of governmental action, the Honorable William G. McAdoo was the right man to assume direct administrative control of this new executive task. At our request, he consented to assume the authority and duties of organizer and Director General of the new Railway Administration. He has assumed those duties and his work is in active progress.

It is probably too much to expect that even under the unified railway administration which will now be possible sufficient economies can be effected in the operation of the railways to make it possible to add to their equipment and extend their operative facilities as much as the present extraordinary demands upon their use will render desirable without resorting to the national treasury for the funds. If it is not possible, it will, of course, be necessary to resort to the Congress for grants of money for that purpose. The Secretary of the Treasury will advise with your committees with regard to this very practical aspect of the matter. For the present, I suggest only the guarantees I have indicated and such appropriations as are necessary at the outset of this task. I take the liberty of expressing the hope that the Congress may grant these promptly and ungrudgingly. We are dealing with great matters and will, I am sure, deal with them greatly.[3]

Printed reading copy (WP, DLC).

[1] WWhw.

[2] T. W. Sims, on January 4, 1918, introduced the administration's bill (H.R. 8172) to provide for the operation of the transportation systems while under federal control, for the compensation of their owners, and for other purposes. *Cong. Record*, 65th Cong., 2d sess., p. 617.

[3] There is a WWT outline; a WWsh draft; and a WWT draft with numerous changes by Wilson, Baker, and McAdoo, all in WP, DLC; a CLST draft of the WWT draft with WWhw emendations, in the C. L. Swem Coll., NjP; WWsh drafts of additions, WP, DLC; and a final CLST draft with WWhw emendations and additions in the C. L. Swem Coll., NjP.

From Newton Diehl Baker

Dear Mr. President: Washington. January 4, 1918.

I took up at once with the Surgeon General the letter of Mr. John Palmer Gavit, which you sent me under date of January 2 and which I received yesterday, January 3.

The statement made is that large numbers of young men are being shipped north from southern camps, barely convalescent from attacks of measles, that the hospital at Englewood has pneumonia cases in it, "most, if not all of which, are barely cured measles cases from the South." General Gorgas tells me that the total number of pneumonia cases at Hoboken, which includes the hospital at Englewood and covers 13,838 men in the several camps, is 23, only 6 of whom were admitted during the previous week. This is regarded as a very small number of pneumonia cases for so large a body of men.

Most of the 13,838 men at Camp Merritt were moved there from Long Island, where they were in a less desirable camp at Camp Mills pending the completion of the construction of Camp Merritt, which was designed for their reception. Very few men, and those in small groups selected for special purposes, were moved from the South to New York during the month of December. General Gorgas is now endeavoring to find out how many of the pneumonia cases are convalescent measles patients from the South, and I will report the figure to you as soon as it is given to me. In the meantime, I have asked General Gorgas to draw an order for me to sign, directed to all Division Commanders, that in the preparation of any men for shipment from the South to the North, the certificate of the chief medical officer at the camp shall be required as to any individual convalescent from any illness that, in the opinion of such medical officer, the convalescent has progressed sufficiently to make the journey safe, and that all such persons are to be left to continue their convalescence in the absence of such a certificate from the medical officer.

On December 10, General Gorgas issued a general order to all division surgeons, requiring the holding of all measles patients on sick report two weeks longer than the usual quarantine period, in order to prevent the subsequent development of pneumonia. This order, with the one I have just suggested, will prevent the exposure of convalescents to a change in climate before they are able to stand it.

In the meantime, pending the receipt of further information, it seems to me that the pneumonia cases referred to by Mr. Gavit could not in any large number be either from the South or measles convalescents, but as soon as I have an accurate statement of the facts I will report it to you, and also draft a letter for you to send to Mr. Gavit, giving him the complete situation.

Respectfully yours,   Newton D. Baker

TLS (WP, DLC).

From George Parmly Day

New Haven, Connecticut

My dear Mr. President,   January 4, 1918.

I write to thank you for your interest in "The Chronicles of America," now in preparation for publication by the Yale University Press, and to assure you that we appreciate the more, if possible, the thought given by you to our suggestion in regard to dedicating the series to you, and your prompt answer thereto, because of the immense burden of matters requiring your immediate attention. It is my hope that you will pardon my not writing you before now in reply to your note, since I have waited to discuss the situation with members of the Council's Committee on Publications of Yale University.

We cannot, of course, but be disappointed at being unable to dedicate the work to you, as we had planned and hoped to do with your permission. We shall not, however, trespass on your good nature by asking you to reconsider your decision in view of your statement that you would be greatly embarrassed by such a dedication as we propose. It is, however, a satisfaction to us that you at least will know of our desire to dedicate the volumes to you, and it will add to our pleasure if you will permit us to present to you a set of the books for your private library. It should, we feel, prove an inspiration to the printers and binders to know that the first set of "The Chronicles of America" to come from the press is being made for the President of the United States.

With high regard and every good wish for the New Year, believe me,   Sincerely yours,   Geo. Parmly Day

TLS (WP, DLC).

From Franklin Knight Lane

My dear Mr. President: Washington January 4, 1918.

I had a conference yesterday with Senator Myers, Chairman of the Public Lands Committee of the Senate, and Mr. Ferris, with regard to the oil bill.

Mr. Ferris thought that the House Committee would stand for it, and later he informed me that Mr. Lenroot, to whom he had talked, agreed with him. These two can handle the Land Committee of the House. Senator Myers, however, was unwilling to introduce the amendment in the Senate, though he said that in the end he might vote for it. He felt himself pledged to support the bill that the Senate Committee had reported out. He said it was understood that no relief provision was to be passed regarding Naval reserves, and that this arrangement had been arrived at by agreement with Senator Swanson who had another scheme in mind and had conferred with the Attorney General regarding it touching Naval reserve lands. It was my impression from what he said that he thought the Senate Committee would not support this measure.

I then sent for Senator Swanson whom I have just seen, and asked him to introduce it; and he thought that he should see you first before doing so, and said he would try to see you tomorrow. He told me that this provision of his had been presented to Senator Pittman and rejected by the latter, but that it was his idea that this bill should only apply as to Naval reserves. Since that time he and Senator Pittman have agreed together that the relief provisions in the Senate bill should not be made to apply to Naval reserves.

I shall try to see Senator Pittman immediately upon his return from the West. In the meantime I shall await your conference with Senator Swanson.[1]

Cordially and faithfully yours,   Franklin K. Lane

I have since seen Pittman. He will talk with Swanson but has little hope of any possibility of change in the Senate.

TLS (WP, DLC).
[1] Wilson did not confer with Swanson until January 9, at which time Gregory and Daniels were also present.

A Letter and a Telegram from
Sir Cecil Arthur Spring Rice to Arthur James Balfour

Dear Mr. Balfour,   Washington. January 4th 1918.

The President gave me an audience yesterday. I communicated to him your telegram announcing Lord Reading's appointment here.[1] He read it and said that he fully understood the circumstances. I pointed out to him how necessary it was to have some one who had been in close touch with the British government to be present here and that he must have full control. He expressed himself in

[1] Reading had just been appointed to succeed Spring Rice as the British Ambassador to the United States.

the kindest language to me personally and in fact nothing could exceed his cordiality. We passed at once from the personal question to wider topics.

He said that when he had first seen me after the war began he had told me that his chief preoccupation was not external but internal. There was imminent danger of civil discord, the country was divided into groups which did not understand one another, which were of different origin and which at any moment might fly at each other's throats. There was evidence of a long planned agitation which might at any time lead to most serious results. The nation was only nominally united. That at least was the substance of the reports which had reached him. That was his main preoccupation during the first year of the war. Now he said the country had not been so thoroughly united for years. Except for a small and no doubt dangerous minority, the whole country was united in defence of the flag. Disloyalty was not an element to be feared any longer. I told him that Bishop Hamilton of the Methodist Episcopal Church,[2] which Church with its affiliations numbers about one third of the whole American population, had only the day before used almost precisely the same language to me. Speaking of the Catholic clergy the Bishop had recognised the fact that some of them, especially those of German and Irish origin, were probably inclined to be disloyal, but that the great majority were ready to follow Cardinal Gibbons who insisted on sole allegiance to the flag. The President said that he had received similar information from representatives of all the Churches and all sections of society. He went on to say that the problem which an American President had to face was in the main a psychological one. He had to gauge public opinion. He had to take the course which commended itself to the great majority of the American people whose interpreter he was bound to be. No action could be taken or at least usefully taken unless it received the support of the great majority. It was not so much a question of what was the right thing to do from the abstract view-point as what was the possible thing to do from the point of view of the popular condition of mind. It was his duty to divine the moment when the country required action and to take that action which the great majority demanded. It was from this point of view that certain considerations had lately presented themselves to him with great force. He himself with the full consent of the American people and with their express approval had made an appeal to the German people behind the back of the German government. The Bolsheviki in Russia were now adopting the same policy. They had

[2] John William Hamilton, retired as bishop in 1916; at this time, Chancellor of American University in Washington.

issued an appeal to all the nations of the world to the peoples and not to the governments. He was without information at present or at least without certain information as to what reception had been given to this appeal. But there was evidence at hand that certainly in Italy and probably also in England and France the appeal had not been without its affect. In the United States active agitation was proceeding. It was too early yet to say with positive certainty how successful this agitation had been. But it was evident that if the appeal of the Bolsheviki was allowed to remain unanswered, if nothing were done to counteract it, the effect would be great and would increase. The main point of the appeal was this. War should not be waged for purposes of aggression. The war should be brought to an end but not on a basis of conquest. The proper basis was satisfaction of legitimate desires of the separate peoples who had a right to satisfy those desires. They should be allowed to live their own lives according to their own will and under their own laws. In point of logic, of pure logic, this principle which was good in itself would lead to the complete independence of various small nationalities now forming part of various Empires. Pushed to its extreme the principle would mean the disruption of existing governments, to an undefinable extent. Logic was a good and powerful thing but apart from the consideration of existing circumstances might well lead to very dangerous results. These were only general considerations. He would not enter into details. But he could express the following general conclusions which I must not take to be enunciated by him as President but merely as the interpreter of certain phases of opinion which had recently come before him. The American people were engaged in this war with all their heart. They were convinced that no course was open to them with honour except to engage in the war. But they would not engage in a war in which America was involved except on American principles. They would not fight this war for private ends either for themselves or for any one else. Their object was a stable peace and they did not believe that a stable peace could be based upon aggression. The German people had been worked upon by their government which had persuaded them that they were fighting not for conquest but for defence and that the object of the allies was to crush and disrupt the German empire and place German peoples under foreign rule. A formidable weapon was in the hands of the German government as long as the German people could be brought to believe that such was the object of the alliance which they had to face. It was also very widely felt here that the allies now fighting in Europe would find it extremely difficult to agree on any definite programme which did not look on the face of it as if its object and its main object was aggression and conquest. In any case it was felt in this country that an agreement among the allies would be a very difficult thing to bring about and in the process very serious differences of opinion would develop themselves. There was considerable fear here that should the Allies agree upon a common statement of claims the effect in Germany and Russia of the claims agreed upon would be such as to create the impression that the allies were prosecuting the war for conquest.

Thus speaking in general terms it seemed to him that the American people were inclined to receive with favour a statement of a moderate and unaggressive character and would welcome such a statement. He had already in general terms indicated the general lines on which he thought American policy should be based. These statements had met with general approval. Each one had been more detailed than the last and it might become necessary as, the war continued, to define even more clearly those objects for which America was waging war. In drawing up this statement it would be necessary not only to follow the rules of logic and to draw reasoned conclusions from accepted principles but also so far as was possible to give due consideration to the circumstances and the facts which actually existed.

I made at once a telegraphic and more detailed report[3] but I put the above on record as an indication of what he said was passing in his mind. He begged me to remember that our conversation was wholly unofficial and that he was not speaking as President. I said that as soon as Lord Reading arrived he would have the advantage of speaking freely with one who could interpret the policy of the British government. Speaking only for myself I said that I knew quite well what your personal wishes were and what was your personal conviction. I knew that you believed the hope and salvation of the world lay in a close and cordial understanding between the free nations, more especially between those who were of the household of our language. I said that we could almost endure with equanimity all the horrors of this terrible struggle if they led in the end to a close sure and permanent understanding between the English speaking peoples. If we stood together we were safe, if we did not stand together nothing was safe.

The conversation ended with renewed and most cordial assurances from the President.

(Signed) Yours sincerely   C. Spring-Rice.

TL (A. J. Balfour Papers, FO 800/209, PRO).

[3] It is missing in all collections.

Washington. 4 January 1918.

PERSONAL & MOST SECRET.

My telegram No.: 31 represents the President's own language, but he begs me to tell you this for your personal information only.

He spoke with great earnestness, but only on the understanding that his words should not be quoted as his own. Please observe this understanding, but warn the Prime Minister that the source of information is not to be despised.

If you approve of the idea that the President should again, as before, make a solemn answer without consulting the Allies, you might tell me so in confidence, or say nothing. In any case, I beg that you will not directly or indirectly allow my promise to be broken. I shall see him again on January 9.

Situation here is such that the President must in self-defence make some answer to the Bolshevists' appeal. Country, he told me, has never been so solid in any cause, and there is no hostile element beyond the violent and criminal pro-German minority, who are dangerous, but not politically so. But it is absolutely essential to prevent a rift from beginning, for it would quickly spread, and the President can do nothing without the support of the peoples' will, of which as you know he is an excellent judge.

T telegram (A. J. Balfour Papers, FO 800/205, PRO).

From the Diary of Colonel House

The White House, January 4, 1918.

I came to Washington today on the 12.08. The train was three hours late although I had been told that Washington would ask them to try and have it on time. I did not reach the White House until nine o'clock. They had saved dinner for me, but I touched it lightly and went into immediate conference with the President concerning the proposed message to Congress on our war aims which I have urged ever since my return, and upon which I advised by cable from Paris that nothing be said by the President until after he had seen me. I did not wish the President to state our case in piecemeal, and I was sure he would not cover the ground I thought necessary.

We were in conference until half past eleven discussing the general terms to be used, and looking over data and maps which I had brought with me, some of which the Peace Inquiry Bureau had prepared at my request. These maps and documents were so voluminous that it was necessary to bring with me to Washington

Professor Knight, of the Wyoming University, now associated with Columbia and the American Geographical Institute.[1]

Both Mrs. Wilson and I, before going to bed, insisted that we should not get to work until ten o'clock tomorrow in order that the President should have a good night's rest.

[1] Samuel Howell Knight, a geologist.

A Memorandum by Sidney Edward Mezes, David Hunter Miller, and Walter Lippmann[1]

THE PRESENT SITUATION: THE WAR AIMS AND PEACE TERMS IT SUGGESTS.

OUR OBJECTIVES.

The Allied military situation and Berlin-Bagdad.

The Allies have had various opportunities to destroy Middle Europe by arms, to wit: the Russian invasion of Galicia, the protection of Serbia, the intervention of Rumania, the offensive of Italy, the expedition of Gallipoli, the expedition to Saloniki, the Mesopotamian campaign, and the Palestinian campaign. The use made of these opportunities has produced roughly the following results: The Russian army has ceased to be an offensive force, and Germany occupies a large part of that territory of the Russian Empire which is inhabited by more or less non-Russian peoples; Rumania is occupied to the mouth of the Danube; Serbia and Montenegro are occupied; the Austrian and German are deep into Italian territory. As the Russian, Rumanian, Serbian, and Italian armies cannot be expected to resume a dangerous offensive, the invasion of Austria-Hungary has ceased to be a possibility. The Allies hold Saloniki, which they are unable to use as a base for offensive operations.

[1] This memorandum was prepared at some time during December before December 22, 1917, by these three members of the executive committee of The Inquiry, at the request of Colonel House. Lawrence E. Gelfand, *The Inquiry: American Preparations for Peace, 1917-1919* (New Haven, Conn., 1962), p. 136; Ronald Steel, *Walter Lippmann and the American Century* (Boston, 1980), pp. 133-34. House brought the memorandum to the White House on December 23, but, as the entry from the House Diary printed at December 30 reveals, Wilson and House did not discuss the memorandum during the Houses' Christmas visit to Washington. Nor is there any evidence that Wilson read the memorandum between December 23, 1917, and January 4, 1918.

House also brought with him on January 4 a revision and enlargement of Part 3 of the first report: S. E. Mezes, D. H. Miller, and W. Lippmann, "Memorandum, January 2, 1917 [1918]. A SUGGESTED STATEMENT OF PEACE TERMS," T MS (WP, DLC). There is no evidence that Wilson ever read this long document, and it is not printed.

The "data" to which House refers in his diary entry was, among other things, The Inquiry's report of December 22, 1917. It is printed here because Wilson and House went through it first on January 4.

There is danger that they may be driven from it. If they are able to hold it, and to keep it from Austrian hands, they have made a blind alley of one subordinate part of the Berlin-Bagdad project, which has always included a branch line to Saloniki, and then to the sea. By the capture of Bagdad they not only control the rich resources of Mesopotamia but have made a blind alley of the main Berlin-Bagdad line, so far as that line was aimed to be a line of communication to the Persian Gulf as a threat against India. By the capture of Palestine the British have nullified a subordinate part of the Berlin-Bagdad scheme, that is, the threat to the Suez Canal. By the almost complete separation of Arabia from Turkey, the Turks have not only lost the Holy Cities, but another threat to the Red Sea has been removed. Germany has therefore lost the terminals of her project, and if Saloniki, Jerusalem, Bagdad, and Arabia remain in non-German hands the possibilities of defense against the politico-military portions of the Bagdad scheme exist.

The problem of Berlin-Bagdad.

The problem is therefore reduced to this: How effectively is it possible for Germany to organize the territory now under her political and military influence so as to be in a position at a later date to complete the scheme and to use the resources and the man-power of Middle Europe in the interests of her own foreign policy? She faces here four critical political problems: 1) The Poles; 2) the Czechs; 3) the South Slavs; and 4) Bulgaria. The problem may be stated as follows: If these peoples become either the willing accomplices or the helpless servants of Germany and her political purposes, Berlin will have established a power in Central Europe which will be the master of the continent. The interest of the United States in preventing this must be carefully distinguished before our objectives can become clear. It can be no part of our policy to prevent a free interplay of economic and cultural forces in Central Europe. We should have no interest in thwarting a tendency toward unification. Our interest is in the disestablishment of a system by which adventurous and imperialistic groups in Berlin and Vienna and Budapest could use the resources of this area in the interest of a fiercely selfish foreign policy directed against their neighbors and the rest of the world. In our opposition to Middle Europe, therefore, we should distinguish between the drawing together of an area which has a certain economic unity, and the uses of that unity and the methods by which it is controlled. We are interested primarily in the nature of the control.

The chief binding interests in Middle Europe.

The present control rests upon an alliance of interest between the ruling powers at Vienna, Budapest, Sofia, Constantinople, and Berlin. There are certain common interests which bind these ruling groups together. The chief ones are: 1) the common interests of Berlin, Vienna, and Budapest in the subjection of the Poles, the Czechs, and the Croats; 2) from the point of view of Berlin the present arrangement assures a control of the external affairs and of the military and economic resources of Austria-Hungary; 3) from the point of view of Vienna and Budapest it assures the German-Magyar ascendency; 4) the interest that binds Sofia to the alliance lay chiefly in the ability of Germany to exploit the wrong done Bulgaria in the treaty of Bucharest; 5) the interest of Constantinople is no doubt in part bought, in part coerced, but it is also in a measure due to the fact that in the German alliance alone lies the possibility of even a nominal integrity for the Turkish Empire; 6) at the conclusion of the war, the greatest tie which will bind Austria-Hungary, Bulgaria, and Turkey to Germany will be the debts of these countries to Germany.

The disestablishment of a Prussian Middle Europe.

It follows that the objectives to be aimed at in order to render Middle Europe safe are the following:

1. Increased democratization of Germany, which means, no doubt, legal changes like the reform of the Prussian franchise, increased ministerial responsibility, control of the army and navy, of the war power and foreign policy, by representatives responsible to the German people. But it means something more. It means the appointment to office of men who represent the interests of south and west Germany and the large cities of Prussia—men who today vote Progressive, Centrist, or Social Democrat tickets—in brief, the men who stood behind the Bloc which forced through the Reichstag resolution of July.[2]

2. In addition to increased democratization of Germany, we have to aim at an independent foreign policy in Austria-Hungary.

3. We must aim at preventing the military union of Austria-Hungary and Germany.

4. We must aim at the contentment and friendship of Bulgaria through a satisfactory solution of the Balkan frontiers.

5. We must aim at the neutralization and the internationalization of Constantinople and the Straits.

[2] That is, the "Peace Resolution."

6. We must see that the control of the two military terminals of Berlin-Bagdad remain in the hands of an administration friendly to the western nations.

7. As a result of the accomplishment of the foregoing, we must secure a guaranteed autonomy for the Armenians, not only as a matter of justice and humanity but in order to re-establish the one people of Asia Minor capable of preventing economic monopolization of Turkey by the Germans.

These being our objectives, what are our present assets and liabilities?

ASSETS.

Our economic weapon.

The commercial control of the outer world, and the possibility of German exclusion both from the sources of raw materials and the richer markets, and from the routes of communication, lie in our hands. The possibility of a continued commercial exclusion weighs heavily, in fact, most heavily of all, upon the German mind at present, because upon the conclusion of peace a successful demobilization is possible only as there are raw materials and markets for the resumption of German industry. Without these the army would become a discontented and dangerous body. If the possibility of exclusion from economic opportunity is associated with a vision of a world co-operation realized, the double motives of fear and hope can be used upon the German people. *This is our strongest weapon, and the Germans realize its menace. Held over them, it can win priceless concessions.* It should be noted that this weapon will be of special advantage after the peace conference has assembled. Our ability to protract the discussion at the industrial expense of Germany and to our own benefit, and [sic] will give us a bargaining power of great advantage. Skilfully handled, this asset can be used both to threaten and to lure them; and its appeal is wellnigh universal, as the utterances and comment from Germany clearly show. To the dynasty and the ruling classes, it presents the most tangible threat of revolution, because it is obvious that the danger of revolution will be enormously increased upon the conclusion of peace, when the patriotic motive subsides. To the commercial classes it presents the obvious picture of financial ruin and of disorder. To the army it presents the picture of a long period following the conclusion of the war in which government will not dare to demobilize rapidly. To the poorer classes generally it presents the picture of a long period after the war in which the present hardships will continue.

II. Our assets in Austria-Hungary.

In Austria-Hungary we have a number of assets which may seem contradictory at first, but which can all be employed at the same time. There is the nationalistic discontent of the Czechs and probably of the South Slavs. The increase of nationalistic discontent among the Czechs and the possibility of some kind of Poland will tend to break the political coalition which has existed between the Austrian Poles and the German Austrians. On the part of the Emperor and of the present ruling powers in Austria-Hungary there is a great desire to emerge from the war with the patrimony of Francis Joseph unimpaired. This desire has taken two interesting forms: 1) it has resulted in the adoption of a policy of no annexations, which is obvious enough; and 2) in the adoption, evidently with much sincerity, of a desire for disarmament and a league of nations. The motive here is evidently a realization that financially Austria cannot maintain armaments at the present scale after the war, and a realization that in a league of nations she would find a guarantee of the *status quo*. It follows that the more turbulent the subject nationalities become and the less the present Magyar-Austrian ascendency sees itself threatened with absolute extinction, the more fervent will become the desire in Austria-Hungary to make itself a fit partner in a league of nations. *Our policy must therefore consist first in a stirring up of nationalist discontent, and then in refusing to accept the extreme logic of this discontent, which would be the dismemberment of Austria-Hungary.* By threatening the present German-Magyar combination with nationalist uprisings on the one side, and by showing it a mode of safety on the other, its resistance would be reduced to a minimum, and the motive to an independence from Berlin in foreign affairs would be enormously accelerated. Austria-Hungary is in the position where she must be good in order to survive.

It should be noted that the danger of economic exclusion after the war affects Austria-Hungary as well as Germany very seriously, and no amount of ultimate trade in transit to Turkey will be able to solve for her the immediate problem of finding work for her demobilized army, of replenishing her exhausted supplies, and of finding enough wealth to meet her financial burdens.

III. Our assets in Bulgaria.

In regard to Bulgaria our greatest asset is the possibility of satisfying her just claims, now that the threat of an imperialistic Russian occupation of Constantinople is removed. A satisfied Bulgaria would no doubt share in the economic advantages of Middle Europe, but without a strong national grievance of her own, her exploitation for political and military purposes is improbable. To this should be added the consideration that the reverberations of the Russian revolution are sure to be felt in Bulgaria.

IV. Our assets in Turkey.

In regard to Turkey our primary assets are our military successes, already commented upon above. These military successes should have a religio-political effect upon the Ottoman Turk. The great financial and economic weakness of Turkey immediately after the war and her need of assistance are also assets to be considered.

V. Our assets outside of Europe.

The German colonies are obvious material to bargain with, as is Germany's exclusion from the Pacific and from Central and South America.

VI. The radicalism of Russia.

It is often overlooked that the Russian revolution, inspired as it is by deep hatred of autocracy, contains within it at least three other great motives of serious danger to German domination: 1) anticapitalist feeling, which would be fully as intense, or more intense, against German capitalism; 2) a religious love of Russia which is spiritually antagonistic to Protestant Germany; and 3) a powerful nationalist feeling among the Moderates, who will either return to power or at least exercise a strong influence in Russia. The revolution, therefore, must be regarded not only as inherently difficult for the Germans to manage and to master, but as being in itself a great dissolving force through its sheer example. Note in this regard the reported interpellation of a deputy in the Austrian parliament, who wanted to know when the Austrian and Hungarian landed estates were to be broken up upon Bolsheviki principles, seeing that the government had recognized the Bolsheviki.

VII. The Vatican.

The Vatican has been rightly regarded as pro-German in its neutrality. But we should not be misled in regard to it as we have been misled in regard to the Russian revolution. The Germans have been skilful enough to use it. The Vatican is one of those forces in the world which require exceedingly skilful handling and contains within it the possibility of great assistance to our cause, as is shown, for example, by the opportunity it offered the President to carry on the first successful diplomatic offensive made by the Allies since the beginning of the war.

VIII. American resources.

The fact that with time the man-power and resources of this country, added to the present forces of the Entente, render a complete and crushing military victory over the Central Powers a certainty.

IX. The intangibles.

To be counted on our side if skilfully used are certain intangibles which the President undoubtedly had in mind when he warned the statesmen of the world in his last message that they were living "in this midday hour of the world's life." These are: 1) the universal longing for peace, which under the circumstances should not be handed over to Germany as something for them to capitalize; 2) the almost universal feeling on the part of common people of the world that the old diplomacy is bankrupt, and that the system of the armed peace must not be restored. This is a sentiment fundamentally anti-Prussian in its nature, and should be capitalized for our side; 3) there is then, too, a great hope of a league of nations which has the approbation of disinterested people everywhere; 4) there is the menace of social revolution all over the world, and as a factor in it a realization by the governing political and financial groups that the meeting of the war debts is virtually insoluble without revolutionary measures about property. In a war fought for democratic aims, these fears should be made to fight on our side.

X. The changed direction of German policy.

In estimating the objects of German policy, as well as the concessions which Germany offers, it should be borne in mind that her first economic and political penetration pointed due south through Italy, that later it swerved southeast towards Constantinople, Bagdad, and the Persian Gulf, and that at present, in view of the Russian *debacle*, its direction of easiest advance is due east. The present is the best time for Germany to seize the opportunities offering themselves there, and this may very well cause her to decide that she will accept sacrifices towards the southeast, the west, on other continents, and in distant seas, in order to assure her control of the Russian opportunities.

Balanced off against these assets are our liabilities. They are, briefly:

I. The military impotence of *Russia*.

II. The *strategic impossibility* of any military operation which will cut to the heart of Middle Europe.

III. The *costs and dangers* of a war of attrition on the western front, and the improbability of anything more than a slow withdrawal by the Germans, leaving behind them an absolute devastation of western Belgium and of northern France.

IV. The *possession* by the Germans at this time of the occupied areas.

V. The concentration of France upon *Alsace-Lorraine*, which opens at least as a possibility an attempt by the Germans to cause an almost complete rupture of the western alliance by offering France an attractive compromise solution. In case the Germans should decide within the next few months that they could compensate themselves in the east, they may offer France enough in the west to force either a peace or so keep a schism of French opinion as to render France impotent.

VI. In regard to *Italy*, our liabilities are also heavy. There is the obvious danger of social revolution and disorganization.

VII. Another liability lies in the present unwillingness of the dominant opinion of Great Britain to discuss modifications of *sea power*.

A PROGRAM FOR A DIPLOMATIC OFFENSIVE.

Bulgaria, Serbia, and Italy.

Attention may first be directed to Bulgaria as a weak section of the German line. The Allies should publicly recognize Bulgaria's just national claims and Serbia's right to independence and to access to the sea. This should be accompanied by a strong public move in the direction of Italy, emphasizing Italy's just claims to a rectification of her frontier, both for defensive and for nationalistic reasons. The abandonment by Italy of her imperialist claims can be covered by strong assurances that her territory shall be evacuated and her pressing economic needs now and after the war assured.

Austria-Hungary.

Towards Austria-Hungary the approach should consist of references to the subjection of the various nationalities, in order to keep that agitation alive, but coupled with it should go repeated assurances that no dismemberment of the Empire is intended, together with allusions to the humiliating vassalage of the proudest court in Europe. It will probably be well to inject into the discussion a mention of the fact that Austria-Hungary is bound to Germany by huge debts expended in the interest of German ambition. In regard to Austria-Hungary it will probably not be wise to suggest frankly the cancellation of these debts, as in the case of Turkey. Reference to their existence and to the bondage which they imply will, however, produce a useful ferment. The desire of Austria-Hungary to discuss the question of disarmament should not be ignored. The discussion should specifically be accepted and the danger of disarmament in the face of an autocratic Germany explained again.

Germany.

As against Germany the lines of the offensive have already been laid down by the President. There should be more explicit assertion that the penalty of a failure to democratize Germany more adequately must mean exclusion from freedom of intercourse after the war, that the reward for democratization is a partnership of all nations in meeting the problems that will follow the peace. This offensive should of course contain the explicit assurance that we do not intend to dictate the form of responsible government in Germany, and that we are quite within the justified limits of intercourse with nations if we take the position that our attitude towards a responsible Germany would be different from our attitude towards the present Germany.

Russia.

Towards Russia our best success will lie: 1) in showing that we are not unwilling to state war aims; 2) in a hearty propaganda of the idea of a league of nations; and 3) in a demonstration to them that the diplomatic offensive is in progress, and that the Allies are not relying totally upon force.

France.

For the sake of the morale of France it will perhaps be wise to indicate an interest in the solution of the problem of Alsace-Lorraine.

The western Allies in general.

All of the western Allies should be braced: 1) by an energetic movement for economic unity of control; 2) by utterances from the United States which will show the way to the Liberals in Great Britain and in France, and therefore restore their national unity of purpose. These Liberals will readily accept the leadership of the President if he undertakes a liberal diplomatic offensive, because they will find in that offensive an invaluable support for their internal domestic troubles; finally 3) such a powerful liberal offensive on the part of the United States will immensely stimulate American pride and interest in the war, and will assure the administration the support of that great mass of the American people who desire an idealistic solution. Such a liberal offensive will do more than any other thing to create in this country the sort of public opinion that the President needs in order to carry through the program he has outlined.

A SUGGESTED STATEMENT OF PEACE TERMS.

What follows is suggested as a statement of peace terms in case a general statement of terms at this time is desired. The different items are phrased, both with a view to what they include and exclude, in their relationship to the present military and diplomatic situation. The purpose is to make them serve both as the bases of an ultimate just peace and as a program of war aims which would cause the maximum disunity in the enemy and the maximum unity among our associates.

BELGIUM.

BELGIUM MUST BE EVACUATED AND RESTORED BY GERMANY, WITHOUT ANY ATTEMPT TO LIMIT THE SOVEREIGNTY WHICH SHE ENJOYS IN COMMON WITH ALL OTHER FREE NATIONS.

NORTHERN FRANCE.

THE INVADED PORTIONS OF[3] NORTHERN FRANCE MUST BE EVACUATED AND RESTORED.

LUXEMBURG.

This question should be ignored at this time and left to negotiation.

ALSACE-LORRAINE.

EVERY ACT OF GERMANY TOWARDS ALSACE-LORRAINE FOR HALF A CENTURY HAS PROCLAIMED THAT THESE PROVINCES ARE FOREIGN TERRITORY, AND NO GENUINE PART OF THE GERMAN EMPIRE. GER-

[3] WWhw.

MANY CANNOT BE PERMITTED TO ESCAPE THE STERN LOGIC OF HER OWN CONDUCT. THE WRONG DONE IN 1871 MUST BE UNDONE.

This paragraph is phrased so as to avoid making the return of Alsace-Lorraine to France an essential aim of the United States in the war, while giving all possible moral support to France in her effort to regain the provinces. It is our belief that the recovery of Alsace-Lorraine is highly desirable and practically essential to the successful recovery of France. It is also our belief that the relinguishment of Alsace-Lorraine would be the final seal upon the destruction of German militarism. At the same time, we recognize that America cannot insist upon fighting for Alsace-Lorraine longer than France herself is willing to fight, and therefore if Germany should offer France a compromise which France herself was willing to accept, it would be unwise for us to have a committment on record which we could not fulfill.*

Italy

WE RECOGNIZE THAT ITALY IS ENTITLED TO RECTIFICATIONS OF HER BOUNDARIES ON THE BASIS OF A JUST BALANCE OF DEFENSIVE AND NATIONALIST CONSIDERATIONS. THIS RIGHT WAS RECOGNIZED IN PRINCIPLE BY AUSTRIA-HUNGARY BEFORE ITALY ENTERED THE WAR AND JUSTICE TOWARDS ITALY IS IN NO WISE ALTERED BY ANY SUBSEQUENT MILITARY EVENTS. WE RECOGNIZE ALSO THAT THE PORT OF TRIESTE SHOULD BE COMMERCIALLY FREE AND THAT THE INHABITANTS OF THE CITY DESERVE THEIR CULTURAL AUTONOMY.

It is our belief that the application of this plank will meet the just demands of Italy, without yielding to those larger ambitions along the eastern shore of the Adriatic for which we can find no substantial justification.

THE BALKANS.

NO JUST OR LASTING SETTLEMENT OF THE TANGLED PROBLEMS CONFRONTING THE DEEPLY WRONGED PEOPLES OF THE BALKANS CAN BE BASED UPON THE ARBITRARY TREATY OF BUCHAREST. THAT TREATY WAS A PRODUCT OF THE EVIL DIPLOMACY WHICH THE PEOPLES OF THE WORLD ARE NOW DETERMINED TO END. THAT TREATY WRONGED EVERY NATION IN THE BALKANS, EVEN THOSE WHICH IT APPEARED TO FAVOR, BY IMPOSING UPON THEM ALL THE PERMANENT MENACE OF WAR. IT UNQUESTIONABLY TORE MEN AND WOMEN OF BULGARIAN

* Mr. Miller dissents in part and submits a separate memorandum. See appendix.

LOYALTY FROM THEIR NATURAL ALLEGIANCE. IT DENIED TO SERBIA THAT ACCESS TO THE SEA WHICH SHE MUST HAVE IN ORDER TO COMPLETE HER INDEPENDENCE. ANY JUST SETTLEMENT MUST OF COURSE BEGIN WITH THE EVACUATION OF RUMANIA, SERBIA, AND MONTENEGRO BY THE ARMIES OF THE CENTRAL POWERS, AND THE RESTORATION OF SERBIA AND MONTENEGRO. THE ULTIMATE RELATIONSHIP OF THE DIFFERENT BALKAN NATIONS MUST BE BASED UPON A FAIR BALANCE OF NATIONALISTIC AND ECONOMIC CONSIDERATIONS, APPLIED IN A GENEROUS AND INVENTIVE SPIRIT AFTER IMPARTIAL AND SCIENTIFIC INQUIRY. THE MEDDLING AND INTRIGUING OF GREAT POWERS MUST BE STOPPED, AND THE EFFORTS TO ATTAIN NATIONAL UNITY BY MASSACRE MUST BE ABANDONED.

It would obviously be unwise to attempt at this time to draw frontiers for the Balkan states.**[4] Certain broad considerations, however, may tentatively be kept in mind. They are in brief these: 1) that the area annexed by Rumania in the Dobrudga*** is almost surely Bulgarian in character and should be returned; 2) that the boundary between Bulgaria and Turkey should be restored to the Enos-Midia line, as agreed upon at the conference of London;† 3) that the south boundary of Bulgaria should be the Aegean Sea coast from Enos to the gulf of Orfano, and should leave the mouth of the Struma river in Bulgarian territory; 4) that the best access to the sea for Serbia is through Saloniki; 5) that the final disposition of Macedonia cannot be determined without further inquiry; 6) that an independent Albania is almost certainly an undesirable political entity.

We are strongly of the opinion that in the last analysis economic considerations will outweigh nationalistic affiliations in the Balkans, and that a settlement which insures economic prosperity is most likely to be a lasting one.

POLAND.

AN INDEPENDENT AND DEMOCRATIC POLAND SHALL BE ESTABLISHED. ITS BOUNDARIES SHALL BE BASED ON A FAIR BALANCE OF NATIONAL AND ECONOMIC CONSIDERATIONS, GIVING DUE WEIGHT TO THE NECESSITY FOR ADEQUATE ACCESS TO THE SEA. THE FORM OF POLAND'S GOVERNMENT AND ITS ECONOMIC AND POLITICAL RELATIONS SHOULD BE LEFT TO THE DETERMINATION OF THE PEOPLE OF POLAND ACTING THROUGH THEIR CHOSEN REPRESENTATIVES.

** a tentative map is appended.
*** In the Treaty of Bucharest
† and in the Treaty of San Stefano
[4] The map is missing.

The subject of Poland is by far the most complex of all the problems to be considered. The present distribution of Poles is such as to make their complete unification impossible without separating East Prussia from Germany. This is probably not within the bounds of practical politics. A Poland which consists essentially of Russian and perhaps Austrian Poland would probably secure its access to the sea through the Vistula River and the canals of Germany which run to Hamburg and Bremen. This relationship would very probably involve both the economic subjection of Poland and the establishment of an area of great friction. If Russia is to remain weak the new Poland will lie in an exceedingly exposed position. The experiment must no doubt be made, however, but in order to assure it a fair start, it is necessary to insist at the outset upon a democratic basis for the Polish state. Unless this is loyally observed, the internal friction of Poles, Ruthenians, and Jews is likely to render Poland impotent in the presence of Germany.

AUSTRIA-HUNGARY.

WE SEE PROMISE IN THE DISCUSSIONS NOW GOING ON BETWEEN THE AUSTRO-HUNGARIAN GOVERNMENTS AND THE PEOPLES OF THE MONARCHY, BUT THE VASSALAGE OF AUSTRIA-HUNGARY TO THE MASTERS OF GERMANY, RIVETED UPON THEM BY DEBTS FOR MONEY EXPENDED IN THE INTERESTS OF GERMAN AMBITION, MUST BE DONE AWAY WITH IN ORDER THAT AUSTRIA-HUNGARY MAY BE FREE TO TAKE HER RIGHTFUL PLACE AMONG THE NATIONS.

The object of this is to encourage the present movement towards federalism in Austria, a movement which, if it is successful, will break the German-Magyar ascendency. By injecting the idea of a possible cancellation of the war debts to Germany, it is hoped to encourage all the separatist tendencies as between Austria-Hungary and Germany, as well as the social revolutionary sentiment which poverty has stimulated.

TURKEY.

IT IS NECESSARY TO FREE THE SUBJECT RACES OF THE TURKISH EMPIRE FROM OPPRESSION AND MISRULE. THIS IMPLIES AT THE VERY LEAST AUTONOMY FOR ARMENIA AND THE PROTECTION OF PALESTINE, SYRIA, MESOPOTAMIA, AND ARABIA BY THE CIVILIZED NATIONS. IT IS NECESSARY ALSO TO ESTABLISH FREE INTERCOURSE THROUGH AND ACROSS THE STRAITS. TURKEY PROPER MUST BE JUSTLY TREATED AND FREED FROM ECONOMIC AND POLITICAL BONDAGE. HER WAR DEBTS TO GERMANY MUST BE CANCELLED. NONE OF THE MONEY

INVOLVED WAS SPENT IN THE INTEREST OF TURKEY, AND NONE OF IT SHOULD BE REGARDED AS A TURKISH OBLIGATION. AN ADJUSTMENT OF HER PRE-WAR DEBT IN ACCORDANCE WITH HER TERRITORIAL LIMITATIONS IS ALSO REQUIRED BY THE CONSIDERATIONS OF JUSTICE. MOREOVER, IT WILL UNDOUBTEDLY BE FEASIBLE TO ARRANGE ADVANCES OF MONEY TO TURKEY IN ORDER TO ENABLE HER UNDER SUITABLE SUPERVISION TO INSTITUTE AND MAINTAIN SATISFACTORY EDUCATIONAL AND SANITARY CONDITIONS, AND TO UNDERTAKE HER ECONOMIC REHABILITATION. THUS TURKEY CAN BE FREED FROM INTERMEDDLING AND ENABLED TO DEVELOP INSTITUTIONS ADAPTED TO THE GENIUS OF HER OWN PEOPLE.

This will appear on the surface to be a drastic solution of the Turkish problem, but it is one which the military situation enables us to accomplish, and it can hardly be doubted that no principle of justice requires the return of occupied portions of Turkey to the German-Turkish alliance. The cancellation of Turkey's debt to Germany is the one final way to abolish German political and commercial penetration. It is also the one method by which Turkey can be given a new start, considerably reduced in size, without power to misgovern alien races, and therefore free to concentrate upon the needs of her own population. It should be noted in this regard that only a few days ago it was announced that Germany had agreed to forego interest on the Turkish debt for a period of twelve years after the war. This implies a realization on Germany's part that if she insists upon the interest payments a repudication [repudiation] is possible, carrying with it a destruction of German influence in Turkey.

THE LEAGUE OF NATIONS

FROM THE NATIONS AT PRESENT ENGAGED IN RESISTANCE TO GERMANY'S EFFORT TO DOMINATE THE WORLD THERE IS GROWING A LEAGUE OF NATIONS FOR COMMON PROTECTION, FOR THE PEACEFUL SETTLEMENT OF INTERNATIONAL DISPUTES, FOR THE ATTAINMENT OF A JOINT ECONOMIC PROSPERITY, INCLUDING EQUAL OPPORTUNITY UPON THE HIGHWAYS OF THE WORLD AND EQUITABLE ACCESS TO THE RAW MATERIALS WHICH ALL NATIONS NEED. WHETHER THIS LEAGUE IS TO REMAIN ARMED AND EXCLUSIVE, OR WHETHER THERE IS TO BE A REDUCTION OF ARMAMENTS AND A CORDIAL INCLUSION OF GERMANY, WILL DEPEND UPON WHETHER THE GERMAN GOVERNMENT IS IN FACT REPRESENTATIVE OF THE GERMAN DEMOCRACY.

This is of course simply another statement of the alternative before Germany.

Conclusion

We regard all of the terms mentioned as essential to any final agreement. It may well be, however, that some of the provisions other than those relating to Belgium and northern France, the evacuation of Italy and Rumania, and the evacuation and restoration of Serbia and Montenegro, do not require assent as a preliminary to discussion at the conference. And this is due to the fact that we have the power to compel Germany's assent at the peace conference by our ability to bar her indefinitely from access to supplies and to protract the negotiations at her cost and at our own benefit.

We emphasize our belief that no surrender of this power, even by inference, should be considered until all the terms stated above are definitely agreed to, in detail as well as in principle, by Germany at the peace conference. This involves adopting as our policy the reserving of the discussion of economic peace until our political, social, and international objects are attained.

We might well adopt as our slogan "No economic peace until the peoples are freed."

Appendix I

Mr. Miller's Memorandum.

ALSACE-LORRAINE

It is an essential part of any peace plan which looks to the end that Germany shall not, either politically or economically, either dominate the world, or terrify the world with the threat of such domination, that Alsace-Lorraine should be *wholly restored to France*.

1. That Alsace-Lorraine is not and never was a part of Germany is conclusively proved by the German treatment and government of that province for nearly fifty years as a conquered and French frontier and not as German territory.

2. Any peace, with a free Poland, involves the possibility of German dominion over Europe, first economically and then politically. For with Poland, as she may be, drawn to Germany by commercial agreements and with Russia open to German penetration directly and through Poland, the possibilities of German power are almost boundless.

3. France is the one country, which in man power and in economic sacrifice, has given the most to the cause of liberty and democracy. Indeed, France is the one country in Europe, (ex-

cept possibly Italy) near to economic ruin from the war. She can never be in any position even to attempt world domination. And even with Alsace-Lorraine, her recovery from disaster will be slow—without it—almost impossible.

4. Neither nationally nor historically is there the slightest ground for any solution of the Alsace-Lorraine question (after its separation from Germany) except the return of the territory as a whole, to France. If the British held Calais for fifty years a far stronger case could be made against France as to Calais than as to Alsace-Lorraine

5. Announcement to the French people that the end of German autocracy means the restoration of Alsace-Lorraine to France, would insure the successful completion of the war, as a military proposition.

6. Conversely, failure to state as an essential term of peace, the restoration of Alsace-Lorraine to France will end the war with a German victory, for France will believe that nothing is left worth her blood and treasure.

It is useless, and worse than useless, in any statement of war aims, to disguise or attempt to disguise by vague diplomatic language, the real purpose as to Alsace-Lorraine, for the French will not be deceived, and anything but plain language with a definite meaning belongs to a past era of history.

T MS (WP, DLC).

From the Diary of Josephus Daniels

Jan 4 1918

Talked again with Thompson. He put a million dollars of his own money in propaganda in Russia because he believed if they understood America they would stand against German propaganda. In English house, during Kerensky's rule, a toast was drunk to the Czar. The E Ambassador & others so afraid of losing their perquisites & place they sympathize with autocracy. "I have been in Wall Street, but Russia gave me a new idea, & I have come home a better Democrat." Later L said he was a crank. WW said spending money in R for propaganda was like pouring water in a bottomless hole. Crane says no cement is left in Russia. We are with E & F giving all aid possible to those in "Little Russia," where there is a fight against Germany & Anarchy. Summers, consul at Moscow, says the only hope is in the men fighting in So. Russia. Baker said War College proposed, not recognition of the Bolsheviki but acceptance as the best way to keep Russia from coming under the dominion of Germany.[1] One Army report recommended giving $25 million dollars a month to a certain General with ample power to do any & all things in Germany. WW was astounded that any one would suggest such a thing.

[1] The Editors have been unable to find this document and the one mentioned below.

The First Versions of the Fourteen Points[1]

The Present Situation: Page twenty-seven.

A SUGGESTED STATEMENT OF PEACE TERMS.

What follows is suggested as a statement
of peace terms in case a general statement of
terms at this time is desired.   The different
items are phrased, both with a view to what they
include and exclude, in their relationship to
the present military and diplomatic situation.
The purpose is to make them serve both as the
bases of an ultimate just peace and as a program of war aims which would xxxxxxx cause the
maximum disunity in the enemy and the maximum
unity among our associates.

BELGIUM.   BELGIUM MUST BE EVACUATED AND RESTORED
BY GERMANY, WITHOUT ANY ATTEMPT TO LIMIT THE
SOVEREIGNTY WHICH SHE ENJOYS IN COMMON WITH
ALL OTHER FREE NATIONS.
                  The invaded portions of
NORTHERN FRANCE. NORTHERN FRANCE MUST BE EVACUATED AND
RESTORED.

LUXEMBURG.   This question should be ignored at this
time and left to negotiation.

All French territory must be freed and the invaded portions restored.

[1] We reproduce these and all other drafts of the Fourteen Points Address (except the printed reading copy) as integral parts of the text. All documents come from WP, DLC. The following pages from the Mezes-Miller-Lippmann memorandum are the ones on which Wilson drafted in shorthand some of the Fourteen Points. Transcripts of his shorthand outlines are printed at the bottom of the pages on which they appear. Wilson's first typed drafts of the points are printed following the shorthand versions.
House tells the story of the drafting of the address in some detail in the extract from his diary printed at January 9, 1918. We have subjected that entry to critical analysis and have concluded that, although it may be somewhat self-serving, it is correct in all

The Present Situation: Page twenty-eight.

ALSACE-LORRAINE.   EVERY ACT OF GERMANY TOWARDS ALSACE-
LORRAINE FOR HALF A CENTURY HAS PROCLAIMED
THAT THESE PROVINCES ARE FOREIGN TERRITORY,
AND NO GENUINE PART OF THE GERMAN EMPIRE.
GERMANY CANNOT BE PERMITTED TO ESCAPE THE
STERN LOGIC OF HER OWN CONDUCT.   THE WRONG
DONE IN 1871 MUST BE UNDONE.

   This paragraph is phrased so as to
avoid making the return of Alsace-Lorraine
to France an essential aim of the United
States in the war, while giving all possible
moral support to France in her effort to regain the provinces.   It is our belief that
the recovery of Alsace-Lorraine is highly
desirable and practically essential to the
successful recovery of France.   It is also
our belief that the relinguishment of Alsace-
Lorraine would be the final seal upon the
destruction of German militarism.   At the
same time, we recognize that Americacannot
insist upon fighting for Alsace-Lorraine

Alsace-Lorraine should be restored to France but without excluding
Germany from the use of the economic resources of those provinces.

its important details. The reader should bear in mind that, since this entry is retro-
spective, House sometimes does not relate events in strict chronological order. We will
not repeat House's account; hence the reader is advised to read it before he or she goes
through the drafts of the Fourteen Points Address.

So much has been said and written about this address that it would be gratuitous for
us to write at length about it. The context of the address and the source of Wilson's
ideas about and suggestions for the reconstruction of the world community are well
explicated in volumes in this series that go back to his early manhood.

The Present Situation: Page twenty-nine

longer than France herself is willing to
fight, and therefore if Germany should
offer France a compromise which France
herself was willing to accept, it would be
unwise for us to have a committment on
record which we could not fulfill.*

Italy

WE RECOGNIZE THAT ITALY IS ENTITLED
TO RECTIFICATIONS OF HER BOUNDARIES ON THE BASIS
OF A JUST BALANCE OF DEFENSIVE AND NATIONALIST
CONSIDERATIONS. THIS RIGHT WAS RECOGNIZED
IN PRINCIPLE BY AUSTRIA-HUNGARY BEFORE ITALY
ENTERED THE WAR AND JUSTICE TOWARDS ITALY
IS IN NO WISE ALTERED BY ANY SUBSEQUENT
MILITARY EVENTS.   WE RECOGNIZE ALSO THAT
THE PORT OF TRIESTE SHOULD BE COMMERCIALLY
FREE AND THAT THE INHABITANTS OF THE CITY
DESERVE THEIR CULTURAL AUTONOMY.

It is our belief that the application
of this plank will meet the just demands of
Italy, without yielding to those larger
ambitions along the eastern shore of the Adriatic
for which we can find no substantial justification.
* Mr. Miller dissents in part and submits a separate
memorandum.   See appendix.

The readjustment of the frontiers of Italy along clearly recognized lines
of nationality.

THE BALKANS.   NO JUST OR LASTING SETTLEMENT

OF THE TANGLED PROBLEMS CONFRONTING

THE DEEPLY WRONGED PEOPLES OF THE BAL-

KANS CAN BE BASED UPON THE ARBITRARY

TREATY OF BUCHAREST.   THAT TREATY WAS

A PRODUCT OF AN EVIL DIPLOMACY WHICH

THE PEOPLES OF THE WORLD ARE NOW DETER-

MINED TO END.   THAT TREATY WRONGED EVERY

NATION IN THE BALKANS, EVEN THOSE WHICH

IT APPEARED TO FAVOR, BY IMPOSING UPON

THEM ALL THE PERMANENT MENACE OF WAR.   IT

UNQUESTIONABLY TORE MEN AND WOMEN OF BUL-

GARIAN LOYALTY FROM THEIR NATURAL ALLEGI-

ANCE.   IT DENIED TO SERBIA THAT ACCESS

TO THE SEA WHICH SHE MUST HAVE IN ORDER TO

COMPLETE HER INDEPENDENCE.   ANY JUST

SETTLEMENT MUST OF COURSE BEGIN WITH THE

EVACUATION OF RUMANIA, SERBIA, AND MONTE-

NEGRO BY THE ARMIES OF THE CENTRAL POWERS,

AND THE RESTORATION OF SERBIA AND MONTE-

NEGRO.   THE ULTIMATE RELATIONSHIP OF THE

Rumania, Serbia, and Montenegro must be evacuated; occupied territories restored; Serbia accorded free and secure access to the sea; and the relationships of the several Balkan states to one another determined by friendly counsel along historically established lines of allegiance and nationality. International guarantees should be entered into of the political independence and territorial integrity of all the Balkan states.

The Present Situation: Page thirty-two

THE BALKANS.

lines to the gulf of Orfano, and should leave the mouth of the Struma river in Bulgarian territory; 4) that the best access to the sea for Serbia is through Saloniki; 5) that a plausible frontier between Bulgaria and Serbia may be based upon the secret treaty between Bulgaria and Serbia prior to the First Balkan War; 5) that the final disposition of Macedonia cannot be determined without further inquiry; 6) that an independent Albania is ~~probably~~ *almost certainly* an undesirable political entity.

We are strongly of the opinion that in the last analysis economic considerations will outweigh nationalistic affiliations in the Balkans, and that a settlement which insures economic prosperity is most likely to be a lasting one.

POLAND.   AN INDEPENDENT AND DEMOCRATIC POLAND SHALL BE ESTABLISHED. ITS BOUNDARIES SHALL BE BASED ON A FAIR BALANCE OF NATIONAL AND ECONOMIC CONSIDERATIONS, GIVING DUE WEIGHT TO THE NECESSITY FOR ADEQUATE ACCESS TO THE SEA. THE FORM OF POLAND'S GOVERNMENT AND

An independent Polish state must be established, whose political and economic independence and territorial integrity shall be guaranteed by international covenant. It shall include the territories inhabited by an indisputably Polish population, and shall be granted a free and secure access to the sea.

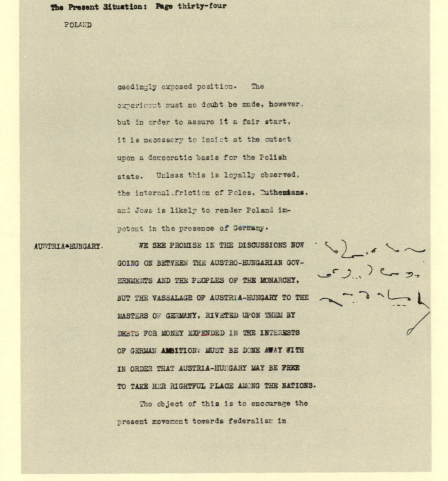

The Present Situation: Page thirty-four

POLAND

ceedingly exposed position.   The
experiment must no doubt be made, however,
but in order to assure it a fair start,
it is necessary to insist at the outset
upon a democratic basis for the Polish
state.   Unless this is loyally observed,
the internal friction of Poles, Ruthenians,
and Jews is likely to render Poland impotent in the presence of Germany.

AUSTRIA-HUNGARY.   WE SEE PROMISE IN THE DISCUSSIONS NOW
GOING ON BETWEEN THE AUSTRO-HUNGARIAN GOV-
ERNMENTS AND THE PEOPLES OF THE MONARCHY,
BUT THE VASSALAGE OF AUSTRIA-HUNGARY TO THE
MASTERS OF GERMANY, RIVETED UPON THEM BY
DEBTS FOR MONEY EXPENDED IN THE INTERESTS
OF GERMAN AMBITION, MUST BE DONE AWAY WITH
IN ORDER THAT AUSTRIA-HUNGARY MAY BE FREE
TO TAKE HER RIGHTFUL PLACE AMONG THE NATIONS.
          The object of this is to encourage the
present movement towards federalism in

The peoples of Austria-Hungary, whose place among the nations of the
world we wish to see safeguarded and assured, must be accorded the
freest opportunity of autonomous development.

The Present Situation: Page Thirty-five.

AUSTRIA-HUNGARY.

in Austria, a movement which, if it is
successfull will break the German-Magyar
ascendency. By injecting the idea of a
possible cancellation of the war debts, it *to Germany*
is hoped to encourage all the separatist
tendencies as between Austria-Hungary and
Germany, as well as the social revolutionary
sentiment which poverty has stimulated.

TURKEY.

IT IS NECESSARY TO FREE THE SUBJECT
RACES OF THE TURKISH EMPIRE FROM OPPRESSION
AND MISRULE. THIS IMPLIES AT THE VERY
LEAST AUTONOMY FOR ARMENIA AND THE ~~MIN-~~
~~TENANCE OF A~~ PROTECTOR*ION OF* ~~ATE~~ OVER PALESTINE, *SYRIA,*
MESOPOTAMIA, AND ARABIA BY THE CIVILIZED
NATIONS. IT IS NECESSARY ALSO TO ESTAB-
LISH FREE INTERCOURSE THROUGH *AND ACROSS* THE STRAITS.
TURKEY ~~XXXXXXX~~ *PROPER* MUST BE JUSTLY TREATED
AND FREED FROM ECONOMIC AND POLITICAL
BONDAGE. HER WAR DEBTS TO GERMANY MUST
BE CANCELLED. NONE OF THE MONEY INVOLVED
WAS SPENT IN THE INTEREST OF TURKEY, AND

The Turkish portions of the present Turkish Empire must be assured a
more secure sovereignty, and the other nationalities which are now
under Turkish rule must be assured full opportunity of autonomous
development.

6   A free and even-handed adjustment of all colonial
      claims.

----

7   The evacuation of all Russian territory and such a
      settlement of all questions concerning Russia
      as will secure the best and freest cooperation
      of the other nations of the world in obtaining
      for her an absolutely unrestricted opportunity
      for the independent determination of her own
      policy and political development and assure
      her of a sincere welcome into the society of
      free nations under institutions of her own
      choosing, and, more than a welcome, assistance
      also of every kind that she may need and may herself desire.

----

2   Absolute freedom of navigation of the seas outside
      territorial waters in peace and in war.

----

14   A league of nations for the purpose of affording
      a mutual guarantee of political independence
      and territorial integrity.

----

1   All the processes of this peace to be open and
      involve and permit no secret understandings
      of any kind.

----

5   Guarantees given and taken that national armaments
     will be reduced to the lowest point consistent
     with domestic safety.

----

4   Removal, so far as possible, of all economic bar-
     riers and equality of trade conditions among
     all the nations consenting to this peace and
     uniting in the league of nations.

----

8   Belgium to be evacuated and restored without any
     attempt to limit the sovereignty which she
     enjoys in common with all other free nations.

----

9   All
     A French territory to be freed and the invaded
     portions restored.

----

9   Alsace-Lorraine to be restored to France , but
     without excluding Germany from the use of the
     economic resources of those provinces.

----

10   Readjustment of the frontiers of Italy along
     clearly recognised lines of nationality.

----

12   Roumania, Serbia, and Montenegro to be evacuated;
     occupied territories restored; Serbia accord-
     ed free and secure access to the sea; and the
     relationships of the several Balkan states to

one another determined by friendly counsel
along historically established lines of allegiance and nationality. International
guarantees to be entered into of the political
and economic independence and territorial integrity of all
the Balkan states.

An independent Polish state to be established
Whose political and economic independence
and territorial integrity shall be guaranteed by international covenant; which shall
include the territories inhabited by indisputably Polish populations; and which shall
be accorded a free and secure access to the
sea.

The peoples of Austria-Hungary, whose place among
the nations of the world we wish to see safeguarded and assured, to be accorded the free-
est opportunity of autonomous development.

The Turkish portions of the present Turkish Empire to be assured a secure sovereignty and
the other nationalities which are now under
Turkish rule must be assured an unmolested
opportunity of autonomous development.

Edward Mandell House to Arthur James Balfour

[The White House, Jan. 5, 1918]

The President wishes me to let the prime minister and you know that he feels that he must presently make some specific utterance as a counter to the German peace suggestions and that he feels that in order to keep the present enthusiastic and confident support of the war quick and effective here that utterance must be in effect a repetition of his recent address to the Congress in even more specific form than before. He hopes that no utterance is in contemplation on your side which would be likely to sound a different note or suggest claims inconsistent with what he proclaimed the objects of the United States to be. The president feels that we have so far been playing into the hands of the German military party and soli[di]fying German opinion against us and he has information which seems to open a clear way to weakening the hands of that party and clearing the air of all possible misrepresentations and misunderstandings.

This is the cable the President and I agreed to send to Lloyd George today. The President typed it.
Washington Jan'y. 5, 1918. E. M. House[1]

WWT telegram (E. M. House Papers, CtY).
[1] EMHhw.

From the British Embassy, with Enclosure

Telegram from Mr. Balfour, January 5, 1918.
Following for information of the President, private and secret:[1]

Negotiations have been going on for some time between the Prime Minister and the Trades Unions. The main point was the desire of the Government to be released from certain pledges which were made to the labour leaders earlier in the war. This release is absolutely indispensible from the military point of view for the development of man power on the western front. Finally the negotiations arrived at a point at which their successful issue depended mainly on the immediate publication by the British Government of a statement setting forth their war aims. This statement has now been made by the Prime Minister. It is the result of consultations with the labour leaders as well as the leaders of the Parliamentary Opposition.[2]

Under these circumstances there was no time to consult the Allies as to the terms of the statement agreed on by the Prime Minister and the above-mentioned persons. It will be found on examination to be in accordance with the declarations hitherto made by the President on this subject.

Should the President himself make a statement of his own views, which in view of the appeal made to the peoples of the world by the Bolsheviki might appear a desirable course, the Prime Minister is confident that such a statement would also be in general accordance with the lines of the President's previous speeches, which in England as well as in other countries have been so warmly received by public opinion. Such a further statement would naturally receive an equally warm welcome.

T telegram (WP, DLC).

[1] For other versions of this telegram, see A. J. Balfour to C. A. Spring Rice, Jan. 5, 1918, Hw telegram (FO 115/2432, pp. 37-38, PRO), and Foreign Office to C. A. Spring Rice, Jan. 5, 1918, T telegram (A. J. Balfour Papers, FO 800/205, PRO).

[2] Lloyd George made his statement of war aims before a conference of the Trades Union Congress in Caxton Hall in London on January 5. In addition to the general statements quoted in the Enclosure, he made a number of more specific declarations. He insisted that Britain was not fighting to destroy Germany, Austria-Hungary, or Turkey. Nor did the British specifically intend to alter or destroy the Imperial constitution of Germany: they considered it "a dangerous anachronism," but the adoption of a more democratic constitution was a question for the German people to decide. The first requirement of British war aims was still "the complete restoration, political, territorial and economic, of the independence of Belgium and such reparation as can be made for the devastation of its towns and provinces." Similar restoration and "reparation for injustice done" would have to take place in the cases of Serbia, Montenegro, and the occupied portions of France, Italy, and Rumania. Lloyd George pledged to stand by the French government "in the demand they make for a reconsideration of the great wrong of 1871" in regard to Alsace-Lorraine. He was even more circumspect on the subject of Russian territories occupied by the Germans: "The present rulers of Russia are now engaged without any reference to the countries whom Russia brought into the War, in separate negotiations, with their common enemy. . . . If the present rulers of Russia take action which is independent of their Allies we have no means of intervening to arrest the catastrophe which is assuredly befalling their country." He called for "an independent Poland, comprising all those genuinely Polish elements who desire to form part of it." He declared that the breakup of the Austro-Hungarian Empire was not part of the British war aims but said that, unless "genuine self-government on true democratic principles" was granted to nationalities within the empire who had long desired it, there was little hope for the removal of the unrest in those areas which had long threatened the peace of Europe. He also urged the satisfaction of the "legitimate claims of the Italians for union with those of their own race and tongue" and that "justice be done" to Rumanians in their "legitimate aspirations." The British government did not "chal-

lenge the maintenance of the Turkish Empire in the homelands of the Turkish race with its capital at Constantinople" but believed that Arabia, Armenia, Mesopotamia, Syria, and Palestine were "entitled to a recognition of their separate national conditions." Lloyd George also made an indirect reference to the secret treaties: "Much has been said about the arrangements we have entered into with our Allies on this and on other subjects. I can only say that as new circumstances, like the Russian collapse and the separate Russian negotiations, have changed the conditions under which these arrangements were made, we are, and always have been, perfectly ready to discuss them with our Allies."

The full text of Lloyd George's speech appears in David Lloyd George, *War Memoirs of David Lloyd George* (6 vols., Boston, 1933-37), V, 63-73. For discussions of the background, motivation, authorship, and content of the speech, see Arno J. Mayer, *Political Origins of the New Diplomacy, 1917-1918* (New Haven, Conn., 1959), pp. 313-28; David R. Woodward, "The Origins and Intent of David Lloyd George's January 5 War Aims Speech," *The Historian*, XXXIV (Nov. 1971), 22-39; and George W. Egerton, *Great Britain and the Creation of the League of Nations: Strategy, Politics, and International Organization, 1914-1919* (Chapel Hill, N.C., 1978), pp. 57-61. For an item-by-item comparison of the speech with Wilson's Fourteen Points Address of January 8, see Kernek, *Distractions of Peace during War*, pp. 72-77.

E N C L O S U R E

The British premier said in his January address that before framing his statement he had "taken special pains to ascertain the view and attitude of representative men of all sections of thought and opinion in the country"; and:

"I am glad to be able to say, as a result of all these discussions, that, although the government are alone responsible for the actual language I purpose using, there is a national agreement as to the character and purpose of our war aims and peace conditions, and in what I say to you to-day, and through you to the world, I can venture to claim that I am speaking not merely the mind of the government, but of the nation and of the empire as a whole. * * *

"We feel that government with consent of the governed must be the basis of any territorial settlement in this war.

"With regard to the German colonies, I have repeatedly declared that they are held at the disposal of a conference whose decision must have primary regard to the wishes and interests of the native inhabitants of such colonies. * * * The general principle of national self-determination is, therefore, as applicable in their cases as in those of the occupied European territories.

"It is desirable and essential that the settlement after this war shall be one which does not in itself bear the seeds of future war.

"The crushing weight of modern armaments, the increasing evil of compulsory military service, the vast waste of wealth and effort involved in warlike preparation—these are blots on our civilization of which every thinking individual must be ashamed. For these and other similar reasons we are confident that a great attempt must be made to establish, by some international organization, an alternative to war as a means of settling international disputes.

"If, then, we are asked what we are fighting for, we reply, as we have often replied. We are fighting for a just and lasting peace, and we believe that before permanent peace can be hoped for, three conditions must be fulfilled: First, the sanctity of treaties must be re-established; secondly, a territorial settlement must be secured based on the right of self-determination or the consent of the governed; and, last, some, international organization to limit the burden of armaments and diminish the probability of war."[1]

T MS (WP, DLC).
 [1] For Wilson's reaction, see the extract from the House Diary, printed at January 9, 1918.

From Newton Diehl Baker, with Enclosure

Dear Mr. President: Washington. January 5, 1918.

On yesterday, Friday, afternoon, after the Cabinet meeting, the Council of National Defense directed a summary to be made of the shipping situation, based on studies just concluded by representatives of the Shipping Board, the Council of National Defense, and the War Department. Enclosed herewith is the summary. It shows practically the minimum needs of the Army, Navy, the Allies for food and other essential materials which we are undertaking to ship for them, and the necessary trade in nitrates, chrome, manganese, etc., which must be maintained, the aggregate of which is 7,700,000 dead-weight tons. Our resources are shown to be 4,400,000 tons, of which an undetermined part is made up of ships which can not be used in trans-Atlantic trade, either on account of their speed or because of the conditions under which they were acquired. The balance to be supplied from some source is thus 3,300,000 tons.

This summary does not take into account possible sinkings, nor is it affected by new tonnage which may be acquired from the neutrals or elsewhere, and which, if acquired, would correspondingly decrease the gross amount needed.

The statement is for tonnage needed to carry out the agreed

minimum military program of transporting 24 divisions with their necessary supplies to France by the first of July, and maintaining the other essential trades indicated to that time.

By direction of the Council, I am transmitting this summary to you with our joint recommendation that this statement be presented by General Bliss, or in such other way as you may prefer, to the Allied authorities abroad, with a view to securing by common consent of the nations interested an agreement either that the necessary tonnage of 3,300,000 tons will be supplied, or that it can not be supplied; and in the latter event that this Government, in conference with the Allies, determine what part of our military program shall be modified, and to what extent.

The Council believes that unless an immediate answer to these questions can be given by common consent among the Governments interested, you should determine the question as a basis of our further activities, since practically all questions of military preparation, armament, and food and munition supplies for ourselves and our Allies are involved.

The supporting data upon which these conclusions as to tonnage are made are all at hand, and it is our thought that General Bliss should take with him these data, so that he would be able to exhibit in the conference a full and detailed basis for the conclusions thus summarized.

General Bliss expects 48 hours notive [notice] before leaving for his port of embarkation. The notice has not come as yet, but depends upon the coaling of his ship, which is temporarily delayed by ice.

If you would care to discuss this matter with General Bliss before he goes he is, of course, available at any moment.[1]

Respectfully yours,   Newton D. Baker

TLS (WP, DLC).
[1] Wilson did not see Bliss at this time. However, he probably discussed the matter with Baker when he conferred with him at the White House from 2:45 p.m. to approximately 4 p.m. on January 5.

ENCLOSURE

SHIPS FOR THE EXPEDITIONARY FORCE

Needs	Deadweight tonnage
Army	4,000,000
Navy	500,000
Allies	1,500,000
Necessary trade	1,700,000
Total needs	7,700,000

Resources

American fleet	2,600,000
New Ships	800,000
Foreign ships under	
American charter	1,000,000
Total Resources	4,400,000

Balance to be supplied   3,300,000

The needs do not take into account any sinkings.

The resources do not take into account foreign shipping or sailing vessels that will carry part of our "Necessary Trade."

If the program of transporting an army of 1,000,000 men and the necessary cargo to France before the first of July is to be carried out, and the needs of our Navy and our Allies are to be met, it appears that there must be furnished 3,300,000 deadweight tons of shipping in addition to present resources, including new ships to be built. This figure might be reduced by several hundred thousand tons by using neutral ships now idle in American harbors.

A determination of the military program and of the total shipping which will be available for meeting that program as well as the other necessary needs will enable a Director of Shipping to allocate the ships from time to time so as to insure the most effective use of each, including the use of neutral ships in coastwise or regular import trade, the maximum use of sailing vessels, and the discontinuance of the use of ships for unnecessary trade.

T MS (WP, DLC).

From Newton Diehl Baker

Information

My dear Mr. President: Washington. January 5, 1918.

General Gorgas has just brought me information to the effect that no troops have gone to New York from any Southern camp later than December 1st, except certain contingents from Fort Myer, Virginia, St. Asaphs, Virginia, and Newport News.

Inquiry has been made in New York at the hospital referred to in Mr. Gavit's letter, and it develops that there are in all forty soldiers in and about New York suffering from pneumonia. Of these only two are from the South, or have come from Southern camps; neither case ever having had measles. Mr. Gavit's information, therefore, seems to have been erroneous.

I am returning Mr. Gavit's letter to you, but have retained a copy and have written him directly.

Respectfully yours,   Newton D. Baker

TLS (WP, DLC).

From Gutzon Borglum

New York, January 5, 1918.

Your communication just received. I will reach Washington to-morrow.[1]   Gutzon Borglum.

T telegram (WP, DLC).
[1] WWhw notation on this telegram: "Please arrange an appointment at once for Mr. B. with Dr. Stratton, Bureau Standards W.W." Samuel Wesley Stratton was the founder and first Director of the Bureau of Standards.

William Graves Sharp to Robert Lansing

Paris. Jan. 5, 1918.

3002, Confidential. My telegram to the President number 2900, December 15th.[1] Mr. Cambon, now in the office of the Ministry of War in charge of matters under Mr. Clemenceau having to do with American Army, following a recent talk with him, has just sent over to me a note from which I quote the material part as follows. "(Blue) As I told you this question of gasoline for motors is of great gravity and can influence heavily the very conduct of the struggle and the result of the war. The only remedy to the critical situation from the point of view of the French Armies which are holding the greater part of the Occidental front, is the permanent and definite assignment to the importations into France of tank tonnage permitting the transport of eighty thousand seven hundred and ninety-two tons per month (fifty-five thousand two hundred ninety-two tons of gasoline and twenty-five thousand five hundred tons of petroleum) total of nine hundred sixty-nine thousand tons per year.

But France at this moment scarcely possesses half the tonnage which would be necessary to reach this total amount annually of importation. The United States alone can cover this deficit by the assignment of a part of the ships which are today in Pacific or coastwise traffic. It is a decision vital for the war which the Government of Washington must here face. I ask you to again call its attention in the most pressing manner to the urgency of arriving in the shortest possible delay at a practical result. Actual necessity compels us to know as soon as possible the reply of your Government."   Sharp.

T telegram (SDR, RG 59, 763.72/8428, DNA).
[1] W. G. Sharp to WW, Dec. 15, 1917.

The Shorthand Draft of the Fourteen Points Address[1]

[Jan. 6, 1918]

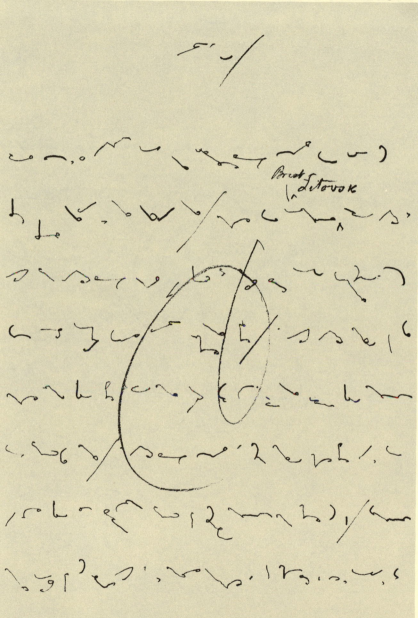

[1] Following Wilson's and House's discussions on Sunday, January 6, Wilson (as the Head Usher's Diary reveals) closeted himself in his study all day. This was when he wrote this shorthand draft and typed the transcript which is printed as the next document.

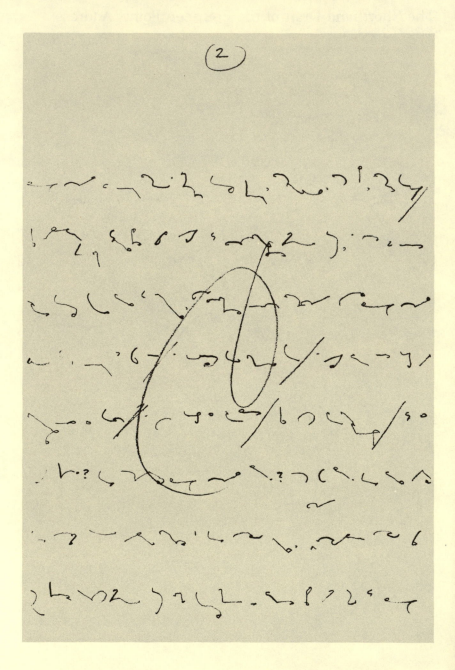

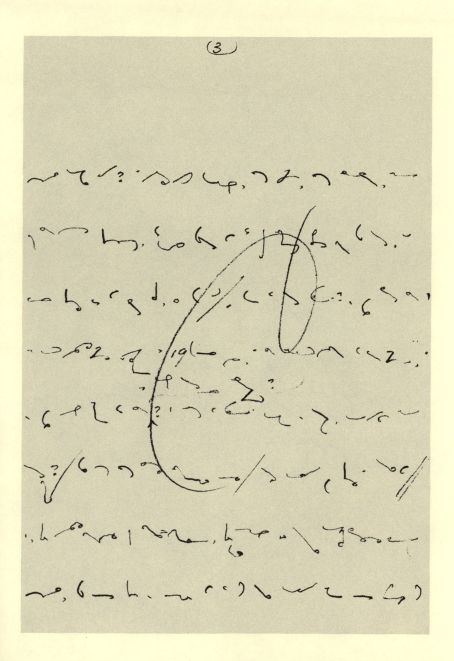

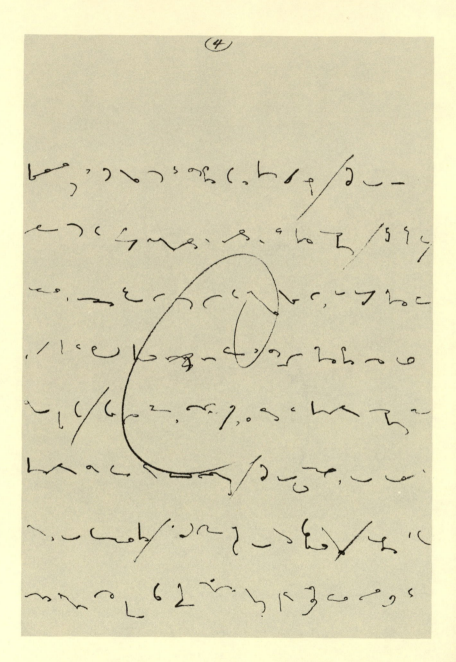

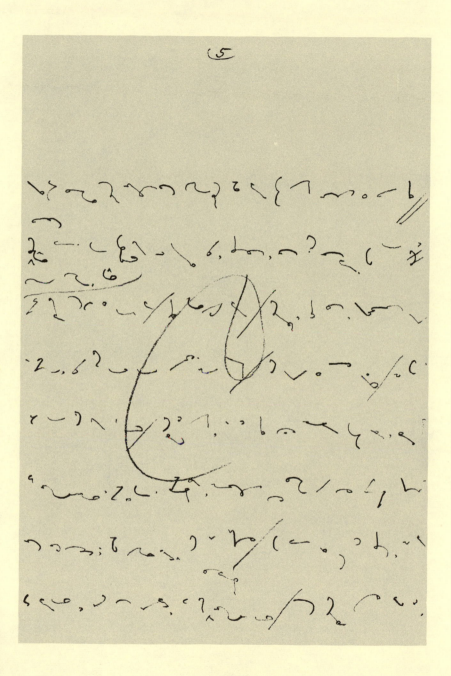

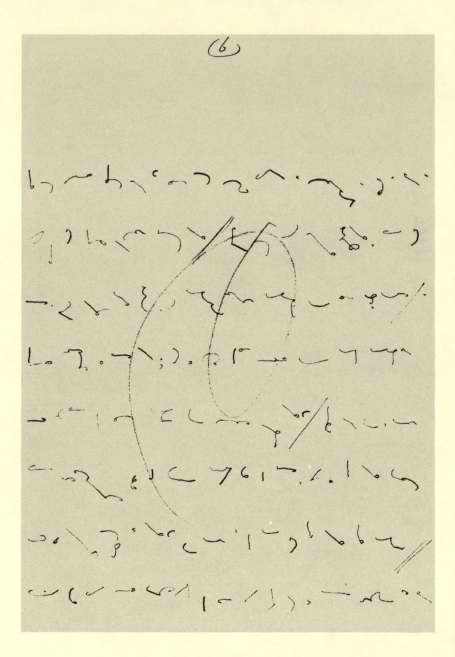

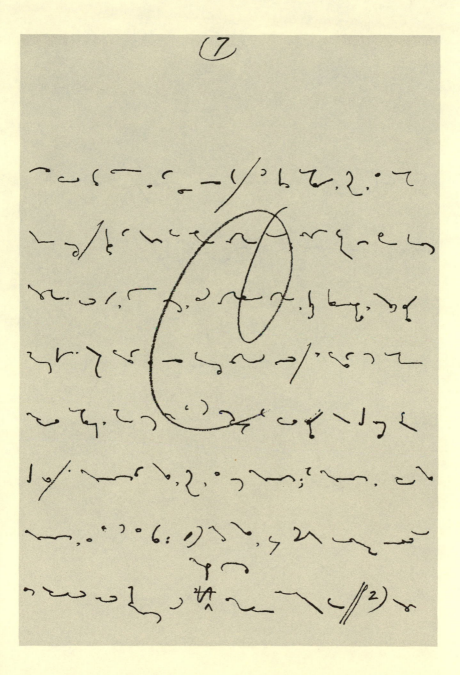

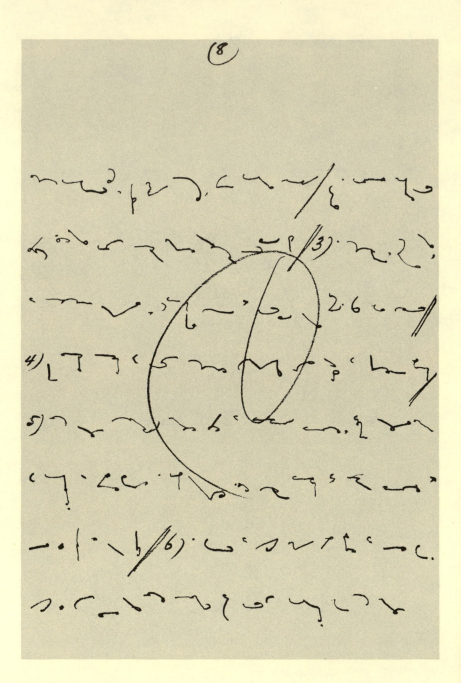

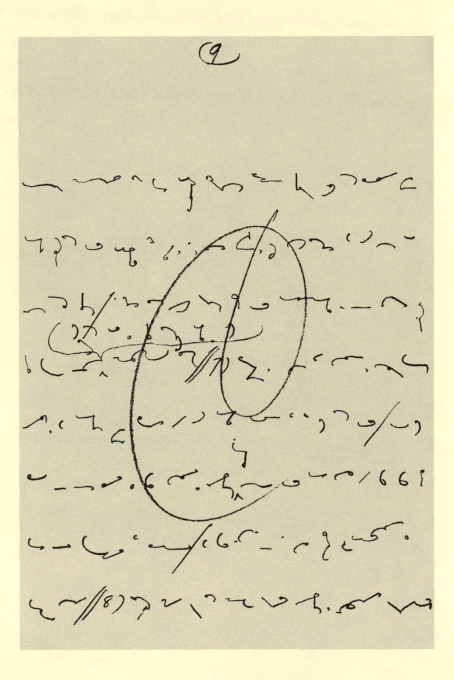

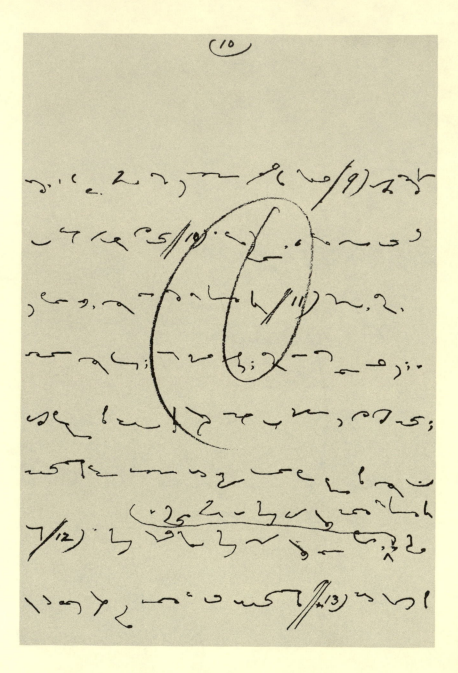

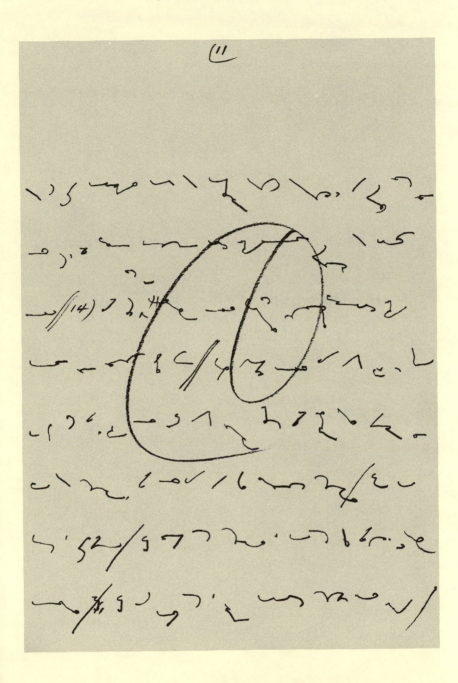

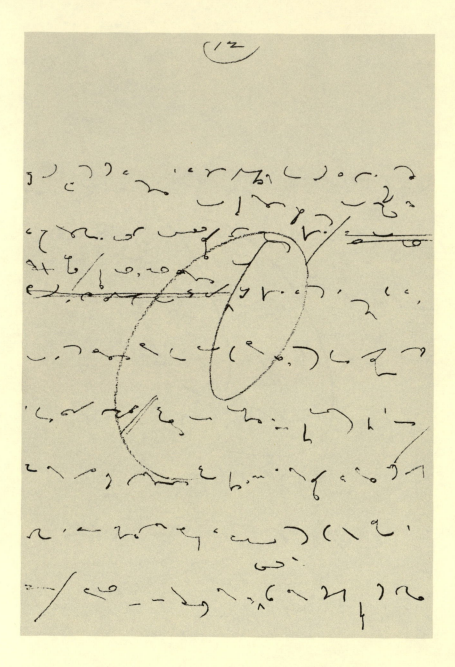

Wilson's Transcript of His Shorthand Draft[1]

Address to Congress
8 January, 1918

Once more, as repeatedly before, the spokesmen of the Central Empires have indicated their desire to discuss the objects of the war and the possible, bases of a general peace. Parlies have been in progress at Brest-Litovsk between representatives of the Russian people and representatives of the Central Powers to which the attention of all the belligerents has been invited. for the purpose of ascertaining whether it may be possible to extend *these parlies* into a general conference with regard to terms of peace and settlement. The Russian representatives presented at these parlies *not only* a perfectly definite statement ~~not only~~ of the principles upon which they would be willing to conclude peace but also an equally definite programme of the concrete application of those principles. The representatives of the Central Powers, on their part, presented an outline of settlement which, if much less definite, seemed susceptible of liberal interpretation until their specific programme of practical terms was added. That programme proposed no concessesions at all either to the sovereignty of Russia or to the preferences of the populations with whose fortunes it dealt, but meant, in a word, that the Central Empires were to keep every foot of territory their armed forces had occupied, — every province, every city, every

---

[1] The reader should bear in mind that this is the draft which Wilson and House went over together on Monday, January 7. House, in his diary entry for January 9, explains Wilson's and his discussions about certain major issues and the changes which Wilson made. Wilson probably made most of the purely literary changes before he read the transcript to House.

-2-

point of vantage, — as a permanent addition to
their territories and their power. It is a reasonable conjecture that the general principles
of settlement which they at first suggested originated with the more liberal statesmen of Germany and Austria, the men who have begun to feel
the force of their own peoples' thought and purpose, while the concrete terms of final actual
arrangement came from the military leaders who
have no thought but to keep what they have got.
The negotiations have been broken off. The Russian representatives were sincere and in earnest.
They cannot entertain such proposals of conquest
and domination.

     The whole incident is full of significance.
It is also full of perplexity. With whom ~~is Rus-
sia~~ *are the Russian representatives* dealing? For whom are the representatives of
the Central Empires speaking? Are they speaking
for the majorities of their respective parliaments or for the minority parties, that military
and imperialistic ~~majority~~ *minority* which has so far dominated their whole policy and controlled the affairs of Turkey and of the Balkan states which
have felt obliged to become their associates in
this war? The *Russian* representatives ~~of Russia~~ have insisted, very justly, very ~~sensibly~~ *wisely*, and in the
true spirit of modern democracy, that the conferences they have been holding with the Teutonic

Wilson and House had completed their review at least by 3 P.M., when Wilson called
in Lansing and read the revised draft to him. As House writes: "Lansing accepted it in toto,
although he made several suggestions as to words which the President adopted." There seems
to be no way to determine what these changes were.

-3-

and Turkish statesmen should be held within open,
not closed, doors, and all the world has been
audience, as they wished.   To whom have we been
listening, then?   To those who speak the spirit
and intention of the Resolutions of the German
Reichstag of the *ninth of July*   last,
the spirit and intention of the liberal leaders
and parties of Germany, or to those who resist
and defy that spirit and intention and insist
upon conquest and subjugation?   Or are we listening, in fact, to both, unreconciled and in
open and hopeless contradiction?   These are very
serious and pregnant questions.   Upon the answer
to them depends the peace of the world.

But, whatever the results of the parlies
at Brest-Litovsk, whatever the confusions of
counsel and of purpose in the utterances of the
spokesmen of the Central Empires, they have a-
gain attempted to acquaint the world with their
objects in the war and have again challenged
their adversaries to say what their objects are
and what sort of settlement they would deem just
and satisfactory.   There is no good reason why
that challenge should not be responded to, and
responded to with the utmost candour.   We did
not wait for it.   Not once, but again and again,
we have laid our whole thought and purpose before the world, not in general terms only but
each time with sufficient definition to make it

-4-

The only secrecy of counsel, the only lack of fearless frankness, the only failure to make definite statement of the objects of the war lies with Germany and her Allies.

clear what sort of actual terms of settlement
must necessarily spring out of them. Within the
last week Mr. Lloyd George has spoken with admir-
mirable candour and in admirable spirit for the
people and government of Great Britain. There is
no confusion of counsel among the adversaries of
the Central Powers, no uncertainty of principle,
no vagueness of detail. The issues of life and
death hang upon these definitions. of purpose.
No statesman who has the least conception of his
responsibility ought for a moment to permit himself to continue this tragical and appaling *outpouring* pouring out of blood and treasure unless he is sure
beyond a peradventure that the objects of the vital sacrifice are part and parcel of the very
life of Society and that *the* his people think *for whom he speaks* them
right and imperative as he does.

There is, moreover, a voice calling for
these definitions of principle and of purpose
which is, it seems to me, more thrilling and
more compelling than any of the many moving
voices with which the troubled air of the world
is filled. It is the voice of the Russian people. They are prostrate and all but helpless,
it would seem, before the grim power of Germany,
which has hitherto known no relenting and no
pity. Their power *apparently* is shattered. And yet their
soul is not subservient. They will not yield
either in principle or in action. Their concep-*tion*

-5-

of what is right, of what it is humane and honourable for them to accept, has been stated with
a frankness, a largeness of view, a generosity of
spirit, and a universal human sympathy which
must challenge the admiration of every friend of
mankind; and they have refused to compound their
ideals or desert others that they themselves may
be safe. They call to us to say what it is that
we desire, in what, if in anything, our purpose
and our spirit differ from theirs, and I believe
that the people of the United States would wish
me to respond, with utter simplicity and franknes:
Whether their present leaders believe it or not,
it is our heartfelt desire and hope that some way
may be opened whereby we may be privileged to assist the people of Russia to attain their utmost
hope of liberty and ordered peace.

It will be our wish and purpose that the processes of peace, when they are begun, shall be
absolutely open and that they shall involve and
permit henceforth no secret understandings of
any kind. The day of conquest and aggrandizement is gone by; so is also the day of secret
covenants entered into in the interest of particular governments and likely at some unlooked
for moment to upset the peace of the world. It
is this happy fact, now clear to the view of

-6-

every public man whose thoughts do not still linger in an age that is dead and gone, which makes
it possible for every nation whose purposes are
consistent with justice and the peace of the
world to avow now or at any other time the objects it has in view.

     We entered this war because violations of
right had occurred which touched us to the quick
and made the life of our own people impossible
unless they were corrected and the world secured
once for all against their recurrence. What we
demand in this war, therefore, is nothing peculiar to ourselves. It is that the world be made
fit and safe to live in; and particularly that
it be made safe for every peace loving nation
which, like our own, wishes to live its own life,
determine its own institutions, be assured of
justice and fair dealing by the other peoples of
the world as against force and selfish aggression.
All the peoples of the world are in effect partners in this interest, and for our own part we
see very clearly that unless justice be done to
others it will not be done to us. The programme
of the world's peace, therefore, is our programme;
and that programme, the only possible programme,
as we see it, is this:
     I. Open covenants of peace, openly arrived at, after which there

-7-

shall be no private international understandings
of any kind but diplomacy shall proceed always
frankly and in the public view.

II. Absolute freedom of navigation upon the
seas, outside territorial waters, alike in peace
and in war, except as the seas may be closed in
whole or in part by international action for the enforcement of international covenants.

III. The removal, so far as possible, of all
economic barriers and the establishment of an e-
quality of trade conditions among all the nations
consenting to the peace and associating themselves
for its maintenance.

IV. Adequate guarantees given and taken that
national armaments will be reduced to the lowest
point consistent with domestic safety.

V. A free, open-minded, and absolutely impartial adjustment of all colonial claims, based upon a strict observance of the principle that in
determining all such questions of sovereignty the
interests of the populations concerned must have
equal weight with the equitable claims of the
government whose title is to be determined.

VI. The evacuation of all Russoan territory
and such a settlement of all questions affecting

-8-

Russia as will secure the best and freest cooperation of ~~all~~ the other nations of the world in obtaining for her an ~~absolutely~~ unhampered and unembarrassed opportunity for the independent determination of her own political development and national policy and assure her of a sincere welcome
into the society of free nations under institutions
of her own choosing, and, more than a welcome, assistance also of every kind that she may need and
may herself desire. The treatment accorded Russia
by her sister nations in the months to come will
be the acid test of their good will, of their comprehension of her needs as distinguished from their
own interests, and of their intelligent and unselfish sympathy.

     VII. Belgium, the whole world will agree, must
be evacuated and restored, without any attempt to
limit the sovereignty which she enjoys in common
with all other free nations. No other single act
will serve as this will serve to restore confidence among the nations in the laws which they
have themselves set and determined for the government of their relations with one another. Without
this healing act the whole structure and validity
of international law is forever impaired.

     VIII. All French territory _should_ ~~must~~ be freed and
the invaded portions restored, ~~and Alsace-Lorraine~~ _and the wrong done_
~~should~~ to France by Prussia in 1871 in the matter of
~~must be reunited to France, but without excluding~~

in order that — *—o— be made*

~~and~~ that peace ▄▄▄ once more secure in the interest
of all.

Alsace-Lorraine, which has unsettled the peace of
~~Germany from the use of the economic resources of~~
~~the world for~~ nearly fifty years, should be righted.

IX. A readjustment of the frontiers of Italy
should ~~must~~ be effected along clearly recognizable lines
of nationality.

X. The peoples of Austria-Hungary, whose place
among the nations we wish to see safeguarded and
assured, ~~must~~ *should* be accorded the freest opportunity
of autonomous development.

XI. Rumania, Serbia, and Montenegro ~~must~~ *should* be
evacuated; occupied territories restored; Serbia
accorded free and secure access to the sea; and
the relations of the several Balkan states to one
another determined by friendly counsel along historically established lines of allegiance and nationality; and international guarantees of the
political and economic independence and territorial integrity of the several Balkan states ~~must~~ *should*
be entered into.

XII. The Turkish portions of the present ~~Tur-~~
~~kish~~ *Ottoman* Empire ~~must~~ *should* be assured a secure sovereignty,
but the other nationalities which are now under
Turkish rule ~~must~~ *should* be assured an undoubted security
of life and an absolutely unmolested opportunity
of autonomous development, and the Dardanelles
~~must~~ *should* be permanently opened as a free passage to
the ships and commerce of all nations under international guarantees.

-10-

XIII. An independent Polish state ~~must~~ *should* be e-
rected which ~~shall~~ *should* include the territories inhabited by indisputably Polish populations, which
~~shall~~ *should* be assured a free and secure access to the
sea, and whose political and economic independence
and territorial integrity ~~shall~~ *should* be guaranteed by
international covenant.

XIV. A general association of nations must be
formed under specific covenants for the purpose
of affording mutual guarantees of political independence and territorial integrity to great and
small states alike.

For such arrangements and covenants we are
willing to fight and to continue to fight until
they are achieved; but only because we wish the
right to prevail and desire a just and stable
peace such as can be secured only by removing the
provocations to
chief ~~causes of~~ war which this programme does remove. We have no jealousy of German greatness,
and there is nothing in this programme that impairs it. We grudge her no achievement or distinction of learning or of pacific enterprise
such as have made her record very bright and very
enviable. We do not wish to injure her or to
block in any way her legitimate influence or power. We do not wish to fight her either with arms
or with hostile arrangements of trade if she is
willing to associate herself with us and the o-
~~ther peoples of the world.~~

[marginal note, printed vertically:] In regard to these essential rectifications of wrong and assertions of right we feel ourselves to be intimate partners of all the governments and peoples associated together against the imperialists. We cannot be separated in interest or divided in purpose. We stand together until the end.

-11-

ther peace loving nations of the world in covenants of justice and law and fair dealing. We wish
her only to accept a place of equality among the
peoples of the world,—the new world in which we
now live,—instead of a place of mastery.

Neither do we presume to suggest to her any
alteration or modification of her institutions.
But it is necessary, we must frankly say, and necessary as a preliminary to any intelligent dealings with her on our part, that we should know
whom her spokesmen speak for when they speak to us
whether for the Reichstag majority or for the military party and the men whose creed is imperial
domination.

We have spoken now, surely, in terms too concrete to admit of any further doubt or question.
An evident principle runs through the whole programme I have outlined. It is the principle of
justice to all peoples and nationalities, and
their right to live on equal terms of liberty and
safety with one another, whether they be strong
or weak. The people of the United States could
act upon no other principle; and to the vindication of this principle they are ready to devote
their lives, their honour, and everything that
they possess.   The moral climax of this the order

[left margin, rotated] Unless this principle,be made its foundation no part of the structure
of international law can stand.

-12-

culminating and final war for human liberty has
come, and they are ready to put their own strength,
their own highest purpose, their own integrity and
devotion to the test.

From George Francis O'Shaunessy[1]

Dear Mr. President: Washington, D. C. January 6, 1918.

The Suffrage Amendment comes up for consideration in the House next Thursday. I have always advocated it in the belief that its adoption and subsequent ratification by the States would add to the sum of human progress and freedom. I believe that the vote will be a close one, and I appreciate thoroughly the impetus the movement would obtain by your endorsement.

With cordial good wishes, believe me,

Sincerely yours,   G. F O'Shaunessy.

TLS (WP, DLC).
    [1] Democratic congressman from Rhode Island.

Sir Cecil Arthur Spring Rice to Arthur James Balfour

Washington January 6th, 1918.

Personal and Secret.

Colonel House told me that President had at first been somewhat mystified by the Premier's detailed statement of War Aims, but that your explanation would make the matter perfectly plain. He was aware of the President's personal message to you,[1] and asked me to tell you that the situation as therein described was not changed by the Prime Minister's speech. If you have a further message, please send it before January 9th, but please bear in mind the extremely personal and confidential nature of his message.

T telegram (A. J. Balfour Papers, FO 800/205, PRO).
    [1] That is, the message embodied in C. A. Spring Rice to A. J. Balfour, Jan. 4, 1918.

The Final Draft of the Fourteen Points Address[1]

[Jan. 7, 1918]

Once more, as repeatedly before, the spokesmen of the Central Empires have indicated their desire to discuss the objects of the war and the possible bases of a general peace. *Parleys* have been in progress at Brest-Litovsk between representatives of the Central Powers to which the attention of all the belligerents has been invited for the purpose of ascertaining whether it may be possible to extend these *parleys* into a general conference with regard to terms of peace and settlement. The Russian representatives presented not only a perfectly definite statement of the principles upon which they would be willing to conclude peace but also an equally definite programme of the concrete application of these principles. The representatives of the Central Powers, on their part, presented an outline of settlement which, if much less definite, seemed susceptible of liberal interpretation until their specific programme of practical terms was added. That programme proposed no concessions at all either to the sovereignty of Russia or to the preferences of the populations with whose fortunes it dealt, but meant, in a word, that

the Central Empires were to keep every foot of territory their armed forces had occupied,—every province, every city, every point of vantage,—as a permanent addition to their territories and their power. It is a reasonable conjecture that the general principles of settlement which they at first suggested originated with the more liberal statesmen of Germany and Austria, the men who have begun to feel the force of their own peoples' thought and purpose, while the concrete terms of actual *settlement* came from the military leaders who have no thought but to keep what they have got. The negotiations have been broken off. The Russian representatives were sincere and in earnest. They cannot entertain such proposals of conquest and domination.

[1] This is the draft which Wilson sent to the Public Printer. Markings, cuttings, and pastings by the typesetter.

The whole incident is full of significance. It is also full of

perplexity. With whom are the Russian representatives dealing? For whom 2)

are the representatives of the Central Empires speaking? Are they speak-

ing for the majorities of their respective parliaments or for the minority

parties, that military and imperialistic minority which has so far domi-

nated their whole policy and controlled the affairs of Turkey and of the

Balkan states which have felt obliged to become their associates in this

war? The Russian representatives have insisted, very justly, very wisely,

and in the true spirit of modern democracy, that the conferences they have

been holding with the Teutonic and Turkish statesmen should be held within

open, not closed, doors, and all the world has been audience, as ~~they wished~~ *was desired*.

To whom have we been listening, then? To those who speak the spirit and

intention of the Resolutions of the German Reichstag of the ninth of July

last, the spirit and intention of the liberal leaders and parties of Germany,

or to those who resist and defy that spirit and intention and insist upon

conquest and subjugation? Or are we listening, in fact, to both, unrecon-

ciled and in open and hopeless contradiction? These are very serious and

pregnant questions. Upon the answer to them depends the peace of the world.

But, whatever the results of the *parleys* at Brest-Litovsk, whatever

the confusions of counsel and of purpose in the utterances of the spokes-

men of the Central Empires, they have again attempted to acquaint the world

with their objects in the war and have again challenged their adversaries   ③

to say what their objects are and what sort of settlement they would deem

just and satisfactory. There is no good reason why that challenge should

not be responded to, and responded to with the utmost candor. We did not

wait for it. Not once, but again and again, we have laid our whole thought

and purpose before the world, not in general terms only, but each time with

sufficient definition to make it clear what sort of *definitive* terms of settle-

ment must necessarily spring out of them. Within the last week Mr. Lloyd

George has spoken with admirable candor and in admirable spirit for the

people and Government of Great Britain. There is no confusion of counsel

among the adversaries of the Central Powers, no uncertainty of principle,

no vagueness of detail. The only secrecy of counsel, the only lack of

fearless frankness, the only failure to make definite statement of the ob-

jects of the war, lies with Germany and her Allies. The issues of life

and death hang upon these definitions. No statesman who has the least

conception of his responsibility ought for a moment to permit himself to

continue this tragical and appalling outpouring of blood and treasure un-

less he is sure beyond a peradventure that the objects of the vital sacri-

fice are part and parcel of the very life of Society and that the people

for whom he speaks think them right and imperative as he does.

There is, moreover, a voice calling for these definitions of

principle and of purpose which is, it seems to me, more thrilling and more

compelling than any of the many moving voices with which the troubled air of

the world is filled. It is the voice of the Russian people. They are

prostrate and all but helpless, it would seem, before the grim power of

Germany, which has hitherto known no relenting and no pity. Their power,

apparently, is shattered. And yet their soul is not subservient. They will

not yield either in principle or in action. Their conception of what is

right, of what it is humane and honorable for them to accept, has been stated

with a frankness, a largeness of view, a generosity of spirit, and a

universal human sympathy which must challenge the admiration of every friend

of mankind; and they have refused to compound their ideals or desert others

that they themselves may be safe. They call to us to say what it is that

we desire, in what, if in anything, our purpose and our spirit differ from

theirs; and I believe that the people of the United States would wish me to

respond, with utter simplicity and frankness. Whether their present leaders

believe it or not, it is our heartfelt desire and hope that some way may

be opened whereby we may be privileged to assist the people of Russia to at-

tain their utmost hope of liberty and ordered peace.

It will be our wish and purpose that the processes of peace, when they are begun, shall be absolutely open and that they shall involve and permit henceforth no secret understandings of any kind. The day of conquest and aggrandizement is gone by; so is also the day of secret covenants entered into in the interest of particular governments and likely at some unlooked-for moment to upset the peace of the world. It is this happy fact, now clear

5

to the view of every public man whose thoughts do not still linger in an age that is dead and gone, which makes it possible for every nation whose purposes are consistent with justice and the peace of the world to avow now or at any other time the objects it has in view.

We entered this war because violations of right had occurred
which touched us to the quick and made the life of our own people impossible
unless they were corrected and the world secured once for all against their
recurrence. What we demand in this war, therefore, is nothing peculiar to
ourselves. It is that the world be made fit and safe to live in; and particularly that it be made safe for every peace-loving nation which, like our
own, wishes to live its own life, determine its own institutions, be assured
of justice and fair dealing by the other peoples of the world as against
force and selfish aggression. All the peoples of the world are in effect
partners in this interest, and for our own part we see very clearly that
unless justice be done to others it will not be done to us. The programme
of the world's peace, therefore, is our programme; and that programme, the

only possible programme, as we see it, is this:

I. Open covenants of peace, openly arrive^d at, after which there shall be no private international understandings of any kind but diplomacy shall proceed always frankly and in the public view.

II. Absolute freedom of navigation upon the seas, outside territorial waters, alike in peace and in war, except as the seas may be closed in whole or in part by international action for the enforcement of international covenants.

III. The removal, so far as possible, of all economic barriers and the establishment of an equality of trade conditions among all the nations consenting to the peace and associating themselves for its maintenance.

IV. Adequate guarantees given and taken that national armaments will be reduced to the lowest point consistent with domestic safety.

V. A free, open-minded, and absolutely impartial adjustment of all colonial claims, based upon a strict observance of the principle that

in determining all such questions of sovereignty the interests of the populations concerned must have equal weight with the equitable claims of the government whose title is to be determined.

VI.   The evacuation of all Russian territory and such a settlement of all questions affecting Russia as will secure the best and freest
cooperation of the other nations of the world in obtaining for her an unhampered and unembarrassed opportunity for the independent determination
of her own political development and national policy and assure her of a
sincere welcome into the society of free nations under institutions of her
own choosing; and, more than a welcome, assistance also of every kind that
she may need and may herself desire. The treatment accorded Russia by her
sister nations in the months to come will be the acid test of their good
will, of their comprehension of her needs as distinguished from their own
interests, and of their intelligent and unselfish sympathy.

VII. Belgium, the whole world will agree, must be evacuated and
restored, without any attempt to limit the sovereignty which she enjoys in

common with all other free nations. No other single act will serve as
this will serve to restore confidence among the nations in the laws which
they have themselves set and determined for the government of their relations with one another. Without this healing act the whole structure and
validity of international law is forever impaired.

VIII. All French territory should be freed and the invaded portions restored, and the wrong done to France by Prussia in 1871 in the matter of Alsace-Lorraine, which has unsettled the peace of the world for nearly fifty years, should be righted, in order that peace may once more be made secure in the interest of all.

IX. A readjustment of the frontiers of Italy should be effected along clearly recognizable lines of nationality.

X. The peoples of Austria-Hungary, whose place among the nations we wish to see safeguarded and assured, should be accorded the freest opportunity of autonomous development.

-11-

XI. Rumania, Serbia, and Montenegro should be evacuated; occupied territories restored; Serbia accorded free and secure access to the sea; and the relations of the several Balkan states to one another determined by friendly counsel along historically established lines of allegiance and nationality; and international guarantees of the political and economic independence and territorial integrity of the several Balkan states should be entered into.

XII. The Turkish portions of the present Ottoman Empire should be assured a secure sovereignty, but the other nationalities which are now under Turkish rule should be assured an undoubted security of life and an absolutely unmolested opportunity of autonomous development, and the Dardanelles should be permanently opened as a free passage to the ships and commerce of all nations under international guarantees.

XIII. An independent Polish state should be erected which should
include the territories inhabited by indisputably Polish populations, which

should be assured a free and secure access to the sea, and whose political
and economic independence and territorial integrity should be guaranteed
by international covenant.

XIV. A general association of nations must be formed under
specific covenants for the purpose of affording mutual guarantees of political independence and territorial integrity to great and small states alike.

In regard to these essential rectifications of wrong and assertions
of right we feel ourselves to be intimate partners of all the governments
and peoples associated together against the Imperialists. We cannot be
separated in interest or divided in purpose. We stand together until the
end.

For such arrangements and covenants we are willing to fight and
to continue to fight until they are achieved; but only because we wish the
right to prevail and desire a just and stable peace such as can be secured
only by removing the chief provocations to war, which this programme does remove. We have no jealousy of German greatness, and there is nothing in this

programme that impairs it. We grudge her no achivement or distinction of
learning or of pacific enterprise such as have made her record very bright
and very enviable. We do not wish to injure her or to block in any way
her legitimate influence or power. We do not wish to fight her either with
arms or with hostile arrangements of trade if she is willing to associate
herself with us and the other peace-loving nations of the world in covenants
of justice and law and fair dealing. We wish her only to accept a place of
equality among the peoples of the world,—the new world in which we now live,—
instead of a place of mastery.

Neither do we presume to suggest to her any alteration or modification of her institutions. But it is necessary, we must frankly say, and
necessary as a preliminary to any intelligent dealings with her on our part,
that we should know whom her spokesmen speak for when they speak to us,
whether for the Reichstag majority or for the military party and the men
whose creed is imperial domination.

We have spoken now, surely, in terms too concrete to admit of any

further doubt or question. An evident principle runs through the whole

programme I have outlined. It is the principle of justice to all peoples

and nationalities, and their right to live on equal terms of liberty and

safety with one another, whether they be strong or weak. Unless this princi-

ple be made its foundation no part of the structure of international justice

can stand. The people of the United States could act upon no other

principle; and to the vindication of this principle they are ready to devote

their lives, their honor, and everything that they possess. The moral

climax of this the culminating and final war for human liberty has come,

and they are ready to put their own strength, their own highest purpose,

their own integrity and devotion to the test.

From William Gibbs McAdoo, with Enclosures

Dear Mr. President: Washington January 7, 1917.

Referring to my note of January 2, with which I sent you copy of a letter I had written to the Secretary of War, making a suggestion in reference to the forthcoming visit of General Bliss to Europe, I now beg to send you the enclosed copy of a reply to my letter from the Secretary of War, together with a copy of a cable which I have asked the Secretary of State to have sent to Mr. Crosby.

Cordially yours,   W G McAdoo

TLS (WP, DLC).

E N C L O S U R E   I

Newton Diehl Baker to William Gibbs McAdoo

Dear Mr. Secretary,   Washington January 4th, 1918.

I am in receipt of your letter of January 2nd in which you express the hope that there may be a discussion of the whole military program with the military authorities of the Allied Governments with a view to determining what restriction should be imposed upon expenditures by our War Department due to the restrictions imposed by the shipping problem upon the transportation of our troops and supplies. You also refer to the effect which such expenditures by the War Department have upon the advances which might otherwise be made available by the United States Treasury to the Allies.

I agree with you that this is a most important study and should be made without delay. This study should result in the coordination of the demands of the other Allied Governments and of the United States with reference to the shipping problem and to the financial problem. To do this effectually, there is no doubt as to the desirability of having a representative of the War Department on the Inter-Ally Council.

As you have requested, I have instructed the Chief of Staff to confer with Mr. Crosby and to cooperate with him along the lines suggested in your letter. The position of General Bliss on the Supreme War Council will enable him to determine with exactness the demands which the other Allied Governments will make upon our military resources and should he find that he could perform full duty upon both the Supreme War Council and the Inter-Ally Council, it might be well to assign him as our military representative upon the latter. The practicability of this, he could probably ascertain soon after conferring with Mr. Crosby in London and, in making any further suggestion to you on the subject, I shall be guided by his recommendation.

Meanwhile, as I have said above, I have very gladly given him instruction to proceed on the line indicated in your letter.

Cordially yours,   Newton D. Baker

ENCLOSURE   II

William Gibbs McAdoo to Robert Lansing

Dear Mr. Secretary: [Washington] January 5, 1918.

May I ask that you kindly have the following cable sent to Mr. Crosby, the substance of which has the approval of Secretary Baker:

Treasury Number 50. I have presented to Secretary War the need for a full discussion of the whole military program with the military authorities of the Allied Governments with a view to determining whether an unrestricted expenditure upon the part of our War Department is advisable having in mind the restrictions which the shipping problem will impose upon the transportation of troops and supplies and the limitations which such expenditures by our War Department will necessarily impose upon the advances which might otherwise be made available by the United States Treasury to the Allies. Secretary of War fully in accord with the pressing need for a study along these lines and agrees also that to do this effectually there should be a United States military representative on the Inter-Ally Council. He has accordingly instructed General Bliss, Chief of Staff, on his return to Europe shortly to confer with you and to cooperate in every way. As American military representative on the Supreme War Council, General Bliss will be in a position to determine with exactness the demands which the other allied governments will make upon our military resources, and should he find that he could perform full duty on both the Supreme War Council and the Inter-Ally Council, the Secretary of War feels that it might be well to assign him as our military representative on the Council. He will await action on this pending recommendation from General Bliss after conference with you.

Cordially yours,   W. G. McAdoo

CCL (WP, DLC).

An Address to a Joint Session of Congress

8 Jan'y, 1918.[1]

Gentlemen of the Congress: Once more, as repeatedly before, the spokesmen of the Central Empires have indicated their desire to discuss the objects of the war and the possible bases of a general peace. Parleys have been in progress at Brest-Litovsk between representatives of the Central Powers, to which the attention of all the belligerents has been invited for the purpose of ascertaining whether it may be possible to extend these parleys into a general conference with regard to terms of peace and settlement. The Russian representatives presented not only a perfectly definite statement of the principles upon which they would be willing to conclude peace, but also an equally definite programme of the concrete application of those principles. The representatives of the Central Powers, on their part, presented an outline of settlement which, if much less definite, seemed susceptible of liberal interpretation until their specific programme of practical terms was added. That programme proposed no concessions at all either to the sovereignty of Russia or to the preferences of the populations with whose fortunes it dealt, but meant, in a word, that the Central Empires were to keep every foot of territory their armed forces had occupied,—every province, every city, every point of vantage,—as a permanent addition to their territories and their power. It is a reasonable conjecture that the general principles of settlement which they at first suggested originated with the more liberal statesmen of Germany and Austria, the men who have begun to feel the force of their own peoples' thought and purpose, while the concrete terms of actual settlement came from the military leaders who have no thought but to keep what they have got. The negotiations have been broken off. The Russian representatives were sincere and in earnest. They cannot entertain such proposals of conquest and domination.

The whole incident is full of significance. It is also full of perplexity. With whom are the Russian representatives dealing? For whom are the representatives of the Central Empires speaking? Are they speaking for the majorities of their respective parliaments or for the minority parties, that military and imperialistic minority which has so far dominated their whole policy and controlled the affairs of Turkey and of the Balkan states which have felt obliged to become their associates in this war? The Russian representatives have insisted, very justly, very wisely, and in the true spirit of modern democracy, that the conferences they have been holding

[1] WWhw.

with the Teutonic and Turkish statesmen should be held within open, not closed doors, and all the world has been audience, as was desired. To whom have we been listening, then? To those who speak the spirit and intention of the Resolutions of the German Reichstag of the ninth of July last, the spirit and intention of the liberal leaders and parties of Germany, or to those who resist and defy that spirit and intention and insist upon conquest and subjugation? Or are we listening, in fact, to both, unreconciled and in open and hopeless contradiction? These are very serious and pregnant questions. Upon the answer to them depends the peace of the world.

But, whatever the results of the parleys at Brest-Litovsk, whatever the confusions of counsel and of purpose in the utterances of the spokesmen of the Central Empires, they have again attempted to acquaint the world with their objects in the war and have again challenged their adversaries to say what their objects are and what sort of settlement they would deem just and satisfactory. There is no good reason why that challenge should not be responded to, and responded to with the utmost candor. We did not wait for it. Not once, but again and again, we have laid our whole thought and purpose before the world, not in general terms only, but each time with sufficient definition to make it clear what sort of definitive terms of settlement must necessarily spring out of them. Within the last week Mr. Lloyd George has spoken with admirable candor and in admirable spirit for the people and Government of Great Britain. There is no confusion of counsel among the adversaries of the Central Powers, no uncertainty of principle, no vagueness of detail. The only secrecy of counsel, the only lack of fearless frankness, the only failure to make definite statement of the objects of the war, lies with Germany and her Allies. The issues of life and death hang upon these definitions. No statesman who has the least conception of his responsibility ought for a moment to permit himself to continue this tragical and appalling outpouring of blood and treasure unless he is sure beyond a peradventure that the objects of the vital sacrifice are part and parcel of the very life of Society and that the people for whom he speaks think them right and imperative as he does.

There is, moreover, a voice calling for these definitions of principle and of purpose which is, it seems to me, more thrilling and more compelling than any of the many moving voices with which the troubled air of the world is filled. It is the voice of the Russian people. They are prostrate and all but helpless, it would seem, before the grim power of Germany, which has hitherto known no relenting and no pity. Their power, apparently, is shattered. And yet their soul is not subservient. They will not yield either in principle or in action. Their conception of what is right, of what is humane and honorable for them to accept, has been stated with a frankness, a largeness of view, a generosity of spirit, and a universal human sympathy which must challenge the admiration of every friend of mankind; and they have refused to compound their ideals or desert others that they themselves may be safe. They call to us to say what it is that we desire, in what, if in anything, our purpose and our spirit differ from theirs; and I believe that the people of the United States would wish me to respond, with utter simplicity and frankness. Whether their present leaders believe it or not, it is our heartfelt desire and hope that some way may be opened whereby we may be privileged to assist the people of Russia to attain their utmost hope of liberty and ordered peace.

It will be our wish and purpose that the processes of peace, when they are begun, shall be absolutely open and that they shall involve and permit henceforth no secret understandings of any kind. The day of conquest and aggrandizement is gone by; so is also the day of secret covenants entered into in the interest of particular governments and likely at some unlooked-for moment to upset the peace of the world. It is this happy fact, now clear to the view of every public man whose thoughts do not still linger in an age that is dead and gone, which makes it possible for every nation whose purposes are consistent with justice and the peace of the world to avow now or at any other time the objects it has in view.

We entered this war because violations of right had occurred which touched us to the quick and made the life of our own people impossible unless they were corrected and the world secured once for all against their recurrence. What we demand in this war, therefore, is nothing peculiar to ourselves. It is that the world be made fit and safe to live in; and particularly that it be made safe for every peace-loving nation which, like our own, wishes to live its own life, determine its own institutions, be assured of justice and fair dealing by the other peoples of the world as against force and selfish aggression. All the peoples of the world are in effect partners in this interest, and for our own part we see very clearly that unless justice be done to others it will not be done to us. The programme of the world's peace, therefore, is our programme; and that programme, the only possible programme, as we see it, is this:

I. Open covenants of peace, openly arrived at, after which there shall be no private international understandings of any kind but diplomacy shall proceed always frankly and in the public view.

II. Absolute freedom of navigation upon the seas, outside territorial waters, alike in peace and in war, except as the seas may be closed in whole or in part by international action for the enforcement of international covenants.

III. The removal, so far as possible, of all economic barriers and the establishment of an equality of trade conditions among all the nations consenting to the peace and associating themselves for its maintenance.

IV. Adequate guarantees given and taken that national armaments will be reduced to the lowest point consistent with domestic safety.

V. A free, open-minded, and absolutely impartial adjustment of all colonial claims, based upon a strict observance of the principle that in determining all such questions of sovereignty the interests of the populations concerned must have equal weight with the equitable claims of the government whose title is to be determined.

VI. The evacuation of all Russian territory and such a settlement of all questions affecting Russia as will secure the best and freest cooperation of the other nations of the world in obtaining for her an unhampered and unembarrassed opportunity for the independent determination of her own political development and national policy and assure her of a sincere welcome into the society of free nations under institutions of her own choosing; and, more than a welcome, assistance also of every kind that she may need and may herself desire. The treatment accorded Russia by her sister nations in the months to come will be the acid test of their good will, of their comprehension of her needs as distinguished from their own interests, and of their intelligent and unselfish sympathy.

VII. Belgium, the whole world will agree, must be evacuated and restored, without any attempt to limit the sovereignty which she enjoys in common with all other free nations. No other single act will serve as this will serve to restore confidence among the nations in the laws which they have themselves set and determined for the government of their relations with one another. Without this healing act the whole structure and validity of international law is forever impaired.

VIII. All French territory should be freed and the invaded portions restored, and the wrong done to France by Prussia in 1871 in the matter of Alsace-Lorraine, which has unsettled the peace of the world for nearly fifty years, should be righted, in order that peace may once more be made secure in the interests of all.

IX. A readjustment of the frontiers of Italy should be effected along clearly recognizable lines of nationality.

X. The peoples of Austria-Hungary, whose place among the nations we wish to see safeguarded and assured, should be accorded the freest opportunity of autonomous development.

XI. Rumania, Serbia, and Montenegro should be evacuated; occupied territories restored; Serbia accorded free and secure access to the sea; and the relations of the several Balkan states to one another determined by friendly counsel along historically established lines of allegiance and nationality; and international guarantees of the political and economic independence and territorial integrity of the several Balkan states should be entered into.

XII. The Turkish portions of the present Ottoman Empire should be assured a secure sovereignty, but the other nationalities which are now under Turkish rule should be assured an undoubted security of life and an absolutely unmolested opportunity of autonomous development, and the Dardanelles should be permanently opened as a free passage to the ships and commerce of all nations under international guarantees.

XIII. An independent Polish state should be erected which should include the territories inhabited by indisputably Polish populations, which should be assured a free and secure access to the sea, and whose political and economic independence and territorial integrity should be guaranteed by international covenant.

XIV. A general association of nations must be formed under specific covenants for the purpose of affording mutual guarantees of political independence and territorial integrity to great and small states alike.

In regard to these essential rectifications of wrong and assertions of right we feel ourselves to be intimate partners of all the governments and peoples associated together against the Imperialists. We cannot be separated in interest or divided in purpose. We stand together until the end.

For such arrangements and covenants we are willing to fight and to continue to fight until they are achieved; but only because we wish the right to prevail and desire a just and stable peace such as can be secured only by removing the chief provocations to war, which this programme does remove. We have no jealousy of German greatness, and there is nothing in this programme that impairs it. We grudge her no achievement or distinction of learning or of pacific enterprise such as have made her record very bright and very enviable. We do not wish to injure her or to block in any way her legitimate influence or power. We do not wish to fight her either with arms or with hostile arrangements of trade if she is willing to associate herself with us and the other peace-loving nations of the world in covenants of justice and law and fair dealing. We wish her only to accept a place of equality among the peoples of the world,—the new world in which we now live,—instead of a place of mastery.

Neither do we presume to suggest to her any alteration or modification of her institutions. But it is necessary, we must frankly say, and necessary as a preliminary to any intelligent dealings with her on our part, that we should know whom her spokesmen speak for when they speak to us, whether for the Reichstag majority or for the military party and the men whose creed is imperial domination.

We have spoken now, surely, in terms too concrete to admit of any further doubt or question. An evident principle runs through the whole programme I have outlined. It is the principle of justice to all peoples and nationalities, and their right to live on equal terms of liberty and safety with one another, whether they be strong or weak. Unless this principle be made its foundation no part of the structure of international justice can stand. The people of the United States could act upon no other principle; and to the vindication of this principle they are ready to devote their lives, their honor, and everything that they possess. The moral climax of this the culminating and final war for human liberty has come, and they are ready to put their own strength, their own highest purpose, their own integrity and devotion to the test.

Printed reading copy (WP, DLC).

To Raymond Poincaré

My dear Mr. President: [The White House] 8 January, 1918

The French Ambassador was kind enough to communicate to me your Excellency's important message with regard to the use to which the American troops were to be put in cooperating with the troops of France, and I want to assure your Excellency that the question is one to which we have been giving a great deal of careful and anxious thought and with regard to which we are all not only willing but anxious to do the best and most effective thing for the accomplishment of the common purpose to which we are devoting our arms.

General Bliss, who is kindly conveying this letter to you for me, is, as your Excellency probably knows, to be the representative of the United States in the Supreme War Council, and I have instructed him that this particular question which you have very properly called to my attention ought to be discussed with the greatest fullness and frankness in that Council. The judgment of the Council with regard to it will, I need hardly assure you, be conclusively influential with the Government of the United States. Our only desire is to do the best thing that can be done with our armed forces, and we are willing to commit ourselves to the general counsel of those with whom we have the honor to cooperate in this great enterprise of liberty.

Meantime, let me assure you that this question seems to us quite as pressing and important as it does to yourself, and our own desire is to settle it promptly as well as wisely.

May I not again convey to you the greetings of the Season and express the hope that our cooperation in arms may soon lead to the results for which we all pray and hope?

With much respect and regard,

Sincerely yours,   [Woodrow Wilson]

CCL (WP, DLC).

To Frank J. Hayes

My dear Mr. Hayes: [The White House] 8 January, 1918

If it were possible for me with a clear conscience to leave Washington next week, you may be sure I would accept with real pleasure the invitation so kindly conveyed by your letter of December thirtieth[1] to address the International Convention of the United Mine Workers of America; but, in view of the many things that are daily demanding my attention and which it would be absolutely wrong for me to turn away from, it is impossible for me to come, and I can only ask you if you will not convey to the assembled delegates a very warm and cordial greeting from me for the New Year and say to them that I would like to be present to say something, if I could, which would make them realize how much the safety of America and the whole honor and dignity and success of her action in the present crisis of the world depends upon their fidelity and energy and devotion. I do not doubt that they will rise to the occasion, but I do want them to realize how deeply and sincerely interested the Government is in their welfare and how anxious it is to be instrumental in doing anything that it is possible to do to further it.   Cordially and sincerely yours,   Woodrow Wilson

TLS (Letterpress Books, WP, DLC).
  [1] It is missing.

To George Parmly Day

My dear Mr. Day: [The White House] 8 January, 1918

Thank you very much for your kind letter of January fourth.

Of course, I cannot decline your very generous offer to send me a set of the "Chronicles of America," but I do not honestly feel that I am entitled to them except by your very gracious courtesy.[1]

Cordially and sincerely yours, Woodrow Wilson

TLS (Letterpress Books, WP, DLC).
[1] The Wilson Library, DLC, includes many, although not all, of the volumes of this series published during Wilson's lifetime.

From Joseph Patrick Tumulty, with Enclosure

Dear Governor: [The White House] January 8, 1918.

I think this is the worst sort of impudence and does not merit a reply. J.P.T.

Quite right W.W.

TL with WWhw (WP, DLC).

ENCLOSURE

Chicago, Ill., Jan. 8, 1918.

Are alcoholic liquors still served in White House after Capitol has gone dry. We must believe reports that they are served unless officially denied. Wire answer our expense.

Prohibition National Committee.

T telegram (WP, DLC).

From Robert Latham Owen

Washington, D. C., January 8, 1918.

I deeply rejoice at your magnificent statement of our American war aims. It was most opportune. I beg you to have it circulated through Russia thoroughly and by speaker to address the people face to face and thus meet German propaganda.

Robert L. Owen.

T telegram (WP, DLC).

From Lillian D. Wald

New York, January 8, 1918.

We think your message to Congress expresses the broadest understanding and profoundest insight and that your program would

bring about the possibility of nations harmonized in their relationship with each other, each developing according to its best traditions
and resources. We are particularly moved by the generous conception of America's obligation and responsibility to the new Russia.
May your high hopes for a speedy termination of the present situation and for a settlement that will preserve the world from a
reoccurence of war be realized.   Lillian D. Wald.

T telegram (WP, DLC).

From John Spargo

New York, January 8, 1918.

Your statement of our war aims is magnificent and will be a great
inspiration to the believers in democracy in all all [sic] lands, including the enemy nations. I tender my respectful and heartfelt
congratulations.   John Spargo.

T telegram (WP, DLC).

From Elizabeth Merrill Bass

My dear Mr. President: Washington, D. C. January 8th, 1918.

I know you do not need me to tell you how fixed and how high
is your permanent place in the history of this epoch of the world,
but I wonder if you know how a word or two from you today or
tomorrow, said to a few Democratic Congressmen or printed in the
public press, would enthrone you forever in the hearts of the women
of the United States as the second Great Emancipator. Their eyes
are turned to you from all over the country and they believe you
will say that word. In these days, when all foundations are shifting,
methods do not seem to matter so very much, and the most extreme
advocates of state rights abandoned their position entirely and passed
the Prohibition Amendment.

If I may say a word as to party policy, the Republican management is treating this entirely as a political matter and are striving
for tactical positions. Do not let us give them the advantage of our
silence to carry with them into the congressional campaigns next
year when asking for the votes of the enfranchised women. They
will lose this, whatever the result of Thursday's vote, if you say this
word of encouragement.

Respectfully yours,   Elizabeth Bass

TLS (WP, DLC).

A Memorandum by Basil Miles

[c. Jan. 8, 1918]

MEMORANDUM FOR THE SECRETARY OF STATE

RUSSIAN POLICY

The attached telegrams[1] show that Mr. Francis has received an invitation from the Bolshevik Government to participate in peace negotiations. In other words, this Government is concerned with some necessity to announce its Russian policy.

The following course of action is suggested:

(1) This Government should direct an address to the Russian people reiterating the war aims of the United States; its determination to help Russia reorganize; its firm belief that the Russian Revolution is an epoch-making event, whose first fruits the United States is unwilling to see stifled by Germany; the sympathetic feeling of the United States for the people of Russia and its purpose to recognize any Government accepted by the Russian people, by democratic procedure registering the expressed will of the people; finally, the confidence of the people of the United States, that Russia, having freed herself from her own autocracy, will not throw herself into the hands of a foreign autocracy, such as that of military Germany.

(2) This address to be presented to the Bolshevik Minister of Foreign Affairs[2] by the Counselor of the American Embassy at Petrograd,[3] with a verbal statement that this is one of several means adopted by this Government to communicate with the Russian people; that the United States has no hostility toward the Bolshevik leaders and does not desire to isolate them, but cannot recognize their legal authority until they secure some democratic basis through democratic methods.

(3) The withdrawal of the American Ambassador at Petrograd to this country, either on grounds of health or for purposes of consultation, leaving Embassy under Chargé d'Affaires.

(4) The immediate undertaking of measures to deliver and distribute considerable quantities of Red Cross supplies, already bought and paid for in this country and ready for shipment such as boots, condensed milk and other articles of purely non-military character. To distribute these supplies, the Red Cross organization at Petrograd, under Raymond Robbins, assisted by Messrs. Thatcher and Wardwell, should be further developed.[4]

(5) Along with this, Mr. Creel's Propaganda Bureau, now in charge of Mr. Sisson should be extended rapidly. Yesterday American moving picture films were shown in twenty-seven Petrograd theatres. The film service should be further extended. Russian patriotic

speakers should be engaged on the spot and circulated through the country. Mr. Sisson's news service should forge ahead rapidly, etc., etc.

(6) The United States to continue its support of elements of law and order in the south, but on the definite and expressed basis of preserving Russia from Germany and not exploiting Russia to carry on a civil war.

It would seem possible to reiterate at this time that the United States regards the Russian Revolution as the latest expression of the vast world movement toward democracy; that its sympathy for the Russian people consequently is inherent in the political ideals of the people of the United States.

NOTE:

The situation in Russia has become additionally a military one. The armistice will enable Germany and Austria to throw to the western front *more troops than the United States can put in France for the next eight months.*

If the armistice achieves full success, the entrance of the United States into the war will be nullified for a year. The consequent additional sacrifice of life and treasure will be enormous.

France was caused to withdraw from Mexico by direct intimation of military intervention on the part of the United States.[5] The President gave General Sherman written instructions to go to the Mexican border and organize an army which should intervene to preserve Mexican intervention [independence] and the ultimate cost of whose maintenance was to devolve on Mexico.

It should be considered whether full power should not be given to the American Military Attaché at Petrograd to take such measures as he deems necessary regarding the Russian situation as a purely military problem; the Military Attaché at Roumania to be under his direction; the withdrawal of the Ambassador, leaving the Embassy under the Chargé d'Affaires, would facilitate such a measure. The Military Attaché would then have complete power to prosecute propaganda, direct and recommend the distribution of relief, the disposition of accumulative military supplies, the support of surviving military Russian units, etc., etc.

There seems to be a definite parallel, not only suggested by the instructions to General Sherman cited above, but also by the instructions and authority which appear to have been given to the head of the British Military Mission which is now in the south of Russia and in touch with the South-Eastern Confederation.[6] Consideration of giving the Military Attaché this power would in no way modify, but it would rather centralize the other recommendations contained in this memorandum. The military Attaché would be at once put on a war basis and would use his discretion as to how far he should act openly or how far he should continue his present course.

This suggestion does not apply if Ambassador be not withdrawn.

Basil Miles

CCS MS (SDR, RG 59, 861.00/935½, DNA).
[1] See D. R. Francis to RL, Dec. 31, 1917, and D. R. Francis to WW, Jan. 3, 1917.
[2] That is, Leon Trotsky (Lev Trotskii).
[3] That is, J. Butler Wright.
[4] Thomas Day Thacher and Allen Wardwell, both lawyers of New York.
[5] That is, in 1866.
[6] See WHP to RL, Dec. 31, 1917, printed as an Enclosure with WW to RL, Jan. 1, 1918 (third letter of that date), and Richard H. Ullman, *Anglo-Soviet Relations, 1917-1921* (3 vols., Princeton, N. J., 1961-72), I, 40-57.

To Elizabeth Merrill Bass

My dear Mrs. Bass: [The White House] 9 January, 1918

It is extremely hard to reply to generous letters like yours of January eighth without seeming to do violence to my real personal sentiments, but the most I have felt at liberty to do (for reasons which I have explained to you) has been to give my advice to members of Congress when they have asked for it. Not as many have asked as I could wish. When they do ask, you may readily conjecture what the advice is.

Personally, I am not afraid of the strategy of the Republican management. It can be counted upon to be stupid, and it is always stupid to be insincere, as in this instance I am sure it is.

Cordially and sincerely yours,   Woodrow Wilson

TLS (Letterpress Books, WP, DLC).

A Statement

[*Jan. 9, 1918*]

The committee found that the President had not felt at liberty to volunteer his advice to members of Congress in this important matter, but when we sought his advice he very frankly and earnestly advised us to vote for the amendment as an act of right and justice to the women of the country and of the world.[1]

Printed in the *New York Times*, Jan. 10, 1918.
[1] This was embodied in a front-page report with the headline "WILSON BACKS AMENDMENT FOR WOMAN SUFFRAGE" in the *New York Times*, Jan. 10, 1918. The report, written from Washington on January 9, told about Wilson's meeting with the Democratic members of the Suffrage Committee of the House of Representatives. About this meeting and what Wilson said to the congressmen, see the Enclosure printed with WW to JPT, Jan. 23, 1918.

To William Gibbs McAdoo

My dear Mac: [The White House] 9 January, 1918

I have your note of the seventh sending me the message which you asked the Secretary of State to send to Mr. Crosby about General Bliss's consulting with the Inter-Allied Council.

I hope, my dear Mac, that hereafter you will let me see these messages before they are sent and not after, because they touch matters of vital policy upon which it is imperative that I should retain control. My particular job is to keep things properly coordinated and if they are coordinated without my advice, some very serious consequences might ensue. In this case, so far as I can see, nothing is likely to go wrong, except that I must frankly say to you again that I am very much afraid of Mr. Crosby's inclination to go very much outside his bailiwick, an inclination of which I have many evidences.

Always   Affectionately yours,   [Woodrow Wilson]

CCL (WP, DLC).

To Newton Diehl Baker, with Enclosure

My dear Mr. Secretary: The White House 9 January, 1918

Do you think that I could with any degree of wisdom or prudence comply with the request of the enclosed telegram?

Cordially and faithfully yours,   Woodrow Wilson

TLS (N. D. Baker Papers, DLC).

E N C L O S U R E

Atlantic City, N. J., Jan. 7, 1918.

We regret more than you can ever know any incident caused by our people that discredits the glorious record of a people always true to their country and its splendid tradition from Bunker Hill to Carrizal and we feel keenly and suffer because a few members of our race so far forget themselves as to actually kill those whom they had sworn to protect. We sincerely believe in law and order and pray for its full enforcement everywhere and no one sin can justify another. We make no excuse for their guilt. We plead no extenuating circumstances. We come to you praying that you may commute the death sentence of the soldiers lately condemned to be hanged for participating in the recent Houston riot, to life imprisonment.[1] We would regard this a magnificent gift to the race and nation at this critical time and hope that the race's gratitude to you and renewed devotion to our common country and its cause may, in a small measure, atone for the sins of those for whom we sincerely pray and plead. Sincerely and prayerfully,

W. F. Cozart, Chairman,

Rev. J. P. Gregory,

George S. Walls,

Dr. E. B. Terry,

F. Daniels,

Dr. P. L. Hawkins,

Secretary committee.[2]

T telegram (WP, DLC).
[1] Thirteen soldiers had already been hanged on December 11, 1917, for their participation in the Houston riot. The soldiers referred to in the above letter had been condemned to death by a second court-martial. See Robert V. Haynes, *A Night of Violence: The Houston Riot of 1917* (Baton Rouge, La., 1976), pp. 1-7, 254-84.
[2] The signers of this letter were Winfield F. Cozart, hairdresser; the Rev. Jeremiah P. Gregory, pastor of the Union Baptist Church; George H. Walls, proprietor of a boardwalk bathhouse; Edward B. Terry, M.D.; Frederick Daniels, chef; and Pompey Long Hawkins, M.D., all of Atlantic City.

To Newton Diehl Baker

My dear Mr. Secretary: The White House 9 January, 1918

Here is a matter which you will agree with me is of great and pressing importance, and I send it to you at once for your consideration and advice.[1]

In haste

Cordially and faithfully yours,   Woodrow Wilson

TLS (N. D. Baker Papers, DLC).
[1] H. A. Garfield to WW, Jan. 9, 1918, TLS, enclosing "Proposed Additions to Selective Service Regulations of November 8, 1917," T MS, both in the N. D. Baker Papers, DLC. As Garfield explained in his covering letter, the "Proposed Additions" provided for the deferment from the military draft of men employed in the mining of coal, upon specific request from the United States Fuel Administrator or any state Fuel Administrator.

From Thomas William Lamont

Personal.

Dear Mr. President: [New York] January 9th, 1918.

May I venture to congratulate you upon your wonderful message to Congress outlining America's peace terms; and may I say too that I am especially moved by your sympathetic references to the Russian people? I am certain that the hand that you hold out to them from America will be powerful in assisting the solution of the whole Russian situation.

In the last week of my recent stay in London, I spent much time in introducing Colonel W. B. Thompson, who had just arrived from Petrograd, to the various Government officials, so that they might have the benefit of any fresh point of view that he could present. I may say to you that in the course of these visits in London, we found the temper of the officials decidedly changing there. The whole thought had apparently been that sheer force was the only thing that would serve to restore order in Russia; but gradually a more sympathetic feeling for what the people of Russia are striving for—even though perhaps blindly—began to creep in. This change of sentiment was crystallized by Mr. Lloyd George in what he said privately to Colonel Thompson and me at luncheon, the gist of which was summed up in the memorandum recently prepared and presented to you for your perusal.

Permit me to add one more thing, not with reference to Russia, but with reference to the feeling of the English people as a whole. I found over there, outside of Government circles, much more sympathy with the Lansdowne point of view than newspaper reports would indicate. In other words, the people as a whole seemed to have reached a point where, though just as steadfast as ever, they could not endure to fight on *blindly*—when, for all they knew, Germany had already reached the point where she might make terms almost as favorable to-day as three years hence. In other words, English people were asking for further definitions of war aims and peace terms. Mr. Asquith, with whom I lunched and who is still a powerful figure in English politics, seemed to feel this.

The result of this growing feeling has shown in Mr. Lloyd George's recent utterance, and now you have followed up this with your wonderful exposition of the situation. I can assure you, even from my comparatively brief study of conditions in both England and France, that your message to Congress will have a stimulating and powerful effect upon those two peoples.

I must apologize for inflicting upon you such a long letter, when I started out simply to express my feelings upon your message and especially upon its references to Russia.

With great respect, believe me,
                    Sincerely yours,   [Thomas W. Lamont]

CCL (T. W. Lamont Papers, MH-BA).

Sir Cecil Arthur Spring Rice to the Foreign Office

Washington Jan. 9 1917 [1918]

private

Following are notes of Presidents private conversation with Governor General[1] and myself today at audience of reception and private lunch.

President's desire in making his statement was to call Germany's bluff and force the German govt to declare its terms in unmistakable language. He thought this would force the issue between the G G on the one hand and with the Russians and the German Parliament on the other. He had made arrangements for immediate publication in Russia of what he had said. He was struck by good sense of all of the Russian proposals except the absurd one for joint compensation for damages caused by Germany. He hoped that underground measures would be taken in Germany for making his speech known. Switzerland was a whispering [place and he hoped] that I would at once communicate any message that I might receive. He approved of the channel made use of.

Speaking generally he said he had always known that the U S would be drawn into the war. But it was plainly worse than useless to join with a disrupted and disunited nation. Reports which had come in from all parts of the country left no doubt whatever in his mind that the country was not united on the question of intervention until the final moment came when he had acted in conformity with the wishes of the vast majority of the people.

Speaking of the British Empire he said Germany wholly failed to understand that such an empire was entirely different from the German conception of Empire, and was a union of free peoples acting on free impulses. G B had to keep a strong fleet for preservation of means of subsistence and also for police purposes.

He talked at length and with great force on the shipping question which he said was the central fact of the present situation. He was devoting to this question the entire energies of the govt. The govt was devoting to naval work men now employed on bridges and construction work. He regarded the next few weeks as extremely critical in this respect but hoped that afterwards there would be an improvement.

He told Governor General that he had studied German books in the university and had always had a great dislike for German political institutions.

Hw telegram (FO 115/2432, pp. 43-44, PRO).
[1] Victor Christian William Cavendish, 9th Duke of Devonshire, Governor General of Canada.

A Translation of a Letter from Jean Jules Jusserand to Stéphen Jean Marie Pichon

[Washington] January 9, 1918.

The French text of the presidential message on the conditions of peace having been cabled to Europe at the very same time when the original was read to Congress, it is in order only that I here enclose a copy of the original document, the tenor of which is already known to Your Excellency.

The President prepared this document in the greatest secrecy. However, I had been able to discover that a favorable declaration concerning Alsace-Lorraine would probably be made soon by him, but the form that it would take had not been indicated to me. One of the President's intimates had asked me if an American affirmation along the lines of Mr. Lloyd George's would be agreeable to us. I hardly need tell you what my response was; I simply refer to the indications that I furnished Your Excellency on this subject on the sixth of the month by telegram No. 21.

The President with whom, as I have already said, I talked about his message and some other questions, in the course of the same afternoon, told me that he had had to hasten his work and its publication, on account of the sudden changes in Russia, which might give, unexpectedly, an untimely character to this or that of his observations. In fact, the hour at which he spoke had been assigned, he told me, to the Serbian mission, which was put off only at the last moment and which was received afterward by the House.

The reception accorded the message by Congress has been especially a triumph for France; no passage was more ardently applauded than the one on Alsace-Lorraine; the same passage on Belgium, which preceded and which was warmly applauded, did not excite an equal enthusiasm. . . .   [Jusserand]

CCL (Papiers Jusserand, Vol. 17, pp. 20-21, FFM-Ar).

From the Diary of Colonel House

New York, January 9, 1918.

Saturday[1] was a remarkable day. I went over to the State Department just after breakfast to see Polk and others, and returned to the White House at a quarter past ten in order to get to work with the President. He was waiting for me. We actually got down

[1] That is, January 5.

to work at half past ten and finished remaking the map of the world, as we would have it, at half past twelve o-clock.

We took it systematically, first outlining general terms, such as open diplomacy, freedom of the seas, removing of economic barriers, establishment of equality of trade conditions, guaranties for the reduction of national armaments, adjustment of colonial claims, general associations of nations for the conservation of peace. Then we began on Belgium, France and the other territorial readjustments. When we had finished, the President asked me to number these in the order I thought they should come. I did this by placing the general terms first and territorial adjustments last. He looked over my arrangement and said it coincided with his own views with the exception of the peace association which he thought should come last because it would round out the message properly, and permit him to say some things at the end which were necessary.

In discussing these questions, I insisted, and made a strong argument, for open diplomacy. I told him there was nothing he could do that would better please the American people and the democracies of the world, and that it was right and must be the diplomacy of the future. I urged him to lay deep stress upon it and to place it first.

I then suggested the removal, as far as possible, of trade barriers. He argued that this would meet with opposition, particularly in the Senate. Nevertheless, I thought that since the document was to be a readjustment of world conditions, that it would not be a complete structure unless this was in it. I thought the two great causes of war were territorial and commercial greed, and that it was just as necessary to get rid of the one as it was the other. He made no argument against this, and we proceeded to frame a paragraph to cover it. He wrote this almost wholly himself.

I then suggested a discussion of the freedom of the seas. He asked my definition of this term. I answered that I went further than anyone I knew, for I believed that in time of both war and peace a merchantman should traverse the seas unmolested. He agreed to this, and the paragraph as framed read something like this: "Absolute freedom of navigation upon the seas, outside territorial waters, alike in peace and in war."

After the message had been entirely written and we had read it over three or four times, wondering how England would receive this particular paragraph, I suggested that he add to it that "the seas might be closed by international action in order to enforce international covenants." The President seized this suggestion with avidity and added it. I gave as my reason for this that I had discussed the matter in England and I believed with this addition it might be acceptable to them.

One of the points we discussed was the reduction of armaments. We played with this sometime before we could get it into its present form which satisfied us both. I need not go into the difficulties of that question because they are apparent to anyone who has tried to work out something satisfactory.

We had less trouble with the colonial question. At first it was thought we might have to evade this entirely, but the President began to try his hand on it and presently the paragraph which was adopted was acceptable to us both, and we hoped would be to Great Britain.

We took up Belgium, and that paragraph was written without difficulty. Then a long discussion followed on France and whether Alsace and Lorraine should be touched upon. I was in favor of not mentioning it specifically, if it were possible not to do so, therefore, at first, we put in "All French territory should be freed and the invaded portions restored." We left it there and went on to other territorial readjustments, but came back to it time and again. The President convinced me that it was necessary to say something about it, since the message was so specific as to other nations, and I could see he was right. I suggested then that it should read "If Alsace and Lorraine were restored to France, Germany should be given an equal economic opportunity," and it was written this way and remained so until Monday morning.

On Monday, after we had eaten lunch, the President said as we were walking toward his study, "the only thing about the message that worries me is in regard to Alsace and Lorraine. I am wondering how that will be taken." I replied that it was practically the only point that disturbed me and I suggested that we try our hands on it again. As it was, I was afraid it would neither suit France nor Germany. I thought he might leave out the economic part and put in the assertion that it had been for fifty years a cause of unrest in Europe, and that a just settlement of the question was as much in the interest of Germany as it was to the balance of the world.

Taking this suggestion, he then wrote the paragraph as it now stands with the exception that he had "*must* be righted" instead of "*should* be righted" as I thought best. We then went into a discussion of where "should" and where "Must" should be used, and we agreed that, where there was no difference as to the justice of a question, the word "must" ought to be used, and where there was a controversy, the word "should" was correct. He went through the entire message and corrected it in this way. He wondered whether that point would be caught. I thought it was certain it would be.

My argument was this, the American people might not consent to fight for the readjustment of European territory, therefore, in suggesting these readjustments, with the exception of Belgium, the word "should" ought to be used.

As to Russia, I urged him to be at his best. I read him a sentence that I had prepared regarding Russia, which I had submitted to the Russian Ambassador who thoroughly approved. I told the President that it did not make any difference how much we resented Russia's action, the part of wisdom was to segregate her, as far as we were able, from Germany, and that it could only be done by the broadest and friendliest expressions of sympathy and a promise of more substantial help. There was no argument about this because our minds ran parallel, and what he wrote about Russia is I think, in some respects, the most eloquent part of his message.

We spent sometime on Poland. I gave him the memoranda which the Polish National Council in Paris had given me, containing a paragraph which they wished the Interallied Conference to adopt, but which was refused.[2] We read this over carefully and both concluded that it could not be used in full, but the paragraph as framed came as near to it as we felt was wise and expedient.

After the Turkish paragraph had been written, the President thought it might be made more specific, and that Armenia, Mesopotamia, Syria and other parts be mentioned by name. I disagreed with this, believing that what was said was sufficient to indicate this, and it finally stood as originally framed.

The paragraph about Roumania, Serbia and Montenegro is interesting in as much as the President asked me to submit it to Vesnitch, head of the Serbian Mission to this country, and Serbian Minister at Paris. He wished to get Vesnitch's reaction on it. The idea was for me to tell Vesnitch that I had prepared it for the

[2] R. Dmowskí to W. G. Sharp, Nov. 13, 1917, *FR-WWS 1917*, 2, I, 786-90. Dmowskí said that the main hope of the Allies lay in the nationalistic aspirations of the Poles and of the subject peoples of Austria-Hungary. Allied support of these aspirations might lead to movements which would paralyze the Austro-Hungarian war effort. Most helpful to the Allied cause would be a pledge by the Allies and the United States "to rebuild the Polish state on the whole national territory of Poland."

"We take the liberty," Dmowskí concluded, "of submitting to the Government of the United States of America the proposition that the great powers in war against Germany make an agreement which they would include in their war aims.

"1. The reconstitution of an independent Polish state comprising Polish territories which before the war belonged to Russia, Germany and Austria. This Polish state to be in possession of the Polish part of Silesia and of a part of the Baltic coast with the mouths of the Vistula and the Niemen; to have proper extension and a sufficiently large population to enable it to become an efficient factor of European equilibrium.

"2. The emancipation of nationalities in Austria-Hungary which remain actually under German and Magyar supremacy: the incorporation of the Polish, Italian, Serbo-Croatian and Roumanian territories into the national states to which they belong on account of their nationality; the creation of an independent Czechish state comprising Bohemia, Moravia, the Czechish part of Silesia and the northern part of Hungary inhabited by the Slovaks."

President's consideration and that the President was desirous of knowing what he thought of it.

I sent for Vesnitch to meet me at Gordon's home as I did not think it advisable to have him come to the White House. Much to my surprise, he totally disagreed with what had been written and said it would not satisfy Serbia. He also said that peace should not be made at this time and that the discussion of peace should be frowned upon. I told him that since Russia, Germany, Austria and Great Britain were actually discussing peace it was not worth while to argue as to whether a discussion was advisable or not, therefore, I asked him to concretely set forth what he would suggest in preference to what I submitted to him. He wrote with some difficulty, underneath the paragraph which the President and I had framed the following:

"There will and there cannot be in Europe any lasting peace with the conservation of actual Austria-Hungary. The nations kept in it, as well as Serbian, Croats and Slovenes, as Turks and Slovaks, as Roumanians and Italians, will continue to combat the Germano-Magya[r] domination. As to Bulgaria, Serbia stands firm on the Treaty of Buc[h]arest. The Allied Powers have guaranteed to her these frontiers. It will be morally and materially impossible to get so rapidly an understanding of Balkan nations, which is of course desirable, and which may come. Bulgarian treachery can and shall not be rewarded. I sincerely believe that serious negotiations for the peace at this moment of the war would mean the complete failure of the policy of Allies and a grave collapse of the civilization of mankind."*

Vesnitch gave me a history of the Balkans, particularly that of Serbia, and I had to check him, saying I had an engagement with the President.

The President was rather depressed at this first and only attempt to obtain outside opinion regarding the message. I had not been in favor of going to Vesnitch, and told him so. I have had so much experience with foreigners and others who are obsessed with an idea that I felt it would be hopeless to expect a reasonable viewpoint. I advised the President not to change the paragraph in the slightest, and to go ahead as if no objection had been made, and this he did. There was not one word or line changed, as will be seen from the little memorandum which the President wrote, and which Vesnitch added to in his own handwriting, and which I make a part of the record.

No one was consulted, either directly or indirectly, concerning

* I have put this down just as he wrote it.

this message on War Aims, and Lansing was not called in until Monday afternoon at three o-clock when he was told of it and it was read to him. Lansing accepted it in toto, although he made several suggestions as to words which the President adopted.

I was in favor of giving notice to the world in Tuesday morning's papers that the President would go before Congress in order to give America's war aims. My idea being to have the whole world expectant. He argued against this, but came to no decision, and it was not done. He told Mrs. Wilson, however, on Monday night, that he had talked me out of my position. Mrs. Wilson repeated this to me when we were driving to the Capitol to hear the speech.

I returned from the Capitol in the motor with the President, and I told him what Mrs. Wilson had said and added that he was mistaken in thinking he had changed my views; and I thought it was a mistake to have made it so secret. I noticed that the Diplomatic Corps were not present, excepting those who had come to hear the Serbian address, and that some of the Cabinet were also absent. The President's argument was that in giving out such a notice as I suggested, the newspapers invariably commented and speculated as to what he would say and that these forecasts were often taken for what was really said.

The thing was done so secretly that his Private Secretary knew nothing of it until half past ten o-clock Tuesday morning, just two hours before the message was delivered. I had an engagement with Secretary Lane on Tuesday at two o-clock at the White House. I asked him how he liked the President's address. He replied "what speech do you mean, his message to Congress?" He was dumbfounded when I told him that the President had just delivered what was perhaps the most important utterance since he had been in office. Lane thought it was the limit of humiliation as far as the Cabinet was concerned. I later found that neither Lane, Houston nor Secretary Wilson had been notified and knew nothing of it until they were told of it in the afternoon. This I think was unfair, and I feel some resentment myself at such treatment of them.

Lane went on to say that Burleson and Tumulty had poisoned the President's mind against him. Burleson, he thought, was angry because he, Lane, had not made an appointment which Burleson requested. He asked if I would not find out from the President what his feeling was toward him. I promised to do this, and before I left on Tuesday I asked the President. His reply was that "Lane has stood still." That at the beginning of his administration he was considered a progressive, but that he had not advanced at all and was now a conservative. He noticed that he was recommended for the Supreme Court and other places of honor by conservatives only.

He condemned his action in regard to the leasing of oil lands in the West, declaring that Lane was acting contrary to his, the President's policy. He would lease oil lands, or hang them up in such a way that they could be denuded of the oil before they could be recovered by legal action.

I said if this were the case, he had better give Lane another office. He expressed a willingness to do so, but wanted to know what I had in mind. I thought any executive place in the Cabinet that did not have to do with the things he was objecting ot [to], for example, the War or Navy. What I had in mind was that Lane could replace Baker and Baker could go to the Interior. . . .

Spring-Rice gave me a cable which had just come from Lloyd George, which he asked me to take to the President.[3] I have no copy of this, but the substance of it was that the reason Lloyd George felt called on to make his speech before the Labor Conference on Friday was that the labor situation in England was critical, and in order to get them to consent to the demands of the Government regarding further recruiting among them, it was necessary for him to state a liberal set of war aims. I have my doubts as to the truth of this, but I am giving him the benefit of the doubt. He was evidently uneasy as to its reception by the President. Lloyd George also said in the message that he had tried to conform to the well known views of the President as expressed in his several public messages on the subject.

And this reminds me that the President was uneasy Friday night lest George might anticipate his forthcoming address, and he asked me to send a cable to George telling him that he, the President, felt it necessary to say something further upon the subject of American war aims, and that he hoped nothing in the meantime would be said on their side that would affect the situation here.

My cable to Balfour about this on Saturday the fifth explains itself.[4] Also my cable of congratulations to George upon his speech which I sent on the sixth. When George's speech came out in Washington Saturday afternoon the President was depressed. He thought the terms which Lloyd George had given were so nearly akin to those he and I had worked out that it would be impossible for him to make the contemplated address before Congress. I insisted that the situation had been changed for the better rather than for the worse. I thought that Lloyd George had cleared the air and made it more necessary for the President to act. I also insisted that after the President had made his address, it would so smother

[3] The British Embassy to WW, Jan. 5, 1917.
[4] E. M. House to A. J. Balfour, Jan. 5, 1917.

the Lloyd George speech that it would be forgotten and that he, the President, would once more become the spokesman for the Entente, and, indeed, the spokesman for the liberals of the world. The President was greatly heartened by this opinion, and set to work again with renewed zest.

After luncheon Sunday I went to the French Embassy to see Jusserand. He had a number of questions he wished to ask, the answers to which he desired to transmit to his Government. He read them off seriatim and I answered as quickly as they were read, for I was in a hurry to get back to the President.

When I reached the White House, the President had not finished the conclusion of his message and, since Gregory wanted to see me, I motored to his house and took him for a short drive. When I returned, the President was waiting and he read to me the message as a whole. I again congratulated him and felicitated with him. I thought it was a declaration of human liberty and a declaration of the terms which should be written into the peace conference. I felt that it was the most important document that he had ever penned, and I laughingly remarked that we would either be on the crest of the wave after it had been delivered, or reposing peacefully in the depths.

The point we were most anxious about was as to how this country would receive our entrance into European affairs to the extent of declaring *territorial* aims.

I suggested to the President that a possible criticism Germany might make was that since the United States refused to permit European nations to interfere in any way with affairs in the Western Hemisphere, European nations should be equally insistent that the affairs in the Eastern Hemisphere be left to the nations therein. He admitted that this would be probably said, and the reply that he expected to make in that event would be that we were perfectly willing for the same principles to govern in the Western Hemisphere as we had outlined as being desirable for the Eastern Hemisphere.

He was quite insistent that nothing be put in the message of an argumentative nature, and once or twice I suggested making an argument in favor of some of the terms, but each time he thought it in[ad]visable because it would merely provoke controversy. I saw the reasonableness of this view and accepted it as wise.

The other points we were fearful of were Alsace and Lorraine, the freedom of the seas and the leveling of commercial barriers. However, we were both resolute in the determination that all these things should be said, and there was not the slightest hesitation on his part in saying them. The President shows an extraordinary courage in such things, and a wisdom in discussing them that places him easily in a rank by himself, as far as my observations go. The more I see of him, the more firmly am I convinced that there is not a statesman in the world who is his equal. He is the only one who measures up to the requirements of the day when the world is in such agony.

I am struck by the difference between the President and Lloyd George. I tried to get Lloyd George to do at Paris what the President has now done, but he was not big enough to realize the necessity for it, and has only seen the light since he returned to England and the necessity of the situation there compelled him to act, and upon the very same lines I urged upon him. The President, on the other hand, needed no arguments or urging but saw the opportunity at once. He saw that he had not adequately covered the case in his message to Congress in December, 1917, and went cheerfully to work to reconstruct and reconsider our war aims.

On Sunday evening we did nothing except to talk and listen to the President read aloud. He read a bacalaureate sermon which he had written at Princeton in 1909.[5] It is a remarkable production and I call particularly attention to it as being a classic as far as its objects are concerned. He also read some short stories from Stephen Leacock and we talked and rested in this way.

Monday evening I went to dinner with Secretary and Mrs. McAdoo. There was no one present except the family and McAdoo and I conferred afterward concerning his presidential prospects. He does not conceal from me his keen desire to be President, although he declares he does not exhibit this feeling to anyone else. I cautioned him against it. He generously offered me the Secretaryship of State when he became President and I as generously declined. I told him I would be glad to help him as I had helped Wilson and that he, perhaps, was the only man I would be willing to serve again in such a capacity.

When I returned to the White House the President was waiting for me. I could not get him to go to bed, although it was nearly eleven o-clock. He insisted upon talking and reading from Wordsworth. We did not go to bed until half past eleven. We urged him to play golf in the morning and he agreed to do so even though he is to deliver his speech at 12.30 on Tuesday.

I shall not go into the conversations I had in Washington with an innumerable number of people, such as General Bliss, Benjamin Strong, Norman Hapgood, Lansing, Polk, etc. etc. It has been an exceedingly busy and fruitful visit, and the President, when I left, expressed his gratitude and pleasure at having me with him.

[5] It is printed at June 13, 1909, Vol. 19.

In speaking of the message in the family after it had been delivered, the President constantly and generously referred to it as "our message."

I left Washington at one o'clock last night and reached New York this morning around nine. I am delighted at the reception the address has received from all classes and conditions. The extreme radicals, even the socialists, approve it, and so do the conservatives and reactionaries. I am including in the diary some of the current newspaper comment, and I particularly commend for consideration the extraordinary editorial in the New York Tribune.

From the Diary of Josephus Daniels

1918 Wednesday 9 January

Swanson, Gregory & I called to see WW about oil bill & he approved bill we had drawn for the Navy to take over all lands in oil reserve No 2 & to operate, paying to present claimants what is right, & if they decline compensation offered to offer them 75% & if they decline permit them to go into the courts. We will oppose the jokers in the bill that passed the Senate. I am to see Ferris & ask to have Swanson amendment incorporated in the bill.

Before discussing oil, Swanson congratulated the President upon his message to Congress, & WW discussed various reasons that prompted him to state his war claims. "They never beat me to it if I see it first" quoting Johnston Cornish.[1] I doubted his recommendation to let the Turks control Turkey in Europe. He said we could not undertake to dictate the form of government of any country or dismember. His autonomy in Austria-Hungary would permit the peoples to resolve their own governt.

[1] A Democratic politician of New Jersey, about whom see the index references in Vol. 26.

An Address and a Reply[1]

[Jan. 10, 1918]

[Phelan] Mr. President, to be called upon at the last moment to perform an always very delightful task on behalf of this committee [is difficult?], but Judge Dowling[2] is unavoidably detained in New York and could not be here, but on behalf of this committee it falls to me as chairman of a subcommittee of the association for the monument of Robert Emmet to present to you this reduced figure of the heroic statue which you accepted for the National Museum last summer.[3]

Robert Emmet was a poor potter, and he died for his country. And the men of Irish blood of America, American citizens here represented, think it is most opportune in the history of the world that attention should be called to his sacrifice, and more particularly to the cause in which he made the sacrifice.

There should be a good feeling among all nations, especially among those allied in the war—and they have all made professions. In fact, Mr. President, you have been their spokesman in favor of recognizing the national right of a country of homogeneous people to independence and autonomy—certainly autonomy. And we feel that, at this time, while presenting to you the image of an Irish rebel, from our point of view, we are presenting to you the representative of a nation in rebellion against the oppression which has been put upon them for centuries. And I don't think it is inappropriate here to say, from my knowledge of history, that no greater indignity, no more atrocious acts, have ever been committed against a people as have been committed against the people of Ireland. That is all back in the past. The world up to the beginning of the war had become enlightened, and we are willing to forget the past if we can be the beneficiaries of that enlightenment which you, sir, are endeavoring to preserve and treasure.

I, therefore, in this spirit, have very great pleasure in presenting to you, on behalf of the committee, this beautiful image, sculptured by an Irish American, Mr. O'Connor[4] who is honored and admired.

[Wilson] Senator and gentlemen: I am very much complimented that you should have come in so representative and important a committee to present this very beautiful work of art to me. And I am complimented that Mr. O'Connor should be present himself.

You will, I think, all agree with me that it would not be in good taste for me to say anything about the particular Irish cause, because at the present moment a convention is meeting to which will be left, as I understand it, the very free right of determining the fundamental questions of the relations between Great Britain and Ireland. Being one of the men who are in a position in which I must be guarded and mind my own business, I know you will excuse me from saying anything about that.

At the same time, I am at liberty to say, not only that I appreciate this gift, as a gift of a work of art, which I shall always value, but also, as I look at the statue, the thing that impresses me most is that it is in the costume of a past age. And I believe that that is not without its significance. What Robert Emmet did in his time would not be necessary to do in our time, and we can, all of us, appreciate, without any partisanship of any kind, the spirit of a man like that— the spirit of self-forgetfulness, the spirit of devotion, the spirit of idealism, the spirit which leads a man to go the full length of sacrifice for the purpose that he holds most dear.

In that sense, if not in order, Robert Emmet represents some of the finest traits of human nature. And, for my part, I believe that the struggle we are going through now will result in the assertion of some of the finest instincts of human nature. The mere revulsion of the war from the barbaric things that have been done—the violations of principle, the violations of every law of humanity that have characterized the aggressions of Germany—will, in the long run, accrue to the benefit of the world by way of reaction.

After the Napoleonic wars, there was a great intellectual and spiritual renaissance. I believe that that renaissance will be still more powerful and still more widespread, and that it will affect all parts of the world, and that, in the light of the days to come, we shall see international questions as we never saw them before, and, having seen that, have national ambitions and have national autonomy that we have never entertained before.

So that, even as the official spokesman of a government, I am at liberty to accept this statue with the greatest pleasure and with the greatest admiration for the self-sacrifice and traits of the man whose interesting and spirited figure it represents.

I thank you very much, indeed, gentlemen, for your courtesy. I shall value it always.

JRT transcript (WC, NjP) of CLSsh (C. L. Swem Coll., NjP).
[1] In a ceremony at the White House at 2:30 P.M., Wilson accepted a small bronze replica of the statue of Robert Emmet recently placed in the National Museum in Washington.
[2] That is, Victor James Dowling.
[3] See J. D. J. Moore to WW, Aug. 17, 1917, n. 4, Vol. 43.
[4] Andrew O'Connor, Jr.

To William Gibbs McAdoo

Personal.

My dear Mac: The White House 10 January, 1918

The enclosed regulations[1] are all right except for Section 5, which seems to leave to the Collector of Customs the right to judge whether the departure of "any person on board, either as officer, member of the crew, or passenger" would be inimical to the interests of the United States in the conduct of the war, and places in the hands of the Secretary of the Treasury the authority to issue all permits to travel.

No single matter has been giving me more perplexity recently than the question of how to settle this very question of who shall leave the United States and who shall not, and there is an elaborate body of regulations which was drafted by the State Department and has been going the round of the Departments of Commerce, Justice, War, etc., without any definitive conclusion having been arrived at. The whole matter will have to be digested by common counsel.

Always   Affectionately yours,   Woodrow Wilson

TLS (WP, DLC).
[1] WGM to "Collectors of Customs and others concerned," Feb. 1, 1918, TLS (WP, DLC). This was originally enclosed in WGM to WW Jan. 8, 1918, TLS (WP, DLC). The regulations dealt with the control of all shipping and personnel in American harbors by the Treasury Department in accordance with the requirements of the Espionage Act of June 15, 1917. Both Wilson, in the above letter, and McAdoo, in WGM to WW, Jan. 14, 1918, explain Section 5 very fully.

To Thomas Watt Gregory

My dear Gregory: [The White House] 10 January, 1917 [1918]

I would be very much obliged if you would look over the enclosed papers.[1] If true, they state a very grave situation and it is thoroughly worth our while to consider what, if anything, should and can be done about the influences proceeding from Seattle. Perhaps you will be kind enough to speak to me about the matter when we see each other again.

Cordially and faithfully yours,   [Woodrow Wilson]

CCL (WP, DLC).
[1] The Editors have not found them.

From Robert Lansing, with Enclosure

My dear Mr. President: Washington January 10, 1918.

You will recall that after Cabinet meeting Tuesday you suggested, upon reading a memorandum which I showed you in regard to our attitude toward Russia,[1] that it would be well to draft a telegram to Francis which could be, through unofficial channels, transmitted to the Bolshevik Government.

I considered the matter and consulted with Mr. Polk on the subject and we both reached the conclusion that the object would not be as well attained by a telegram of that sort as it would for me to issue a public statement of our attitude here and let Mr. Creel transmit it to Russia to his representatives there and we send it to Francis for his information. In that way it would obtain greater publicity and would, I think, accomplish every purpose that could be accomplished by unofficially delivering it to the Bolshevik Government, which would have a measure of danger and might cause irritation—while a statement would not.

I therefore drafted a proposed statement and would be glad to have your views as to this method of stating our attitude, and also as to the language of the statement.

I am leaving tomorrow noon, as I told you, for New York and will return Sunday night. Possibly by that time you will have had the opportunity to pass upon the statement.

Faithfully yours,   Robert Lansing.

TLS (WP, DLC).
¹ The memorandum by Basil Miles, printed at Jan. 8, 1918.

ENCLOSURE

January 10, 1918.

STATEMENT.

In view of the fact that there seems to be some confusion in the public mind as to the attitude of this Government in regard to the present Russian situation it seems to me advisable to make at this time a statement upon the subject.

Although Russia appears at the present time to be separated or to be separating into distinct political groups, each of which claims authority over a portion of the territory of the nation, the Government of the United States is convinced that the spirit of democracy continues to dominate the entire Russian nation. With that spirit the United States feels a profound sympathy and believes in the ultimate effect of its cohesive power upon the Russian people as a whole.

The separate independent authorities functioning in different sections of Russia present a situation to the Government of the United States which causes it to pause before formally recognizing any one of those authorities as the *de facto* Government of the Russian nation. The evidence of the possession of a right to exercise sovereignty over all Russia by a particular group of citizens must be substantially conclusive before recognition, otherwise a foreign government might reasonably be charged with exercising through recognition an influence in favor of a group and with improperly interfering with the internal political affairs of Russia.

In applying this principle the Government of the United States awaits the full manifestation of the will of the Russian people because it is convinced that it is its imperative duty to avoid any interference or any appearance of interference with the domestic affairs of Russia, denying at the same time that the adoption of this course is in any way influenced by partiality for or opposition to any particular group or body. The determination of an agency to exercise the sovereign power of the nation belongs wholly and solely to the Russian people. As to that they ought to be supreme. With the popular determination of the governmental agency of all the Russian nation the United States, in accordance with its conception of independence and national sovereignty, has nothing and will have nothing to do. When undoubted proofs of the will of the Russian people are manifest the Government of the United States will gladly recognize the agents of the sovereign people of Russia as the Russian Government and enter into relations with that Government.

Even while the question of the governmental agency remains undecided the United States, appreciating the dominance of the democratic spirit in Russia and inspired by the most friendly and unselfish motives, is desirous of rendering such aid as it is able, provided its aid is acceptable to the Russian people, to relieve their reported needs which have unavoidably arisen out of the social and industrial disorganization consequent upon a radical change in political institutions.

The United States has only the kindliest feelings for Russia. Its policy as to recognition or non-recognition of a government at the present time is founded on the principle that the Russian people are sovereign and have the right to determine their own domestic organization without interference or influence by other nations. Its desire to aid the people of Russia rests solely upon the fraternal spirit which it possesses for a great democracy which has endured so much in its struggle against autocracy both within and without its borders.

T MS (WP, DLC).

From Edward Mandell House

Dear Governor: New York. January 10, 1918.

I want to congratulate you and felicitate with you over the astounding success of your address to Congress.

I was never so happy over the outcome of anything as I am over this. It took tremendous courage, but the reward is great, as indeed it should be.   Your devoted,   E. M. House

TLS (WP, DLC).

Helen Hamilton Gardener to Joseph Patrick Tumulty

My dear Mr Tumulty: Washington, D. C. January 10, 1918

I was so excited last evening when the inevitable happened—and you know that I have believed all the time that the President *would* do something of the kind at the psychological moment,[1] as he always does with big questions—but I was so excited and overwhelmed by the meaning of it all to us and to democracy, that I did not fully realize that you had proposed a most gracious thing when you said that you would ask the President to let me have that little penciled document.[2]

Afterward I did realize it and want to not only thank you, from the bottom of my heart for thinking of it, but to urge you please not to forget it and to ask him to sign it and let me have it just as it is. Then if he is willing perhaps we may like to photograph it and use it in our little Woman Citizen.

The women of the country would, I am sure, be glad to see it and to know just how it was done. It will be an historic document and the very simplicity of it adds to its value.

Dont let it be folded, please, and when you get it ready for me (you see I am assuming that he will do, as always, the gracious thing) I shall come for it or ask you to send it to me here at my home.

I, of course, shall write to thank him (as Mrs Catt will) when this historic day is done.[3] I am just starting for the Capitol now and want to mail this "lest you forget" that document.

With gratitude and respect, I remain,

Very Sincerely, Helen H. Gardener

TLS (WP, DLC).

[1] About Wilson's action, see n. 1 to the statement printed at Jan. 9, 1918.

[2] This was the penciled version of the statement printed at Jan. 9, 1918.

[3] The House of Representatives, in the early evening of January 10, adopted the federal woman-suffrage amendment by a vote of 274 to 136, exactly the two-thirds majority needed, after a five-hour debate on the measure. This was followed by an emotional scene in which women in the gallery and corridors of the House sang the hymn, "Old Hundred." See *Cong. Record*, 65th Cong., 2d sess., pp. 762-811; *New York Times*, Jan. 11, 1918; and Eleanor Flexner, *Century of Struggle: The Woman's Rights Movement in the United States* (Cambridge, Mass., 1959), pp. 291-93.

Sir Cecil Arthur Spring Rice to the Foreign Office

Washington. 10th January 1918.

Personal and Secret.

I gather that President would have been glad of an expression of opinion from H. M. Government about his speech.

Press comments have given much satisfaction here.

T telegram (A. J. Balfour Papers, FO 800/209, PRO).

To George Earle Chamberlain

Personal.

My dear Senator: [The White House] 11 January, 1918

When you and Senator Hitchcock were at the White House the other evening[1] we were discussing various suggestions of coordination and means of speeding up the military programme and among other things you told me that you had in mind a bill for the creation of a munitions ministry.

That, of course, set my mind to work on that particular suggestion, and I feel that I ought to say to you, now that the matter is clear in my mind, that I hope sincerely no such re-coordination will be attempted. For one thing, it would naturally include the Navy as well as the Army and would, so far as the Navy is concerned, bring about, I fear a dislocation of activities which would cause delay where there is none that is avoidable; and in regard to the Army, I think that nothing substantial would be accomplished. Indeed, I believe that delay would inevitably be produced by such a measure.

I have had in the last few months a great deal of experience in trying to coordinate things, and upon every fresh coordination delay inevitably results and not only delay, but all sorts of cross currents of demoralization which are very serious impediments to the effective conduct of business.

Rather intimate information from the other side of the water convinces me that the munitions ministries which have been set up there have not fulfilled the expectations of those who advocated them, and the structure of those governments is so utterly different from our own that we could not, if we would, create any such parity of power and influence between the head of such a bureau and the heads of the permanent departments as can be created under such political arrangements as the French and English.

In short, my dear Senator, my judgment is decidedly that we

would not only be disappointed in the results, but that to attempt such a thing would greatly embarrass the processes of coordination and of action upon which I have spent a great deal of thought and pains, and which I believe are more and more rapidly yielding us the results we desire.

I felt that I ought not to keep you in ignorance of what had been going on in my mind with regard to this important matter.

Cordially and sincerely yours,   Woodrow Wilson

TLS (Letterpress Books, WP, DLC).
[1] At 8:30 P.M. on December 28.

To Stephen Samuel Wise

My dear Rabbi Wise: [The White House] 11 January, 1918

Your friendship always cheers me and your praise always encourages me very much, and I want you to know how deeply I appreciate your judgment of my last address to Congress.[1] I hope from the bottom of my heart that it will clear the air and lead to saner attitudes of mind.

Cordially and sincerely yours,   Woodrow Wilson

TLS (Letterpress Books, WP, DLC).
[1] Wise's letter is missing.

To Andrew Jackson Montague[1]

[The White House]
My dear Governor Montague: 11 January, 1918

None of the messages I have received about my recent address to Congress has gratified me more than yours of the eighth[2] and I want you to know how warmly and deeply I appreciate it. I value your judgment most highly and am very much heartened to receive such assurances.

I had not known that your son[3] was in the war. I know how that must tug at your heart, but to speak perfectly frankly I think I ought to congratulate you.

Cordially and sincerely yours,   Woodrow Wilson

TLS (Letterpress Books, WP, DLC).
[1] At this time, a Democratic congressman from Virginia.
[2] It is missing.
[3] Robert Latané Montague, a second lieutenant in the United States Marine Corps.

To John Hollis Bankhead

My dear Senator:　　　　　[The White House] 11 January, 1918

I am writing to enlist your help, if I may, in straightening out the coal mining situation in Alabama. I am exceedingly loath to take over the mines and have them operated by the Government, and yet I must frankly say that I see no other alternative if the mine owners should remain unwilling to accept the settlement which Doctor Garfield has so laboriously worked out after conference with all parties and in the sincere desire to be just to each and prejudice the future in no respect.[1] I myself think the proposed settlement the right one; I know it is the only practicable one, and I am sure you would be rendering a very great service to the country in this critical time of the war if you would lend your valuable counsel to obtain the assent of the coal operators.

　　　　　Cordially and sincerely yours,　[Woodrow Wilson]

CCL (WP, DLC).

[1] After several days of negotiations in Garfield's office in Washington between representatives of the Alabama Coal Operators' Association (one of whom was John Hollis Bankhead, Jr.) and the United Mine Workers, Garfield proposed a settlement of the matters in dispute on December 14, 1917. The settlement included recognition of the workers' right to join any union and provided machinery for the settlement of grievances. All questions of wages were to be postponed until July 1, 1918. All disputes which could not be resolved on the company level were to be referred to an "umpire" chosen by the judge for the United States District Court for the Northern District of Alabama from a list of three names nominated by the coal operators and three names proposed by the workers. In addition, Garfield strongly urged the operators to accept the eight-hour day, at least for the duration of the war. The settlement was to be subject to ratification by "the coal operators of Alabama, or those who indicate their acceptance by their signature," and by the mine workers of Alabama. The settlement was embodied in Rembrandt Peale to the mine workers of Alabama, Dec. 14, 1917, printed in United States Fuel Administration, *Final Report of the United States Fuel Administrator, 1917-1919.* . . . (Washington, 1921), pp. 211-12.

To John Grier Hibben

　　　　　　　　　　　　　　　[The White House]
My dear President Hibben:　　　　　11 January, 1918

I am in receipt of your telegram of January tenth[1] conveying the very generous resolution adopted by the Board of Trustees of the University at their session on January tenth.[2] I beg that as the first opportunity presents itself you will convey to the Trustees my warm appreciation of that message and my hope that the address to Congress which it so generously supports may bear some substantial fruit in the year which has just opened.

　　　　　Sincerely yours,　Woodrow Wilson

TLS (Letterpress Books, WP, DLC).

[1] It is missing.

To Ignace Jan Paderewski

[The White House] 11 January, 1918

I warmly appreciate your message of yesterday[1] and wish to convey to you my warmest thanks not only but also my hope that the year just opening may bring to the people of Poland a real fruition of their hopes.   Woodrow Wilson.

T telegram (Letterpress Books, WP, DLC).
[1] It is missing.

To Samuel Reading Bertron

My dear Mr. Bertron: [The White House] 11 January, 1918

Just a line to thank you very warmly for your letter of yesterday.[1] I am heartily glad that you think the passages in my recent address about Russia are the sort that will do good in that disturbed and distressed country.

With sincere regard,

Cordially yours,   Woodrow Wilson

TLS (Letterpress Books, WP, DLC).
[1] It is missing.

To Thomas William Lamont

My dear Mr. Lamont: The White House 11 January, 1918

There was certainly no reason why you should apologize for your generous letter of January ninth, which I warmly appreciate. I need not tell you that my address to Congress the other day came from the deepest sources in me, and I pray with all my heart that it may bear some sort of substantial fruit.

I was aware of the feelings in England to which you refer, and I felt that it was imperatively necessary to give definition at every point to the situation. The Germans can now never pretend that we have not stated our position and that they do not know where we stand.

I have been much interested in what I have heard of Colonel Thompson's activities in Russia.

With much appreciation,

Sincerely yours,   Woodrow Wilson

TLS (T. W. Lamont Papers, MH-BA).

To George Foster Peabody

My dear Mr. Peabody: The White House 11 January, 1918

Your judgments about my public utterances I always await with keen interest, and you may be sure that I have been most deeply gratified by your opinion of my last address to Congress.[1] I hope with all my heart that it may clear the air of the world and bring us into the presence of some sane counsels, even in Germany.

Cordially and sincerely yours,   Woodrow Wilson

TLS (G. F. Peabody Papers, DLC).
    [1] It is missing.

To James Oscar Boyd[1]

My dear Doctor Boyd: The White House 11 January, 1918

Thank you for your letter of January ninth.[2] The suggestion it contains interests me very much, but this objection seems to me to have very considerable force against the use of the word "ecumenical," namely, that while in its real meaning it is unlimited it has in usage been generally limited to the entire Christian Church and has assumed in the general mind an ecclesiastical aspect. Undoubtedly we are in need of some such word and it is possible that we might rescue the word "ecumenical" from its narrower environment.

Cordially and sincerely yours,   Woodrow Wilson

TLS (NjPT).
    [1] Pastor of the Church of the Redeemer (Presbyterian) in Paterson, N. J. He had received the Ph.D. from Princeton University in 1905 and had taught at Princeton Theological Seminary from 1900 to 1915.
    [2] It is missing.

From Newton Diehl Baker

My dear Mr. President: Washington January 11, 1918.

At a conference of the Council of National Defense with Mr. Hoover, Dr. Garfield, and Mr. Willard, on January 9, it was decided to transmit to you, with our approval, two tentative bills, copies of which are enclosed. These bills have to do with legislation covering price fixing, and the conservation of food.[1]

Respectfully yours,   Newton D. Baker

TLS (WP, DLC).
  [1] See WW to ASB, Jan. 16, 1918.

From Newton Diehl Baker, with Enclosure

Information

Dear Mr. President: Washington. January 11, 1918.

The enclosed is General Pershing's reply to my cablegram on the subject presented to you by the French Ambassador.[1]

Respectfully yours,   Newton D. Baker

TLS (WP, DLC).
  [1] See R. Poincaré to WW, Dec. 28, 1917; J. J. Jusserand to the Foreign Ministry, Dec. 29, 1917 (two telegrams); NDB to WW, Jan. 3, 1918, and its Enclosures; and WW to R. Poincaré, Jan. 8, 1918.

E N C L O S U R E

[Chaumont] January 9, 1918.

Number 467. January 8. Confidential. For the Chief of Staff.

Reference your cablegrams 558 and 588, am in conference and communication on subject mentioned. French have not been entirely frank, as unofficial information indicates they really want to incorporate our regiments into their divisions for such service in the trenches as they desire. As to our instruction, a certain amount of work with French troops is beneficial and this we are having and expect to have. We are following closely latest developments and are using French and British instructors as *they are* best. Our men are working hard and instruction is progressing favorably. Have expressed a willingness to aid in any way in an emergency but do not think good reason yet exists for us to break up our own divisions and scatter regiments for service among French and British, especially under the guise of instruction. As we are now at war ourselves the integrity of our own forces should be preserved as far as possible. Shall see M. Clemenceau Wednesday the ninth instant and expect to hold joint conference with Field Marshal Haig and General Petain within a few days. Shall have frank discussion of whole subject. The President and the Secretary of War may depend upon it that every endeavor will be made to arrive at satisfactory agreements consistent with maintenance of our own national military identity.   Pershing.

TC telegram (WP, DLC).

Two Telegrams from Sir Cecil Arthur Spring Rice to the Foreign Office

[Washington] Jan 11. 1918.

No. 158. Jews here after careful thought considered that British govt. had perhaps gone rather far to one side in slighting the Bolsheviki whilst the President had done the same on the other in praising them, so that while the former had offended them the latter had aroused their suspicion for they would be wondering 'what do the bourgeois want of us now?' But on the whole it seemed wiser to send the desired message through U. S. channels which has never been done. See my next tel. Message was approved by President and House though they eliminated last sentence. "Please leave etc."

[Washington] Jan 11. 1918.

No. 159. My immediately preceding telegram.

Following is text of message signed by Wise, Epstein and de Haas[1] sent yesterday through State Dept. addressed to Ussischkin, Barbasch & Weinstein in Odessa, Rosoff & Zlatopolski in Petrograd, Halperin in Kieff, Tchlenow in Copenhagen & Motzkin[2] in same place with instructions to forward to all interested & influential men in Russia.

"According to advices received here, Germany's peace proposals at Brest Litovsk now leave no doubt as to her imperialistic aims. As stated in the Leipziger Volkszeitung Germany aims at a peace providing for an enormous increase in Germany's military, political and economic strength, and she intends really to annex all the territories she now holds. Surely the Jews of Russia will not lend themselves to further such imperialistic designs, not even by appeals to their pity. We have learned with grave apprehension that the Imperialistic Govt. is seeking to provision her army through Southern Russia, and is seeking to accomplish this purpose through Russian Jews. We refuse to believe that the Jews of Russia will allow themselves thus to be used as cats paws by Imperialistic Germany. It would greatly imperil the cause of the Jews and particularly in Palestine. Please leave no effort untried to prevent this latest move of the Imperialistic Govt. from succeeding."

Please inform Weizman

Hw telegrams (FO 115/2399, pp. 200-202, PRO).
[1] That is, Stephen S. Wise, Lewis Epstein, and Jacob de Haas.
[2] Those who can be identified with certainty are Abraham Menahem Mendel Ussishkin, engineer and publicist; Samuel Barbash, banker; Israel Benjamin Rosov, director of oil and mining companies in Russia; Hillel Zlatopolsky, industrialist, philanthropist, and man of letters; Jehiel Tschlenow, physician, formerly of Moscow but at this time in London; and Leo Motzkin, journalist and author, at this time head of the Copenhagen office of the World Zionist Organization. "Weinstein" may have been Aaron Weinstein,

a socialist leader at this time living in Minsk. "Halperin" may have been Yehiel Halperin, an educator who specialized in Hebrew kindergartens. All but Weinstein were leaders of the Zionist movement.

From the Diary of Josephus Daniels

1918 Friday 11 January

Cabinet—Discussed military minister. The President said he wished Americans could learn their country was not like Britain. Baker explained mistake of Minister of Munitions in England. Baker detailed grilling to which he was subjected in the House. WW indignant at speech by Phelan, in presenting small bust of Emmett, wishing the President to help Ireland secure its rights. At this time, with England fighting with us, such talk almost treasonable. President said he was so mad he could hardly restrain himself. Trots[k]y, it is said, will ask all allied nations to join in giving self-rule to Ireland, Egypt, India along with Belgium and Servia. That is playing into hands of Germans, but is shrewd move.

WW: ["]Preacher in Orkney islands prayed for the people of this land & adjacent islands of England, Scotland and Ireland"

Why does Englishman wear monocle? So he cannot see more than he can understand.

Spring Rice & Capt Harts: What is White House made of? Va sandstone. That is not white? No. It must be painted. Why? To cover up the burns &c after the fire. What caused the fire? The British.

Saw Dublin after catastrophe:[1] "I did not know Ireland had home rule"

[1] For Wilson's description of his visit to Dublin, see WW to EAW, Aug. 20, 1899, Vol. 11.

From Walter Evans Edge

My dear Mr. President: [Trenton] January 12th 1918

At a recent meeting of the New York, New Jersey Port and Harbor Development Commission, Governor Whitman and I generally approved plans prepared by the Commission providing for an exhaustive investigation of the Port's present facilities with a view to formulating a policy for the further development of the Port; relieving congestion and proper control of the Port by the two States cooperating with the Federal Government, so that future improvements shall be along consistent and regulated lines.

To make a proper survey and collect the information the Commission estimates will require approximately four hundred thousand dollars. Governor Whitman and I each agreed that one hundred thousand dollars be appropriated by the respective Legislatures now in session. As the work will probably require two years, we will ask a similar appropriation next year provided the work would seem to warrant and justify it.

It seems particularly important in view of the Federal Government's control of transportation lines, that when Port transportation is considered, that that phase of control should be taken up with this Port Commission, before any important changes of policy are promulgated. This Commission has already been designated by the Secretary of War as a war board of the Port of New York, thereby giving it federal recognition. Of course, New Jersey and New York do not want to authorize and begin the expenditure of four [hundred] thousand dollars with the design of ultimately controlling the development of the Port, unless we can be reasonably assured that plans of the Government will not ultimately interfere with such control. Both Governor Whitman and I will be glad to go to Washington to discuss this with you and Mr. McAdoo as we consider it of sufficient importance and we would be pleased if you would suggest a time in the near future convenient to you. I would say Wednesday or Thursday of next week would meet our plans if it could be arranged.   Very sincerely,   Walter E Edge

TLS (WP, DLC).

From William Royal Wilder, with Enclosure

My dear Wilson: New York January 12, 1918.

The master stroke of your speech or message to Congress related to the Bolsheviki, and I heartily congratulate you and the world. When, some months ago you made the distinction between the German Government and the German People, I thought it was politic, but meticulous. It did not take long to realize that even if the distinction then did not exist in fact, it would have to be made a fact sooner or later, for I am convinced that if not *in esse* it is *in posse*.

Lloyd George and our friends are a little too close to Russia to realize that it is both politics and truth to strike through and past the Bolsheviki phase of the Russian Revolution, and carry hope and inspiration to the real Russian people,—and you have done it.

You never will know how much literature I have prevented getting to you, for I have not hesitated to fill the office of censor. It occurs to me, however, that among recent letters that my indefatigable and patriotic Polish friend, General Sosnowski, has written, it may be worth your while to peruse the enclosure. I am quite sure that his view of the Bolsheviki is yours. It is senseless to pronounce an anathema against the Russians, because this evolutionary element in the Revolution is just now on top, for while both the cream and the scum rise to the top, there is much "saving grace" in this scum. The Bolsheviki represent something a little better than protoplasm. They are grown-up children, and children are simple, selfish and savage, until they at least reach adolescence.

As to General Sosnowski's recommendation, I fear he is premature; but the time is certainly coming when this seething caldron will cease to boil over, and instead of merely wtaching [watching] it at a distance it may be safe to approach nearer and take an active part in arranging and ordering and disposing of its contents.

Of course you know of the recent and sad death of Charlie Mitchell. Bridges, Halsey and I went down from New York. It was a terrible trip on a terrible Sunday. He is the fourth of the class to die this fall, and the best to go.

Faithfully yours, Wm. R. Wilder

ENCLOSURE

From George Jan Sosnowski

Dear Mr. President: New York. January 11, 1918

The "Bolshevikis" are a very delicate but powerful instrument which has been used skilfully up to the present time for the accomplishment of certain ends—but not by the Allies. And why not? Because the Allies do not know Russia and they do not know Germany; they do not understand the problems with which they are dealing; they do not know how or in what manner to manipulate such an instrument—and a most wonderful one it is—as the "Bolshevikis."

They do not even dream that such an instrument is in preparation on their own soil and will be ready for delivery between June and September next.

I call "Bolshevikis" an instrument because after performing certain work it will disappear in the same manner in which it appeared. The makers, although not the originators, of this tool of destruction of civilization are the superstatesmen and governments of the Allies. They unceasingly and unconsciously labor on this instrument in the same manner as somnambulists take their midnight strolls on the roofs and cornices of houses. The Allied statesmen will give to mankind that instrument in a more perfect form than Russia poses—more destructive in power. The Westerners of Europe are always more thorough in their conceptions than the Easterners.

The "Bolshevikis" recognize themselves for what they are; they have no aspirations nor do they believe they can establish their power or their doctrine at any place for any length of time. The "Bolshevikis" know perfectly well that they are only an instrument with which the present system of government in Europe might be destroyed in order to establish democracy.

They are destructive but not constructive and are as dangerous to autocracy as to real democracy.

Up to now Germany has been making use of them.

By stating the aims of the war, as you did, Mr. President, on the 8th instant, you postponed the development of "Bolshevikism" in the Allied countries. Now is the proper time to STIMULATE its development on the soil of the Central powers. All democracies of Europe, labor parties and socialists support the Wilson Doctrine. You can be sure of them. And being so assured of their support, why not deal a mortal blow to German supremacy among the Socialists and Internationalists and take the bull—Russian Bolshevikis—by the horn at the same time?

This can be done if YOU will call an International Conference of Democracy, including Socialists of all shades, at Washington or at Stockholm—Washington preferred—for the CONSIDERATION of the American and Allied war aims.

If I am not mistaken Germany will not grant passports for such a conference, neither will Austria-Hungary. At such Conference the Bolshevikis' real power and importance in Russian affairs will be shown in the truest light. In your invitations you must insist that no restriction will be tolerated in granting the passports to elected delegates of Socialists or other democratic bodies.

In calling such a Conference there is no danger whatsoever except to the Central Powers, who will recognize that their delegates will be outnumbered and outvoted. The refusal to grant passports for such a Conference must result in the internal labor troubles of the Central Powers. It will quickly develop the "Bolshevikism" in Austria-Hungary and in Germany.

The separate Russian-Bulgarian peace opened the most important way of trading in and tapping Russia's enormous mineral and food resources via the Black Sea and the Danube—a very clever diplomatic achievement for the Central Powers—who at their will can protract peace negotiations with Russia.

I am, your Excellency,

Most respectfully,   G. J. Sosnowski

TLS (WP, DLC).

Charles Curtis[1] to Joseph Patrick Tumulty

Dear Tumulty: Washington, D. C. January 12, 1918.

I am handing you herewith a letter from Nick Chiles,[2] Editor of the Topeka Plaindealer, Topeka, Kansas, which is one of the leading colored papers in the central west. Mr. Chiles is very deeply interested in the trial and conviction of the members of the 24th Infantry, and is desirous of receiving the findings of the court martial.[3] He has a large amount of the evidence and thinks he should have the balance of it as well as the findings. I took this matter up with the Secretary of War and under date of January 2, 1918, the Adjutant General advised Mr. Chiles through me that he was directed by the Secretary of War to inform him it was regretted that it was impracticable to furnish the desired copy. The colored people of our section are very much worked up over the affair and I believe it would be only fair to the interested parties to give them a copy of the findings. I hope you will present this matter to the President and that he may feel justified in ordering that the findings be furnished.

With personal regards, I am

Very truly yours,   Charles Curtis[4]

TLS (WP, DLC).
[1] Republican senator from Kansas.
[2] N. Chiles to C. Curtis, Jan. 8, 1918, TLS (WP, DLC). Curtis paraphrases it well.
[3] For the results of the two courts martial held thus far, see n. 1 to the Enclosure printed with WW to NDB, Jan. 9, 1918 (first letter of that date). A third and final court martial did not begin until February 18, 1918. Subsequent documents will reveal its outcome and Wilson's action concerning the condemned men.
[4] "Please tell Senator Curtis that this matter is going to be very seriously handled by us and that I do not think it will contribute to the settlement of it to comply with Mr. Chiles' desire." WW to JPT, c. Jan. 17, 1918, TL (WP, DLC).

Sir Eric Drummond to Sir Cecil Arthur Spring Rice

[London] 12 January 1918.

PERSONAL & SECRET.

Your personal & secret telegram of January 11.

You will see that Mr. Balfour, speaking at Edinburgh on the 10th, dwelt on and recognized to the full the admirable character of the President's speech.[1]

If however you think any further message desirable, you may inform the President that the Prime Minister is grateful for his declaration, and is happy to find that the peace policies of the two nations as expressed by the President and himself are so entirely in harmony.

PRIVATE.

You will no doubt realize that there are certain obstacles to a more precise endorsement, as there are naturally some slight divergencies between the two speeches.

T telegram (A. J. Balfour Papers, FO 800/209, PRO).
    [1] Balfour, in an address to a mass meeting in Edinburgh on the evening of January 10, had declared that Wilson's address of January 8 was a "magnificent pronouncement" and went on to hail its virtues at some length. However, he asserted that both Wilson's speech and that of Lloyd George on January 5 did not represent a new policy on the part of the Allies. The Allies had long stood for the war aims which the President and the Prime Minister had so eloquently restated. Moreover, he, Balfour, could see no noticeable improvement in the attitude of the German leaders in their recent public statements, with the single exception that they now seemed prepared to concede that future wars should be avoided. Balfour could see no modification of Germany's aggressive war aims. He warned that no league of nations or other world organization could succeed unless based upon a settlement of questions of territory and nationality far different from those envisaged by the German government. Balfour's speech is summarized in the *New York Times*, Jan. 11, 1918; the full text appears in the London *Times*, Jan. 11, 1918.

Sir Cecil Arthur Spring Rice to Arthur James Balfour

Washington Jan 12 1918

private. Your speech about the President's statement will I am sure give him great satisfaction. I called his attention to the text today.

Hw telegram (FO 115/2432, p. 51, PRO).

From Colville Adrian de Rune Barclay

Private & Confidential.

My dear Mr. President,   Washington January 13. 1918

Since Sir Cecil left Washington this morning a telegram has been received by us from London, the contents of which I venture to communicate to you as supplementing the Ambassador's letter of yesterday which accompanies these lines.

The Prime Minister hopes you will have seen the report of Mr. Balfour's speech in Edinburgh on January 10, which gave him a welcome opportunity of recognizing to the full and dwelling on the admirable character of your address to Congress on January 8. Mr. Lloyd George desires me to add that he is grateful for your declarations, and is happy to find that the peace policies of the United States and Great Britain as expressed by yourself are so entirely in harmony.

I have the honour to be, my dear Mr. President, with the highest respect,   Your obedient servant,   Colville Barclay

ALS (WP, DLC).

From Newton Diehl Baker, with Enclosure

My dear Mr. President: Washington. January 13, 1918.

I have your letter of January 9th,[1] and herewith return the telegram from the Committee with regard to the soldiers convicted of participation in the Houston riots. I have taken the liberty of drafting a reply for your signature if it meets with your approval.[2]

Respectfully yours,   Newton D. Baker

TLS (WP, DLC).
[1] WW to NDB, Jan. 9, 1918 (first letter of that date).
[2] Wilson signed a copy of this; it is printed as the Enclosure.

E N C L O S U R E

To Pompey Long Hawkins

My dear Dr. Hawkins: [The White House] January 13, 1918

I have received your telegram of January 7th, with regard to certain soldiers upon whom the death sentence has been imposed by court martial for participation in the so-called Houston riot.

The Secretary of War informs me that in time of war Division Commanders are authorized to carry into execution sentences of courts martial, and that pursuant to this power the verdict of the court martial in the first group of cases was promptly executed when approved by the Division Commander.

The Secretary of War further advises me that every safeguard was thrown around the men tried, and executed, in that a special investigation was made by the Inspector General of the Army; the court martial most carefully selected in order that it might be composed of men of character, experience and courage, and that a Judge Advocate of great experience was assigned to supervise the trial.

Nevertheless, the Secretary of War feels, and I concur in his judgment, that however appropriate this power of summary execution may be to our Army actually in the field in time of War, it is not necessary thus to foreclose the possibility of review so far as those parts of our Army are concerned which are remote from the scene of actual operations.

The Secretary of War has, therefore, directed in my name that all subsequent convictions involving capital punishment shall be suspended until a careful judicial review of the records can be made by the Judge Advocate General, and the Secretary of War in person.

So far as the particular cases to which you call my attention are concerned I cannot, of course, anticipate the action I shall feel called upon to take when these papers are officially brought to my attention; but I can, and do assure you of my understanding of the spirit in which your appeal is made, and shall not allow myself to forget when I come to act upon these cases the loyalty of the people in whose name you speak, and whose interest I have greatly at heart.   Very truly yours,   Woodrow Wilson

TLS (Letterpress Books, WP, DLC).

To George Creel, with Enclosure

My dear Creel: The White House 14 January, 1918

Here is the report[1] and my letter concerning it. I hope that you will feel at liberty to publish the report *in extenso* and to use my letter if you wish.

By the way, I would be obliged to you if you would send me a complete set of the pamphlet and book publications.

Always   Faithfully yours,   Woodrow Wilson

[1] United States. Committee on Public Information, *The Activities of the Committee on Public Information* (Washington, 1918). Wilson's letter to Creel, printed as the Enclosure with this letter, appeared on p. 3 of the report.

ENCLOSURE

To George Creel

My dear Mr. Creel: The White House 14 January, 1918

I have just finished reading the report of the Committee on Public Information which you were kind enough to bring me last week, and I want to say how much it has gratified me and how entirely the work being done by the Committee meets with my approval. I have kept in touch with that work, piece by piece, as you know, in our several interviews, but had not realized its magnitude when assembled in a single statement.

I feel confident that as the work of the Committee progresses it will more and more win the public approval and confidence.

                    Cordially and sincerely yours,   Woodrow Wilson

TLS (G. Creel Papers, DLC).

To Herbert Bayard Swope

My dear Mr. Swope: [The White House] 14 January, 1918

Your letter of the tenth[1] has touched me very deeply. I hope you know how I value and appreciate your judgment, and that you should feel as you do about my address of last week to the Congress gives me a deep sense of encouragement. I thank you for your letter with all my heart. You have certainly interpreted my purpose and if I have rightly addressed myself to its accomplishment, I am profoundly thankful.

I have been hearing from time to time of the work you have been doing here in Washington and have been very much interested. If I can help in any way, let me know.

With the best wishes for the New Year,

Cordially and sincerely yours,   Woodrow Wilson

TLS (Letterpress Books, WP, DLC).
    [1] It is missing.

To Cleveland Hoadley Dodge

My dear Cleve: The White House 14 January, 1918

Please never refrain from writing me when you feel like it.[1] Your letters are always a joy to me. They bring such a breath of reassuring friendship as keeps me in spirits for many days together, and I can assure you I need all the tonic I can get during these anxious days.

I have been as much reassured and heartened as I have been surprised at the reception of my recent address to Congress and your own approval of it gives me the keenest pleasure, for I know that you have thought of many phases of the subject for a long time and are competent to judge whether I have proposed the wise programme or not.

Bless you, my dear fellow! May all the best things of the New Year come to you and yours is the wish of all of us.

Affectionately yours,   Woodrow Wilson

TLS (WC, NjP).
    [1] His letter is missing.

To Lucy Marshall Smith

My dear Cousin Lucy: [The White House] 14 January, 1918

Your and Cousin Mary's letters always give us genuine joy, and it was with real delight that I opened yours of January seventh.[1] Our friendships seem to mean more to us than ever in these days of stress and anxiety, and I was so much delighted to learn from Margaret how well you were looking and that Cousin Mary, too, was well, though Margaret reported her as looking tired. Please above all things take care of yourselves.

I hardly have time to think of my own personal affairs these days, but there are two friends to whom my thoughts turn very often with unalloyed joy. May God bless you both for the year to come is the prayer of us all, and particularly of

Your friend,   Woodrow Wilson

TLS (Letterpress Books, WP, DLC).
 [1] Lucy M. Smith to WW, Jan. 7, 1918, ALS (WP, DLC).

From the White House Staff

The White House.
January 14, 1918.

Memorandum for the President:

Senator Owen telephoned that Senator Stone, Senator Calder, Senator Borah and himself, Mr. Flood, Chairman of the Foreign Affairs Committee, and Mr. Cooper, leading Republican on that Committee, have been working on a proposition in regard to Russia and wish to have an opportunity to talk with the President about it. Senator Owen said that he regarded this as most important and hoped the President could fix an early hour when he could see them.[1]

T MS (WP, DLC).
 [1] Wilson conferred with the group at the White House at 2:30 p.m. on January 17. There seems to be no contemporary record of the meeting, but it clearly dealt with the plan which Owen later proposed in the Enclosure printed with WW to RL, Jan. 24, 1918.

From Newton Diehl Baker, with Enclosure

[Washington, c. Jan. 14, 1918]

For the President's information

The cablegram no 487 referred to has not yet been received[1]

Baker

ALS (WP, DLC).
 [1] It is printed as Enclosure I with NDB to WW, Jan. 16, 1918.

ENCLOSURE

[Chaumont] January 14, 1918.

Number 488. January 13th. Confidential. For the Chief of Staff.

Paragraph 1. With reference to your cablegram 558 and 588 and my cablegram 457 have had entirely frank conference with Prime Minister Clemenceau and General Petain. Have now a definite understanding with the French satisfactory to them and to me that our divisions now in France shall complete their training as already begun. In the future divisions arriving in zone of French *army* are to have a period of training with the French, each regiment in a French division. When sufficiently experienced by training in a quiet sector with French, our divisions are to be united under their own commanders and will be placed in the line in our own sector.

Paragraph 2. To avoid reduction by French of number of organizations in their divisions have offered them four colored regiments now here or about to arrive and offer has been accepted. This offer conditioned on return of these troops to our forces when circumstances make it possible to incorporate them into our divisions.

Paragraph 3. At the same conferences secured agreement by Clemenceau and Petain to our acceptance of British proposition outlined in my cablegram number 487. Discussion with both Prime Minister and General Petain was characterized by utmost frankness on both sides and it is believed we have a complete understanding. Expect within a few days to have meeting at my headquarters with Field Marshal Haig and General Petain.   Pershing.

TC telegram (WP, DLC).

From Newton Diehl Baker

My dear Mr. President: Washington. January 14, 1918.

On the 9th of January you sent me a letter from Mr. Garfield[1] suggesting a plan of deferred classification for miners, similar to that instituted by us to meet the necessities of the Emergency Fleet Corporation.

I later had a letter from Mr. McAdoo with regard to a deferred classification for railroad operatives.

Secretary Houston has presented to me a plan for deferred classification for agricultural experts, and I have also before me a statement from Mr. Hurley, of the Shipping Board, to the effect that skilled men in certain trades already in the Army will be needed by the Emergency Fleet Corporation, probably to the extent of three or four thousand men. Incidentally, General Pershing's forces in

France, in their various subdivisions, are requesting very large numbers of trained and skilled mechanics to man railroad construction enterprises and various ordnance and supply repair and construction shops.

The questions which arise out of all these considerations are first, the extent to which it is possible to meet the Army's own needs for trained mechanics, and second, the extent to which the several industries of the United States can be accorded preferential consideration without disorganizing the Army on the one hand, or creating very serious demands for similar recognition on the part of other industries.

So far as I am able to judge, the draft already operated cannot be said to have borne heavily upon industrial workers. The total industrial population engaged in coal mining in 1917 was 600,148 men. Of these, 225,109 were registered as of draft age. Of that number, 74,109 were called for examination before local boards, but many of them were exempted and the actual number drafted for service was only 18,710, or 3.12% of the total number so engaged. Undoubtedly, a number of mine workers enlisted during the period of volunteer enlistment, but that source of trouble is now substantially disposed of, and in view of the fact that under the new form of classification only unskilled common laborers in the mines will be included in Class 1, it seems quite unlikely that there will be much, if any, additional burden placed upon miners.

With regard to railroad operatives, the experience of the first draft discloses that out of a total industrial population of 1,236,867 persons engaged in steam railroading only 277,000 were registered, only 87,780 called for examination, and only 22,089 called for military service; or, in other words, the draft took only 1.76% of the railroad operatives, which seems to me to be a very small number. The same considerations with regard to the reclassification obtain in the matter of railroad operatives as are above discussed in the case of miners. Under the new classification only unskilled labor on the railroads will be included in Class 1, and skilled train operatives will have an automatic deferred classification.

Much of the same situation will exist with regard to skilled agriculturalists, and it would therefore seem that the completion of the present first draft, or even the addition of another increment of 500,000, would have a far less serious effect on the industries of mining, railroading and agriculture than is probably feared by those who are specially attending to the needs of those services. If, however, an actual deferred classification were awarded in any of these three cases, the result would be that persons desiring to avoid the draft would immediately seek employment in that industry and there would be a consequent dislocation of other industries, including those engaged in the manufacture of munitions and necessary supplies.

Under all the circumstances, it seems to me better for me to explain this situation to Mr. McAdoo, Secretary Houston and Mr. Garfield, and ask their concurrence in my judgment against the wisdom of the establishment of class exemptions or class deferred classifications.

The request of Mr. Hurley seems to me to stand on a different ground. I have for some time been meeting every request from Mr. Hurley for ship-building mechanics included in the Army either by draft or by volunteering. A large number of men have been turned over to him for work in the shipyards. His present request, however, is not for technical shipbuilding mechanics but for electricians, pipe-fitters, and men who have had mechanical experience and training of a similar character to that needed by actual shipyard employees.

In view of the urgency of the shipbuilding program, I think it ought to be regarded as in a class by itself, and men ought to be furloughed to the Emergency Fleet Corporation almost without delay so that every man who can be used effectively in shipbuilding will be so employed. I have asked the military affairs committees of the House and the Senate to pass as early as possible a bill giving the War Department power to furlough men without pay, a power which we do not now have. Both committees have promised immediate action on the measure. When it is passed it will be possible for us to furlough mechanics during such time as they are actually employed in shipbuilding operations.

There is one danger in this plan, however. If we furlough men on condition that they continue their work in a particular industry, and bring them back into the Army when they cease to be so employed, the labor union leaders feel that we are in effect drafting men for industry and holding out the threat of a return to military service as a means of preventing men from demanding redresses of grievances as to wages and conditions in the industrial occupations to which we have furloughed them. The point is really difficult and embarrassing, but in the shipbuilding program I should be entirely willing to face it boldly and agree with any man who makes such a claim that shipbuilding was military in its necessity and that I was perfectly willing to use the military draft in furtherance of shipbuilding.

If these general ideas meet with your approval, I will endeavor to reconcile those who ask deferred classifications, and will act as I have indicated with regard to the shipbuilding program.

                    Respectfully yours,   Newton D. Baker

TLS (WP, DLC).
  ¹ See WW to NDB, Jan. 9, 1918 (second letter of that date), n. 1.

From Jane Addams

My dear Mr. President: [Chicago] January 14, 1918.

In transmitting to you the resolutions adopted by our Board last Saturday, may I express my personal appreciation of your courage and far-sightedness in thus making so clear the great principles of a democratic peace.

"The National Board of the Woman's Peace Party desires to give public expression to its admiration and gratitude for the President's statement of January 8th.

We are glad to see in the fore front of this statement the fundamental bases of the new order—democratic diplomacy, freedom of the seas, equality of trade conditions, the greatest possible reduction of armaments, prime regard in colonial matters for the welfare of the population themselves, co-operation with the New Russia and finally formation of a general association of nations.

As the Section for the United States of the International Committee of Women for Permanent Peace, we are inviting all the other national sections organized in 21 countries to study this,—the most profound and brilliant formulation as yet put forth by any responsible statesman of the program of international reorganization."

                    Very sincerely yours   Jane Addams

CCLS (J. Addams Papers, PSC).

From Charles Richard Van Hise

                    Madison, Wis., January 14, 1918.

It gives pleasure to transmit to you a statement unanimously adopted by the Wisconsin Faculty today, reading as follows:

"The Faculty of the University of Wisconsin welcomes and indorses President Wilson's recent message to Congress in which he speaks for the American people upon the issues of the war. He recognized that the independence of all nations under modern conditions requires the United States to assume world responsibility. He sets forth with perfect clearness the principle and purposes for which we are fighting. We pledge unswerving and enthusiastic support to his program for securing world peace and for establishing the rights of nations great and small."

Chas. R. Van Hise.

T telegram (WP, DLC).

Two Letters from William Gibbs McAdoo

My dear Mr. President: Washington January 14, 1918.

I have your letter of the 10th, relative to the proposed regulations under Section 1 of Title II of the Espionage Act, with particular reference to Section 5.

The authority vested in the Secretary of the Treasury to prevent the embarkation of persons "not specifically authorized by him" served to clarify a situation which has heretofore been uncertain and productive of much confusion. Section 5 of the proposed regulations is intended to remove this confusion and to make clear the authority under which the Government is acting.

It is true that the Espionage Act does not cover all the requirements of the present situation as it deals only with the departure of persons on vessels leaving the United States. Conferences have been held with representatives of the Department of State and the Department of Justice, and I am informed that it is the intention to recomment [recommend] further legislation in order to cover departures by land, especially on the Mexican frontier.

The proposed regulations, however, embody the provisions which will permit the Government to go as far as existing legislation now permits in regulating departures by sea. These regulations were submitted to the Secretary of War and the Secretary of the Navy and have received their full approval.

Customs officers are now viseing the passports of all departing passengers and are requiring the identification of seamen on vessels in foreign trade and refusing to permit seamen whose identity is not established to depart. They are also preventing the departure of American citizens within the draft age. These measures have been taken to meet an emergency and without full legal authority. The purpose of the proposed regulations is to establish such control in conformity with the requirements of Title II, section 1, of the Espionage Act, and to remove all doubt concerning the legality of the authority now being exercised.

I hope, Mr. President, that this explanation will dispel any doubts that may have existed with reference to the proposed regulations. Their early issuance will enable the Government to act with full legal authority in performing duties demanded by the present situation. If, however, any further doubt exists in your mind with reference to Section 5, I would suggest that we omit from this section all that follows the word "navigation" in the fourth line thereof. This will enable us to issue the other regulations which are so urgently needed.   Respectfully,   W G McAdoo

Dear Mr. President: Washington January 14, 1918.

I received your letter of the 9th instant[1] about the cable which I asked the Secretary of State to forward on January 5 to Mr. Crosby, concerning the suggestion that General Bliss confer and cooperate with Mr. Crosby on his return to Europe.

I am distressed that you should have the impression that I did not consult you about this matter before the Secretary of State was asked to send the cable. This obliges me to review the situation somewhat at length, as I should like you to know exactly how it came about.

On January 2, I wrote you[2] in reply to your letter of December 26,[3] in which I outlined the problem confronting the Treasury Department in the allocation of credits to the Allies, and emphasized the importance of a related study of the expenditures of the War Department and other Departments of our Government and the expenditures of the Allies for the general purposes of the war. I attach copy of that letter marked "Exhibit A."[4] Not having received a reply from you, I fear you may have overlooked it, and it is for that reason that I bring it again to your attention.

On the same date, I took the liberty of writing the Secretary of War, suggesting that General Bliss' return to Europe offered, it seemed to me, the opportunity of a coordinated study of the financial problems as related to joint military operations of the Allies and the United States and of the shipping facilities that would be available for the carrying out of any plans that might be determined upon. The Treasury cannot meet the demands now being made upon it indiscriminately unless those demands have relation to the ability of all the Governments concerned to translate them into actual power or force upon the battlefronts. A copy of my letter to the Secretary of War dated January 2, together with a copy of my letter to you of the same date, transmitting for your information a copy of said letter to the Secretary of War, are attached hereto as "Exhibit B" and "Exhibit C" respectively.[5]

[1] WW to WGM, Jan. 9, 1918.
[2] WGM to WW, Jan. 2, 1918.
[3] WW to WGM, Dec. 26, 1917 (first letter of that date).
[4] Not reprinted.
[5] WGM to NDB, Jan. 2, 1918, and WGM to WW, Jan. 2, 1918, both TCL (WP, DLC).

By reference to page 3 of my letter to the Secretary of War, you will observe that I merely made a suggestion to the Secretary of War as to the manner in which I thought General Bliss could cooperate with Mr. Crosby and the Inter-Ally Council in a way which would be highly beneficial not alone to the United States Treasury, but to the general situation, and I said specifically:

"If you and the President should think well of it, I should be glad to have the United States represented by a military officer, as well as by a financial secretary upon the Inter-Ally Council. Meanwhile, it seems to me that this second trip of General Bliss to Europe will offer an opportunity for obtaining some light upon the problems which I have suggested, informally if you like. Needless to say, Mr. Crosby will be glad to cooperate in every way with General Bliss if you should determine to instruct the General to take action on the lines suggested.

"I am sending a copy of this letter to the President, so that he may be informed, if you think it worthy of discussion with him."

On the 4th instant I received from the Secretary of War a letter expressing his entire approval of my suggestions (copy attached as "Exhibit D").[6] In view of the fact that I had sent you a copy of my letter of January 2 to the Secretary of War and had suggested that he take the matter up with you if he thought it worthy of discussion, I assumed upon receipt of the Secretary of War's letter that he had consulted you and that I was free to act upon his letter.

Therefore, on the 5th of January I requested the Secretary of State to cable Mr. Crosby. Copy of that cable is attached marked "Exhibit E."[7] You will observe that Mr. Crosby was advised that General Bliss, Chief of Staff, on his return to Europe had been instructed by the Secretary of War "to confer with you and to cooperate in every way" and that the cable concluded with this sentence: "He (the Secretary of War) will await action on this pending recommendation from General Bliss after conference with you." The whole matter was left in position to be dealt with by yourself, the Secretary of War and myself after a full report of the conferences between General Bliss and Mr. Crosby had been received.

On the 7th of January I sent to you a copy of the Secretary of War's reply to my letter of the 2d instant, together with a copy of the cable which I had asked the Secretary of State to send to Mr. Crosby (copy attached marked "Exhibit F").[8]

On the 8th of January I received through the Secretary of State

[6] NDB to WGM, Jan. 4, 1918, TCL (WP, DLC).

[7] WGM to RL, Jan. 5, 1918, TCL (WP, DLC). The telegram to Crosby was embodied in this letter.

[8] WGM to WW, Jan. 7, 1918.

copy of a cable from Mr. Crosby dated January 7 (copy attached marked "Exhibit G").[9]

I sincerely hope that you will read these Exhibits in their order because they tell a connected story, a full knowledge of which on your part I regard as of genuine importance.

Perhaps I was not justified in assuming, after the receipt of the Secretary of War's letter of January 4, that he had consulted you, but I think you will agree with me that it was a natural presumption. In my eagerness to despatch business and get things forward, I perhaps jumped to the conclusion that you and the Secretary of War had conferred about the matter and that he was advising me not only as to his own views, but as to yours as well.

The problem presented by this correspondence is of a very grave and pressing character. It must be settled and settled promptly, and I earnestly hope that you will give the whole subject as prompt consideration as you possibly can and advise me as to the course you wish to have pursued.

What concerns me deeply is the renewed expression of your feeling that Mr. Crosby is disposed to go too far afield. The work which the Inter-Ally Council was intended to accomplish in coordinating demands upon the United States Treasury obliges consideration of the available supply of ships and the military plans and is of such vital importance and of such urgent necessity in order to relieve the Treasury of some of the stupendous and unbearable demands now being made upon it that the representative of the United States in attendance upon the Inter-Ally Council must not only take all these subjects into consideration in determining what credit demands shall be satisfied by the United States Treasury, but he must be as well a person having your entire confidence.

I am obliged to say in all candor that unless a more effective and intelligent check can be imposed upon the expenditures now being made by the different Departments of our own Government and upon the demands being made upon the Treasury by the Allied Governments, it will be impossible to meet these demands. It is absolutely impossible for the Secretary of the Treasury unaided to assume the great responsibility of determining which demands shall be refused and which shall be granted in view of the grave consequences, military and otherwise, which such determinations carry.

Mr. Crosby's experience as Assistant Secretary of the Treasury and the admirable work he did here, in combination with his unusual qualifications for the important mission upon which he was

[9] O. T. Crosby to WGM, Jan. 7, 1918, CC telegram (WP, DLC).

sent to Europe, fit him preeminently for this service, but unless he can enjoy your complete confidence and command your full support, it would be wise, in my judgment, to recall him and to substitute another representative. I confess I have no one in mind who is suitable for the task or who can approach Crosby in the matter of qualifications.

Personally, it would be a great relief to me to have Crosby returned to the Treasury. He is invaluable here. I need at least two Assistant Secretaries in charge of financial matters, one of whom shall give his attention primarily to loans to foreign governments, and the other to domestic finance.

I have spoken to you of my desire that Crosby should be designated High Commissioner of the United States, partly in order that he might have the prestige and rank which are necessary to the efficient performance of his duties as the representative of the United States upon the Inter-Ally Council, and also with a view to enabling me to accept his resignation as an Assistant Secretary of the Treasury and to appointing another Assistant here who could give me further much needed assistance. For these reasons I am disposed to recommend that Crosby be recalled and another substituted who will have your entire confidence, or that if I have over-estimated the significance of what you have written me about Crosby and if he does really enjoy your confidence in fundamental matters, you strengthen his position by giving him the suitable rank and title of High Commissioner of the United States, or some similar title, and leave me free to choose another Assistant Secretary of the Treasury.

I should like to repeat that I know of no one whose qualifications to represent the United States on the Inter-Ally Council are at all comparable with his. The work Mr. Crosby is doing is extremely difficult. In fact, I know of no more difficult position for an American to occupy in Europe, and I fear that you are likely to do him unconsciously an injustice as a result of hearing one sided accounts of his activities and reading his cables without being fully informed of all the details and ramifications of the financial problems with which those cables deal.

Please forgive me for instancing in this connection your comment in your note to me of November 19[10] on Crosby's telegram No. 5 dated November 16, concerning the Italian situation. When I explained the facts at the time,[11] you were quick to recognize that they threw another light on the matter of Crosby's cable,[12] and I may add that a substantial part of the credit of $230,000,000 which

[10] It is missing.
[11] WGM to WW, Nov. 19, 1917, TLS (WP, DLC).
[12] WW to WGM, Nov. 23, 1917, TLS (Letterpress Books, WP, DLC).

had been established for Italy at that time remains unavailed of. The matter is unimportant in itself, but shows how a message from Crosby, which appeared unsympathetic on its face, gave me, in fact, precisely the information which I had to have in order to know how to meet the demands which the Italian Ambassador here was at the moment pressing, but which he subsequently withdrew and which actual experience has shown were without any basis.

Similarly, I am confident that in every instance a full exposition of the situation to you would convince you that the subjects discussed by Mr. Crosby in his cables are most intimately and directly connected with precisely the problems he was sent over to Europe to handle. In the light of my own knowledge of the financial problems, I have found Crosby's cables intelligent, wise and relevant to his duties. The single departure from what I should regard as his immediate affair—the suggestion in relation to the Italian shipping problem—he has explained in his cable No. 36, to which I have already referred, and which is attached as "Exhibit H"[13] and which I hope you will be careful to read. This cable was sent in reply to one I have sent to Crosby by your direction, cautioning him against mixing in too many matters.

This seems a very long letter. I am under such pressure that I have not time to compact it into something more brief. The situation is of such fundamental and grave importance that I have felt obliged to review it somewhat at length.

With the earnest hope that it may receive your prompt and thoughtful consideration, I am, as always

Cordially yours,   W G McAdoo

TLS (WP, DLC).
[13] O. T. Crosby to WGM, Dec. 21, 1917, TC telegram (WP, DLC). This telegram discussed Italy's dire need of fuel and the inability of the British shipping authorities to remedy the situation. Crosby suggested the creation of an "inter-ally shipping board" to deal with this and similar problems and that he be authorized temporarily to represent the United States during the establishment of this board.

To Walter Evans Edge

My dear Governor Edge: [The White House] 15 January, 1918

Immediately upon reading your letter of January twelfth, I took the matter of the conference you proposed up with the Secretary of the Treasury who is, of course, deeply and directly interested. I have this morning a note from him[1] in which he says he thinks that the proposed meeting would be very desirable but hopes that it may be deferred until a later date, when he has had a chance to mature his views on some of the matters involved. I wonder if this suggestion would commend itself to you and Governor Whitman?

In haste   Sincerely yours,   Woodrow Wilson

TLS (Letterpress Books, WP, DLC).
  [1] It is missing.

To Charles Richard Van Hise

My dear Doctor Van Hise: The White House 15 January, 1918

The resolutions of the faculty of the University of Wisconsin which you were kind enough to send me in your telegram of January fourteenth have given me very great and sincere pleasure, and I hope that you will express to your colleagues my very deep and heartfelt appreciation.

Very sincerely yours,   Woodrow Wilson

TLS (C. R. Van Hise Papers, WU).

To Lincoln Steffens

My dear Mr. Steffens: The White House 15 January, 1918

I am heartily glad you liked the message[1] and you evidently approve of the parts for which I hoped the most by way of influencing a complicated situation.

Cordially and sincerely yours,   Woodrow Wilson

TLS (NNC).
  [1] Steffens' letter is missing in all collections.

To Jane Addams

My dear Miss Addams: The White House 15 January, 1918

It gives me peculiar gratification that you and your associates should feel as you do about my recent address to the Congress and I thank you most warmly for your kindness in transmitting to me the resolutions of the National Board of the Woman's Peace Party.

Cordially and sincerely yours,   Woodrow Wilson

TLS (J. Addams Papers, PSC).

To Newton Diehl Baker

My dear Mr. Secretary: The White House 15 January, 1918

You are undoubtedly quite right about the question of deferred classifications in connection with the draft, and with regard also to the exception which ought to be made in promotion of the ship-building programme. I think it would dispose of the matter entirely if you would send a copy of your letter of January fourteenth to me to Mr. Garfield, Mr. McAdoo, and Mr. Houston.

Cordially and faithfully yours,   Woodrow Wilson

TLS (N. D. Baker Papers, DLC).

From Newton Diehl Baker, with Enclosure

Dear Mr. President: Washington. January 15, 1918.

I enclose a copy of the confidential semi-weekly summary just received from General Pershing. I think you will find its details interesting.   Respectfully yours,   Newton D. Baker

TLS (WP, DLC).

E N C L O S U R E

Received at the War Department, January 14, 1918. For the Chief of Staff.

Paragraph 1. Arrangements completed for putting first division into the line. Sector selected north of Toul. Relief of French troops now in sector will probably begin on night of nineteenth and twentieth instant.

Paragraph 2. Arrival of 4 additional divisions from Russia make total of 160 divisions on the Western front. Indications point to the arrival of 1 additional division. 70 Divisions are credited with being in Russia but the *veterans* are old and unreliable. Three German divisions Macedonia and 8 in Italy. Present distribution of Austrian infantry divisions is Eastern Theatre 35, Balkans 2, Italy 42 and one-half, total 79 and one-half.

Paragraph 3. In England Mr. Lloyd George's speech[1] receives the most cordial indorsements from all sections of the press. Even the Pacifists have not criticised it in principle. The papers which have been suspicious of allied war aims and have been demanding a restatement express themselves entirely satisfied. Lord Reading's appointment obtains great favor. Press opinion is that the government has made an excellent choice.

Paragraph 4. In France President's speech to Congress has been received with unqualified approval by the French Press. The reference to Alsace and Lorraine and the doing away with secret treaties are especially commended. Oat shortage in France is great and no relief is in sight from imports as full capacity of shipping must be employed for wheat.

Paragraph 5. Italy. Government begun examination and enrollment of class of 1920 which is expected to furnish 600,000 recruits for the army. 1919 classes furnished 350,000 men. 800,000 previously exempted have been combed out.

Paragraph 6. Russia. British War Office states that British and French Governments will recognize de facto government of Ukraine.

Paragraph 7. Basle newspapers announce that the German-Swiss and German-Holland frontiers will probably be closed both *passenger and freight* traffic for a period of two months. Military Attache Berne reports today German-Swiss frontier closed indefinitely.

Paragraph 8. German press unitedly demands modifications of conciliatory policy of Kuhlman in Russian peace negotiations.[2] Ludendorf's threat to resign roused widespread rally to General Staff control. Von Hertling said to have accepted General Staff views and to be taking more active part in resumed negotiations.[3]

Paragraph 9. Violation of food control in Germany threatens to undermine whole system. Confidential reports from Neukoelln[4] disclosed that municipal authorities there had been obliged to buy at prices in excess of legal rates to compete with other municipalities paying four and five times American market rate. Big industries also buy at excessive rates with results that crops are sold before reaching open market. Prussian food commissioner Waldow[5] attacked for incompetency. Violation facilitated by official underestimate of crops made prior to harvest. Germany army rations average 600 grams per day compared with 750 in peace times; meat 6 days per week; grease rations irregular.   Pershing.

TC telegram (WP, DLC).

[1] About which see British Embassy to WW, Jan. 5, 1918, n. 2.

[2] For the beginning of the negotiations at Brest-Litovsk, see H. R. Wilson to RL, Dec. 28, 1917, n. 2. Von Kühlmann's allegedly conciliatory policy was embodied in Czernin's speech of December 25, discussed and quoted in the note just cited. However, even Czernin's proposals had been predicated on the unlikely event that the Entente Allies would agree to participate in the peace conference. Moreover, further preliminary talks before the first adjournment of the conference on December 28 had revealed that the German and Austrian negotiators took a very hard-nosed view of the details of any proposed agreement, and that their idea of what constituted "annexations" of territory differed radically from that of the Russians. See John W. Wheeler-Bennett, *Brest-Litovsk: The Forgotten Peace, March 1918* (London, 1938), pp. 116-29.

[3] The threat of Ludendorff and Hindenburg to resign grew out of an attempt by General Max Hoffmann, chief of staff of the German army on the eastern front and military representative at the Brest-Litovsk negotiations, to persuade William II, in an audience on January 1, to accept a Polish frontier line which would leave only a minimal number of Poles within Germany. William agreed, at least provisionally, and on the following

day presented a map including the proposed line to Hindenburg and Ludendorff at a meeting of the Crown Council. The two generals reacted most unfavorably, and William postponed a decision. At Ludendorff's instigation, Hindenburg sent to the Emperor on January 7 a letter in which he bitterly attacked the proposed boundary line, as well as Hoffmann and Kühlmann, and broadly hinted that he and Ludendorff would resign if the policy was not reversed. The Emperor did in effect reverse the policy, although he did not dismiss Hoffmann and Kühlmann. However, news of the letter leaked out, and the position of the two negotiators became much more difficult when they returned to Brest-Litovsk on January 9. Moreover, Adolf Joffe had been replaced by the much more inflexible Trotsky as head of the Russian delegation. Finally, it was by then apparent that the Entente powers had no intention of participating in the peace talks. Consequently, the negotiations soon became stalemated, as both sides assumed much more rigid stances. See *ibid.*, pp. 129-40, 151-75.
    4 A working-class residential area in south Berlin.
    5 Wilhelm von Waldow, Secretary of the War Food Office.

From George Creel, with Enclosures

MEMORANDUM

My dear Mr. President,   [Washington] January 15, 1918.

    I attach herewith cable just received from Sisson. He reports utmost harmony and is not concerning himself with anything but the presentation of America's aims and objects.

    The British sounded me out recently with regard to having James M. Beck make a speaking tour in England some time in March or April. Mr. Beck is willing to go if we have no objections.

    I enclose a speech that he made in 1916 that seems to prove that he acted very decently even before the war, while ever since he has been your very devoted follower.[1]

    I enclose also a letter from Mr. Roy Howard, which was drawn up in conference with Colonel House—so Mr. Howard tells me. I gather that he wants some sort of an answer that he can use.

                                        Respectfully,   George Creel

TLS (WP, DLC).
    [1] This enclosure is missing. Beck was a prolific public speaker. However, the Editors have found no speech among those reported in the *New York Times* in 1916 which fits the characterizations given by Creel and by Wilson in his reply to Creel on January 16. Morton Keller, *In Defense of Yesterday: James M. Beck and the Politics of Conservatism, 1861-1936* (New York, 1958), pp. 96-124, does not indicate that Beck modified his highly critical view of the Wilson administration to any considerable extent either before or after the entrance of the United States into the war.

E N C L O S U R E   I

Cable from Sisson: Petrograd, January 13th.

    President's speech placarded on walls of Petrograd this morning. One hundred thousand copies will have this display within three days. Three hundred thousand handbills will be distributed here within five days. Proportionate display Moscow by end of week.

Y.M.C.A. agree distribute million Russian and million German copies along line. Other channels into Germany being opened. Is-
vestia, official Government newspaper, with nearly a million circulation through Russia, printed speech in full Saturday morning
with comment, welcoming it as sincere and helpful. Much of their
newspaper comment still cynical, but shifting rapidly as speech
makes its own mighty appeal. German version in hands of printer.

T MS (WP, DLC).

E N C L O S U R E   I I

From Roy Wilson Howard

Dear Mr. President: New York City January 12th, 1918.

I am leaving January 26th for another tour of the South American
countries on a mission which will bring me in contact with the
leading statesmen and journalists of Latin America.

That I may the better and the more accurately reflect the attitude
and the purposes of our government as a patriotic American abroad
should reflect them, may I request some direct expression from
you on one or two points which my correspondence has indicated
are the subject of very serious consideration on the part of our
fellow Americans south of Panama.

Your suggestion that the other neutrals unite with the United
States in the fight to make the world safe for democracy has been
so adroitly distorted by the German propagandist in South America
that your real objective has been completely lost sight of in many
quarters. Is it possible for you to state the conditions and the hopes
on which your appeal to other neutrals was predicated, especially
so far as it affected other American democracies?

Has the war and the participation by the United States served to
strengthen the common bond between the democracies of the western hemisphere? Since our participation you have crystallized interest in the moral issues in the war. The sincerity of your policy
of no aggression in Mexico is no longer questioned. Do you believe
these facts will suffice to thwart those propagandists who are endeavoring to sow the seeds of suspicion and envy among the great
republics of South America because of the more important role in
world affairs which the war has forced upon the United States?

Have you in mind any specific plan whereby the friendships
which have given our nation nearly a century of uninterrupted
peace with other American nations can be intensified? What part
can the press and the commercial interests of the Americas play
in strengthening these bonds?

Can we hope for a peace which will insure to the whole world a condition which obtains throughout the Americas?

Thanking you in advance for such light as you can give me on the foregoing questions which I know are subjects of the deepest consideration throughout Latin America, I am, my dear Mr. President,   Very sincerely yours,   Roy W. Howard.

TLS (WP, DLC).

From the Duke of Devonshire

Dear Mr. President.   Ottawa. Jan 15. 1918.

I hope you will accept my most grateful thanks for the extremely kind and courteous reception which you gave me during my visit to Washington.[1]

In ordinary circumstances I should have deeply appreciated it, but at a time like the present it had special significance and meaning.

It was also a great pleasure to me to have the opportunity of making the acquaintance of the Members of the Cabinet and others who are doing such invaluable work, but if I might mention one out of many I am especially grateful to the Secretary of State for the generous references which he made to Canada at the Bar Association dinner[2] and in saying this I am only echoing what is in the mind of all true Canadians.

He is, I know, very busy but if he could possibly find time to pay us a visit here we shall be delighted to see him and I can assure you that he will receive a most warm hearted welcome in Ottawa.

It has occurred to me that there might be occasions when it would be mutually convenient if I might write to you personally and privately and I hope I may be allowed to do so, although I promise you that I shall not add to your work with needless correspondence.

May I ask you to convey my best wishes to Mrs. Wilson.

Believe me,   Yours v. sincerely   Devonshire.

ALS (WP, DLC).

[1] Devonshire's visit to Washington was not covered extensively by the press. Wilson received him in the Blue Room of the White House at noon on January 9 and then entertained him at luncheon. On the following day, Devonshire spoke before the National Press Club. *Washington Post*, Jan. 10, 1918 and *New York Times*, Jan. 11, 1918.

[2] The dinner of the New York State Bar Association at the Hotel Astor in New York on January 12. Devonshire attended the event. *New York Times*, Jan. 13, 1918.

From William Jennings Bryan

My dear Mr. President,   Miami, Florida Jan. 15th. 1918.

I have just read in the Official Bulletin (whose publication I hope will be continued after war is over) your recent message *complete* and it is even more satisfactory than the summary given in the local papers.

Am sure it will strengthen the people of this country as well as lay the foundations of an enduring peace.

While the conditions set forth seem revolutionary, when judged by international standards of the past, they meet the requirements of today. The world is ready for the abolition of secret agreements between nations—concealed weapons, so to speak. Acting on the theory that I may be honored with a place on the peace commission,[1] am devoting all my time this winter to study of European politics of the past century and the more important treaties and am sure your demand for publicity is supported by history. It was an appropriate proposition with which to begin, and "f[r]eedom of the seas" naturally follows it. Without such freedom permanent peace would be impossible.

The third proposition ought to appeal powerfully to the commercial classes of Germany; they have exerted an increasing influence on the government and have furnished the militarists with a plausible pretext for their propaganda.

Disarmament will make, I believe, another war almost impossible. It will suppress the rivalry that finally makes overburdened peoples welcome war as a means of putting an end to intolerable expense and to unbearable strain. (The French Yellow Book shows that that argument was used in Germany in 1913) With disarmament accomplished no nation can make special preparation without advertizing its purpose.

The provisions with regard to Belgium, Alsace-Lorraine, and the colonies are in harmony with the fundamental doctrines of democracy toward which the world is moving.

Some may not applaud your treatment of the Russian situation, but you are entirely right. The people of Russia are emerging from a long, dark night of despotism and deserve encouragement; they are stumbling toward the dawn. Their case is far from hopeless. Even if they, unhappily, negotiate a separate peace they will strengthen the hands of the democratic element in Germany rather than the military party.

I am convinced that your clear statement of the nation's war aims, while stimulating the American people to fight as long as fighting is necessary will hasten peace negociations by showing the people of Germany that they can secure more by peace on such terms than they can hope for from a continuation of hostilities.

Mrs. Bryan joins in kind regards to Mrs. Wilson.

With assurances of respect, I am, my dear Mr. President,

Very truly yours,   W. J. Bryan

TLS (WP, DLC).
¹ "Dear Tumulty: What *do* you think of this and what possible answer can I make, for, of course, the assumption he is acting on will never be realized." WW to JPT, c. Jan. 18, 1918, TL (WP, DLC). For Wilson's reply, see WW to WJB, Jan. 22, 1918.

Daniel Willard to Joseph Patrick Tumulty, with Enclosure

My dear Mr. Tumulty: Washington January 15, 1918.

I enclose, with this, a letter addressed to the President, which I would be glad to have you lay before him to be acted upon at his convenience. I talked with him about the subject Sunday afternoon, and he understands why I feel impelled to make this request.

Sincerely yours,   D Willard

E N C L O S U R E

From Daniel Willard

My dear Mr. President: Washington January 11, 1918.

The taking over of the railroads by the Government has naturally raised many unforeseen and intricate questions, and it seems clear to me that I ought now to give my whole time to the affairs of the Baltimore & Ohio Company. Further, the Baltimore & Ohio Railroad, because of its location, is one of the heavy coal carriers and also serves many of the industries engaged in the manufacture of materials necessary for the prosecution of the war, and in common with all other American railroads its operating organization has been considerably weakened during the last year because of the large number of officers and skilled employes who have gone to France and Russia.

With all this in mind it has seemed to me best that I should ask you to relieve me, at least temporarily, of the duties of Chairman of the War Industries Board in order that I may devote my whole time to the Baltimore and Ohio service. If I felt that my resignation would interfere with the usefulness of the Board, I should hesitate to make this request, but I am confident that there are many others much better qualified than I am to perform the duties of that important position.

I appreciate greatly the honors you have shown me and the confidence which you have placed in me, and I regret that it has seemed to me necessary to ask you to accept my resignation, but my sense of obligation to the Baltimore & Ohio Company, together with the very strong feeling which I have that under existing circumstances I can actually contribute more toward winning the war as President of that Company than in any other capacity, convinces me that I am taking the right course. While I feel that it is in the best interests of all that the change should be made as soon as possible, I shall of course expect to yield to your wishes and endeavor to meet your views.

I wish to assure you again of my undivided confidence and support, and of my willingness and desire to be of service. I earnestly hope that you may continue to have good health and strength to sustain the great responsibility that rests upon you.

I remain,

Respectfully and sincerely yours,   Daniel Willard

TLS (WP, DLC).

From the Diary of Josephus Daniels

1918 Tuesday 15 January

WW   One woman had 2 stars, for her nephews & this caused Mrs. W to tell her story of a Jew merchant who had 75 stars. Why   It was not for his family in war but for the 75 customers he had lost because of the war.

WW. "I saw a good adv. Sense—Common and Preferred["]

Lansing fearful introduction by Lewis of resolution endorsing WW's speech on war aims.[1] WW not perturbed. Thought *it* a good thing if ⅔ should vote for it.

WW asked Lansing to see Chamber of Commerce and ask them not to send out interrogatory as to whether American business men would refuse to trade with Germany when it established a Democratic form of governt. We could not go so far & Pres. said such a referendum if in the affirmative would be embarrassing.[2]

WW handed Baker petition from "Bible Students"—conscientious objectors. B said "They read the petition to me & also read the 17th & 18 Chap. of Revelations. WW said "They did not read to me, thinking I knew them by heart." B. said they had no such presumptions as to him. "File it with your curious" said WW

McAdoo wished to know how much money each Dept. would draw from the treasury by July 1 Necessary to know how many bonds to sell Discussed RR plan & Baker agreed to advance money for Russian engines

[1] Senator Lewis, on January 11, had presented a resolution (S. Res. 181) to the effect that the Senate approved Wilson's statement of peace terms in his address of January 8. The resolution also said that the Senate would "cooperate with the President in every way consistent with its duty to the public to obtain the acceptance of the terms presented by the President, or such other terms as will serve the objects set forth by the President, as will bring peace consistent with the welfare of the United States and justice to the contending parties." At that time, Lewis himself asked that the resolution lie on the table. On January 31, Lewis requested, in view of the fact that several senators had since presented resolutions regarding peace terms and had had them transmitted to the Committee on Foreign Relations, that his resolution be sent to that committee also. None of these resolutions ever emerged from the committee during that session of Congress. *Cong. Record*, 65th Cong., 2d sess., pp. 817, 1500.
[2] See E. A. Filene to WW, Jan. 16, 1918.

ADDENDUM

To Robert Lansing

My Dear Mr. Lansing: Princeton, N. J. March 7th, 1907.

I am sincerely obliged to you for remembering my interest in your discussion of Sovereignty, and I am sure that I shall derive a great deal of pleasure from reading your article.[1]

I look back with the greatest interest to our intercourse in Bermuda and wish very much that it might have been longer. I shall hope that some good fortune will bring us together again.

Cordially and sincerely yours,   Woodrow Wilson

TLS (R. Lansing Papers, DLC).
[1] R. Lansing, "Notes on Sovereignty in a State," *The American Journal of International Law*, I (Jan. 1907), 104-28.

INDEX

NOTE ON THE INDEX

THE alphabetically arranged analytical table of contents at the front of the volume eliminates duplication, in both contents and index, of references to certain documents, such as letters. Letters are listed in the contents alphabetically by name, and chronologically within each name by page. The subject matter of all letters is, of course indexed. The Editorial Notes and Wilson's writings are listed in the contents chronologically by page. In addition, the subject matter of both categories is indexed. The index covers all references to books and articles mentioned in text or notes. Footnotes are indexed. Page references to footnotes which place a comma between the page number and "n" cite both text and footnote, thus: "418,n1." On the other hand, absence of the comma indicates reference to the footnote only, thus: "59n1"—the page number denoting where the textual reference occurs.

The index supplies the fullest known form of names and, for the Wilson and Axson families, relationships as far down as cousins. Persons referred to by nicknames or shortened forms of names can be identified by reference to entries for these forms of the names.

All entries consisting of page numbers only and which refer to concepts, issues, and opinions (such as democracy, the tariff, the money trust, leadership, and labor problems) are references to Wilson's speeches and writings. Page references that follow the symbol Δ in such entries refer to the opinions and comments of others who are identified.

Two cumulative contents-index volumes are now in print: Volume 13, which covers Volumes 1-12, and Volume 26, which covers Volumes 14-25. Volume 39, covering Volumes 27-38, is in preparation.

INDEX